MW01625287

Ancient Israel and Its Neighbors

Ancient Israel and Its Neighbors

Interaction and Counteraction

Collected Essays
Volume 1

Nadav Naʾaman

Winona Lake, Indiana
Eisenbrauns
2005

Printed in the United States of America.

Library of Congress Cataloging-in-Publication Data

Na'aman, Nadav.
Ancient Israel and its neighbors : interaction and counteraction : collected essays / by Nadav Na'aman.
v. cm.
Includes bibliographical references and index.
ISBN 1-57506-108-2 (hardcover : alk. paper)
1. Jews—History—To 70 A.D. 2. Palestine—History—To 70 A.D.
3. Jews—History—953–586 B.C. 4. Assyria—History, Military. I. Title.
DS121.3.N33 2005
933—dc22

2005009376

The paper used in this publication meets the minimum requirements of the American National Standard for Information Sciences—Permanence of Paper for Printed Library Materials, ANSI Z39.48-1984. ♾

Dedicated to the memory of my beloved wife

Ilana Na'aman

Contents

Preface

This volume is the first in a series of three, each containing a number of my articles that deal with particular well-defined periods and themes. The present volume focuses on the theme of Israel and Assyria, from their first clash in the time of Shalmaneser III and Ahab to the destruction of Assyria in the time of Josiah. The last two articles (nos. 24–25) extend this period and deal with the period of the Babylonian and the early Persian empires. Most of the articles deal, at least in part, with Assyria's relationship with the kingdoms of Israel and Judah, but a few focus entirely on the relationship of Assyria with other neighboring kingdoms (nos. 6, 10-11, 22, 24). The choice of period and theme is meant to lend the collection a certain coherence. There is some overlap where articles discuss related matters. This is due to the length of time over which the collected articles were written, as new archaeological and documentary evidence came to light and new questions arose that called for new discussions of old problems.

The articles were published beginning in the mid-1970s; the earliest were written nearly 30 years ago. The question always arises, in these circumstances, whether or not to revise the articles to take account of more recent works and the present state of knowledge. I have decided against revision, except in a few instances, and the revisions are acknowledged in the first note to a few articles (nos. 1, 12, 13). Similarly, I did not update the bibliography either, except for a few cases in which I considered it necessary to point out a more recent innovative work on the subject under discussion. Thus, readers may follow the gradual shift in my outlook on the history of Israel. As is well known, since the 1970s, the scholarly view of the early history of Israel has undergone great changes, and, since the 1990s, researchers have raised serious doubts concerning the historicity of the biblical descriptions of the United Monarchy. Scholars are more conscious today of the many problems inherent in the study of the Bible as a source for the history of Israel and the need for a thorough literary critical analysis of the text before taking it as evidence of the ancient reality. A similar critical approach has developed in the study of the ancient Near Eastern documents, in particular, the complicated problems involved in the study of royal inscriptions. It is not only the state of knowledge that has changed in the last decades, but also the fundamental approach to texts, whether biblical or Near Eastern. Leaving the articles unrevised should enable readers not only to read them in the state of knowledge in which they were originally published, but also to look into the more general developments that have taken place in the study of the history of Israel in recent years.

All the articles in the volume were edited according to a unified style for references and bibliography. The system selected was that of *Tel Aviv*, so only articles previously published in this journal did not receive some modifications. In many articles, this has meant changes in the enumeration of the footnotes, because strictly bibliographical references that appeared in the original publications are now included in the text.

The preparation of the book for publication was made with the generous financial support of the Chaim Rosenberg School of Jewish Studies of Tel Aviv University, and its directors, Prof. Yair Hoffman and Prof. Ziva Shamir.

It remains for me to thank those who have helped me carry out the project. The initiative to collect the articles came from Dr. Oded Lipschits — my former student and now colleague — who was also instrumental in bringing current technology into this endeavour. Ms. Liat Steir undertook the task of unifying the style for references and bibliographies. Ms. Susan Efrat prepared a camera-ready version of the volume. Ms. Rachel Yurman prepared the indices. Special thanks are due to Ms. Yael Lotan, who edited many of the articles reproduced in this collection and, with her skills and clarity, made them more accessible for a wider audience. Finally, I would like to thank Mr. Jim Eisenbraun for accepting the book for publication and for bringing the project to fruition.

Nadav Na'aman
Tel Aviv University

Acknowledgments

Thanks are due, as indicated below, for permission to republish the following articles:

To the editor of *Tel Aviv* for 1. "Ahab's Chariot Force at the Battle of Qarqar," *Tel Aviv* 3 (1976), 89–106; 5. "Tiglath-Pileser III's Campaigns against Tyre and Israel (734–732 BCE)," *Tel Aviv* 22 (1995), 268–278; 6. "Two notes on the History of Ashkelon and Ekron in the Late Eighth-Seventh Century BCE," *Tel Aviv* 25 (1998), 219–227; 9. "Hezekiah and the Kings of Assyria," *Tel Aviv* 21 (1994), 235–254; 16. "Population Changes in Palestine following Assyrian Deportations," *Tel Aviv* 20 (1993), 104–124; 18. "The Brook of Egypt and Assyrian Policy on the Border of Egypt," *Tel Aviv* 6 (1979), 68–90; 19. "The Shihor of Egypt and Shur that is Before Egypt," *Tel Aviv* 7 (1980), 95–109; 20. "An Assyrian Residence at Ramat Raḥel?" *Tel Aviv* 28 (2001), 260-280, and 23. "The Kingdom of Judah under Josiah," *Tel Aviv* 18 (1991), 3–71.

To Israel Exploration Society for 2. "Jehu Son of Omri — Legitimizing a Loyal Vassal by his Lord," *Israel Exploration Journal* 48 (1998), 236–238.

To the Hebrew University Magnes Press for 3. "Forced Participation in Alliances in the Course of the Assyrian Campaigns to the West," in M. Cogan and I. Eph'al (eds.), *Ah, Assyria . . . Studies Presented to Hayim Tadmor* (Scripta Hierosolymitana 33), Jerusalem 1991, 80-98.

To the editors of *Zeitschrift des Deutschen Palästina-Vereins* for 4. "Rezin of Damascus and the Land of Gilead," *ZDPV* 111 (1995), 105–117.

To the Editrice Pontificia Università Gregoriana and the Editrice Pontificia Istituto Biblico for 7. "The Historical Background to the Conquest of Samaria (720 BC)," *Biblica* 71 (1990), 206–225; 10. "Sargon II and the Rebellion of the Cypriot Kings against Shilṭa of Tyre," *Orientalia* 67 (1998), 239–247, and 14. "New Light on Hezekiah's Second Prophetic Story (2 Kings 19:9b-35)," *Biblica* 81 (2000), 393–402.

To the editor of *State Archive of Assyria Bulletin* for 8. "The Historical Portion of Sargon II's Nimrud Inscription," *SAAB* 8/1 (1994), 17–20.

To the CDL Press for 11. "The Conquest of Yadnana according to the Inscriptions of Sargon II," in T. Abusch, et al. (eds.), *Proceedings of the XLV[e] Rencontre Assyriologique Internationale*, Part. 1: *Historiography in the Cuneiform World*, Bethesda 2001, 365–372.

To the Publication Office of the American Schools of Oriental Research Publications for 12. "Sennacherib's 'Letter to God' on his Campaign to Judah," *Bulletin of the American Schools of Oriental Research* 214 (1974), 25–39, and 13. "Hezekiah's Fortified Cities and the LMLK Stamps," *Bulletin of the American Schools of Oriental Research* 261 (1986), 5–21.

To the director of *Rivista di Studi Fenici* for 15. "Esarhaddon's Treaty with Baal and Assyrian Provinces along the Phoenician Coast," *RSF* 22 (1994), 3–8.

To the editor of the series *Quaderni di Geografia Storica* for 17. "Province System and Settlement Pattern in Southern Syria and Palestine in the Neo-Assyrian Period," in M. Liverani (ed.), *Neo-Assyrian Geography* (Quaderni di Geografia Storica 5), Rome 1995, 103–115.

To the Secretary-Treasurer of the American Oriental Society for 21. "Ḫabiru-Like Bands in the Assyrian Empire and Bands in Biblical Historiography," *Journal of the American Oriental Society* 120 (2000), 621–624.

To Walter de Gruyter for 22. "Chronology and History in the Late Assyrian Empire (631–619 BC)," *Zeitschrift für Assyriologie* 81 (1991), 243–267.

To the editor of *Biblische Notizen* for 24. "Nebuchadnezzar's Campaign in the Year 603 BCE," *Biblische Notizen* 62 (1992), 41–44.

To the editor of *Henoch* for 25. "Royal Vassals or Governors? On the status of Sheshbazzar and Zerubbabel in the Persian Empire," *Henoch* 22 (2000), 35–44.

List of Abbreviations

AASOR Annual of the American Schools of Oriental Research
AfO Archiv für Orientforschung
AJA American Journal of Archaeology
AJSL American Journal of Semitic Languages and Literature
ANET Pritchard, J. B. ed. 1955. *Ancient Near Eastern Texts.* Princeton.
AnOr Analecta Orientalia
AnSt Anatolian Studies
AOAT Alte Orient und Altes Testament
ARM Archives Royales de Mari.
ARMT Archives Royales de Mari Transcrites et Traduites
ArOr Archiv Orientálni
BA Biblical Archaeologist
BASOR Bulletin of the American Schools of Oriental Research
BIES Bulletin of the Israel Exploration Society; continuation of BJPES
BiOr Bibliotheca Orientalis
BJPES Bulletin of the Jewish Palestine Exploration Society
BMB Bulletin du Musée de Beyrouth
CAD Assyrian Dictionary of the University of Chicago
CAH Cambridge Ancient History
EI Eretz-Israel
Enc. Miqr. Encyclopaedia Miqra'it (Encyclopaedia Biblica). Jerusalem (Hebrew)
ICC International Critical Commentary
IEJ Israel Exploration Journal
JAOS Journal of the American Oriental Society
JBL Journal of Biblical Literature
JCS Journal of Cuneiform Studies
JEA Journal of Egyptian Archaeology
JNES Journal of Near Eastern Studies
JPOS Journal of the Palestine Oriental Society
Kbo Keilschrifttexte aus Boghazköi 1916–. Leipzig and Berlin
KUB Keilschrifttexte aus Boghazköi 1912–. Berlin
MDOG Mitteilungen der Deutschen Orient Gesellschaft
MVAG Mitteilungen der Vorderasiatisch-Ägyptischen Gesellschaft
New Enc Arch. Exc. Encyclopedia of Archaeological Excavations in the Holy Land. Jerusalem 1993
OLZ Orientalistische Literaturzeitung
Or Orientalia
PEFQSt Palestine Exploration Fund, Quarterly Statement
PEQ Palestine Exploration Quarterly, continuation of *PEFQSt*
PJb Palästinajahrbuch
QDAP Quarterly of the Department of Antiquities in Palestine
RA Revue d'Assyriologie et d'Archéologie Orientale
RB Revue Biblique
RHA Revue Hittite et Asianique
RLA Reallexikon der Assyriologie
VT Vetus Testamentum
WO Die Welt des Orients
ZA Zeitschrift für Assyriologie
ZAS Zeitschrift für die ägyptische Sprache und Altertumskunde
ZAW Zeitschrift für die alttestamentliche Wissenschaft
ZDMG Zeitschrift der Deutschen Morgenländischen Gesellschaft
ZDPV Zeitschrift des Deutschen Palästina-Vereins

200, not 2000 chariots (one of numerous scribal errors in this text)

Ahab's Chariot Force at the Battle of Qarqar[1]

The Kurkh Monolith as a Provincial Stele

In the year 1861, J.C. Taylor, the British Consul at Diarbekir, made an excursion to Kurkh, a site located on the southern bank of the Tigris, about 20 km. southeast of Diarbekir. While exploring the tell, he found two inscribed stelae, one of Ashurnaṣirpal II and the other of Shalmaneser III, both of which came to be known in scholarly circles as the Monolith from Kurkh (Taylor 1865:22–23). Both inscriptions were originally published by George Smith (1870:pls. 6–8).

The first intensive study of the Shalmaneser inscription (the subject under discussion here), including a collation of the original in the British Museum, was published by Craig (1886–87). Over the years, the text has been re-examined numerous times, in part or in whole, in a long series of scholarly papers for which a bibliography is furnished by Schramm (1973:70–72). A study of this inscription raises a number of fundamental questions, the first being: When was the inscription composed and the stele erected?

The last section of the text describes the events of Shalmaneser III's sixth regnal year (853 BCE), when he set forth for Syria and clashed with a coalition of southern Syrian states near the city of Qarqar; it is most unlikely that Shalmaneser was able, during that campaign, to erect a stele at Kurkh, situated far to the north on the Upper Tigris. However, in the following year (852 BCE), the Assyrian monarch's campaigning was directed to the Upper Tigris region, and, presumably, it was during this expedition that the monolith was erected.

It is, however, curious that Shalmaneser fails to mention the erection of this stele in any other inscription referring to his seventh year, particularly considering his penchant for recording each stele he set up. For example, in

---

1. *Tel Aviv* 3 (1976), 89–106 [89–91, 97–106]

Reprinted with permission. This is a revised version of an article originally published under the title: "Two Notes on the Monolith Inscription of Shalmaneser III from Kurkh," *Tel Aviv* 3 (1976), 89–106 [89–91, 97–106]. Part of the original article (pp. 92–97) was omitted, and the text was revised in some places.

his inscription referring to his seventh year he relates that he erected a stele at the sources of the Tigris to commemorate his heroic deeds,[2] and, indeed, four rock-hewn inscriptions were found in this area at the confluence of the Tigris and Sebeneh-Su rivers, two each from his seventh and 15th years[3]; one of these may be the inscription to which he referred. Why, then, was the Kurkh inscription ignored in all subsequent inscriptions of Shalmaneser III?

An explanation may be deduced when we consider the sources available to us: for Shalmaneser's seventh year only brief summaries are extant; the detailed inscription recording the events of this year is yet to be discovered. The implication of this lack maybe demonstrated by a comparison of the two editions of the annals recording Shalmaneser's 15th year (when he campaigned in the same region): the detailed annals, composed in year 16 (i.e., one year after the events), refer explicitly to *three* stelae set up during the course of the campaign (Michel 1952:468–471), whereas the later editions (referring to the same expedition) mention only *one*. By analogy, one may assume that during the campaign of his seventh year, Shalmaneser likewise erected several monuments, but not all were considered of sufficient importance to be mentioned in the less-comprehensive later editions. One such stele may have been that found at Kurkh, the city Tušḫan of the Assyrian texts.[4] However, another explanation may be that, because Tušḫan had already become the seat of an Assyrian province in the days of Ashurnaṣirpal II (Forrer 1920:22, 27–28, 33), the erection of a royal stele at an Assyrian administrative capital (unlike those set up on the battlefield) did not rate a reference in the annals. It is even likely that, only at the end of the campaign of the year 852, were instructions given to inscribe and set up the stele at this important administrative center on the northern border of the Assyrian empire.

At this point, the question naturally arises as to why the stele does not make any reference to the campaign conducted in the seventh year to the Upper Tigris. If we compare this text to the Kurkh Monolith of Ashurnaṣirpal, we note that the latter inscription is devoted entirely to the expedition that

2. The most detailed source for the seventh year of Shalmaneser III is the inscription on the Black Obelisk written in his 31st year (Michel 1955–56:148, line 67–72). For historical description, see Olmstead 1921:367 ff. For detailed list of the texts describing the seventh year of Shalmaneser, see Schramm 1973:87–90.

3. Unger (1920:31 ff., 53) and Schramm (1973:84–85) are certainly justified in their assertion that Shalmaneser carved his inscriptions from his seventh and 15th years in one and the same place. A different opinion was expressed by Michel 1954:33 n. 11 and 1964: 148–149.

4. Kurkh was identified with the city of the Tušḫan by Henry C. Rawlinson (Taylor 1865: 23). See also G. Rawlinson 1864:338 n. 5. For detailed treatment, see Olmstead 1918:228 and n. 43.

concluded with the erection of the monument.[5] Likewise, on the two stelae of Tiglath-pileser III and Sargon II found in Iran, full details appear regarding the campaign conducted in the respective year in which each stele was set up (Levine 1972; Herrero 1973). The texts on the stelae erected by Nergal-eresh in the name of Adad-nirari III were also apparently composed immediately after the victory over Damascus in the year 796 BCE, an event that is described in detail in both of the stelae (Tadmor 1973:147–148). The stele from Larnaka seems to have been prepared just after Sargon received tribute from the kings of Cyprus, as noted in the text (Winckler 1889:174–185; Luckenbill 1927:§§179–189), and it would appear that the Zincirli stele was also inscribed immediately upon the return of Esarhaddon from the Egyptian campaign of 671, which is the central theme of its historical narrative (Borger 1956:96–100). Thus, the *lapsus* in the Monolith inscription concerning the campaign of 852, the year in which the stele was erected at Tušḫan (Kurkh), is rather curious.

An additional difficulty is the absence of a building inscription in the text under discussion, *viz.* a passage in which the king describes the quarrying of the stele, its erection, and invocation of curses upon whoever might desecrate it. Similarly, if the text had been composed in honor of a newly dedicated building, one would expect such fact to be mentioned. Admittedly, this type of passage is also missing on the Ashurnaṣirpal monolith from Kurkh, but it appears on all other stelae mentioned above. In his article on the stele fragments from Ashdod, Tadmor (1967:241–242) has suggested that the rulers of Ashur may have solved the difficulty of preparing stelae while on expeditions to far distant lands by having a prefabricated stock on hand, which naturally bore no reference to the places in which they were eventually to be set up. However, it should be remembered that the Kurkh Monolith was found at Tušḫan, an administrative center that had been annexed to Assyria in the days of Ashurnaṣirpal II, Shalmaneser's predecessor, and, therefore, Tadmor's plausible solution is not applicable in the case under consideration. One must seek elsewhere for an explanation of the sudden break in the description of the events for the year 853 BCE and for the absence of a record concerning events in 852 (when the stele was set up), as well as the lack of a "building inscription" in the final section of the text.[6]

5. A second stele of Ashurnaṣirpal has been found at Babil by Lehmann-Haupt and was published by Hawkins 1969. As the lower half of the stele is missing, it cannot be determined whether or not it contained an historical or building description.

6. It must be remembered that those scholars who claim that the Monolith inscription was written at the end of 853 BCE, the last year described therein, encounter the same dif-

In this connection, an additional characteristic of the text should be noted, i.e., the large number of scribal errors it contains. Many scholars who have studied this text have been forced to resort to emendation in one place or another (Craig 1886–1887:*passim*; Balkan 1957:34 ff.; Tadmor 1961a:143–145, and n. 10; Genge 1965:*passim*; Schramm 1973:71–72). In my opinion, the poor execution of the inscription suggests the direction in which we should seek an explanation for the anomalies of the Monolith inscription discussed thus far.

It would seem that the Monolith text was carved by a provincial scribe dwelling in Tušḫan (Kurkh), who was insufficiently skilled in his profession. It may be assumed that this scribe recorded the events of the first seven years of Shalmaneser III's reign by copying a standardized text furnished to him, but, as he did not space his work properly, he had to break off in the middle, thus, omitting both the narrative of the campaign of 852 BCE and the building inscription that should have concluded the text.

In this light, we may re-examine a passage that has been the subject of controversy in the past: the passage concerning Ahab's chariot force at the battle of Qarqar in his sixth year.

The Chariot Force of Ahab According to the Kurkh Monolith

After he had annexed the kingdom of Bīt Adini to the territory of Assyria and had subjugated the rulers of northern Syria, Shalmaneser set forth in the year 853 BCE on another campaign to the west. Along his route, he collected tribute from the vassal kings of northern Syria, and, from there, the Assyrian army continued southward, reaching the border of the kingdom of Hamath and destroying several of its towns. Then, near the city of Qarqar, he encountered the combined forces of the kingdoms of central and southern Syria (the "southern league").[7] In the description of the ensuing battle, the Assyrian scribe lists the forces of the allies assembled for battle: heading the roster is Hadadezer (Adad-idri), the king of Damascus, with 1,200 chariots, 1,200 cavalry and 20,000 troops; second is Irḫuleni, king of Hamath, with 700 chariots, 700 cavalry and 10,000 troops; the third is Ahab, king of Israel,

---

ficulty. In 853, a campaign was conducted to the west and not to the northern Tigris region; if the stele had been set up in this year, it must have been associated with building activity carried out at the Assyrian administrative center itself, and the text would have been accompanied by the customary building inscription.

7. For the battle of Qarqar, see Hommel 1888:608 ff.; Kraeling 1918:73 ff.; Olmstead 1921: 365 ff.; 1931:383 ff.; Elliger 1947:80–84; Tadmor 1961b:239–248; Malamat 1964: 246ff.: Elat 1975.

with 2,000 chariots and 10,000 troops. Among the other participants,[8] Irqata provided 10 chariots and 10,000 troops, Siannu had 30 chariots and x-thousand troops, and the other cities along the coast sent foot soldiers only and in much smaller numbers. In addition, there were x-thousand troops furnished by Ba'asa the ruler of Beth-rehob and Amana,[9] and 1,000 camels supplied by Gindibu' the Arab.

The fact that the greatest chariot force is listed only in third place presents a considerable difficulty; furthermore, in all later editions providing a summarized version of the events, Hadad-ezer of Damascus and Irḫuleni of Hamath invariably head the list, accompanied by 12 kings from the sea coast, whose names and countries are not included (Michel 1947:57–58; 1964:152; Oppenheim 1969:279; Hulin 1963:52). It should be noted that the Assyrians generally used one of two ways: either they mention only the head of the enemy coalition, or they list all of the participants in detail. Inasmuch as all of the later editions list only these same two leaders who come at the head of the roster in the Monolith inscription, it is obvious that these two kings headed the alliance. But how is it that the Kurkh text should assign the vast

8. According to the Monolith inscription, 12 kings participated in the coalition, but in the detailed list we have only 11. Weidner (in: Michel 1947:70 n. 13) suggested that part of one name had been inadvertently deleted from the list and that the last name, *Ba'sa mār Ruḫūbi māt Amanayu*, actually represents two: Ba'asa of Beth-rehob and a ruler of the Ammonites (whose name has been lost). For additional discussion, see Malamat 1964:258 n. 22; 1973:144, 152 n. 26. It is preferable, however, to assume that the number 12 is only schematic, because it recurs many times in the inscriptions from the reign of Shalmaneser (see Michel 1947:70 n. 13, with earlier literature).

9. The location of KUR *Amana* requires extensive discussion. In the early days of research, scholars assumed that the kingdom of Ammon in Transjordan was intended, see Delitzsch 1881:294; Schrader 1885:127. However, the kingdom of Ammon is consistently rendered in Neo-Assyrian sources as *Bīt Ammān*, with the *bīt* element and with doubled *–mm–*. Winckler (1895:141–143; 1900:216–217; 1901:150) was the first to note the parallel between Hadad-ezer son of Rehob king of Zobah mentioned in 2 Sam. 8:3, 12 and Ba'asa the son of Rehob from *māt* Amana in the Monolith inscription. In his opinion, Ba'asa was the king of Aram Beth-rehob, a kingdom located in Transjordan whose area included the districts of Zobah, Rehob and Ṭob, who had subjugated the neighboring kingdom of Ammon. Meyer (1906:539; 1931:252), on the other hand, suggested that Aram Beth-rehob and Aram Zobah may have been situated in the Lebanon region. As a consequence, Forrer (1932a:134; 1932b) proposed to identify KUR *Amana* with Mt. Amana = the Anti-Lebanon range, located in the same geographical region; he thus felt that the inscription was referring to the kingdom of Zobah located there. This proposal has been accepted by a number of scholars (Mazar 1950: 436 [but see, Mazar 1962:108–109, 114]; Malamat 1950:577; 1964:258 n. 22; 1973:144, 152 n. 26; Tadmor 1961b:245. Admittedly, Amana does not appear in any other source as a kingdom, but it might have been a second name of the kingdom of Zobah, located north and northwest of Mount Anti Lebanon. [For recent discussion, see Na'aman 1995:385–386].

number of chariots to the third-ranking ruler in the list, i.e., Ahab, king of Israel?

To clarify this problem, one must explore, first of all, the economic and military (both technical and logistic) significance of a chariot force numbering 2,000. In the two editions of Shalmaneser III's annals from the years 16 (843 BCE) and 20 (839 BCE), the Assyrian monarch reports in the summary passage that he furnished the army with 2,002 chariots and 5,542 cavalry (year 16), 2,001 chariots and 5,242 cavalry (year 20) (Michel 1952:474, lines 47–48; 1954:44, lines 2–3). Elat (1975:26–29), in a detailed study of these two passages, has demonstrated that these numbers represent the sum total of the Assyrian chariot forces for those years. It must be remembered that, in 839 BCE, the kingdom of Assyria had reached the peak of its power after Shalmaneser defeated the kingdom of Damascus, reaching southward even to the borders of Israel, and westward beyond the Amanus range. Is it really feasible that the kingdom of Israel by itself had at its disposal a chariot force equal in strength to that of the Assyrian Empire at the height of its greatness under Shalmaneser III? In this respect, one may also recall that, at the Battle of Qadesh, the Hittites committed a force of 2,500 chariots, recruited from the vast expanses of their empire (Gardiner 1960:9–10, 39).[10] Once again, we must ask: Could the Israelite chariotry under Ahab have been almost equal to that fielded by the Hittite Empire at its greatest?

The next point that requires elucidation is whether the Israelite monarchy had the means to acquire horses for such a chariot force. A study of the Assyrian data from the time of Ashurnaṣirpal shows that an Assyrian chariot was harnessed to four horses in those days (Nagel 1966:53 ff.). Although we do not know how many horses were required by an Israelite chariot, it is obvious, in any case, that a force numbering 2,000 chariots would necessitate several thousand horses, which would undoubtedly have to be imported.

It should be noted that horses were extremely expensive in the ancient Near East; according to 1 Kgs. 10:29, a horse cost 150 shekels of silver in the days of Solomon. Most of the information concerning the price of horses is from the second half of the 2nd millennium BCE; the relevant evidence has been collected by Salonen (1956:39–40; see also Lacheman 1950:no. 12:4–7; Nougayrol 1970:no. 7B:6–14). According to a text from Nuzi (Chiera 1934:no. 553), the price of a horse was equal to that of an ox plus three goats and six sheep, and, from this entry alone, it is obvious that the value of a horse was immeasurably higher than that of any other animal. From the 1st millen-

10. On the sizes of various Egyptian expeditions during the 2nd and 1st millennia BCE, see Herrmann 1964:70–72; Kitchen 1973:295 nn. 288–289.

nium BCE we have no records of horse transactions in the Assyrian Empire, but in Babylonia — although only three sales of horses are documented — horses went for a very high price indeed (Meissner 1936:17; 1937:6 and n. 1; Dubberstein 1939:32 and n. 57). However, the available data does not permit one to establish a standard price for a horse, owing to the great variability in price from place to place, for different breeds and ages of horses, etc.

We have already noted that no evidence has come down regarding the sale of horses throughout the Assyrian Empire in the 1st millennium BCE, which would seem to indicate that private ownership of horses was not prevalent in Assyria. Securing a supply of horses was first and foremost the task of the royal bureaucracy, which had to muster the resources of the entire empire for this purpose. The material for clarification of this question was collected and analyzed in detail by Postgate[11], and the following are his principal conclusions: horses were acquired by Assyria as booty, as tribute rendered by vassal kings, and as contributions extracted from the provinces throughout the empire. The horses were collected in the districts by the commissioners and then transferred to Assyria under the care of officials appointed especially for this task. The numbers sent by various districts are most impressive: in one case, 1,840 draft horses and 787 cavalry were brought to Assyria in a period of 100 days! In the lists of booty appearing in Assyrian royal inscriptions, thousands of horses are mentioned; particularly outstanding are the great numbers taken from Media: 5,000 during the reign of Tiglath-pileser III and 8,609 under Sargon II (Luckenbill 1926:§812; Gadd 1954:177:56; see Luckenbill 1926:§§466, 802; and 1927:§§24, 39, 274). In addition to the above sources, the Assyrian administration had numerous other methods for an uninterrupted supply of horses for the royal chariotry,[12] and it is obvious that vast efforts were expended by the empire towards this goal.

Obviously, the kingdom of Israel did not have any empire from which to acquire the necessary horses without resorting to some means of payment. Israel was evidently forced to purchase the horses at their full market price, as may be inferred from 1 Kgs. 10:29.[13] Is it at all conceivable that as small a kingdom as Israel could have mustered the resources required for the purchase of sufficient horses to maintain a force of 2,000 chariots?

Naturally, this was not the end of the outlay, because, first of all, there was

---

11. Postgate 1974:7–18, 102–103, 143–144, 208–213. The horse lists from Nineveh were treated most recently by Fales 1974.

12. See the diagram of horse movements in Postgate 1974:212–213.

13. The problem of *'ereṣ Miṣraim*, mentioned in 1 Kgs. 10:28 as a supplier of horses to Solomon — alongside the country of Que — now finds its solution in Assyrian documents. Since the days of Winckler, not a few scholars have assumed that this *'ereṣ Miṣraim* must be

the cost of stabling, grooming and feeding the horses. The horse-trappings and chariots must also be included in any reckoning, and, according to 1 Kgs. 10:29, the price of a chariot was four times the price of a horse. Furthermore, their maintenance required an extensive technical cadre to repair and refurbish the chariots after field exercises and battle. Finally, one cannot ignore the charioteers. In the 2nd millennium BCE, these comprised a unique group within the ruling class that was granted special means of support (land and other awards) to enable its members to devote themselves exclusively to fulfilling their military functions.[14] Furthermore, chariot warfare required intensive training for the horses and charioteers alike in order to develop teamwork within the chariot, co-ordination between chariot units, field tactics, etc. In short, the use of chariotry required the maintenance of professional personnel whose sole occupation was to man the chariots and fight from them, and the government had to provide their financial support.

The question, therefore, is unavoidable as to whether the kingdom of Israel in the days of Ahab was at all capable of meeting such heavy expenses and whether it had the means of assuring a steady supply of horses and vehicles for such a large chariot force. The answer is self-evident: it is inconceivable that Israel would have had the power to maintain a chariot force of 2,000 or even a major portion thereof. Even the suggestion that the chariot force ascribed to Ahab may have included those of neighboring countries (of Judah in particular) (Olmstead 1931:384; Malamat 1964:249–250) cannot in any way account for such a large figure or explain the strange fact that the leader of

sought in southern Anatolia (for discussion and bibliography, see Montgomery 1951:227–228). However, it has been demonstrated that the land of Muṣri in Anatolia was nothing but a scholarly invention and lacks all support (see Tadmor 1961a; Garelli 1971). On the other hand, we now have a series of testimonies to the effect that horses that were evidently famous for their size were, in fact, imported from Egypt to Assyria: In the inscriptions of Tiglath-pileser III, horses from Egypt are mentioned twice as tribute to Assyria from rulers in the West (Wiseman 1951:23:7; 1956:125 rev.9); moreover, Shilkanni (Osorkon IV), king of Egypt, sent 12 large horses as a gift to Sargon II (Weidner 1941–44:42–46; Tadmor 1958: 77–78), and in his annals there are also several references to such Egyptian horses that were used to draw the Assyrian chariots; Ashurbanipal, likewise, brought horses of unusual size as booty from Egypt (for references, see Weidner 1941–1944:44 n. 14). It would appear that these large horses were of the type denoted in Assyrian administrative records as *māt Kūsayu*. Such horses were delivered in great numbers as contributions to Assyria; Postgate (1974:11), who discussed this problem in detail, has shown that *māt Kūsayu* refers to a special breed of horses from Nubia, namely *māt Kūsi*, (i.e., the land of Cush). Therefore, the cuneiform sources fully confirm the text of 1 Kgs. 10:28, in which Egypt is pictured as an exporter of horses to neighboring countries in the 1st millennium BCE.

14. O'Callaghan 1950–51:309 ff.; Alt 1956; Mayrhofer 1966:41 ff. and full bibliography there; Dietrich and Loretz 1969; Heltzer 1969:41–42; Reviv 1972.

the largest chariot force appears in third place on the list of allied rulers, according to the earliest source, and, in later editions, Israel is included only within the group of 12 minor allies and — not even mentioned by name.

The assumption that Ahab's chariotry numbered 2,000 raises some inexplicable problems. For example, the revolt of Mesha, king of Moab, occurred after the death of Ahab, a few years after the battle of Qarqar. Nevertheless, the kingdom of Israel, even with the aid of Judah, did not succeed in repressing that revolt. Can one conceive of such success on the part of a rebel against a power possessing this alleged chariot capability? Furthermore, during the campaign of Shalmaneser in 841 BCE Jehu, king of Israel,[15] capitulated without a fight and rendered tribute to the Assyrians, and during the reign of his successor, Jehoahaz, when the kingdom of Israel was sorely pressed by Aram-Damascus, only 50 cavalry and ten chariots and ten thousand infantry remained at its disposal (2 Kgs. 13:7). Did this allegedly vast Israelite chariot force melt away within so short a period with hardly a trace? Or may it not be more plausible to assume that the kingdom never really enjoyed such tremendous military might?

In conclusion, it is obvious that the number of 2,000 chariots mentioned in the Monolith Inscription from Kurkh is not historically feasible. Tadmor has pointed out at least ten scribal errors in the passage dealing specifically with the battle of Qarqar (Tadmor 1961a:144–145 and n. 10), and we may assume that the number 2,000 is also a mistake. Did the scribe write 2,000 when he originally intended 200?[16] It seems to me that the number 200 is much more suitable to the reality of that period than the number 2,000, and, by this emendation, the history of Israel may be placed on a more realistic footing.

15. The recent proposal by McCarter (1974) to interpret the name *Ia-ú-a/Ia-a-ú* in these passages as a shortened form of Jehoram (based on a hypocoristic PN Yaw!) is unsound. Furthermore, hypocoristic names are rare exception in the Assyrian royal inscriptions; such a solution is *a priori* inadequate. It is preferable to adhere to the original interpretations, which consider the above cuneiform spellings as attempts to approximate the pronunciation of the biblical name Jehu. Ungnad (1906) showed that the name *mār* PN (e.g., *mār Ḫumri*) actually denotes (*ša*) *bīt* PN ("which is of the house PN"). The Assyrians were accustomed to denote countries by the name of the founder of the ruling dynasty at the time of their first acquaintance with it (e.g., *Bīt Baḫiani, Bīt Agusi, Bīt Ḫumri,* regardless of which dynasty was in power at the time. Thus, the name *mār ḫumri* for Jehu poses no problem. Accordingly, the synchronization between Jehu and Shalmaneser III in 841 BCE remains valid.

16. Katzenstein (1973:168) pointed out that the numbers of the soldiers sent by Irqata (10,000) and Siannu ([x],000) are too high and suggested the former number is probably a scribal error for 100.

[Recently De Odorico (1995:104–105) argued that some of the numbers of chariotry and troops were deliberately exaggerated. He further assumed that the numbers relating to the cavalry and troops of Damascus, Hamath and Israel, the troops of Irqata and the camels of the Arabs, were intentionally multiplied by 10.]

References

Alt, A. 1956. Bemerkungen zu den Verwaltungs- and Rechtsurkunden von Ugarit und Alalach. *WO* 2: 234–243.

Balkan, K. 1957. *Letter of King Anum-hirbi of Mama to King Warshama of Kanish.* Ankara.

Borger, R. 1956. *Die Inschriften Asarhaddons, Königs von Assyrien.* (AfO Beiheft 9). Graz. (Reprint 1967. Osnabrück).

Chiera, E. 1934. *Joint Expedition with the Iraq Museum at Nuzi. V. Mixed Texts.* Philadelphia.

Craig, J.A. 1886–87. The Monolith Inscription of Shalmaneser II. *Hebraica* 3: 201–232.

De Odorico, M. 1995. *The Use of Numbers and Quantifications in the Assyrian Royal Inscriptions.* (State Archives of Assyria Studies 3). Helsinki.

Delitzsch, F. 1881. *Wo lag das Paradies?* Leipzig.

Dietrich, M. and Loretz, O. 1969. Die Soziale Struktur von Alalaḫ and Ugarit (II). *WO* 5: 57–93.

Dubberstein, W.H. 1939. Comparative Prices in Later Babylonia (625–400 B.C.). *American Journal of Semitic Languages and Literature* 56: 20–43.

Elat, M. 1975. The Campaign of Shalmaneser III Against Aram and Israel. *IEJ* 25: 25–35.

Elliger, K. 1947. Sam'al and Hamat in ihrem Verhältnis zu Hattina, Unqi and Arpad. Ein Beitrag zur Territorialgeschichte der norsyrischen Staaten im 9. und 8. Jahrhundert v. Chr. In: Fück, J. ed. *Festschrift für Otto Eissfeldt zum 60. Geburtstag.* Halle: 69–108.

Fales, F.M. 1974. Notes on some Nineveh Horse Lists. *Assur* I/3: 28–47.

Forrer, E. 1920. *Die Provinzeinteilung des assyrischen Reiches.* Leipzig.

Forrer, E. 1932a. Aramu, *RLA* I: 131–139.

Forrer, E. 1932b. Ba'asa, *RLA* I: 328.

Gadd, C.J. 1954. Inscribed Prism of Sargon II from Nimrud. *Iraq* 16: 173–201.

Gardiner, A.H. 1960. *The Qadesh Inscriptions of Ramesses II.* Oxford.

Garelli, P. 1971. Nouveau. coup d'oeil sur Muṣur. In: Caquot, A. and Philonenko, M. eds. *Hommages à André Dupont-Sommer.* Paris: 37–48.

Genge, H. 1965. *Stelen neuassyrischer Könige. Eine Dokumentation and philologische Vorarbeit zur Würdigung einer archäologischen Denkmälergattung. 1. Die Keilschriften.* (Ph.D. Thesis). Freiburg.

Hawkins, J.D. 1969. The Babil Stele of Assurnasirpal. *Anatolian Studies* 19:111–120.

Heltzet, M. 1969. Problems of Social History of Syria in the Late Bronze Age. In: Liverani, M. ed. *La Siria nel Tardo Bronzo.* Roma: 31–46.

Herrmann, S. 1964. Operationen Pharao Schoschenks I. im östlichen Ephraim. *ZDPV* 80: 55–79.

Herrero, P. 1973. Un fragment de stèle néo-assyrienne provenant d'Iran. Delegation Archéologique Française en Iran 3: 105–111.

Hommel, F. 1888. Geschichte Babyloniens and Assyriens. Berlin.

Hulin, P. 1963. The Inscription on the Carved Throne-base of Shalmaneser III. Iraq 25: 48–69.

Katzenstein, H.J. 1973. *The History of Tyre, from the Beginning of the Second* Millennium B.C.E. until the Fall of the Neo-Babylonian Empire in 538 B.C.E. Jerusalem.
Kitchen, K.A. 1973. *The Third Intermediate Period in Egypt (1100-650 B.C.).* Oxford.
Kraeling, E.G.H. 1918. *Aram and Israel.* New York.
Lacheman, E.R. 1950. *Miscellaneous Texts from Nuzi II. The Palace and Temple Archives.* Cambridge (Mass.).
Levine, L.D. 1972. *Two Neo-Assyrian Stelae from Iran.* (Royal Ontario Museum, Art and Archaeology Occasional Paper 23). Toronto.
Luckenbill, D.D. 1926. *Ancient Records of Assyria and Babylonia* I. Chicago.
Luckenbill, D.D. 1927. *Ancient Records of Assyria and Babylonia* II. Chicago.
McCarter, P.K. 1974. Yaw, son of 'Omri. A Philological Note on Israelite Chronology. *BASOR* 216: 5–7.
Malamat, A. 1950. Aram Beth–rehob. *Encyclopaedia Biblica* I. Jerusalem: 577 (Hebrew).
Malamat, A. 1964. The Wars of Israel and Assyria. In: Liver, J. ed. *The Military History of the Land of Israel in Biblical Times.* Tel Aviv: 241–260 (Hebrew).
Malamat, A. 1973. The Aramaeans. In: Wiseman, D.J. ed. *People of Old Testament Times.* Oxford: 134–155.
Mayrhofer, M. 1966. *Die Indo-Arier im Alten Vorderasien.* Wiesbaden.
Mazar (Maisler), B. 1950. Amana. *Enc. Miqr.* I: 436 (Hebrew).
Mazar, B. 1962. The Aramean Empire and its Relations with Israel. *BA* 25:98–120.
Meissner, B. 1936. *Warenpreise in Babydonien.* (Abhandlungen der Preussischen Akademie der Wissenschaften, philosophisch-historische Klasse 1). Berlin.
Meissner, B. 1937. Nachträge zu *Warenpreise in Babylonien. Sitzungsberichte der Preussischen Akademie der Wissenschaften, philosophisch-historische Klasse.* Berlin: 5–8.
Meyer, E. 1906. *Die Israeliten and ihre Nachbarstämme.* Halle.
Meyer, E. 1931. *Geschichte des Altertums.* II/2 — *Der Orient vom zwölften bis zur Mitte des achten Jahrhunderts.* (2nd ed.). Stuttgart and Berlin.
Michel, E. 1947. Die Assur-Texte Salmanassars III. (858–824). *WO* 1: 5–20, 57–71.
Michel, E. 1952. Ein neuentdeckter Annalen-Text Salmanassars III. *WO* 1/6: 454–475.
Michel, E. 1954. Die Assur-Texte Salmanassars III. (858–824). 6. Fortsetzung. *WO* 2/1: 27–45.
Michel, E. 1955–56. Die Assur-Texte Salmanassars III. (858–824). 7. Fortsetzung. *WO* 2/2-3: 137–157.
Michel, E. 1964. Die Assur-Texte Salmanassars III. (858–824). 10. Fortsetzung. *WO* 3: 146–155.
Montgomery, J.A. 1951. *A Critical and Exegetical Commentary on the Books of Kings.* (*International Critical Commentary*) . Edinburgh.
Na'aman, N. 1995. Hazael of 'Amqi and Hadadezer of Beth-rehob. *Ugarit-Forschungen* 27: 381–394
Nagel, W. 1966. *Der mesopotamische Streitwagen und seine Entwicklung in Ostmediterranen.* Berlin.
Nougayrol, J. 1970. *Le Palais Royal d'Ugarit* VI. Paris.
O'Callaghan, R.T. 1950–51. New Light on the Maryannu as "Chariot Warrior." *Jahrbuch für Kleinasiatische Forschung* 1: 309–324.
Olmstead, A.T.E. 1918. The Calculated Frightfulness of Ashur-nasir-apal. *JAOS* 38:209–259.
Olmstead, A.T.E. 1921. Shalmaneser III and the Establishment of the Assyrian Power. *JAOS* 41: 345–382.
Olmstead, A.T.E. 1931. *History of Palestine and Syria.* London.
Oppenheim, A.L. 1969. Babylonian and Assyrian Historical Texts. In: *ANET*: 265–317.
Postgate, J.N. 1974. *Taxation and Conscription in the Assyrian Empire.* Rome.

Rawlinson, G. 1864. *The Five Great Monarchies of the Ancient Eastern* World II. London.
Reviv, H. 1972. Some Comments on the Maryannu. *IEJ* 22:218–228.
Salonen, A. 1956. *Hippologica Accadica.* Helsinki.
Schrader, E. 1885. *The Cuneiform Inscriptions and the Old Testament.* London.
Schramm, W. 1973. *Einleitung in die assyrischen Königsinschriften, Zweiter Teil 934-722 v. Chr.* (Handbuch der Orientalistik). Leiden.
Smith, G. 1870. *The Cuneiform Inscriptions of Western Asia* III. London.
Tadmor, H. 1958. The Campaigns of Sargon II of Assur: A Chronological-historical Study. *JCS* 12: 22–40, 77–100.
Tadmor, H. 1961a. Que and Muṣri. *IEJ* 11: 143–150.
Tadmor, H. 1961b. Azriyau of Yaudi. *Scripta Hierosolymitana* 8: 232–271.
Tadmor, H. 1967. Fragments of a Stele of Sargon II from the Excavations of Ashdod. *Eretz Israel* 8: 241–245 (Hebrew).
Tadmor, H. 1973. The Historical Inscriptions of Adad-nirari III. *Iraq* 35: 141–150.
Taylor, J.G. 1865. Travels in Kurdistan. *Journal of the Royal Geographical Society* 35: 21–58.
Unger, E. 1920. Die Wiederherstellung des Bronzetores von Balawat. *Mitteilungen des Deutschen Archäologischen Instituts, Athenische Abteilung* 45: 1–105.
Ungnad, A. 1906. Jaua, mâr Humrî. *OLZ* 9: 224–226.
Weidner, E.F. 1941–44. Šilkan(ḫe)ni König von Muṣri, ein Zeitgenosse Sargons II. *AfO* 14: 40–53.
Winckler, H. 1895–1900. *Geschichte Israels in Einzeldarstellungen,* I–II. Leipzig.
Winckler, H. 1889. *Die Keilinschrifttexte Sargons nach den Papierabklatschen and Originalen neu herausgegeben* 1. Leipzig.
Winckler, H. 1901. Besprechungen zu Kittel, R. Die Bücher der Könige übers. u. erklärt. *OLZ* 4: 141–152.
Wiseman, D.J. 1951. The Historical Inscriptions from Nimrud. *Iraq* 13: 21–26.
Wiseman, D.J. 1956. A Fragmentary Inscription of Tiglath-Pileser III from Nimrud. *Iraq* 18: 117–129.

Jehu Son of Omri: Legitimizing a Loyal Vassal by His Lord[1]

The name of Jehu is recorded in the inscriptions of Shalmaneser III as *Iu-ú-a*[2] *mār Ḫumri* (Michel 1949:266 lines 25–26; Michel 1955–1956a:140, paragraph 8; Kinnier Wilson 1962:95, lines 29–30; see Michel 1954:38, line 11). There is a contradiction (either apparent or real) between the references to Jehu as "son of Omri" and the biblical story in 2 Kings 9–10, according to which Jehu killed all members of the dynasty of Omri and seized the throne. Scholars have observed that the designation "son of PN" in the Assyrian royal inscriptions refers to the ancestral founder of the dynastic house and not to the ruler's father (Ungnad 1906; Brinkman 1968:247). New West Semitic kingdoms that emerged in the Fertile Crescent in the early first millennium BCE are called by the eponymic/dynastic name "Bīt/Beth-PN" (e.g., Bīt-Adini, Bīt-Agusi, Beth-Rehob, Beth-David), and the "son" (*mār*) of a tribal eponym or of the founder of a dynasty is called (in the Assyrian royal inscriptions) "son (of Bīt)-PN" (Liverani 1961; Sader 1987: 272–273; Rendsburg 1995; Na'aman 1995: 19–24). Bīt-Ḫumri, "the house of Omri," is a designation for the Kingdom of Israel after the founder of its dynasty; Jehu's affiliation (*Iu-ú-a mār Ḫumri*) in Shalmaneser's inscriptions, accordingly, may be rendered "Jehu son of (Beth)-Ḫumri."

No other Israelite king is designated "*mār* PN" in the Assyrian royal inscriptions. Ahab is called "the Israelite," and Joash and Menahem are designated "the Samarian." Moreover, the Assyrians were certainly aware that Jehu seized the throne by force and that he was an illegitimate ruler. Why did they call the usurper by a designation that conveys a message of continuity with the former dynasty of Israel?

Schneider has recently suggested that Jehu was the descendant of some branch of the Omride dynasty, a suggestion that, in her opinion, may explain his important position in the Israelite army and his designation as "son of Omri" (Schneider 1995; 1996). However, Jehu was the son of Jehoshaphat and

1. Reprinted with permission. *Israel Exploration Journal 48* (1998), 236–238.

2. For the rendering of the name as *Iu-ú-a*, rather than the accepted form *Ia-ú-a*, see Na'aman 1997; Zadok 1997.

the grandson of Nimshi (2 Kings 9:2, 14). At the most, he could have been a remote relative of Joram, son of Ahab, the reigning king of Israel. Moreover, as demonstrated below, the Assyrians did not consider usurpers affiliated with an eliminated royal house as legitimate kings. The theory that Jehu was dynastically affiliated with the house of Omri is not well founded and does not explain adequately the Assyrian references to the usurper as *mār Ḫumri*.

Unlike Jehu, Hazael of Damascus, who illegitimately seized the throne of Damascus, is called "son of a nobody" (*mār la mammana*) (Michel 1954:57 line 26). Surri of Patina, who, like Jehu, killed the reigning king and seized the throne, is described as a ruler "who has no right to the throne" (*la bēl kussi*) (Michel 1955–1956b:226 line 151). Marduk-bēl-usate, who revolted against his elder brother Marduk-zakir-shumi, is designated in the Assyrian sources (the Synchronistic History and the Balawat Gate inscription of Shalmaneser III) as "the usurper" (*šar ḫamma'i*).

The three kings described by Shalmaneser III as usurpers were all his enemies. Their negative portrayal was deliberately selected to discredit them and to justify the Assyrian operations against them. Of the three usurpers, Marduk-bēl-usate was the younger brother of the reigning king. Hazael was, apparently, of a royal family, as indicated by the new Aramaic stela from Tel Dan, in which he refers three times to his predecessor as "my father" (Biran and Naveh 1995:9–11, 17–18 and n. 26; Yamada 1995:613; Na'aman 1995). The origin of Surri is unknown. It is clear that royal ancestry played no part in the Assyrian designation of a king as usurper. What mattered was the propagandistic objects of the Assyrian king in the inscriptions he wrote.

With this background in mind, Jehu's designation as *mār Ḫumri* is easily explained. Ahab and Joram, his predecessors on the Israelite throne, were enemies of Assyria and participated in the coalition of kings that fought against Shalmaneser in the years 853, 849, 848 and 845 BCE. When Jehu seized the throne, he immediately reversed the former anti-Assyrian policy of the Omrides. He refused to cooperate with Hazael, the new king of Aram, so that the latter was forced to stand alone against the advancing Assyrian troops (841 BCE). When, in that year, the Assyrian army reached the northern border of Israel, Jehu surrendered and paid his tribute. No wonder Shalmaneser looked upon him favourably. Although Shalmaneser must have been aware of Jehu's non-royal origin, his description of the king was motivated by the desire to portray him positively and to legitimize his reign. The designation selected for Jehu, *mār Ḫumri*, fulfilled these requirements. On the one hand, the designation presented Jehu as a ruler of the kingdom called by the eponymic/dynastic name "Bīt Ḫumri," and, on the other, it described him as a "son" of the former dynasty, thereby legitimizing him and acknowledging his new policy towards Assyria.

References

Biran, A. and Naveh, J. 1995. The Tel Dan Inscription: A New Fragment. *IEJ* 45:1–18.

Brinkman, J.A. 1968. *A Political History of Post-Kassite Babylonia 1158-722 B.C.* (Analecta Orientalia 43). Rome.

Kinnier Wilson, J.V. 1962. The Kurba'il Statue of Shalmaneser III. *Iraq* 24: 90–115.

Liverani, M. 1961. Bar-guš e Bar-rakib. *Rivista degli Studi Orientali* 36: 185–187.

Michel, E. 1947. Die Assur-Texte Salmanassars III. (858–824). 2 Fortsetzung. *WO* 1: 5–20, 57–71.

Michel, E. 1949. Die Assur-Texte Salmanassars III. (858–824). 3. Fortsetzung. *WO* 1/4: 255–271.

Michel, E. 1954. Die Assur-Texte Salmanassars III. (858–824). 6. Fortsetzung. *WO* 2/1: 27–45.

Michel, E. 1955–56a. Die Assur-Texte Salmanassars III. (858–824). 7. Fortsetzung. *WO* 2/2-3: 137–157.

Michel, E. 1955–56b. Die Assur-Texte Salmanassars III. (858–824). 8. Fortsetzung. *WO* 2/2-3: 221–233.

Na'aman, N. 1995. Hazael of 'Amqi and Hadadezer of Beth-rehob. *Ugarit-Forschungen* 27: 381–394.

Na'aman, N. 1995. Beth-David in the Aramaic Stela from Tel Dan. *Biblische Notizen* 79: 17–24.

Na'aman, N. 1997. Transcribing the Theophoric Element in North Israelite Names. *Nouvelles Assyriologiques Brèves et Utilitaires.* 1997/1: No 19.

Rendsburg, G.A. 1995. On the Writing *byt dwd* in the Aramaic Inscription from Tel Dan. *IEJ* 45: 22–25.

Sader, H. 1987. *Les états Araméens de Syrie depuis leur fondation jusqu'à leur transformation en provinces Assyriennes.* Beirut.

Schneider, T.J. 1995. Did King Jehu Kill his own Family. *Biblical Archeology Review* 21/1: 26–33, 80.

Schneider, T.J. 1996. Rethinking Jehu. *Biblica* 77: 100–107.

Ungnad, A. 1906. Jaua, mār Ḫumrî. *Orientalische Literaturzeitung* 9: 224–225.

Yamada, S. 1995. Aram-Israel Relations as Reflected in the Aramaic Inscription from Tel Dan. *Ugarit-Forschungen* 27: 611–625.

Zadok, R. 1997. Jehu. *Nouvelles Assyriologiques Brèves et Utilitaires* 1997/1: No. 20.

Forced Participation in Alliances in the Course of the Assyrian Campaigns to the West[1]

Introduction

The Assyrian thrust to the west in the 9th century BCE marked a new political and military situation in the history of the southern Anatolian and Syro-Palestinian kingdoms. This whole area was divided in the 14th-13th centuries BCE between two major powers — Hatti and Egypt — each dominating its own vassals and defending its sphere of influence by fighting external enemies and curbing internal rebellions. These two powers collapsed in the course of the 12th century: the Hittite empire was entirely destroyed and Egypt lost its Asian province and suffered growing internal weakness. The urban culture within the Syro-Palestinian area suffered a heavy blow at that time, and almost all the kingdoms were destroyed, many of them disappearing from the historical arena. The new array of kingdoms that gradually developed in the course of the 11th–10th centuries emerged in a world that was devoid of great powers. The campaigns of Tiglath-pileser I and Ashur-bel-kala to the Mediterranean during the first half of the 11th century were no more than episodes that had no effect on the history of Syria. After the middle of the 11th century, Assyria gradually withdrew from its western and northern provinces, which fell, step by step, in to the hands of the nomadic and semi-nomadic groups, notably the Arameans. From the point of view of the people living west of the Euphrates, Assyria ceased to be a major power for about 150 years. The campaign of Pharaoh Shishak to Palestine in one of his late years (ca. 926 BCE) was likewise no more than an episode that had no long-term effect on the history of Israel and Judah. Thus, no external great power played an important role in the history of southern Anatolia and Syria-Palestine in the 11th–10th centuries. The struggles for hegemony in various parts of this area were fought among kingdoms that either survived the destruction of the "Sea Peoples" or had crystallized during the course of this period.

1. Reprinted with permission. Cogan, M. and Eph'al , I. (eds.), *Ah, Assyria . . . Studies in Assyrian History and Ancient Near Eastern Historiography Presented to Hayim Tadmor.* (Scripta Hierosolymitana 33). Jerusalem (1991), 80–98.

This situation drastically changed with the recovery of Assyria after a long period of external and internal weakness. Assyria started its re-expansion in the days of Ashur-dan II (932–912) and gradually conquered and annexed its lost western territories during the reigns of Adad-nirari II (911–891) and Tukulti-Ninurta II (890–884). It first crossed the Euphrates in the late years of Ashurnaṣirpal II (883–859), threatening to conquer and subdue the neighboring Syrian states.

The appearance of a great power near their borders obliged the western states to find military solutions to the new threat. No single kingdom was able to stand alone against Assyria. Consequently, a coalition of states was formed, in the hope that their common power would equal that of Assyria. Several alliances of this kind are known, e.g., the Syro-Hittite kingdoms that fought Shalmaneser III in his first year (858 BCE); the 12 kingdoms of south Syria and Palestine that fought 4 times against Assyria in the years 853–845; and the Syro-Hittite states that fought Adad-nirari III in 805 BCE. Another solution to the military problem was participation with another great power, whose troops served as a counter-balance to Assyrian military superiority. Alliances of this kind are known in the second half of the eighth century and the first half of the seventh century. A well-known example is the coalition of Syro-Hittite kings, headed by Urartu, that fought Tiglath-pileser III (743 BCE). Egypt and Elam likewise started playing the same role on the Palestinian and Babylonian fronts, beginning in the last quarter of the eighth century BCE.

The fundamental study of these alliances was written by the jubileer in his article "Azriyau of Yaudi" (Tadmor 1961:239–248; Tadmor 1975:36–40). The alliances' historical background was investigated in detail and then compared with similar coalitions that are known from the Old Babylonian period. The role of these leagues in the history of Syro-Palestine in the 9th–8th centuries was amply discussed and clarified. This study served as a point of departure for other scholars investigating the history of the "west" in this period.

As cooperation was the only way to retain independence, it is clear that an all-inclusive participation in the alliances was essential for their members. No wonder that refusal to participate was not acceptable and even may have been regarded as an act of hostility. This is particularly true of the largest and strongest kingdoms, whose armies contributed considerably to the military strength of the alliance. And, indeed, there are several cases in which the leading parties of the south Anatolian and Syro-Palestinian areas tried to enforce participation on refusing kingdoms. This was done by assembling the troops of several states and attacking the unwilling king. Such measures were either intended to force him to change his policy and send his troops to the battlefield or to replace him by someone who was willing to cooperate militarily with his neighbors. It goes without saying that breaking the military power of the refusing king or devastating his country was not intended, because both were essential for the alliance. Such campaigns were directed mainly against the king and his supporters, rather than against the entire kingdom, its army and inhabitants.

It is the purpose of this article to investigate various historical episodes in which kings were attacked because of refusal to participate in an alliance. The article is presented to my teacher, Prof. Hayim Tadmor, who opened the gates to the history of the Assyrian empire for me in his lectures and detailed seminars and who himself has contributed so much to our understanding of the relations of Assyria with the west.

1. *Joram of Israel and Hazael of Aram-Damascus*

Ahab king of Israel participated in the battle of Qarqar in 853 as one of the partners of a coalition of 12 (or 11) members. The league was headed by Adad-idri (Hadadezer) of Damascus; the two other most powerful members were Irḫuleni of Hamath and Ahab of Israel. In subsequent years, Shalmaneser conducted three further campaigns to central Syria (849, 848, 845), during which he clashed with the same Syro-Palestinian coalition. A detailed enumeration of the alliance's members appears only in the Kurkh Monolith Inscription of 853; the descriptions of the later alliances are shorter and schematic. However, these coalitions were again headed by Adad-idri of Damascus and Irḫuleni of Hamath and included "twelve kings of the seacoast." Scholars assumed, therefore, that Joram king of Israel (852/1–842/1) carried on the policy of his father, Ahab, and sent his troops to fight the invading Assyrian army (Jepsen 1941/44:154–155; Astour 1971:387; Elat, 1975: 30–31; Lipiński 1979:75–76).

According to biblical tradition, Israel and Aram fought several times in the days of the Omride dynasty. It has been demonstrated, however, that the battles against Aram — assigned by the editor(s) of the books of Kings to the time of Ahab and Joram (1 Kgs. 20; 2 Kgs. 5–7) — should all be dated to the dynasty of Jehu, more accurately to the days of Jehoahaz and Jehoash.[2] The authenticity of the battle of Ramoth-gilead (1 Kgs. 22), in which Ahab was wounded and died, is in dispute, and many scholars believe that such battle never took place (Jepsen 1941/44:155–156; Whitley 1952:147–149; Miller 1966: 444–448; 1968:339–341; Astour 1971:387; Lipiński 1979:76–78; de Vries 1980; Rofé 1988:142–152). Be it as it may, it is clear that there were peaceful rela-

2. The fundamental study of this problem was written by Jepsen 1941/44:155–158. For further discussions, see Whitley 1952; Miller 1966; 1968; Lipiński 1969; Schmitt 1972:60–63; Rofé 1988:63–74.

tions between Israel and Aram-Damascus throughout the time of the Omride dynasty and that the two kingdoms fought in an alliance against the common enemy, the king of Assyria.

In view of this picture, it is surprising to find Joram, king of Israel, defending his kingdom against Aram in his last year(s). 2 Kgs. 9:14b: "Now Joram with all Israel had been on guard at Ramoth-gilead against Hazael king of Syria." Joram went to war with his close ally Ahaziah, the son of Jehoram king of Judah (2 Kgs. 8:28), and was wounded in battle (2 Kgs 8:28; 9:15). While he returned to be healed, the army continued to stay at Ramoth-gilead in a state of alert, expecting another Aramean attack (2 Kgs 8:29; 9:1–5, 11–16).

The change in the relations of the two kingdoms is the result of the coup of Hazael, who murdered Adad-idri (Hadadezer), the head of the alliance, and crowned himself in Damascus (2 Kgs 8:7–15).[3] Alliances in the ancient Near East were made between dynasties, and, with the cessation of the dynasty, the agreement came to an end. The enthronement of Hazael marked the end of the alliance that successfully fought Shalmaneser in years 853–845. This is evident from Shalmaneser's inscription, which describes the campaign of his 18th *palû* and mentions Hazael of Damascus as the only enemy (Oppenheim, 1969:280, with earlier literature; Lipiński 1979:77–78, note 89, with earlier literature). Hamath and Israel, Aram's former allies, did not take part in the battle. From a later inscription of Sargon II, we can infer that Hamath surrendered to Assyria, apparently without battle.[4] It is, therefore, logical to assume that Joram, likewise, refused to send his troops and, thus, was attacked by Hazael, who tried to force him to join his army against the invading Assyrians. Though Joram was wounded in the battle, the Israelite army was able to curb the attack. The Assyrian campaign of 841 soon forced the Arameans to retreat and defend their own territory, and the Israelite army stayed home on alert.[5]

Jehu, one of Joram's commanders, took advantage of the situation, rushed with his troops and killed Joram, his family and his supporters, as well as his close ally, the king of Judah. It must be remembered that Joram was an enemy of Assyria for almost a decade; eliminating the anti-Assyrian party

3. For the usurpation of Hazael as is witnessed by Shalmaneser's summary inscription, see Oppenheim 1969:280b; Michel 1947:57–61.

4. Finet 1973:12–13, note 48; Hawkins 1982:393. The new text proves that Astour's presentation of Hamath as an independent state that came to an agreement with Assyria (1971:note 3, 384) is untenable. Following the campaign of 841 BCE, Hamath became a vassal state, like all the other Syro-Hittite kingdoms.

5. Astour's suggestion (1971:383–389) that Joram was wounded while fighting the Assyrians (and not the Arameans) is not convincing. His explanation for Hosea 10:14 is open for criticism; see Elat 1975:31–32, note 25; Lipiński 1979:76, note 83.

in both Israel and Judah may well have been one of the motives behind the rebellion of 841 (Astour 1971:388). When the Assyrian army arrived to the Israelite border, Jehu immediately surrendered and paid the tribute.[6] Thus, a new Israelite policy was initiated, characterized by submission and loyalty to the great power in the east. Enmity of the close neighbor in the north, Aram-Damascus, was the immediate result of the new policy. No wonder that the Israelite-Aramean relations in the time of the dynasty of Jehu were entirely different from those of its predecessor, the dynasty of Omri — subjugation and vassaldom took the place of an alliance, and enforced participation in campaigns replaced the cooperation by free will.

2. Zakkur of Hamath and Bar-Hadad of Aram-Damascus

The campaigns of Adad-nirari III to the west have been the subject of many articles since the publication of the Tell ar-Rimaḥ stele in 1968 (Dalley 1968:139–153; Lipiński 1979:80–93, with earlier literature in notes 117–120; Hawkins 1982:399–405). The place of the episode of Zakkur, king of Hamath and Luʿash, within the chain of events was sometimes discussed in these treatments. Zakkur's inscription relates the story of the siege of his capital city, Hadrach, by a coalition of kingdoms headed by Bar-Hadad, son of Hazael. Among its members were most of the Syro-Hittite kingdoms (Arpad, Que, Unqi, Gurgum; Sam'al, Melid and one or two others, whose names are broken).[7] Arpad (*brgš*) appears first in this list; thus, it may safely be regarded as the leader, second only to Damascus who had assembled the anti-Hamathean coalition. The king of Kummuh is missing, and, as I will suggest, this is not accidental.[8]

Of all the Syro-Hittite states, Kummuh was the only one that did not take part in the struggle against Assyria in the 9th–8th centuries (Hawkins 1974: 79–80, with earlier literature; 1983:338–340, with earlier literature). Qatazilu, king of Kummuh, paid his tribute both to Ashurnaṣirpal II and Shalmaneser III. Significantly, he did not participate in the alliance that fought Shalmaneser in his first campaign to the west (858). Moreover, Qatazilu is the only king, who, in the next year (857), paid Shalmaneser a relatively low yearly tribute, whereas other kings paid him both a heavy subjugation tribute and yearly tribute (Craig 1886/87:210–213, lines 21–30; Luckenbill 1926:

6. For the tribute of Jehu, see Lipiński 1979:77–78, notes 90–91, with earlier literature; Tadmor 1961:146–147; Elat 1975:32–34; Green 1979:35–39.

7. For translation of the text see, e.g., Rosenthal 1969:655–656; Gibson 1975:6–17; Lipiński 1978:229–232.

8. Hawkins 1982:400, 403. Gibson's tentative restoration of the name Kummuh in line 8 (ibid., 14) is not well founded.

§601). The same policy of submission and loyalty to Assyria was continued by Ushpilulme, king of Kummuh, in the days of Adad-nirari III and Shalmaneser IV. According to the Pazarcik stele, Adad-nirari crossed the Euphrates at the instigation of the king of Kummuh and, at Paqarḫubuna, defeated a coalition of eight kings headed by Atarshumki, king of Arpad (Millard and Tadmor 1973:57–61; Hawkins 1972–75:157; 1983:338–339).[9] The similarity of this alliance to that cemented by the king of Damascus against Zakkur is hardly accidental. One may suggest that the Assyrian offensive in the early days of Adad-nirari brought about the crystallization of a coalition of the Syro-Hittite states under the leadership of the king of Arpad. Ushpilulme of Kummuh refused to participate in the league and, thus, was attacked. At his call for help, Adad-nirari crossed the Euphrates and defeated the alliance. He further established the border between Kummuh and Gurgum, certainly in favor of the former (Hawkins 1972:157; 1983:339; 1982:400).

The Zakkur Stela reflects a similar situation: Bar-Hadad of Damascus tried to crystallize an anti-Assyrian alliance, but was confronted by the refusal of Zakkur, king of Hamath. "Persuasion" by force soon took the place of negotiation.

The date of the siege of Hadrach is in dispute among scholars, and several solutions have been offered. We may safely dismiss the old proposal to date the episode later than Adad-nirari's campaigns to the west, because, at that late time, Damascus had lost its hegemonic standing in the area (Lidzbarski 1915:8–9; Kraeling 1918:101–102; Noth 1929:128–130; 1937:48; Albright 1942: 23–25; Millard 1962:42–43; 1973:163–164; cf. Unger 1957:85–89). One possible solution is to date the event shortly before 796 BCE, on the eve of Adad-nirari's campaign against Damascus (Jepsen 1941/44:164–170; Mazar (Maisler) 1948:126–127; Mazar 1962:111, note 29; Lipiński 1971:393–399; 1979:88–93; Ikeda 1977:208–209; Hawkins 1982:400, 403–404; Lemaire 1984: 346–347). According to this hypothesis, Damascus tried to re-establish its hegemony in the Syro-Palestinian area after the Assyrian retreat from the west in 803. The king of Hamath was attacked, because he had refused to participate in the coalition. The campaign of 796 was directed against Damascus and is the historical background for the "miraculous deliverance" of Zakkur from his strong enemies (Jepsen 1941/44:170; Lipiński 1971:397–399; 1979:93, note 141; Hawkins 1982:403–404).

However, it is inconceiveable that Arpad and her allies were able to join Bar-Hadad of Damascus several years after they were defeated in battle (805) and subdued by Adad-nirari (805–803). Crystallization of an alliance in which

9. [The Pazarcik stela was published by Donbaz 1990:8–10.]

Anatolian kingdoms like Melid and Gurgum took part hardly suits a date after 803. Furthermore, no coalition of states is mentioned in the part of Adad-nirari's inscriptions that describes the attack on Damascus in 796.[10] For these reasons, another solution has been offered: the "miraculous deliverance" should be placed shortly before 805, i.e., prior to Adad-nirari's Syrian expeditions. Such an early date would fit a Syro-Hittite coalition headed by Aram and Arpad (Dupont-Sommer 1949:47; Cazelles 1969:113; Millard and Tadmor 1973:63 –64).

However, Adad-nirari's campaign of 805 was directed against the Syro-Hittite coalition headed by Arpad and, according to the Pazarcik stele, was conducted at the instigation of the king of Kummuh. The decisive battle was fought at Paqarḫubuna, near the northern border of Kummuh. The "miraculous deliverance" of Zakkur hardly can be combined with the events of 805 BCE. It seems that the episode described in the Zakkur Stela reflects the efforts of Damascus to unite an all-inclusive Syro-Hittite coalition against Assyria immediately after the defeat of the northern alliance in 805. This may explain the initiation of Damascus and its leading role in the new coalition. One may assume that, following the battle of Paqarḫubuna, it became clear that even a partial coalition of kingdoms was not strong enough to hold back the Assyrian war machine. Thus, Bar-Hadad tried to consolidate an overall Anatolian-Syrian (and Palestinian?) coalition that would fight Assyria. Zakkur of Hamath, possibly encouraged by the events of the 805 campaign, refused to join the alliance and was attacked. The Assyrian campaigns of 804–803 forced the Syro-Hittite kingdoms to hurry northward to defend their homeland and, thus, Hamath was saved. The details of the Assyrian campaigns remain unknown, though Damascus, the strongest kingdom in Syria at that time, must have played an important role in the chain of events.

3. *Jehoash of Israel and Bar-Hadad of Damascus*

Two sieges of Samaria by Bar-Hadad king of Aram are described in the books of Kings (1 Kgs. 20:1–21; 2 Kgs. 6:24–7:20). Both may be classified as prophetic legends. The former was assigned by the editor(s) of the book of Kings to the days of Ahab, and the latter was attached to the description of the days of Joram, his son. However, scholars have demonstrated that both should be dated to the time of the Jehu dynasty (see above, note 2). The evidence for the re-dating of these episodes is so conclusive that no further

10. For the campaign of 796 against Damascus in Adad-nirari's summary inscriptions, see Dalley (Page) 1968:142:6–7; Tadmor 1973:145:18–20; 148–149:14–21. Cf. Millard and Tadmor 1973:61–64; Tadmor.1973:147–148.

comments are necessary. Assigning both to the time of rulers of this dynasty — either Jehoahaz or Jehoash, as scholars suggested — is the point of departure for our discussion.

The two stories differ in the point of interest of their respective narrators.[11] The might of the Lord who can deliver his people by the hand of few, as against the military power of human beings, is the central motif of the first legend (1 Kgs. 20:13, 28). To illustrate this, the narrator emphasized the enormous military strength of Aram on the eve of the two battles (vv. 1, 10, 13, 18, 25, 28, 29), as against the overwhelming inferiority of the Israelites (vv. 2–9, 14–15, 27). The prophecy of Elisha and its embodiment by a miraculous act of the Lord are the essence of the second legend. The narrator described in great detail the inner situation in the besieged city and the harsh time due to the siege; the entire story is immersed with folkloristic and legendary motifs. In spite of the many differences between the two stories, which are well explained by their legendary character and the different outlook of the two narrators, I concur with Lipiński that both refer to one and the same historical event: the siege of Samaria by Bar-Hadad and his allies (Lipiński 1979:85, 90). Indeed, one hardly would think of two miraculous deliverances of the Israelite capital within the reign of the same king of Aram.

Two parallel descriptions are presented for the beginning of the siege. 1 Kgs. 20:1: "Ben-Hadad the king of Syria gathered all his army together; thirty two kings were with him, and horses and chariots; and he went up and besieged Samaria and fought against it." 2 Kgs. 6:24: "Afterward Ben-Hadad king of Syria mustered his entire army, and went up and besieged Samaria." A major campaign against Samaria was undertaken, in which the king of Aram and his vassals took part. This brings to mind the inscription of Zakkur, in which the siege of Hadrach by an alliance of kings headed by Bar-Hadad of Aram is portrayed.[12]

What may be the date of the siege of Samaria? Lipiński (1979:81–93) suggested that Jehoahaz was an Aramean vassal and that it was his son, Jehoash, who took advantage of the Assyrian campaigns of 805–804 to Syria and rebelled. Bar-Hadad reacted by besieging Samaria. The Assyrian campaign of 803 was conducted against Damascus, and the Aramean king was forced to retreat to defend his kingdom. After his victory over the Arameans, Adad-

11. For alternative presentations of a particular situation in different accounts, see Ackroyd 1968.

12. A different interpretation for the 32 kings mentioned in 1 Kgs. 20:1 was suggested by scholars, who assumed that the prophetic legend refers to an event of the time of Ahab. See Alt 1934:245–248 (= 1959:223–225); Mazar 1948:106–107; Gray 1970:420–422. For criticism, see Jepsen 1941/44:169, note 48.

nirari proceeded southward and reached the northern border of Israel (Ba'li = Ba'li-ra'si). There Jehoash paid him the tribute that is mentioned in the Tell ar-Rimaḥ Stela (Dalley 1968:142:8, 144–145, 148–149). Soon after the Assyrian retreat (802 BCE), Bar-Hadad tried, for the second time, to invade Israel. This time he was defeated at Aphek (1 Kgs. 20:23–34; 2 Kgs 13:17). A treaty then was signed between the two rivals, in which the strength and achievements of Jehoash were recognized officially by the king of Aram (1 Kgs 20:31–34).

There are several points with which I agree in this historical reconstruction. The king of Israel in whose time Samaria was besieged must have been Jehoash. This is evident from what is said about the battle of Aphek: it was conducted one year after the siege (1 Kgs. 20:26) and was won by Jehoash (2 Kgs. 13:17). The secondary nature of the passage that refers to Jehoahaz' repentance and Israel's delivery from the hand of Aram (2 Kgs. 13:4–5) is also clear.[13] The verses (and also v. 23) came from the quill of a post-exilic editor who wanted to exemplify, to his own generation, the power of repentance. The transition from the time of Jehoahaz, in whose days Israel reached its lowest ebb (2 Kgs. 13:3, 7, 22), to the time of Jehoash, when Israel recovered and started the anti-Aramean offensive (2 Kgs. 13:14–25), fitted his theological lesson perfectly. Thus, he expanded vv. 2–3 and formed a description that has the typical structure of the stories of the book of Judges and ends with a delivery from the hands of the oppressing enemy (see McCarthy 1973:409–410; Rehm 1982:129). The identity of the "savior" is disputed among scholars.[14] One may very much doubt whether Adad-nirari III is intended, because the late Judaean editor hardly knew either his name or his relationship to these events. We may conclude that Israel's liberation from the Aramean yoke started in the days of Jehoash son of Jehoahaz (800–786/5).

Lipiński's proposed identification of Ba'li, mentioned in the Eponym Chronicle for 803 BCE, with Ba'li-ra'si of Shalmaneser III's inscriptions is possible, though cannot be verified.[15] Ba'li-ra'si was safely identified with Mt. Carmel, which marked the border between Tyre and Israel (Aharoni 1970:1–7; Astour 1971:385–388 and note 16). It was suggested above that Damascus was deeply involved in the struggles of the years 804–803 against Assyria, and Adad-nirari may well have reached the northern border of Israel after he

13. This was commonly accepted by all scholars. See, e.g., Montgomery 1951:433–434; Lipiński 1979:84–85; Rehm 1982:128–130, with earlier literature.

14. For a survey of the suggestions offered for the identity of the deliverer, see Gray 1970: 594–595; Lipiński 1979:88, note 129; Rehm 1982:129–130.

15. Lipiński 1969:165–166; 1971:84–92. For a survey of the literature on the identification of Ba'li-ra'si and Ba'li, see Puech 1981:550–552, notes 34, 41.

defeated his enemies. The kingdoms located on both sides of the Jordan immediately surrendered: they were only too happy to become vassals of the remote king of Assyria, rather than remaining vassals of their next-door oppressing neighbor, the king of Aram.

However, the relief was only temporary. Assyria was absent from the west in years 802–797 BCE, and Damascus had enough time to recover and to try to regain its former influence. The Syro-Hittite states were under Assyrian rule, and the crystallization of a new Syro-Anatolian coalition hardly was possible at that time. Bar-Hadad tried to strengthen his position by restoring his former alliance of subjugated kingdoms in South Syria and Palestine, but encountered the refusal of Jehoash, Israel's new king, to take part in the anti-Assyrian league. The latter may well have addressed the king of Assyria for help.

It is against this background that the siege of Samaria (ca. 797/6) — in which the king of Aram and his allies (1 Kgs. 20:1) participated — should be interpreted. In spite of the inferiority of his troops, the military pressure and the severe famine, Jehoash stubbornly resisted, hoping, no doubt, for the intervention of Assyria. The help indeed came in time: the Assyrian army under the command of Nergal-eresh marched against Damascus (796 BCE).[16] The troops of Aram and her allies left Samaria in haste (2 Kgs. 7:3–16). The sudden retreat was interpreted in the prophetic legend as a miraculous deliverance by the hand of the Lord (2 Kgs. 7:6; compare 2 Kgs. 19:35). In the first story (1 Kgs. 20:13–21), the same episode was portrayed as a miraculous victory of the few over the many.

Historically, the circumstances of the campaign of 796 were not dissimilar to those of Shalmaneser III's campaign of 841: Damascus alone was unable to withstand the Assyrian war machine and was defeated in battle, possibly in the Valley of Lebanon (near Manṣuate).[17] Bar-Hadad surrendered and paid a heavy tribute to save his kingdom from devastation.

16. For the place of Nergal-eresh in the 796 campaign, see Dalley 1968:150–151; Tadmor 1973:147–148. Hawkins' assumption (1982:403–405) that Shamshi-ilu played an important role in the campaign is problematic. The latter held the office of *turtānu* in 780, 770 and 752, and his office may well have been terminated by Tiglath-pileser III after 745 (Hawkins 1982: 404). It hardly is conceiveable that he was *turtānu* for a term that exceeded 50 years. One may suggest that he was nominated during the later years of Adad-nirari III, his intervention in the boundary dispute between Arpad and Hamath in favor of the former (Hawkins 1982:400, 404) taking place about the same time. His anti-Hamathean policy may well have provoked the change in the relations of Assyria and Hamath since that time, as is evident from the three campaigns launched by the Assyrians against Hadrach in 772, 765 and 755 (see below).

17. Various suggestions have been offered for the exact location of Manṣuate. See the comprehensive discussion of Lipiński 1971:393–398, with earlier literature in notes 9–15; Millard and Tadmor 1973:63, note 21; Zadok 1977/78:56, with earlier literature.

The next stage in the chain of events was probably initiated by the king of Israel. In the following year (795 BCE; see 1 Kgs. 20:26), Jehoash took advantage of the Aramean defeat and attacked. The two armies clashed near Aphek, a city whose location is not clear.[18] The Aramean army, severely weakened by the struggle with Assyria, was unable to curb the Israelite offensive and suffered a second defeat (1 Kgs. 20:26–30; 2 Kgs. 13:17). As a result of his victory, Jehoash regained all the former Israelite territories (2 Kgs. 13:25) and acquired a privileged status in the capital of Israel's former overlord (1 Kgs. 20:34).

Summing up the discussion, it seems that three episodes of enforced participation in alliances are known from the time of Adad-nirari's campaigns to the west:

(a) On the eve of the Assyrian campaign of 805, the Syro-Hittite kingdoms, under the leadership of Arpad, tried to force Kummuh to participate in the league. Kummuh was rescued by the intervention of Adad-nirari, who defeated the allies at Paqarḫubuna.

(b) Following the Assyrian victory of 805, Bar-Hadad of Damascus, while trying to organize a larger coalition that might stand against Assyria, attacked Zakkur of Hamath, who refused to participate in that stand. Hamath was rescued by the Assyrian campaigns of 804–803 BCE.

(c) Following these campaigns, Bar-Hadad tried to re-unite his former vassals of the South Syrian-Palestinian area, attacking Jehoash of Israel, who refused to join him. Israel was rescued by the Assyrian campaign against Aram in 796 BCE. The Aramean defeat at Manṣuate and the heavy tribute paid by Damascus opened the way to a new period in which Israel acquired hegemonic status in its relations with Aram.

4. Kushtashpi of Kummuh and Sarduri II of Urartu

The second half of the eighth century BCE witnessed a new development in the western alliances: a growing trust on the troops of great powers as a counter-balance to the strength of Assyria. This must have been the logical inference from the failure to withstand Assyria in the battlefield. The overwhelming military power of Assyria reached such a peak that even a coalition of many of the western kingdoms was unable to compete with it. The ex-

---

18. For the various localizations proposed for the city of Aphek, see Lipiński 1979:91–92, note 137; North 1960:52–53. No Iron Age city has been discovered in any of the sites that actually are called by the name Aphek. As the name is so common in the Syro-Palestinian toponymy, one hardly can be certain as to the exact location of the city mentioned in 1 Kgs. 20:26–30 and 2 Kgs. 13:17.

ternal powers that became involved in the fighting were Urartu in the north, Egypt in the south-west and Elam in the east. That this was conceived as a new stage in the history of the wars is indicated by the appearance of a new term, *kitru*, by which the scribes of the Assyrian royal inscriptions derogatorily started to call the anti-Assyrian alliances that were concluded between enemy kings (Liverani 1982:43–66).

The new alliance that Tiglath-pileser III met in his first campaign to the west (743 BCE) included Urartu and the Syro-Hittite kingdoms. A few years earlier (ca. 746 or 745), Sarduri II of Urartu attacked Kummuh, destroyed several important cities (Uita, Ḫalpa and Parala) and subdued Kushtashpi, its king, who was forced to pay him a heavy tribute (Astour 1979:73–74, with earlier literature). One may suggest that the destructive campaign conducted against Kummuh and the emphasis on its subjugation by Sarduri were the outcomes of its long standing pro-Assyrian policy and that by this means Kushtashpi was "persuaded" to join Urartu.

According to Tiglath-pileser's summary inscriptions, Sarduri of Urartu "made common cause with Mati'ilu of Bīt-Agusi (Rost 1893:50, lines 29–31; see 44, lines 20–21). By joining the new alliance, the king of Arpad had transgressed his former treaty with Assyria. Tiglath-pileser's campaign of 743 was directed against this powerful coalition that endangered the entire Assyrian supremacy in the west.

The decisive battle was waged "between Kishtan and Ḫalpi" in the land of Kummuh.[19] The list of participants, according to the fragmentary inscriptions of Tiglath-pileser, includes Urartu, Melid and Gurgum.[20] Kummuh was subdued by Sarduri, and the battle was waged in its territory. Thus, scholars assumed that Kummuh took part, possibly unwillingly, in the anti-Assyrian alliance (Garelli and Nikiprowetzky 1974:110–111; Astour 1979:8; Hawkins 1974:339; Weippert 1982:2, 396). However, according to the (yet unpublished) stele of Tiglath-pileser III from Iran, the king of Kummuh seems to have directed the Assyrian king to the place of the Urartian camp.[21] It is evident that Sarduri's attack on Kummuh, a long standing loyal vassal of Assyria, was an important motive for the Assyrian campaign of 743. Kushtashpi, who was

19. Rost 1893:44, line 21; 50–52, lines 31–32; 66, line 47. For the location of Kishtan and Ḫalpi, see Astour 1979:9–14, with earlier literature. The Eponym Chronicle for this year has "A defeat on Urartu was inflicted in Arpad" (see Tadmor 1961:252–254). No appropriate explanation has been offered for the contradiction of sources, unless the scribe of the Eponym Chronicle mistakenly wrote Arpad for Kummuh

20. The kingdom of Tabal also participated in the coalition, according to Tadmor 1982: 422.

21. For the published part of the stele, see Levine 1972:11–24. [The stele was published by Tadmor 1994: 91–110.]

forced to join the anti-Assyrian coalition, seems to have betrayed his allies and helped Tiglath-pileser gain the victory. Indeed, the surprise attack on the Urartian camp decided the fortune of the campaign: Sarduri was severely defeated and fled back to his country, and the way was opened for Assyria to deal with the west without the intervention of the other rival power. Kushtashpi appears, in the first place, in the three tribute lists of Tiglath-pileser of years 740, 738 and 734/33; his position well reflects his status as the most loyal Assyrian vassal in the west.

The place of Hamath in the campaigns of Tiglath-pileser is not entirely clear. Elsewhere, I have suggested that Azriyau was the ruler of Hamath and Hadrach, who led the rebellion against Assyria in 738 and was defeated by the Assyrian king (Na'aman 1974:36–39; Na'aman 1977/78:229–230, 238). According to the Eponym Chronicle, the Assyrians launched three campaigns against Hadrach in 772, 765 and 755 (Ungnad 1938:432). This may well indicate a turn in the policy of Hamath, which was possibly the result of the anti-Hamathean decision of the *turtānu* Shamshi-ilu in the border dispute between Hamath and Arpad (see note 16 above). The growing hostility between Hamath and Assyria, whose policy in the west in the time of Shalmaneser IV, Ashur-dan III and Ashur-nirari V was directed by the powerful *turtānu* (for the career of Shamshi-ilu, see Hawkins 1982:404–405; Lemaire and Durand 1984:37–58, with earlier literature), possibly culminated in the clash of 738 BCE. After the conquest of this kingdom, its northern part was turned into an Assyrian province (Hatarikka), and the southern areas under a new king, Eni-ilu, became tributary to Assyria.

5. *The Syro-Ephraimite War*

The sources for the historical reconstruction of the Syro-Ephraimite war are the Assyrian royal inscriptions and certain biblical passages (2 Kgs. 15:23–31, 37; 16:1–9; Isa. 7:1–9). Tiglath-pileser's annals for the years 734–732 are almost completely lost, and his summary inscriptions are our main external sources. The scope of the alliance and the date and historical background of its crystallization are the main problems debated by scholars.[22] They will be discussed in order to relate the episode more closely to the subject at hand.

It seems reasonable to assume that the plans for the new alliance came into effect with the accession of Pekah to the throne of Israel (736 BCE), after the Assyrian withdrawal from the western front at the end of the 738 cam-

22. The fundamental studies of the Syro-Ephraimite war are Begrich 1929:213–237; Mowinckel 1932:182–195. For further literature, see Weippert 1973:53, note 110. For further discussions, see Cazelles 1978:70*–78*; Tadmor and Cogan 1979:491–508; Lipiński 1979: 97–101.

paign. The murder of Pekahiah, who apparently continued the pro-Assyrian policy of his father (Menahem), and Pekah's coronation were the first steps in the formation of the anti-Assyrian coalition. This fits well with the words of 2 Kgs. 15:37, according to which Rezin's and Pekah's hostile acts against Judah had begun in the days of Jotham, Ahaz's father (749–734). The pressure on Judah at this stage, probably intended to lead to both a change in the Judaean policy towards Assyria and the nomination of a regent who would support their strategy, did not bring the hoped-for results. The new heir to the throne, Ahaz (734/3–715/4), pursued his father's policy and refused to join the anti-Assyrian alliance. He was attacked soon afterward, the attackers trying to take advantage of the transfer of power in the kingdom, hoping either to force the new king to change his policy or to replace him by a rival candidate to the throne (Isa. 7:6).

The leadership of the alliance was held by the king of Damascus, who is mentioned first in the biblical tradition (2 Kgs. 15:37; 16:5, 7; Isa. 7:1, 5, 8–9; 8:6). Small kingdoms in the neighborhood joined Aram and Israel. This is evident from Assyrian accusations of either joining Damascus (e.g., Hiram of Tyre) (Wiseman 1956:125, rev. 5; Borger 1967:639) or of breaking the loyalty oath (e.g., Mitinti of Ashkelon and Samsi, queen of the Arabs) (Rost 1893:36, line 210; 38, lines 235–236). Damascus, Tyre, Israel, Gaza and the Arabs appear side by side in Tiglath-pileser's summary inscriptions and apparently took part in the preparations for rebellion.[23] The Transjordanian kingdoms are mentioned alongside Judah and other vassal kingdoms in the list of tribute payers of 734/3 and did not participate in the alliance. 2 Chr. 28:17 ("For the Edomites had again invaded and defeated Judah, and carried away captives") is probably no more than a rework of the Chronicler of the account of 2 Kgs. 16:6 and cannot be considered as evidence for the participation of Edom in the rebellion and the anti-Judaean expedition.

How could an alliance of such poor military potential hope to stand against the enormous Assyrian war machine? The only explanation that may be offered is that Egypt was also actively involved in the negotiation and that the two leaders had reasonable hopes for Egyptian military aid (this was suggested by Begrich 1929:218). This may well explain the reaction of the Assyrian king to the new danger in the west: a campaign to the Egyptian bor-

23. For the passage in III R 10, 2, see Rost 1893:78–82, lines 5–26 (Damascus, Gaza, Israel, Samsi). ND 400 is either a duplicate or a "long distance join" of II R 67 (Na'aman, 1979:69, note 4). For the texts of ND 400 and II R 67, see Wiseman 1951:23–24; Rost 1893:70, lines 1–2 ([Damascus], Tyre, Israel, Gaza, Ashkelon(?), Egypt, Me'unites, Samsi). For the passage in ND 4301+, see Wiseman 1956:125–126, lines 3–5 (Damascus, Tyre, Israel, Ashkelon(?), Gaza, Samsi, Egypt).

der (naḫal Muṣur = the Brook of Egypt) in order to block the possible advance of the Egyptian troops to the coast of Philistia.[24] This move, dated to 734, decided the fortune of the new alliance. Hanunu of Gaza, one of the members of the coalition, fled to Egypt, only to return soon and become an Assyrian vassal. The "tribute" (i.e., gift) sent by the Egyptian Pharaoh to Assyria, according to Tiglath-pileser's summary inscriptions, may reflect the temporary renouncement of his former plans to send his troops northward. The gift was meant to express goodwill towards his new northern neighbor, the Assyrian kings.[25]

When did the Syro-Ephraimite war and the siege of Jerusalem take place? Did it happen after the Assyrian campaign of 734, or immediately before it? No definite answer can be offered, because the order of events during the Assyrian campaigns of years 734–732 is entirely unknown. The probability, in my opinion, is for the second alternative. The preparation for rebellion, apparently started in ca. 736, culminated with a campaign against the new king of Judah, who refused to take part in the revolt (ca. 734). Tiglath-pileser immediately reacted to this sign of unfaithfulness by conducting a campaign to the coast of Philistia, conquering and destroying cities of the rebels along the route of his advance. The list of tribute payers of 734/3 possibly reflects those who surrendered and swore fealty at that time (Na'aman 1986:81–82, with earlier literature; Aharoni 1970:1–7; Astour 1971:385–388 and note 16).

The campaigns of years 734–732 can probably be taken as one continuous expedition in which Tiglath-pileser was determined to remodel the south Syrian-Palestinian area according to his own plans, just as he had remodeled the south Anatolian-north Syrian area during his campaigns of years 742–738. Indeed, the Judaean historiographer described the episode as one event in which the Assyrian monarch marched to rescue the attacked king of Judah, thus, telescoping the campaigns of 734–732 to one expedition whose climax was the conquest of Damascus and the deportation of its inhabitants (2 Kgs. 16:7–9). Historically, the annexation of Damascus and Israel is directly connected with their attack on Judah, which remained loyal to Assyria. Therefore, one may conclude that, in this particular case, the perspectives of the Judaean historiographer fit well into the overall picture of the campaign,

24. For Tiglath-pileser's campaign to Philistia, see Begrich 1929:218–220; Mowinckel 1932:182–189; Alt 1953:150–162; Tadmor 1964:263–269 1966:87–90; 1972 222–230; Elat 1978: 26–30; Na'aman 1979:68–70, 80–86; Spieckermann 1982:325–330; Borger and Tadmor 1982: 250–251.

25. For the "tribute" of Egypt, see Wiseman 1951:23:20–21; Wiseman 1956:126:23–25. For the restoration of the text, see Tadmor 1964:223.

although the Assyrian king must have many more considerations and motives in this operation than the rescue of his loyal vassal, the king of Judah.

How can we explain the fact that Israel was not annexed in its entirety? It is worth noting that the same policy was applied to the kingdom of Hamath in 738: most of its areas were annexed, but the reduced kingdom of Hamath remained vassal under its new king, Eni-ilu (Na'aman 1974:238–239). The particular policy in the two kingdoms may be explained by their long standing loyalty to Assyria, from the days of Shalmaneser III. That the historical memory of this act of loyalty was remembered in the Assyrian court can be deduced from an inscription of Sargon II relating the annexation of Hamath: "I imposed upon them tribute, the bearing of the basket (and) the service on campaign like that which the kings my fathers imposed upon Irḫuleni of Hamath."[26] S. Dalley (1985:31–42) recently pointed out that the Samarians were treated favourably by Sargon II as well, after the capture and annexation of the city in 720 BCE. The Assyrian policy toward the kingdom of Kummuh is another indication for this assumption. It was shown above that Kummuh was a loyal vassal of Assyria throughout the 9th–8th centuries BCE and never participated willingly in anti-Assyrian coalitions. Indeed, the kingdom was expanded by territories detached by Assyrian kings from Kummuh's neighbors and was the last of the Syro-Anatolian states to be annexed to Assyria (only ca. 708 BCE) (Olmstead 1908:91–96; Naster 1938:59–67; Landsberger 1948:72–79; Tadmor 1958:96; Hawkins 1974:339–340). Therefore, we may suggest that the rebellions against Assyria in Hamath (740) and Israel (734) were regarded by Tiglath-pileser as deviations from the kingdoms' past policy. Both kingdoms were severely punished by drastic reductions of their territories. Nevertheless, they were given another chance to behave "properly." It was only after the next rebellion that they were eliminated and turned into Assyrian provinces.

6. Hezekiah and the Philistine Kingdoms

Upon the death of Sargon II on the battlefield in 705 BCE, rebellions broke out simultaneously in Anatolia, Babylonia and southern Palestine. The unification of Egypt under the kings of the XXVth Dynasty and the new, more aggressive, policy of the Cushite kings toward Assyria opened new opportunities for the anti-Assyrian forces in this area. Hezekiah changed his prede-

---

26. Finet 1973:12–13, note 48, lines 9–12. A similar description appears in a detailed summary inscription of Sargon II relating the annexation of Samaria: "I set my governor over them, and I imposed upon them the (same) tribute as the previous king." See Winckler 1899:100, lines 24–25; Oppenheim, 1969:285a.

cessors' policy of submission and loyalty to Assyria and led a coalition that tried to break the Assyrian yoke.[27]

The military weakness of the small number of kingdoms that survived the western campaigns of Sennacherib's predecessors was a serious obstacle in the way of the new alliance. Hezekiah must have tried to include in his alliance as many kingdoms as possible to broaden his military strength. Refusal to participate was not accepted as the last word, and, in certain cases, he tried to force kingdoms to take part in the rebellion.

One such episode referring to the kingdom of Ekron appears in the annals of Sennacherib that relate the events of year 701: "The officials, the patricians and the (common) people of Ekron — who had thrown Padi, their king, into fetters (because he was) loyal to (his) solemn oath (sworn) by the god Ashur, and had handed him over to Hezekiah, the Judahite — (and) he (Hezekiah) held him in prison, unlawfully, as if he (Padi) be an enemy. . . ." After the conquest of Ekron, Sennacherib "made Padi, their king, come from Jerusalem and set him as their lord on the throne, imposing upon him the tribute (due) to me (as) overlord" (Oppenheim 1969:287b–288a).

The imprisonment of the king of Ekron in Jerusalem illustrates well one of the measures taken against those who refused to participate: the management and power were transferred to the anti-Assyrian party who supported the rebellion.

Another episode is related to Ashkelon: its king, like the king of Ekron, refused to join the rebellion and was deposed and replaced by Ṣidqa, possibly his younger brother (Tadmor 1964:276–277; 1966:96–97).

According to the Bible, Hezekiah "smote the Philistines as far as Gaza and its territory, from watchtower to fortified city" (2 Kgs. 18:8). This description is a précis of the military events that took place on the eve of the battle (Na'aman 1979:67). Significantly, the city of Gaza is not mentioned either in the list of tribute payers near Sidon or in the description of the fighting. On the other hand, the king of Gaza appears among the Philistine rulers to whom Sennacherib assigned Judaean territories at the close of the campaign. Taking into account the strategic position of Gaza on the way to Egypt, the evidence of the cited biblical verse and the fact that the Assyrian army did not immediately march southward to block the route leading from Egypt (as was done by Tiglath-pileser [734] and Sargon [720]), one may assume that Gaza was likewise forced to participate in the anti-Assyrian alliance and that

27. The fundamental studies on Sennacherib's campaign of 701 are Honor 1926; Childs 1967. For recent studies, see Na'aman 1974:34–36; Na'aman 1979:61–86; Na'aman 1986:5–21; Spalinger 1978:33–41; Yurco 1980:221–240; Ussishkin 1982; Kitchen 1983:243–253; Eph'al 1984:60–70; Tadmor 1985:65–80; Vogt 1986.

Egyptian troops were stationed in the city. Thus, the Cushite king was able to send a second task force, headed by Taharqa, to reinforce the troops that were defeated at Eltekeh.[28] Later on, however, the king of Gaza tacitly surrendered to Assyria and, like the other Philistine rulers that were forced to take part in the anti-Assyrian coalition, was treated favourably and even received his share from the territory of the kingdom of Judah. The episode of the city of Gaza was ignored in the official annals, just as the fate of the city of Tyre (Luli's capital) was disregarded: neither was captured by the Assyrian army and, thus, did not fit the literary and ideological conventions of the Assyrian royal inscriptions.[29]

No further anti-Assyrian western alliances are mentioned in the inscriptions of the days of Esarhaddon and Ashurbanipal. This is due to the overwhelming success of Sennacherib in his campaign against Judah. The assumption, so common among scholars, that Sennacherib intended to annex Judah and did not succeed in his goal is not supported by evidence. His policy in the south-western and north-western fronts of the empire was designed to gain a balance of power, not to expand the Assyrian territory. The annexation of Judah would have been regarded as a serious threat in the eyes of the Egyptians and, thus, would hardly fit Sennacherib's policy of reconciliation. He intended, rather, to break and weaken Judah, the strongest kingdom that remained near the Egyptian border. To achieve this, he systematically destroyed as many Judaean places as possible and deported thousands of its inhabitants. The words of the Rabshakeh near the walls of Jerusalem (2 Kgs. 18: 31–32) reflect a plan for mass deportation, as was already taking place in the Shephelah. The severance of large evacuated Judaean territories to its western neighbors is a further step in the same direction (Alt 1929:80–88 [=1953: 242–249]; 1945:145–146 [=1953:240–241]; Na'aman 1974:35–36). A drastic deterioration of urban life at the end of the eighth century was observed in the ar-

28. Na'aman 1979:65; Yurco 1980:224–228. Kitchen (1983:250) correctly observed that "Gaza then served Taharqa as his HQ, as base for operations." However, his assumption that the Cushite prince stayed at Gaza even before the battle of Eltekeh and sent only one of his divisions to battle is not very likely. The pitched, open field battle demanded all the troops available (see Eph'al 1983:91–92), and a commander hardly would let most of his troops stay out of battle. Kitchen's other assumption (1983:250 n.32) that "the two episodes cannot have been more that a week or two apart" is likewise problematic. The siege of the Judaean towns apparently lasted several months (cf. Eph'al 1984:63–64), and the timetable of the campaign hardly suits such an assumption. It is more reasonable to suggest that Taharqa reached Gaza sometime after the battle of Eltekeh and that, in the meantime, the city was held by the division that was defeated at Eltekeh.

29. For the structure and historiographic motifs of the Assyrian account of Sennacherib's campaign, see Tadmor 1985.

chaeological excavations conducted in the Shephelah; the kingdom of Judah did not recover from the Assyrian systematic destruction and depopulation of 701 BCE until the Babylonian captivity.[30] Sennacherib's success in his campaign against Judah enabled his heirs to dominate the western territories without being threatened by local rulers.

Ironically, the biblical historiographers employ entirely different criteria in their judgement of past events than modern historians use and describe Ahaz and Hezekiah in a way that is contrary to their real place in the history of Judah (Ackroyd 1984). Ahaz's policy of loyalty to Assyria and avoidance of participation in anti-Assyrian coalitions — even with the risk of war and siege — kept his kingdom safe and sound in a period of widespread annexations and total loss of political existence. Hezekiah's new policy of trusting the power of Egypt and the formation of anti-Assyrian alliances in order to liberate Judah from the Assyrian yoke[31] brought, in its wake, large-scale destruction and loss of territory and population (compare Isa. 1:4–9; 22:1–7, 12–14; Mic. 1:8–16), achieving nothing less than worse subjection and heavier taxation than previously.

At the close of the discussion I would like to emphasize three points of interest for the subject at hand.

(a) Episodes in which the enforcement was successfully achieved and kingdoms, though unwillingly, joined coalitions were not recorded and may have been lost forever. The scribes of the Assyrian annals and summary inscriptions often ignored this aspect of forced participation, and our historical information is sometimes dependent on casual findings (e.g., local stelae). Thus, there may have been many more cases of enforced participation in alliances than those that have been discussed in this paper.

(b) The motif of conducting campaigns to rescue loyal vassals sometimes appears in the Assyrian royal inscriptions, but is not common. It is not one of the prominent motifs that constituted the formal code designed by the scribes to justify the undertaking of military expeditions. This can be explained by the kind of agreement that Assyria formed with her vassals. Only in a few cases were the relations established by a treaty in which the obligations were formulated in writing. Usually the vassals were bound by an oath sworn before the gods of the two countries to be loyal to Assyria and to ful-

30. Zimhoni 1985:63–90, with earlier literature; Na'aman 1987:12–14. The place of the kingdom of Judah in the northern Shephelah area was taken by the kingdom of Ekron, as is evident from the sudden flourishing of the city in the seventh century BCE.

31. On the plans to form an alliance with Egypt and other neighboring kingdoms in Hezekiah's early years (ca. 713 BCE), see Winckler 1899:188, lines 28–36; Oppenheim 1969: 287a; Na'aman 1974:32 and notes 29–31.

fill all duties incumbent upon them. The relations were more that of imposed vassalage and of dependence (*ardūtu*) than of a treaty (Tadmor 1982:141–152, with earlier literature). Coming to the rescue of attacked vassals was not formally laid on the Assyrian kings, and, therefore, the motif is not common among the fixed set of reasons for conducting campaigns that were formulated by the scribes.

(c) The rarity of the motif in Assyrian historiography does not mean that it was not an important motive in historical reality. To secure the loyalty of vassals even in harsh times and in situations of severe external pressure, it was essential that the vassals could trust the support of the overlord. An attack on a loyal vassal was an ominous sign for his lord, meaning that an anti-Assyrian coalition had been formed. Thus, it was in the interest of Assyria to rescue him and break the power of his enemies before final consolidation. The biblical description of Ahaz addressing Tiglath-pileser by the words "Come up, and rescue me from the hand of the king of Aram and from the hand of the king of Israel, who are attacking me" (2 Kgs. 16:7) and the Assyrian reaction to this plea (v. 7 "And the king of Assyria hearkened to him; the king of Assyria marched up against Damascus, and took it. . . .") faithfully reflect the rescued king's point of view. In this and other cases, the Assyrians indeed came to help the attacked loyal vassal, but treated the case in such radical ways that far exceeded the limited intentions of the latter.

References

Ackroyd, P.R. 1968. Historians and Prophets. *Svensk Exegetisk Åarsbok* 33: 18–54.

Ackroyd, P.R. 1984. The Biblical Interpretation of the Reigns of Ahaz and Hezekiah. In: Barrick, W.B. and Spencer, J.R. eds. *In the Shelter of Elyon: Essays on Ancient Palestinian Life and Literature in Honor of G. W. Ahlström*. Sheffield: 247–259.

Aharoni, Y. 1970. Mount Carmel as Border. In: Kuschke, A. and Kutsch, E. eds. *Archäologie und Altes Testament. Festschrift für K. Galling*, Tübingen: 1–7.

Albright, W.F. 1942. A Votive Stele Erected by Ben-Hadad I of Damascus to the God Melcarth. *BASOR* 87: 23–29

Alt, A. 1929. Nachwort über die territorialgeschichtliche Bedeutung von Sanheribs Eingriff in Palästina. *PJB* 25: 80–88. (Reprint: Alt 1953: 242–249).

Alt, A. 1934. Die Syrische Staatenwelt vor dem Einbruch der Assyrer. *ZDMG* 88: 233–258 (Reprint: Alt 1959: 214–232).

Alt, A. 1945. Neue assyrische Nachrichten über Palästina und Syrien. *ZDPV* 67:128–159 (Reprint: Alt 1953: 226–241).

Alt, A. 1953. *Kleine Schriften zur Geschichte des Volkes Israel* II. München.

Alt, A. 1959. *Kleine Schriften zur Geschichte des Volkes Israel* III. München.

Astour, M. 1971. 841 B.C.: The First Assyrian Invasion of Israel. *JAOS* 91: 383–389.

Astour, M.C. 1979. The Arena of Tiglath-pileser III's Campaign against Sarduri II (743 B.C.). *Assur* 2: 69–91.

Begrich, J. 1929. Der Syrisch-Ephraimitische Krieg und seine weltpolitischen Zusammenhänge. *ZDMG* 83: 213–237.
Borger, R. 1967. *Handbuch der Keilschriftliteratur* I. Berlin.
Borger, R. and Tadmor, H. 1982. Zwei Beiträge zur alttestamentlichen Wissenschaft aufgrund der Inschriften Tiglathpilesers III. *ZAW* 94: 244–251.
Cazelles, H. 1969. Une nouvelle stèle d'Adad-nirari d'Assyrie et Joas d'Israël. *Compte rendus de l'Academie des Inscriptions et Belles Lettres:* 106–114.
Cazelles, H. 1978. Problèmes de la guerre Syro-Ephraimite. *Eretz Israel* 14: 70*–78*.
Childs, B.S. 1967. *Isaiah and the Assyrian Crisis.* (Studies in Biblical Theology, Second Series 3). London.
Craig, J.A. 1886/87. The Monolith Inscription of Shalmaneser II. *Hebraica* 3:201–232.
Dalley (Page), S. 1969. A Stela of Adad-nirari III and Nergal-ereš from Tell al Rimah. *Iraq* 30: 139–153.
Dalley, S. 1985. Foreign Chariotry and Cavalry in the Armies of Tiglath-Pileser III and Sargon II., *Iraq* 47: 31–48.
Donbaz, V. 1990. Two Neo-Assyrian Stelae in the Antakya and Kahramanmaraş Museums. *Annual Review of the Royal Inscriptions of Mesopotamian Project* 8: 5–24
Dupont-Sommer, A. 1949. *Les* Araméens. Paris.
Elat, M. 1975. The Campaigns of Shalmaneser III against Aram and Israel. *IEJ* 25:25–35.
Elat, M. 1978. The Economic Relations of the Neo-Assyrian Empire with Egypt. *JAOS* 98: 20–34.
Eph'al, I. 1983. On Warfare and Military Control in the Ancient Near Eastern Empires: A Research Outline. In: Tadmor, H. and Weinfeld, M. eds. *History, Historiography and Interpretation. Studies in Biblical and Cuneiform Literatures.* Jerusalem: 88–106.
Eph'al, I. 1984. The Assyrian Siege Ramp at Lachish: Military and Lexical Aspects. *Tel Aviv* 11: 60–70.
Finet, A. 1973. Le trône et la rue en Mésopotamie: l'exaltation du roi et les techniques de l'opposition. In: Finet, A. ed. *La voix de l'opposition en* Mésopotamie. Colloque organisé par I'Institut des Hautes Études de Belgique. Bruxelles: 2–27.
Garelli, P. and Nikiprowetzky, V. 1974. *Le Proche-Orient asiatique. Les empires* Mésopotamiens. Israël. (Nouvelle Clio, l'histoire et ses problèmes). Paris.
Gibson, J.C.L. 1975. *Textbook of Syrian Semitic Inscriptions* 2. Oxford.
Gray, J. 1970. *I & II Kings: A Commentary.* 2nd revised edition. (Old Testament Library). Philadelphia.
Green, A.R. 1979. Sua and Jehu: The Boundaries of Shalmaneser's Conquest. *PEQ* 111: 35–39.
Hawkins, J.D. 1974. Assyrians and Hittites. *Iraq* 36: 67–83.
Hawkins, J.D. 1972–75. Hatti, the 1st Millennium B.C. *RLA* IV: 152–162.
Hawkins, J.D. 1982. The Neo-Hittite States in Syria and Anatolia. *The Cambridge Ancient History* III/1, Cambridge: 372–435.
Hawkins, J.D. 1983. Kummuh. *RLA* VI: 338–340.
Honor, L.L. 1926. *Sennacherib's Invasion of Palestine. A Critical Source Study.* New York.
Ikeda, Y. 1977. *The Kingdom of Hamath and Its Relations with Aram and Israel.* (Ph.D. Thesis). Jerusalem (Hebrew).
Jepsen, A. 1941–44. Israel und Damaskus. *AfO* 14: 153–172.
Kitchen, K.A. 1983. Egypt, the Levant and Assyria in 701 BC. In: Görg, M. ed. *Fontes atque Pontes. Eine Festgabe für H. Brunner* (Ägypten und Altes Testament 5). Wiesbaden: 243–253.
Kraeling, E. 1918. *Aram and Israel* (Columbia University Oriental Studies 13). New York.
Landsberger, B. 1948. *Sam'al. Studien zur Entdeckung der Ruinenstaette Karatepe.* Ankara.

Lemaire, A. 1984. La stèle araméenne de Barhadad. *Orientalia* 53: 337–349.
Lemaire, A. and Durand, J.-M. 1984. *Les inscriptions araméennes de Sfiré et l'Assyrie de Shamshi-ilu*. Genève and Paris.
Levine, L.D. 1972. *Two Neo-Assyrian Stelae from Iran*. Toronto.
Lidzbarski, M. 1915. *Ephemeries für Semitische Epigraphik* 3. Giessen.
Lipiński, E. 1969. Le Ben-Hadad II de la bible et l'histoire. *Proceedings of the Fifth World Congress of Jewish Studies* 1. Jerusalem: 157–173.
Lipiński, E. 1971. The Assyrian Campaign on Manṣuate, in 796 B.C., and the Zakur Stela. *Annali dell'Istituto Orientale di Napoli* 31: 393–399.
Lipiński, E. 1971. Note de topographie historique: Ba'li-Ra'ši et Ra'šu Qudšu. *RB* 78:84–92.
Lipiński, E. 1978. North Semitic Texts from the First Millennium BC. In: Beyerlin, W. ed. *Near Eastern Religious Texts Relating to the Old Testament* (OTL). Philadelphia: 227–268.
Lipiński, E. 1979. Aram et Israël du Xe au VIIIe siècle av. N.È. *Acta Antiqua Academiae Scientiarum Hungaricae* 27: 49–102.
Liverani, M. 1982. Kitru, katāru. *Mesopotamia* 17: 43–66.
Luckenbill, D.D. 1926. *Ancient Records of Assyria and Babylonia* 1. Chicago.
McCarthy, D.J. 1973. 2 Kings 13,4–6. *Biblica* 54: 409–410.
Mazar (Maisler), B. 1948. The Historical Background of the Samaria Ostraca. *JPOS* 21: 117–133.
Mazar, B. 1962. The Aramaean Empire and Its Relations with Israel. *BA* 25: 97–120.
Michel, E. 1947. The Assur-Texte Salmanassars III. (858–824). *WO* 1: 5–20, 57–71.
Millard, A.R. 1962. Alphabetic Inscriptions on Ivories from Nimrud. *Iraq* 24: 41–54.
Millard, A.R. 1973. Adad-nirari III, Aram, and Arpad. *PEQ* 105: 161–164.
Millard, A.R. and Tadmor, H. 1973. Adad-nirari III in Syria. Another Stele Fragment and the Date of His Campaigns. *Iraq* 35: 57–64.
Miller, J.M. 1966. The Elisha Cycle and the Accounts of the Omride Wars. *JBL* 85: 441–454.
Miller, J.M. 1968. The Rest of the Acts of Jehoahaz. *ZAW* 80: 337–342.
Montgomery, J.A. 1951. *A Critical and Exegetical Commentary on the Books of Kings* (ICC). Edinburgh.
Mowinckel, S. 1932. Die Chronologie der israelitischen und jüdischen Könige. *Acta Orientalia* 10: 161–277.
Na'aman, N. 1974. Sennacherib's "Letter to God" on His Campaign to Judah. *BASOR* 214: 25–39.
Na'aman, N. 1977–78. Looking for KTK. *WO* 9: 220–237.
Na'aman, N. 1979a. Sennacherib's Campaign to Judah and the Date of the LMLK Stamps. *VT* 29: 61–86.
Na'aman, N. 1979b. The Brook of Egypt and Assyrian Policy on the Egyptian Border. *Tel Aviv* 6: 68–90.
Na'aman, N. 1986. Hezekiah's Fortified Cities and the KMLK Stamps. *BASOR* 261:5–21.
Na'aman, N. 1987. The Negev in the Last Century of the Kingdom of Judah. *Cathedra* 42: 3–15. (Hebrew).
Naster, P. 1938. *L'Asie Mineure et l'Assyrie aux VIIIe et VIIe siècles av. J.C. d'après les annales des rois assyriennes*. Louvain.
North, R. 1960. Ap(h)eq(a) and 'Azeqa. *Biblica* 41: 41–63.
Noth, M. 1929. La'asch und Hazrak. *ZDPV* 52: 124–141. (Reprint: Noth 1971:135–147).
Noth, M. 1937. Das Reich von Hamath als Grenznachbar des Reiches Israel. *PJB* 33:36–51. (Reprint: Noth 1971: 148–160).
Noth, M. 1971. *Aufsätze zur biblischen Landes- und Altertumskunde I. Archäologische, exegetische und topographische Untersuchungen zur Geschichte Israels*. Neukirchen-Vluyn.

Olmstead, A.T.E. 1908. *Western Asia in the Days of Sargon of Assyria, 722–705 B.C.: A Study in Oriental History.* New York.

Oppenheim, A.L. 1969. Babylonian and Assyrian Historical Texts. In *ANET*: 265–317.

Puech, E. 1981. L'ivoire inscrit d'Arslan Tash et les rois de Damas. *RB* 88: 544–562.

Rehm, M. 1982. *Das zweite Buch der Könige. Ein Kommentar.* Würzburg.

Rofé, A. 1988. *The Prophetical Stories: The Narratives about the Prophets in the Hebrew Bible; Their Literary Types and History.* Jerusalem.

Rosenthal, F. 1969. Canaanite and Aramaic Inscriptions. In: *ANET*: 653–662.

Rost, P. 1893. *Die Keilschrifttexte Tiglath-Pilesers III, nach den Papierabklatschen und Originalen des Britischen Museums* I-II. Leipzig.

Schmitt, H.-C. 1972. *Elisa, Traditionsgeschichtliche Untersuchungen zur vorklassischen nord-israelitischen Prophetie.* Gütersloh.

Spalinger, A. 1978. The Foreign Policy of Egypt Preceding the Assyrian Conquest. *Chronique* d'Égypte 53: 22–47.

Spieckermann, H. 1982. *Juda unter Assur in der Sargonidenzeit* (FRLANT 129). Göttingen.

Tadmor, H. 1958. The Campaigns of Sargon II of Assur: A Chronological-Historical Study. *JCS* 12: 22–40, 77–100.

Tadmor, H. 1961a. Que and Muṣri. *IEJ* 11: 143–150.

Tadmor, H. 1961b. Azriyau of Yaudi. *Scripta Hierosolymitana* 8: 232–271.

Tadmor, H. 1964. The Assyrian Campaigns to Philistia. In: Liver, J. ed. *The Military History of the Land of Israel in Biblical Times.* Tel Aviv: 261–285 (Hebrew).

Tadmor, H. 1966. Philistia under Assyrian Rule. *BA* 29: 86–102.

Tadmor, H. 1972. The Me'unites in the Book of Chronicles in the Light of an Assyrian Document. In: Uffenheimer, B. ed. *Bible and Jewish History, Studies in Bible and Jewish History Dedicated to the Memory of Jacob Liver.* Tel Aviv: 222–230 (Hebrew).

Tadmor, H. 1973. The Historical Inscriptions of Adad-nirari III. *Iraq* 35: 141–150.

Tadmor, H. 1975. Assyria and the West: The Ninth century and Its Aftermath. In: Goedicke, H. and Roberts, J.J.M. eds. *Unity and Diversity. Essays in the History, Literature and Religion of the Ancient Near East.* Baltimore and London: 36–47.

Tadmor, H. 1982a. Treaty and Oath in the Ancient Near East. A Historian's Approach. In: Tucker, G.M. and Knight, D.A. eds. *Humanizing America's Iconic Book: Society of Biblical Literature Centennial Addresses 1980.* Chico.

Tadmor, H. 1982b. Tiglath-Pileser III. *Enc. Miqr.* VIII: 415–430. (Hebrew).

Tadmor, H. 1985. Sennacherib's Campaign to Judah: Historical and Historiographical Considerations. *Zion* 50: 65–80 (Hebrew).

Tadmor, H. 1994. *The Inscriptions of Tiglath-pileser III King of Assyria.* Jerusalem.

Tadmor, H. and Cogan, M. 1979. Ahaz and Tiglath-Pileser in the Book of Kings. Historiographic Considerations. *Biblica* 60: 491–508.

Unger, M.F. 1957. *Israel and the Aramaeans of Damascus.* London.

Ungnad, A. 1938. Eponymen. *RLA* II: 412–457.

Ussishkin, D. 1982. *The Conquest of Lachish by Sennacherib.* Tel Aviv.

Vogt, E. 1986. *Der Aufstand Hiskias and die Belagerung Jerusalems 701 v. Chr.* Rome.

de Vries, S.J. 1980. *Prophet against Prophet: The Role of the Micaiah Narrative (1 Kings 22) in the Development of the Early Prophetic Tradition.* Grand Rapids.

Weippert, M. 1973. Menahem von Israel und seine Zeitgenossen in einer Steleninschrift des assyrischen Königs Tiglathpileser III. aus dem Iran. *ZDPV* 89: 26–53.

Weippert, M. 1982. Zur Syrienpolitik Tiglathpilesers III. In: Nissen H.J. and Renger, J. eds. *Mesopotamien and seine Nachbarn: Politische und kulturelle Wechselbeziehungen im Alten Vorderasien vom 4. bis 1. Jahrtausend v. Chr.* (Berliner Beiträge zum Vorderen Orient 1). Berlin: 395–408.

Whitley, C.F. 1952. The Deuteronomic Presentation of the House of Omri. *VT* 2:137–152.

Winckler, H. 1899. *Die Keilschrifttexte Sargons nach den Papierabklatschen and Originalen neu herausgegeben* I. Leipzig 1899.

Wiseman, D.J. 1951. Two Historical Inscriptions from Nimrud. *Iraq* 13: 21–26.

Wiseman, D.J. 1956. A Fragmentary Inscription of Tiglath-pileser III from Nimrud. *Iraq* 18: 117–129.

Yurco, F.J. 1980. Sennacherib's Third Campaign and the Coregency of Shabaka and Shebiktu. *Serapis* 6: 221–240.

Zadok, R. 1977–78. Historical and Onomastic Notes. *WO* 9: 35–56, 240–241.

Zimhoni, O. 1985. The Iron Age Pottery of Tel Eton and its Relation to the Lachish, Tel Beit Mirsim and Arad Assemblages. *Tel Aviv* 12: 63–90.

Rezin of Damascus and the Land of Gilead[1]

1. The Southern Border of Aram in the Time of Tiglath-Pileser III

The annexation of Aram Damascus (Bīt Ḫazaili) is recorded in two summary inscriptions of Tiglath-pileser III. One is a stone fragment from Calah (Nimrud) (III R 10, 2), known only through paper squeezes made by Layard and published by Smith (1870:pl. 10, 2; see Smith 1875:253. 284). It was recopied by Rost (1893 I:78; II:pl. XXV), who checked the squeezes and published a textual edition. The other inscription is found on a broken tablet unearthed at Calah (ND 4301+) and published by Wiseman (1956:125, Rev. lines 3–4). Tadmor (1962) combined the two fragmented texts (and K 2649 as well) (For K 2649, see Tadmor 1962:117; Borger 1967:639; Oded 1968a:65–66 and pl. 1) to produce a coherent description of the borders of the newly annexed territory, and he added a historical and geographical commentary. His edition and interpretation have been accepted by all scholars save for some minor textual corrections (Walker in: Ottoson 1969:20, n. 30; Weippert 1972:152, 154–155; Kessler 1975:60–61, n. 52).

To introduce the present discussion, I suggest a new translation for the two passages:

(a) "[From] the town of Kashpuna which is on the shore of the Upper Sea [as far as the town of *mi?-in?*]*-ni-te*, the town of *ga-al-'a-/a/-*[*di*] and the town of *a-bi-il-šiṭ-ṭi* which is on the border of Bīt Ḫumri, the widespread [land of Bīt Hazai]li in its entirety, I restored to the territory of Assyria . . ." (III R 10,2) (Tadmor 1962:114–115; Walker in: Ottoson 1969:20, n. 30; Weippert 1972:154–155).

(b) "The widespread [land of Bīt] Ḫazaili in its entirety, from the t[own of Kashp]una as far as the town of Gilea[d and the town of Abel-šiṭṭi which is on the bor]der of Bīt-Ḫumri, I [restored] to the territory of Assyria . . ." (ND 4301+) (Tadmor 1962:117–119; Weippert 1982:405, n. 21).

According to the above textual restorations, the southern border of Aram Damascus (Bīt Ḫazaili) reached the towns of [Min]nite, Gilead and Abel-šiṭṭi. Weippert (1972:152) suggested restoring ^{uru}*A-bi-il-šiṭ-ṭi* and compared it with

1. Reprinted with permission. *ZDPV* 111 (1995), 105-117.

biblical Abel-shittim. As the latter is located in southern Gilead, in Wādi el-Kefrein, east of Jericho,[2] he assumed that it is too far south for the frontier between Aram and Israel. Therefore, he regarded them as different homonymous places. It seems to me that the opposite is the case and that the identity of the two names is an important clue for the correct delineation of Aram's southern border.

The town of Gilead may be identified safely with biblical Mizpeh-Gilead located on the Jabbok river (Gen. 31:48–49), near the northwestern border of the kingdom of Ammon (Judg. 10:17; 11:29). Note that the disjoined names Galeed and Mizpah in Gen 31:48–49 are combined in the place name Mizpeh-Gilead of Judg 11:29 (de Vaux 1941:31–32; Ottoson 1969:24, 27–28, 31–32, 42–43). Mizpeh-Gilead is sometimes identified with Tell el-Maṣfa, northwest of Jerash (Steuernagel 1925:108, 269; Lemaire 1981:44). However, the identification is by no means certain, and, rather, one should look for a site closer to Mahanaim and the Jabbok river on the one hand and the border of Ammon on the other.[3]

In light of these site identifiations, I have suggested restoring the third toponym as [*Mi-in*]-*ni-te* = Minnith (For the cuneiform signs, see Tadmor 1967: 65, n. 29). The town is mentioned once in the Jephtah story (Judg. 11:33) and, generally, is located at Umm el-Ḥanafish (= Umm el-Basatin), near the southwestern border of Ammon.[4]

According to these site identifications, the "widespread land of Bīt Ḫazaili" encompassed the Israelite Transjordanian territories up to the boundaries of Ammon, Moab and Israel. Mizpeh-Gilead and Minnith mark the northwestern and southwestern limits of Ammon, and Minnith and Abel-shittim mark the northheast and northwest limits of Moab. Significantly, of the three towns, only the location of Abel-šiṭṭi is described in reference to a neighboring territory ("on the border of Bīt Ḫumri"). The elaboration is due to the importance of "Bīt Ḫumri" and its role in the two summary inscriptions (III R 10,2 lines 15–19; ND 4301+ rev. lines 9–11). We may conclude that the entire land of Gilead is presented in the Assyrian inscription as a Damascenean territory, contrary to 2 Kgs. 15:29, according to which the Gilead was captured from Pekah, king of Israel.

2. For the identification of Abel-šiṭṭim with Tell el-Ḥammam, see Neef 1984:100-101, with earlier literature in notes 60-61; Slayton 1992.

3. For other identification of Mizpeh-Gilead, see de Vaux 1941:31-33; Abel 1938:390; North 1959: 36; Oded 1968b: 242-243, with earlier literature; Mittmann 1969:66; Kallai 1986: 300-301.

4. For the identification, see Mittmann 1969:71-73, with earlier literature; Hübner 1992: 133-136, with earlier literature.

My analysis of Tiglath-pileser's inscriptions contests the scholarly consensus about the location of the borders of Israel in the third quarter of the eighth century BCE. It calls for a new evaluation of the role of Rezin in the events that preceded the Syro-Ephraimite war and for a reappraisal of numerous biblical border descriptions that show similarity to the delineation of the borders in the Assyrian inscriptions.

2. The Early Career of Rezin of Damascus

Rezin is mentioned in the Bible and in the inscriptions of Tiglath-pileser III.[5] His lineage is unknown. Scholars sometimes assume that he usurped the throne of Damascus, because his home town is given as [*x*]-*ḫa-a-da-ra*, rather than Damascus. The date of his enthronement is not known. He is mentioned for the first time in a list of Anatolian and Syro-Palestinian kings who paid tribute to Tiglath-pileser in the years 740 and 738 BCE (Tadmor 1961:57–58; Cogan 1973; Weippert 1973:33–39; Shea 1978).

The date of the rise of Aram and Israel's decline after the expansion in the days of Joash and Jeroboam II remains unknown. Provided that the oracle on Damascus in Amos 1:3–5 is a realistic portrayal of circumstances at the time of the prophet, the Aramaic offensive began in the late years of Jeroboam II or soon afterward (Vogelstein 1945:19; Cohen 1965:155; Wolff 1969:181–184; Rudolph 1971:130–131; Barton 1980:30–31). Recently, I have suggested reading ". . . and the war(s) of Judah against Israel" in the epilogue to the reign of Jeroboam II (2 Kgs. 14:28) (Na'aman 1993:230–231). Judah's success in its struggle with Israel may be interpreted as an indication of the latter's decline in the time of Jeroboam II.

The inscriptions of Tiglath-pileser III indicate that the Assyrian king regarded the conquered and annexed Transjordanian areas as part of Rezin's territory. Their evidence is consistent with the text of 2 Kgs 16:6: "At that time Rezin, the king of Aram, recovered Elat for Aram, and drove the men of Judah from Elat; and the Edomites (with *qerē*) came to Elat, where they dwell to this day" (for the text, see Barthélemy 1982:406 with earlier literature). The Aramaic expansion to Elat must have followed the subjugation of the Gilead and the Transjordanian kingdoms. The chronological opening "at that time" does not indicate an exact date. Although the episode is included within the history of Ahaz, it interrupts the narrative sequence of v. 5 and 7–9 and may be regarded as a parentheticed note. Rezin's conquest of Elat may have antedated the reign of Ahaz and may have been assigned to Ahaz's time,

5. For discussions and literature, see Oded 1972:161-164; Oded 1976:432-434; Miller and Hayes 1986:323-330; Donner 1986:303-313; Pitard 1987:179-189; 1992.

due to historiographical and theological considerations.

Aram's relationship with the inhabitants of the Gilead prior to the time of Rezin remain a matter of conjecture. What is known is that Hazael and Bar-Hadad subjugated the Gilead (ca. 835–796 BCE) and that the Aramaic influence was strongly felt there, even after the Damascene withdrawal from the area. This is borne out by the linguistic and cultural evidence of the plaster inscription unearthed in a mid-eighth stratum at Tell Deir 'Alla (see Hoftijzer and Van der Kooij 1991, with earlier literature) and the official stone weight and jar measure inscribed in Aramaic discovered in the same stratum (Eph'al and Naveh 1993). How profoundly "Aramaized" was the Gilead in the first half of the eighth century BCE? What was the political attitude of the Gileadites *vis à vis* Aram at that time? Only with an answer to these questions will we have a better understanding of the circumstances that led to the Damascene reconquest of the Gilead in the time of Rezin.

Some scholars suggest that Rezin established "Greater Syria" in the mid-eighth century BCE, similar in scope to the great kingdom of Hazael in the second half of the ninth century BCE. According to this analysis, Rezin annexed all of Israel, except the central hill country, and dominated Philistia and Transjordan (Vogelstein 1945:19–20; Oded 1972:162–164; Miller and Hayes 1986:324–325; Hayes and Irvine 1987:38–39; Irvine 1990:103–106, 298). A critique of the concept of Rezin's "Greater Syria" will appear in the concluding section below.

3. Rezin of Damascus and Pekah of Israel

Pekah's conspiracy against the king of Israel is described thus (2 Kgs. 15: 25): "And Pekah the son of Remaliah, his captain, conspired against him and stroke him in Samaria in the citadel of the king's house *'t 'rgb w't h'ryh*, and with him fifty men of the Gileadites, and slew him and reigned in his stead."

Scholarly attempts to interpret the four enigmatic words ("and Argob and the Arieh") have not met with general acceptance (see Barthélemy 1982: 405 with earlier literature; Viviano 1992). Geller (1976) suggested rendering this phrase as "by the eagle and the lion," i.e., portal figures of sphinxes at the gates of the palace. However, such detail would be an exception within the context of the short, terse accounts of court rebellions in the histories of Israel and Judah. Moreover, the suggestions that biblical *'rgb* is cognate to Ugaritic *hrgb* (which might mean "eagle") and that the sphinx was depicted by the combination of *'rgb*+lion (rather than by the noun "cherub") are not convincing. Another solution should be sought for the incomprehensible words.

Remarkable in the text is the mention of the 50 Gileadites who helped Pekah in his conspiracy. Such detail does not appear in other accounts of court rebellions. Why was it included? The answer may be found in the enigmatic four words which, with all due reserve, I would suggest rendering *'t gbr(y)w w't hkry* ("his mighty men and the Carites"). According to this *ad sensum* textual emendation, *'rgb* is a metathesis of *gbrw*, the *waw* being dropped due to dittography. I further assume that *h'ry(h)* is a scribal error for original *hkry*. The *gibbōrîm* ("mighty men"), as an organized military unit, are attested several times in the Bible (2 Sam. 10:7; 16:6, 9; 20:7; 23:8; 1 Kgs. 1:8, 10; Jer 26:21; Neh 3:16; l Chr. 28:1; 29:24; 2 Chr. 32:3) (see de Vaux 1961:123–124, 218–222; Na'aman 1988:74). The Carites are mentioned in 2 Sam 20:23 and 2 Kgs. 11:4, 19. They must have served as a bodyguard of the king and were possibly of foreign origin.[6] The pair of terms *kārī* and *rāṣîm* in 2 Kgs 11:4, 19 portrays a royal bodyguard composed of local and foreign soldiers. It seems to me that the bodyguard of Pekahiah was depicted by a similar pair of terms, *gibbōrîm* and *kārī* (compare 2 Sam. 20:7; 1 Kgs. 1:10, 38, 44).

The reconstructed text of 2 Kgs. 15:25 runs as follows: "And Pekah . . . his captain (*šālîš*), conspired against him and stroke him in Samaria in the citadel of the king's house, (also) the mighty men and the Carites, and with him fifty men of the Gileadites, and slew him. . . ." The author has mentioned the 50 Gileadites to explain how Pekah was able to overcome the strong bodyguard of Pekahiah. There must have been a fierce battle in the palace with the king and his bodyguard trying to find shelter in the citadel, but finally being vanquished and killed.

According to 2 Kgs. 15:27, Pekah reigned for 20 years. Scholars have observed that Pekah could not have had a reign of 20 years in Samaria, and they have advanced various suggestions to solve the problem. According to one hypothesis, he reigned as a Damascene vassal in Transjordan, in rivalry with the king ruling in Samaria.[7] However, this hypothesis entails the assumption of a long schism in the Northern Kingdom, shortly before its final destruction, and there is no evidence for such an assumption. Furthermore, Pekah is explicitly described as an officer (*šālîš*) of Pekahiah, who conspired against his lord and slew him (2 Kgs. 15:25).[8] The episode is depicted as a *coup d'état* initiated by an ambitious officer, rather than a struggle between two com-

6. The Carites have nothing to do with the Carian mercenaries, who appear in the east only from the late seventh century BCE onward. See Cogan and Tadmor 1988:126, with earlier literature.

7. Vogelstein 1945:5-17, 13-20; Thiele 1965:123-126, with earlier literature in p. 124, n. 6; 1966:87-90; Cook 1964; Shea 1977:21; Miler and Hayes 1986:324; Hayes and Hooker 1988: 54, 60; Irvine 1990:105-106; Becking 1992.

8. For the title *šālîš*, see Mastin 1979:125-154, with earlier literature; Na'aman 1986:71-79, with earlier literature; Schley 1990.

peting kings. Its author used the same vocabulary as in other descriptions of conspiracies in the history of the Northern Kingdom. The "divided kingdom" theory rests solely on the length of Pekah's reign, a datum that can be interpreted in other ways (Na'aman 1986:74–82, with earlier literature in notes 9, 14–16).[9] The theory creates many more problems than it solves and, in my opinion, should best be abandoned. Pekah may have served as a high officer in the Gilead, thus, having a unit of 50 Gileadites under his command. It is definitely possible that his *coup d'état* was initiated and supported by Rezin, although that hypothesis cannot be corroborated. Concrete details of the relationship between Rezin and Pekah prior to the latter's rebellion and enthronement in Samaria are yet to be found.

The earliest evidence for the crystallization of the Syro-Ephraimite coalition is found in the history of Jotham (2 Kgs. 15:37): "In these days YHWH began to send Rezin the king of Aram and Pekah son of Remaliah against Judah." Ben Zvi (1990) suggested that the text reflects a prophetic source that was written before the collapse of the coalition of Aram and Israel. The note is identical in form to 2 Kgs 10:32, the two notes serving as a kind of preface for the more detailed descriptions of the Aramaic offensives under Hazael and Rezin. The years of Jotham's reign are disputed among scholars, and I have suggested dating him to about 749–734 BCE (Na'aman 1986:89). Pekah ascended the throne in about 736 BCE, and the Syro-Ephraimite coalition must have been formed during the years 736–735 BCE.

According to the chronological scheme suggested here, Ahaz ascended the throne in 734 BCE. Upon his enthronement, the young king faced a decision of the utmost importance. He was severely pressed to take part in the coalition under the leadership of Rezin, but refused to join it. Thus, Ahaz was attacked and his capital besieged. Rezin and Pekah tried either to force him to join the coalition or to replace him with the son of Tabeel (Isa. 7:6), certainly a scion of David's House (Oded 1972:161), who had just lost his chance to succeed Jotham as king of Judah and who was willing to join the coalition in exchange for a second chance at the throne. But Ahaz had better judgement and correctly appreciated the risks of joining an anti-Assyrian coalition. He resisted the military pressure and saved Judah from the fate of its northern neighbors.

How can we account for the conflicting words of Tiglath-pileser III's summary inscriptions and 2 Kgs. 15:29? The latter text runs as follows:

"In the days of Pekah king of Israel Tiglath-pileser king of Assyria came and captured Ijon, Abel-beth-maacah, Janoah, Qedesh, Hazor, Gilead,

9. For a recent summary of the evidence, see Olson 1992.

and Galilee, all the land of Naphtali; and he carried the people captive to Assyria."

Commentators have noted that the term Galilee appears here in its late Hebrew, Aramaized form, *haggālīlā* (Cogan and Tadmor 1988:174), and that Gilead does not accord with the list of place names. Thus, it was suggested that the geographical designations Galilee and Gilead are glosses (Montgomery 1951:452; Würthwein 1984:383; Cogan and Tadmor 1988:174). The original text summarized the list of towns by the phrase "all the land of Naphtali." The formula of numerous conquered towns and an inclusive geographical term has an exact parallel in 1 Kgs 15:20 "And Ben-Hadad . . . conquered Ijon, Dan, Abel-beth-maacah, and all Chinneroth, with all the land of Naphtali." It seems that both texts originally mentioned the conquest of "all the land of Naphtali." I would suggest that the text of 2 Kgs. 15:29 was later expanded to encompass the entire "traditional" territory of the Northern Kingdom.

It may further be suggested that the source upon which the author of the Book of Kings (the Deuteronomistic Historian) drew contained only the names of the five captured towns and that he added the summarizing words "all the land of Naphtali." The area of Gilead would not have been included in the source material that came down to the historian.

Gilead is mentioned again in 2 Kgs 10:32–33. Ben Zvi (1990:102–104) has noted that v. 32 reflects a prophetic source, which is different from the numerous archival notes that constituted a major source for the Book of Kings and is closely related to 2 Kgs 15:37. Verse 33, which is written on the basis of the biblical descriptions of conquest and settlement, apparently was composed by a redactor to fill in the missing data of Hazael's attack mentioned in v. 32. The two texts that detailed the fate of Gilead within the history of the Northern Kingdom, thus, are not part of the original Deuteronomistic History.

We may conclude that the Deuteronomistic Historian had no concrete data for reconstructing the history of Gilead. He, thus, left its fate out of his history of the Northern Kingdom. It was only later that a redactor filled in some of the missing gaps by inserting Gilead into 2 Kgs. 10:33 and 15:29.

Against this background, the importance of Tiglath-pileser's inscriptions becomes more clear. They indicate that the entire Israelite territory east of the Jordan was then in Aramaic hands and was annexed to Assyria following the conquest of Damascus in 732 BCE.[10] Whether Rezin officially annexed the Gilead to his territory or held it as a tribute-paying area remains unknown.

---

10. There is no textual support for the assumption that Gilead was the name of an Assyrian province. Alt (1929:238-241) has suggested that Tiglath-pileser's conquests and annexations of 733-732 are the historical background for the mention of "the way of the

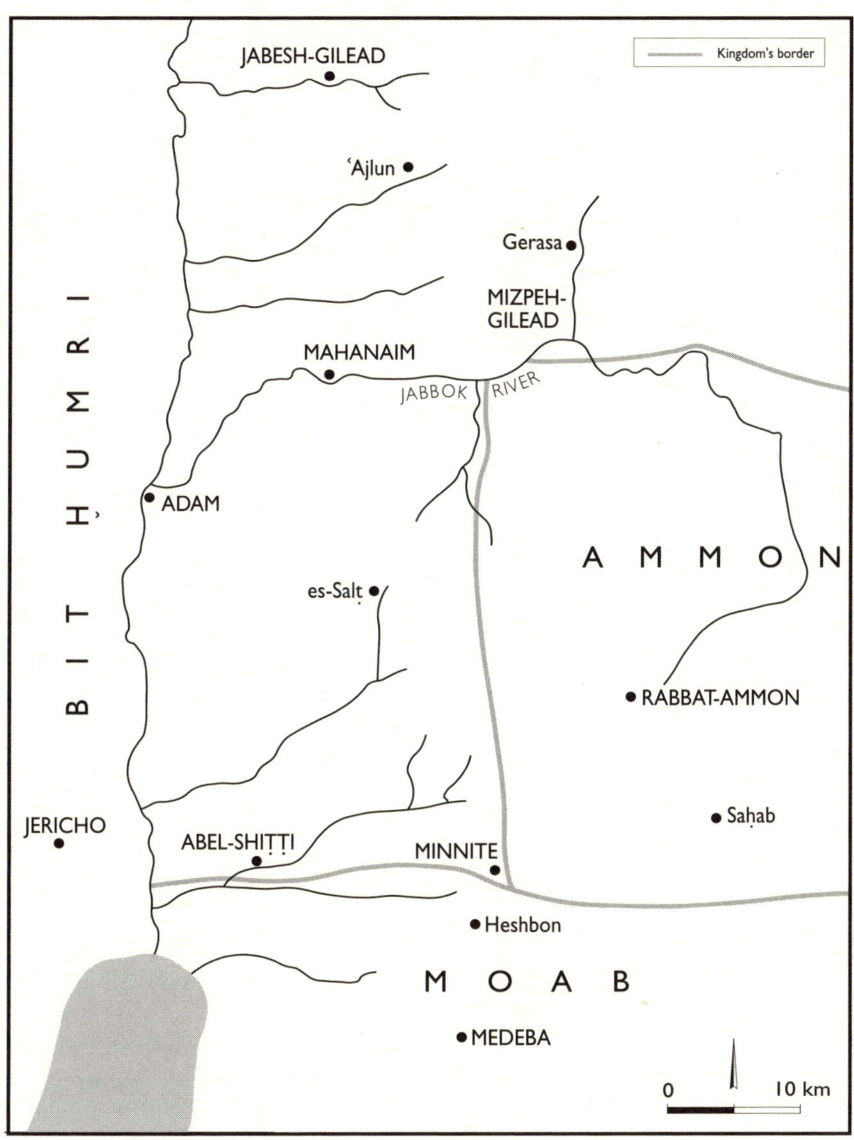

The Land of Gilead in the Late 8th-7th Centuries BCE

4. *The "Southern Border of Aram" in the History of Pre-Monarchial Israel*

Tiglath-pileser III annexed the Transjordanian territory up to the borders of Ammon and Moab, the three border points of Abel-shittim, Mizpeh-Gilead and Minnith becoming key locations on the new boundaries of the empire. The boundary system established by Tiglath-pileser after his conquest apparently followed the earlier configuration of borders and must have survived up to the Assyrian withdrawal from the area during the second half of the seventh century BCE. Indeed, recent investigation into the distribution of Ammonite settlements of the seventh century indicates that this distribution exactly matches the data of the Assyrian inscriptions (Kletter 1991; Hübner 1992:137–157; 330–331). In what follows, I will try to show that this boundary system, which was established no later than the early eighth century and survived at least until the late seventh century BCE, appears in the Bible and can be traced in numerous biblical descriptions that depict pre-monarchial Israel.

(a) The most obvious example is the place of Abel-shittim (or, in its abbreviated form, Shittim) and the Plains of Moab in the narratives of the wandering and conquest. The Plains of Moab, that is, the northern Moabite territory, appear in many accounts as the area where the Israelites encamped before crossing the Jordan (Num. 22:1; 26:3, 63; 31:12; 33:48–50; 35:1; 36:13; Deut. 34: 1, 8; Josh. 13:32). Its counterpart on the other side of the Jordan is called "the plains of Jericho" (Josh. 4:13; 5:10). Abel-shittim is the last station before the crossing of the Jordan and the entrance into the Land of Canaan (Num. 25:1; 33:49; Josh. 2:1; 3:1), and Gilgal and Jericho are the first stations within the Promised Land. The location of *Abel-šiṭṭi(m)* "on the border of Bīt Ḫumri" exactly matches its presentation in the biblical narratives.

(b) The story of Jephthah opens with the mobilization of the two armies and their deployment one against the other (Judg. 10:17): "Then the Ammonites were called to arms, and they encamped in Gilead; and the people of Israel came together, and they encamped at Mizpah." The deploy-

sea, Transjordan, and Galilee of the nations" in Isa 8:23b. He has identified "the way of the sea" and "Galilee of the nations" with the provinces of Du'ru and Magidu, reconstructing a single Transjordanian district called Gilead. His suggestion has been followed by the majority of scholars; see e.g., Tadmor 1962; Aharoni 1967:331-332; Weippert 1982:308; Miller and Hayes 1986:332-333. Forrer (1920:64), on the other hand, holds that, at a later date, the province of Gilead was split into two provinces: Gilead in the north and Hamath in the south. For another suggestion, see Oded 1970:179-181. Unfortunately, there is no concrete evidence to support any of these conflicting reconstructions. The same uncertainty involves the organization and administration of Transjordan in the Persian period. See Lemaire 1990: 67-73.

ment reminds us of the encampment of Jacob and Laban (Gen. 31:25b): "Now Jacob had pitched his tent in the hill country and Laban with his kinsmen encamped in the hill country of Gilead." As was pointed out by de Vaux (1941: 31–33; see Ottoson 1969:23–24, 29–32, 41–43), the actual site at which Jacob and Laban concluded their treaty is referred to in vv. 48–49 as both Mizpeh and Gilead.[11] Mizpah appears in both stories as a place on the border of Israel facing either the Ammonites (Judg. 11) or the Arameans (Gen. 31).

The location of Mizpah near the Ammonite border finds further support in the description of Jephthah's offensive. According to the story, he took his vow at Mizpah (Judg. 11:11), assembled an army from all the Israelite Transjordanian areas (v. 29a) "and passed on to Mizpeh-Gilead, and from Mizpeh-Gilead he passed on to the Ammonites" (v. 29b). After his victory over the Ammonites he returned to Mizpah, his home town (v. 34).

Jephthah smote the Ammonites "from Aroer to the neighborhood of Minnith, twenty cities, and as far as Abel-keramim, with a very great slaughter" (v. 33). The words "twenty cities" are clearly a later addition, intended to magnify the victory. Mittmann (1969:64–71) suggested that the words "from Aroer to the neighborhood of Minnith" are also a late insertion; the original text would have run thus: "And he smote them as far as Abel-keramim, with a very great slaughter." His suggestion was accepted by some scholars (Wüst 1975:170–174; Soggin 1981:214; Hübner 1992: 134, n. 31).[12] However, he failed, in my opinion, to give due consideration to the prepositional construction *mi(n) . . . we'ad . . . we'ad . . .*, which presents a place on one side and then two on the other, the second of which lies beyond the first (Ginsberg 1951a; 1951b; Dorsey 1980:185–186; Demsky 1990:78–81).[13] The description of Jephthah's victory over the Ammonites should be translated thus: "And he smote them from Aroer and unto Minnith > < and unto (i.e., as far as) Abel-keramim. . . ." This may be compared with Joshua's pursuit of the fleeing Canaanites in Josh 10:10 and the Israelite pursuit of the fleeing Philistines in 1 Sam 17:52 (cf. Josh. 16:3; Neh. 3:16, 24, 31). Mittmann's assumption of the interpolation of material on the line of pursuit and toponyms goes too far; the combination of victory and pursuit is an integral part of the original Jephthah narrative.

The three toponyms are arranged roughly in a north-south line. According to Josh. 13:25, Aroer is located "in front of (*'al-p^{e}nē*) Rabbah."[14] Verse 25 is one

11. Whether the identification is part of the original story or was attached to it at a later stage is not my concern here.

12. Knauf 1984:119, n. 1 has assigned to the original text only the words "and he smote them with a very great slaughter."

13. For a possible parallel in an el-Amarna letter, see Na'aman 1992:28.

14. For a possible reconstruction of the original text of Josh 13: 25, see Oded 1971. Compare Drinkard 1979:28.

of three Deuteronomistic descriptions in which Transjordanian territories are delineated by southern, northern and northeastern/eastern demarcations.[15] In the two other descriptions (Deut. 3:16 and Josh. 12:2), the eastern boundary is demarcated by the northwestern border point of Ammon on the Jabbok river, possibly along Wādi Umm ed-Dananir.[16] In Josh. 13:25, the boundary is demarcated more precisely, i.e., by a town located on Ammon's eastern border (cf. the LXX rewriting of Num. 21:24 "for Jazer was the boundary of the Ammonites"). Aroer should be sought south of Wādi Umm ed-Dananir, in a prominent high place overlooking Rabbah from some distance (for the identification of Aroer, see Wüst 1975:168–174; Kallai 1986:251–252; Hübner 1992, 133, with earlier literature in n. 19). The demarcation accords with the words of Deut 2:36–37, according to which Israel did not transgress the land of Ammon and did not enter "to all the banks of the river Jabbok and the cities of the hill country" (cf. Num. 21:24; Deut. 2:18–19; Judg 11:15).

Minnith is generally located at Umm el-Ḥanhfish (Umm el-Basatin), on the southwestern border of Ammon (Mittmann 1969:71–73; Hübner 1992:133 with earlier literature in n.19).

Knauf (1984:119–121; see Hübner 1992:135) has suggested locating Abel-keramim at Saḥab, northeast of Minnith. Unfortunately, the identification is mainly dependent on Redford's proposal (1982) to locate toponyms nos. 93–102 of Thutmose III's topographical list along the "King's Highway" in Transjordan, a proposal that seems inadequately grounded.[17] Provided that Abel-keramim is identical to a site in the Saḥab area, the author of Judges 11 depicted Jephthah pursuing the fleeing Ammonites along the western and southern borders of the kingdom.

It is evident that the delineation of borders in the Jephthah story reflects a boundary configuration similar to that of Transjordan in the time of the Assyrian conquest. This may help us date the story, although the time-span of the border system is too broad for an exact chronological determination.

15. For the Ammonite point of view and the delineation of the territory by southern, northern and western demarcations, see Judg 11:13.

16. Some scholars have identified the Jabbok river referred to in these verses with the Upper Jabbok, which flows from south to north and passes near Rabbah. See, e.g., Glueck 1939:242-247; 1940:139-140; Wüst 1975:12-20; Kallai 1986:251-252. However, not only were the Israelites warned not to enter the Ammonite territory (Deut. 2:18-19), but there are explicit statements that they reached the border of Ammon and did not transgress it (Num. 21:24; Deut. 2:37; Josh. 13:10; Judg. 11:15). It seems to me that none of the texts mentioning the Jabbok river refer to the Upper Jabbok; they all refer to either Ammon's western border (Num. 21:24; Deut 2:37; Josh. 13:10, 25) or its northwestern border (Wādi Umm ed-Dananir) (Deut. 3:16; Josh 12:2).

17. For a preliminary criticism of Redford's article, see Na'aman 1994:184 n. 7.

(c) The biblical Mishor (*mîšōr*; "the plain") encompassed the area of southern el-Belqa (Liver 1962; Simons 1959:63–64, 128; Ottoson 1969:113). Its borders are identical to the deployment of the Reubenite towns listed in Josh. 13:16–21. Its northern border is delimited by the town of Beth-haram (Tell Iktanu), which is included in Gad's inheritance (Josh. 13:27; see Num. 32:36) and was located at Tell Iktanu, south of Wādi el-Kefrein (Ottoson 1969:86 with earlier literature), as well as by the Gadite town of Jazer (Josh 13:25; see Num 32:3, 35), which may be identified with Tell el-ʿAremeh (Rendtorff 1960: Kallai 1986:268–270, n.356; Hübner 1992:143 with earlier literature in n. 76). The Mishor's northeastern border is set at the southern border of Ammon. The Mishor and the inheritance of Reuben, according to Josh. 13:16–21, encompassed the area from the Arnon up to the line of Wādi el-Kefrein and Ammon's southern border. The major towns of the Mishor, according to Josh. 13:9, were Madeba and Dhiban. The same area is covered by the towns enumerated in Jer. 48:21–24. It is evident that the demarcation of these areas reflects the political boundaries of Transjordan in the eighth-seventh centuries BCE. The Mishor and Reuben's allotment encompass the Moabite territory north of the Arnon, whereas the inheritance of Gad was confined to the areas of the Assyrian Transjordanian province. Abel-shittim, which is located near Beth-haram, and Minnith, located at Ammon's southwestern border, are situated along the line that separates the Mishor and Reuben's allotment from the inheritance of Gad.

5. Conclusions

The two summary inscriptions of Tiglath-pileser (III R 10,2; ND 4301+) have been known for many years, yet their implications for the history and historical geography of Transjordan have not been fully appreciated. The two inscriptions were written only a few years after the Assyrian conquest and annexation of Aram Damascus and Israel and, according to their author(s), the Gilead was, at that time, part of the "widespread land of Bīt Ḫazaili" bordering on the west with "Bīt Ḫumri." This evidence can serve as a point of departure for a reevaluation of the relationship between Damascus and Israel in the late years of the two kingdoms.

Details of the early stages of Rezin's career are still missing. When evaluating all the known data, it is clear that he was the dominant figure in the south Syrian-Palestinian arena, possibly from the mid-eighth century BCE. onward. Aramaic cultural (and political?) influence was felt strongly in the Gilead, even in the time of Joash and Jeroboam II, and may have helped Rezin in his dealings with the area. Apparently, he was involved in Pekah's rebellion and enthronement, though the conjecture that the latter had previously been a puppet king in the Gilead must be rejected. In his last years, Rezin put together an anti-Assyrian coalition, a deed that brought about his defeat, his death and the annexation of his and his main ally's kingdoms by Assyria. Overall, Rezin expanded his realm and exerted influence in the entire area of Palestine and Transjordan, but his power and influence could hardly match those of Hazael. The influence of the latter reached the Euphrates, and he was the dominant figure in the entire Syro-Palestinian arena, as is evident from epigraphic material and the Bible.[18] Rezin's power and influence were more restricted, and it would be advisable to avoid using the term "Greater Syria" (for the term, see Miller and Hayes 1986:323–325) to describe his realm.

The Assyrian province in Transjordan seems to have replaced the Israelite/Damascene district of Gilead, and it apparently remained unchanged until the Assyrian withdrawal in the second half of the seventh century BCE. This long enduring boundary configuration was well known to biblical authors, and they took it as a basis for their anachronistic depiction of the territorial "reality" of various episodes in the pre-monarchial history of Israel.

References

Abel, F.M. 1938. *Géographie de la Palestine* II. Paris.

Aharoni, Y. 1967. *The Land of the Bible: A Historical Geography.* Philadelphia.

Alt, A. 1929. Das System der assyrischen Provinzen auf dem Boden des Reiches Israel. *ZDPV* 52: 220–242. (Reprint: Alt 1953: 188–205).

Alt, A. 1953. *Kleine Schriften zur Geschichte des Volkes* Israel II. München.

Barton, J. 1980. *Amos's Oracles Against the Nations: A Study of Amos 1.3–2.5.* Cambridge.

Barthélemy, D. 1982. *Critique textuelle de l'Ancien Testament. 1. Josué, Juges, Ruth, Samuel, Rois, Chroniques, Esdras, Néhémie, Esther.* (Orbis Biblicus et Orientalis 50/1). Fribourg and Göttingen.

Becking, B. 1992. *The Fall of Samaria. An Historical and Archaeological Study.* Leiden.

Ben Zvi, E. 1990. Tracing Prophetic Literature in the Book of Kings. The Case of II Kings 15,37, *ZAW* 102: 100–105.

Borger, R. 1967. *Handbuch der Keilschriftliteratur* I. Berlin.

Bron, F. and Lemaire, A. 1989. Les inscriptions Araméennes de Hazaël. *RA* 83: 35–44.

Cogan, M. 1973. Tyre and Tiglath-pileser III. Chronological Notes. *JCS* 25: 96–99.

Cogan, M. and Tadmor, H. 1988. *II Kings. A New Translation with Introduction and Commentary.* (The Anchor Bible). Garden City.

Cohen, S. 1965. The Political Background of the Words of Amos. *Hebrew Union College Annual* 36: 153–160.

Cook, H.J. 1964 Pekah. *VT* 14: 121–135.

18. Donner and Röllig 1968:204-211 with earlier literature; Kyrieleis and Röllig 1988; Eph'al and Naveh 1989; Bron and Lemaire 1989; Na'aman 1991:84-89; Lemaire 1991 with earlier literature.

Demsky, A. 1990. "From Kezib unto the River near Amanah" (Mish. Shebi'it 6:1; Halla 4:8): A Clarification of the Northern Border of the Returnees from Egypt. *Shnaton: An Annual for Biblical and Ancient Near Eastern Studies*: 10: 71–81. (Hebrew).

Donner, H. 1986. *Geschichte des Volkes Israel und seiner Nachbarn in Grundzügen* II. Göttingen.

Donner, H. and Röllig, W. 1968. Kanaanäische und Aramäische Inschriften 1–3. (2nd revised edition). Wiesbaden.

Dorsey, D.A. 1980. The Location of Biblical Makkedah. *Tel Aviv* 7: 185–193.

Drinkard, J.F. 1979. 'al pĕnê as "east of." *JBL* 98: 285–286.

Eph'al, I. and Naveh, J. 1989. Hazael's Booty Inscriptions. *IEJ* 39: 192–200.

Eph'al, I. and Naveh, J. 1993. The Jar of the Gate. *BASOR* 289: 59–65.

Forrer, E. 1920. *Die Provinzeinteilung des assyrischen Reiches*. Leipzig.

Geller, M. 1976. A New Translation for 2 Kings XV 25. *VT* 26: 374–377.

Ginsberg, H.L. 1951a. A Preposition of Interest to Historical Geography. *BASOR* 122: 12–14.

Ginsberg, H.L. 1951b. Postscript to Bulletin No. 122, pp. 12–14. *BASOR* 124: 29–30.

Glueck, N. 1939. *Explorations in Eastern Palestine* III. (AASOR 18–19). New Haven.

Glueck, N. 1940. *The Other Side of the Jordan*. New Haven.

Hayes, J.H. and Irvine, S. A. 1987. *Isaiah, the Eighth Century Prophet: His Time and His Preaching*. Nashville.

Hayes, J.H. and Hooker, P. K. 1988. *A New Chronology for the Kings of Israel and Judah*. Atlanta.

Hoftijzer, J. and Van Der Kooij, G. eds. 1991. *The Balaam Text from Deir ʿAlla Re-evaluated*. Leiden.

Hübner, U. 1992. Die Ammoniter. *Untersuchungen zur Geschichte, Kultur und Religion eines transjordanischen Volkes im 1. Jahrtausend v. Chr.* Wiesbaden.

Irvine, S.A. 1990. *Isaiah, Ahaz, and the Syro-Ephraimitic Crisis*. Atlanta.

Kallai, Z. 1986. *Historical Geography of the Bible. The Tribal Territories of Israel*. Jerusalem and Leiden.

Kessler, K. 1975. Die Anzahl der assyrischen Provinzen des Jahre 738 v. Chr. im Nordsyrien. *WO* 8: 49–63.

Kletter, R. 1991. The Rujm el-Malfuf Buildings and the Assyrian Vassal State of Ammon. *BASOR* 284: 33–50.

Knauf, E.A. 1984. Abel Keramim. *ZDPV* 100: 119–121.

Kyrieleis, H. and Röllig, W. 1988. Ein altorientalischer Pferdeschmuck aus dem Heraion von Samos. *Mitteilungen des Deutschen Archaologischen Instituts Athenische Abteilung* 103: 37–75.

Lemaire, A. 1981. Galaad et Makîr. *VT* 31: 39–61.

Lemaire, A. 1990. Populations et territoires de la Palestine a l'époque perse. *Transeuphratène* 3: 31–74.

Lemaire, A. 1991. Hazaël de Damas, roi d'Aram. In: Charpin, D. and Joannès, F. eds. *Marchands, diplomates et empereurs. Études sur la civilization Mésopotamienne offertes à Paul Garelli*. Paris: 91–108.

Liver, J. 1962. Mishor, Land of Mishor. *Enc. Miqr.* IV. Jerusalem: 919–920 (Hebrew).

Mastin, B.A. 1979. Was the *šālîš* the Third Man in the Chariot? *Supplement to VT* 30: 125–154.

Miller, J.M. and Hayes, J. H. 1986. *A History of Ancient Israel and Judah*. Philadelphia.

Mittmann, S. 1969 Aroer, Minnit und Abel Keramim (Jdc. 11, 33). *ZDPV* 85: 63–75.

Montgomery, J.A. 1951. *A Critical and Exegetical Commentary on the Books of Kings*. (ICC). Edinburgh.

Na'aman, N. 1986. Historical and Chronological Notes on the Kingdoms of Israel and Judah in the Eighth Century BCE. *VT* 36: 71–92.

Na'aman, N. 1988. The List of David's Officers (*šālîšîm*). *VT* 38: 71–79.

Na'aman, N. 1991. Forced Participation in Alliances in the Course of the Assyrian Campaigns to the West. In: Cogan, M. and Eph'al, I. eds. Ah, Assyria . . . Studies in Assyrian History and Ancient Near Eastern Historiography Presented to Hayim Tadmor. (*Scripta Hierosolymitana* 33). Jerusalem: 80–98.

Na'aman, N. 1992. Canaanite Jerusalem and Its Central Hill Country Neighbours in the Second Millennium BCE. *Ugarit-Forschungen* 24: 275–291.

Na'aman, N. 1993. Azariah of Judah and Jeroboam II of Israel. *VT* 43: 227–234.

Na'aman, N. 1994. The Hurrians and the End of the Middle Bronze Age in Palestine. *Levant* 26: 175–187.

Neef, H.-D. 1984. Die Ebene Achor — das "Tor der Hoffnung." *ZDPV* 100: 91-107.

Noth, N. 1959. Gilead und Gad. *ZDPV* 75: 14–73.

Oded, B. 1968a. Israelite Transjordan during the Period of the Monarchy (to the Fall of Samaria). (Ph.D. Thesis). Jerusalem (Hebrew).

Oded, B. 1968b. Mizpeh-gilead. *Enc. Miqr.* V. Jerusalem: 242–243 (Hebrew).

Oded, B. 1970. Observations on Methods of Assyrian Rule in Transjordania after the Palestinian Campaign of Tiglath-Pileser III. *JNES* 29: 177–186.

Oded, B. 1971. A Note on Josh. xiii 25. *VT* 21: 239–241.

Oded, B. 1972. The Historical Background of the Syro-Ephraimite War Reconsidered. *Catholic Biblical Quarterly* 34: 153–165.

Oded, B. 1976. Rezin. *Enc. Miqr. VII.* Jerusalem: 432–434 (Hebrew).

Olson, D.T. 1992. Pekah. *The Anchor Bible Dictionary* 5. New York: 214–215.

Ottoson, M. 1969. *Gilead, Tradition and History.* (Coniectanea Biblica, Old Testament Series 3). Lund.

Pitard, W.T. 1987. *Ancient Damascus. A Historical Study of the Syrian City State from Earliest Times unto Its Fall to the Assyrians in 732 B.C.E.* Winona Lake.

Pitard, W.T. 1992. Rezin. *The Anchor Bible Dictionary* 5. New York: 708–709.

Redford, D.B.1982. A Bronze Age Itinerary in Transjordan (Nos 89–101 of Thutmose III's List of Asiatic Toponyms). *Journal of the Society for the Study of Egyptian Antiquities* 12: 55–74.

Rendtorff, R. 1960. Zur Lage von Jaser. *ZDPV* 76: 124–135.

Rost, P. 1893. *Die Keilschrifttexte Tiglath-Pilesers III, nach den Papierabklatschen und Originalen des Britischen Museums* I-II. Leipzig.

Rudolph, W. 1971. Joel-Amos-Obadja-Jona (*Kommentar zum Alten Testament* XIII/2). Gütersloh.

Schley, D.J. 1990. The *šālîšîm*: Officers or Special Three-Man Squads? *VT* 40: 321–326.

Shea, W.H. 1977. The Date and Significance of the Samaria Ostraca. *IEJ* 27: 16–27.

Shea, W.H. 1978. Menahem and Tiglath-Pileser III. *JNES* 37: 43–49.

Simons, J. 1959. *The Geographical and Topographical Texts of the Old Testament.* Leiden.

Slayton, J.C. 1992. Shittim. *The Anchor Bible Dictionary* 5. New York: 1222–1223.

Soggin, J.A. 1981. *Judges, A Commentary.* (*Old Testament Library*). Philadelphia.

Steuernagel, C. 1925. Der 'Adschlun. *ZDPV* 48: 1–144, 201–392.

Smith, G. 1870. *The Cuneiform Inscriptions of Western Asia* III. London.

Smith, G. 1875. *Assyrian Discoveries.* London.

Tadmor, H. 1961. Azriyau of Yaudi. *Scripta Hierosolymitana* 8: 232–271.

Tadmor, H. 1962. *The Southern Border of Aram. IEJ* 12: 114–122.

Tadmor, H. 1967. The Conquest of Galilee by Tiglath-Pileser III, King of Assyria. In: Hirschberg, H.Z. ed. *All the Land of Naphtali. The Twenty-Fourth Archaeological Convention.* Jerusalem: 62–67 (Hebrew).

Thiele, E.R. 1965. *The Mysterious Numbers of the Hebrew Kings* (2nd edition). Grand Rapids.

Thiele, E.R. 1966. Pekah to Hezekiah. *VT* 16: 83–103.

de Vaux, R. 1941. Notes d'histoire et de topographie Transjordaniennes. *RB* 50: 16–47.

de Vaux, R. 1961. *Ancient Israel. Its Life and Institutions.* London.

Viviano, P.A. 1992. Argob and Arieh. *The Anchor Bible Dictionary* 1. New York: 376.

Vogelstein, M. 1945. *Jeroboam II: The Rise and Fall of his Empire.* Cincinnati.

Weippert, M. 1972. Review of S. Parpola, Neo-Assyrian Toponyms, Kevelaer und Neukirchen-Vluyn 1970. *Göttingische gelehrte Anzeigen* 224: 150–161.

Weippert, M. 1973. Menahem von Israel und seine Zeitgenossen in einer Steleninschrift des assyrischen Königs Tiglathpileser III. aus dem Iran. *ZDPV* 89: 26–53.

Weippert, M. 1982. Zur Syrienpolitik Tiglathpilesers III. In: Nissen, H.J. and Renger, J. eds. *Mesopotamien und seine Nachbarn: Politische und kulturelle Wechselbeziehungen im Alten Vorderasien vom 4. bis 1. Jahrtausend v. Chr.* (Berliner Beiträge zum Vorderen Orient 1). Berlin. 395–408.

Wiseman, D.J. 1956. A Fragmentary Inscription of Tiglath-Pileser III from Nimrud. *Iraq* 18: 117–129.

Wolff, H.W. 1969. *Joel und Amos.* (Biblischer Kommentar. Altes Testament XIV/2). Neukirchen-Vluyn.

Würthwein, E. 1984. *Die Bücher der Könige. 1. Kön. 17-2. Kön. 25.* (Das Alte Testament Deutsch XI,2). Göttingen.

Wüst, M. 1975. *Untersuchungen zu den siedlungsgeschichtlichen Texten des Alten Testament* I. Ostjordanland. Wiesbaden.

Tiglath -pileser III's Campaigns Against Tyre and Israel (734–732 BCE)[1]

H. Tadmor's long-awaited edition of the inscriptions of Tiglath-pileser III has just appeared, marking a new stage in the research of the time of the founder of the Assyrian empire (Tadmor 1994). All the extant texts are published, and the entire corpus of inscriptions is carefully edited. All the available data are presented in the plates and can be checked and compared with the textual evidence. Numerous detailed studies appear under the veil of "excurses" and "supplementary studies," complementing the textual edition and clarifying details that were either unknown or disputed among scholars. The book will serve both as a definitive publication of Tiglath-pileser's inscriptions for many years to come and as a point of departure for all future studies of this crucial period in the history of the ancient Near East.

The publication of a comprehensive edition of texts is always an ideal opportunity to examine them once again, in an effort to shed more light on old problems. It is the purpose of this article to re-examine some texts referring to the Assyrian campaigns against Tyre and Israel in the years 734–732 BCE, as well as the closing lines of the debated episode of Azriyau's rebellion in 738 BCE. The textual restorations of Ann. 19*:2–3 and Ann. 24 suggested below and the historical inferences drawn from them were made known to Prof. Tadmor when he prepared the edition of Tiglath-pileser's inscriptions. As an edition of texts is no place for tentative restorations, they naturally were not included. I hope that the elucidation of the fragmented texts restored below will contribute to a better understanding of Tiglath-pileser's campaigns to the west during the decisive years of 738–732 BCE.

1. The Conquest of Tyre According to Summ. 8:1–9

Wiseman (1951:21–22), in his *editio princeps*, did not suggest a clear identification of the kingdoms mentioned in lines 1–13 of ND 400 (=Summ. 8; see photograph in Tadmor 1994: Pl. LVI). Alt (1953:151–157) suggested that the coastal kingdom referred to in lines 1–9 is Arvad and that the kingdom men-

1. Reprinted with permission. *Tel Aviv* 22 (1995), 268–278.

tioned in lines 9–13 is Israel. According to Vogt (1964:349–350), lines 1–9 refer either to Arvad or Tyre. Katzenstein (1973:215–216) adopted Alt's suggestion for lines 1–9; Katzenstein identified the enemy of Assyria mentioned in lines 10–13 with either Damascus or Israel. Oded (1974:46) suggested that "lines 1–7 in the fragment refer to Arvad and lines 10–13 refer to the region south of Kashpuna, which may be Tyre or some country on the coast of Palestine." Eph'al (1982:30) identified the first kingdom with Tyre and the second with either Damascus, a Phoenician city-state, or Israel. Tadmor (1994:282), in his new edition, concluded that "the episodes in Summ. 8:1–9 and 10–13 may refer to Arvad and Tyre, respectively."

It seems to me that the kingdom referred to in lines 1–9 is Tyre, and the one mentioned in lines 10–13 is Israel. Following is some of the evidence in support of these geographical attributions.

(a) The following sequence of episodes is related in Summ. 9 (=ND 4301+) rev. 5–31: Tyre; Israel; Ashkelon; Gaza; Samsi queen of the Arabs; Egypt; Metenna of Tyre; Ḫulli of Tabal; Arabian tribes[2] (Tadmor 1994:181). It may be compared with the sequence of episodes that appears in Summ. 8 + Summ. 7:rev. 1–16: GN_1 (lines 1–9); GN_2 (lines 10–13); Gaza; Ashkelon; Egypt; Siruatti the Me'unite; Samsi queen of the Arabs; Arabian tribes; summary list of vassal kings; Ḫulli of Tabal; and Metenna of Tyre (Tadmor 1994:156–157). The identity of episodes and the close similarity of their order in the two texts is self-evident, and one would naturally identify GN_1 with Tyre and GN_2 with Israel. We may go even one step further and assume that the four episodes of Bīt-Agusi, Unqi,[3] Ḫatarikka and Bīt-Ḫaza'ili, which are depicted in Summ. 9 (obv. 24–27; rev. 1–4) before the list of episodes enumerated above, also appeared once, in the same order, within the missing part at the beginning of Summ. 8.

(b) There is no evidence that the island kingdom of Arvad occupied continental territories in the time of the Assyrian expansion to the west, in the ninth-seventh centuries BCE. According to the Kurkh Monolith of Shalmaneser III, Arvad sent only 200 soldiers to the battle of Qarqar (Oppenheim 1969:279a), a number befitting the limited extent of its island territory.[4] Moreover, the province of Ṣimirra, established by Tiglath-pileser

2. Summ. 9:rev. 30–31 probably refer to the Arabian tribes mentioned in Summ. 7:rev. 3–5. Thus, line 30 possibly opens with a list of tribal names, and the end of line 31 may be restored with a plural pronoun (*ta-mar-ta-šú-*[*nu am-ḫur*]).

3. One may restore at the beginning of Summ. 9:27 [KUR *šú-a-t*]*ú*, "that country." The same restoration may also be suggested for the end of line 24.

4. In his 21st campaign, Shalmaneser III attacked Hazael of Damascus. He then marched westward against a certain king named Ba'il, received his tribute and set up his royal image in the city of Laruba, his stronghold (Laessoe 1959:154–155). Astour (1979:19) suggested restoring the damaged name of Ba'il's country [*Ar-ma-d*]*a-a-a* = Arvad. However, the broken

III in 738 BCE, covered the entire coastal area opposite the island of Arvad, up to Kashpuna (modern Kusba, situated southeast of Tripoli; see Na'aman 1978: 231) in the south. No Arvadite territory is mentioned there (for the text, see Tadmor 1994:58–63, lines 4–11). Thus, the assumption that an Arvadite continental fortified city and its territory were conquered by Tiglath-pileser in his 734–732 BCE campaigns is untenable. Lines 1–9 of Summ. 8 refer to some other coastal kingdom.

(c) There is no similarity whatsoever between the description of the subjugation of Tyre in Summ. 9:rev. 5–8 and the text of Summ. 8:10–13. Noteworthy is the 3rd person sing. in the former description, as opposed to the 3rd person pl. in the latter. The conquest of some other kingdom is evidently being described in the latter text (for further discussion of Summ. 8: 10–13, see Part 2 below).

(d) There is a marked similarity between the episode of Tyre in Summ. 9:5–8 and the more detailed description of the Tyrian episode in Summ. 8: 1–9. The city whose conquest is related in Summ. 8:3 is Maḫalab, described in Summ. 9:r. 6 as "his (i.e., Hiram's) fortified city" (*āl dannūtišu*). Its name is spelled Maḫalliba in the Annals of Sennacherib (Luckenbill 1924:29 line 42). The city is situated south of the mouth of the Liṭani river (today Khirbet el-Maḥalib), on the main road leading to Tyre from the north. In my opinion, Maḫalab/Maḫalliba is referred to in Josh. 19:29 with the descriptive name "the fortress of Tyre" (*'īr mibṣar ṣôr*; 2 Sam. 24:7 *mibṣar ṣôr*), a designation that befits its strategic location.[5] Biblical *'īr mibṣar* ("fortified city") is an accurate

sign in line 17 does not look like a *da*-sign. As far as I am aware, there is no evidence that in the Iron Age, the island kingdom of Arvad occupied territories on the Phoenician coast.

5. For recent discussions of the tribal territory of Asher, see Kallai 1986:37–40, 212–224, with earlier literature; Na'aman 1986b:50–60; Lemaire 1991:135–137, 143; Lipiński 1991: 162–165. The northern boundary of Asher is described in detail (Josh. 19:28–29) and can be delineated accurately. The assumption of some scholars (Alt 1927:69, n. 3; Noth 1935: 222–225; Lemaire 1991:136) that the phrases "unto great Sidon" and "and to the fortress of Tyre" were inserted to Josh. 19:28–29 is arbitrary and is founded on Noth's obsolete idea of an original unified document that was formulated as a list of border points (*Grenzfixpunkte*) (for a critical discussion, see Kallai 1986:7–9, 99–102, and *passim*). The two phrases are integral parts of the original description of Asher's borders. The northern boundary of Asher reached the *Liṭani* river, turned sharply (*šāb*) along its southern bank to Ramah (Lemaire [1991:136] and Lipiński [1991:163–164] read *hayyammāh* ["to the sea"] instead of *hārāmāh*) and reached the fortress of Tyre (*'īr mibṣar ṣôr*). The identification of the "fortress of Tyre" with the fortified city (*āl dannūti*) of Maḫalab/Maḫalliba located south of the mouth of the Liṭani river is self-evident. At this point, the boundary turned sharply (šāb) southward, passed through a place called Hosah that must be sought east of the city of Ushu ("Old Tyre"; today Tell er-Rashidiyeh) and reached the sea, leaving a small continental territory for the kingdom of Tyre (Na'aman 1986b:54–56). The town list that follows runs "from *ḥbl*

equivalent of Akkadian *āl dannūti*; both descriptive terms refer to the same city.

On the basis of Summ. 9:rev. 6–7, lines 3–6 of Summ. 8 may be restored thus:

3. [. . . their weapons?] I dispersed. That city to[gether with (other) large cities I captured].

4. [Their spoil. . . . The rest of them] I devastated in the midst of the sea and anni[hilated them].

5. [. . . he fear]ed ([*ip-la*]*ḫ-ma*) and was frightened. He put on sackcloth, [(. . .) came before me and kissed my feet].

6. [20 talents of gold . . .].

The tribute list is long and covers lines 6–7. Lines 8–9 detail the administrative arrangements of Tiglath-pileser along the Phoenician coast. Lines 8–9 open with a territorial definition: "from Kashpuna, which is on the shore of the [Upper] Sea," possibly continue with a list of towns situated along the coast, and end with the words "[I placed it] under the control of my eunuch, the governor of Ṣi[mirra]." Kashpuna is located on the southernmost end of the province of Ṣimirra (see Ann. 19*:5); thus, the entire Phoenician coast south of it, including the kingdom of Gubla and the continental areas of Tyre, must have been entrusted to the supervision of the governor of Ṣimirra.

(e) Tiglath-pileser's administrative arrangements along the Phoenician coast are illuminated by the letters of Qurdi-Aššur-lāmur (Saggs 1955:127–133; 1963:76–78). This Assyrian official built Kashpuna and settled it with Babylonian deportees (ND 2715 lines 30–49; Postgate 1974:391–393), appointed tax-collectors over the quays of all Mount Lebanon and levied taxes on anyone who brought down wood to the quays (ND 2715 lines 1–29; Postgate 1974:390–391), inspected the affairs of Tyre and Sidon (ND 2715 lines 1–29; ND 2686), and defended the Phoenician coast against Greek pirates (ND 2370; Saggs 1963:76–78). Qurdi-Aššur-lāmur must have been the governor of Ṣimirra, who was appointed as inspector of the southern areas of the Phoenician coast following the Assyrian campaign of 734 BCE. His letters are other evidence that lines 1–9 of Summ. 8 indeed refer to the kingdom of Tyre.

---

to Achzib." Some MS of the Old Greek translates *mḥbl* "from Oleb" (Barthélemy 1982:57–59). In light of Judg. 1:31, it should best be rendered "from Ahlab." The town may tentatively be located at Ras el-Abyad (the Promotorium Album of Pliny), 12 km. south of Tyre, and has nothing to do with the town of Maḫalab/Maḫalliba ("the fortress of Tyre"), situated further to the north (Kallai 1986:221–223; Na'aman 1986b:57–60).

2. Tiglath-pileser's Campaigns Against Israel (734–732 BCE)

Tadmor (1994:279–282; cf. 1990), in his edition, summarizes all the available evidence of the Assyrian campaigns against Israel in the years 734–732 BCE. Recently, I also discussed some aspects of these campaigns (1986a:71–74; 1993:105–106). However, the relationship of (a) the two annal fragments that describe the Assyrian 733 BCE campaign against Israel, to (b) the summary inscriptions in which the events of several years are combined together, is not entirely clear and needs to be investigated further.

The major obstacle for the discussion is the fragmentary condition of the two relevant sections (Ann. 18 and 24). Moreover, the original slabs were left in the mound, and Layard's original copies, now published by Tadmor (1994: Pls. XV and XXIII), are our main source for the episode. Ann. 23, which relates the events of the Assyrian campaign of year 733 against Damascus, and Ann. 24, which describes the campaign against Israel and the submission of Ashkelon, were originally two columns on one slab (Tadmor 1994:220–221). Thus, the length of lines of the two columns was probably the same. With the help of the text of Ann. 18, one may tentatively reconstruct the text of Ann. 24. Admittedly, the reconstruction is highly speculative because, in particular, there are certain variant readings in the two texts. Also, there may have been expanded details of certain towns (compare, e.g., Tadmor 1994 72:11, 80:13–14, 186:3–4), and the captives of two towns are sometimes (though not often) grouped together (see, e.g., Tadmor 1994 80:15–16). Nevertheless, the reconstructed text, hypothetical as it is, may give us a better idea of the overall structure and contents of the annalistic account and may help estimate the number of toponyms enumerated in the original text.

Ann. 24 restored:

ša la [. . . kima {im-ba-ri as-ḫ}u-up . . . {-šú}]
ša la [. . . xx URU^{meš}]
ša 16 na-[{ge-e ša KUR É Ḫu-um-ri] qa}-[qqariš amnû x ME xx]
šal-la-[at ^{uru}Da-{ba-ra-a 6 ME 25 šallat ^{uru}x-a}-. . .]
2 ME 26 [šallat $^{uru}GN_3$ x ME xx šallat $^{uru}GN_4$ x ME xx]
šal-la-at [^{uru}{Ḫi-na-tu-na 6 ME 50 šallat ^{uru}Ku}-. . .]
4 ME+x [šallat $^{uru}GN_7$ x ME xx šallat ^{uru}Ia-{aṭ-bi-te]
6 ME 56 šal-[la-at ^{uru}Sa-a}m-ḫu-na x ME xx šallat $^{uru}GN_{10}$]
13 LIM 5 ME 20 [Un$^{meš??}$ šallat $^{uru}GN_{11}^{??}$ {^{uru}A-ru-ma-a ^{uru}Ma-ru-um}]
a-di mar-ši-ti-šú-nu [alpēšunu ṣēnīšunu$^{?}$ imērēšunu$^{?}$ ašlula]
KUR-e mar-ṣu-ti [. . . ana KUR . . . ú-ra-a]
^{m}Mi-ti-in-ti KUR As-[{qa-lu-na-a-a ina a-de}-e DINGIR^{meš} GAL^{meš} iḫ-ṭi-ma]
it-ti-ia it-ta-[bal-kit . . . . . .^{m}Ra-{ḫi-a-ni}]
e-mur-ma ù iplàḫ [libbašu {ina mi-qit} ṭēmi$^{?}$ . . .]

15. ḫa-at-ti ra-ma-ni-[šú imqussu . . .]
ᵐRu-ú-kib-tu DUMU-[šú? {ina ᵍⁱˢGU.ZA-šú ú-šib a-na} . . .]

Translation

[. . . like a fog I covered. His xxx] without [. . . xx cities] of the 16 di[stricts of Bīt-Ḫumri I razed to the ground. xx] captives [from the city of Dabara, 625 captives from GN_2], 226 [captives from GN_3, xx captives from GN_4, xx] captives [from the city of Ḫinatuna, 650 captives from the city of Ku . . .], 400+x [captives from GN_7, xx captives from the city of Yaṭbite], 656 cap[tives from the city of Shamḫuna?, xx captives from GN_{10}], 13,520 [people??, captives from the cities of GN_{11}, Aruma, Marum], with their belongings, [their cattle, their sheep, their asses I took as spoil. I had them cross??] difficult mountains [and carried off to the land of . . .].

Mitinti of Ash[kelon broke the loyalty oath (sworn) by the great gods] and re[volted] against me. [. . . the defeat of Rezin] he saw and was fri[ghtened. In an attack of desperation/panic? . . . he fe]ared for his life [. . .]. Rukibtu [his?] son [sat on his throne. In order to . . .].

Notes to the Text

The length of the restored lines is about the same as that of Ann. 23. Identical signs that are common to Ann. 18 and 24 are italicized. The estimated location of the text of Ann. 18 in each line is marked by the signs { }. According to the reconstruction, one line of Ann. 18 covers about one and a half lines of Ann. 24. Line 11 of Ann. 24 probably was omitted from the text of Ann. 18. Also, the episode of Mitinti is longer in Ann. 24 (compare line 9 of Ann. 18 with line 14 of Ann. 24).

For the toponyms, see recently Na'aman 1993:105-106; Tadmor 1994:82–83.

Line 9: the restoration is highly uncertain. Tadmor (1994:281) suggests that the figure of 13,520 people may be "the sum total of the deported in one or several campaigns to northern Israel." This is a plausible suggestion, although the sum total does not match the preceding numbers of deportees; there is no other text in Tiglath-pileser's inscriptions in which an exact total follows a detailed list of captives. As the cities of Aruma and Marum appear in Ann. 18, I suggest that a short list of cities followed the sum total of 13,520, showing that the scribe indicated that the overall number of captives includes many more people than the preceding detailed list of deportees and their original locations.

Line 10: the restoration is based on Ann. 23:14–15 and Summ. 8:11.

Line 12: see Ann. 25:3; Summ 7:19.

Line 16: the episode continues in Ann. 18. It describes how Rukibtu wandered around (*idūl)* seeking the support of the Assyrian king and was obliged to pay his lord a tribute of "500 [talents of silver]" in return for recognition of his kingship. For a recent discussion of the episode, see Ehrlich 1991:56–58.

The reconstruction clarifies the structure of the account of the Assyrian 733 BCE campaign against Israel. It may be divided into three parts: (a) a description of an attack and conquest (lines 1–3); (b) a long list of places and the numbers of their deportees (lines 4–8); and (c) a conclusion of the episode (lines 9–11). Sections (a) and (c) agree well with the first portion of both the "Israelite passages" in Tiglath-pileser's four summary inscriptions and the account of the Assyrian campaign in the Book of Kings. This is illustrated by the following five citations:

(a) Summ. 4:15–17 — "The land of Bīt-Ḫumria [to its full extent I captured]. The host? (*illūt*) [of its troops? I killed/scattered??]. All its people [I captured] and carried off [to] Assyria."

(b) Summ. 9:rev. 9 — "[The land of Bīt-Ḫumria] to its fu[ll extent I captured. All its people together with] their belongings [I carried off to Assyria]."

(c) Summ. 8:10–11 — "[. . .] I filled [the plain] with the bodies of their warriors [like gr]ass [. . . All its people with] their belongings, their cattle, their sheep, their asses [I took as spoil]."

(d) Summ. 13:17–18 — "[The land of Bīt-Ḫumria], all [of whose] cities I had [devastated] in my former campaigns, [all its people with] its livestock I had despoiled and had spared Samaria alone."

(e) 2 Kgs 15:29 — "In the days of Pekah king of Israel Tiglath-pileser king of Assyria came and captured Ijon, Abel-beth-maacah, Janoah, Kedesh, Hazor . . . all the land of Naphtali; and he carried the people captive to Assyria."[6]

The text of Summ. 13:17–18 indicates that Tiglath-pileser conducted several campaigns against Israel (Tadmor 1994:281). However, the close similarity among the text of the annals of year 733 and all four summary inscriptions implies that this was the major campaign in which Israel's power was broken, and a massive deportation took place. One may further assume that the north Galilean towns enumerated in 2 Kgs. 15:29 were also captured and their inhabitants deported during the 733 BCE campaign.

In his 734 campaign, Tiglath-pileser subjugated the Philistine coast up to its southernmost border (Naḫal Muṣur, today Wādi Ghazzeh and Wādi Shelaleh), and, on his way southward, he must have conquered the Phoenician coast between Kashpuna and Mount Carmel and the Israelite coast between

6. Commentators have noted that Gilead does not accord with the list of towns and that the term Galilee appears here in its late Hebrew, Aramaized form (Cogan and Tadmor 1988: 174). Thus, they suggest that the geographical designations Galilee and Gilead are glosses. The original text summarized the list of towns by the phrase "all the land of Naphtali." See Montgomery 1951:452; Würthwein 1984:383; Cogan and Tadmor 1988:174.

Mount Carmel and the Yarkon river. In his 732 campaign, Tiglath-pileser conquered and annexed the kingdom of Damascus, as well as the Transjordanian areas east of the Jordan river (on the status of Transjordan on the eve of the Assyrian campaign, see Na'aman 1995). The "sparing" of Samaria alone (Summ. 13:18) reflects exactly the state of affairs following the three Assyrian campaigns in the years 734–732 BCE and the probable annexation of the three provinces of Dor, Megiddo and Gilead to the Assyrian territory.

In Hosea 9:13, the prophet declares that what has happened to Tyre would likewise befall Israel ("Ephraim, just as I have seen Tyre planted in a pleasant place, so Ephraim must lead his children out to the slaughter"). J. Kuan (1991) suggested that the prophecy refers to the rebellion of Israel and Tyre during the time of Shalmaneser V (726–722) and cited as evidence the text of Menander as quoted by Josephus (*Antiquities* IX, 277–287). Provided that Menander indeed referred to Shalmaneser, the interpretation is certainly possible. However, the political situation as reflected in Hosea 9:13 could also refer to Israel's involvement in the Syro-Ephraimite alliance in 734–732 BCE (as correctly noted by Wolff 1982:166). Tiglath-pileser's destructive campaign against Tyre in 734 might have formed the background for Hosea's prophecy and, just as the "planted in a pleasant place" Tyre was struck, so Ephraim would bring out his children to the slaughter.

The episode of the removal of Pekah and the installation of Hoshea on the throne follows the episode of conquest and deportation in all four Assyrian summary inscriptions and in the Book of Kings. Following is a translation of this second episode:

(a) Summ. 4:17–19 — "Pekah, their king, died (DU (*illik*) /*nam*/-[*m*]*u*-[*ši*]-*šú*[!]). I installed Hoshea [as king] over them. 10 talents of gold, 1000 (sic!) talents of silver, their [tribu]te ([*ta-mar*]-*ti-šú-nu*) I received from them and [car]ried them [to Assyria]."

Notes to the Text

The original fragmentary slab was left on the mound. On the basis of several squeezes, Smith first made rough copies and then restored the text and published it in III R 10,2 (see the discussion in Tadmor 1994:136–137). The reading *illik nammušišu* is based on Smith's early draft, now published by Tadmor (1994:Pl. L Fr. d, line 17). It should be noted that the cuneiform signs of line 17 in Smith's rough copy look quite different from those in the composite restored text (1994:Pl. LI).

The reading 10 (talents of gold) and 1000 (talents of silver) (also Tadmor 1994:276) follows a pattern, according to which the weight of the silver is either a multiplication of 10 or 100 of the gold; see Ann. 10:6; Summ. 7:rev. 15; Ann. 21:5 ("30[!] talents of gold and 300 talents of silver").

The restoration [*ta-mar*]-*ti-šú-nu* matches exactly the missing space (Pl. LI line 18) and fits the context of a heavy tribute paid by a newly installed king in return for the recognition of the Assyrian king (see Tadmor 1994:276).

(b) Summ. 9:rev. 10–11 — "[. . . I installed Hoshea] as king over them. [. . . he/they went] before me to the city of Sarrabanu [and kissed my feet]."

(c) Summ. 8:12–13 — "[. . . They have killed$^{?}$ Pekah$^{?}$, their king$^{?}$], within his palace [. . .]. I accepted their plea to [forgive] their sin and sp[ared] their country."

Note to the Text

The restoration of line 12 is uncertain. Another possible restoration: "[. . .] within his palace [I set up my throne]." See Ann. 25:8.

(d) Summ 13:18 — "[Pek]ah, their king, [. . .]."

(e) 2 Kgs. 15:30 — "Then Hoshea the son of Elah made a conspiracy against Pekah the son of Remaliah and struck him down, and slew him, and reigned in his stead. . . ."

The slaying of Pekah and the installment of Hoshea as king of Israel should be dated to 731 BCE, when Tiglath-pileser was engaged in Babylonia after the termination of his Syro-Palestinian campaigns (Na'aman 1986a:71–74). The author of Summ. 4 uses a general expression to relate the rise of a new king in Samaria, and it remains uncertain whether any of the summary inscriptions explicitly refers to the slaying of Pekah by Hoshea (note the alternative possible restorations of Summ 8:12). The author of the Book of Kings, on the other hand, had a better source before him and was able to describe in detail the background for the installation of Hoshea, the last king of Israel, on the throne of Samaria.

3. The End of Azriyau's Rebellion (Ann. 19:2–3)*

The original slab was left in the mound, and Layard's original copy, now published by Tadmor (1994:Pl. XVI), is our main source. The slab was also copied by Rawlinson (see Tadmor 1994:Pl. XVII). It was collated and prepared for publication by Smith, who first made rough copies (Tadmor 1994:Pls. XXVII–XXVII) and, finally, a reconstructed text (III R 9,3; see the detailed discussions in Tadmor 1994:32–33, 216–219).

In his edition of Ann. 19*:2–3, Tadmor (1994:58, n. 2) followed the text of Layard and noted some variant readings in Smith's facsimile and translation of line 2. He further commented (*ibid.*:216) that "it seems that Smith also incorporated in III R 9,3 some improved readings . . . derived from consulting the squeeze (or Rawlinson's rough copy of the slab made *in situ*)." There is no apparent motivation for Smith to replace Layard's cuneiform signs by his own readings. It seems that he had observed the improved readings either in the squeeze or in Rawlinson's rough copy and integrated them into his draft and lithographic copy of the text.

In light of some parallels (Ann. 17:9; 23:7; Summ. 7:19), the beginning of line 2 may safely be restored thus: ᵐ*Az-ri-a-ú* [*a-di . . . ina qātē ú*]-ṣab-*bit-ma*.[7] Smith's copy of the *ma*-sign as a GAL indicates that he saw a horizontal wedge after the *ma* and it may be interpreted as an AŠ-sign. He further copied Layard's ZA-sign as an *a* and the AD-sign as a *ia*. Smith's *ia*-sign may possibly be deciphered as an *ad*-sign+the beginning of a *di*, but this remains uncertain. In this light, the second half of line 2 may be restored thus: *ina*! [*bi-ra*]-*a-ti ad*-[*di-šú-nu-ti*] (compare Summ. 7:19–20).

In line 3, I suggest restoring [ᵐ*e-ni*-DINGIR *ana* LUGAL]-*ú-ti ina*! [UGU-*šú-nu aškunma biltu*] *ma-da-at-tu ki-i šá* [*. . . ēmissu*].

A suggested translation for lines 2–3: "I seized Azriyau [together with his nobles? with (my) hands], I pl[aced them in fet]ters [and took them to Assyria. (. . .) I installed Eni-ilu as k]ing ov[er them. I imposed upon him] tribute like that [of an earlier? king?]."[8]

Tiglath-pileser's annexation and organization of the two provinces of Ḫatarikka and Ṣimirra are described in detail in Ann. 19*:58–63 lines 4–11. It is clear that lines 2–3 refer to different matters. According to the above-suggested restorations, line 2 relates the end of Azriyau's rebellion and the captivity of its leader and his supporters, whereas line 3 recounts the installment of Eni-ilu on the throne of the reduced kingdom of Hamath. These textual restorations support my former suggestion (Na'aman 1974:39; 1979: 229–230, 238–239) that Azriyau was king of Ḫatarikka+Hamath, was possibly of Aramean origin, who stood at the head of the rebellion against Assyria in 738 BCE, was defeated, lost his kingdom and, probably, lost his life.

---

7. Smith (1875:276, line 12) translated: "Azriau my hand greatly captured." In Ann. 25:6–7 one may restore thus: "Tutammu, together with his nobles, [I seized with (my) hands and took them to Assyria]. I captured Kinalua . . ." (compare Ann. 17:8). The number of signs restored at the beginning of line 7 equals the numbers of signs restored at the beginning of line 3 (see Tadmor's note to line 3').

8. The formula *kī ša Aššurī ēmissunūti* restored by Tadmor (1994 58:3) refers to territories that were annexed to Assyria. I believe that line 3 refers to a vassal king (Eni-ilu) and, therefore, suggest a different restoration based on Sargon II's inscription that relates the organization of the province of Hamath following its rebellion and annexation (Fuchs 1994 197:24). For another possible restoration, see Lambert 1981:125 lines 10–12.

References

Alt, A. 1927. Eine galiläische Ortsliste in Jos 19. *ZAW* 45: 59–81.

Alt, A. 1953. Tiglathpilesers III. erster Feldzug nach Palästina. *Kleine Schriften zur Geschichte des Volkes Israel* II. München: 150–162.

Astour, M.C. 1979. The Kingdom of Siyannu-Ušnatu. *Ugarit-Forschungen* 11: 13–28.

Barthélemy, D. 1982. *Critique textuelle de l'Ancien Testament. 1. Josué, Juges, Ruth, Samuel, Rois, Chroniques, Esdras, Néhémie, Esther.* (Orbis Biblicus et Orientalis 50/1). Fribourg and Göttingen.

Cogan, M. and Tadmor, H. 1988. *II Kings. A New Translation with Introduction and Commentary.* (The Anchor Bible). Garden City.

Ehrlich, C.S. 1991. Coalition Politics in Eighth Century B.C.E. Palestine: The Philistines and the Syro-Ephraimite War. *ZDPV* 107: 48–58.

Eph'al, I. 1982. *The Ancient Arabs. Nomads on the Borders of the Fertile Crescent 9th-5th Centuries B.C.* Jerusalem and Leiden.

Fuchs, A. 1994. *Die Inschriften Sargons II. aus Khorsabad.* Göttingen.

Kallai, Z. 1986. *Historical Geography of the Bible. The Tribal Territories of Israel.* Jerusalem and Leiden.

Katzenstein, H.J. 1973. *The History of Tyre from the Beginning of the Second Millennium B.C.E. until the Fall of the Neo-Babylonian Empire in 538 B.C.E.* Jerusalem.

Kuan, J. 1991. Hosea 9:13 and Josephus, *Antiquities* IX, 277–287. *PEQ* 123: 103–108.

Lambert, W.G. 1981. Portion of Inscribed Stela of Sargon II, King of Assyria. In: Muscarella, O.W. ed. *Ladders to Heaven. Art Treasures from Lands of the Bible.* Ontario.

Laessoe, J. 1959. A Statue of Shalmaneser III, from Nimrud. *Iraq* 21: 147–157.

Lemaire, A. 1991. Asher et le Royaume de Tyr. In: Lipiński, E. ed. *Phoenicia and the Bible. Proceedings of the Conference Held at the University of Leuven on the 15th and 16th March 1990.* (Orientalia Lovaniensia Analecta 44; Studia Phoenicia XI). Leuven: 135–152.

Lipiński, E. 1991. The Territory of Tyre and the Tribe of Asher. In: Lipiński, E. ed. *Phoenicia and the Bible. Proceedings of the Conference Held at the University of Leuven on the 15th and 16th March 1990.* (Orientalia Lovaniensia Analecta 44; Studia Phoenicia XI). Leuven: 153–166.

Luckenbill, D.D. 1924. *The Annals of Sennacherib.* (Oriental Institute Publications 2). Chicago.

Montgomery, J.A. 1951. *A Critical and Exegetical Commentary on the Books of Kings.* (ICC). Edinburgh.

Na'aman, N. 1974. Sennacherib's "Letter to God" on his Campaign to Judah. *BASOR* 214: 25–39.

Na'aman, N. 1977–78. Looking for KTK. *WO* 9: 220–239.

Na'aman, N. 1986a. Historical and Chronological Notes on the Kingdoms of Israel and Judah in the Eighth Century B.C. *VT* 36: 71–92.

Na'aman, N. 1986b. *Borders and Districts in Biblical Historiography. Seven Studies in Biblical Geographical Lists.* Jerusalem.

Na'aman, N. 1993. Population Changes in Palestine following Assyrian Deportations. *Tel Aviv* 20: 104–124.

Na'aman, N. 1995. Rezin of Damascus and the Land of Gilead. *ZDPV* 111: 105–117.

Noth, M. 1935. Studien zu den historisch-geographischen Dokumenten des Josuabuches. *ZDPV* 58: 185–255. (Reprint: 1971. *Aufsätze zur biblischen Landes- und Altertumskunde* I. Neukirchen-Vluyn: 229–280).

Oded, B. 1974. The Phoenician Cities and the Assyrian Empire in the Time of Tiglath-pileser III. *ZDPV* 90: 38–49.

Oppenheim, A.L. 1969. Babylonian and Assyrian Historical Texts. In: *ANET*: 265–317.

Postgate, J.N. 1974. *Taxation and Conscription in the Assyrian Empire*. (Studia Pohl, Series Maior 3). Rome.

Saggs, H.W.F. 1955. The Nimrud Letters, 1952 — Part II. *Iraq* 17: 126–154.

Saggs, H.W.F. 1963. The Nimrud Letters, 1952 — Part VI. *Iraq* 25: 70–80.

Smith, G. 1875. *Assyrian Discoveries*. London.

Tadmor, H. 1990. Tiglath-pileser III in Palestine. *Shnaton — An Annual for Biblical and Ancient Near Eastern Studies* 10: 179–187. (Hebrew) .

Tadmor, H. 1994. *The Inscriptions of Tiglath-Pileser III King of Assyria. Critical Edition, with Introductions, Translations and Commentary.* Jerusalem.

Vogt, E. 1964. Die Texte Tiglath-Pilesers III. über die Eroberung Palästinas. *Biblica* 45: 348–354.

Wolff, H.W. 1982. *Hosea. A Commentary on the Book of the Prophet Hosea.* (Hermeneia). Philadelphia. (English translation of 1965. *Dodekapropheton.* 1:*Hosea.* [Biblischer Kommentar Altes Testament XIV/1]. Neukirchen-Vluyn).

Wiseman, D.J. 1951. Two Historical Inscriptions from Nimrud. *Iraq* 13: 21–26.

Würthwein, E. 1984. *Die Bücher der Könige. 1. Kön. 17–2. Kön. 25.* (Das Alte Testament Deutsch XI,2). Göttingen.

Two Notes on the History of Ashkelon and Ekron in the Late Eighth-Seventh Centuries BCE[1]

The Ashkelon Episode in the Annals of Tiglath-pileser III

The publication of a new edition of the inscriptions of Tiglath-pileser III by H. Tadmor (1994) marked a new stage in the study of the Assyrian king and his time. Tadmor collected all the inscriptions, collated all the extant texts and established the texts of other inscriptions that had perished, on the basis of the original drafts made by Layard, Rawlinson, Smith and Boutcher. Thus, he was able to assemble all the evidence in its most original manifestations. The edition is complemented by a number of excursuses and supplementary studies, many of which are detailed analyses of literary, historiographical and historical problems emanating from the corpus of texts.

An edition of texts is no place for tentative reconstructions. Therefore, some broken passages are published with minimal restorations. However, in some cases, it is tempting to try and reconstruct the texts, even when the restorations are not free from doubt (see Na'aman 1995). This is particularly true for episodes in which Tiglath-pileser's inscriptions are our only source for the history of a particular kingdom or tribal group.

Ashkelon is a case in point. The city is mentioned in two badly broken passages that are part of the royal annals (Ann. 18 and 24 according to Tadmor's system of numbering). Tadmor (1994:178, note on line 19; 181) further attributed to Ashkelon two broken passages that are included in Tiglath-pileser's summary inscriptions (Summ. 8 line 19; Summ. 9 rev. line 12). Their attribution to Ashkelon is quite certain, because these passages appear either before the Gaza episode or immediately after it, and because no other western kingdom is missing from these summary inscriptions (Summ. 7+8, 9), .

The preserved texts of the two summary inscriptions are identical and run as follows: "[. . .] x+100 talents of silver I removed (*assuḫamma*) and [carried/brought] to Assyria." The use of the verb *nasāḫu* (see CAD N/2 5a) probably indicates that the broken booty list included people as well as silver (cf. Summ. 8:15–16).

---

1. Reprinted with permission. *Tel Aviv* 25 (1998), 219–227.

Layard (1851: Pls. 72b+73a and also 29b) published the two annal slabs that mention Ashkelon among his drawings of the Nimrud (Calah) reliefs. Rost (1893: Pls. XVIIIa and XVIIIb) drew the slabs separately in his plates, but he treated them as a single text in his edition of the annals (1893:38–41, lines 229–240). Tadmor published the two slabs separately (1994:80–84, 220–221; Pls. XV and XXIII), each in its own right, and my transliteration follows his textual enumeration.

Ann. 24

12. ^{m}Mi-ti-in-ti KUR As-[qa-lu-na-a-a ina a-de-e DINGIR^{meš} GAL^{meš} iḫ-ṭi-ma]
13. it-ti-ia it-ta-[bal-kit itti$^{?}$ nakriya$^{?}$ iškuna$^{?}$ pi-i-su$^{?}$ dab-de ^{m}Ra-ḫi-a-ni]
14. e-mur-ma ù ip-làḫ [libbāšu ina mi-qit$^{?}$ ṭēmi$^{?}$ . . .]
15. ḫa-at-ti ra-ma-ni-[šu imqussu . . . šadāšu$^{?}$ ēmid$^{?}$]
16. ^{m}Ru-ú-kib-tu DUMU-[šu$^{?}$ ina ^{gis}GU.ZA-šu ú-šib a-na ^{URU}GN . . .]

Ann. 18

8. [. . . ^{m}Mi-ti-in-ti KUR As]-qa-lu-na-a-a ina a-de-[e DINGIR^{meš} GAL^{meš} iḫ-ṭi-ma it-ti-ia it-ta-bal-kit itti$^{?}$ nakriya$^{?}$]
9. [iškuna$^{?}$ pi-i-šu$^{?}$ dab-de ^{m}Ra]-ḫi-a-ni e-mur-ma ina mi-qit [ṭēmi$^{?}$ . . . ḫa-at-ti ra-ma-ni-šu imqussu . . .]
10. [šadāšu$^{?}$ ēmid$^{?}$ ^{m}Ru-ú-kib-tu DUMU-šu$^{?}$] ina ^{giš}GU.ZA-šu ú-šib a-na [^{URU}GN]
11. [. . . a-di maḫ-ri-ia] i-dul-ma ú-ṣa-la-ni 500 [GÚ.UN KÙ.BABBAR ta-mar-ta-šu kabittu ūbilānimma unaššiqa šēpēya]
12. [ana ašri-šu$^{?}$ utir-šu$^{?}$]-ma a-na URU-šu TU-ub 15 URU[^{meš}-ni ša ina . . .]
13. [. . . ina qātīšu apqid ^{MI}]-di-bi-'i-i-lu KUR A-ru-bu [a-na ^{LÚ}atûti ina muḫḫi KUR Muṣri aškun]

Translation of Ann. 18 (combined with Ann. 24)

Mitinti of Ashkelon [broke] the loyalty oath [of the great gods], revo[lted] against me [and joined$^{?}$ with my enemy$^{?}$]. The defeat of Re]zin he saw and in an attack of [insanity. . . . He was stricken] with panic, [. . . and died].

Rukibtu, [his$^{?}$] son, sat on his throne. To [the city of GN . . . in front of me] he wandered around and implored me. 500 [talents of silver he brought and kissed my feet. I restored$^{?}$ him to his place$^{?}$] and he entered his city. Fifteen town[s located$^{?}$ in the . . . I entrusted in his hands].

Idibi'ilu, the Arabian, [I appointed as the "Gatekeeper" over (the area) facing Egypt].

Notes on the Text of Ann. 18

The length of the restored lines of Ann. 24 is about the same as that of Ann. 23. According to my estimation, one line of Ann. 18 covers about one and a half lines of Ann. 24 (see Na'aman 1995: 272–273).

For a recent discussion of the Ashkelon episode, see Ehrlich 1996: 98–102, 176–180.

Line 8: For the restoration, see Summ. 7 line 19; cf. Ann. 25, note on line 3.

Line 10: the restoration *šadāšu ēmid* (or *illik nammušišu*; see Na'aman 1995: 274–275), "he died" is *ad sensum*. The family relation of Mitinti and Rukibtu cannot be established with certainty. Smith (1875: 284) suggested restoring *mār*-[*šu*] (cf. Borger 1984: 373). Tadmor (1994: 83, note on line 10) presented two other restorations: "Rukibtu, the son [of Mitinti]" and "Rukibtu, the son [of his (i.e., Mitinti's) brother]." All three restorations are possible. On the basis of Summ. 5 line 15 and Summ. 9 line 28, Ehrlich (1996:179 and n. 56) suggested restoring *mār* [*la mammāna*], "son of [a nobody]." However, it is doubtful that the Assyrian king would emphasize the illegitimacy of a ruler that he set on the throne of Ashkelon. On the contrary, in the case of Hoshea (Ausi'), the king of Israel, whom Tiglath-pileser III installed as king and vassal of Assyria, Tiglath-pileser III deliberately ignored Hoshea's illegitimacy, although Tiglath-pileser III must have known that Hoshea was a usurper who took the throne by force. Regardless of whether Rukibtu was a usurper or not, the royal scribe would have presented Rukibtu in a way that fit the Assyrian ideological aims, rather than the exact factual accuracy (on this problem, see Na'aman 1998).

Lines 10–11: for the restoration, see Summ. 9 rev. 10–11 (and see below). It solves the problem of the verbal form *ūšib* ("sat") in line 10. Rukibtu first set himself on the throne, but holding the throne of Ashkelon required an act of submission to the Assyrian king and recognition of his status as an Assyrian vassal.

Line 12: The restoration at the beginning of the line is *ad sensum*. Another possible restoration is *rēmu aršīšu* ("I showed mercy upon him").

Line 13: for the restoration, see Summ. 7 rev. 6.

Discussion

The restorations, uncertain as they are, may help us understand the Ashkelon episode. Ann. 23 relates the events of the Assyrian campaign of year 733 BCE against Damascus (Tadmor 1994:78–80, 235). Ann. 24, which relates the struggle with Samsi, the campaign against Israel and the submission of Ashkelon (Tadmor 1994:220–221), describes some other episodes that took place in this year.

Mitinti of Ashkelon joined the anti-Assyrian coalition headed by Rezin of Damascus, which included, at least, Israel, Tyre, Samsi and Gaza. We may safely assume that Egypt was actively involved in the negotiation and that Rezin had hopes for Egyptian military aid (Begrich 1929:218; Alt 1953:157–161). The preparation for rebellion must have started in ca. 736 (Begrich 1929; Na'aman 1991:91–94, with earlier literature). The Assyrian campaign of 734

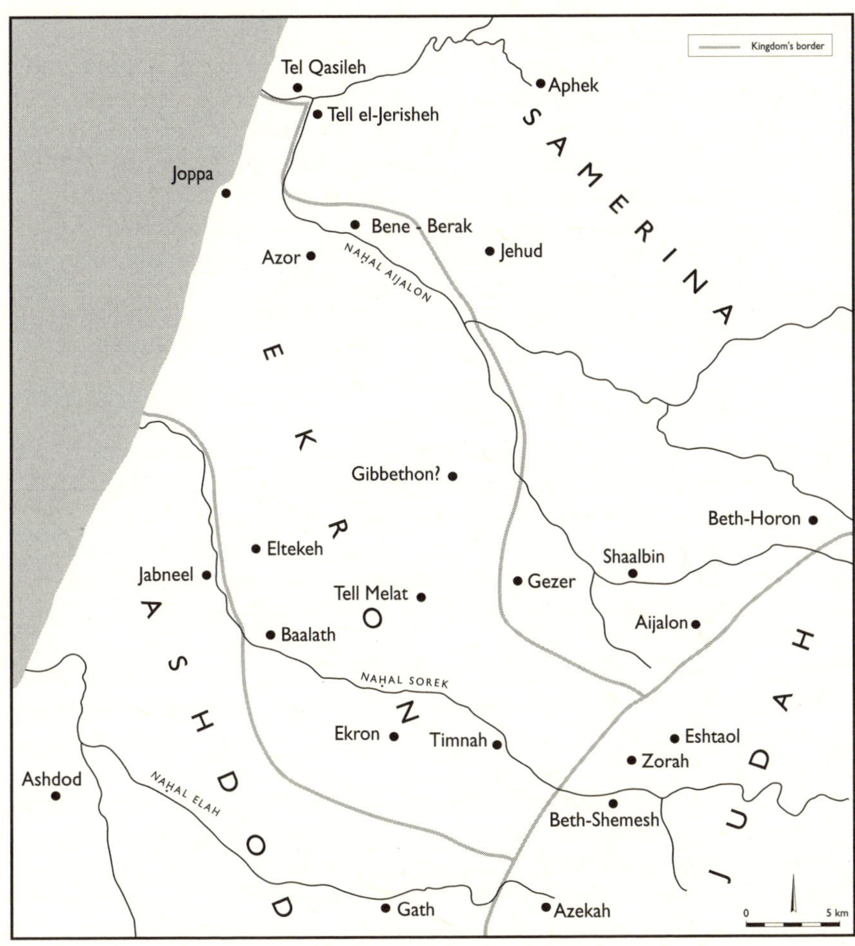

The Kingdom of Ekron in the Seventh Century BCE

to the Brook of Egypt (*Naḫal Muṣur* = Naḥal Besor) on the southern border of Gaza, which was aimed at blocking the possible approach of an Egyptian task force to Philistia, took the coalition by surprise (Na'aman 1991:92–93). Hanunu of Gaza fled to Egypt, only to return and become an Assyrian vassal (Tadmor 1994:222–225; Ehrlich 1996:94–98, with earlier literature). Mitinti must have paid his tribute to Assyria at that time, as indicated by the list of tribute-bearers in Summ 7 rev. 7–13 (for the date, see Tadmor 1994: 268).

Shortly afterward, Mitinti fell victim to a *coup d'état* initiated by his son[?], Rukibtu. To justify Tiglath-pileser's recognition of Rukibtu as a legitimate king in Ashkelon, the author of the annals described the infidelity of the former king and how he died, stricken by panic and madness. The author further described how the new king wandered around seeking to be recognized as an Assyrian vassal and how the Assyrian king finally installed him on the throne of Ashkelon, but not before he paid a heavy tribute of 500 talents of silver (Eph'al 1982:25). Tadmor (1994:171, note to line 16; 276) has demonstrated that a series of newly installed kings, most of them usurpers, paid Tiglath-pileser huge sums in return for recognition of their rule. Among these rulers are Hoshea of Israel (10 talents of gold and 1000? talents of silver), Hulli of Tabal (10 talents of gold, 1000 talents of silver and 2000 horses) and Metenna of Tyre (50 or 150 talents of gold and 2000 talents of silver). Rukibtu is another example of someone who paid heavy tribute in return for recognition. The different figures of the tribute of Ashkelon in Tiglath-pileser's annals (500 talents) and summary inscriptions (x+100 talents) illustrate the inconsistency of the Assyrian scribes in drawing numbers in their inscriptions (cf. the tribute of Metenna of Tyre in Summ. 7 rev. 16 and 9 rev. 26).

The restoration of lines 12–13 is guesswork. The basis for my restoration is the appearance of an Ashkelonite enclave east of Joppa (namely, Joppa, Beth-dagan, Bene-berak and Azor) in the time of Sennacherib's campaign to Palestine (Luckenbill 1924: 31 lines 68–72; Oppenheim 1969: 287b). No reasonable explanation was offered for the surprising status of the king of Ashkelon in the Joppa area, far north of the kingdom of Ashkelon. Assuming that Tiglath-pileser transferred the coastal territory east of Joppa to Rukibtu may explain this territorial anomaly, as well as Rukibtu's long enduring loyalty to Assyria, until he was deposed by Ṣidqa shortly before Sennacherib's campaign of 701 BCE.

The nomination of Idibi'ilu to supervise the area that "faces Egypt," south of Naḥal Besor (*Naḫal Muṣur*), is associatively related to the entrusting of the northernmost coast of Philistia to Rukibtu (for the references to Idibi'ilu in Tiglath-pileser III's inscriptions, see recently Na'aman 1997).

What happened to the Ashkelonite enclave after Sennacherib's campaign is not related in any source. Tentatively, I would suggest that the area was transferred to the king of Ekron, who enjoyed a favored status in the late Assyrian empire. The expansion of Ekron's territory and its possible access to the Mediterranean (via the port of Joppa) may partly explain the remarkable prosperity of the city in the seventh century BCE (Gitin 1997, with earlier literature).

Dan's Inheritance and the Kingdom of Ekron in the Seventh century BCE

To have a better understanding of the territorial scope of Ekron in the seventh century, we should analyze another source, which has been discussed many times in the past, but never in conjunction with Ekron's territory.

The inheritance of Dan is demarcated in the Book of Joshua by a town list and a fragmentary border description (Josh. 19:40–46). Some of Dan's eastern towns are mentioned in the border descriptions and town lists of neighboring tribes (i.e., Zorah, Eshtaol, Beth-shemesh, Timnah and Baalath). This is not exceptional, and I have already noted that there are numerous cases in which the same toponyms appear in border descriptions of neighboring tribes (Na'aman 1986:108–110). I have further suggested that the inheritance of Dan is an integral part of the boundary system of the Israelite tribes (Josh. 13–19) and that Dan's allotment was drawn after the delineation of the inheritances of Judah, Benjamin and Ephraim, because its borders presuppose the demarcation of its three neighbors (Na'aman 1986:102–106).

Many scholars have analyzed in detail the town list of Dan (e.g., Noth 1953:118, 121–123; Mazar 1960; Strange 1966; Kallai 1986:361–371; Na'aman 1986:107–114; Fritz 1994:197–200), and there is agreement on the identification of most of the towns. The list may be divided into six small geographical sub-groups, and I will list the names of towns and add a short note where either the version or the identification is controversial.

1. Along the western border: Zorah, Eshtaol (see recently Lehmann, Niemann and Zwickel 1996: 384–386) and 'Ir-shemesh (=Beth-shemesh).
2. Along the northeastern border: Shaalabin, Aijalon and Yitlah (see Barthélemy 1982: 59–60).
3. Along the southeastern border: Elon (=Elon Beth-hanan — 1 Kgs. 4:9), Timnah and Ekron.
4. In the mid-west: Eltekeh (Tell esh-Shallaf?), Gibbethon (Ras Abu Ḥamid; Schmitt 1980: 107–109) and Baalath.
5. In the west: Yehud, Bene-berak, Azor (see Barthélemy 1982: 60) and Gath-rimmon (location unknown).
6. V. 46 "And the Water of Yarkon and Rakkon with the coastal line over against Joppa." (see Barthélemy 1982:60–61). Rakkon (or should we transcribe <Ya>rkon and assume that the town was called after the river?) possibly may be identified with either Tell el-Jerisheh or Tell Qasileh.

There is a close similarity of names among the towns mentioned in Sennacherib's Annals (Joppa, Bene-berak, Azor, Eltekeh, Timnah and Ekron) and the western half of the town list of Dan. The town of Gibbethon (Gabbutunu) is mentioned alongside Ekron in Sargon II's reliefs (Tadmor 1958:83 n. 243; Franklin 1994:255–263; contra Schmitt 1989). Seven out of the ten western towns of Dan's allotment are mentioned in Assyrian inscriptions of the late eighth century BCE. The city of Gimtu/Gath (Tell eṣ-Ṣafi), on the other hand, was included in the territory of Ashdod, as indicated by Sargon II's royal inscriptions (Oppenheim 1969:286a; Fuchs 1994:134 line 250; 220 line 104). Hence, the area along Naḥal Elah (Wādi Samt) was included in Ashdod's territory. Assuming that Sennacherib transferred the Ashkelonite towns east of Joppa to the king of Ekron, we may suggest that Ekron's territory in the seventh century BCE roughly overlaps the inheritance of Dan in the boundary system of the Israelite tribes. Its southern border ran south of Naḥal Sorek (Wādi eṣ-Ṣarar), and its northern border ran along Naḥal Aijalon (Wādi el-Kabir). Each town had a territory, and the capital city of Ekron must have encompassed a vast agricultural land. Therefore, we suggest that the limits of the southern towns of Dan's allotment (Elon, Timnah, Ekron, Baalath and Eltekeh) reflect the southern border of the kingdom of Ekron (see map — Fig. 1).

With this reconstruction in mind, we may speculate how the town list of Dan was formed. The author of the tribal system has already delineated the tribal allotments of Judah, Benjamin and Ephraim. This author attributed the territorial gap among these three allotments to the tribe of Dan, which, according to the biblical tradition, originally settled in this area. To demarcate this artificial tribal territory, the author first selected some eastern towns located on the borders of neighboring tribes (i.e., Beth-shemesh, Zorah, Eshtaol, Shaalabin and Aijalon) to demarcate Dan's eastern border. He then added a list of western towns whose scope roughly overlaps the territory of the kingdom of Ekron, thus, filling in the gap among the above-mentioned three tribal allotments.

Provided that my reconstruction, admittedly highly conjectural, is acceptable, then the biblical inheritance of Dan may help us configure the territorial scope of the kingdom of Ekron in its zenith in the seventh century BCE.

References

Alt, A. 1953. Tiglathpilesers III. erster Feldzug nach Palästina. *Kleine Schriften zur Geschichte des Volkes Israel* II. München: 150–162.

Barthélemy, D. 1982. *Critique textuelle de l'Ancien Testament.* 1. *Josué, Juges, Ruth, Samuel, Rois, Chroniques, Esdras, Néhémie, Esther.* (Orbis Biblicus et Orientalis 50/1). Fribourg and Göttingen.

Begrich, J. 1929. Der Syrisch-Ephraimitische Krieg und seine weltpolitischen Zusammenhänge. *Zeitschrift der Deutschen Morgenländischen Gesellschaft* 83: 213–237.

Borger, R. 1984. Historische Texte in akkadischer Sprache. In: Kaiser, O. ed. *Texte aus der Umwelt des Alten Testaments* I/4. Gütersloh: 354–410.

Ehrlich, C.S. 1996. *The Philistines in Transition: A History from ca. 1000-730 BCE.* Leiden.

Eph'al, I. 1982. *The Ancient Arabs. Nomads on the Borders of the Fertile Crescent 9th-5th Centuries B.C.* Jerusalem and Leiden.

Franklin, N. 1994. The Room V Reliefs at Dur-Sharrukin and Sargon II's Western Campaigns. *Tel Aviv* 21: 255–275.

Fritz, V. 1994. *Das Buch Josua.* (Handbuch zum Alten Testament I/7). Tübingen.

Fuchs, A. 1994. *Die Inschriften Sargons II. aus Khorsabad.* Göttingen.

Gitin, S. 1997. The Neo-Assyrian Empire and its Western Periphery: The Levant, with a Focus on Philistine Ekron. In: Parpola, S. and Whiting, R.M. eds. *Assyria 1995.* Helsinki: 77–103.

Kallai, Z. 1986. *Historical Geography of the Bible. The Tribal Territories of Israel.* Jerusalem and Leiden.

Layard, A.H. 1851. *Inscriptions in the Cuneiform Character from Assyrian Monuments.* London.

Lehmann, G., Niemann, H. M. and Zwickel, W. 1996. Zora und Eschtaol. Ein Archäologischer Oberflächensurvey im Gebiet nördlich von Bet Schemesch. *Ugarit Forschungen* 28: 343–442.

Luckenbill, D.D. 1924. *The Annals of Sennacherib.* (Oriental Institute Publications 2). Chicago.

Mazar, B. 1960. The Cities of the Territory of Dan. *IEJ* 10: 65–77.

Na'aman, N. 1986. *Borders and Districts in Biblical Historiography. Seven Studies in Biblical Geographical Lists.* Jerusalem.

Na'aman, N. 1991. Forced Participation in Alliances in the Course of the Assyrian Campaigns to the West. In: Cogan, M. and Eph'al, I. eds. *Ah, Assyria . . . Studies in Assyrian History and Ancient Near Eastern Historiography Presented to Hayim Tadmor.* (Scripta Hierosolymitana 33). Jerusalem: 80–98.

Na'aman, N. 1995. Tiglath-pileser III's Campaign against Tyre and Israel (734–732 BCE.). *Tel Aviv* 22: 268–278.

Na'aman, N. 1997. Siruatti the Me'unite in a Second Inscription of Tiglath-pileser III. *Nouvelles Assyriologiques Brèves et Utilitaires.* 1997/4: 139.

Na'aman, N. 1998. Jehu Son of Omri — Legitimizing a Loyal Vassal by his Lord. *IEJ* 48:236–238.

Noth, M. 1953. *Das Buch Josua.* (Handbuch zum Alten Testament I/7). Tübingen.

Oppenheim, A.L. 1969. Babylonian and Assyrian Historical Texts. In: *ANET* 265–317.

Rost, P. 1893. *Die Keilschrifttexte Tiglat-Pilesers III., nach den Papierabklatschen und Originalen des Britischen Museums* I–II. Leipzig.

Schmitt, G. 1980. Gat, Gittaim und Gitta. In: Cohen, R. and Schmitt, G. ed. *Drei Studien zur Archäologie und Topographie Altisraels.* Wiesbaden: 77–138.

Schmitt, G. 1989. Gabbutunu. *ZDPV* 105: 56–69.

Smith, G. 1875. *Assyrian Discoveries.* London.

Strange, J. 1966. The Inheritance of Dan. *Studia Theologica* 20: 120–139.

Tadmor, H. 1958. The Campaign of Sargon II of Assur: A Chronological-Historical Study. *JCS* 12: 22–40, 77–100.

Tadmor, H. 1994. *The Inscriptions of Tiglath-Pileser III King of Assyria. Critical Edition, with Introductions, Translations and Commentary.* Jerusalem.

The Historical Background to the Conquest of Samaria (720 BCE)[1]

The chain of events leading to the conquest of Samaria by the Assyrians and the deportation of its people is delineated in 2 Kgs. 17:3–6 as follows (*RSV*):

> (3) Against him came up Shalmaneser king of Assyria; and Hoshea became his vassal, and paid him tribute. (4) But the king of Assyria found treachery in Hoshea; for he had sent messengers to So, king of Egypt, and offered no tribute to the king of Assyria, as he had done year by year; therefore the king of Assyria shut him up, and bound him in prison. (5) Then the king of Assyria invaded all the land and came to Samaria, and for three years he besieged it. (6) In the ninth year of Hoshea the king of Assyria captured Samaria, and he carried the Israelites away to Assyria and placed them in Halah, and on the Habor, the river of Gozan, and in the cities of the Medes.

Only one Assyrian king is called by name in this passage (v. 3). It is, however, clear that the reference is to two different kings, Shalmaneser V and Sargon II. According to the latter's inscriptions, he had deported 27,290 of the inhabitants of Samaria. The deportation of the Israelites to northern Mesopotamia and Media as mentioned in v. 6b is, doubtless, the same as that undertaken by Sargon after his campaign to the west in 720 BCE. Thus, whereas v. 3 refers explicitly to Shalmaneser, v. 6b implicitly refers to Sargon II, his successor to the throne. One may ask where in the account the deeds of Shalmaneser come to an end and where those of his successor begin, or in other words, which of the two kings besieged and conquered Samaria and to is referred in vv. 5–6a.

I. Criticism of the Commonly Accepted Reconstruction of the Fall of Samaria

In his inscriptions, Sargon II repeats, several times, that he conquered Samaria at the beginning of his reign. For many years scholars interpreted

1. Reprinted with permission. *Biblica* 71 (1990), 206–225.

2. Borger (in Galling 1968:60) suggested transcribing *ik-me-lu-ma* and taking the verb as *kamālu* "to become angry" (*CAD* K 109). This rendering of the verb was also adopted by Spieckermann (1982:349–350 and n. 93) and Dalley (1984:36). In this light, we may restore [ŠÀ-*šu-n*]*u* at the beginning of line 28. Compare lines 249–250 of Sargon's annals (Lie 1929: 38) PN *ana la našê bilti libbašu ikpudūma* with lines 25–28 of our passage *Samerinaya . . . ana la epēš ardūti [u la na]šê bilti [libbašun]u ikmelūma*. However, the verb *kamālu* appears only in

2 Kgs. 17:6 in light of Sargon's claim in his inscriptions. Only a very few denied the authenticity of Sargon's claim and assigned the fall of Samaria to Shalmaneser (Olmstead 1904/5:179–182; Olmstead 1908:45–47, n. 9; Thiele 1965:122–128). A turning point in the direction of the research came when H. Tadmor published his detailed discussion of the inscriptions of Sargon (Tadmor 1958:33–40). He critically analyzed the royal annals and demonstrated that Sargon's first campaign to the West was conducted only in the second year of his reign (720 BCE). During this campaign, he defeated a coalition of states headed by the king of Hamath and recaptured the rebellious Syrian provinces of Arpad, Ṣimirra and Damascus. Subsequently, he conquered Gaza and defeated Re'e, "the *turtānu* of Egypt," near Raphia. After the conclusion of the campaign, he established new provinces at Hamath and Samaria, deported thousands of their inhabitants and rebuilt their centers.

Tadmor further suggested that the city of Samaria was conquered two years earlier, by Shalmaneser V (722 BCE), after a siege that lasted three years (724–722 BCE). The episode of the long siege and conquest as described in 2 Kgs. 17:5–6a and 18:9–10 refers to Shalmaneser; the campaign and conquest of the Assyrian king was recorded in the Babylonian Chronicle as well ([uru]*šamara'in iḫtepi*). Sargon's capture of the city was hardly a glorious operation — the glory for the military achievement should be attributed to his predecessor, Shalmaneser V (Tadmor 1958:36–40; Tadmor 1976:713–715).

The hypothesis of the two conquests of Samaria — by Shalmaneser (722 BCE) and by Sargon (720 BCE) — was accepted by many scholars and, with minor variations, was defended recently by B. Becking in his detailed study of the sources referring to the fall of Samaria (Becking 1985. For a list of works that followed the two-conquest hypothesis, see Becking 1985:69–70, notes 241–242; Dalley 1985:33–36; Na'aman 1986:74; Laato 1986:217–218; Donner 1986:314–315).

However, this reasonable and well-constructed historical reconstruction is not free from uncertainty. Most obvious, of course, is the hypothesis of two separate conquests taking place within two (or three) years by two Assyrian kings, when the Bible and the Assyrian inscriptions refer to a single conquest. The problems arising out of the two-conquest reconstruction is outlined in the following seven points:

religious contexts and has only the gods as subject (see Becking 1985:52). As an alternative reading, we may suggest here that [*lemutt*]*i ig-me-lu-ma* be transcribed, translating it in the light of West Semitic *gml r'h*: "to repay evil," "to treat badly." Compare Gen. 50:15.17; 1 Sam. 24:17; Isa. 3:9; Ps. 7:4[5]; Prov. 3:30; 31:12. Admittedly, the reading has no parallel in the corpus of Akkadian literature.

(A) Literary sources, reliefs and archaeological excavations agree that the conquest of non-submissive cities by the Assyrians was always an extremely destructive event. If Samaria were besieged for three years (with all the terrible effects of such a long siege) and then conquered by the Assyrians in 723/22 BCE, one would hardly expect its weakened surviving inhabitants to be able to participate in a rebellion that broke out shortly afterwards. Yet, according to Sargon's earliest inscription (the "Ashur charter") — from his second year — the Samarians participated in the alliance formed by the king of Hamath alongside the older provinces that had been annexed by Tiglath-pileser III (Olmstead 1908:45–49; Tadmor 1958:37, n. 137; Saggs 1975:11–20; Dalley 1985:34; Hawkins 1982:416–417). Furthermore, the episode of the conquest of Samaria occupied a central place in Sargon's inscriptions composed in his later years, after he had conquered and annexed vast areas and had expanded the Assyrian empire to its maximal extent. Thus, it is clear that the king and his scribes regarded the former as a major event of the king's early years. The participation of the Samarians in the rebellion of 720 BCE and the place of the city's conquest in Sargon's inscriptions do not accord well with the assumption that Samaria was captured by Shalmaneser after a long siege and that Sargon recaptured a weakened, ruined city.

(B) The excavators of Samaria attributed burned layers covering the later buildings of the Israelite period to the Assyrian conquest of the city (Crowfoot, Kenyon, and Sukenik 1942:110–112). The layer of debris of destruction that was found, however, was restricted to a relatively small area. Furthermore, the city walls continued to be in use over a long period of time (Crowfoot, Kenyon, and Sukenik 1942:116–118; Avigad 1978:1046). Few remains have survived from level VII, which the excavators attributed to the period of the Assyrian dominion in Samaria (Crowfoot, Kenyon, and Sukenik 1957:97–98; Avigad 1978:1046). One wonders what would have been written in the archaeological report if the excavators had not been influenced by historical records. The relatively few signs of destruction revealed in Samaria are at variance with the findings from other cities that were captured by the Assyrians after much shorter sieges; signs of utter destruction are remarkably clear at all these sites. Lack of accord between the assumed three years of intensive siege and conquest as recorded in 2 Kgs. 17:5–6a; 18:9–10 and the results of the archaeological excavations conducted at Samaria should warn us against a literal interpretation of the biblical text.

(C) The description of the capture of Samaria in the Nimrud prism opens, thus, (Gadd 1954:179, 181–182 and pl. XLV–XLVI; Tadmor 1958:33–35; Borger in Galling 1968:60–61; Borger 1984:382, note; Dalley 1985:36; Spieckermann 1982:349–350; Becking 1985:51–55): "The Samarians, whose [hearts]? became angry?" ([ŠÀ-*šu-n*]*u*? *ikmelūma;* or "who had repaid? [evil]?"

– [*lemutt*]*i*? *igmelūma)*[2] "against/to the king my [predecessor] ([*ālik pāni*]-*ia*) – not to endure servitude nor to bring tribute – and did battle, with the strength of the great gods, my lords, I fought with them. . . ." Sargon explicitly refers here to the time of his predecessor, stating that the rebellion of the Samarians had begun during the latter's reign. The reasonable inference is that he suppressed a rebellion that had broken out in the time of Shalmaneser. Would Sargon's scribe have linked a rebellion started during the reign of Shalmaneser with the conquest of the rebellious city by his lord, if the rebellion was suppressed and the city conquered by the previous king?

Noteworthy also is the perfect accord between the words of Sargon's inscriptions, according to which the rebellion of the Samarians was involved with "evil doing" and the cessation of the tribute, and the words of 2 Kgs. 17: 4, according to which Hoshea started conspiring with the king of Egypt and did not bring his yearly tribute. The agreement of the two sources gives further support to Sargon's inscription of the early stage of the rebellion and its suppression.

(D) The Babylonian Chronicle, in which the "ravaging" of Šamara'in under Shalmaneser is recorded, plays a central role in the currently accepted reconstruction of the capture of the city by the Assyrians (for the Babylonian Chronicle see Grayson 1975:69–87). However, the text of the chronicle is organized throughout in a chronological order, with each and every event accurately dated within a specific year of the king of Babylonia and a transverse line marked to separate the years of reign. The "ravaging" of Šamara'in is included within the accession year of Shalmaneser and, accordingly, should be assigned to that year.[3] The claim that the conquest of Samaria should be assigned to the fourth/fifth year of Shalmaneser has no foundation in the listing of the episodes in the Babylonian Chronicle.

(E) The selection of the verb *ḫepû* to describe the capture of Samaria after a long siege is also problematic.[4] The author of the Babylonian Chronicle uses this verb to describe the plundering of vast areas or of groups of towns, whereas the capture of the larger cities is described by the verbs *ṣabātu*, *erēbu* and *kašādu*. Of the five references where the verb *ḫepû* appears, three refer to extensive areas (I, 21 Bit-Amukanni; I, 44 Bit-xxx; III, 10–11 "from Rashi to Bit Buranki"), one refers to two towns (II, 24–25) and one mentions four towns

3. The dating of the "ravaging" of Šamara'in to 727 BCE was taken by H. Winckler as an important piece of evidence against the identification of the city with Samaria. See Winckler 1887:351–352; Winckler 1903:62. See further n. 4 below.

4. The verb *hepû* in this context was formerly discussed by Dalley 1985:33, 36 and by Becking 1985:43.

(III, 37–38). The last episode is described in the annals of Sennacherib by the words: "The cities which were in those districts I completely destroyed, I burned with fire and turned (them) into heaps of ruins" (Luckenbill 1924:38, IV, 44–46). The fourth episode is also portrayed in detail in Sennacherib's annals, and it is clear that an unconditional surrender rather than a siege or a breaking of the walls of the two cities had taken place (Luckenbill 1924:25–26, I, 54–56).

This analysis indicates that the verb *ḫepû* appears in the Babylonian Chronicle, in the connotation of "to plunder" or "to ravage," and that other verbs were selected to designate the breaking of walls after a siege. Thus, it is questionable whether the Babylonian scribe would have used this verb to describe the breaking of the walls and the conquest of Samaria after a long siege. Another explanation for the notation "Šamara'in was ravaged" should be sought.

(F) There is a marked contrast between the text of 2 Kgs. 17:4, according to which Hoshea was arrested and imprisoned before the siege of Samaria, and the text of v. 6 (and 18:10), according to which the city was captured in the ninth year of Hoshea. The assumption that Samaria was conquered in Hoshea's ninth year involves denial of both the sequence of events as described in 2 Kgs. 17:3–6 (on this problem, see below) and the explicit statement that Hoshea was imprisoned before the beginning of the siege of Samaria.

(G) The conquest of Samaria is described, thus, in v. 6: "In the ninth year of Hoshea the king of Assyria captured Samaria, and he carried the Israelites away to Assyria, and placed them in Halah. . . ." All scholars agree that Sargon is the king who deported the Samarians. Thus, according to the two-conquest hypothesis, two different kings, Shalmaneser and Sargon, are referred to in this verse under the title "the king of Assyria." Accepting the hypothesis necessarily involves the assumption that the author of the passage lived a long time after the conclusion of the events and was unaware of the historical reality, to the extent that he combined the actions of two Assyrian kings in one sentence.

In light of the many problems involved in the commonly accepted reconstruction of the siege and fall of Samaria, a fresh examination of the data is desirable. The biblical and Assyrian sources are examined in this article in order to clarify their structure and contents and to try to suggest a better description of the chain of events culminating in Sargon's conquest of the city in 720 BCE.

II. The Conquest of Samaria by the Assyrians: A Suggested Reconstruction

Our point of departure is the text of 2 Kgs 17:3–6. V. 3 states that Shalmaneser "came up" (*'ālāh*) against Hoshea and that the latter became his vassal. Inasmuch as this episode is at the beginning of the description, one would naturally assume that it describes an event during the early years of Shalmaneser's reign, prior to the episodes delineated in vv. 4–6.

Strangely enough, the plain and clear sequence of events in vv. 3–6 was discredited by many scholars, who suggested that vv. 3–4 and vv. 5–6 are two parallel accounts of the same historical event, originating from different archives. The assumption that two different sources were combined in vv. 3–6 was first suggested by H. Winckler, mainly on historical grounds (Winckler 1892a:16–25). He suggested that vv. 3a and 5a refer to one and the same episode — Shalmaneser's campaign against Hoshea in his later years. Thus, Winckler claimed that vv. 3–4 depend on archival documents of the Northern Kingdom, whereas vv. 5–6 (and also 2 Kgs. 18:9–11) were extracted from the archives of the Kingdom of Judah. Although Winckler (1903:269) himself later abandoned this hypothesis, other scholars have followed this line of research. There are, of course, many variations in their analyses of the text, but they all confine the events described in vv. 3–6 to a single historical episode that took place in Hoshea's later years (Becking 1985:25–29, with earlier literature in 24, n. 93; Šanda 1912:217; Rehm 1982:167; Hentschel 1985:77; Laato 1986:217–218).

When examining vv. 3–6, we must note, first of all, that the chain of events, as related there, is reasonable and that there are no stylistic or linguistic differences between the two assumed sources. The passage is written in the same verbal pattern as many other passages in the book of Kings, including the other episodes that refer to the campaigns of Assyrian kings against the kingdoms of Israel and Judah (2 Kgs. 15:19–20:29–30; 18:13–15; cf. Isa. 7:1). First comes a verb in the *qaṭal* form and, subsequently, there appears a series of verbs, all in the *wayyiqṭol* form. The two-sources one-episode hypothesis is not supported by textual criteria and is based only on a preconceived reconstruction of the historical chain of events. Methodologically (and, in my opinion, also historically), it is better, first, to try to follow the sequence of events as related in 2 Kgs. 17:3–6.

First, we must look for the historical background of Hoshea's early act of disobedience, as related in v. 3. As this act was directed against Shalmaneser, we may well assume that it refers to the time of unrest that followed the death of Tiglath-pileser III, the founder of the Assyrian empire, in 727 BCE.[5]

5. Lehmann(-Haupt) 1902:128–129, 466–472; Goedicke 1963:64 (but see Goedicke 1977:4); Katzenstein 1973:226.

Rebellions that broke out following death of the founders of empires are so well known that it is redundant to look for examples. However, it is worth noting that similar rebellions broke out several times, immediately after the deaths of later Assyrian kings, with the southwestern frontier of the Assyrian empire always being an important center for unrest and revolts (e.g., after the death of Shalmaneser V),[6] Sargon II,[7] Sennacherib,[8] and Esarhaddon (Spalinger 1974:316–325, with earlier literature; Grayson 1980:244–245). It also should be recalled that Tiglath-pileser's last campaigns to the West were conducted in the years 734–732 and that, in his last years, he stayed in Babylonia and Assyria and, as far as we know, did not return to the conquered southwestern regions. The surviving kingdoms, thus, had enough time to negotiate and conspire against Assyria. We may conclude that v. 3 most probably refers to unrest and perhaps even rebellion that broke out in the West upon the death of the great emperor and the accession of his son, Shalmaneser V.

In this context we may further note the prophecy of Isaiah (14:29–32) that echoes the hopes of the Philistine kingdoms, as the news broke of the death of their subjugator, possibly Tiglath-pileser (Wildberger 1978:573–579, with earlier literature). Far-sighted politicians like Isaiah, who warned against vain hopes at this delicate moment, were rare among the rulers of his time. Hoshea was a typical, short-sighted politician and, like the kings of Philistia, he nourished a vain hope for a turn of fortune following the breaking of "the rod which smote."

Further evidence for the events of 727 BCE, presumably, may be derived from the account of Menander as related by Josephus (*Ant.* IX 283–287).[9] Menander recounted the history of Tyre during the reign of Eloulaios, the sequence of events in his account being somewhat parallel to the chain of events in the history of Hoshea (2 Kgs. 17:3–4). According to Menander's description, Selampsas (in the Latin text Salmanasar) king of Assyria invaded Phoenicia and "made a treaty" with the Phoenician cities. The Tyrians, however, did not submit to him, and he came back and attacked the city of Tyre.

6. Olmstead 1908:31–35, 40–41, 43–51; Tadmor 1958:37–38; Tadmor 1966:90–91; Hawkins 1982:416–417; Becking 1985:56–63.

7. For the rebellion that broke out upon the death of Sargon on the battlefield in 705 BCE, see Landsberger 1948:80–82; Tadmor 1958:97 and notes 311–313; Na'aman 1974:32–34; Hawkins 1982:422, 426–427.

8. For the murder of Sennacherib and the western campaign of Esarhaddon in his second year (679 BCE), see Hirschberg 1932:5–16, 42–45; Spalinger 1978:22–33, 41–43; Parpola 1980:171–181, with earlier literature.

9. For an analysis of the passage, see Lehmann(-Haupt) 1902:125–140; Katzenstein 1973:222–230, with earlier literature.

When he retreated, he placed guards on the mainland and blockaded the isle of Tyre for 5 years.

Common to the histories of Eloulaios, the king of Tyre, and Hoshea are the two-stage encounters with Selampsas/Shalmaneser (Lehmann(-Haupt) 1902: 128–129, 466–472; Šanda 1912:212–213; Katzenstein, 1973:222–230). The first stage related by Menander may well be combined with the campaign of 727 BCE, a campaign that was designed to pacify the western front, quell all possible rebellion and manifest the hegemonic status of Assyria in all areas up to the border with Egypt. The second stage may possibly be synchronized with Hoshea's conspiracy with Egypt and the withholding of the tribute (2 Kgs. 17: 4) in ca. 724/23 BCE (see below).

The above reconstruction also fits the account of the Babylonian Chronicle, according to which Shalmaneser "ravaged (*iḫtepi*) Šamara'in" in his accession year. Assuming that the city of Šamara'in is indeed Samaria,[10] we may suggest that soon after his accession, when news of unrest and disobedience in the western vassal states reached Assyria, the new king immediately sent his troops to pacify the region. He, himself, may have participated in the campaign, although this cannot be verified. The extent of the unrest is not clear, but it was certainly limited and included Israel, the Phoenician coast and possibly also the Philistine kingdoms (Isa. 14:29–32). Shalmaneser's immediate reaction was successful: all the disobeying kings

10. Several arguments raised by Winckler (1887:351–352; Winckler 1903:62), against the identification of Šamara'in (or Šabara'in) with Samaria are worthy of consideration. Winckler dated the "ravaging" of the city to the accession year of Shalmaneser (727 BCE), thus, commenting that "die betreffende sta[d]t wurde im antrittsjahre Sargon's zerstört, während II Reg. 17, 5 deutlich sagt, dass Sargon Samaria drei jahre lang belagert babe." He further noted that the Babylonian Chronicle reports only events that were of interest to the Babylonians, which can hardly be said of the conquest of Samaria. Indeed, no western place is mentioned in the first part of the Chronicle, up to the time of Esarhaddon, with the exception of the land of Tabal, where Sargon was killed in battle. The chronicler described only the Assyrian-Babylonian-Elamite relations; the city of Samaria is an exception within this geographical region. Finally, Winckler (1887:352) correctly asked: "was ist das von Sargon eroberte Samirina, wenn Samaria schon 5 jahre vorher fiel?"

Winckler's claim that Šam/bara'in must be sought in Babylonia may be sustained by the Ashur Ostracon, which refers to the deportation of captives of Bit-Adini (a Babylonian toponym) by Ululai, i.e., Shalmaneser V (Donner and Röllig 1968:No. 233, line 15). Thus, it is evident that the Assyrian king or his commander conducted a campaign into Babylonia, a campaign that would otherwise have been left out of the Babylonian Chronicle.

However, no city by the name Šam/bara'in is so far known in Babylonia, whereas there is a perfect accord between this name and the name of Samaria in the Babylonian-Aramaic tradition (Tadmor 1958:39–40; Becking 1985:42, with earlier literature in n. 151). In the present state of our knowledge, and in spite of the above observations, we must conclude that the city of Samaria is the one mentioned in the Babylonian Chronicle.

immediately surrendered and paid their tribute; Samaria, possibly the center of resentment, was ravaged. How long the entire operation lasted cannot be established, but it certainly did not take long. According to the Eponymic Chronicle, Shalmaneser was in Assyria during the first year of his reign, so that, even if he himself commanded the operation, he was soon able to return to his own country.

The next stage should be dated c. 724/23 BCE and is recounted in 2 Kgs. 17:4: Hoshea sent envoys to "So, king of Egypt" and withheld his tribute. The identity of the king of Egypt is disputed among scholars (see recently Christensen 1989:140–153, with earlier literature). Of the various solutions raised so far for *sô'*, the suggestion to regard it as a title, as an inaccurate rendering of the Egyptian appellation for "king" (*nj-św·t* > *nśw-t* > *nśw*), seems preferable (Donner 1977:433; Krauss 1978:49–54). R. Krauss (1978:51–52) drew attention to the analogical title of *t3-ḥmt-nj-św·t* "the king's wife," i.e., "queen," which was likewise regarded in the Book of Kings as a personal name (1 Kgs. 11:19). Another case of the rendering of the Egyptian title *t3-ḥmt-nj-św·t* as a personal name (Daḫamunzu) is known from the annals of Shuppiluliuma, King of Hatti (Federn 1960:33). There are quite a number of instances in the Bible (Arawna/Awarna) (McCarter 1984:512; Abramski 1985:55–56. For another suggestion, see Cody 1965:381–393), in the Amarna letters (Albright 1946:14, no. 16, 20–21, no. 53) and in the Assyrian royal inscriptions (Borger 1957:8–10)[11], in which foreign titles or designations of officials are taken as proper names. The interpretation of the "name" *sô'* as a title is well supported by these examples. Thus, it is clear that the identity of the Egyptian king who tried to form an anti-Assyrian alliance can be clarified only by way of historical analysis.

We suggest that the conquest of Samaria and the quelling of the rebellion, which started by negotiations with an Egyptian king and the withholding of tribute (17:4a), should be assigned to Sargon II. Egypt was involved in the rebellion against Sargon, and an Egyptian commander with an army was sent to the Philistine coast to support the rebels. Thus, we may well assume that the Egyptian king who sent the task force in 720 *BCE* is the same king of Egypt mentioned in 2 Kgs. 17:4. In the period of the Sargonids, it is only the Ethiopian rulers of the 25th Dynasty who are known to have sent their troops across the Sinai peninsula to fight the Assyrians.[12] Thus, Pi(ankhy),

11. For further suggested parallels, see Eilers 1964/66:137–140; Singer 1988:247.

12. A. Spalinger has pointed out that the Sargonids regarded the Nubian monarchs of the 25th Dynasty as foreign conquerors who had imposed themselves on the local princes. Thus, there is a clear distinction in their presentation between the local and the Cushite kings. See Spalinger 1973:95–101; Spalinger 1974:307–308, 320–326; Na'aman 1979:65.

who, according to several scholars invaded Lower Egypt in 724–22 BCE and conquered it (Christensen 1989:146 153, with earlier literature), was probably the king who conspired with Hoshea and later sent his commander with a task force to support the anti-Assyrian rebellion.[13]

When Shalmaneser heard of the conspiracy, he sent troops under his own or his general's command and ordered the conspirator to appear before him. Hoshea did so and "the king of Assyria shut him up, and bound him in prison" (v. 4b). In a somewhat similar situation, Josiah appeared before his overlord, Necho king of Egypt, and was slain (2 Kgs. 23:29). Hoshea probably was deported to Assyria, and his subsequent fate remains unknown. The last king of the Northern Kingdom, thus, disappeared from the historical arena (723/22 BCE). Whether the city of Samaria was besieged or the countryside plundered at that time cannot be established (see n. 16 below).

Shalmaneser died shortly afterwards and his heir to the throne, Sargon II, met serious opposition at home; he was able to put down the rebellion only with great difficulty. All Assyrian military operations in the West necessarily came to an abrupt end. Only in his second year (720 BCE) was Sargon able to conduct a campaign to the West. At Qarqar, he defeated a coalition of former Assyrian provinces and vassal states and won a second battle against an Egyptian task force near Raphia. His hands were then free to punish the Samarians who had participated in the anti-Assyrian coalition that fought him at Qarqar, and he besieged and conquered the city of Samaria.

This is the background against which we should interpret 2 Kgs. 17:5–6. V. 5 states, "The king of Assyria invaded all the land and came to Samaria and . . . besieged it." This "king of Assyria" is no other than Sargon II, and the verse refers to his western campaign of 720 BCE. The invasion of "all the land" accurately reflects the wide scope of the Assyrian campaign, which had fateful consequences for the Northern Kingdom. In its importance for Israelite history, it may be compared to Tiglath-pileser III's campaigns of 734–32 BCE and to Sennacherib's campaign of 701 BCE, both reported in the Book of Kings (2 Kgs. 15:29; 16:9; 18:13–16). The sequence of events as described in 17:5–6 (invasion of the land, siege and conquest of Samaria) is identical with the se-

13. The appearance of black soldiers in Assyrian reliefs depicting the campaign of Sargon II to the Philistine coast in 720 BCE supports and corroborates the assumption that the Egyptian army was dispatched by a king of the 25th (Cushite) Dynasty. See Unger 1932: 310 and pl. 38b, with earlier literature; Unger 1957–71:129–130; El-Amin 1953:35–36; Wäfler 1971:33–34, with earlier literature on p. 27, n. 102. In n. 142 Wäfler noted that "Der Zyklus Ḫorsābad . . . der die Schlacht von Rapiḫu darstellen dürfte — zeigt, sowohl noch erkennbar — ausschliesslich Äthiopier." A similar conclusion, based on entirely different foundations, was reached by Trebolle 1981:147–149, 152.

quence of events as inferred from Sargon's inscriptions. Thus, it is clear that the reference in these verses was to the same king, i.e., Sargon II.

The Deuteronomistic Historian, who described the fall of the Northern Kingdom in 2 Kgs. 17:3–6, in his sources had most probably found only one name of an Assyrian king (i.e., Shalmaneser). Therefore, he erroneously assigned to him (though only implicitly) all the operations associated with the fall of Samaria. The campaigns and operations of the two Assyrian kings were combined by him in correct chronological order, but he was unable to draw a line between them, due to the lack of clarity in his sources. We may conclude that "the king of Assyria" in vv. 3–4 is Shalmaneser, whereas the king in vv. 5–6 is Sargon, his successor.

The description of the conquest of Samaria in the annals of Sargon is damaged; it may be partly restored on the basis of parallel accounts.[14] In his detailed display inscription, Sargon wrote thus: "I besieged and captured the city of Samaria" (Winckler 1899:100–101, line 23; Luckenbill 1927:§55). In the Nimrud prism, on the other hand, no siege is mentioned, only a fight against the Samarians (Gadd 1954:179–180, lines 29–30).[15] In a display inscription, Sargon wrote: "I plundered the city of Shinuḫtu, the city of Samaria and the whole land of Bit Ḫumri" (Winckler 1889:82–83 line 15; Luckenbill 1927:§80). In several pavement inscriptions, Sargon described himself as "conqueror of the city of Samaria and the whole land of Bit Ḫumri" (Winckler 1889:2, pl. 38–40, lines 31–32; Luckenbill 1927:§99); in a bull inscription, he is portrayed as "(he) who overthrew the city of Samaria (and) all the land of Bit Ḫumri" (Lyon 1883:40–41, line 21; Luckenbill 1927:§92). Siege operations are not emphasized in Sargon's inscriptions, and no king of Israel is ever mentioned. Thus, it is evident that there was no king either in Samaria or in any other Northern Israelite city at that time.

S. Dalley has suggested that the Samarians were treated favourably by Sargon after the capture of the city and the annexation of the land in 720 BCE (Dalley 1985:33–42). Her analysis of the Assyrian documents fits well into the historical reconstruction suggested here. It is not clear whether Samaria was severely damaged in the course of its conquest; the scanty archaeological ev-

14. For restoration of the badly mutilated passage in the Khorsabad annals, see Tadmor 1958:33–35. The similarity of this passage (lines 11–17) with the description of the conquest of Samaria on the Nimrud prism (IV 25–41) is clear and should not be questioned (contra Becking 1985:44–47). The following broken episode in the annals (line 18) also has a parallel passage on the Nimrud prism (IV 46–49).

15. For further literature, see Gadd 1954:182 and pl. XLV–XLVI; Tadmor 1958:33–35; Borger in Galling 1968:60–61; 1984:382, note; Spieckermann 1982:349–350; Dalley 1985:36; Becking 1985:51–55.

idence hardly supports the claim of overall destruction. Rather, we may assume a continuity of urban life and rapid reconstruction of the city under the Assyrians, when Samaria became the capital of the province of Samerina.

How should we interpret the data about three years of siege and the capture of Samaria in the ninth year of Hoshea? It is these data that led so many scholars to believe that Shalmaneser conquered Samaria, in disregard of the claim to the contrary in contemporary inscriptions of Sargon and the contradictory statement of v. 6b, which has the same subject as v. 6a ("the king of Assyria"), but indisputably refers to Sargon. Are these really historical data derived directly from archival sources? In my opinion, the answer to this crucial question is negative. The three years of siege (v. 5b) and the date in v. 6a are both historical deductions by the Deuteronomistic Historian, who, in his sources, had found a datum that Samaria was besieged and conquered by the Assyrians three years *after* its rebellion and the imprisonment of its king.[16] He mistakenly interpreted the datum to mean that the city fell — after three years of siege — in Hoshea's last year, thus, combining his last year with the fall of Samaria.

A short note on the author of the passage is desirable for a better understanding of his mistaken historical deduction. It must be realized that he was, in the first place, a historian struggling with the source material available to him, trying to write a history of Israel according to his best understanding of past events and in accordance with his guiding historiographical concepts. He lived long after the conclusion of the events he portrayed and, thus, he depended heavily on his source material.[17] The results of his interpretation of the sources may be read and appreciated today, in the light of many sources not available to him. Side by side with admiration for his achievement as a historian, we must also remember that his work, like that of all human beings, is not free of mistakes caused by misinterpretation of source material.

16. One may ostensibly suggest that Shalmaneser laid siege to Samaria immediately after the imprisonment of Hoshea and that the three years of siege (v. 5b) were counted from this early siege (723/22) until Sargon's conquest (720). According to this hypothesis, v. 5 refers to Shalmaneser and v. 6 refers to Sargon. It is better, however, to assume that the two verses (5–6) refer to the same Assyrian king (i.e., Sargon)

17. My analysis of 2 Kgs. 17:3–6 clashes with the conclusions of Weippert (1972:304–323), according to which the first edition of the DtrH was written in the time of Hezekiah and also included 2 Kgs. 17:1–6. It is inconceivable that an author living at the time of the conquest of Samaria would have confused the operations of the king who had captured the city, deported its people and annexed it to Assyrian territory with those of his predecessor. Such confusion could have occurred only long after the conclusion of the events recorded in the passage.

The mistaken dates in vv. 5–6 were the basis for a later redactor (possibly DtrN) who composed 2 Kgs. 18:9–12 (Šanda 1912:244–245; Würthwein 1984: 410). The passage is entirely dependent on 17:5–6 and is the result of the desire of the redactor to incorporate the fall of Samaria within the chronological framework of the reign of Hezekiah (Montgomery 1951:482).

The redactor removed all the obscurities involved in the understanding of the text of 17:5–6 and composed a clear and consistent chronology of the stages in the fall of Samaria. Needless to say, the passage in 18:9–12 is worthless for historical reconstruction; it contributes instead to our understanding of the way in which scribes in the post-exilic period worked with the old texts, trying to interpret them, smooth difficulties and fill gaps in the chain of events.

V. 24 of 2 Kgs. 17 originally most probably came after v. 6 (Trebolle 1981: 150–151; Mayes 1983:126). It described the deportation of people from Babylonia and the peripheral areas east of the Tigris by the "king of Assyria," i.e., Sargon II (Na'aman and Zadok 1988:44–46).[18] A later author, writing a polemical composition against the Samarians, detached the verse from its original place and used it as an introduction for his work. verses 6, 24, thus, recounted the episode of the conquest of Samaria by Sargon and the following two-way deportation: from Samaria to northern Mesopotamia and Media and from Babylonia and its peripheral areas to Samaria.

Conclusion

Amalgamation of biblical and extra-biblical data always involves great difficulties arising from differences of outlook, divergence of literary genres and differences in the aims of the scribes. Attempts to combine them into a unified historical picture involves reconstructions and hypotheses; the best reconstruction is one that best fits the majority of evidence and is not contradicted by any unequivocal testimony. It is in this light that we must examine the problem at hand. No reconstruction fits all the documentary evidence — every proposed solution must include a detailed explanation for those sources that either contradict it or are at variance with it.

In the first part of this article, we have critically examined the widely accepted reconstruction, according to which Samaria was conquered twice — once after three years of siege by Shalmaneser V (723 or 722 BCE) and for the second time by Sargon II (720 BCE). The reconstruction rests mainly on the

18. For a different dating of the deportation of the Babylonians and Cuthians to Samaria, see Winckler 1892b:97–107; Cogan 1974:101, n.23, with earlier literature; Tadmor 1983:4–6.

chronological data of 2 Kgs. 17:5b–6 and 18:9–10, according to which Samaria, after three years of siege, was captured by Shalmaneser in Hoshea's ninth year. Sargon explicitly claimed, in his inscriptions, that he had conquered Samaria; therefore, a two-conquest hypothesis was necessary to reconcile the conflicting sources. The hypothesis, however, involves rejection of various details that appear in Sargon's inscriptions and in the Book of Kings.

As shown in the discussion, Sargon's inscriptions can hardly be reconciled with the two-conquest hypothesis. The prominent place of the conquest of Samaria in inscriptions composed in Sargon's later years, his statement that the rebellion of the Samarians had already started in the time of his predecessor, the place of the Samarians in the struggle of 720 BCE and Sargon's claim that it was he who suppressed the rebellion and conquered Samaria — all these data do not accord well with the hypothesis that Samaria was conquered by Shalmaneser after a long siege. The archaeological excavations of Samaria hardly support a theory of a long siege that culminated with the conquest of the city. Likewise, these excavations can be interpreted as evidence for a conquest after a short siege and limited destruction. The Babylonian Chronicle sets the "ravaging" of Šamara'in in Shalmaneser's accession year. Provided that the ravaged city is indeed Samaria (see note 10 above), the Chronicle may refer to a western campaign conducted by Shalmaneser at the beginning of his reign, a campaign that is also mentioned in 2 Kgs. 17:3 and is probably referred to in the Tyrian history of Menander. The notation in the Babylonian Chronicle hardly can refer to a conquest after a long siege in Shalmaneser's last year, as was suggested by the two-conquest hypothesis.

Similar problems arise out of the interpretation of the account in 2 Kgs. 17:3-6. The text of v. 4b, according to which Hoshea was arrested before the siege of Samaria, contradicts the dates in 17:6a and 18:9–10. Dividing the operations related in v. 6 between two Assyrian kings, Shalmaneser (v. 6a) and Sargon (v. 6b), although only one "king of Assyria" is mentioned, is likewise problematic. Division of the account in vv. 3–6 into originally two parallel sources (vv. 3–4 and 5–6) also is not supported by analysis of the text.

As noted above, the chronological datum in v. 6a (and in 18:9–10) and the statement that Samaria was besieged for three years are the cornerstones of the two-conquest hypothesis. We suggest that the dates are not of archival source, but rather historical inferences based on interpretation of the source material by the Deuteronomistic Historian. Unfortunately, his chronological interpretation of the sources was mistaken, and a later redactor, trying to convert DtrH's dates into a chronological sequence of events, expanded the error into a scheme of mistaken dates (18:9–10). When removing the cornerstones of the two-conquest hypothesis, we are left with only one conquest of Samaria mentioned both in the Bible and in the Assyrian royal inscriptions.

Eliminating the erroneous dates enabled us to suggest a new reconstruction of the events leading to the fall of Samaria, and this reconstruction fits all the available data much better. The history of Hoshea as related in 17:3–4 accords well with the Assyrian, Babylonian and Tyrian sources. According to the description in the book of Kings, Hoshea clashed twice with the Assyrians, once in Shalmaneser's accession year (v. 3) and once toward the end of the latter's reign (v. 4). Hoshea's (and possibly Eloulaios') second act of rebellion was encouraged by the king of Egypt, apparently Pi(ankhy) of the 25th (Cushite) Dynasty.

When the Assyrian army (under Shalmaneser or his general) reached the Land of Israel, Hoshea appeared before him and was arrested (v. 4b). Shortly afterwards, Shalmaneser died, and it is not clear whether a siege of Samaria was under way during his last year. When Sargon ascended the throne, he was detained for a year and a half in Assyria, trying to curtail the inner rebellion and consolidating his rule. The Samarians, whose king was held in prison (as a hostage?), were then able to join the coalition of Assyrian vassal states and provinces crystallizing under the leadership of the king of Hamath and supported by Egypt. Only after Sargon's victories in the north and south did the city of Samaria come under a siege, one which apparently did not last long. Three years passed between Hoshea's imprisonment and the conquest of Samaria by Sargon, a period regarded by the Deuteronomistic Historian as years during which the city was under siege.

Sargon II is the king who conquered Samaria, annexed it to the Assyrian territory, deported its people and brought in others to take their place. His inscriptions give many accurate details about the history of Samaria in its last stage; the fact that the episode was artificially dated in the royal annals to the beginning of the king's reign (Tadmor 1958:22–26, 30–36) does not reduce the accuracy of the account. Conquest, annexation and deportation were stages in one and the same historical episode and should be assigned to Sargon's reconquest of the West in the year 720 BCE. The Deuteronomistic Historian likewise described these stages in sequential order (2 Kgs. 17:5–6, 24); it is only his erroneous chronological data that marred the accuracy of his account of the final stage of the Northern Kingdom.

References

Abramski, S. 1985. The Attitude toward the Amorites and Jebusites in the Book of Samuel: Historical Foundation and Ideological Significance. *Zion* 50: 27–58 (Hebrew).
Albright, W.F. 1946. Cuneiform Material for Egyptian Prosopography 1500–1200 B.C. *JNES* 5: 7–25.
Avigad, N. 1978. Samaria. *Enc. Arch. Exc.* 4: 1032–1050.
Becking, B. 1985. *De Ondergang van Samaria.* (Ph.D. Thesis). Utrecht.
Borger, R. 1957. Assyriologische and altarabistische Miszellen. *Orientalia* 26: 1–10.
Borger, R. 1984. Historische Texte in akkadischer Sprache. In: Kaiser, O. ed. *Texte aus der Umwelt des Alten Testaments,* 1/4. Gütersloh: 354–410.
Christensen, D.L. 1989. The Identity of "King So" in Egypt (2 Kings xvii 4). *VT* 39: 140–153.
Cody, A. 1965. Le titre égyptien et le nom propre du scribe de David. *RB* 72: 381–393.
Cogan, M. 1974. *Imperialism and Religion. Assyria, Judah and Israel in the Eighth and Seventh Centuries B.C.E.* (Society of Biblical Literature Monograph Series 19). Missoula.
Crowfoot J.W. and Kenyon, M. and Sukenik, E.L. 1942. *The Buildings at Samaria.* London.
Crowfoot J.W. and Kenyon, M. and Sukenik, E.L. 1957. *The Objects from Samaria.* London.
Dalley, S. 1985. Foreign Chariotry and Cavalry in the Armies of Tiglath-Pileser III and Sargon II. *Iraq* 47: 31–48.
Donner, H. 1977. The Separate States of Israel and Judah. In: Hayes, J.H. and Miller, J.M. (eds) *Israelite and Judaean History.* Philadelphia: 381–434.
Donner, H. 1986. *Geschichte des Volkes Israel and seiner Nachbarn in Grundzügen* 2. Göttingen.
Donner, H. and Röllig, W. 1968. *Kanaanäische and Aramäische Inschriften* 1–3 (2nd revised ed.). Wiesbaden.
Eilers, W. 1964–66. Zur Funktion von Nominalformen. Ein Grenzgang zwischen Morphologie und Semiologie. *WO* 3: 80–145.
El-Amin, M. 1953. Die Reliefs mit Beischriften von Sargon II in Dûr-Sharrukin. *Sumer* 9: 35–59, 214–228.
Federn, W. 1960. Daḫamunzu KBo V 6 iii 8. *JCS* 14: 33.
Gadd, C.J. 1954. Inscribed Prisms of Sargon II from Nimrud. *Iraq* 16: 173–201.
Galling, K. 1968. *Textbuch zur Geschichte Israels*[2]. Tübingen.
Goedicke, H. 1963. The End of "So, King of Egypt." *BASOR* 171: 64–66.
Goedicke, H. 1973. 727 vor Christus. *Wiener Zeitschrift für die Kunde des Morgenlandes* 69: 1–19.
Grayson, A.K. 1975. *Assyrian and Babylonian Chronicles.* Locust Valley.
Grayson, A.K. 1980. The Chronology of the Reign of Ashurbanipal. *ZA* 70: 227–245.
Hawkins, J.D. 1982. The Neo-Hittite States in Syria and Anatolia. In: Boardman, J. et al. eds. *The Cambridge Ancient History* 3/1. Cambridge: 372–435.
Hentschel, G. 1985. *2 Könige.* (Die Neue Echter Bibel). Würzburg.
Hirschberg, H. 1932. Studien zur Geschichte Esarhaddons König von Assyrien (681–669). Ohlau in Schlesien.
Katzenstein, H.J. 1973. *The History of Tyre, from the Beginning of the Second Millennium B.C.E. until the Fall of the Neo-Babylonian Empire in 538 B.C.E.* Jerusalem.
Krauss, R. 1978. Sō', König von Ägypten — ein Deutungsvorschlag. *MDOG* 110: 49–54.
Laato, A. 1986. New Viewpoints on the Chronology of the Kings of Judah and Israel. *ZAW* 98: 210–221.
Landsberger, B. 1948. *Sam'al. Studien zur Entdeckung der Ruinenstaette Karatepe.* Ankara.
Lehmann (-Haupt), C.F. 1902. Menander and Josephos über Salmanassar IV. *Klio* 2: 125–140, 466–472.

Lie, A. G. 1929. *The Inscriptions of Sargon II King of Assyria.* Part I: *The Annals Transliterated and Translated with Notes.* Paris.

Luckenbill, D.D. 1924. *The Annals of Sennacherib.* Chicago.

Luckenbill, D.D. 1927. *Ancient Records of Assyria and Babylonia* 2. Chicago.

Lyon, D.G. 1883. *Keilschrifttexte Sargon's, Königs von Assyrien (722–705 v. Chr.).* Leipzig.

McCarter, P.K. 1984. *II Samuel. A New Translation with Introduction and Commentary.* (Anchor Bible 9). Garden City.

Mayes, A.D.H. 1983. *The Story of Israel between Settlement and Exile. A Redactional Study of the Deuteronomistic History.* London.

Montgomery, J.A. 1951. *A Critical and Exegetical Commentary on the Books of Kings.* (ICC). Edinburgh.

Na'aman, N. 1974. Sennacherib's "Letter to God" on his Campaign to Judah. *BASOR* 214: 25–39.

Na'aman, N. 1979. Sennacherib's Campaign to Judah and the Date of the LMLK Stamps. *VT* 29: 61–86.

Na'aman, N. 1986. Historical and Chronological Notes on the Kingdoms of Israel and Judah in the Eighth Century BC. *VT* 36: 71–92.

Na'aman, N. and Zadok, R. 1988. Sargon II's Deportations to Israel and Philistia (716–708 BC). *JCS* 40: 36–46.

Olmstead, A.T.E. 1904/5. The Fall of Samaria. *American Journal of Semitic Languages and Literatures* 21: 179–182.

Olmstead, A.T.E. 1908. *Western Asia in the Days of Sargon of Assyria, 722–705 BC.* New York.

Parpola, S. 1980. The Murderer of Sennacherib. In: Alster, B. ed. Death in Mesopotamia. (Mesopotamia 8). Copenhagen: 171–181.

Rehm, M. 1982. *Das zweite Buch der Könige.* Würzburg.

Saggs, H.W.F. 1975. Historical Texts and Fragments of Sargon II of Assyria. 1. The Aššur Charter. *Iraq* 37: 11–20.

Šanda, A. 1912. *Die Bücher der Könige übersetzt und erklärt. 2. Das zweite Buch der Könige.* (Exegetisches Handbuch zum Alten Testament 9/2). Münster.

Singer, I. 1988. The Origin of the Sea Peoples and Their Settlement on the Coast of Canaan. In: Heltzer, M. and Lipiński, E. eds. *Society and Economy in the Easter Mediterranean (c. 1500-1000 B.C.).* (Orientalia Lovaniensia Analecta 23). Leuven: 239–250.

Spalinger, A. 1973. The Year 712 B.C. and its Implications for Egyptian History. *Journal of the American Research Center in Egypt* 10: 95–101.

Spalinger, A. 1974. Esarhaddon and Egypt: An Analysis of the First Invasion of Egypt. *Orientalia* 43: 295–326.

Spalinger, A. 1974. Assurbanipal and Egypt: A Source Study. *JAOS* 94: 316–328.

Spalinger, A. 1978. The Foreign Policy of Egypt Preceding the Assyrian Conquest. *Chronique d'Égypte* 53: 22–47.

Spieckermann, H. 1982. *Juda unter Assur in der Sargonidenzeit.* (Forschungen zur Religion und Literatur des Alten und Neuen Testaments 129). Göttingen.

Tadmor, H. 1958. The Campaigns of Sargon II of Assur: A Chronological-Historical Study. *JCS* 12: 22–40, 77–100.

Tadmor, H. 1966. Philistia under Assyrian Rule. *BA* 29: 86–102.

Tadmor, H. 1979. The Chronology of the First Temple Period. In Malamat, A. ed. *The Age of the Monarchies: Political* History. (The World History of the Jewish People IV/1). Jerusalem: 44–60.

Tadmor, H. 1976. Shalmaneser V. *Enc. Miqr.* VII. Jerusalem: 714–715 (Hebrew).

Tadmor, H. 1983. Some Aspects of the History of Samaria during the Biblical Period. *The Jerusalem Cathedra* 3: 1–11

Thiele, E.R. 1965. *The Mysterious Numbers of the Hebrew Kings*. Grand Rapids.

Trebolle, J.C. 1981. La caida de Samariá. Critica textual, literaria e história de 2 Re 17,3–6. *Salmanticensis* 28: 137–152.

Unger, E. 1932. Äthiopier in assyrischer Darstellung. *RLA* I: 310.

Unger, E. 1957–71. Gabbutunu. *RLA* III: 129–130.

Wäfler, M. 1975. *Nicht-Assyrer neuassyrischer Darstellungen* (AOAT 26). Kevelaer and Neukirchen-Vluyn.

Weippert, H. 1972. Die "deuteronomistischen" Beurteilungen der Könige von Israel and Juda and das Problem der Redaktion der Königbücher. *Biblica* 53: 301–339.

Wildberger, H. 1978. *Jesaia, 2. Jesaja* 13–27 (Biblischer Kommentar 10/2). Neukirchen-Vluyn.

Winckler, H. 1887. Nachtrag. *ZA* 2: 351–352.

Winckler, H. 1892a. Beiträge zur Quellenscheidung der Königsbücher. In: Winckler, H. *Alttestamentliche Untersuchungen*. Leipzig: 1–54.

Winckler, H. 1892b. Die samaritanischen Ansiedler. In: Winckler, H. *Alttestamentliche Untersuchungen*. Leipzig: 97–107.

Winckler, H. 1899. *Die Keilschrifttexte Sargons nach den Papierabklatschen und Originalen neu herausgegeben* 1. Leipzig.

Winckler, H. 1903. In: Schrader, E. (ed) *Die Keilinschriftten und das Alten Testament*[3], *mit Ausdehnung auf die Apokryphen, Pseudepigraphischen und das Neue Testament neu bearbeitet von H. Zimmern und H. Winckler*. Berlin.

Würthwein, E. 1984. *Die Bücher der Könige. 1. Kön. 17-2. Kön.* 25. (Das Alte Testament Deutsch 11,2). Göttingen.

The Historical Portion of Sargon II's Nimrud Inscription[1]

The account of Sargon's restoration of Ashurnaṣirpal's palace appears on two slabs from Calah (Nimrud) — one in Assyrian, the other in Babylonian characters (Layard 1851:pls. 33–34; Winckler 1889:168–173; Luckenbill 1927: §§136–138; Tadmor 1958:38–39, n. 146). The inscription is not dated, but was clearly written in Sargon's early years. It is a summary inscription divided into four parts: (a) An introduction consisting mainly of the ruler's titles; (b) Sargon's achievements in his campaigns; (c) the restoration of Calah's *duprānu* palace; (d) the placement of the Carchemish booty in the palace's treasure-house.

The following analysis of the "historical" part of the inscription seeks to clarify the principle underlying the organization of its material and to establish an accurate date for the consecration of the restored palace.

For the sake of convenience, I will first translate this part of the inscription (lines 7–12):

> Exalted prince, who met with Ḫumbanigash, king of Elam, in the district of Der and defeated him; subduer of the land of Judah, which lies far away; who deported the people of Hamath, capturing Jaubi'idi, their king, in his hands; who repulsed the land of Kakme, the wicked enemy; who set in order the disordered land of Mannai; who gladdened the heart of his land; who extended the border of Assyria. Diligent ruler, snare of the unsubmissive, whose hand captured Pisiri, king of Ḫatti, and set his official over Carchemish, his city; who deported (the people of) Shinuḫtu, bringing Kiakki, king of Tabal, to Ashur, his city, and placing his yoke on the land of Mushki; who conquered the land of Mannai, Karalla and Pattiru; who avenged his land; who defeated the far away land of Media as far as the rising sun.

The passage is clearly divided into two sections, each of which opens with a royal title: "exalted prince" in the first, "diligent ruler" in the second. A foreign king captured by Sargon is mentioned in each section. Each cites the deportation of a group of people, and each names a land that lies far away: Judah — located in the southwestern end of the empire — in the first section,

1. Reprinted with permission. State *Archives of Assyria Bulletin* 8/1 (1994), 17–20

and Media — situated in the northeastern end of the empire — in the second. The land of Mannai is mentioned twice, once in each section.

The division of the passage into two parallel sections requires an explanation. It seems to me that the basis for the partition is chronological and that each section presents events of a well defined period.

The episodes mentioned in the text can be dated by reference to these campaigns recorded in the Khorsabad Annals, whose dates are well established. But the ensuing chronology should be completed by reference to Sargon's Stela from Najafehabad in Iran (Levine 1972:25–50). Tadmor (1958: 22–40, 77–94) has demonstrated that Sargon's scribes sometimes shifted historical episodes from one year to another (for another example, see Na'aman and Zadok 1988:42–43). The Najafehabad Stela was composed during the king's campaign against Media in 717 and, thus, belongs to the small group of inscriptions written in Sargon's early years. Comparison of the dates of campaigns as they appear in the Stela and in the much later Khorsabad Annals (707 BCE) gives further support to Tadmor's argument and indicates how cautiously one should treat the later organization of the historical material in the Annals.

Following is a chronology of the episodes that appear in the Nimrud Inscription:

(a) The battle against Ḫumbanigash at Der and the subjection of Ḫamath and Judah took place in year 720 BCE.

(b) The first campaign against the cities of Mannai that revolted against their king was conducted in 719. The land of Kakme is located in the northwestern part of the Iranian plateau, east or northeast of Mannai. A campaign against the land of Kakme is not mentioned in Sargon's other inscriptions. In his Cylinder Inscription from Khorsabad, composed a short time after 713, Sargon is designated "destroyer of the seats of the cities Papa, Lallukna, Sukkia, Bala and Abitikna, who conspired treacherously(?) with the land of Kakme."[2] In the Khorsabad Annals composed in Sargon's late period (707 BCE), this episode appears in two different *palûs* and is combined with the motif of deportation as the final stage of a campaign. The third *palû* (719) records that the men of Sukkia, Bala and Abitikna conspired with Ursa of Urartu and were deported and resettled in Syria (*Ḫatti*) (Lie 1929:10–11, lines 66–68); and the fifth *palû* (717) indicates that the men of Papa and Lallukna plotted with the land of Kakme and were deported to Damascus (Lie 1929:12–13, lines 76–78). It seems to me that Kakme was an ally of Urartu and, thus, was involved in

2. Lyon 1883:32, line 28; Luckenbill 1927:§118; CAD N/1 262b. For the date of composition of the Cylinder Inscriptions from Khorsabad, see Tadmor 1958:36, n. 124.

the rebellion that broke out in Mannai in the year 719. Therefore, it was described in the Nimrud Inscription as a kingdom "repulsed" by Sargon when he suppressed the rebellion of Mannai. The scribe of the Khorsabad Annals edited the historical material in a way that fitted his overall scheme. He, thus, artificially combined the land of Kakme with the deportation, which he assigned to the fifth *palû*, while connecting the kingdom of Urartu with the deportation assigned to the king's third *palû*.

(c) The campaign against Carchemish and its annexation was conducted in 717 BCE.

(d) The campaign against Shinuḫtu, in which the ruler (Kiakki) and many of his subjects were deported, was conducted in the year 718. According to the Najafehabad Stela (lines 17–19), this campaign was conducted against the land of Tabal, and its rulers were obliged to pay tribute. According to a late prism of Sargon from Calah, "Kiakki of the town of Shinuḫtu [conspired with] Mita, king of Mushki."[3] It goes without saying that Sargon's claim of "placing his yoke" on the land of Mushki is a vain boast. It is evident that the enmity between Sargon and Mita of Mushki began as early as 718 BCE and that the above-mentioned campaign against Shinuḫtu and Mushki should be assigned to this year.

(e) The conquest of Mannai, Karalla, Pattiru and Madai may be safely dated to the year 717, as is evident from the Najafehabad Stela (lines 20ff). This is contrary to the Khorsabad Annals, in which the campaign was assigned to the sixth *palû*. The major campaign in 717 was conducted to the east; the conquest and annexation of Carchemish at the beginning of the year was more administrative than military in nature.

Summing up the discussion, it is evident that the author of the Nimrud Inscription divided its historical part into two sections: the events of the years 720–719 and the events of the years 718–717. Moreover, even within the two sections, the events are chronologically arranged with one exception: the conquest of Carchemish (717) is prior to the conquest of Shinuḫtu (718). Locating the conquest of Carchemish at the beginning of the second section may be due to the scribe's desire to underline the event, because the placement of the booty of Carchemish in the treasure-house of the restored palace forms the last episode in the inscription. It is clear that our inscription was written either in late 717 or in early 716, when the new palace was consecrated and the treasures of Carchemish deposited there.[4]

3. Gadd 1954:180, lines 50–52, and p. 182. For a comparison of the various descriptions of Sargon's campaign against Kiakki of Shinuḫtu, see Renger 1986:144.

4. Dating the Nimrud Inscription to either 717 or 716 BCE is not uncommon in scientific literature. See Winckler 1889:VI, n. 2; Olmstead 1908:17; Tadmor 1958:36, n. 127; 1989:

In conclusion, the Nimrud Inscription may be regarded as a summary inscription whose historical part is mainly arranged according to a chronological principle. With all due caution, it may be used as an additional source for the campaigns of Sargon in the years 720–717 BCE.

References

Becking, G. 1992. *The Fall of Samaria: An Historical and Archaeological Study.* (Studies in the History of the Ancient Near East 2). Leiden.

Gadd, C.J. 1954. Inscribed Prisms of Sargon II from Nimrud. *Iraq* 16: 173–201.

Layard, A.H. 1851. *Inscriptions in the Cuneiform Character from Assyrian Monuments.* London.

Levine, L.D. 1972. *Two Neo-Assyrian Stelae from Iran.* (Royal Ontario Museum, Art and Architecture, Occasional Papers 23). Totonto.

Lie, A.G. 1929. *The Inscriptions of Sargon II, King of Assyria.* Part I: *The Annals Transliterated and Translated with Notes.* Paris.

Luckenbill, D.D. 1927. *Ancient Records of Assyria and Babylonia* II. Chicago.

Lyon, D.G. 1883. *Keilschrifttexte Sargon's, Königs von Assyrien (722–705 v. Chr.).* (Assyriologische Bibliothek 5). Leipzig.

Na'aman N. and Zadok R. 1988. Sargon II's Deportations to Israel and Philistia (716–708 B.C.). *JCS* 40: 36–46.

Olmstead, A.T.E. 1908. *Western Asia in the Days of Sargon of Assyria, 722–705 B.C.* New York.

Renger, J. 1986. Neuassyrische Königsinschriften als Genre der Keilschriftliteratur. Zum Stil und zur Kompositionstechnik der Inschriften Sargon II. von Assyrien. In: Hecker, K. and Sommerfeld, W. eds. *Keilschriftliche Literaturen* (Berliner Beiträge zum Vorderen Orient 6). Berlin: 109–128.

Tadmor, H. 1958. The Campaigns of Sargon II of Assur: A Chronological-Historical Study. *JCS* 12: 22–40, 77–100.

Tadmor, H. 1989. The Historical Background. *State Archives of Assyria Bulletin* 3/1: 25–32.

Winckler, H. 1889. *Die Keilschrifttexte Sargons nach den Papierabklatschen und Originalen neu herausgegeben* I-II. Leipzig.

26–27. The attribution of the subjection of the kingdom of Judah to Sargon's campaign of the year 715 (Becking 1992:54–55) is, in my opinion, untenable.

Hezekiah and the Kings of Assyria[1]

Sargon II and the Kingdom of Judah: the Problem of the Sources

According to the Book of Kings, Rezin of Aram and Pekah of Israel laid siege to Jerusalem. Ahaz, the king of Judah, sought the help of the Assyrian king Tiglath-pileser III, who subsequently conducted a campaign, killed Rezin and conquered Aram and Israel (2 Kgs. 15:29; 16:1–9; see Isa. 7:1–9). Following the Assyrian campaign, Ahaz became an Assyrian vassal (2 Kgs. 16:5, 7–18). Judah rebelled in the days of Hezekiah, the son of Ahaz, and was attacked by Sennacherib in Hezekiah's 14th year (2 Kgs. 18:7, 13–16). The name of Sargon II, king of Assyria (721–705 BCE), does not appear in the Book of Kings and is mentioned only once in the Bible (Isa. 20:1).

According to Sargon II's inscriptions, he conducted a large-scale campaign to the west in 720 BCE, conquered the coast of Philistia to its southernmost border, captured Samaria, deported many of its inhabitants and annexed it to Assyria (see 2 Kgs. 17:5–6). In the Nimrud Inscription, he is called "subduer of the land of Judah which is far away" (Winckler 1889 I:168, line 8). The subjection of Judah may safely be dated to the same campaign. In the following years, Sargon brought deportees to the coast of Philistia, replaced the ruler of Ashdod, quelled a rebellion that broke out there and annexed the rebellious kingdom. Is it possible that Sargon also attacked the kingdom of Judah, but the attack was mentioned neither in the Bible nor in Sargon's royal inscriptions? Or does the absence of Judah from these sources indicate that Judah was not attacked by Sargon and remained a loyal vassal throughout his reign?

Some scholars interpreted the silence of the sources as an indication that Sargon did not clash with the kingdom of Judah. The main controversy involves the interpretation of the "Azekah Inscription." A fragment of the text (BM 82-3-23, 131) was published by Winckler (1899:570–574) and discussed in detail by Tadmor (1958a:80–84). Tadmor dated the inscription to the year 712 BCE and combined it both with Sargon's campaign against Ashdod of the

1. Reprinted with permission. *Tel Aviv* 21 (1994), 235–254.

same year and with several Assyrian reliefs unearthed in Khorsabad (Dur-Sharrukin). The suggestion was adopted by some scholars (Eph'al 1968:1124; Ginsberg 1968:48–49; Wäfler 1975:27–32), but was abandoned after the first fragment was combined with another (K 6205), and it was argued that the combined inscription describes Sennacherib's campaign against Judah in 701 BCE (Na'aman 1974:25–31; 1979a:61–63 and n. 4). Nonetheless, some scholars still hold the opinion that the inscription should be attributed to Sargon II and that it refers to the king's punitive campaign against Judah in 711 BCE (Cogan and Tadmor 1988:261–262, n. 6; Galil 1992; cf. Borger 1979:134; Timm 1989: 356, n. 50).[2]

In this article, I will re-examine the sources referring to the relationship of Sargon II with Hezekiah of Judah to better understand Hezekiah's foreign policy prior to his rebellion of 705 BCE. The Deuteronomistic Historian's view of Hezekiah's reign will be examined in the final part of the article, in an effort to better understand the way the Deuteronomistic Historian evaluated his sources and judged the chain of events within his historical composition.

The Date of Hezekiah's Throne Tenure

There are obvious contradictions in the Book of Kings regarding Hezekiah's enthronement, and the dates of his 29-year reign are disputed among scholars. Some give priority to the synchronisms (2 Kgs. 18:1, 9–10), according to which Hezekiah ascended the throne in the 3rd year of Hoshea, the son of Elah, and, thus, reigned 727–698 BCE (Gonçalves 1986:52–54, with earlier literature; Miller and Hayes 1986:350–351; Hayes and Hooker 1988: 64–80; Becking 1992:47–56). Others give more weight to the text of 2 Kgs. 18:13 (and Isa. 36:1), according to which Sennacherib conducted his campaign in Hezekiah's 14th year (701 BCE) and, thus, date Hezekiah to ca. 715/14–686 BCE (Thiele 1965:118–161; Gonçalves 1986:54–58, with earlier literature). Sennacherib's campaign corresponds to the story of the miraculous recovery of Hezekiah from illness, following which YHWH added 15 years to Hezekiah's life (2 Kgs. 20:1–11), which shortly antedated the Assyrian attack on Jerusalem (see 2 Kgs. 20:6). Those who adhere to the first chronological system dismiss the synchronism between Hezekiah's 14th year and Sennacherib's campaign and the chronological conclusion drawn from the story of the miraculous recovery of the king; supporters of the second alternative dismiss the synchronism between Hezekiah's and Hoshea's reigns,

2. Becking (1992:3, n. 8; 54, n. 30) recently suggested that the "Azekah Inscription" reflects events in 715 BCE.

regarding them as artificial calculations of the throne tenures of the Israelite and Judean kings by later scribes.[3]

The selection of a certain chronological system for Hezekiah's reign has an important bearing on the overall evaluation of his reign. According to one chronology, Hezekiah was an Assyrian vassal for more than two decades. It was only in his later years that he rebelled, and he died a few years after Sennacherib's campaign. According to the second chronology, the rebellion broke out less than 10 years after his enthronement, and Sennacherib's campaign was conducted in the middle of his reign. Unfortunately, there is no conclusive evidence for either chronological system.

I would like to raise two points in support of the second chronology, according to which the death of Ahaz and Hezekiah's enthronement took place in the year 715/14 BCE.

(A) It seems that almost all the data concerning Hezekiah's reign in the Book of Kings must be attributed to the time of his anti–Assyrian rebellion and the campaign of 701 BCE. These data include the notes of the revolt and the conquest of Philistia (2 Kgs. 18:7b-8), the illness and miraculous recovery (20:1–11), Merodach-baladan's embassy (20:12–19) (see below) and the episodes of Sennacherib's campaign (18:13–19:36). The critical period of the rebellion and Assyrian campaign must have been engraved in the collective historical memory and later put down in writing, either in the late Monarchial or the early Exilic period. When the author (the Deuteronomistic Historian) composed the history of Hezekiah, he used his sources in two different ways: (a) the chronographic sources (e.g., 2 Kgs. 18:7b-8, 13–16) served as a basis for the outline of Hezekiah's reign, and (b) the literary sources and verbal memories formed the core of the narratives through which the author transmitted his religious messages to his audience. The contents and presentation of these long narratives (2 Kgs. 18:17–19:36; 20:1–11) reflect the author's view of these events and the roles played by Hezekiah and Isaiah. The story of the Babylonian embassy (20:12–19) was apparently added later, in the post-Exilic period (McKenzie 1991:106–109, with earlier literature).

Due to compositional considerations, the narratives of Hezekiah's illness and recovery follow those of the campaign and miraculous delivery. The hypothesis that the date in 2 Kgs. 18:13 ("In the fourteenth year of King Hezekiah") originally stood before the story of the illness and recov-

3. According to another chronological system, Hezekiah ascended the throne of Judah as a co-regent (728/27); the year 715/14 marks the beginning of his sole reign. See Gonçalves 1986:58–60, with earlier literature; Na'aman 1986:83–85, with earlier literature in n. 44.

ery (Tadmor and Cogan 1982; Hutter 1982:67–69; Cogan and Tadmor 1988: 228, 260–263; Ruprecht 1990:33–52, 65–66) seems doubtful. There is no textual support for breaking v. 13 into two different sources. Moreover, prophetic narratives in the Book of Kings never open with such an accurate date, and the date in v. 13 can hardly serve as an introduction to the prophetic narrative in Chapter 20. On the other hand, numerous chronographic passages that describe the invasion of Israel/Judah by foreign rulers open with such a chronological note, followed by the verb *bw'/'lh* — with a human being (not a god) as the subject of the verb (2 Kgs. 12:18; 14:25; 15:29; 16:5; 18:9, 13; 23:29; 24:1, 10; 25:1, 8) (see Ben Zvi 1990). It is clear that the date in 2 Kgs. 18:13 is an integral part of the description in 2 Kgs. 18:13 ff.

We may conclude that the author of the story of the King's illness and recovery assumed that it had happened on the eve of the Assyrian campaign and that the king reigned long afterwards. The author, therefore, calculated the number of years that the prophet had promised to Hezekiah (15 years) in reference to the year in which, according to the author's source, the campaign had been conducted (year 14). He further combined the prophecy of recovery ("behold, I will heal you . . . and I will add fifteen years to your life") with the promise of divine protection to the king and his capital ("I will deliver you and this city out of the hand of the king of Assyria, and I will defend this city for my own sake and for my servant David's sake") (2 Kgs. 20:5–6).

(B) The assumption that Hezekiah reigned many years after the Assyrian campaign of 701 BCE may be supported by a comparison of the fates of Luli, king of Sidon, and Hezekiah, as described in Sennacherib's inscriptions.

The earliest annalistic edition of Sennacherib's campaign to the Phoenician coast and Palestine was written in 700 BCE (the Rassam Cylinder). The text runs as follows: "Luli, king of Sidon, the terrifying splendor of my sovereignty overcame him and far off into the midst of the sea he fled." In later inscriptions written from 697 BCE onward, the scribes added "and he died." The motif of Luli's death was expanded in detailed summary inscriptions written in the years 696–694 BCE and was presented as a divine punishment for the rebellion: "Luli, king of Sidon, was afraid to fight me and fled to Yadnana, which is in the midst of the sea, and there sought a refuge. In that year, by the splendor of the weapons of Ashur, my lord, he died" (Luckenbill 1924:77, lines 17–19). It is clear that when the author of the early inscription wrote his text he did not know of Luli's death. Later, when it was found that Luli had died some time after his flight, the motif of the rebel's death was inserted into the text. Some scribes even showed a direct relationship between rebellion and death as a divine punishment for the revolt.

According to one chronology, Hezekiah reigned in the years 727–698 BCE and died about 3 years after the rebellion. If these dates are valid, one would expect the Assyrian scribes to recall the death of the leader of the rebellion, as in the case of Luli. However, nothing of this kind is mentioned in inscriptions composed after Hezekiah's assumed death in 698 BCE. In the latest edition of the annals written in 691 BCE (with a copy dated to 689), Hezekiah is depicted exactly as in the early edition of 700 BCE. Moreover, an entirely new, shortened description of the campaign against Judah was composed in 696–694 BCE. It runs thus: "I laid waste the large district of Judah and made the stubborn (*šepṣu mitru*) Hezekiah, its king, bow in submission" (Luckenbill 1924:77, lines 20–22). In a summary inscription written in 691 (or 690) BCE, the event is presented thus: "I laid waste the large district of Judah and put the straps of my yoke upon Hezekiah, its king" (Luckenbill 1924:86, line 15). The way in which Hezekiah is portrayed in inscriptions composed 4–10 years after the campaign suggests that the Assyrians knew that, in spite of his rebellion, he remained ruler of Judah in the years to come. To minimize and obscure this fact, they emphasized the utter failure of the rebellion, the utter destruction that overcame the rebellious kingdom, and the unconditional submission of the rebel ruler.

The evidence presented here is inconclusive, but seems to tip the scales in favor of the late chronology. Ahaz died in 715/14 BCE, and Hezekiah succeeded him and remained on the throne for approximately 15 years after the Assyrian campaign. His son, Manasseh, was possibly a co-regent in the final decade of his reign, Hezekiah being forced to pay the price of his abortive rebellion by sharing his reign with his son and heir.[4]

Ashdod's Rebellion and Annexation

The Ashdod episode is described in detail in Sargon II's annals and summary inscriptions (Weissbach 1928; Weidner 1941–1944:49–50; Alt 1945:138–146; Tadmor 1958a:79–84; 1966:90–95; Spalinger 1973; Mattingly 1981, with earlier literature; Kapera 1987; Galil 1992). The chain of events is not my concern here, and I will discuss only the part played by the kingdom of Judah in the revolt.

The background of the rebellion is as follows: Sargon suspected that Azuri, king of Ashdod, was plotting with his neighbors, so he removed him from the throne, and replaced him with his brother, Aḫimeti, who must have supported Assyrian interests on the coast of Philistia. However, the Ashdodites

4. Manasseh's co-regency with Hezekiah may be compared with the nomination of Uzziah as co-regent with his father Amaziah, following the latter's defeat in the battle of Beth-shemesh (Thiele 1965:77–81).

refused to recognize the Assyrian nominee, overthrew him and enthroned a commoner called Yamani.[5]

The Nineveh Prism describes the Ashdodites' preparations in anticipation of the Assyrian campaign as follows (lines 25–33) (for transliteration and translation, see Winckler 1889 I:188, lines 28–38; II:44D; Oppenheim 1969:287; Na'aman 1974:32 and notes 29–31):

(25) To the k[ings] (L[UGAL^{MEŠ}-*ni*]) of Philistia, Judah, Ed[om] (and) Moab, who dwell by the sea, payers of tribute and gifts to Ashur, my lord, (they sent) evil words and unseemly speeches, (30) to set (them) at enmity with me. To Pharaoh, king of Egypt, a prince who could not save them, they sent their presents and asked him for (military) aid (*kitru*).[6]

No more than three signs are missing at the end of Line 25, as is evident from a collation of the original tablet in the British Museum by Prof. R. Zadok. The restoration L[UGAL^{MEŠ}-*ni*] fits the space at the end of the line and the traces of the broken sign and is doubtless correct.

The rulers of the neighboring states are described as "payers of tribute and gifts to Ashur, my lord," a positive characteristic from the point of view of the Assyrian king. It is the Ashdodites who tried to incite them to rebel, just as they tried to seduce the king of Egypt to send troops to their aid. The motif of inciting neighboring kings to join an anti-Assyrian revolt is common in the Assyrian royal inscriptions and is used as justification for conducting a campaign against the king who stirs the rebellion (Oded 1992:46–50). The dethronement of Azuri of Ashdod is explained in the same way (Lie 1929:38–41 lines 249–251): "Azuri, king of Ashdod, had schemed not to deliver tribute any more and sent messages (full) of hostilities against Assyria, to the kings (living) in his neighborhood." The two Ashdodite kings are accused of inciting their neighbors to rebel, but it is not stated that they succeeded. The opposite is true: Azuri was dethroned for this deed, and a campaign was conducted against Yamani, during the course of which his towns were captured, and he was forced to flee. Moreover, the king of Cush — who was supposed to lead the anti-Assyrian coalition and to whose country Yamani fled in face of the Assyrian onslaught — delivered the rebel into Assyrian hands. There is no

5. Yamani must have been an officer in the service of Aḫimeti before his enthronement. This is borne out by the text of the Nineveh Prism (Winckler 1889 I:186, lines 18–20; Oppenheim 1969:287a): "Yamani, a comm[oner, without claim to the throne, they have exalted] to kingship above themselves and made [him] sit [in the throne] of his lord (bēlišu)."

6. The term *kitru* in the Sargonid inscriptions designates military aid requested by an enemy king from a foreign power, in contrast to the king of Assyria, who trusted in divine support and needed no human aid (Liverani 1982).

indication that any other country except Ashdod was attacked in the course of the 711 BCE campaign. We may conclude that Ashdod alone was punished for opposing Assyrian policy on the coast of Philistia.

Sargon's inscriptions indicate that, following the campaign, Ashdod became an Assyrian province (Winckler 1889 I:116, lines 104–109; Weissbach 1918:178, lines 12–14; Lie 1929:40, lines 259–262; Weidner 1941–1944:50 lines 6–11). Indeed, the governor of Ashdod was an eponym (*limmu*) in the year 669 BCE (Ungnad 1938:428–429, 455; Alt 1945:145–146). On the other hand, a king is mentioned in Ashdod in 701 BCE. This may be explained by the assumption that the annexation of Ashdod was the first step in an overall plan to annex the entire coast of Philistia up to the border with Egypt. However, Sargon II was killed on the battlefield (705 BCE) before he was able to accomplish this. His son, Sennacherib, adopted a different policy and let the royal house of Ashdod rule over the kingdom. Ashdod, thus, remained an isolated Assyrian province ruled by a local king, side by side with an Assyrian governor, surrounded by vassal kingdoms (Alt 1945:141–146; Na'aman 1979b:71–72 n. 7).

Scholars agree that the Babylonians and Persians adopted the administrative system prevailing in Palestine when they conquered it. The annexation of Ashdod by the Assyrians well explains the adoption of the name "Ashdod" for the Persian (and possibly Babylonian) province on the coast of Philistia.

The Reliefs from Room V of Sargon II's Palace

The reliefs discovered in Room V of Sargon II's palace at Khorsabad play a central role in any discussion of his campaigns to the west. These reliefs have already been studied by scholars (Botta and Flandin 1849:pls. 84–100; Botta 1849:iii, pl. 180, line 3; El-Amin 1953:35–39, 214–228; Guterbock 1957: 68; Tadmor 1958a:83, n. 243; Wäfler 1975:27–35; Reade 1976:99–102; Mattingly 1981:49–50; Albenda 1986:82–86, 140–142; pls. 91–103; Schmitt 1989). I will discuss only those reliefs that scholars attribute to Sargon's campaigns on the coast of Philistia.

It must be emphasized that the reliefs were arranged according to a geographical, rather than chronological, order. Illustrations of campaigns conducted in different years to a certain region may appear side by side in the same room (Guterbock 1957:68; Winter 1983; Marcus 1989). One may ask: is there conclusive evidence that the reliefs from Room V portray episodes from Sargon's campaigns of 720 and 711 BCE, or are they episodes of a single campaign?

The city of Gabbutunu is portrayed in Relief 5-L. Ambidextrous Nubians each holding two long spears are depicted on the city's wall. Similar Nubians, each holding two long spears, are depicted in Reliefs 2–4 (Unger 1932:310; Pl. 38b; 1957–71; El-Amin 1953:35–36; Wäfler 1975:33–34 and n. 142). Neither ambidextrous soldiers nor Nubians are depicted on other reliefs in Room V, hence, reliefs 2–5 form a closed unit and represent a single scene.

Sargon fought a Nubian army only in his campaign of 720 BCE, when he defeated an Egyptian army under the command of Re'u near the city of Raphia; captured his ally Hanunu, king of Gaza; and conquered Raphia. Some scholars identify the nameless city in Relief 2-L as Raphia (El-Amin 1953:35–41; see Schmitt 1989:62).

The majority of scholars identify biblical Gibbethon with Gabbutunu of Relief 5-L. However, the identification is problematic. Gibbethon was situated on the border of Philistia and Israel (1 Kgs. 15:27; 16:15), within the inheritance of Dan (Josh. 19:44), and, thus, is located far from the field of battle. Schmitt (1989) instead placed Gabbutunu of the relief in the area of Raphia and presented evidence that a town bearing a similar name was situated here in the Roman and Byzantine periods and the late 15th century CE. He, thus, disassociated Gabbutunu form biblical Gibbethon. Admittedly, the late date of the documents and the lack of contemporaneous evidence for a town named Gabbutunu in the area of Raphia preclude an unequivocal identification. On the other hand, very little is known of the names of settlements in southern Philistia in the Iron Age. It is entirely possible that a town named Gabbutunu was situated in the Raphia area without being mentioned in contemporaneous documents. In any case, it is clear that the conquest of Gabbutunu, a town on whose walls ambidextrous Nubian soldiers are depicted, is closely related to the battle near Raphia and should be dated to 720 BCE.

One may recall that the Phoenician coast was conquered in 720 BCE and that the battle of Raphia was waged in the same year. Reade (1976:100–101) has noted that Sargon led only the campaign of 720 BCE, and the campaign against Ashdod in 711 was led by the Turtanu. In Reade's opinion, the appearance of the king standing on his chariot as captives are brought before him (Reliefs 2 in Door O and 13) indicates that the king participated, and, thus, must represent the campaign of 720 BCE. Although these scenes may reflect an artistic convention, Reade's argument adds weight to the assumption that not only Scenes 2–5a, 14–17, but also Scenes 5b-2 of Door O, and 10–13 (including the siege of the city of Ekron) took place during Sargon's campaign to the west in 720 BCE. We may conclude that there is no conclusive evidence that episodes of the 711 BCE Assyrian campaign against Ashdod are depicted on the lower walls of Room V of Sargon's palace at Khorsabad.

The Prophecies of Isaiah

In some of his prophecies, Isaiah expresses a strong opposition to political ties with Egypt and the seeking of its military aid. In Isa. 18:1–6, he preaches that the Nubian envoy who had arrived in Jerusalem should be sent back, predicting that a disaster would soon befall Cush (vv. 5–6). He criticizes the Judean court for seeking shelter "in the shadow of Egypt" and for not consulting YHWH (through his prophet, Isaiah) on this important matter (Isa. 30: 1–5). He describes Egypt as "a people that cannot profit them." The prophet portrays a dangerous journey through the desert by a caravan carrying gifts from the king of Judah to the Pharaoh (Isa. 30:6–7). Egypt is again called "a people that cannot profit them," a tiger made of paper (*rahab ha-mašbāt* [sic!]), whose help is "worthless and empty." In Isa. 31:1–3, the prophet emphasizes that the appeal for Egyptian help will bring disaster on Judah ("and helper will stumble, and he who is helped will fall, and they will all perish together") and calls for seeking support from YHWH alone.

The majority of these prophecies (and others) expresses Isaiah's reaction to Hezekiah's international activity of the years 705–702 BCE (Gonçalves 1986:31–33, 137–186, with earlier literature; Høgenhaven 1988:132–140).[7] Extensive political and diplomatic activities took place in those years to secure the military support of the king of Cush and the Egyptian princes for the anti-Assyrian coalition. Indeed, the diplomatic efforts were fruitful, and an Egyptian-Nubian army arrived to the battlefield in 701 BCE, but suffered a defeat and retreated, leaving Judah exposed to the Assyrian military machine. Isaiah's warnings were not vain words.

It is possible that contacts between the courts of Jerusalem and Nubia/ Egypt had already taken place in the time of Sargon II and that some of the anti-Egyptian Isaianic prophecies should be dated to this time. Yet, even if such anti-Assyrian plots were negotiated, there is no evidence that they were implemented, or that Assyria operated against the kingdom of Judah. Tension between Assyria and Judah in the days of Sargon is neither mentioned in Assyrian sources nor in the Bible. Judah was a vassal kingdom that paid tribute to Assyria and, as far as we know, did not clash with Assyria until Sargon's death in 705 BCE.

The introductory words to the prophecy in Isa. 20 run thus: "In the year that the Tartan, who was sent by Sargon king of Assyria, came to Ashdod and fought against it and took it." Isaiah is mentioned in the third person in vv. 2–3, which indicates that the original prophecy was re-worked at some later stage (Wildberger 1978:753–754; Høgenhaven 1988:135–136). The walking of

7. The concluding words of Gonçalves (1986:33) are worth being cited in full: "Bref, on ne dispose pas de renseignments sûrs au sujet de la politique suivie par Juda lors du soulevèment mené par Ashdod en 713–712. En tout cas, ni les documents assyriens ni les textes bibliques ne permettent d'affirmer, comme on le fait souvent, que Juda a pris part, voire une part importante, dans le soulèvement de 713–712, et qu'il en a subi les conséquences." A somewhat similar conclusion was reached by Miller and Hayes 1986: 352–353.

the prophet naked and barefoot for 3 years is presented in the prophecy as "a sign and a portent" that Egypt and Nubia shall also go into exile (vv. 3–4). It will cause a great panic to the "inhabitants of this coastland," namely, the inhabitants of the coast of Philistia who put their trust in the southern power, and their hope will be in vain (vv. 5–6; compare the prophecy over Philistia in Isa. 14:29–32).[8] The prophet's message is clear: an imminent disaster shall soon befall Egypt and Nubia; the inhabitants of Judah should not trust them (compare Isa. 18:1–6), or they will fear for their own future, as do the inhabitants of the coast of Philistia.

It goes without saying that the titles of the prophecies in Isaiah are not an integral part of them, but were added to the text at a later stage to establish a better historical or theological background. However, in the prophecy of Isa. 20, the title fits its contents. Following the Assyrian campaign, Ashdod became an Assyrian province and the border of Assyria reached the southern coast of Philistia. No wonder the extensive Assyrian operations on the border of Egypt suggested to the prophet that the fate of Egypt and Nubia would be the same. The prophet's fundamental belief that Israel must trust its god and no earthly power was supported by a practical political consideration that the fates of Egypt and Nubia were sealed. Israel should neither trust them, nor seek their military aid.

The prophecy (vv. 2–6) is predicting what will happen in the future, rather than describing current events. It echoes the fears of the inhabitants of Judah in the face of Assyrian operations on their western front, but reveals nothing of the role of Judah in the political events of 711 BCE.

The Date of Merodach-baladan's Embassy

The story of the dispatch of the Babylonian envoy to Jerusalem is related in 2 Kgs. 20:12–19 and Isa. 39. The historical authenticity of the prophecy has been discussed many times and is not my concern (e.g., Clements 1983; Ockinga 1983; Gonçalves 1986:332–337, with earlier literature; Begg 1986; 1987a; 1987b; 1988; McKenzie 1991:107–108). Scholars generally assume that the sending of an embassy by Merodach-baladan to Hezekiah is a historical event motivated by political-military considerations (rather than a polite gesture on the occa-

8. Some scholars suggested that the words "the inhabitants of this coastland" (v. 6) refer to the kingdom of Judah. See Marti 1900:140–141; Duhm 1914: 125; Kaiser 1974:116. However, it is unlikely that a Judean author would describe his own country by the noun "island (ʾy)." One would naturally assume that the noun "island" refers to Philistia, which is situated along the sea coast and whose inhabitants arrived, according to biblical tradition, from the Mediterranean islands. See Gray 1912:347; Wildberger 1978:759; Clements 1982: 176, with earlier literature.

sion of the king's recovery as related in the Bible). The arrival date is debated among scholars. Some attribute it to the first throne tenure of Merodach-baladan (722–710 BCE) (Clements 1980:67; Hutter 1982:69–71; Tadmor and Cogan 1982; Cogan and Tadmor 1988:260–262) and others to his second tenure (704–703 BCE) (Brinkman 1964:31–33, with earlier literature in n. 184).

According to the first view, the arrival of the envoy is linked to Hezekiah's preparations for rebellion against Assyria in 712/11 BCE. However, it has been demonstrated that there is no concrete evidence that Hezekiah planned a revolt at this time. Moreover, Ashdod's rebellion was of a local nature and was subjugated before the crystallization of an anti-Assyrian coalition. The remoteness of Babylonia from the arena and the local nature of the episode are incompatible with the assumption of political contacts between rulers situated on the two extreme ends of the Assyrian empire. It is far more logical to assume that the Babylonian embassy arrived in Jerusalem in 705–703 BCE. The anti-Assyrian revolt, at that time, encompassed vast areas on the southeast, north and southwest borders of the empire, and the dispatch of an envoy of the leader of the rebellion in the southeast (Merodach-baladan) to the coalition's leader in the southwest (Hezekiah) was appropriate. Such a date would fit the biblical story, according to which Hezekiah recovered from illness on the eve of the Assyrian campaign (see above). The Babylonian embassy can safely be dated to about 704/703 BCE and is another example of Hezekiah's extensive diplomatic activity in anticipation of the Assyrian campaign against his kingdom.

The Date of the "Azekah Inscription"

The first part of the "Azekah Inscription" is broken, and the surviving fragment begins with a description of a large-scale attack conducted by an Assyrian king against the kingdom of Judah: "[With the mig]ht of Ashur, my lord, the province of [Hezek]iah of Judah like [. . .]." The city of Azekah and another city, whose name is broken and is described as "a royal [city] of the Philistines, which H[ezek]iah (/^{m}*Ha/-[za-<qi>-i]a-a-u*) had captured and strengthened for himself," were captured in the course of the campaign. The continuation of the text, unfortunately, is broken (Na'aman 1974; 1979a 61–62; Borger 1979:134–135).

When did the Assyrians conduct such a major campaign against the kingdom of Judah? No campaign waged by Sargon against Judah, or even tension between the two kingdoms, is mentioned in our sources. On the other hand, there is a vast corpus of evidence for Sennacherib's campaign against Judah and its disastrous results. Thus, there can be no doubt that the "Azekah Inscription" refers to the campaign of 701 BCE, and the suggestion to date it to 711 BCE should be dismissed.

The second city, whose name is broken, was identified in the original publication as Gath of the Philistines (Na'aman 1974:34–35). Recently, Mittmann (1990:98–99) suggested identifying it with Ekron, a Philistine city-state located near the western border of Judah.[9] Ekron is mentioned in Sennacherib's annals as a city that joined Hezekiah's rebellion and was conquered during the campaign. In its political-strategic position, it fits well the inscription's unnamed "royal city of the Philistines." But there is a considerable gap between the description of the conquest of Ekron in the annals and that described in the "Azekah Inscription." Furthermore, as mentioned above, no evidence of a destruction level was found during the current excavations of Ekron. Although Mittmann's suggestion is not free from doubt, I tend to accept it. The difference between the descriptions in the two sources may be the result of the literary character of the "Azekah Inscription." The city most probably resisted the Assyrians for some time and then surrendered. Sennacherib severely punished the leaders and their supporters from among the citizens, but did not destroy the city (contrary to his policy in his campaign against Judah).

Some literary aspects of the "Azekah Inscription" were discussed in the original publication (Na'aman 1974:28–31). Only two points need further elaboration:

(A) Azekah is described as a city located "between my [bo]rder and the land of Judah" (for a different rendering, see Borger 1979:134).[10] "My border" ([*mi-i*]*ṣ-ri-ia*) refers to the encampment of the king and his army before the attack on Judah. According to the annals, Sennacherib operated on the coast of Philistia before the attack on Judah; this same region apparently appeared

---

9. Mittmann's arguments in favor of the identification of the Philistine city with Ekron are as follows: (a) the city is called "a royal city of the Philistines," but Gath was a secondary city within the territory of Ashdod (for the term "royal city" [*āl šarrūti*] in the Assyrian royal inscriptions, see Ikeda 1979); (b) the participation of Ekron in the rebellion is explicitly mentioned in Sennacherib's annals; and (c) the Assyrian royal inscriptions give selective information, and we must be careful not to draw conclusions from what is not explicitly said. It is possible that, following the siege, Ekron surrendered and opened its gates, thus, avoiding a total destruction. There are, however, certain difficulties in Mittmann's suggestion: (a) Ekron's location on flat land does not correspond with the topographical features of the city under siege as described in the inscription; and (b) the assumption of a surrender rather than conquest does not fit the detailed description of a siege and conquest in the "Azekah Inscription." No evidence of a destruction in the late 8th century BCE was detected in the course of the site's excavations, contrary to what one would expect from the text of the inscription.

10. Recently, Frahm (1997:230a) suggested restoring it as [*ki-i*]*ṣ-ri-ia*, "contingent." According to this interpretation, Azekah was located between the camp of his troops and the kingdom of Judah.

in the missing part of the "Azekah Inscription." Thus, the inscription fits the evidence of the other sources referring to the campaign of 701 BCE.

(B) The name of the god Ashur is written AN.ŠÁR in the inscription. Tadmor (1958a:82 n. 231; 1958b:159–160; Tadmor, Landsberger and Parpola 1989:27–28) has pointed out that this writing appears for the first time in several royal inscriptions of Sargon II, but, in most inscriptions, the name of Ashur is given in the regular spelling ^{d}A-šur, ^{d}Aš-šur. In Sennacherib's inscriptions, it appears only in those found in the city of Ashur and in the inscriptions from Nineveh relating the building of the *bīt akītu*. Thus, the writing AN.ŠÁR in the "Azekah Inscription" was regarded as evidence that the inscription dates to Sargon's, rather than Sennacherib's, time.

Numerous recently published inscriptions of Sennacherib have the ideographic writing AN.ŠÁR (e.g., Walker 1980; Watanabe 1985; George 1986:133–135, 144–145). Landsberger (1965:25–26 and n. 40) has suggested that a copy of inscriptions that Sennacherib engraved on the throne of Marduk and the bed of Ṣarpanitu, in which the name of Ashur is written AN.ŠÁR, were included in a dedicatory inscription of Ashurbanipal. It must be emphasized that the spelling AN.ŠÁR is common neither in Sargon's inscriptions, nor in those of Sennacherib. Its use in the "Azekah Inscription" cannot establish a date for the inscription.

The significance of the sudden appearance of a new ideographic writing of the national Assyrian god's name must be clarified. Parpola (1993:205–206) has pointed out that AN.ŠAR has the meanings of "universal God" (*il kiššati*) and "totality of Heaven" (*kiššat šamê*). Its earliest attestation is in the late 14th century BCE, and it was revived in the time of Sargon II to designate the national Assyrian God who became, under Tiglath-pileser III and Sargon II, the major god of a vast empire ("universal God") (Parpola 1993:189–190, n. 106). The new ideographic spelling, with its ideological meaning, was first adopted in the city of Ashur, probably by scribes attached to Esharra, the major temple of the God. From Ashur, it gradually spread and was used by scribes operating in other Assyrian centers. In the time of Sargon and Sennacherib, it mainly appeared either in inscriptions composed in the city of Ashur, or in reference to building activity in this city. Only under the late Sargonids (Esarhaddon and Ashurbanipal) did it become a common way of writing the national god's name.

An outstanding development in the theology of the god Ashur appeared in the days of Sennacherib. In the Assyrian version of the *Enūma eliš*, Ashur (written ideographically AN.ŠÁR) substitutes Marduk, the national god of Babylon. The identification creates a certain ambiguity between Ashur (AN.ŠÁR) and the god Anshar, a deity of the primordial Babylonian theogony (Zimmern 1917:218–219; Tadmor 1958b:160; Machinist 1984–85:359–360;

Livingstone 1986:230–235). The identification of Ashur and Anshar is evident from a few texts in which Ashur is described as a god "who creates himself, the father of the great gods whose figure was shaped in the Abyss" (Ebeling 1954:4, lines 8–9; see Luckenbill 1924:149, lines 1–2). In other texts, Ashur (written AN.ŠÁR) substitutes Marduk in both titles and cult (Zimmern 1917: 219–220; Tadmor 1958b:160–161; Machinist 1984–85, with earlier literature; Watanabe 1985:381–382; George 1986:139–144). This cultic and literary development was part of an anti-Babylonian polemic, which emerged in the course of Sennacherib's struggle with Babylonia and culminated in the destruction of Babylon in 689 BCE. Thus, Sargon's new ideographic spelling of the name Ashur gave birth to a sophisticated theology, which served political and cultic objectives in the time of Sennacherib.

It should be noted that only a fragment of the "Azekah Inscription" was preserved, and it remains unknown to which god it was dedicated and under what circumstances it was written. Was it composed as part of the building and restoration activities conducted by Sennacherib in the city of Ashur in his early years?[11] Or was it written in another city in honor of the god Ashur?

In conclusion, there is no evidence to support the view that the "Azekah Inscription" dates to the time of Sargon II. All the available evidence indicates that it describes an early stage of Sennacherib's campaign against Judah, and its data should be integrated with all other data concerning the Assyrian campaign of 701 BCE.

Hezekiah's Policy in Historical Context and in Biblical Historiography

Ahaz, Hezekiah's father, held the throne of Judah in the years 734–715/14 BCE. Soon after his enthronement, Rezin and Pekah tried to consolidate an anti-Assyrian coalition and pressured Ahaz to join their league (Hayes and Hooker 1988:59, with earlier literature; Irvine 1990, with earlier literature; Na'aman 1991b:91–94). Following Ahaz's refusal, Jerusalem was besieged in an attempt either to force him to join the coalition, or to replace him with the son of Ṭob-El (Isa. 7:6), possibly a scion of the House of David, who, having lost hope of succeeding Jotham on the throne of Judah, was willing to support the allies in exchange for coronation. Ahaz, however, correctly evaluated the dangers involved in participation in the coalition and stood firm, in spite of the military threat. In the years 734–732 BCE, the kingdom of Damascus and most of the kingdom of Israel became Assyrian provinces. All the kingdoms in

11. For the making of the images of the god Ashur (*AN.ŠÁR*) and the great gods in Sennacherib's early years, see Tadmor 1958b:160; Tadmor, Landsberger and Parpola 1989: 30.

the Syro-Palestinian arena became Assyrian vassals. Ahaz's loyalty certainly gained him a favorable position in the eyes of his Assyrian lord.

Throughout his reign, Ahaz was a loyal Assyrian vassal and kept the Judean territory intact in a period in which the larger kingdoms of Hamath, Damascus and Israel were annexed, and Judah's western neighbors (Gaza, Ashkelon and Ashdod) were conquered and plundered. Contrary to the non-historical picture presented in 2 Chr. 28 (see Welten 1973:174–175), one must emphasize Ahaz's success in ensuring the safety of his subjects during a tumultuous period.

Hezekiah (reigned 715/14–686 BCE) apparently continued his father's policy in the first decade of his reign, although details of these years are missing. It is possible that soon after his enthronement he attempted to consolidate an anti-Assyrian coalition and opened negotiations with his neighbors and with the ruler(s) of Egypt. However, even if he had begun conspiring (as mentioned above, there is no concrete evidence for such an assumption), he drew back, in time, and his kingdom remained intact during the Assyrian campaign against Ashdod in 711 BCE.

The shift in his policy took place after Sargon's death in 705 BCE. Hezekiah rebelled, organized an anti-Assyrian coalition and secured Egyptian support for the league. This was the reversal of Ahaz's policy of caution, a policy also advocated by the prophet Isaiah.

The disastrous results of Sennacherib's campaign against Judah have been amply documented by archaeological research. Large districts were destroyed, and tens of thousands of people were deported to distant places. Manpower in the kingdom was restricted, and Judah was unable to replace the deportees and settle the deserted areas. There was a drastic reduction in settlement in the kingdom in the 7th century BCE. Even in the late 7th century, following 100 years of recovery, the kingdom's settlement, population and economy were considerably less than in the 8th century BCE (Na'aman 1991a:29–30, 49, 57–58; 1993:112–115, 118; Dagan 1992). The districts of the Shephelah were transferred — at least for some years — to Judah's western neighbors. Hezekiah submitted to Assyria and paid a heavy tribute, in addition to the yearly tribute. Judah remained a tribute-paying Assyrian vassal from this time until the Assyrian withdrawal in the last third of the 7th century BCE.

From the Assyrian point of view, the campaign was an utter success. Sennacherib achieved all his aims, namely, the weakening of Judah, the strongest remaining kingdom in Palestine, and the strengthening of the Assyrian hold along the Egyptian border. Neither the destruction of Jerusalem, nor the annexation of Judah were on the agenda, because the Assyrian king deliberately kept intact the integrity of the kingdoms located on his buffer zone with Egypt. Following the campaign, Sennacherib's hands were free to operate on the Babylonian front and to invest in the royal cities of Assyria. So successful were the results of the campaign that he never returned to the southwestern front of the empire.

Within the Book of Kings, Ahaz and Hezekiah appear as two antithetical figures:

(A) Ahaz is presented as a sinful king, the association of his sins (2 Kgs. 16:2b-4) with the siege of the city (v. 5) being a transparent allusion that the latter event was the result of the former. Ahaz's appeal for help to the Assyrian king (vv. 7–8) is presented negatively (Cogan and Tadmor 1978:58–61; Na'aman 1995:41–48) and, according to the sequence in the Book of Kings, brought, in its wake, the subjugation of Judah to Assyria.

(B) In contrast to Ahaz, Hezekiah carried out a comprehensive and unprecedented cultic reform in his kingdom (2 Kgs. 18:5–7): "He trusted in the Lord the God of Israel; so that there was none like him among all the kings of Judah after him, nor among those who were before him. For he held fast to the Lord . . . And the Lord was with him; wherever he went forth, he prospered. He rebelled against the king of Assyria, and would not serve him." The rebellion against Assyria is mentioned within an extremely positive context.

Not only the beginning of the revolt, but also its results are presented in a favorable light. According to the author of Kings, the revolt ended in complete success: the Assyrian ruler and his army retreated from Judah, and the offensive invader was murdered by his sons. Assyria is not mentioned any further in the Book of Kings. In view of the internal sequence of Kings, anyone who read it would draw the conclusion that Judah fell under the yoke of Assyria in the reign of Ahaz and was freed during the reign of Hezekiah. The latter's standing at the time of siege is presented as opposite to that of Ahaz: Hezekiah initiated the rebellion against the oppressive conqueror; he did not surrender in spite of siege and heavy pressure; in time of danger he addressed YHWH and his prophet; and, thus, he was able to deliver his people and his country from the Assyrian yoke.

How should we account for the enormous discrepancy between the biblical presentation of the days of Ahaz and Hezekiah and the historical reality? There is no doubt that literary and historiographical forms, as well as theological and didactical considerations, played a major role in the shaping of the material. Is it possible that the author of Kings had no interest in history "as it really happened" and was mainly directed by literary-ideological considerations? It goes without saying that the author of Kings (i.e., the Deuteronomistic Historian) had before him some written sources, part of which had been written soon after the event. However, the considerable amount of time that separated the actual events from the time they were written down had distorted the historical perspectives, precluding the possibility of a realistic evaluation of the events of the late 8th century BCE (see Ackroyd 1984). The disastrous results of Sennacherib's campaign had been, by then, largely forgotten. At this later date, Hezekiah became the righteous king who, due to his piety and his trust in YHWH, saved Judah and Jerusalem. Ahaz became, accordingly, the negative of Hezekiah.

Only rarely are such detailed external sources and ample archaeological data available as those that we have for the reigns of Ahaz and Hezekiah. The history of the two kings, thus, teaches us a lesson about the limitation of biblical historiography as a source for the history of Israel. Of the utmost importance is the time span that separates historical events from the time in which they were first described in written form. A contemporaneous author can write a non-historical description, but, in such a case, the author knows a great deal of the event. The authenticity of his description is, to a certain extent, the result of his conscious decision. A later author (and in biblical historiography an author may have lived hundreds of years after the events), on the other hand, may write an entirely mistaken description, even when attempting to reconstruct the event "as it really was," because his knowledge of the earlier event was totally erroneous. Only if we take into account all the above mentioned variables and, above all, the date in which the events were written down, can we attempt to reconstruct the early history of Israel. In this way, we have achieved a better understanding of the contradictions between the historical and biblical figures of Ahaz and Hezekiah and may be able to give "a second chance" to figures who formerly had no grace before the muse of history.

References

Ackroyd, P.R. 1984. The Biblical Interpretation of the Reigns of Ahaz and Hezekiah. In: Barrick, W.B. and Spencer, J.R. eds. *In the Shelter of Elyon. Essays on Ancient Palestinian Life and Literature in Honor of G.W. Ahlström.* (Journal for the Study of the Old Testament Supplement 31). Sheffield: 247-259.

Aharoni, Y. 1967. *The Land of the Bible: A Historical Geography.* Philadelphia.

Albenda, P. 1986. *The Palace of Sargon, King of Assyria.* Paris.

Alt, A. 1945. Neue assyrische Nachrichten über Palästina. *ZDPV* 67: 128–159. (Reprint: Alt 1953: 226–241).

Alt, A. 1953. *Kleine Schriften zur Geschichte des Volkes* Israel II. München.

Becking, B. 1992. *The Fall of Samaria. An Historical and Archaeological Study.* (Studies in the History of the Ancient Near East 2). Leiden.

Begg, C.T. 1986. 2 Kings 20:12–19 as an Element of the Deuteronomistic History. *Catholic Biblical Quarterly* 48:27–38.

Begg, C.T. 1987a. The Deuteronomistic Retouching of the Portrait of Hezekiah in 2 Kgs 20: 12–19. *Biblische Notizen* 37–38:7–13.

Begg, C.T. 1987b. Hezekiah's Display (2 Kgs 20:12–19). *Biblische Notizen* 37–38: 14–18.
Begg, C.T. 1988. Hezekiah's Display: Another Parallel. *Biblische Notizen* 41: 7–8.
Ben Zvi, E. 1990. Tracing Prophetic Literature in the Book of Kings. The Case of II Kings 15,37. *ZAW* 102: 100-105.
Borger, R. 1979. *Babylonisch-assyrische Lesestücke* (2nd ed.). Rome.
Botta, P.É. 1849. *Monument de Ninive.* III–IV: *Inscriptions.* Paris. (Reprint 1972. Osnabrück).
Botta, P.É. and Flandin, E. 1849. *Monument de Ninive.* I–II: *Architecture et sculpture.* Paris. (Reprint 1972. Osnabrück).
Bright, J. 1965. *Jeremiah. A New Translation with Introduction and Commentary.* (The Anchor Bible). Garden City.
Brinkman, J.A. 1964. Merodach-Baladan II. In: Biggs, R.D. and Brinkman, J.A. eds. *Studies Presented to A. Leo Oppenheim.* Chicago: 6–53.
Clements, R.E. 1980. *Isaiah and the Deliverance of Jerusalem. A Study of the Interpretation of Prophecy in the Old Testament.* Journal for the Study of the Old Testament Supplement 13). Sheffield.
Clements, R.E. 1982. *Isaiah 1-39.* (New Century Bible Commentary). Grand Rapids and London.
Clements, R.E. 1983. The Isaiah Narrative of 2 Kings 20:12–19 and the Date of the Deuteronomic History. In: Rofé, A. and Zakovitch, Y. eds. *Isac Leo Seeligmann Volume* III. Jerusalem: 209–220.
Cogan M. and Tadmor, H. 1988. *II Kings. A New Translation with Introduction and Commentary.* (The Anchor Bible). Garden City.
Dagan, Y. 1992. *The Shephelah during the Period of the Monarchy in Light of Archaeological Excavations and Survey.* (M.A. Thesis). Tel Aviv University. (Hebrew).
Duhm, B. 1914. *Das Buch Jesaja.* (Göttinger Handkommentar zum Alten Testament, III/1). Göttingen.
Ebeling, E. 1954. *Stiftungen und Vorschriften für assyrische Tempel.* Berlin.
El-Amin, M. 1953. Die Reliefs mit Beischriften von Sargon II. in Dûr-Sarrukîn. *Sumer* 9: 35–59, 214–228.
Eph'al, I. 1968. Sargon. *Enc. Miqr.* V: 1121–1126. (Hebrew).
Frahm, E. 1997. *Einleitung in die Sanherib-Inschriften* (AfO Beiheft 26). Horn.
Galil, G. 1992. Judah and Assyria in the Sargonid Period. *Zion* 57: 113–133 (Hebrew).
George, A.R. 1986. Sennacherib and the Tablet of Destinies. *Iraq* 48: 133–146.
Ginsberg, H.L. 1968. Reflexes of Sargon in Isaiah after 715 BCE. In: Hallo, W.W. ed. *Essays in Memory of E.A. Speiser.* (American Oriental Series 53). New Haven: 47–53.
Gonçalves, F.J. 1986. *L'expédition de Sennachérib en Palestine dans la literature hébraïque ancienne.* Louvain-la-Neuve.
Gray, G.B. 1912. *A Critical and Exegetical Commentary on the Book of Isaiah I-XXVII.* (ICC). New York.
Güterbock, H.G. 1957. Narration in Anatolian, Syrian and Assyrian Art. *AJA* 61: 62–71.
Hayes, J.H. and Hooker, P.K. 1988. *A New Chronology for the Kings of Israel and Judah and its Implication for Biblical History and Literature.* Atlanta.
Høgenhaven, J. 1988. *Gott und Volk bei Jesaja. Eine Untersuchung zur biblischen Theologie.* (Acta Theologica Danica 24). Leiden.
Hutter, M. 1982. *Hiskija, König von Juda.* Graz.
Ikeda, Y. 1979. Royal Cities and Fortified Cities. *Iraq* 41: 75–87.
Irvine, S.A. 1990. *Isaiah, Ahaz, and the Syro-Ephraimite Crisis.* Atlanta.
Kaiser, O. 1974. *Isaiah 13-39, A Commentary.* (Old Testament Library). London.

Kapera, Z.J. 1987. The Oldest Account of Sargon II's Campaign against Ashdod. *Folia Orientalia* 24: 29–39.

Landsberger, B. 1965. *Brief des Bischofs von Esagila an König Asarhaddons.* (Mededlingen der Koninkluke Nederlandse Akademie van Wetenschappen, afd Letterkunde. Nieuwe Reeks 28/6). Amsterdam.

Lie, A.G. 1929. *The Inscriptions of Sargon II King of Assyria.* Part I. *The Annals Tranliterated and Translated with Notes.* Paris.

Liverani, M. 1982. Kitru, Katāru. *Mesopotamia* 17: 43–66.

Livingstone, A. 1986. *Mystical and Mythological Explanatory Works of Assyrian and Babylonian Scholars.* Oxford.

Luckenbill, D.D. 1924. *The Annals of Sennacherib.* (Oriental Institute Publications 2). Chicago.

Luckenbill, D.D. 1927. *Ancient Records of Assyria and Babylonia* II. Chicago.

Machinist, P. 1984–85. The Assyrians and Their Babylonian Problem: Some Reflections. *Wissenschaftskolleg zu Berlin—Jahrbuch.* Berlin: 353–364.

Marcus, M.I. 1989. Geography as an Organizing Principle in the Imperial Art of Shalmaneser III. *Iraq* 49: 77–90.

Marti, K. 1900. *Das Buch Jesaja* (Kürzer Hand-Commentar zum Alten Testament X). Tübingen, Freiburg and Leipig.

Mattingly, G.L. 1981. An Archaeological Analysis of Sargon's 712 Campaign against Ashdod. *Near Eastern Archaeological Society Bulletin* 17: 47–64.

McKenzie, S.L. 1991. *The Trouble With Kings. The Composition of the Book of Kings in the Deuteronomistic History.* Leiden.

Miller, J.M. and Hayes, J.H. 1986. *A History of Ancient Israel and Judah.* Philadelphia.

Mittmann, S. 1990. Hiskia und die Philister. *Journal of Northwest Semitic Languages* 16: 91–106.

Na'aman, N. 1974. Sennacherib's "Letter to God" on his Campaign to Judah. *BASOR* 214: 25–39.

Na'aman, N. 1979a. Sennacherib's Campaign to Judah and the Date of the LMLK Stamps. *VT* 29: 61–86.

Na'aman, N. 1979b. The Brook of Egypt and Assyrian Policy on the Border of Egypt. *Tel Aviv* 6: 68–90.

Na'aman, N. 1986. Historical and Chronological Notes on the Kingdoms of Israel and Judah in the Eighth Century B.C. *VT* 36: 71–92.

Na'aman, N. 1991a. The Kingdom of Judah under Josiah. *Tel Aviv* 18: 3–71.

Na'aman, N. 1991b. Forced Participation in Alliances in the Course of the Assyrian Campaigns to the West. In: Cogan, M. and Eph'al, I. eds. *Ah, Assyria... Studies in Assyrian History and Ancient Near Eastern Historiography Presented to Hayim Tadmor.* (Scripta Hierosolymitana 33). Jerusalem: 80–98.

Na'aman, N. 1993. Population Changes in Palestine Following Assyrian Deportations. *Tel Aviv* 20: 104–124.

Na'aman, N. 1995. The Deuteronomist and Voluntary Servitude to Foreign Powers. *Journal for the Study of the Old Testament* 65: 37–53.

Ockinga, B.O. 1983. Hiskias "Prahlerei," In: Görg, M. ed. *Fontes atque Pontes. Eine Festgabe für Hellmut Brunner.* (Ägypten und Altes Testament 5). Wiesbaden: 342–346.

Oded, B. 1992. *War, Peace and Empire: Justification for War in Assyrian Royal Inscriptions.* Wiesbaden.

Oppenheim, A.L. 1969. Babylonian and Assyrian Historical Texts. In: Pritchard, J.B. ed. *Ancient Near Eastern Texts Relating to the Old Testament.* Princeton: 265–317.

Parpola, S. 1993. The Assyrian Tree of Life: Tracing the Origins of Jewish Monotheism and Greek Philosophy. *JNES* 52: 161–208.

Reade, J.E. 1976. Sargon's Campaigns of 720, 716 and 715 B.C.: Evidence from the Sculptures. *JNES* 35: 95–104.

Ruprecht, E. 1990. Die ursprungliche Komposition der Hiskia-Jesaja-Erzählungen un ihre Umstrukturierung durch den Verfasser des deuteronomistischen Geschichtswerkes. *Zeitschrift fur die Theologie und Kirche* 87: 33–66.

Schmitt, G. 1989. Gabbutunu. *ZDPV* 105: 56–69.

Spalinger, A. 1973. The Year 712 B.C. and Its Implications for Egyptian History. *Journal of the American Research Center in Egypt* 10: 95–101.

Tadmor, H. 1958a. The Campaigns of Sargon II of Assur: A Chronological-Historical Study. *JCS* 12: 22–40, 77–100.

Tadmor, H. 1958b. The "Sin of Sargon." *Eretz Israel* 5: 150–162. (Hebrew).

Tadmor, H. 1966. Philistia under Assyrian Rule. *BA* 29: 86–102.

Tadmor, H. and Cogan, M. 1979. Ahaz and Tiglath-Pileser in the Book of Kings. Historiographic Considerations. *Biblica* 60: 491–508.

Tadmor, H. and Cogan, M. 1982. Hezekiah's Fourteenth Year: The King's Illness and the Babylonian Embassy. *Eretz Israel* 16: 198–201. (Hebrew).

Tadmor, H. Landsberger, B. and Parpola, S. 1989. The Sin of Sargon and Sennacherib's Last Will. *State Archives of Assyria Bulletin* 3: 3–51.

Thiele, R.E. 1965. *The Mysterious Numbers of the Hebrew Kings*. Grand Rapids.

Timm, S. 1989. *Moab zwischen den Mächten. Studien zu historischen Denkmälern und Texten.* (Ägypten und Altes Testament 17). Wiesbaden.

Unger, E. 1932. Äthiopier in assyrischer Darstellung. *RLA* I: 310.

Unger, E. 1957–1971. Gabbutunu. *RLA* III: 129–130.

Ungnad, A. 1938. Eponymen. *RLA* II: 412–457.

Wäfler, M. 1975. *Nicht-Assyrer neuassyrischer Darstellungen* (AOAT 126). Kevelaer and Neukirchen and Vluyn.

Walker, C.B.F. 1980. Some Mesopotamian Inscribed Vessels. *Iraq* 42: 84-86.

Watanabe, K. 1985. Die Sieglung der "Vasallenverträge Asarhaddons" durch den Gott Assur. *Baghdader Mitteilungen* 16: 379–392.

Weidner, E. 1941–44. Šilkan(ḫe)ni, König von Muṣri, ein Zeitgenosse Sargons II. *AFO* 14: 40–53.

Weissbach, F.H. 1918. Zu den Inschriften der Säle im Palaste Sargon's II. von Assyrien. *Zeitschrift der Deutschen Morgenländischen Gesellschaft* 72: 161–185.

Weissbach, F.H. 1928. Sargons II. Feldzug nach Asdod. *Zeitschrift der Deutschen Morgenländischen Gesellschaft* 82: lvii–lvix.

Welten, P. 1973. *Geschichte und Geschichtsdarstellung in den Chronikbuchern* (Wissenschaftliche Monographien zum Alten and Neuen Testament 42) Neukirchen-Vluyn.

Wildberger, H. 1978. *Jesaja. 2. Jesaja 13-27* (Biblischer Kommentar X/2). Neukirchen and Vluyn.

Winckler, H. 1889. *Die Keilschrifttexte Sargons nach den Papierabklatschen und Originalen neu herausgegeben* I–II. Leipzig.

Winckler, H. 1899. *Altorientalische Forschungen* II. Leipzig.

Winter, I.J. 1983. The Program of the Throneroom of Assurnasirpal II. In: Harper, P.O. and Pittman, H. eds. *Essays in Near Eastern Art and Archaeology in Honor of Charles Kyrle Wilkinson*. New York: 15–31.

Zimmern, H. 1917. Marduks (Ellils, Aššurs) Geburt im babylonischen Weltschopfungsepos. *Mitteilungen der Vorderasiatischen Gesellschaft* 21: 213–225.

Sargon II and the Rebellion of the Cypriot Kings Against Shilṭa of Tyre[1]

The episode of the submission of the seven kings of Cyprus to Sargon II of Assyria and the sending of their tribute is described in detail in his royal inscriptions. The text of the summary inscriptions is clear, and the sequence of events is easy to understand. Yet the historical interpretation of the episode is fraught with difficulty, and scholars have offered various suggestions to explain how Sargon was able to reach and conquer the remote island of Cyprus and what might have been the background of the operation. The text of the Annals, on the other hand, is badly damaged, and its interpretation involves enormous difficulties. Therefore, it has played only a minor role in the reconstruction of the historical event.

As will be suggested below, deciphering the text of the Annals is the key to the correct historical interpretation of the episode. I will first discuss briefly the summary inscriptions and their contribution and then suggest a new reconstruction of the text of the Annals. The newly reconstructed text will serve as a basis for a re-evaluation of the episode of Sargon and the Cypriot kings.

The Evidence of Sargon's Summary Inscription

The most detailed descriptions of the Cypriot episode appear in Sargon's stele from Kition (Messerschmidt and Ungnad 1907:No. 71; Borger 1967:351, No. 71, with earlier literature; Tadmor 1996), in the so-called great Display Inscription (German *Prunkinschrift*) (Winckler 1889:126:145–149; Fuchs 1994: 232–233, 352) and in Sargon's prisms from Calah (Nimrud) (Gadd 1954:191:25–44 and pl. XLIX). The latter text runs as follows:

> A[nd seven kings] of the land of Ia' — a dis[trict of the land of Yadnana], which [is situated] a seven days' journey away [in the middle of the] western [sea and its] location is distant, so that since far-off days [and until now], none among the kings, my ancestors, of Assyria and Babylonia, had heard the name of their land — from far off in the middle of the sea [they heard] the deeds which I had performed in the lands of Chaldea [and Hatti], their hearts palpitated and [fright] fell upon them. They brought to me in

1. Reprinted with permission. *Orientalia* 67 (1998), 239-247.

> Babylon gold, silver, furniture (made) of ebony and boxwood, the manufacture of their land, and kissed my feet.
>
> I caused to inscribe upon a stele the victory and the conquests of my hands which, by the strength of the great gods, I achieved over all my enemies, and left it for the future in the land of Ia', a district of the land of Yadnana.

The summary inscriptions relate how the seven kings of Yadnana were overwhelmed by the great victories of Sargon and sent him their tributes. This is sheer propaganda and hardly can explain the willingness of the Cypriot rulers to send tribute to Sargon and to allow him to erect his monument on the island. The stele was erected on a mount as indicated by the Kition stele: "I set it up [at the t]op ([*i-na re*]-*eš)* of the land of Adnana" (Messerschmidt and Ungnad 1907:No. 71, left face, line 53; Winckler 1889: 182:53; Tadmor 1996:287). Thus, it is clear that, at later time, the stele was removed from its original location to the city of Kition, where it was dicovered (on the site where the Kition stele was found, see Schrader 1882:4; Olmstead 1908:10–11, n. 41).

Scholars attempting to reconstruct the background of the Cypriot submission to Sargon have combined it with the king's operations along the eastern Mediterranean coast and his fight with the Iamneans/Ionians (Winckler 1897:363–369; Olmstead 1908:98–102; 1938:57–59; Bing 1969:77–78; Katzenstein 1973:237–244; Elayi and Cavigneaux 1979; Helm 1980:180–190; Briquel-Chatonnet 1992:184–186.). According to the Annals, the struggle with Mita of Mushki (Phrygia) and the conquest of some of his towns along the western coast of Cilicia took place in Sargon's 7th and 13th years of reign (*palû*). The Annals of Sargon's 7th *palû* relates that the Iamneans "since far off days had killed the men of Tyre (and) the land of Que and [had blocked?] the (naval) routes" (Fuchs 1994:109–110, lines 117–120 (cited from p.109, line 118). For discussions of the passage, see Winckler 1897:365, 368; Olmstead 1930/31:266). Sargon's Cylinder inscription describes him as "the one who caught the Iamneans (*Iamnāia*) in the midst of the sea like a fish in a net and pacified the land of Que and the city of Tyre" (Fuchs 1994:34, line 21). The same episode appears in four other summary inscriptions of Sargon but without the reference to Que and Tyre (see the references in Fuchs 1994:440, s.v. Jamnaju; Gadd 1954:199, line 19). The episode of the capture of the Iamneans appears in three summary inscriptions side by side with the episode of the submission of the seven Cypriot kings, thus, clearly referring to a different historical event. In addition, whereas the struggle with the Iamneans is dated to Sargon's 7th *palû*, the Cypriot episode is included within the operations of the 13th *palû*. The two episodes are dated to different stages in the wars of Sargon and, contrary to the suggestions of some scholars (for the history of research, see Helm 1980:183–190), there is no apparent connection between the wars with the Iamneans in Cilicia and the Assyrian involvement in the affairs of Cyprus.

The Evidence of Sargon's Annals

In his detailed commentary of Lie's edition of the Annals of Sargon, Olmstead noted that the account of the Cypriot episode "is the most difficult in the Annals" (Olmstead 1930/31:278). Indeed, ever since the publication of Winckler's and Lie's text editions, Luckenbill's translation, and Olmstead's commentary, no significant progress has been made in deciphering and understanding this account.

The facsimile of the text of Hall II was published by Botta on pl. 91 and of Hall V on pl. 108 (Botta 1849). Winckler and Abel (henceforth, W+A) collated and copied the text of Hall V (pl. 23 No. 48) and reproduced without collation the text of Hall II (pl. 12 No. 26). However, the collated copy of W+A's edition must be treated with caution, as is evident even from a superficial comparison with Botta's facsimile. In the words of Olmstead (1930/31:259): "Unfortunately, it is often too uncertain whether Winckler actually read the correct sign on the squeeze or whether it was his own correction, while the brackets which should have indicated a restoration were often misplaced or even omitted."

Recently, A. Fuchs published a new edition of Sargon II's inscriptions from Khorsabad. He has collated the squeezes of Halls II and V (now in the Louvre Museum) and published a new transliteration and detailed textual notes (Fuchs 1994:175–177, lines 393–398, 337). Thanks to the new edition, the textual situation is now much more clear. However, the understanding of the sequence of events and its contribution to historical research has remained basically unchanged. Botta's copies and Fuchs' transliteration and notes must be taken as a basis for the restoration of the length of lines and the estimation of the gaps within the text.

In what follows, I will refer to the text according to the number of plates and lines in Botta's facsimile.

Remarkable in the text of the Annals is the presence of someone who is referred to in the third person. Note: *mandattašu* and *iššamma* (pls. 91, line 6; 108, line 13); *ašpuršūma* (pl. 91, line 8); *ana turri gimillišu* (pls. 91, line 8; 108, line 14). This anonymous figure, who seems to have played a central role in the episode, is, in my opinion, the key to the correct understanding of the episode. This was realized by Fuchs, and he appended the following interpretive note to the last sentence of the text (Fuchs 1994: 337, n. 387):

> Ich vermute in ihr den Name eines Landstriches oder Volkes auf Zypern, dessen Fürst ähnlich wie vor ihm Daltā von Ellipi um Waffenhilfe der Assyrer ersucht und auch bekommt. Die sieben Könige von Jā', wohl Aufständische, gegen die sich die Aktion

richtet, ergeben sich noch vor dem Kampf und werden diesem Land oder Volk wieder$^{?}$ unterstellt.

Scholars assumed that the episode opens with names of some Cypriot kings (Silda, Qura, xx-Ashur) (Luckenbill 1927:44; Olmstead 1930/31:278; Elayi and Cavigneaux 1979:65). However, not only is there not enough space for seven names, but the last assumed name ends with the god Ashur, which is improbable for a Cypriot king. Moreover, the second line of Hall II is almost completely preserved and no DIŠ sign appears there. Some other solution for the introduction to the episode must be sought.

When examining the episodes of Sargon's 13th *palû*, it is evident that three out of five open with a ruler's name and his country: "Uperi king of Dilmun," "Mitâ of Muski (^{kur}*Muskāia*)," and "Mutallu of *Kummuḫu* (^{kur}*Kummuḫāia*)." It seems to me that the Cypriot episode opens in the same manner: ^{m}*Si-il-ṭa* [^{uru}*Ṣu*]r$^{!}$-ra-a-a, "Silṭa of Tyre" (Botta pl. 108, line 11; W+A pl. 23 No. 48). The assumed broken [KU]M sign may equally stand for a *ṣur* sign; a restoration of an URU sign in the gap (compare Annals, line 118; Cylinder inscription, line 21) is self-evident. In Assyria, a well-known shift is that of the West Semitic shin represented by a cuneiform *s* (e.g., Ya'asu, Sibittiba'il, Manasi, Samerina, Ursalimmu, Asdudu/i, Saba'). The name Shilṭa may be analyzed as a *qitl* formation of Š-L-Ṭ "to dominate, rule."[2] Shilṭa of Tyre is the person referred to in the third person in the text of the Annals.

In the light of this suggestion, I will present a new transliteration and translation of the Cypriot episode as it appears in Sargon's Annals. The two recensions of Halls II and V will be presented separately, each in its own right, but, for the sake of completeness, restorations borrowed from one text to the other will be allowed when they seem befitting to the missing gaps. The restorations are based on an estimate of the number of missing signs in each line according to Botta's facsimile and Fuchs' notes.

Botta IV t. 108 = Winckler pl. 23 No. 48 (Saal V)

11. ^{m}*Si-il-ṭa* [^{uru}*Ṣu*]*r*$^{!}$*-ra-a-a* [*x x x x x x x x a-na* KUR] ^{d}Aš-šur[^{ki} 7 LUGAL]^{meš}*-ni* [*ša* KUR] *Ia-a' na-ge-e* [*ša* KUR *Ad-na-na*]
12. *ša ma-lak* 7 UD*-me i-na* MURUB$_4$ *tam-*[*di e-reb*] ^{d}UTU*-ši šit-ku-n*[*u-ma šu-bat-su-un né-sa*]*-at ša* [*ul*]*-tu* UD*-me ul-lu-ti a-na* [*x*]*-ta*$^{?}$*-šu-ma i-x-ma*$^{?}$ *ir*$^{?}$ [*x* (*x*) ŠID$^{?}$]
13. *mit-ḫa*$^{?}$-riš$^{?}$ [*kàd*$^{?}$*-ra*$^{?}$]*-/a/-šu-*[*u*]*n*$^{??}$ */ú/*$^{?}$*-*[*šab*$^{?}$*-ṭi*$^{?}$*-lu*$^{?}$*-*(*ma*)] *ik-lu-ú* [*bi-lat-sún*$^{?}$ *ù* ^{m}*Si-il-ṭ*]*a man-da-ta-š*[*ú*] *ka-bit-tú* [*iš*]*-šam-ma* [*a*]*-na šuk-nu-uš il-*[*la-at x x x x x*]

---

2. For the root Š-L-Ṭ in personal names, see Zadok 1990:262, with earlier literature; cf. Benz 1972:416. An alternative solution was offered to me by Dr. A. Fuchs: Silṭa "ein missverstandener Titel ist, wie etwas Pir'u von Ägypten, Janzu von Hubuškia, Mari' von Damaskus. Sozusagen der 'Sultan' von Tyros" (letter of 10.8.1997).

14. *e-r[i-ša-an-ni kit-ru* L]Ú *šu-*[u]t SAG-*ia la* [*a-di*]*r ta-ḫa-zi* [*it-ti*] *ki-*[*ṣir* LUGAL]*-ti-ia a-na tur-ri gi-mil-li-šú ú-ma-'*[*e*]*-ra* [*x x x x x x x x*]
15. [*e*$^{?}$*-ti*$^{?}$*-q*]*u*$^{?}$*-*[*ma*$^{?}$ *e*]*-mu-qa-at* ^{d}*Aš-šur e-*[*m*]*u-ru-ma a-*[*na z*]*i-kir* [*š*]*u-me-i*[*a i*]*š-ḫu-tú-ma i*[*r-m*]*a-a i-*[*d*]*a-a-šú-*[*u*]*n* KÙ.GI KÙ.[BABBAR *ú-nu-tu* ^{giš}ESI ^{giš}TÚG]
16. [*né-peš-ti* KUR$^{meš?}$]*-šú-*[*un a*]*-na qé-reb* KA.[DINGIR.RA^{ki} *a-na maḫ-ri-i*]*a iš-*[*šu-nim-m*]*a* [*x*] *il k*[*u*] *x r*[*i*$^{?}$] *am-nu-*[*ú-šú-nu-t*]*i*

Translation

Shilṭa [of] Tyre [. . . to] Assyr[ia. (And) seven kin]gs of the [land] of Ia', a district [of the land of Adnana], who are situated a seven days' journey in the middle of the western sea [and whose abodes are dista]nt, who since old days, to his$^{?}$ [. . .] together s[topped the[ir presents (and)] withhold [their tributes. And Shilṭ]a bro]ught his heavy tribute, and to suppress the ho[st$^{?}$ of . . .] he ap[plied to me for military aid]. I sent my officer, who is fearless in battle, with my royal guard, to avenge him, [and . . . they cros]sed$^{?}$. (When) they saw the strong troops of Ashur, at the mention of my name they became afraid and their arms collapsed. They brought to Babylon, into my presence, gold, silver, ut[ensils of ebony and boxwood, the manufacture] of their land, and [to . . .] I entrusted [them].

Notes:

Lines 12–13: The textual restorations follow Botta's and Winckler's facsimilles, assuming a close similarity to lines 4–5 of Hall II. For a slightly different restoration, see Fuchs 1994: 175–176.

Line 13: For the restoration *il-*[*la-at* . . .], see *CAD* I 82b–83a.

Line 14: For the motif of wreaking venegance (*gimilla turru*), see Fuchs 1994:225, lines 119–120. For the dispatch of officers with a guard (*kiṣir šarrūti*) with orders to quell a rebellion, compare Fuchs 1994:178, line 404; *CAD* A/2 320b.

Line 15: The reading [*e*]*-t*[*i*]*-q*[*u-ma*] is obtained by the combination of signs from the two halls.

Line 16: The gaps at the end of line 11 and the beginning of line 12 of Hall II indicate that the five (or six) undeciphered signs at the end of the episode should be divided to two words. For a possible restoration, compare Tadmor 1958:77–78, lines 6–7 and note 182; *CAD* M/1 225b–226a.

Botta IV t. 91 = Winckler pl. 12 No. 26 (Saal II)

1. [^{m}*Si-il-ṭa*]
2. [^{URU}*Ṣur-r*]*a*$^{?}$*-*[*a-a*] *na-á*[*š*]$^{?}$ [GÚ]$^{?}$.UN *kid* [*x*] *la še /a/-*[*n*]*a*$^{?}$ K[UR$^{?}$ ^{d}*Aš-šur*$^{ki?}$] 7 [LUGAL^{meš}*-ni*]
3. [*ša* KUR *Ia*]*-a' na-ge-e ša* KUR *Ad-na-na ša ma-lak* [7] UD-[*me i-na* MURUB *tam-di*]
4. [*šit-ku-nat š*]*u-bat-s*[*ú*]*n ša ul-tu UD-me ul-lu-ti a-na* [*x x x x x x x*]
5. [*x x*]*-ŠID kàd-ra-a-šú-un mit-ḫa-riš* [*ú-š*]*ab*$^{!}$*-*[*ṭi-lu i*]*k-*[*lu-ú*(*-ma*) *bi*]*-lat-*[*sún ù*]

6. [^{m}*Si-il-ṭa*] *ma-d*[*a*]*-at-ta-šu ka-*[*b*]*it-tu iš-šam-ma a-n*[*a šuk-nu-uš x x x*]
7. [*e*]*-ri-*<*ša*>*-an-ni* [*ki*]*t-ru LÚ šu-u*[*t* S]AG*-ia pit-qu-du la a-di*[*r ta-ḫa-zi it-ti*]
8. [*ki-ṣir* LUGAL*-ti*]*-ia áš-pur-šu-ma a-na tur-ri gi-mil-li-šu* [*x x x x x* (*x*)]
9. [*e*$^{?}$]*-t*[*i*$^{?}$*-qu*$^{?}$*-(ma)*$^{?}$] *e-mu-qa-at* ^{d}[*Aš*]*-šur g*[*a*]*p-šá-a-ti iš-mu-ma a-na z*[*i-kir šu-me-ia iš-ḫu-tú-ma*]
10. *ir-ma-a i-da-a-*[*šu*]*-u*[*n* K]Ù.GI KÙ.BABBAR *ú-nu-tu* ^{giš}ESI [^{giš}TÚG *né-peš-ti*]
11. [KUR^{me}]^{š}*-šú-un a-na* KA.DINGIR.RA^{ki} *a-na maḫ-ri-ia iš-šu-*[*nim-ma x x* (*x*)]
12. [*x x* (*x*)] *am-nu-ú-šu-nu-ti*

Translation:

[Shilṭa of Tyr]e pays$^{?}$ [tri]bute$^{?}$ . . . [t]o$^{?}$ A[ssyria$^{?}$. (And) seven kings of the land of Ia]', a district of the land of Adnana, whose abodes [are situated a seven days'] journey [in the middle of the sea], who since old days to [. . . together [st]op[ped] their presents (and) wi[thhold their tributes. And Shilṭa] brought his heavy tribute, and t[o suppress their$^{?}$ host$^{?}$ he ap]plied to me [for military aid]. I sent him my trustworthy officer, who is fearless [in battle, with] my [royal guard], and to avenge him [. . . they] cr[ossed$^{?}$]. (When) they heard of the strong troops of Ashur, at the me[ntion of my name they became afraid and] their arms collapsed. They brought to Babylon, into my presence, gold, silver, utensils of ebony [and boxwood, the manufacture] of their land, and [to . . .] I entrusted them.

Notes:

Line 2: The suggested restorations, based on Botta's copy, are extremely tentative. For the reading *nāš bilti*, compare Winckler 1889:188, lines 30–31. Dr. A Fuchs suggests (in a letter of 10.8.1997) the following restoration: *arad*(KID) *kan*(LA)*-še* [*š*]*á-di*(UD)*-i*[*d ni-ir*] ^{d}*Aš-šur* [*be-lí-ia*]. Compare Fuchs 1994: 202: 36, and the episode of Dalta of Ellipi in his forthcoming publication of the broken prism of Sargon.

Line 5: For the restoration, see Fuchs 1994: 222–223, line 113.

Line 7: Compare Fuchs 1994:180, line 418. Dr. Fuchs suggests restoring °*e-riš*(RI)*-an-ni*, assuming that Botta copied RI for an original SAG sign.

Lines 9–10: Compare Gadd 1954:179, lines 44–45.

The Annals of Sargon and Menander's History of Tyre

The text of Sargon's Annals as reconstructed above sheds new light on the relations of Tyre and Cyprus and the circumstances of Sargon's conquest of the island. It is evident that, until the late years of Sargon, Tyre governed either large parts of Cyprus or even the island in its entirety. Twenty years after Tiglath-pileser III's annexation of large parts of Syria and Palestine and the subjugation of Tyre under his yoke, the Cypriot kingdoms remained Tyre's tributaries. Neither the part played by Ḫirimmu of Tyre in the anti-Assyrian

Syro-Ephraimite coalition of 734 BCE (Briquel-Chatonnet 1992:152–160, with earlier literature; Irvine 1990; Na'aman 1991:91–94; Ehrlich 1991:48–58; Becking 1992:5–20), nor the Assyrian campaign conducted a few years later against Metenna, his heir (Briquel-Chatonnet 1992:162–163), changed the hegemonic status of Tyre in Cyprus.

The scribes of Sargon's Annals called Cyprus "Ia', region of Adnana." Adnana is called by the name of the Danunians, the inhabitants of the coast of Cilicia in the Late Bronze and Iron Age (Laroche 1958:263–275). Yadnana, the most common name for Cyprus in the Assyrian royal inscriptions, may be interpreted in the sense of "island of Danunians" (Luckenbill 1914:92–99; Hill 1940:106; Lipiński 1991:64).

Most of the Cypriot kings in the time of Esarhaddon and Ashurbanipal have Greek names (Lipiński 1991:58–62). The Tyrians must have ruled an island whose kings and a considerable part of the population were Ionians. This is a clear indication of the military power of the Tyrian navy and its leading role in the naval trade of the eastern Mediterranean in the eighth century BCE.

The rebellion of the Cypriot kings threatened to bring the Tyrian supremacy to an end. The king of Tyre, being unable to subjugate the rebellion, asked his overlord, the king of Assyria, for military support. The fact that Tyre is not mentioned at all in Sargon's inscriptions, save for the reference to the Assyrian offensive against the Iamneans and the "pacifying" of Que and Tyre, in itself is significant. There must have been good relations between Sargon and his vassal, the king of Tyre, and these relations must have suggested to Shilṭa that the Assyrian king would support him. And indeed, Sargon had the power to both compel towns along the eastern Mediterranean coasts to send ships to help quell the rebellion and to man them (at least partially) with competent Assyrian soldiers. Furthermore, Sargon controlled all the ports through which Cyprus conducted trade with the mainland and was able to lay an effective embargo on Cypriot commerce (Smith 1925:56). The Assyrian military operation and economic threat must have brought the immediate surrender of the rebellious kings and their recognition of the hegemony of the Assyrian king and his vassal, the king of Tyre. The Cypriot kings sent tributes to their new overlord (and to the king of Tyre as well) and let Sargon establish his stele at some prominent place in the Kition area.

Identifying Shilṭa as king of Tyre in the late years of Sargon clashes with the commonly held opinion that Lulî was king of Tyre at that time. The latter is known to have rebelled against Assyria after Sargon's death in the battlefield (705 BCE). In Sennacherib's inscriptions, Lulî is consistently called "king of Sidon (*Lulî šar Ṣidunni*)." It must be emphasized that the Assyrians were well aware of the location of Tyre and Sidon and did not mix the two names.

Thus, Ba'al-manzer is referred to in Shalmaneser III's inscription as "of Tyre"; in Tiglath-pileser III's inscriptions Tuba'il (Ithoba'il), Ḫirimmu and Metenna are called "of Tyre"; Tuba'lu (Ithoba'al), who succeded Lulî, is referred to in Sennacherib's inscriptions as "of Sidon"; in Esarhaddon's inscriptions Abdi-milkutti is called "king of Sidon," and Ba'al is called "king of Tyre." The clear distinction between the titles "of Tyre/king of Tyre" and "of Sidon/king of Sidon" may lead to the conclusion that Lulî was king of Sidon, a contemporary of Shilṭa of Tyre.

Such a conclusion may be supported by the fact that, in the face of the advance of Sennacherib's army, Lulî fled to Cyprus (rather than to Tyre). Sennacherib's early inscriptions state that he fled "far off into the midst of the sea." Only one inscription connects Lulî to Tyre, namely, Bull Inscription IV, which was written in c. 694 BCE, about 7 years after Sennacherib's campaign (Luckenbill 1924:68-69, lines 18–19). The text runs as follows: "Lulî king of Sidon — my terrifying splendor overcame him and from Tyre he fled to Cyprus (Yadnana), in the midst of the sea, and died." However, this description sounds odd, because there is no reasonable explanation for Lulî's escape from his assumed island capital, which did not come under threat during the 701 BCE campaign. Had he been the king of Tyre, he would have remained in the island, which gave him the best shelter against future Assyrian pursuit. Lulî's flight to Cyprus indicates that Tyre was not his capital.

Why then did all scholars regard Lulî as king of Tyre? The obvious reason is Menander's account of the history of Eloulaios (i.e., Lulî) as related by Josephus (Ant. IX, 284–287). This account runs as follows:[3]

> And Eloulaios, to whom they gave the name Py(l)as, reigned thirty-six years. This king, upon the revolt of the Kitians, put out to sea and reduced them to submission. Against them sent (ἐπι τούτους πέμψας) the king of Assyria, came up against all Phoenicia and invaded (it) and, after making a treaty of peace with all (its cities), withdrew from the land. And Sidon and A(r)ke and Old Tyre (Palaityrus) and many other cities also revolted from Tyre and surrendered to the king of Assyria. But, as the Tyrians for that reason would not submit to him, the king turned back again and attacked them after the Phoenicians had furnished him with sixty ships and eight hundred oarsmen. . . . But the king of Assyria, on retiring, placed guards at the river and the aqueducts to prevent the Tyrians from drawing water, and this they endured for five years, and drank from wells which they had dug.

The text of Menander was examined in detail by S. Timm (1982:214–224). This scholar has demonstrated that the Greek manuscripts have no names of Assyrian kings in the citation of Menander's words. The name of

3. The text follows the translation of R. Marcus in the *Loeb Classical Library*, with one major change (see below) and a few minor alterations.

Shalmaneser appears only in the text of Josephus (Ant. IX, 287): "This, then, is what is written in the Tyrian archives concerning Salmanasses, the king of Assyria." The correct text, which is supported by the majority of manuscripts, reads ἐπι τούτους πέμψας. The suggestion of B. Niese to correct it and read the name Selamphas has no textual support. Josephus must have drawn his conclusions about the identity of the Assyrian king from the position of the passage within Menander's work and possibly, by inference, from the biblical account of the reign of Hosea and the siege and conquest of Samaria (2 Kgs. 17:3–6).

Many scholars agree that the blockade of Tyre should be attributed to the time of Shalmaneser V (Lehmann 1902:125–140, 466–472; Katzenstein 1973: 222–230; Rebuffat 1976:71–79; Tadmor 1976:714; Na'aman 1990:215; Kuan 1991; Hayes and Kuan 1991:160–162; Briquel-Chatonnet 1992:163–172, with earlier literature). As the latter reigned for only 5 years (726–722 BCE) and, according to Menander, the blockade lasted for 5 years and was laid after the Assyrian king "withdrew from the land," i.e., sometime after his first campaign to the Phoenician coast, it must have ended in Sargon's early years.

Sennacherib's inscriptions make it clear that until the 701 BCE campaign, Lulî held the coastal area between Sidon in the north and Mount Carmel in the south. After his flight to Cyprus, his kingdom was transferred to his heir, Tuba'lu (Ithoba'al). According to Menander, the continental areas of Tyre had been detached prior to the blockade of the city. Thus, scholars who date the blockade to the time of Shalmaneser and assume that Lulî was king of Tyre in the time of Sennacherib have no alternative but to reconstruct a hypothetical stage in which Sargon restored these areas to him (Katzenstein 1973:244; Briquel-Chatonnet 1992:184). It goes without saying that nothing of this kind is known from any source, and, moreover, such a step would be an exception in Sargon's imperialistic policy. Significantly, when describing the suffering during the 5 years of siege, Menander refers only to the Tyrians, whereas Lulî is not mentioned in this context. Thus, it is possible that Lulî surrendered to Shalmaneser and was held in captivity during the blockade, just as Hosea of Israel was held in captivity in the last years of Shalmaneser, and that there was no king in Samaria when it came under siege (2 Kgs. 17:4–5). Be that as it may, when Sargon ended the blockade, he may have released Lulî and transferred to him the continental areas of the former kingdom of Tyre. He further installed Shilṭa on the throne of Tyre. This may explain Shilṭa's application for military aid to his overlord and the willingness of Sargon to help him crush the rebellion. It may also explain Lulî's motives in his second rebellion against Assyria after Sargon's death in the battlefield.

In conclusion, the episode of Sargon and the Cypriot kings as described in the royal Annals sheds new light on the history of Tyre and its relations with

Assyria in the late eighth century BCE. It indicates that Tyre kept its hegemonic position in Cyprus at least until the end of the eighth century BCE. It relates the name of a new king of Tyre and gives some details of his relations with his overlord, the king of Assyria, and with his subjects, the local kings of Cyprus. It allows us to suggest an explanation for Lulî's title "king of Sidon" in Sennacherib's inscription, a title that ostensibly contradicts Menander's account of Luli's history, and to draw some (admittedly conjectural) outlines of his career on the basis of Menander's history and the Assyrian royal inscriptions. Finally, it supplies an answer to the problem presented at the beginning of the article: the way by which Sargon, in spite of lack of navy and maritime knowledge, was able to reach Cyprus and erect his stele on a mount near the city of Kition.

References

Becking, B. 1992. *The Fall of Samaria. An Historical and Archaeological Study.* (Studies in the History of the Ancient Near East 2). Leiden, New York and Köln.

Benz, F.L. 1972. *Personal Names in the Phoenician and Punic Inscriptions* (Studia Pohl 8). Rome.

Bing, J.D. 1969. *A History of Cilicia during the Assyrian Period.* (Ph.D. Thesis). Ann Arbor.

Borger, R. 1967. *Handbuch der Keilschriftliteratur* I. Berlin.

Botta, P.É. 1849. *Monument de Ninive.* III–IV: Inscriptions. Paris. (Reprint 1972. Osnabrück).

Briquel-Chatonnet, J. 1992. *Les relations entre les cités de la côte Phénicienne et les royaumes d'Israël et de Juda.* (Studia Phoenicia XII). Leuven.

Ehrlich, C.S. 1991. Coalition Politics in Eighth Century B.C.E. Palestine: The Philistines and the Syro-Ephraimite War. *ZDPV* 107: 48–58.

Elayi, J. and Cavigneaux, A. 1979. Sargon II et les Ioniens, *Oriens Antiquus* 18: 63–75.

Fuchs, A. 1994. *Die Inschriften Sargons II. aus Khorsabad.* Göttingen.

Gadd, C.J. 1954. Inscribed Prisms of Sargon II from Nimrud. *Iraq* 16: 173–201.

Hayes, J.H. and Kuan, J.K. 1991. The Final Years of Samaria (730–720 BC). *Biblica* 72: 153–181.

Helm, P.R. 1980. *"Greeks" in the Neo-Assyrian Levant and "Assyria" in Early Greek Writers.* (Ph.D. Thesis). Ann Arbor.

Hill, G. 1940. *A History of Cyprus.* Cambridge.

Irvine, S.A. 1990. *Isaiah, Ahaz, and the Syro-Ephraimitic Crisis.* (Society of Biblical Literature Dissertation Series 123). Atlanta.

Katzenstein, H.J. 1973. *The History of Tyre, from the Beginning of the Second Millennium B.C.E. until the Fall of the Neo-Babylonian Empire in 538 B.C.E.* Jerusalem.

Kuan, J. 1991. Hosea 9:13 and Josephus, *Antiquities* IX, 277–287. *PEQ* 123: 103–108.

Laroche, E. 1958. Études sur les Hieroglyphes Hittites. *Syria* 35: 263–275.

Lehmann, C.F. 1902. Menander und Josephos über Salmanassar IV. *Klio* 2: 125–140, 466–472.

Lipiński, E. 1991. The Cypriot Vassals of Esarhaddon. In: Cogan, M. and Eph'al, I. eds. *Ah, Assyria . . . Studies in Assyrian History and Ancient Near Eastern Historiography Presented to Hayim Tadmor.* (Scripta Hierosolymitana 33). Jerusalem: 58–64.

Luckenbill, D.D. 1914. Jadnana and Javan (Danaans and Ionians). *ZA* 28: 92–99.
Luckenbill, D.D. 1924. *The Annals of Sennacherib.* (Oriental Institute Publications 2). Chicago.
Luckenbill, D.D. 1927. *Ancient Records of Assyria and Babylonia* II. Chicago.
Messerschmidt, L. and Ungnad, A. 1907. *Die bildlichen Darstellungen auf vorderasiatischen Denkmälern der königlichen Museen zu Berlin* (Vorderasiatische Schriftdenkmäler der Königlichen Musee zu Berlin 1). Leipzig.
Na'aman, N. 1990. The Historical Background to the Conquest of Samaria (720 BC). *Biblica* 71: 206–225.
Na'aman, N. 1991. Forced Participation in Alliances in the Course of the Assyrian Campaigns to the West, in: Cogan, M. and Eph'al, I. eds. *Ah, Assyria... Studies in Assyrian History and Ancient Near Eastern Historiography Presented to Hayim Tadmor.* (Scripta Hierosolymitana 33). Jerusalem: 80–98.
Naster, P. 1938. *L'Asie Mineure et l'Assyrie aux VIIIe et VIIe siècles av. J.C. d'après les annales des rois Assyriens.* Louvain.
Olmstead, A.T.E. 1908. *Western Asia in the Days of Sargon of Assyria 722-705 B.C.* New York.
Olmstead, A.T.E. 1930/31. The Text of Sargon's Annals. *AJSL* 47: 259–279.
Rebuffat, R. 1976. Une bataille navale au VIIIe siècle. (Josèphe, Antiquités Judaïques, IX, 14). *Semitica* 26: 71–79
Schrader, E. 1882. *Die Sargonsstele des Berliner Museum.* Berlin.
Smith, S. 1925. The Supremacy of Assyria. The *Cambridge Ancient History* III. Cambridge: 32–60.
Tadmor, H. 1976. Shalmaneser V. *Enc. Miqr.* VII: 714–715. (Hebrew).
Tadmor, H. 1996. Notes on the Stele of Sargon II from Cyprus. *Eretz Israel* 25: 286–289. (Hebrew).
Timm, S. 1982. *Die Dynastie Omri. Quellen und Untersuchungen zur Geschichte Israels im 9. Jahrhundert vor Christus.* (Forschungen zur Religion und Literatur des Alten und Neuen Testaments 124). Göttingen.
Winckler, H. 1889. *Die Keilschrifttexte Sargons nach den Papierabklatschen und Originalen neu herausgegeben* 1. Leipzig.
Winckler, H. 1897. Griechen und Assyrer. *Altorientalische Forschungen* I: 356–370.
Zadok, R. 1990. Zut Struktur der nachbiblischen Jüdischen Personennamen semitischen Ursprung. *Trumah* (Hochschule für jüdische Studien Heidelberg 1). Wiesbaden: 243–343.

The Conquest of Yadnana According to Sargon II's Inscriptions[1]

Sargon conquered Cyprus about 707 BCE and erected his stele there. The Cypriot episode is related in numerous Assyrian inscriptions, all written shortly after the island's conquest. Most of the references to Cyprus come from Sargon's new capital, Khorsabad (Dur-Sharrukin). Most of these inscriptions were written on limestone slabs, or other architectural elements, which adorned the palace of Sargon. It is, therefore, not surprising that in depicting this episode, many of these inscriptions share similar motifs and expressions.

The question of typology and terminology is confronted anew in every discussion of the Assyrian royal inscriptions. In the case of the Cypriot episode, a classification by contents is the most appropriate. For the sake of identification, I will use the terms "Annals" and "Summary Inscriptions." In spite of the similarity in motifs and expressions, there are marked differences in content between the two classes, so that their discussion will be kept apart.

The Summary Inscriptions

With the conquest of the island of Cyprus, Sargon pushed Assyria's western border to a limit far beyond the achievements of any of his predecessors. No wonder that in a group of building inscriptions from Khorsabad, which describe the extent of Sargon's empire in his late years, the island of Cyprus opens the delineation of the empire. "From the land of Yadnana in the middle of the western sea, until the border of Egypt . . ." (Fuchs 1994:77, line 22; 194, lines 16–17; 250, lines 7–8; 252, lines 4–5; 255, lines 5-7; 264, lines 63–64; 273, lines 14–15). It may be compared with the description of the empire in Sargon's Cylinder inscriptions of his ninth/tenth year (about 712/711 BCE), a few years before the conquest of the island. The border delineation that begins in the east and ends in the west runs as follows: "From the land of Rashi

1. Reprinted with permission. Abusch, T. et al. (eds). 2001. *Proceedings of the XLV*[e] *Rencontre Assyriologique Internationale, Part 1: Historiography in the Cuneiform.* Bethesda:365-372.

on the border of Elam . . . until the Brook of Egypt, the wide land of Amurru and all the land of Hatti" (Fuchs 1994:33, lines 12–13). The prominent place of Cyprus in the border descriptions of Sargon's late inscriptions is self-evident.

Three inscriptions from Khorsabad relate the conquest of Cyprus in an almost identical short manner: "Subduer of/I subdue the seven kings of the land of Ia', a district of the land of Yadnana, whose abodes are situated a journey of seven days away in the middle of the sea of the setting sun" (Fuchs 1994:64 lines 27–29; 77 lines 17–18; 262–63 lines 41–45). The stock of phrases used by the scribes in these inscriptions also appears in the more detailed inscriptions. The emphasis on the most vital elements of the description directed the choice of these particular phrases in the three short accounts.

Another group of summary inscriptions relates the Cypriot episode in a somewhat similar manner. This group includes Sargon's great display inscription from Khorsabad (Fuchs 1994:232–233, lines 145–149), two prisms from Nimrud (Gadd 1954:191–92, lines 25–38), and the Larnaka stele (Winckler 1889:180–183, lines 28–42). The text of these inscriptions runs as follows:

> And seven kings of the land of Ia', a district of the land of Yadnana, who are situated a journey of seven days away in the middle of the sea of the setting sun and their locations are distant, so that since far-off days (*var.* since the far-off days of the taking over of Assyria) and until now, none among the kings, my ancestors, of Assyria and Babylonia, had heard the name of their land — from far off in the middle of the sea they heard the deeds which I had performed in the lands of Chaldea and Hatti, their hearts palpitated and fright fell upon them. They brought to me in Babylon gold, silver, furniture (made) of ebony and boxwood, the manufacture (*var.* the treasures) of their land, and kissed my feet.

It is clear that all the summary inscriptions share a common stock of phrases, some of which are part of the repertoire of many other royal inscriptions and some coined specifically for this unusual episode.

The following text appears even in the shortest descriptions of the episode:

> *sebe šarrāni ša māt Ia-a' nagê ša māt Yadnana ša mālak sebe umê ina qabal tâmti ēreb* [d]*Šamši šitkunat šubassun/šitkunūma nessat šubassun.*

The phrases of the above text reflect the unusual character of this episode and were chosen to describe this particular situation. After all, Assyria had never before conquered an island far from the coast.

All other elements in the detailed summary inscriptions are drawn from a repertoire of stock phrases that describe actions occurring during the military campaigns of the Assyrian king. These phrases are:

(a) *ša ultu umê ruqūti adi inanna . . . manamma la išmû zikir mātišun.*

(b) *epšet ina qereb māt GN eteppūšu . . . išmūma libbušun itrukūma imqussunūti ḫattu.*

(c) *ḫuraṣu kaspu . . . nepešti mātišun/niṣirti mātišun ana qereb GN adi maḫriya ūbilūnimma unaššiqū šēpēya.*

Thus, it is evident that the scribes who wrote the summary inscriptions composed the Cypriot episode by combining a few basic facts about the event with a stock of phrases they had learned at school and had used to describe many other military campaigns (for the same literary technique in many other inscriptions of Sargon, see Renger 1986). Even the scribe who wrote the Larnaka stele used the same text as all the other scribes who worked in the Assyrian royal cities.

The Annals

The text of the summary inscriptions is clear and the sequence of events is easy to understand. Yet, the historical interpretation of the episode is fraught with difficulty, and scholars have offered various suggestions to explain how Sargon was able to reach and conquer the remote island of Cyprus, and the possible background of the operation. The text of the Annals, on the other hand, is badly damaged and its interpretation involves enormous difficulties. Therefore, it has played only a minor role in the reconstruction of the historical event.

Deciphering the text of the Annals is the key to the correct historical interpretation of the episode. Two recensions of the Cypriot episode appear in Hall II and V and were published in facsimile by Botta (1849:91 and 108). Recently, I suggested a new transliteration and translation of the Cypriot episode as it appears in Sargon's Annals (Na'aman 1998). The two recensions of Halls II and V were presented there separately, each in its own right. However, for the sake of clarity, I will present here only the reconstructed text of Hall V, restored with the help of of the text of Hall II.

> Shilṭa [of] Tyre [pays? tribute? . . . to] Assyr[ia. (And) seven kin]gs of the [land] of Ia', a district [of the land of Adnana], who are situated a journey of seven days away in the middle of the sea of the setting sun [and their locations are dista]nt, who since old days, to his? [. . .] together s[topped the[ir presents (and)] withhold [their tributes. And Shilṭ]a bro]ught his heavy tribute, and to suppress the ho[st? of . . .] he ap[plied to me for military aid]. I sent my officer, who is fearless in battle, with my royal guard, to avenge him, [and . . . they cros]sed?. (When) they saw the strong troops of Ashur, at the mention of my name they became afraid and their arms collapsed. They brought to Babylon, into my presence, gold, silver, ut[ensils of ebony and boxwood, the manufacture] of their land, and [to . . .] I entrusted [them].

Comparing Sargon's annals and summary inscriptions reveals that the annals are far more detailed and were written on the basis of first-hand knowledge. The episode is, in many ways, exceptional. The campaign was set in motion by a request from a loyal vassal, the king of Tyre, to intervene on his behalf in an affair that was not the concern of Assyria, namely, the failure of the foreign kings of Cyprus to pay tribute to the Tyrian. The foreign kings lived in an area that was inaccessible to Assyrian power, and Assyria depended on the Tyrian fleet to get there. According to the Assyrian literary code, on the other hand, Assyria had to be depicted as the dominating power, whose operation depended on its strength alone and whose action led to the enemy's total surrender. Hence, the roundabout manner in which the plot is presented.

The account of the annals opens with the name and city of the allied king, as opposed to many other episodes that open with the name and country of a foreign king. It is followed by a detailed description of the cause of Sargon's action, an account of the call to arms in Assyria and the enemy's surrender. These two parts are missing in the summary inscriptions, because no military operation is mentioned there, and, hence, no cause of action is required. The episode closes with the list of tributes sent to Sargon and a note on the organization of the conquered area.

Like the text of the summary inscriptions, parts of the annals consist of stock phrases common to other Assyrian royal inscriptions. In addition to the phrases already cited, we may note the following examples:

(a) *mitḫāriš kadrâšun ušabṭilūma iklû bilassun*

(b) *Silṭa mandatašu kabittu iššâmma*

(c) *šut rēšiya la adir tāḫazi itti kiṣir šarrūtiya ana turri gimillišu uma'era*

(d) *emūqat* [d]*Aššur emurūma ana zikir šumeya išḫutūma irmâ idāšun*

The episode of Sargon and the Cypriot kings, as described in the Annals, sheds new light on the history of Tyre and its relations with Assyria in the late eighth century BCE. It indicates that Tyre kept its hegemonic position in Cyprus at least until the end of the eighth century. It relates the name of a new king of Tyre and gives some details of his relations with his overlord, the king of Assyria, and with his vassals, the local kings of Cyprus. Finally, it explains the way by which Sargon, in spite of lacking a navy or maritime knowledge, was able to reach Cyprus and subjugate its kings to his rule.

The Larnaka Stele

Sargon's stele was erected in Cyprus shortly after its conquest in 707 BCE. The site where it originally stood is described on the stele as follows (Winckler 1889:180–83, lines 54–57; Borger 1967:351, No 71, with earlier literature; Malbran-Labat 1995; Tadmor 1996):

> [At that ti]me I had a stele fashioned and [the symbols] of the great [gods], my lords, [I engraved] thereon. My royal image [implorin]g for my life I set before them. [I insc]ribed thereon [the names of the lands] that from the rising sun [to the setting]

> sun, with the aid of Ashur, [Nabu] and Marduk, the gods my helpers, I had subjugated [to the yoke] of my rule. I set it up [on] Ba'il-ḫurri, the mountain, (located) [at the to]p of the land of Adnana. [The glory] of the great gods, my lords, [by who]se reliable (oracular) [answer] I marched to and fro, having no [rival], I left [for the king]s, my sons, for all time.

It is clear that the stele was erected on a prominent mountain described as "the head ([*re-e*]*š*) of (Y)adnana." Tadmor (1996) suggested restoring in line 53 [*e-li* KUR] *Ba-il-ḫur-ri* KUR-*i* ("on Ba'il-ḫurri, the mountain") and identified the site as the mountain range overlooking the coastal plain, northeast of Larnaka, on the summit of which today stands the monastery of Stavravouni.

The text does not state where the stele was quarried and inscribed (the problem may easily be solved by petrographic analysis). Either it was quarried and engraved in Syria, after the scribe received exact information of the future site of the stele, or the scribe travelled to Cyprus and inscribed the stele after it was quarried near the place where it was erected.

At some stage, the stele was removed from its original location and brought to Larnaka, where it was unearthed in 1844 (see Schrader 1882:4; Yon 1995).

The discovery of the stele on the island corroborates Sargon's accounts in the annals and summary inscriptions of the conquest of Yadnana. Prisoners from Yadnana are mentioned in Sennacherib's inscriptions (Luckenbill 1924:73 lines 59–60), but this Assyrian king does not mention any campaign that he conducted to the island. The annals of Esarhaddon enumerate ten Cypriot vassals who participated in the construction and embellishment of the royal palace of Nineveh (Borger 1956:60 lines 63–72; see Lipiński 1991). Ashurbanipal enumerates the same list of ten Cypriot vassals in conjunction with his first campaign to Egypt (Streck 1916:II 140 lines 36–50). It is clear that Assyria maintained its hegemonic status in Cyprus from the time of Sargon's conquest onward. After all, it had the means to compel towns along the eastern Mediterranean coast to send ships to help quell any rebellion that might break out, as well as to man them with competent Assyrian soldiers. Moreover, Assyria controlled all the mainland ports with which Cyprus conducted trade and was able to impose an effective embargo on Cypriot commerce. Assyrian military power and economic threat guaranteed the cooperation of both the Tyrian authorities and the local Cypriot kings and their recognition the sovereignty of Assyria over the island.

Assyrian representative(s) either stayed at Kition, the main Tyrian centre on the island, or visited the place from time to time. Their main concern was the regular payment of tribute and the economic cooperation of the Tyrian and local Cypriot authorities. Assyrian presence in other parts of the island was extremely limited, and there are no indications that Assyria conducted commercial relations with the island. The absence of both Assyrian and Assyrian-influenced artifacts in Cypriot sites reflects the one-sided exploitative nature of the relationship. Assyria remained a continental power, with no real maritime policy, and its brief period of control in Cyprus did not leave any mark on the island's history.

References

Borger, R. 1956. *Die Inschriften Asarhaddons Königs von Assyrien.* (AFO Beiheft 9). Graz. (Reprint 1967. Osnabrück).

Borger, R. 1967. *Handbuch der Keilschriftliteratur* I. Berlin.

Botta, P.É. 1849. *Monument de Ninive.* III–IV: *Inscriptions.* Paris. (Reprint 1972. Osnabrück).

Fuchs, A. 1994. *Die Inschriften Sargons II. aus Khorsabad.* Göttingen.

Gadd, C.J. 1954. Inscribed Prisms of Sargon II from Nimrud. *Iraq* 16: 173–201.

Lipiński, E. 1991. The Cypriot Vassals of Esarhaddon. In: Cogan, M. and Eph'al, I. eds., *Ah, Assyria . . . Studies in Assyrian History and Ancient Near Eastern Historiography Presented to Hayim Tadmor.* (Scripta Hierosolymitana 33). Jerusalem: 58–64.

Luckenbill, D.D. 1924. *The Annals of Sennacherib.* (Oriental Institute Publications 2). Chicago.

Malbran-Labat, F. 1995. La stèle de Sargon II à Chypre. Le texte de l'inscription. In: Caubet, A. ed. *Khorsabad, le palais de Sargon II, roi d'Assyrie.* Actes du colloque organisé au musée du Louvre les 21 et 22 janvier 1994. Paris: 169–179.

Na'aman, N. 1998. Sargon II and the Rebellion of the Cypriot Kings against Shilṭa of Tyre. *Orientalia* 67: 239–247.

Renger, J. 1986. Neuassyrische Königsinschriften als Genre der Keilschriftliteratur. Zum Stil und zur Kompositionstechnik der Inschriften Sargons II. Von Assyrien. In Hecker, K. and Sommerfeld, W. eds. *Keilschriftliche Literaturen.* Ausgewählte Vorträge der XXXII. Rencontre Assyriologique Internationale (Berliner Beiträge zum Vorderen Orient 6). Berlin: 109–128.

Schrader, E. 1882 Die Sargonsstele des Berliner Museum. Berlin.

Streck, M. 1916. Assurbanipal und die letzten Assyrischen Könige bis zum *Untergange Niniveh's* I–III. Leipzig.

Tadmor, H. 1996. Notes on the Stele of Sargon II from Cyprus. *Eretz Israel* 25:286–289. (Hebrew).

Winckler, H. 1889. Die Keilschrifttexte Sargons nach den Papierabklatschen und Originalen neu herausgegeben I–II. Leipzig.

Yon, M. 1995. La stèle de Sargon II à Chypre. La decouverte de la stèle à Larnaca (Chypre). In Caubet, A. ed. *Khorsabad, le palais de Sargon II, roi d'Assyrie.* Actes du colloque organisé au musée du Louvre les 21 et 22 janvier 1994. Paris: 161–168.

Sennacherib's "Letter to God" on his Campaign to Judah[1]

The document with which the present paper deals has had a somewhat split personality until now, its two fragments having been ascribed to two different kings: One piece (K 6205) was first published in cuneiform by G. Smith (1870:Pl. 9, 2) and has since been associated with the episode of Azriyau king of Yaudi, in the days of Tiglath-pileser III (Rost 1893:18–20, lines 103–119). The second fragment (BM 82–3–23, 131) was first edited, in transcription only, by H. Winckler (1899:570–574) and republished by H. Tadmor, who treated its literary and historical aspects in detail, suggesting that it be ascribed to the days of Sargon II (Tadmor 1958a:80–84).

The outstanding and characteristic feature of both fragments is the specific literary style, unique among all the documents concerning the Syro-Palestinian region. This peculiar style was the point of departure for associating the two fragments as one document. Through a comparison of the transcriptions and, subsequently, an examination of photographs of the two fragments, it became apparent that they comprise parts of one and the same document, describing, as I shall attempt to demonstrate below, Sennacherib's campaign to Judah in 701 BCE.

The two fragments are presented here, fitted together, along with a transcription and translation.[2]

Transcription

(1) . . .
(2) [   ] ŠID [. . .
(3) [. . . AN.ŠÁR bēli ú-tak-kil-a]n-ni-ma a-na KUR Ia-[ú-di lu al-lik ina] me-ti-iq KASKAL^{II}-ia man-da-at-tu šá LU[GAL^{MEŠ} KUR . . . amḫur . . .
(4) [. . . ina da-n]a-ni šá AN.ŠÁR EN-ia na-gu-u [šá ^{m}Ḫa-za-qi-i]a-a-u KUR Ia-u-da-a-a GIM x[. . .

1. *Bulletin of the American Schools of Oriental Research* 214 (1974), 25–39.

Reprinted with permission. Some parts of the original article have been revised in light of recent research (see notes 2, 12, 21).

2. The transcription and translation were updated according to the collation of the tablet by Borger (1979:134–135) and Frahm (1997:229–232).

(5) [. . .] ^{URU}A-za-qa-a É tuk-la-te-šú šá ina bi-ri [t mi-i]ṣ-ri-ia u KUR Ia-u-di [. . .
(6) [. . .] ṣe-er ŠU.SI KUR-e šá-kin GIM zi-qip GÍR.AN$^{?}$.B[AR$^{?\text{ME}}$]^{Š} la ni-bi ana AN-e šá-qu-u ŠUR [. . .
(7) [dūrānīšu] dun-nu-nu-ma šit-nu-nu KUR-e zaq-ru-ti a-na ni-[ṭil] IGI^{IIMEŠ} ki-i šá ul-tu AN-e [. . .
(8) [ina šukbus a-r]a-am-me qur-ru-bu šu-pe-e da-an ši-pir [xx]-tú [i-n]a mit-ḫu-uṣ zu-ki GIR^{II} q[u-ra-di-ia . . .
(9) [. . . ANŠE.KU]R.RA^{MEŠ}-ia e-mu-ru-ma ri-gim um-na(read ma)-nat A[N].ŠÁR gap-šá-te iš-mu-ma ip-làḫ Š[À-šú-un . . .
(10) [^{URU}A-za-qa-a al-m]e KUR-ud áš-lu-la šal-lat-su ap-pul aq-qur [ina ^{d}Gira aqmu . . .
(11) [^{URU}GN UR]U LUGAL-ti šá KUR Pi-liš-ta-a-a /šá/ /^{m}Ha/-[za-<qi>-i]a-a-u e-ki-mu ú-dan-ni-nu-šú-ma [. . .
(12) [. . .] xx^{II} x /GIŠ$^{?\text{MEŠ}}$/ [. . .]x GIM ^{GIŠ}gap-ni [. . .
(13) [. . . di$^{?}$]-ma-a-ti GAL^{MEŠ} šu-tas-ḫu-u[r-m]a šum-ru-ṣa-at [. . .
(14) [. . . l]i$^{?}$ É.GAL GIM KUR-e pa-nu-uš-šú-u[n] ed-let-ma šá-qa-at [. . .
(15) [. . .] e-kil la na-pi-iḫ-šú ^{d}UTU-šú A^{MEŠ}-šú ina e-ṭ[u]-ti šit-ku-nu-ma mu-ṣa-[šú$^{?}$ . . .
(16) [. . . pi]-i-šá ina qul-mì-i na-kis ḫa-ri-ṣu i-te-[š]á$^{?}$ šá-pil-ma ka-x[. . .
(17) [. . . l]e-'-u-te MÈ ú-še-rib qé-reb-šú ^{GIŠ}TUKUL^{MEŠ}-šú ú-ra-kis a-n[a epēš . . .
(18) [. . . u]m-ma-na-at KUR MAR.TU^{KI} DÙ-šú-un SA[ḪAR^{Ḫ}]$^{\text{I.A}}$ ú-šá-az-bíl-šu-nu-ti-m[a . . .
(19) [. . .] x ṣe-ru-uš-šú-un ina 9-šu x[x d]u–/ri/-šú GAL^{MEŠ} GIM kar-p[at pa-ḫa-ri ú-par-ri-ir . . .
(20) [. . . GU$_{4}^{\text{MEŠ}}$ u ṣe]-e-ni ul-tu qer-bi-šú /ú/-[še-ṣa-am-ma] /šal/-[la-tiš am-nu . . .
(21) [. . .] xxxxxxx [. . .

Translation:

(3) [. . . Ashur, my lord, encourag]ed me and against the land of Ju[dah I marched. In] the course of my campaign, the tribute of the ki[ngs of Philistia? I received . . .
(4) [. . . with the mig]ht of Ashur, my lord, the province of [Hezek]iah of Judah like [. . .
(5) [. . .] the city of Azekah, his stronghold, which is between my [bo]rder and the land of Judah [. . .
(6) [like the nest of the eagle$^{?}$] located on a mountain ridge, like pointed iron daggers without number reaching high to heaven [. . .
(7) [Its walls] were strong and rivaled the highest mountains, to the (mere) sight, as if from the sky [appears its head$^{?}$ . . .
(8) [by means of beaten (earth) ra]mps, mighty$^{?}$ battering rams brought near, the work of [. . .], with the attack by foot soldiers, [my] wa[rriors . . .
(9) [. . .] they had seen [the approach of my cav]alry and they had heard the roar of the mighty troops of the god Ashur and [their] he[arts] became afraid [. . .
(10) [The city Azekah I besieged,] I captured, I carried off its spoil, I destroyed, I devastated, [I burned with fire . . .
(11) [The city of Ekron$^{?}$], a royal [city] of the Philistines, which H[ezek]iah had captured and strengthened for himself [. . .
(12) [. . .] like a tree [standing out on a ridge? . . .
(13) [. . .] surrounded with great [to]wers and exceedingly difficult [its ascent? . . .
(14) [. . .] palace like a mountain was barred in front of them and high is [its top?
(15) [. . .] it was dark and the sun never shone on it, its waters were situated in darkness and [its$^{?}$] overflow [. . .
(16) [. . .] its [mou]th was cut with axes and a moat was dug around it [. . .

(17) [. . .warriors] skillful in battle he caused to enter into it, their weapons he bound (on them) to [offer battle . . .
(18) [. . .] I caused the warriors of Amurru, all of them, to carry earth [. . .
(19) [. . .] against them. In the ninth time the great [. . .] of his wall like a pot [of clays I smashed? . . .
(20) [. . . cattle and she]ep I carried out from its midst [and counted as] spo[il . . .
(21) . . .

I

The inscription can be divided into two parts, both concerning a single episode — the war against Hezekiah king of Judah. The first part, lines 3–10, describes the conquest of the town of Azekah, whereas the second part, lines 11–20, relates the conquest of a kingdom. At this point, the obverse is broken off, reverse is not preserved.

Line 2: The restorations in this line are based on comparisons with Sennacherib's inscriptions, where the same formulae appear (Luckenbill 1924:26, lines 65–68; 39, lines 54–55; 67, lines 7–8).

Lines 4 and 11: The spelling *Ha-za-qi-ia-a-a* appears also in Sennacherib's annals (Luckenbill 1924:76, n. 7).

Line 5: It was this line that led fragment K 6205 to be associated with the Azriyau episode. Rost copied here [*I*]z-*ri-ia-u māt Ia-u-di*, in spite of the obvious difficulty that the spelling *Yaudi* would be an incorrect form of the gentilic. The suggested reading for this line — *ina birīt miṣriya u māt Yaudi* — of course removes this difficulty and removes Azriyau altogether from the picture.

Line 6: At the start of the line we might possibly restore *kima qinni erî,* "like the nest of the eagle," on the basis of the annals of Sennacherib (Luckenbill 1924:36, line 77).

The spelling GIR$^{(MEŠ)}$ AN.BAR, without the plural, appears in the Rassam Cylinder of Sennacherib (see Borger 1963:69).

Lines 12–16: describe, rhetorically and with exaggeration, the strength of a city in Philistia that had been annexed to Judah. The description is more detailed than that concerning Azekah, possibly because it was the more important of the two.

Line 12: At the end of the line, we might possibly restore "like a tree [standing out on a ridge]" (on the basis of Thureau-Dangin 1912:38, line 239), because, on the basis of the structure of the document, we have here the description of the city from afar (see below).

Line 13: The restoration at the start of the line is based on similar spellings in the inscriptions of Sargon and Sennacherib (see *CAD* D 144–145). At the end of the line, we might restore *alaktu.*

Line 14: The scribe seems to depict the palace jutting out from the fortifications on one flank of the city.

Line 15: An authentic description of a water tunnel — one of the most typical features of Palestinian archaeology in the period of the Israelite monarchies (Pritchard 1961; Yadin 1972:172–178, with earlier literature). The inclusion of the water source within the fortifications enabled the besieged to hold out for a very lengthy time. A famous example of such an installation, contemporaneous with the present document, is the tunnel hewn by Hezekiah in Jerusalem (2 Kgs. 20:20), still extant today (Vincent 1911).

Line 16: The subject of this sentence is not clear.

Line 17: Among the preparations for the siege, Hezekiah brought troops within the city, probably because he was not sure of the loyalties of the Philistine inhabitants of the city.

Lines 18–20: describe the siege and conquest of the city.

Line 18: Auxiliary forces of the vassal kings take part in the siege operations.

Line 20: In the cuneiform published by G. Smith (1870:Pl. 9, 2), the sign *šal* appears in its entirety, whereas today only the upper part is visible. This line is restored on the basis of many of Sennacherib's inscriptions in which this expression recurs (Luckenbill 1924:27, lines 75–76; 28, line 21; 33, line 26; etc.).

II

On the basis of its style, Tadmor (1958a:82) assigned the "Azekah inscription" to the type scholars refer to as "Letters to God." (Bauer 1931:250, n. 1; Oppenheim 1960, with earlier literature). The external traits of such documents are the fine literary style, differing from the dry, monotonous style of the annals, and the developed literary structure. Such a structure is evident in the present text, upon comparison of its two parts. First, each place is identified (lines 5,11), then each is described from afar (lines 6, 12), after which details of the fortifications and means of defense are given (lines 7, 13–17), followed, finally, by a description of the fighting and conquest (lines 8–10, 18–20). Also noteworthy is the structure of line 9: . . *ēmurūma* . . . *išmûma* . . . *iplaḫ libbašun,* as well as several descriptions unparalleled in known Akkadian literature (lines 6–7, 14–15). All this points to fine, well-planned writing of a very high standard.

There is no doubt that, stylistically and in lexicon, this text is especially close to the "Letter to God," describing the campaign of Sargon II to Urartu in 714 BCE.

However, a considerable number of expressions would bring us down beyond the time of Sargon, to the days of Sennacherib his son.[3] These specific expressions are treated below in the same order as they appear in the text, together with their parallels in the Sennacherib's annals:

Aššur bēlī utakkilannīma ana māt GN lu allik (see the note to line 2 of the text).
ina mēteq gerrīya[4]
bīt tuklāti[5]
ina šukbus aramme qurrubu/qitrub šupê . . . mitḫuṣ zūk šēpē . . .[6]
ummanāt māt Amurri kališun[7]
alpi u ṣeni ultu qirbīšu ušēṣamma šallatiš amnu[8]

We must note that all these expressions (besides the first) appear specifically in passages describing Sennacherib's campaign to Palestine in 701 BCE[9] — and, indeed, this would seem to hint at the date of the text as well. Several other factors strengthen my ascribing this tablet to Sennacherib rather than Sargon.

(a) In all of Sargon's inscriptions, no mention is ever made of a campaign against Judah. In contrast, such a campaign is quite prominent in all of Sennacherib's inscriptions. The central positioning of Judah here would suit a campaign by Sennacherib, but not one by Sargon.

---

3. Note that only little more than a decade separates Sargon's eighth campaign (714 BCE.) from that of Sennacherib to Palestine (701 BCE), and, thus, it is not surprising that in the writing of such a standard as that of the text there should appear stylistic features and expressions close to those of Sargon.

4. The expression *ina mēteq gerrīya* as an opening of a new paragraph, appears only at the beginning of Sennacherib's reign and is common in his inscriptions (Luckenbill 1924: 25, line 54; 31, line 68; 39, line 58). There is one occurrence where it seems to appear in the inscriptions of Sargon (Gadd 1954:177:54; *AHw* 649b, *s.v. mētequ*), but according to the cuneiform (Gadd 1954:pl. XLVI), we should read *i-na mè-ti-iq ḫ*[*a*!*-ar-ra-ni-ia*]. The appearance of the expression *ina mēteq gerrīya* in Sennacherib's inscriptions stems, in my opinion, from the term *gerru*, "campaign of war," used in his inscriptions to denote his successive campaigns; this term came to replace the conventional *palû*, "regnal year," used by the earlier kings. For the reasons behind the use of the term *gerru* in Sennacherib's inscriptions, see Tadmor 1958a:31–32. The expression *ana mēteq gerrīya* appears once in the annals of Sargon, but in a different meaning. See Lie 1929:44, line 275.

5. Luckenbill 1924:30, line 45; Borger 1963:LI, s.v, bīt tuklāti.

6. Luckenbill 1924:32–33, lines 21–23; 63, lines 10–11.

7. In Sennacherib's inscriptions, the expression *šarrāni māt Amurri kališun* (Luckenbill 1924:30, line 58; 69, lines 19; 132, line 68) is similar to the one occurring in the text, whereas in the inscriptions of Sargon, only the combination *māt Amurri* appears and always as a geographical name.

8. A common expression in Sennacherib's inscriptions. See the note to line 20.

9. Another similarity can be seen in *adi* 4-*šu* "fourfold," appearing in Sennacherib's account of his campaign to Palestine (Luckenbill 1924:30, line 59), as compared with *ina* 9-*šu*, "in the ninth time," in the text.

(b) Sargon himself apparently did not participate in the campaign to Philistia in 711 BCE, his place at the head of the army being taken by the *turtannu* (Alt 1945:141–143; Tadmor 1958a:79–80). We should remember that a "Letter to God" was a sort of personal report of the king to the god Ashur on his activities during campaigns carried out in the god's name, and such texts were composed for only the most outstanding of the campaigns conducted by the king. Thus, it would be difficult to assume that the king would write a report to his god on a campaign in which he did not even participate.

(c) Near the name of the city of Azekah there appears in this text (line 5) the statement "which is between my [bo]rder and the land of Judah." Azekah — Tell Zakariyeh in Judah (Abel 1938:85) — is on the latitude of Ashdod, and it is clear that such a description would have been impossible prior to the annexation of Ashdod as an Assyrian province in 711 BCE. It is difficult to assume that this refers to the campaign in 711 BCE, at the start of which Ashdod was conquered and annexed, the invasion of Judah taking place only later, because it is surely doubtful that, in the description of that very same campaign, such an annexation would appear as if long done. It is much simpler to assume that the text refers to Sennacherib's campaign of 701 BCE, at which time the king of Ashdod, whose territory had been annexed by the Assyrians in the days of Sargon, was among the kings summoned before Sennacherib near Tyre (Luckenbill 1924:30, line 54).

(d) The dating of the "Azekah inscription" to the days of Sargon is based principally on the specific spelling of the name of the god Ashur, which appears as AN.ŠÁR (Tadmor 1958a:82; see Tadmor 1958b:159–160). According to this argument, the same spelling does occur in the documents of Sennacherib, but only in two types of text: those originating in the city of Ashur (mostly building inscriptions) and in two inscriptions from Nineveh dealing with the *bit akītu* in the city of Ashur. Inasmuch as the "Azekah inscription" is a historical text, so the argument runs, it could not be from the time of Sennacherib, becuase in all the other historical texts only the usual spelling *Aššur* appears.

Against this, we must note first the special character of the text, differing considerably from all other of Sennacherib's historical texts. We must further remember that the "Letter to God" was meant to be read before the god Ashur, whose main temple was in the city of Ashur, and it is quite likely that the text either was even originally written there and copied by the scribes of Ashurbanipal, or simply transferred from Ashur to Nineveh during the building up of the library there. Only Sargon's "Letter to God" was found at the city of Ashur (Meissner 1922:113), whereas all the others were found at Kuyunjik, probably in Ashurbanipal's library. In my opinion, the regular historical texts should not be applied to the problem of spelling in the text and, even if a certain difficulty does remain, it definitely is not so serious as to cancel out the cumulative weight of the other evidence for the dating of the document to the time of Sennacherib.

(e) The portion of the campaign described in the text, and apparently also its continuation (which has not been preserved) are described more briefly in Sennacherib's annals, and — besides Jerusalem — no city in Judah is mentioned there by name (Luckenbill 1924:32–33, lines 18–23; 1927:§340; Oppenheim 1969:288). The "Letter to God" either may have served as the source for the shorter version in the annals, or both of the documents may have been composed quite independently. Several typical expressions are common to the text and to the annals of Sennacherib, thus, possibly alluding to the interdependence of the two. Scholars have already noted that the annals is of an unusual literary quality, which might corroborate the assumption that the literary text served as the example. It is clear that a redacted summary or brief report would emphasize specific facets of the campaign and would omit other facets or describe them only in passing.[10] Thus, we cannot accept the argument that the omission of Azekah from Sennacherib's inscriptions (even if composed shortly after his campaign to Judah) might indicate two different campaigns.

The conclusion arising from this can be summed up as follows: The document is to be dated to the days of Sennacherib and is to be considered a "Letter to God" written close upon the termination of his campaign to Palestine in 701 BCE.[11] We can perhaps also assume that it was composed to magnify and glorify the god Ashur, on the one hand, and on the other hand, to explain the results of the campaign to Judah, which did not end with the capture of Jerusalem, the deposition of the rebellious king and his replacement by an Assyrian loyal vassal.[12]

III

The transfer of the "Azekah inscription" to the days of Sennacherib somewhat changes the balance of evidence on the relationship of Judah with

10. Thus, for instance, from the Bible and from Sennacherib's reliefs (Barnett 1958), it is known that Lachish was conquered during Sennacherib's campaign to Judah. Lachish, however, despite having been the second city of the realm, is not mentioned at all in the annals.

11. The fact that we have only a single "Letter to God" from several Assyrian kings (Shalmaneser IV, Sargon II, Sennacherib, Esarhaddon and Ashurbanipal) does not necessarily point to the custom of a king writing only one such "letter" during his reign. The survival of one example only for each king is most probably coincidental.

12. In an article written 5 years later (Na'aman 1979:63 n. 4), I gave up the "letter to God" hypothesis, suggesting that it is "insufficiently supported by documentary evidence."

Assyria in the days of Sargon. We shall try to review here, briefly, the known factors on those relations (for summary articles on Philistia in the days of Sargon, see Alt 1945:128–146; Tadmor 1958a:79–84; Tadmor 1966:90–95).

In an inscription written around 717 BCE, Sargon is termed "the subduer of the land of Judah which lies far away" (Winckler 1889:188, lines 28–36; Tadmor 1958a:38, n. 146). This appellation undoubtedly refers to the rebellion of 720 BCE, at which time Sargon prevailed over an alliance of states headed by Hamath, in which Gaza and Samaria also took part. Hezekiah may have supported this alliance as well,[13] but the term "which lies far away" and the fact that Judah is not mentioned in any inscription relating the events of 720 BCE show that Judah had, at most, a secondary role in this revolt. It would seem that Hezekiah was quick to surrender before the king of Assyria and to pay the demanded tribute so that his country would not be harmed during the Assyrian campaign along the Philistine coast.

Judah is mentioned a second time in one of Sargon's inscriptions, in connection with the revolt of Ashdod which began in 713 BCE. Below is the passage mentioning Judah in this connection (Winckler 1889:188, lines 28–36; Luckenbill 1927:§195; Oppenheim 1969:287): "To the k[ings] of Philistia, Judah, Ed[om and] Moab, who dwell by the sea, payers of tribute and gifts to Ashur my lord, (they sent) evil words and unseemly speeches,[14] to set (him) at enmity with me. To Pharaoh, king of Egypt, a prince who could not save them, they sent their presents and asked him for (military) aid."

According to the description, the Ashdodites tried to incite the rulers of the neighboring states, who were used to pay tribute and gifts to Ashur, to rebel, just as they tried to seduce the king of Egypt to send troops to their aid. Hezekiah appears in this description among the tax payers to Assyria, not as a rebel. Moreover, according to all the Assyrian sources, the campaign of 711 BCE was directed against Ashdod alone, and there is no indication that any other country except Ashdod was attacked in the course of the 711 BCE campaign. I doubt whether the alliance mentioned above ever crystallized, in light of the Egyptian hesitancy to take an active part in the conspiracy against Assyria (Winckler 1889:188: 28–36; Tadmor 1958a:38, n. 146). It can be assumed that all the rulers mentioned hastened to submit to Assyria immediately upon the appearance of Assyrian troops in Philistia, and the main sufferer in the campaign was Ashdod, whose principal towns were conquered. The kingdom of Ashdod was annexed by Assyria, although for unknown reasons, the local dynasty was left in power (Alt 1945:144–146).

13. I have adopted here the dates of 727–698 BCE for the reign of Hezekiah.

14. According to the photograph, we should read in line 29: *da-bab sa-ar-ra-a-ti at*[!]*-me-e nu-ul*[!]*-la-a-ti.*

The border of the Assyrian Empire, thus, was moved twice in the days of Sargon, once in 720 and again in 711 BCE, and it was tangent upon Judah on the north and on the west. The kingdom of Judah appears not to have suffered in the days of Sargon, and, until his death, it remained subservient to Assyria. But the border with the Assyrian provinces and the proximity of Assyrian rule obviously presented a continual pressure on Judah.

The opportunity to throw off the Assyrian yoke came upon the death of Sargon on the battlefield in 705 BCE, following which, rebellion broke out simultaneously in Babylonia, Anatolia[15] and on the border of Egypt, and even Egypt took an active role in the impending struggle. This about-face in Egyptian policy toward Assyria seems to have occurred with the rise to power of the Twenty-fifth (Nubian) dynasty as the sole rulers of Egypt in about 711/10 BCE.[16] We should attempt to ascertain the reasons behind this change in policy. The key to this problem would seem to lie in the Assyrian policy in Philistia, which lies on the main route from the north to Egypt; thus, whoever ruled Philistia ruled the approaches to Egypt (from Raphia, the southernmost borderpoint of Philistia, to the Pelusian branch of the Nile, the northern border of ancient Egypt, is about 175 kms).

The Assyrian hold in Philistia gradually grew, reaching a peak with the

---

15. Sargon seems to have been killed during his campaign against Tabal (see Tadmor 1958a:97–98, nn. 311–313), and, upon his death, many of the Assyrian provinces in Anatolia rebelled. The extent of the rebellion is indicated by the fact that even such a central province as Que was among the rebels (Luckenbill 1927:§§286–289), and Landsberger went so far as to ascribe the destruction of the palace at Sam'al on the Syrian Anatolian border to this war (Landsberger 1948:79–83). Only in 696 BCE, some 10 years after the outbreak, did Sennacherib conduct his first campaign into Anatolia in an attempt to regain control over the Assyrian territories there. He succeeded in Que, but failed in Tilgarimmu (Forrer 1920: 81–82; Luckenbill 1927:§§286–292). All the western Anatolian provinces (Tabal, Ḫilakku and Tilgarimmu) were lost forever. Only after the quelling of the rebellion in Babylonia in 689 was Sennacherib free to deal with Anatolia without hindrance from behind, and, in these years, he consolidated his hold in the eastern provinces (Melid, Kummuh, Gurgum and Que). For a detailed discussion see Landsberger 1948:81–82, nn. 212–215; Bing 1975:89–121, and the bibliography there.

16. The data indicate that, until 711/10 BCE, the rulers of the local dynasties still ruled in Egypt: (a) Hoshea the son of Elah wrote to Tephnakht ruler of the city of So/Sais after 727 BCE (see Goedicke 1963); (b) Osorkon IV, last of the rulers of the Twenty-third dynasty at Tanis, still ruled in 716 BCE (see Albright 1956:23–26); (c) In 711 BCE, Yamani, the ruler of Ashdod, fled to Egypt after failing in his rebellion. The rulers of the Delta refused him aid, and he even wandered to Nubia in search of support; the ruler of Nubia, however, in his desire to preserve peaceful relations with Assyria, turned the rebellious vassal over to the Assyrians (Tadmor 1958a:83). Shortly afterward, in about 711/10 BCE, the Nubian dynasty gained control over all Egypt and subjugated the local princes (Albright 1953:4–8; Horn 1966:1–5).

annexation of Ashdod by Sargon, which was undoubtedly interpreted in Egypt as a threat to Egyptian territory. To this we may add the Egyptian attitude regarding Philistia as within her sphere of influence from earliest times. Fear of Philistia becoming a springboard for an attack on Egypt, and the ambition of again seizing a bridgehead in Asia led to the crystallization of this new Egyptian policy, expressed in the open support given by Egypt to the rebellious movement against Assyria.

The rebellion throughout the Assyrian Empire and the definite Egyptian support are, in turn, the factors behind Hezekiah's revolt, and he now stood at the head of an alliance supported by Egypt.

This discussion leads us to conclude that only at the end of his reign did Hezekiah openly oppose Assyria, he previously having purposely avoided any direct conflict. At this point, Hezekiah abandoned the traditional Judean policy, which pursued a more cautious course in its dealings with Assyria (see the discussion in the final section of this paper).

IV

It remains to ascertain where the new document fits into the scheme of Sennacherib's campaign, because the campaign itself has been dealt with extensively in a long list of papers and books dealing specifically with it (Childs 1967 and bibliography there). Analysis of the annals reveals that Sennacherib's campaign to Palestine was conducted as follows: at first the king conquered the Ashkelonite enclave at Joppa, which had been surrounded by Assyrian territory;[17] from there he proceeded to Ekron, meeting an Egyptian force at Eltekeh on the way; at Ekron he took the city after a short siege, and, at about the same time, Ashkelon surrendered to him. Thus, the conquest of Philistia resulted in the surrender of the rebellious cities and the placing of rulers loyal to Assyria on the local thrones — without the more important cities having been harmed in any actual manner.

After the fall of Philistia, Sennacherib turned toward Judah, and it is at this point in the campaign that we can place the text. We do not know who the ruler or rulers paying tribute to Assyria at the beginning of the text were (line 3), although it may be the kings of Philistia, in whose land Sennacherib had encamped on his way to Judah.[18]

---

17. We should note the detailed description devoted to this region, and it is possible that Sennacherib conquered the Jaffa enclave, which was entirely surrounded by Assyrian provincial territory, by force, intending to annex it to one of the adjacent administrative units.

18. I do not think this refers to the tribute of "all the kings of the land of Amurru" mentioned in the annals (Luckenbill 1924:30, lines 50–60), because this tribute was paid when

In the document there is a quite detailed description of the conquest of two cities belonging to Hezekiah. The first to be mentioned is Azekah (modem Tell Zakariyeh) (Abel 1938:85) at the entrance to the Elah Valley on the route connecting Lachish and Beth-shemesh. The second city is denoted "a royal [city] of the Philistines," which Hezekiah had taken and fortified for his own purposes. The detailed description of the city is indicative of its importance (see the notes to lines 12–16). Among the eastern towns of Philistia, only two would suit the present case: Ekron and Gath of the Philistines. Gath (identified with Tell eṣ-Ṣafi)[19] is located not far from Azekah, lying on a high hill (which would suit my restoration in line 12) and, thus, would have required a water installation (line 15); Gath might have been a large and fortified city in this period.[20] On the other hand, Gath was conquered by Sargon II in his 711 BCE campaign and was possibly destroyed at that time. Moreover, according to Sargon's inscriptions, it was a secondary city within the territory of Ashdod, not "a royal city of the Philistines," as related in line 11.

Originally I identified the city whose name is broken as Gath of the Philistines. Mittmann (1990:98–99), however, suggested identifying it with Ekron, a Philistine city-state located near the western border of Judah.[21] Ekron is mentioned in Sennacherib's annals as a city that joined Hezekiah's rebellion and was conquered during the campaign. In its political-strategic position, it fits well the inscription's unnamed "royal city of the Philistines."

Sennacherib was still near Tyre, and it is difficult to conceive that such a detailed document as ours should skip over the entire first part of the campaign.

19. For the identification, see the discussion and bibliography in Rainey 1966a; 1966b.

20. Tell eṣ-Ṣafi was excavated early in modern archaeological research (Bliss and Macalister 1902), and, thus, its stratigraphy and the dates of the city walls (ascribed by the excavators to Rehoboam) remain vague. The pottery evidence points to a considerable settlement there in the Iron age (for a recent summary, see Stern 1970, with bibliography there). Among the finds (not *in situ*) were five fragments of a small Assyrian limestone relief (Bliss and Macalister 1902:41, fig. 17; Albright 1923:15–16), indicating that there might have been an Assyrian palace there, which was built after the destruction of the city during Sennacherib's campaign of 701 BCE. We may also mention several *lmlk* seal-impressions of the four-winged type (only) found at this same site (Bliss and Macalister 1902:107). If it is proper to ascribe these sealings to the reign of Hezekiah (see Aharoni 1967:340–346), then this might indicate that Gath had been taken into the administrative framework of Judah in that period.

21. Mittmann's arguments in favour of the identification of the Philistine city with Ekron are as follows: (a) the city is called "a royal city of the Philistines," whereas Gath was a secondary city within the territory of Ashdod; (b) the participation of Ekron in the rebellion is explicitly mentioned in Sennacherib's annals; (c) the Assyrian royal inscriptions give selective information, and we must be careful not to draw conclusions from what is not explicitly said. It is possible that following the siege, Ekron surrendered and opened its gates, thus, avoiding a total destruction.

There are, however, certain difficulties in Mittmann's suggestion: (a) Ekron's location on a flat land does not correspond to the topographical features of the city under siege, as described in the inscription; (b) Sennacherib's annals do not explicitly mention the siege and conquest by force of Ekron, which might have surrendered and opened its gates. The assumption of a surrender does not fit well the detailed description of a siege and conquest in the text; and (c) no evidence of a destruction in the late 8th century BCE was detected in the course of the site's excavations. Although Mittmann's suggestion is not free from doubt, I tend to accept it and attribute the incongruities to the boasting style and tendentiousness of the Assyrian royal inscriptions (see Na'aman 1994:245–246).

The identification of the two conquered cities also serves to clarify the Assyrian plan of attack on Judah: penetration through the central and northern Shephelah and conquest of two key cities, thus, opening two main routes that lead into the heart of the land, between the two principal centers of Jerusalem and Lachish.

An additional interesting detail concerning the "warriors of Amurru" (line 18), who took part in the siege operations alongside the Assyrians, is also revealed: These troops are probably to be identified with the payers of tribute to Sennacherib at the beginning of his campaign, as mentioned in the annals (Luckenbill 1924:30, lines 50–56), and who apparently had been forced to send auxiliary units to accompany the Assyrian army.[22]

Both the descriptions in the royal annals and the "Letter to God" indicate the strength of Judah under Hezekiah and the great degree of resistance encountered by Sennacherib during his campaign there. At this time, Judah was undoubtedly the strongest nation on the Assyrian-Egyptian frontier. It is against this background that we are able to understand also the steps taken by Sennacherib during and after this campaign: He avoided destroying the rebellious cities of Philistia and was content to receive their surrender and place loyal rulers in power; in contrast, he fought tooth-and-nail in Judah. Sennacherib even took away western border regions of Judah, transferring them to four Philistine cities, creating a new balance of power between Philistia and Judah. His purpose is revealed as an attempt to create a series of states of equal strength on the Assyrian Egyptian border, headed by rulers loyal to Assyria and, thus, to prevent the possibility of any one of them gaining sufficient power to lead the others against Assyria with Egyptian support.

22. In Ashurbanipal's campaign to Egypt, vassal kings from Syria and Palestine also participated (Luckenbill 1927:§§770, 876). The participation of vassal kings in Assyrian campaigns is also indicated in the stele inscription of Bar Rakib king of Sam'al, dedicated to Panammuwa his father (Donner and Röllig 1967:No. 214).

This step may have been interpreted in Egypt as an Assyrian retreat from the region, and, therefore, a lessening of the threat of an Assyrian invasion into Egypt proper. (Or, could there have been some agreement on the matter between the two rivals?) In any event; we hear little more of the conflict between Assyria and Egypt until the days of Esarhaddon, and the long years of quiet on this border for the remainder of Sennacherib's reign are witness to the success of this policy.

V

Ascribing tablet K 6205 to Hezekiah rather than to Azariah/Uzziah considerably changes the balance of evidence concerning the "Azriyau episode": Instead of two texts describing the events of the war in 738 BCE, we are left with only one. This latter text of the annals of Tiglath-pileser III was published in cuneiform by G. Smith (1870:pl. 9, 3) and was included in the annals of this ruler published by P. Rost (1893:20–24, lines 123–141; Tadmor 1961, with earlier literature). Perusal of this text shows that it describes only the final phase of the events of 738 BCE. It gives details of the territorial arrangements made by the king of Assyria in northern Syria, following his victory (annexation of Hatarikka, the biblical Hadrach, and the northern Mediterranean coast, Rost 1893:20–23, lines 125–132) and the resulting exile of the population (Rost (1893:22–23, lines 132–133). Thus, we have no source either relating the background of the Assyrian campaign to Syria in 738 BCE, or on the actual war conducted in that same year between Assyria and the Syrian alliance, but only the end of the events.

The name Azriyau appears in the fragment twice: in line 123, in the spelling *Az-ri-a-*[*ú*], and in line 131, in the variant spelling *Az-ri-ia-a-ú*. Nowhere in the text, however, does the name of the land of Azriyau appear. Thus, the question of the identity of this person cannot be solved directly, and the answer must be sought elsewhere. Hence, we should review briefly the background of the wars in Syria in 738 BCE in the light of the known facts.

In 740 BCE, Tiglath-pileser III conquered the kingdom of Arpad and annexed it to Assyria (Rost 1893:14–17, lines 82–89). In doing so, Tiglath-pileser III diverged from the policy upheld since the days of Shalmaneser III, according to which the border of Assyria remained along the Euphrates (on both banks), with the Syrian states holding the status of vassals. Upon the annexation of Arpad, Tiglath-pileser moved the border of his kingdom toward the Mediterranean seaboard and included parts of North Syria within the framework of Assyrian territory.

In 739 BCE, Tiglath-pileser III turned northward and conducted a campaign to Ulluba, southwest of Urartu. During this campaign, a rebellion broke out in Syria, in reaction to which there was an Assyrian campaign to Syria, in 738 BCE. According to the description of this episode in the annals, as far as the passages are preserved, Unqi, Hatarikka and the northern coastal cities took part in this rebellion, but it seems possible to identify further elements that joined in the rebellion.

In the Eponym Chronicle for 738 BCE, there appears the entry "Kullania was conquered" (Ungnad 1938:431, CB1 line 36). In my opinion, Kullania (biblical Calneh) is identical to the city of Kinalua/Kunulua, the capital of the land of Unqi, mentioned several times in the annals of the Assyrian kings.[23]

---

23. For the various citings and spellings of Kinalua/Kunulua (i.e., Kinalia, Kulnia and Kullania), see Parpola 1970:206, 213. Forrer suggested regarding these two names as one city, the capital of Unqi; this has been rejected by Gelb (1934/35), who distinguishes between the two names and regards them as two different places. Kullania is identified by Gelb as Kullan-köy, a site north of Arpad, and this has been accepted by most scholars dealing with this period (an exception is Astour 1963:225). The reasons behind the identifications of the two above places have not been noted previously and, thus, are presented here:

(a) The spelling Kunalia appears only in the annals of the Assyrian kings from Ashurnaṣirpal II to Tiglath-pileser III. In contrast, the spelling Kullania appears only in economic and administrative documents and in letters. It can be assumed that the former is the formalistic-traditional spelling used by the scribes in the royal inscriptions, whereas the latter spelling reflects the pronunciation of the name during the 8th and 7th centuries BCE (and also suits the biblical form "Calneh"), explaining the appearance of this form in the Assyrian administrative documents (for a phonetic comparison of the spellings, see Astour 1963:225).

(b) It is known that Unqi was annexed to Assyria by Tiglath-pileser III (Rost 1893:16–19, lines 92–101). But Unqi does not appear in any Assyrian document later than its annexation. Thus, we may assume that the new Assyrian province was not called by its old name, but rather by some other name which should be sought by indirect means (see [c], below).

(c) Within the description of the annexation of Unqi in the annals, there appears the formula "the city of Kinalia I reorganized"; this expression in the Assyrian inscriptions serves to denote the founding of a new provincial capital over the ruins of the former capital. But the place-name Kunalia does not appear in any Assyrian document later than its annexation. In my opinion, the name does appear, but in a slightly different spelling Kullania; this denotes the capital of the province and is extended to refer to the entire province, as is so often the case with such names (Kullania appears in the documents with the determinatives KUR and URU, as well). Kullania is, thus, the name of the Assyrian province, identical to the territory of the former kingdom of Unqi, and under this name it appears in the later Assyrian documents.

(d) In the list of Syrian cities to which Tiglath-pileser sent exiles in 738 BCE, the cities of Unqi appear. The Assyrian campaign in that same year is denoted in the Eponym Chronicle as a campaign during which "Kullani was conquered," which would be quite fitting if we identify this land with Unqi (see below, n. 25).

(e) All the citings of Kullania in the Assyrian documents, as far as they can be related to known places suit admirably the region of Unqi: The name appears between Samaria and

The fact that Kullania appears as the most important destination during the campaign indicates that the rebellion against Assyria broke out in the areas it conquered in 740 BCE. Further indirect evidence for the fact that Kullania was the central aim of the Assyrian campaign of 738 BCE is found in the Bible, in Amos 6:2. There, the city of Calneh is mentioned together with "Hamath the great" as an example and warning to Israel not to rely upon her strength against Assyria. In my opinion, Amos was alluding to Tiglath-pileser's campaign to Syria in 738 BCE, during which the Assyrians conquered Kullania and Hatarikka (the northern part of the land of Hamath). It would seem that the conquest of these two cities echoed throughout the Syro-Palestinian region in this period, and, thus, the prophet chose it as an example that would be familiar to all his audience.[24]

The rebellion of the cities of Unqi can also be deduced from the fact that following the Assyrian campaign of 738 BCE exiles were brought to them on a large scale (Rost 1893:24–25, lines 143–145), whereas Unqi had been annexed to Assyria two years earlier. It would seem that this late exile was the direct result of the rebellion of the cities of Unqi in 739 BCE, following which, Tiglath-pileser decided to break up the internal structure and the identity of this land by settling foreign populations in its cities and, thus, forestalling the possibility of further disturbances.[25] From the data we have gathered here, it is apparent that in the war conducted in north Syria in 738 BCE, the kingdoms of Unqi and Hatarikka took a part, as did the northern coastal cities. In contrast, there is no evidence that even one of the southern Syrian or Palestinian states participated. We must agree with H. Tadmor that the list of payers of

Arpad (ADD 951), and after Ṣimirra (ibid.), between Megiddo and Sam'al (ADD 952), alongside Arpad (ABL 43) and in a list of cities sending horses to Assyria, after Qarnē and Dana but before Arpad (ABL 372; are these places listed here in a geographical order, from south to north?).

Thus, we may assume that Kullania was the capital of Unqi, conquered by Tiglath-pileser III and rebuilt as the Assyrian provincial capital, giving its name to the entire Assyrian province.

24. The prophet Amos generally is placed in the days of Jeroboam II (784–748 BCE), though scholars are divided as to the exact position within this reign. In any event, 738 BCE is later than Jeroboam and, thus, presents a problem as far as Amos' period of activity is concerned. It is beyond the present scope to determine whether this late date points to the intrusive character of Amos 6:2 (or the passage 6:1–7), as some scholars have held, or whether the final date of Amos' prophetic activity is to be reconsidered. See recently Rudolph 1971:95–96, 219, and bibliography there.

25. The exiles to the cities of Unqi were part of the exiles by Tiglath-pileser to Syria in 738 BCE. The region to which the foreign population was sent (Rost 1893:24–27, lines 143–150) corresponds with the territory of the allies who fought against Tiglath-pileser that same year, according to the reconstruction presented here.

tribute to Assyria, appearing in the annals following the exiles to Syria, includes a list of states that did not participate in the alliance and who preferred to pay tribute (Tadmor 1961:266–267, 55; Rost 1893:72, line 11). This list includes such kingdoms as Hamath, Damascus, Byblos and Israel — all southern neighbors of the bloc of states that did rebel against Assyria in 738 BCE.

It is against this background that we must review the question of the identity of Azriyau of the text with Azariah/Uzziah king of Judah. There is nothing to support such an identification, except for the essential identity of names; against this, however, there are several weighty factors which shed considerable doubt on this identity.

(a) The entire episode takes place in northern Syria, and there is no evidence that southern kings took any part in the events. Even such kingdoms as Hamath and Damascus, much closer to the arena of the war, did not join the alliance.

(b) Judah is mentioned only once in the inscriptions of Tiglath-pileser, in a routine list of vassal states paying tribute to Assyria around 732 BCE (Rost 1893:72, line 11). Indeed, Judah does not even appear in the list of payers of tribute in 738 BCE. Had Judah stood at the head of a rebellion against Assyria in this year, she surely would have been severely punished; certainly Judah would not have avoided payment of a tribute demanded even of states which did not participate in the alliance at all. The fact that the king of Assyria mentions Judah only in a routine list from late in his reign and never mentions or even hints that it was his great rival during the years of struggle over rule in Syria, in my opinion, clearly indicates that Assyria had no score to settle with Judah.

(c) Judah is mentioned early in Sargon's reign as a land "which lies far away" (see above), and this is a further indication that it did not take any central role in the struggle against Assyria up to that time.

The cumulative effect of these factors brings us to the conclusion that the Azriyau of the annals of Tiglath-pileser III and Azariah of the Bible — the king of Judah — should be regarded as two separate individuals, and that the identity of names is incidental, a pitfall for the modern historian. The identity of the northern Azriyau remains without solution and will do so till new, relevant documents are found. Was he an Aramean of Hatarikka, like Yaubi'di, the usurper of Hamath, who stood at the head of the rebellion against Assyria in 720 BCE?[26]

26. The name Yaubi'di in northern Syria indicates that the element *Yau-* was found in this region in personal names and in a period quite close to that of Azriyau. On the other hand, the identification of Azriyau as a Syrian ruler strengthens the assumption, upheld since the early days of Assyriology, that there is a connection between the element *Yau* ap-

This separation of Azriyau from Azariah frees us from a stumbling block to the understanding of the Judahite policy toward Assyria in the second half of the eighth century BCE: Ahaz kept to a steady line throughout his reign, including the years in which he was regent under his father Azariah/Uzziah; he accepted the yoke of Assyria and was most cautious in his dealings with her. This policy was also supported unflinchingly by Isaiah the prophet.

As we have attempted to demonstrate above, Hezekiah continued the same line during most of his reign and only in his final years did he change his policy and openly stand at the head of an alliance against Assyria.

References

Abel, F.M. 1938. *Géographie de la Palestine* II. Paris.

ABL = Harper, R.F. 1892–1914. *Assyrian and Babylonian Letters Belonging to the Kouyunjik Collection of the British Museum* I–XIV. London and Chicago.

ADD = Johns, C.H.W. 1898–1923. *Assyrian Deeds and Documents Recording the Transfer of Property, Including the So-Called Private Contracts, Legal Decisions and Proclamations, Preserved in the Kouyunjik Collections of the British Museum, Chiefly of the 7th Century B.C.* I–IV. Cambridge.

Aharoni, Y. 1967. *The Land of The Bible: A Historical Geography.* Philadelphia.

Albright, W.F. 1923. Contribution to the Historical Geography of Palestine. *AASOR* 2–3: 1–46.

Albright, W.F. 1953. New Light from Egypt on the Chronology and the History of Israel and Judah. *BASOR* 130:4–11.

Albright, W.F. 1956. Further Light on Synchronisms between Egypt and Asia in the Period 935–685 B.C. *BASOR* 141: 23–27.

Alt, A. 1945. Neue assyrische Nachrichten über Palästina und Syrien. *ZDPV* 67: 128–159 (Reprint: Alt 1953: 226–241).

Alt, A. 1953. *Kleine Schriften zur Geschichte des Volkes* Israel II. München.

Astour, M.C. 1963. Place-Names from the Kingdom of Alalaḫ in the North Syrian List of Thutmose III: A Study in Historical-Geography. *JNES* 22: 220–241.

Barnett, R.D. 1958. The Siege of Lachish. *IEJ* 8: 161–164.

Bing, J.D. 1969. *A History of Cilicia during the Assyrian Period.* (Ph.D. Thesis). Ann Arbor.

Bliss, F.J. and Macalister, R.A.S. 1902. *Excavations in Palestine 1898-1900.* London.

Borger, R. 1963. *Babylonisch-assyrische Lesestücke.* Rome.

Borger, R. 1967. *Handbuch der Keilschriftliteratur* I. Berlin.

Borger, R. 1979. *Babylonisch-assyrische Lesestücke* (2nd ed.). Rome.

Childs, B.S. 1967. *Isaiah and the Assyrian Crisis.* (Studies in Biblical Theology, Second Series 3). London.

Donner, H. and Röllig, W. 1968. *Kanaanäische und Aramäische Inschriften* 1–3. 2nd revised edition. Wiesbaden.

Forrer, E. 1920. *Die Provinzeinteilung des assyrichen Reiches.* Leipzig.

Frahm, E. 1997. *Einleitung in die Sanherib-Inschriften* (AfO Beiheft 26). Horn.

pearing in Syria and the theophoric element *Yahu* commonly found in Judah. See Olmstead 1908:48, n. 12, and bibliography there.

Gadd, C.J. 1954. Inscribed Prisms of Sargon II from Nimrud. *Iraq* 16: 173–201.
Gelb, I.J. 1934/35. Critical Note: Calneh. *AJSL* 51:189–191.
Goedicke, H. 1963. The End of "So, King of Egypt." *BASOR* 171: 64–66.
Horn, S.H. 1966. Did Sennacherib Campaign Once or Twice against Hezekiah? *Andrew University Seminary Studies* 4: 1–28.
Landsberger, B. 1948. *Sam'al. Studien zur Entdeckung der Ruinenstaede Karatepe.* Ankara.
Lie, A.G. 1929. *The Inscriptions of Sargon II, King of Assyria*. Part I: *The Annals.* Paris.
Luckenbill, D.D. 1924. *The Annals of* Sennacherib. (Oriental Institute Publications 2). Chicago.
Luckenbill, D.D. 1927 *Ancient Records of Assyria and Babylonia* II. Chicago.
Meissner, B. 1922. Die Eroberung der Stadt Ulḫu auf Sargons 8. Feldzug. *ZA* 34:113–122.
Mittmann, S. 1990. Hiskia und die Philister. *Journal of Northwest Semitic Languages* 16: 91–106.
Na'aman, N. 1979. Sennacherib's Campaign to Judah and the Date of the *LMLK* Stamps. *VT* 29: 61–86.
Na'aman, N. 1994. Hezekiah and the Kings of Assyria. *Tel Aviv* 21: 235–254.
Olmstead, A.T.E. 1908. *Western Asia in the Days of Sargon of Assyria, 722-705 B.C.: A Study in Oriental History.* New York.
Oppenheim, A.L. 1960. The City of Assur in 714 B.C. *JNES* 19:133–147.
Oppenheim, A.L. 1969. Babylonian and Assyrian Historical Texts. In *ANET*: 265–317.
Parpola, S. 1970. *Neo-Assyrian Toponyms* (AOAT 6). Kevelaer and Neukirchen-Vluyn.
Pritchard, J.B. 1961. *The Water System of Gibeon*. Philadelphia.
Rainey, A.F. 1966a. Gath of the Philistines. *Christian News from Israel* 17/2–3: 30–38.
Rainey, A.F. 1966b. Gath of the Philistines. *Christian News from Israel* 17/4: 23–34.
Rost, P. 1893. *Die Keilschrifttexte Tiglath-Pilesers III., nach den Papierabklatschen und Originalen des Britischen Museums* I–II. Leipzig.
Smith, G. 1870. *The Cuneiform Inscriptions of Western Asia* III. London.
Stern, E. 1970. Tell Ṣafit. *Enc. Arch. Exc. 2: 608–610.* (Hebrew).
Rudolph, W. 1971. *Joel — Amos — Obadja — Jona* (Kommentar zum Alten Testament XIII/2). Gütersloh.
Tadmor, H. 1958a. The Campaigns of Sargon II of Assur: A Chronological-Historical Study. *JCS* 12: 22–40, 77–100.
Tadmor, H. 1958b. The "Sin of Sargon." *Eretz Israel* 5: 150–162. (Hebrew).
Tadmor, H. 1961. Azriyau of Yaudi. *Scripta Hierosolymitaua* 8: 232–271.
Tadmor, H. 1966. Philistia under Assyrian Rule. *BA* 29: 86–102.
Thureau-Dangin, F. 1912. *Une relation de la huitième campagne de Sargon.* Paris.
Ungnad, A. 1938. Eponymen. *RLA* II: 412–457.
Vincent, L.H. 1911. *Jerusalem sous Terre.* London.
Winckler, H. 1889. *Die Keilschrifttexte Sargons nach den Papierabklatschen und Originalen neu herausgegeben* I–II. Leipzig.
Winckler, H. 1899. *Altorientalische Forschungen* II. Leipzig.
Yadin, Y. 1972. *Hazor The Head of all those Kingdoms, Joshua 11:10* (The Schweich Lectures of the British Academy 1970). London.

Hezekiah's Fortified Cities and the *LMLK* Stamps[1]

The List of Rehoboam's Fortified Cities (2 Chr. 11:5–10): Historical and Archaeological Analysis

In his description of the reign of Rehoboam, the Chronicler has presented a list of 15 cities built to defend the kingdom of Judah. It has long been recognized that the list of cities was originally an independent document, although the precise nature of this document is debated among scholars (e.g., Junge 1937:74–75; Rudolph 1955:227–30; Welten 1973:11–15; Fritz 1981:46*). The 15 towns together formed a well-planned defensive system that covered the area of the Shephelah and the hill country of Judah. They were arranged in groups in a general geographical order, the connection between the groups being mainly associative. An arrangement based on a flexible order according to region is typical of many geographical lists from all over the ancient Near East, and one should avoid looking for a rigid order according to administrative district in this kind of document.[2]

The list is composed of the following groups of towns:

(a) Bethlehem, Etam, Tekoa, and Beth-zur in the central Judean hill country;

(b) Socoh, Adullam, Gath, and Mareshah in the central Shephelah of Judah;

(c) Ziph and Adoraim in the southern Judean hill country;

(d) Lachish and Azekah also in the central Shephelah;

(e) Zorah and Aijalon in the northern Shephelah; and

(f) Hebron, in the hill country between groups (a) and (b).

---

1. Reprinted with permission. *Bulletin of the American Schools of Oriental Research* 261 (1986), 5–21.

2. Kallai's analysis of the list of 2 Chr. 11:6–10 (1971:247–51) is based on the presupposition that the groups of towns were arranged in a territorial administrative order. To prove his hypothesis, he was obliged both to assume alterations in the scope of the districts as compared with the province list of Josh 15:21–62 and to dissociate the Gath in the list (2 Chr. 11:8) from the Gath of the Philistines. However, Kallai's assumption of the nature of this document is hardly justified by the actual grouping of the 15 cities; their enumeration in the list was based on a loose associative geographical order, rather than on a rigid territorial administrative principle.

It is possible that the fortified cities were originally grouped by pairs of towns:

Bethlehem-Etam, Tekoa-Beth-zur, Socoh-Adullam, Gath-Mareshah, Ziph-Adoraim, Lachish-Azekah, Zorah-Aijalon, and Hebron

All 15 towns can reasonably be identified with Judean sites. The only city in this list whose location is in dispute is Gath. Aharoni (1967: 292), followed by Kallai (1971:248–49), proposed identifying Gath with Moresheth-gath, because Philistine Gath (Tell eṣ-Ṣāfi) is located west of the defensive line formed by the other cities. However, identifying the location of the cities must precede the determination of the layout of the towns. Moresheth-gath is unlikely to be Gath of the list, because the place name was shortened to Moresheth by omitting the second element, rather than by dropping the first. This is indicated in an Amarna letter (EA 335:17; see Kallai 1971:249) and in the Bible (Jer 26:18; Mic 1:1). Also the name Gath was the common abbreviated form of the well known city of the Philistines, which appeared many times in the Bible (e.g., Josh 11:22; 1 Sam 5:8; 7:14; 17:4, 52; 27:2–4; 2 Sam 15:18; 21:20–22; 2 Kgs 12:17; Mic 1:10; 2 Chr 26:6).[3] The inclusion of Philistine Gath in a list of Judean fortified towns is one of the main clues to the correct dating and understanding of the list (below).

The Chronicler assigned the list of towns to Rehoboam, and scholars have generally accepted this date (Beyer 1931; Rudolph 1955:227–30; Gichon 1964; Aharoni 1967:290–93; Welten 1969:167–71; Kallai 1971). Junge (1937:75–80) was the first scholar to date the list to the reign of Josiah. He was followed by Alt (1953) and Fritz (1981), although they argued the point differently. Before starting a discussion of the chronology, it should be emphasized that the cities mentioned in the list were inhabited by civilian populations, although they functioned as administrative military centers in which garrisons were stationed and food and armor stored. They certainly were not fortresses and were not necessarily located on the borders of the kingdom. The exterior lines of the defense system should not be regarded as the boundaries of the kingdom.[4] The date and the historical background of the list can only be determined through historical-geographical, archaeological, and literary considerations.

The archaeological excavations at the sites of the fortified cities provide important evidence for dating the list. The problem was recently discussed

3.The identification of the city of Gath (2 Chr. 11:8) with the Gath of the Philistines was generally accepted by German scholars (including Beyer, Elliger, Junge, Welten, Fritz), although they differ with regard to its location.

4. This was rightly demonstrated by Kallai (1971:247–48).

by Fritz (1981:47*–48*), but further discussion of the two key sites of Lachish and Beth-zur is in order.

The history of the fortifications of Lachish has been clarified by the current excavations at the site. Level V, the first Iron Age settlement on the site after the two centuries of desolation that followed the destruction of the Canaanite city of Level VI, was probably reestablished in the 10th century. The city was without walls, and only a small fortified palatial building ("Palace A") was built, probably at a later stage of Level V (Ussishkin 1978: 27–31, 93). It was only in Level IV, during the 9th century BCE, that massive fortifications were constructed (Ussishkin 1978:55–64). This made Lachish a massively fortified city, which endured throughout the 9th and 8th centuries (Levels IV–III); it was destroyed by Sennacherib in 701 BCE. After a period of desolation, the city was rebuilt and fortified in the 7th century BCE (Level II). It was sacked and destroyed by the Babylonians during the conquest of Judah in 587 BCE.

Beth-zur was settled for a short time in the 11th century BCE and was subsequently abandoned. No major settlement of the 10th or 9th centuries was discovered on the site. According to the site report (Sellers et al. 1968:8), Beth-zur was built on a large scale only in the middle of the 7th century, probably (but not definitely) without fortifications. It, too, was destroyed by the Babylonians in the campaign of 587 BCE.

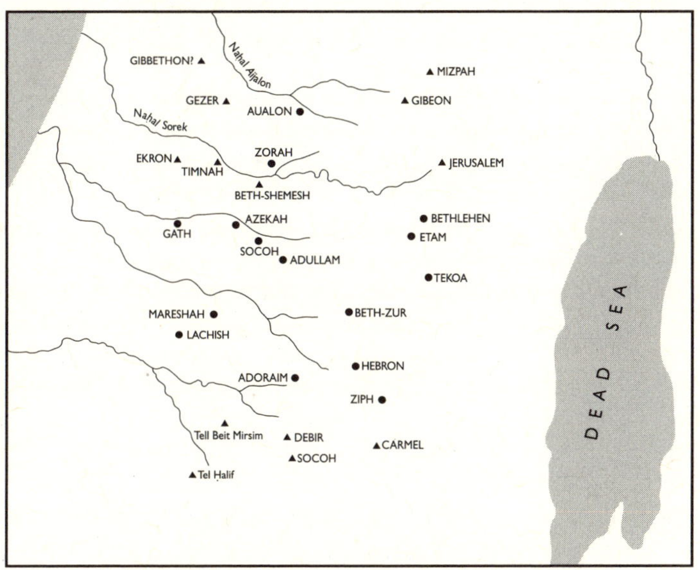

The List of Fortified Cities and Neighboring Sites

The main problem is whether Beth-zur was in fact reestablished only in the mid-7th century. The new excavations at Lachish have definitely demonstrated that Level III of the city was destroyed by Sennacherib in 701 BCE and that the *lmlk* jars discovered therein should be dated to the late 8th century (Ussishkin 1977:54–57). Aharoni (1973:5–6; Aharoni and Aharoni 1976) has further demonstrated that Tell Belt Mirsim Stratum A_2 was destroyed at the same time. The excavators of Beth-zur, however, have erroneously dated the destruction of both Lachish Level III and Tell Beit Mirsim Stratum A_2 — as well as the entire corpus of *lmlk* jars — to the second half of the 7th century. Examination of the typological analysis of the pottery from Beth-zur (as it appears in the site report; Lapp, in Sellers et al. 1968:54–69), reveals that certain pottery types have been compared with vessels found in strata destroyed by Sennacherib in 701 BCE. Furthermore, 11 *lmlk* seal impressions were uncovered at the site (Welten 1969:90–91). Thus, there is enough evidence to date the reestablishment of the settlement in Beth-zur to the second half of the 8th century BCE. The site probably survived the Assyrian campaign of 701 and endured throughout the 7th century, until the campaign of Nebuchadnezzar in 587 BCE.

In light of the archaeological discussion, it seems clear that Beth-zur was desolate in the time of Rehoboam and that the city of Lachish was not fortified until after Rehoboam. It is, thus, clear that the Chronicler was wrong in assigning the list of fortified towns to the days of Rehoboam.

The appearance of the cities of Aijalon and Gath in the list poses similar chronological difficulties.

Aijalon belonged both to the inheritance of Dan, according to the territorial division of the Israelite tribes (Josh. 19:42), and to the second district in the Solomonic administrative system (1 Kgs. 4:9). Both "systems" reflect the historical situation of the United Monarchy of Israel (Kallai 1977). Following the establishment of the Northern Israelite kingdom, parts of the second Solomonic district, including the central city of Gezer, fell into North Israelite hands. Gezer was an Ephraimite city (Josh 16:3; 10; 21: 21; Judg 1:29; I Chr 6:67; 7:28), which was conquered by Tiglath-pileser III and became an Assyrian administrative center on the southwestern border of the province of Samaria. It is reasonable to assume that Aijalon was included in Jeroboam's kingdom and that the campaign of Shishak (945–924 BCE), conducted along the Aijalon-Beth-boron line, passed within the territory of the northern kingdom. Israelite rule over the Aijalon-Gezer area would further explain the siege of Gibbethon in northern Philistia in the days of Nadab, Jeroboam's son (1 Kgs. 15:27) and Elah son of Baasha (1 Kgs. 16:15- 17). The southwestern border of the northern kingdom ran along Naḥal Aijalon (Wādi el-Kabir) and its tributaries up to the Mediterranean

Sea. The kingdom of Judah dominated the western offshoots of Naḥal Sorek (Wādi eṣ-Ṣarar), including the towns of Beth-shemesh, Zorah, and Eshtaol. The territory of the Philistines extended along Naḥal Sorek up to Timnah (Tel Baṭash) and up to Gibbethon (probably Ras Abū Ḥamid) south of Naḥal Aijalon. It is, thus, clear that Aijalon was located outside the confines of Rehoboam's kingdom.

Gath was a vassal kingdom of Israel in the early days of Solomon (1 Kgs 2:39–40); its subsequent history is not clear. According to 2 Chr 26:6, it was a Philistine city in the days of Uzziah, was conquered by Sargon II and, apparently, was designated as "a royal city of the Philistines" in an Assyrian document from the days of Hezekiah (below). Gath probably remained a Philistine city throughout the period of the First Temple, although it was conquered several times by strong Judean kings. By taking into consideration the campaign of Pharaoh Shishak in the early days of Rehoboam, as well as Shishak's hegemonic standing over Philistia at that time, it is hardly conceivable that Rehoboam was able to annex and fortify this strong Philistine center.

A final point concerning the attribution of this list to the time of Rehoboam refers to the Judean king's ability to carry out such an extensive fortification project. As is well known, the rebuilding and fortification of cities and fortresses in ancient Near Eastern kingdoms usually depended on the levy of corvée workers, because this was the only means by which kingdoms were able to supply the necessary manpower for such works. Corvée labor was introduced into Israel by David (2 Sam. 20:24) and was extensively implemented during the days of Solomon to meet the growing needs of the young Israelite kingdom (Crüsemann 1978). The levy and the corvée were the focus of bitterness and deep unrest among the Israelite tribes during Solomon's reign; the demand to lighten "the grievous service of thy father and his heavy yoke which he put upon us" (1 Kgs. 12:4) was raised immediately after Solomon's death. The request for reform in the burden of the corvée and Rehoboam's arrogant refusal (1 Kgs. 12:14) led to a rebellion, which ended in a schism and the coronation of Jeroboam as king of Northern Israel. Rehoboam's kingdom encompassed the tribal territories of Judah, Simeon, and Benjamin. Whether under such circumstances Rehoboam would have been able to enforce an extensive levy to fortify the 15 towns is doubtful. Scholars have already suggested that, subsequent to Absalom's rebellion, Judah gained a preferential status in the kingdom, including relief from the forced labor requirements (Crüsemann 1978:101-104; Tadmor 1982:247–49). It seems unlikely, under the circumstances of the schism and the immediate necessity to secure his control over his severely reduced territory, that Rehoboam would have been able to increase the levy and the burden and to mobilize his country to carry out such an extensive building project.

If the attribution of the fortification of the 15 towns to Rehoboam is untenable, how can we account for this error on the part of the Chronicler?[5]

To answer this question, one may propose that the Chronicler possessed an undated list of towns from the period of the First Temple. One may further suggest that the original list of towns was introduced by the headlines *'rym lmṣwr* ("cities for siege/fortification") and that the Chronicler deliberately interwove this unique expression into his description. In his effort to combine this authentic document into his historical description and to fit it into his historiographical objectives he dated it — according to the best of his knowledge — to the time of Rehoboam.

An analogous case of erroneous dating of an old document by biblical scribe(s) can be seen in the Book of Kings. As has been demonstrated (Miller 1966, with additional bibliography), some of the original prophetic stories of the miraculous deeds of Elisha omitted the name of the king in whose reign the events occurred. The author of the Book of Kings, endeavoring to place these stories into their historical context, assigned them to the reign of Joram, son of Ahab (2 Kgs 4:1–8:15). Analysis of the historical background of these stories makes it evident that they reflect the events of the Dynasty of Jehu: the influential position of Elisha in the royal court of Israel, which is in marked contrast to the hostility of both Elijah and Elisha to the Dynasty of Omri, was due to his prominent role in the rebellion of Jehu (2 Kgs 9:1–3). The hegemonic position of the Arameans within the Israelite kingdom, which is in stark contrast to the situation under the Dynasty of Omri, is due to the victories of Hazael, king of Aram-Damascus, over Jehu and Jehoahaz and the subjugation of the Israelite kingdom (2 Kgs 10:32-33; 12:17–18; 13: 3–4, 7, 22). One could hardly blame the author of the Book of Kings, writing long after the events, for this erroneous identification (Šanda 1912:86–88). Equally, one should not blame the Chronicler, living in an entirely different society and culture at the time of the Second Temple, for incorrectly assigning this undated list of towns from the time of the First Temple. Only the new data gained from archaeological excavations and historical sources enable us to better judge the date of this document.

The Date of the List of Fortified Towns

In an effort to establish the date of the list in 2 Chr. 11:6–10, one must first deal with the problem of its territorial scope and military disposition.

5. Welten (1973:191–94), analyzing the historical descriptions of Chronicles, concluded that all passages originating from documents of the time of the First Temple — including the list of 2 Chr. 11:6–10 — were correctly placed in context by the Chronicler. Accordingly,

As scholars have observed (e.g., Beyer 1931:127–33; Gichon 1964; Fritz 1981: 48*), the cities were situated in strategic locations, controlling access to the Judean hills from the west and south. Together they formed a line of defense on the western side of the kingdom of Judah. Both the Negev and the southernmost Shephelah remained outside the defensive system, and the southern fortified front ran along the Lachish-Adoraim-Ziph line. Cities in the northern part of the kingdom are entirely missing from the list of fortified towns, and, unlike the southern front, no line of defense is recognizable on the northern front. This unusual defensive arrangement was perceived by all scholars dealing with the list, and various explanations have been offered over the years (Beyer 1931:122–33; Alt 1953; Rudolph 1955:227–30; Gichon 1964; Aharoni 1967:290–93; Welten 1969:161–71; Kallai 1971; Fritz 1981:48*).

The most remarkable feature of the "system" of fortification is the absence of a defensive line on the northern front of the kingdom. Beyer (1931: 127–28) believed that the layout of the towns reflects the actual borders of the kingdom, the reduction of territory being the result of the schism. Aharoni (1967:292) proposed that "there were no forts on the boundary with Israel evidently because of Rehoboam's constant desire to expand in that direction." Both proposals were rightly criticized by Kallai (1971:246–47). Elliger (1934:108–9, 149–50) suggested that the list does not mention all the fortified towns of the kingdom, but only those rebuilt by Rehoboam. Kallai (1971) has elaborated further on this thesis. His discussion is based on two studies: Mazar's presentation (1960) of the Levitical cities as fortified administrative cultic centers during the period of the United Monarchy, and Alt's analysis (1953) of the relationship between the distribution of the Levitical cities and the layout of Rehoboam's fortified towns. Accordingly, Kallai has reconstructed Rehoboam's defensive system and borders by combining Solomon's fortified cities, the Levitical cities located within the borders of Rehoboam's future kingdom, and Rehoboam's fortified towns. He, thus, claimed that the northern front was already fortified in the time of the United Monarchy and that Rehoboam could have relied on these fortifications.

Several problems confront this suggestion. Elsewhere (Na'aman 1982), I have suggested that the list of 13 Aaronite cities (Josh. 21:13–19; 1 Chr. 6: 5460) situated within the confines of the kingdom of Judah and dated to the time of Josiah (rather than to the period of the United Monarchy) is the only

he assumed that the Chronicler handled a source of annalistic nature written during the time of the Judean Monarchy. The conclusion reached above, according to which the list of "Rehoboam's Fortresses" was wrongly placed by the Chronicler, calls for a revision of Welten's hypothesis.

part of the list of Levitical cities that reflects the historical reality. The other "Levitical" cities were selected by the author of the list from the inheritances of the 12 tribes. Thus, the complete "system" of Levitical cities has no historical significance, either in the early period or in the author's own time. Furthermore, the 13 Aaronite towns were the residences of the Levitical families, and there is hardly any evidence for the claim that they served as fortified administrative cultic centers. Finally, the border between the inheritances of Benjamin and Ephraim was a peaceful inner line during the days of Solomon, becoming a border of Judah only as a result of the schism. Kallai's suggestion (1971) that Rehoboam found it unnecessary to strengthen the northern front of his kingdom, because it was already fortified (against whom?) during the reign of Solomon, is not very likely.

Junge (1937:76–78), the first scholar who proposed dating the list of fortified towns to the reign of Josiah (639–609 BCE), based his analysis on Alt's presentation (1929) of Sennacherib's campaign to Judah in 701 BCE, whereby the Assyrian king annexed extensive Judean territories to Philistia, leaving Hezekiah only the "city-state" of Jerusalem. According to Junge, this small territory, mainly north of Jerusalem, was fortified during Manasseh's reign. Josiah was able to regain the lost Judean territories in the hill country and the Shephelah, strengthening his rule therein by rebuilding the 15 towns. However, most of the area covered by the fortified towns actually remained in Judean hands even after the Assyrian campaign of 701 BCE (Na'aman 1979a: 83–86); other areas had probably already come under Judean rule in the days of Manasseh. The unusual layout of the 15 towns and the absence of the northern Judean fortified cities require a different explanation.

It seems to me that the absence of fortified towns located north of Jerusalem in the list of 2 Chr. 11:6–10 is due to the Chronicler's deliberate omission. The omission was motivated by his particular presentation of the relationship between the two neighboring kingdoms, Judah and Israel, whereby an increasing flow of people from the north made pilgrimage to Jerusalem to sacrifice in the temple, and the kings of Judah were able to expand their territory northward.[6] According to the Chronicler's description, Rehoboam did not fight the northern kingdom immediately after the schism (2 Chr. 11:1–4). This peaceful situation enabled the priests and Levites staying in the north to return to Judah and Jerusalem (2 Chr. 11:13–14). Immediately after them came many people "out of all tribes of Israel" to sacrifice in the

6. For the Chronicler's concept of the unity of all Israel and his description of the gradual annexation of Northern Israelite tribes to the kingdom of Judah, see Japhet 1977:249–55.

temple (2 Chr. 11:16–17). Rehoboam's son, Abijah, defeated Jeroboam, annexing numerous Ephraimite towns, including the important cultic center of Bethel (2 Chr. 13:3–19). His son Asa was able to hold these towns (2 Chr. 15:8), and many people of the northern kingdom joined Judah during his reign (2 Chr. 15:9). It was only in the wake of Asa's wrongdoing that he was forced to defend himself against Baasha, king of Israel, and to fortify his northern border (2 Chr. 16:1–9). Nevertheless, his son Jehoshaphat remained in control of the Ephraimite towns conquered by Abijah (2 Chr. 17:2). Only in the days of Jehoshaphat's wicked son Jehoram are the conquered Ephraimite towns no longer mentioned. It is clear that, according to the Chronicler's presentation of the history of the kingdom, the northern border of Judah remained unfortified and open to movement, enabling both an uninterrupted pilgrimage to Jerusalem and military expansion northward. To make his sources conform to this concept, the Chronicler must have cut short his original list of fortified towns, omitting the cities north of Jerusalem. The list of northern towns is no longer available to us, but it is important to take it into account when dealing with the overall layout of the system of fortified cities.

As has been noted, the 15 fortified cities were strategically located to protect the kingdom of Judah from an attack on its western front. Scholars who suggested dating the list to the time of Josiah have assumed that it reflects the experience acquired from Sennacherib's attack on the western front. According to this line of reasoning, the list must be later than Sennacherib's campaign of 701 BCE (Junge 1937:78; Fritz 1981: 50*). However, the strategic disposition of the fortified cities hardly can be explained in the context of Josiah's time. During his reign, Egypt was a major power campaigning northward along the Mediterranean coast. The western and southern borders of the Judean kingdom were equally threatened by the Egyptians and were strongly fortified, as is evident from archaeological excavations. The absence of the Negev and the southernmost Shephelah from the array of fortification of 2 Chr. 11:6–10 would hardly suit this situation. Furthermore, both Aijalon and Gath are missing from the list of towns and districts of Judah (Josh 15: 21–62; 18:21–28a), a list that should be dated to the time of Josiah.[7] The omis-

7. Dating the province list of Judah (Josh 15:21–62; 18:21–28a) to the time of Josiah, king of Judah (639–609 BCE), was first suggested by Alt (1925:100–11). The decisive argument raised by Alt in favor of this date was the inclusion of the district of Bethel (Josh 18: 21–24) within the list of Judean districts. The area of Bethel was annexed to the kingdom of Judah only in the days of Josiah, remaining outside the Judean territory before and after Josiah's time. Thus, the province list should be dated to his time. Alt's date can be supported by additional arguments. Two towns included in the district of Bethel — Avvim (Josh. 18:23) and *kpr h'mny* (Josh. 18:24) — were probably called after the name of group of exiles deported by Sargon II to the province of Samaria (Na'aman 1982:249, n. 36). These settlements of ex-

sion of the two cities from this detailed list of towns is hardly accidental; both were apparently situated outside the confines of Josiah's kingdom.

That Aijalon was not included in Josiah's borders can be inferred further from the analysis of the list of Levitical cities. The 13 cities of the Aaronites (Josh. 21:13–19; 1 Chr. 6:54–60), situated in the inheritances of the three tribes of Judah, Simeon, and Benjamin, form the historical core of the list and reflect the situation at the time of Josiah. That only these towns, out of the list of Levitical cities, were included within the confines of Josiah's kingdom is evident from the perfect accord between the scope of the province list of Judah (Josh. 15:21–62; 18:21–28a) and the distribution of the 13 Aaronite towns. On the other hand, Aijalon, Gezer, and Beth-horon, situated according to the list of Levitical cities in the inheritances of Dan and Ephraim, are also absent from the province list. One may suggest that Egypt, which became an ally of Assyria in the second half of the 7th century BCE, was internationally regarded as a kind of "successor state" to the Assyrian empire, inheriting its evacuated territories in the Syro-Palestinian arena. To preclude the possibility of a military clash with Egypt, Josiah did not annex the abandoned Assyrian territories in the Shephelah, claiming for himself only the southern areas of Mount Ephraim (Josh. 18: 21–24; 2 Kgs. 23:15–18).

One must, therefore, conclude that the presence of Aijalon and Gath in the list of 2 Chr. 11:6–10 and the layout of the 15 fortified towns do not at all fit the situation at the time of Josiah.

A comparison of this array of Judean strongholds with the historical sources shows that it clearly matches only one situation: Hezekiah's preparations for the impending campaign of Sennacherib prior to 701 BCE. Contrary to the disposition of the borders in the days of Josiah, both Gath and Aijalon were included in Hezekiah's kingdom. The city of Gath is mentioned in Micah's lament over the destruction of the region of his birth during Sennacherib's campaign (Mic 1:10) and possibly also in a detailed Assyrian description of that same campaign (Na'aman 1974:26–27, 34–35). Aijalon, alongside Gezer and Timnah (Mazar and Kelm 1980: 94–96), was included in the defensive system organized by Hezekiah at that time (Na'aman 1979a:76). The list of fortified towns should be thoroughly investigated in light of the events of the

iles cannot antedate the annexation of the province of Samaria to Ashur (720 BCE) and the subsequent deportation of exiles (probably 710–709 BCE). Also, several places mentioned in the list were established only during the 7th century BCE. To this group of towns belong En-gedi (Josh. 15:62), 'Aro'er (M.T. *'d'dh* = *'r'rh*, Josh. 15:22) and possibly Kinah (Josh 15:22), which might possibly be identified with Ḥorvat 'Uza (Khirbet Ghazzeh; Lemaire 1972:18–22; Mittmann 1977:234–35; Beit Arieh 1982:262–63). The list of districts and towns, thus, reflects the kingdom of Judah in the time of Josiah.

reign of Hezekiah (714–686 BCE; co-regent since 728/27 BCE), particularly the Assyrian campaign of 701 BCE.

Several towns mentioned in 2 Chr. 11:6–10 are known as Judean fortified cities in the days of Hezekiah. Lachish was, at that time, the central city of the Shephelah, second in importance only to the capital city of Jerusalem. Its conquest by the Assyrians is depicted in great detail in a series of reliefs found in Sennacherib's palace at Nineveh (Ussishkin 1980). Azekah and possibly Gath are described as important Judean strongholds in an Assyrian tablet relating the details of Sennacherib's campaign. The latter city is described as "a royal city of the Philistines which Hezekiah had captured and strengthened for himself" (Na'aman 1974:26–27). The prophet Micah, lamenting the destruction of towns in the Shephelah during the Assyrian campaign of 701 BCE (Mic. 1:8–16), mentions Gath, Lachish, Mareshah, and Adullam (Elliger 1934; Na'aman 1979a:67–68, 84–85). Thus, five of the six fortified towns in the Shephelah are mentioned in sources relating to Sennacherib's campaign and its disastrous results.

The absence of the city of Libnah from the list of 2 Chr. 11:6–10 is problematic. The city was besieged by the Assyrian army after the conquest of Lachish (2 Kgs. 19:8), and one would have expected to find its name in the list of fortified towns.[8] It should be emphasized, however, that the list of 2 Chr. 11:6–10 enumerates the towns that were built and fortified at that particular time, not all the walled cities of Judah (as was correctly noted by Elliger 1934:108–9, 149–50). Libnah probably had been fortified earlier and, thus, had no place in the list.

The List of Fortified Cities and The Distribution of the LMLK Seal Impressions

Another source of great importance for the understanding of both Hezekiah's preparations in anticipation of Sennacherib's attack and the results of the Assyrian campaign of 701 BCE is the *lmlk* seal impressions (Na'aman 1979a:70–86). Dating the list of 2 Chr 11:6–10 to this same period requires a thorough examination of the archaeological relationship between the fortified towns and the royal stamps.

The quantity of the *lmlk* jar handles discovered at each site is dependent upon several factors: the extent of excavations, the importance of the town on the eve of the Assyrian attack and its fate during the campaign (Na'aman 1979a:73–74). Most important, of course, is the scope of the archaeological work (digs and surveys) conducted on the site. The significance of these fac-

8. Junge (1937:77, n. 1) has indeed rejected dating the list to the time of Hezekiah on the grounds that Libnah is not mentioned.

tors will be clarified in Table 1, which shows the number of *lmlk* seal impressions found in each of the 15 towns. The sites are divided into two zones; the extent of the archaeological work in each place is also noted (see already: Welten 1969:168).[9]

TABLE 1. Seal Impressions Found in the 15 Cities

Geographical Zone	*City*	*No. Impressions*	*Excavated?*
Hill Country	Bethlehem	2	no
	Etam	0	no
	Tekoa	0	no
	Beth-zur	11	yes
	Ziph	0	no
	Adoraim	0	no
	Hebron	0	"cursorily"
Shephelah	Socoh	"numerous"	no
	Adullam	0	no
	Gath	6	yes
	Mareshah	17	yes
	Lachish	350	yes
	Azekah	17	yes
	Zorah	0	no
	Aijalon	0	no

Of the 15 towns of 2 Chr. 11:6–10 only Beth-zur, Gath, Mareshah, Lachish, and Azekah have been extensively excavated; all produced royal seal impressions. The results of the excavations at Hebron have never been published.[10] All of the other sites were only superficially investigated. The limited nature of the surveys makes the absence of *lmlk* jar handles from these sites understandable.

Also noteworthy is the fact that the three Judean towns whose names appear on the *lmlk* seal impressions — Hebron, Ziph and Socoh — are included

9. The analysis of the *lmlk* jars is mainly based on the corpus of *lmlk* seal impressions assembled by Welten (1969: 57–93 and the table following p. 188) augmented by a number of seal impressions published later (Na'aman 1979a:75, n. 37; Ussishkin 1978:76–81). The large group of royal seal impressions discovered by various scholars in the course of their excavations in Jerusalem are not yet published and, therefore, are not included in my discussion.

10. Not even a preliminary report was ever published of the results of Hammond's archaeological excavations at Hebron. The only sources of information are his short notes published in *Revue Biblique* (Hammond 1965, 1966, 1968).

in the list of the fortified towns. The fourth town whose name appears on *lmlk* seal impressions, *Mmšt,* was probably located north of Jerusalem, as is evident from the distribution of the jar handles bearing its name (Welten 1969:147–56; Lemaire 1975a). Like all other northern sites, it is absent from the list of 2 Chr 11:6–10.

The town of Socoh of the *lmlk* seal impressions usually is located in the Shephelah (Khirbet ʿAbbâd). In a recent article, Rainey (1982:59) suggested identifying the town with Khirbet Shuweikeh in the southern Judean hill country. The evidence supporting this new location, however, is hardly convincing. Rainey's claim that the identification of Socoh in the hill country "would account for the large number of Socoh impressions in the south" is at variance with the facts. Only 11 *lmlk* seal impressions were discovered in the Negev area (Rainey 1982:60b), and, as far as they have been published, two bear the name Ziph (one each from Tel Beer-sheba and Tel ʿAroʿer); only one bears the name Socoh (from Tel Arad). Of the 13 *lmlk* jar handles published from the southern Judean hills (Welten 1969:183; Kochavi 1972:77–78; 1974: 18) Socoh is missing entirely. On the other hand, the number of *lmlk* Socoh seal impressions discovered in the Shephelah is double that of the *lmlk* Ziph. Furthermore, three quarters of all the *lmlk* Socoh impressions discovered so far were found in the Shephelah. Also the list of the 15 fortified towns, corresponding well with both the distribution of the *lmlk* impressions and the names of towns stamped on the jars, clearly shows that Socoh should be located in the Shephelah. Considering the importance of the lowlying Socoh — as is indicated in the Bible — its place in the list of 2 Chr. 11:6–10, and the distribution of the *lmlk* Socoh impressions, one would hardly doubt the generally accepted identification of Socoh of the *lmlk* seal impressions at Khirbet ʿAbbâd. The lack of accord between the *lmlk* seal impressions found in the site and its name (Socoh) will be discussed below in detail.

The close congruence between the distribution of the *lmlk* seal impressions and the layout of the 15 fortified cities can be demonstrated further by what may be designated as "negative evidence": both the Negev and the southernmost Shephelah areas that are not represented in the list of 2 Chr. 11:6–10 have produced only a few *lmlk* impressions. This point requires further elaboration.

The rarity of the *lmlk* impressions is particularly clear for the area of the eastern Negev (Na'aman 1979a:74–75). No *lmlk* impressions were found in the excavations at Tel Malḥata. Only one impression was discovered in Tel Beer-sheba (on a large pithos of Stratum II), despite the extensive excavations conducted throughout the site. At Tell Arad, which was excavated in its entirety, only six stamped handles were discovered. One seal impression was found in Tel ʿIra and three were unearthed at Tel ʿAroʿer, both sites being recently excavated. Thus, only 11 *lmlk* seal impressions were discovered in the Valley of Beer-sheba, in spite of the extensive excavations in almost all the sites located there.

Only a handful of stamped *lmlk* jar handles, likewise, were discovered in the western Negev and the southernmost Shephelah, despite the extensive excavations conducted there. Four *lmlk* impressions were uncovered at Tell Belt Mirsim, which was thoroughly excavated. One *lmlk* jar handle was found at Tel Ḥalif, a site that is being excavated currently. No *lmlk* impressions have been discovered so far at Tell el-Ḥesi, an extensively excavated site, and one *lmlk* jar handle was discovered in the nearby site of Tell esh-Shuqf (Na'aman 1979a:75 n. 37). As will be suggested, the correlation between the distribution of the 15 fortified towns and the royal seal impressions is the key to the proper understanding of the paucity of the *lmlk* jars in the southern areas of the kingdom of Judah.[11]

Dating the list of 2 Chr 11:6–10 to the time of Hezekiah and considering the harmony between the layout of the 15 towns and the distribution of the *lmlk* seal impressions may enable us to reconstruct the manner in which Hezekiah prepared his kingdom for the impending Assyrian attack. Having a limited span of time for his preparations, Hezekiah must have selected several strategically located towns along the main approach and supply lines to his capital, Jerusalem, and the Judean hill country and fortified them against the expected Assyrian advance from the west, storing therein the necessary supplies for a siege. Some of the commodities sent to the fortified cities were stored within the *lmlk* jars, which can now be understood to have been connected with Hezekiah's preparations for war. The general distribution of the *lmlk* impressions reflects the scope of Hezekiah's preparatory activity (below). As was suggested above, several towns in the area north of Jerusalem were originally included within the list of 2 Chr. 11:6–10; the heavy concentration of royal seal impressions in that area accords well with this hypothesis. The *lmlk* jars were not sent exclusively to the newly fortified towns, but to all the fortified cities of Judah that were threatened by the anticipated Assyrian campaign.

The towns of the Negev and the southernmost Shephelah remained outside of this array of fortification and network of supply, presumably because

11. The overall distribution of the *lmlk* jar handles has been taken by scholars as a basis for the general delineation of the territorial scope of the kingdom (e.g., Aharoni 1967:344; Welten 1969:93–102; Na'aman 1979a:75–77). However, Rainey (1982:60b) recently has questioned the validity of such delineation on the grounds that a single *lmlk* seal impression was discovered at Ashdod situated outside the borders of Judah. It should be emphasized that isolated *lmlk* jars may have come to the market or may even have been carried off as

they lay outside the expected Assyrian line of approach. It is for this reason that so few *lmlk* jar handles have been found there. In an earlier article (Na'aman 1979a:74–75, 82–83) I tried to construct a historical picture based on the scarcity of *lmlk* jars in these southern areas. The analysis of Hezekiah's preparations for the impending Assyrian attack requires a revision of my earlier presentation: despite the fact that only four *lmlk* jar handles were unearthed in the excavations of Tell Belt Mirsim, the city apparently was destroyed during Sennacherib's campaign of 701 BCE (Aharoni 1973:5–6; Aharoni and Aharoni 1976:73–84). Tel Ḥalif was probably destroyed in the same campaign, despite the rarity of *lmlk* jar handles found at the site (Seger 1980:224). Also, eastern Negevite sites like Arad might have been destroyed at that same time, possibly by Edomite troops (below).

Tel Beer-sheba (which, in my opinion, should not be confused with biblical Beer-sheba; see Na'aman 1980:149–51) poses a special problem. The site, covering an inhabited area of approximately 1 hectare, was almost entirely excavated, uncovering a densely populated city. Only one *lmlk* seal impression, whose origin is different from all the other *lmlk* jars of Type 484 (Mommsen, Perlman, and Yellin 1984:107–13), was found among the thousands of vessels discovered in the destruction layer of Stratum II. Taking into account the extent of the excavated area and the large number of public and private buildings unearthed on the site, the scarcity of the *lmlk* impressions in Tel Beer-sheba is without parallel among the Judean sites of that period. The question arises as to whether the site was destroyed during the Assyrian campaign of 701 BCE or slightly earlier, by the Assyrians or others. The problem was discussed recently by Rainey (1982:59–61), and I would like to present the following four points:

(a) Rainey has called attention to four sites excavated in the western Negev and the southernmost Shephelah (Tell Jemmeh, Tell el-Far'ah, Tel Sera' and Tell el-Ḥesi) to prove that Tel Beer-sheba was not the only Judean site where *lmlk* seal impressions do not appear. However, two of these sites, Tell Jemmeh and Tell el-Far'ah, were located outside the confines of the kingdom of Judah and were never annexed to it. The third site, Tel Sera', was deserted from the early 9th century until the 7th century (Oren 1982:159–63)

booty from the conquered Judean towns. Thus, a single *lmlk* jar handle was found in Kfar Ata, in the Acco plain (Stern 1975:50, n. 20), in an area far north of the borders of Judah. Sporadic and isolated occurrences of *lmlk* seal impressions, therefore, must be ignored (see Na'aman 1979a:76). The general territorial scope of the kingdom may be delineated only by accounting for both the distribution of the *lmlk* impressions and their number, according to regional criteria.

and is not relevant to the discussion. Tell el-Ḥesi is not only smaller, but also less populated than Tel Beer-sheba and was excavated on a reduced scale. The scarcity of the *lmlk* seal impressions in the densely inhabited site of Tel Beer-sheba, which was so extensively excavated, is without parallel among all excavated sites of the kingdom of Judah dating to this period.

(b) Holding that Tel Beer-sheba could not have been destroyed before Sennacherib's campaign of 701 BCE, Rainey claimed that "silence on such a sensitive issue as Judean control of the Negeb is unthinkable." However, we know that many events of great importance were entirely ignored. Even the final destruction of the towns of the Negev at the end of the First Temple period and the occupation of the Valley of Beer-sheba by the Edomites were passed over in the Book of Kings and Chronicles. Tel Beer-sheba could have been conquered before 701 BCE without being mentioned in the Bible.

(c) The possibility that the Assyrians attacked and destroyed Judean cities prior to Sennacherib (i.e., in the course of the four campaigns conducted under Sargon II to the Philistine coast) should be taken into consideration. The Nineveh Prism, which contains the most detailed description of the Assyrian campaigns to the Philistine coast in the years 716 and 712–711, is, unfortunately, fragmentary (Tadmor 1958:77–80). Moreover, the reliefs of Sargon's palace depict the capture of Gibbethon and Ekron (El-Amin 1953: 35–47). The cities were probably conquered by Sargon during his first campaign to the Philistine coast in 720 BCE (Reade 1976:99–102), but they are not mentioned in the king's annals and summary inscriptions. Other cities as well may have been conquered by Sargon and excluded from his inscriptions (Na'aman 1979b:83–86).

(d) Alongside the Assyrians, the Edomites also threatened the towns of the Negev at the end of the 8th century BCE. In the description of Ahaz's reign, the Chronicler relates that "the Edomites had come and smitten Judah and carried away captives" (2 Chr. 28:17). The Edomite danger is also reflected in a letter discovered at Arad Stratum VIII (Aharoni 1975:72–76; Lemaire 1977: 207–208).

We may conclude that several ethnic elements (i.e., Assyrians, Edomites, and possibly also Arabs) were capable of raiding and destroying southern Judean towns in the period under discussion. Tel Beer-sheba was conquered while its stores were still full, and the city presumably was captured in a surprise attack. Taking into account the rarity of the *lmlk* impressions found in the site, it is not impossible that it was conquered and destroyed prior to Sennacherib's campaign of 701 BCE.

The Four Towns Accompanied by the Designation LMLK

The role of the four towns whose names appear on the *lmlk* stamps and the closely related problem of the origin of the contents of these jars can be reviewed in the light of the above conclusion. It has been suggested that the four towns so designated were part of the system of fortifications established by Hezekiah prior to 701 BCE and that the *lmlk* jars were stored in the fortified cities as part of the official preparations for the anticipated war with the Assyrians.

By tying the *lmlk* jars to the preparations for war, one may first question the widely accepted theory that the *lmlk* jars were produced and stamped solely for the products of the royal estates (Galling 1937:339; Sellin 1943; Tufnell, in Diringer 1949: 80; Lapp 1960: 22; Rainey 1967:41; 1982:57; Welten 1969:133–42, 173–74; Mettinger 1971:95–97; Lemaire 1975b: 680). This suggestion should have been questioned long ago, because the *lmlk* jars were never found in royal stores, as should have been the case for the produce of crown lands; rather, they were found in private houses (Welten 1973:171–72). Furthermore, underlying the "royal estates" theory is a state of peace, during which the yield of the royal estates located near the four towns would have been gradually garnered in special jars and transported to the fortified cities of Judah for storage there. Under such circumstances, it would be logical to mark the yield of the royal farms to specify its origin. This, however, was not the case for the *lmlk* jars, and the emergency situation does not fit well into this theory. After all, the crown lands were mainly intended to furnish the necessary supplies for the king and his household, and there is no evidence that, under ordinary circumstances, they would have been utilized outside this circle, much less used to meet the needs of the entire kingdom.

Although hardly anything is known of the extent of the royal estates in the kingdom of Judah, its production was probably no more than a small fraction of the overall yield of the country. However, on the eve of Sennacherib's campaign, one could hardly doubt that the entire resources of the kingdom would have been mobilized, the crown lands contributing to the preparations for war. In this situation, there was no point in marking or specifying the products of the royal estates to distinguish them from the yield of the other sectors of the kingdom, because all were intended for the same purpose. One would naturally assume that the *lmlk* jars contained products originating from all parts of the kingdom, including, perhaps, the yield of the crown lands.

The hypothesis that the *lmlk* stamps indicated special brands of produce, namely wine, was put forward by Cross (1969:20*–22*). He suggested that the vessels were wine jars and that the four place names specified the location of vineyards. In Cross's words, "Wines are known by their district. It is the key to their taste and quality. But it matters little where grains are grown or where oil is pressed." However, this solution, while very attractive, presupposes a state of peace in the land, which would hardly accord well with the preparations for an impending war. The source of the wine jars was rarely indicated during the time of the First Temple, and an emergency is certainly not the appropriate time to start the systematic recording of the origin of the wine. The *lmlk* jars may have contained wine, but the indication of the four towns was hardly likely to have been intended as a specific reference to the origin of their contents.

Establishing the function of the four towns is a vexing problem due to the random distribution of the *lmlk* jars (Welten 1969:143–56; Na'aman 1979a:81–82). The vast majority of the impressions bearing the name *Mmšt* are concentrated in the northern part of the kingdom. Three quarters of the impressions with the name Socoh have been found in the Shephelah. The distribution of the *lmlk* Ziph and *lmlk* Hebron impressions, however, is problematic. Most of the *lmlk* Ziph impressions have been found in northern Judah. The seal impressions bearing the name Socoh were found only in small numbers in this region, whereas the impressions stamped with the names of the other three towns are more common. The majority of the seal impressions unearthed in the Shephelah and, in particular, at Lachish and Beth-shemesh were stamped by *lmlk* Hebron. Significantly, the number of *lmlk* Socoh impressions discovered in the Shephelah is double those of *lmlk* Ziph. Few *lmlk* impressions of any kind were uncovered in the Judean hill country, where Ziph and Hebron are situated. The distribution of the *lmlk* seal impressions and, in particular, the dispersal of the impressions stamped by *lmlk* Ziph and *lmlk* Hebron require explanation. Also, more than one-third of the entire *lmlk* jar handles are devoid of the name of any town. That an enormous number of *lmlk* jars had seal impressions that did not include the name of a city does not fit well with the commonly held assumption that the four towns were points of origin for general distribution. The *lmlk* jars were stored, together with their contents, for use in a time of siege. As a result of the Assyrian campaign, many places in which the *lmlk* jars were stored were destroyed. Thus, one can hardly posit a large-scale mobility of the jars, because most of them were unearthed in those sites to which they had been originally dispatched.

Also of significance are finds from the actual sites of the four towns (or rather three, as the location of *Mmšt* is unknown). The site of ancient Hebron (Tell er-Rumeideh) was partly excavated, but apparently no *lmlk* jar handles were discovered (Hammond 1965, 1966, 1968; also see note 10). No *lmlk* jar handles have been found in Ziph. Admittedly, the overall number of *lmlk* impressions found in the Judean hill country is very small. However, assuming that Hebron and Ziph were indeed the distribution centers for the *lmlk* jars, as many scholars believe, one would have expected to find some evidence for this on the sites. Moreover, of the numerous *lmlk* jar handles discovered so far at Socoh, none has borne the name of the city (Rainey 1982:59a).[12] The conclusion is inevitable: the four towns were neither the points of origin, nor the planned destinations of the *lmlk* jars. The solution to the problem of the four names must be sought in a regional, rather than a local, framework.

The layout of the 15 fortified towns (2 Chr. 11:610) and the distribution of the *lmlk* jars stamped with the names of the four towns lead to the tentative suggestion that Hezekiah's system of defense and supply was organized on the basis of a fourfold division, with the city of Hebron assigned a central position in this organization. The four military administrative zones, represented by the four place names on the royal stamps, are: the Shephelah (Socoh), the southern Judean hill country (Ziph), the central hill country (Hebron) and the northern hill country (*Mmšt*).[13] Hebron was situated deep in the hill country, in the middle of a rich agricultural area, far from Jerusalem, which was most likely the main target of the Assyrian campaign. Thus, it was selected to be the pivotal town in the distributional and defensive system. For this reason Hebron was set apart from all other fortified towns in the list of 2 Chr. 11:6–10. We may thus suggest that the names of the northern Judean towns, presumably omitted from this list by the Chronicler, were originally registered at the beginning of the *Vorlage* of the fortified cities, and that Hebron closed this hypothetical list of towns.

The reasons behind the selection of Socoh, Ziph, and *Mmšt* from among the fortified towns of Judah to symbolize the three regions are not clear. Scholars have noted that, unlike Hebron, the others are minor towns, and the town of *Mmšt* is not mentioned elsewhere. It was probably destroyed during the Assyrian campaign of 701 BCE and, subsequently, abandoned; therefore, it is absent from the list of Judean towns of the time of Josiah (Josh. 15:21–62; 18:21–28). Sellin (1943:222–23) emphasized David's close links to the towns of Hebron, Ziph, and Socoh, suggesting that parcels of land in their vicinity were turned into crown property in David's time. However, the assumption that David acquired royal estates in Ziph after taking revenge on its inhabitants is not very convincing: his policy of gaining wide support from among

12. The *lmlk* jar handles discovered by visitors on the site of ancient Socoh (Khirbet 'Abbâd) have never been published.

13. Several scholars have already suggested that the four cities represent territorial division of the kingdom of Judah. See Albright 1925:44–53; Yadin 1961, with additional bibliography on p. 6; Aharoni 1967:340–46.

the members of the tribe of Judah would hardly go along with such measures of punishment and revenge. Furthermore, no adequate explanation was offered by the supporters of the "crown land" theory for the problem of why these four towns were selected from among the Judean cities, rather than places like Jerusalem or Bethlehem, where the Davidic dynasty must have held larger parcels of land.[14] The function of Socoh, Ziph, and *Mmšt* within both Hezekiah's defensive system and the organization of the kingdom in his time is not known. It is best to suspend judgment until at least one of them has been excavated and its characteristics clarified.

Since the early days of research on the *lmlk* stamps (see Clermont-Ganneau 1899:206), scholars have noted certain biblical passages in which it is stated explicitly that grain, wine, and oil were stored in the fortified cities of Judah (2 Chr 11:11; 17:12b–13a; 32:38). The letters of Arad displayed for the first time the contents of a royal Judean store and indicated that indeed these three commodities formed the basis of the Arad storehouse (Aharoni 1975: 142–143; Lemaire 1977: 228–232). It is not clear whether grain was stored and stamped in the *lmlk* jars as well, but they certainly would have contained wine and oil for a time of siege.

As has been noted, the Shephelah and the northern Judean hill country, near Jerusalem, were the main targets of the expected Assyrian onslaught. For this reason, they probably would have been a high priority of the Judean kingdom and were the first supplied with provisions for a siege. This may explain the heavy concentration of the *lmlk* jars in these regions, where many towns were destroyed during the Assyrian conquest, leaving the *lmlk* jars buried in the debris. Supplies to these areas were transported in *lmlk* jars from neighboring regions. It is for this reason that so many *lmlk* Hebron jars that were filled in the agriculturally rich olive and grape region of Hebron were found in the neighboring Shephelah. Jars garnered in the Ziph and Hebron areas likewise were transported to the northern Judean front. On the other hand, jars filled in the Shephelah and the area of Jerusalem, which constituted the front, were delivered almost exclusively to the fortified towns located in these regions. Therefore, most of the *lmlk* Socoh seal impressions were found in the Shephelah and hardly any *lmlk Mmšt* seal impressions were found outside the northern Judean hill country. The hypothesis of the fourfold division into areas of defense and supply nicely explains the distribution of the *lmlk* jars.

---

14. Welten's proposal (1969:141–42, 174) that only the yield of the royal estates located in these four towns was assigned for the preparations for the impending war is not very likely.

The recent excavations at Lachish have demonstrated that private seal impressions were stamped on the same vessels that carried royal seal impressions (Ussishkin 1976). Their distribution matches that of the royal seal impressions, and they appear on the same sites that produced a considerable number of *lmlk* jar handles (see Heltzer 1965:23–26; Ussishkin 1976; Mazar and Kelm 1980:95–96). The private stamped handles, therefore, should be examined alongside the royal seal impressions.

The best example of the state's official seals appearing alongside seals that carry personal names is the *Yehud* jars of the 5th century BCE. The following legends have been found on jar handles and body fragments of these storage jars: *yhwd/yhw'zr/pḥw'; l'ḥzy/pḥw'; yhwd/ḥnnh; yhwd/'wryw* (see Avigad 1976a:22–23, with additional bibliography). Thus, side by side with the Aramaic name of the province of Judah under Persian rule (*Yehud*), a personal name (Yeho'ezer) with his official title *pḥw'* ("the governor"; Avigad 1976a: 6–7) appears. It is clear that both Yeho'ezer and Aḥzai were governors of the province of Judah (Avigad 1976a: 33–35). Moreover, three *bullae* of *yhwd/ ḥnnh* were recently discovered. Both Ḥananah and Uriyau were doubtless officials of the province of Judah (Avigad 1976a: 5, 22). In light of these new data, Avigad (1976a: 35) has suggested the following interpretation for the *Yehud* jars:

> The governors who preceded Nehemiah . . . introduced an efficient tax-gathering apparatus using special jars. These, indeed, are the jars stamped with the names of the province, *yhd,* and the names of the governors and their officers, found in excavations on Judean sites. Such a system of concentrating provisions in store-jars was known in Judah already in the period of the First Temple, when the jars bearing the lamelekh stamps were employed. It proved itself then, and it was revived when need called, for whatever purpose. In the Persian period, a similar system was employed at Elephantine in Egypt, as well.

The *lmlk* jars were assigned for the storing of provisions for the anticipated hard time of siege rather than for the gathering of taxes. The legend *lmlk* probably played the same role as the legend *yhd,* both designating that the jars belonged to the state. The formula *lmlk is* an elliptic form of a longer phrase, which should be rendered as "[the seal belonging] to the king" (*pace* Rainey 1965; 1966).[15] The private stamps may theoretically belong to ei-

15. Rainey (1965; 1966:189–90) has claimed that the formula *lmlk* on the royal stamps is a statement of commodity "for the king." Unfortunately, this claim was based on the assumption that the *lmlk* legends referred to standard measure and all the semantic parallels suggested in his articles for the formula *lmlk* pertain to royal weights and measures. The new excavations at Lachish, however, have shown that the Type 484 jars (the *lmlk* jars)

ther royal officials or royal potters (Cross 1968: 232; cf. Avigad 1976a: 6–7). However, not only does the above analogy strongly support the first interpretation, but the title *na'ar* appearing in the seal of *'lyqm n'r ywkn* (Ussishkin 1976: 6–11) would hardly suit potters.[16] Thus, one is tempted to link the private stamps with the royal officers who were involved with the preparations for war and, thus, who were entitled to use the royal seal.

For the sake of completeness, we will try to reconstruct the entire procedure related to the manufacture and distribution of the *lmlk* jars. Many details in the reconstruction are uncertain, but a general outline seems appropriate.

The *lmlk* jars of Type 484 were all produced in a single pottery-making center located somewhere in the Shephelah, probably in the region of Lachish (Mommsen, Perlman, and Yellin 1984).[17] The central workshop of Judah is probably alluded to in 1 Chr 4:23 (see Rothstein and Hanel 1927:66–67; Rudolph 1955:36–37). The *lmlk* seal impressions indicated that the manufactured jars were under royal authority ("belonging to the king"). The private seals stamped on the *lmlk* jars probably belonged to the king's officers supervising the preparations for war, who were entitled to use the official royal seal. From the central workshop the empty jars were sent to the four military administrative districts, where preparations for the war took place. The names of the four towns probably designated the names of the four regions where the empty jars stamped with names would have been sent. Jars bearing the *lmlk* seal impressions with no town name might have been dispatched to towns all over the country. The empty jars were filled in the towns in the four defense and supply areas and then were sent and stored in the fortified cities of Judah. The two-winged insignia and the four-winged insignia were intended to mark the region to which the loaded jars would have been sent. Jars bearing the sun-disc were sent to the northern region of Judah, and those bearing the scarab were sent to the Shephelah. The contents of the jars must have included all the resources of the kingdom: taxes in kind, payments by rich land owners, perhaps even tithes and possibly products from

---

were of varying capacities and, thu,s the "standard measure" theory must be abandoned. Rainey's hypothesis (1966) that the private seals and the *lmlk* stamps belong to separate semantic fields is not corroborated by the evidence. Although Rainey (1982:57, 60) admitted that the *lmlk* stamps did not refer to a standard measure, he still cited his former conclusion of the meaning of the *lmlk* formula.

16. For the title of *na'ar* in the Israelite society at the time of the First Temple, see Avigad 1976b; Macdonald 1976.

17. For the classification of the royal stamps, see Lemaire 1981.

the crown lands. The procedure suggested here—jars of high quality manufactured in a single pottery-making center and distributed to the major defense zones of the kingdom, while the produce garnered there was delivered and stored in the fortified cities—seems to account well for a period of emergency. The system had to have been flexible and the jars with their contents had sometimes to be transported to distant places in accordance with the current requirements. The entire procedure was probably an *ad hoc* device, planned and carried out in an emergency situation.

Summary

The measures taken by Hezekiah to prepare for the impending Assyrian attack may be reconstructed by combining the biblical account of the days of Hezekiah and the list of 15 fortified cities (2 Chr. 11:6–10) with the archaeological evidence and, in particular, with the distribution of the *lmlk* seal impressions. Hezekiah seems to have selected cities in the Judean hill country and the Shephelah, strengthened them and stored provisions there for the anticipated siege. The fortified cities were manned with garrisons and furnished with arms (see 2 Chr. 11:12; 17:2, 19; 26:14; 33:14), a point that has not been discussed in this article. The king and his officials, while organizing and controlling the preparation for war, distributed stamped jars of high quality among the towns of Judah. The jars were filled and loaded in these places and then transported to the fortified cities of Judah in accordance with the order of priorities established by the king. The provisions were collected from all sectors of the population; the king may have added his share from his own estates. The stamps on the jars were probably intended to simplify the allotment of the vessels according to region and to preclude the possible misuse of their contents.

The entire area covered by the defense system was divided into four military-administrative zones: the Shephelah, the southern, the central, and the northern hill country. Hebron was selected as the pivotal town of the entire defense and supply system because of its strategic position and economic importance. The role of the other three towns whose names appear on the *lmlk* jars (Socoh, Ziph, and *Mmšt)* remains unknown.

The towns of the Negev and the southernmost Shephelah were not included in this array of fortifications, which was mainly directed against an attack from the north and west; thus, these towns were outside the system of provisions linked with the distribution of the *lmlk* jars.

The defense system established by Hezekiah was severely shaken by the heavy Assyrian onslaught. Many fortified towns in the Shephelah and the northern hill country were destroyed and even Jerusalem was besieged. The second line of defense, however, located in the Judean hill country and centered around the city of Hebron, was able to resist the Assyrian attack (Na'aman 1979a:73–74, 83–86). The sudden change in the situation and the retreat of the Assyrian army left considerable parts of the kingdom, including most of the Judean hill country, unconquered, enabling the gradual recovery of the kingdom of Judah.

References

Aharoni, M., and Aharoni, Y. 1976. The Stratification of Judahite Sites in the 8th and 7th Centuries B.C.E. *BASOR* 224: 73–90.

Aharoni, Y. 1967. *The Land of the Bible: A Historical Geography.* Philadelphia.

Aharoni, Y. 1973. The Stratification of the Site. In: Aharoni, Y. ed. *Beersheba* I. *Excavations at Tel Beer-sheba, 1969-1971 Seasons.* Tel Aviv: 4–8.

Aharoni, Y. 1975. *Arad Inscriptions* (Judean Desert Studies). Jerusalem. (Hebrew).

Albright, W.F. 1925. The Administrative Divisions of Israel and Judah. *JPOS* 5: 17–54.

Alt, A. 1925. Judas Gaue unter Josia. *PJB* 21: 100–16. (Reprint: Alt 1953: 276–288).

Alt, A. 1929. Nachwort über die territorialgeschichtliche Bedeutung von Sanheribs Eingriff in Palästina. PJb 25: 80–88. (Reprint: Alt 1953: 242–249).

Alt, A. 1953. Festungen and Levitenorte im Lande Juda. In: Alt 1953: 306–315.

Alt, A. 1953. *Kleine Schriften zur Geschichte des Volkes Israel* II. München.

Avigad, N. 1976a. *Bullae and Seals from a Post-Exilic Judean Archive* (Qedem 4). Jerusalem.

Avigad, N. 1976b. New Light on the Na'ar Seals. In: Cross, F.M., Lemke, W.E. and Miller, P.D. eds. *Magnolia Dei. The Mighty Acts of God.* Essays on the Bible and Archaeology in Memory of G. Ernest Wright. New York: 294–300.

Beit-Arieh, I. 1982. Ḥorvat 'Uza. *IEJ* 32:262–263.

Beyer, G. 1931. Beiträge zur Territorialgeschichte von Südwestpalästina im Altertum. 1. Das Festungssystem Rehabeams. *ZDPV* 54: 113–134.

Clermont-Ganneau, C. 1899. Note on the Inscribed Jar-Handle and Weight Found at Tell Zakarîya. *PEQ* 31: 204–209.

Cross, F.M. 1968. Jar Inscriptions from Shiqmona. *IEJ* 18: 226–233.

Cross, F.M.1969. Judean Stamps. *Eretz Israel* 9: 20*–27*.

Crüsemann, F. 1978. *Der Widerstand gegen das Königtum. Die antiköniglichen Texte des Alters Testamentes and der Kampf um den frühen israelitischen Staat.* (Wissenschaftliche Monographien zum Alters and Neuen Testament 49). Neukirchen-Vluyn.

Diringer, D. 1949. The Royal Jar-Handle Stamps of Ancient Judah. *BA* 12: 70–86.

El-Amin, M. 1953. Die Reliefs mit Beischriften von Sargon II. in Dûr-Sharrukîn. *Sumer* 9: 35–59, 214–228.

Elliger, K. 1934. Die Heimat des Propheten Micha. *ZDPV* 57: 81–152.

Fritz, V. 1981. The "List of Rehoboam's Fortresses" in 2 Chr 11: 5–12 — A Document from the Time of Josiah. *Eretz Israel* 15: 46*–53*.

Galling, K. 1937. Krugstempel. *Biblisches Reallexikon.* Tübingen: 337–340.

Gichon, M. 1964. The System of Fortifications in the Kingdom of Judah. In: Liver, J. ed. *The Military History of the Land of Israel in Biblical Times.* Tel Aviv:410–425. (Hebrew).

Hammond, P.C. 1965. Hébron. *RB* 72: 267–270.

Hammond, P.C.1966. Hébron. *RB* 73: 566–569.

Hammond, P.C.1968. Hébron. *RB* 75: 253–258.

Heltzer, M. 1965. Epigraphy on Ancient Palestinian Ceramics as an Important Historical Source. *Epigrafika Vostoka* 17: 18–37. (Russian).
Japhet, S. 1977. *The Ideology of the Books of Chronicles and its Place in Biblical Thought.* Jerusalem. (Hebrew).
Junge, E. 1937. *Der Wiederaufbau des Heerwesens des Reiches Juda unter Josia.* (Beiträge zur Wissenschaft vom Alten and Neuen Testament 75). Stuttgart.
Kallai, Z. 1971. The Kingdom of Rehoboam. *Eretz Israel* 10: 245–254. (Hebrew).
Kallai, Z. 1977. The United Kingdom of Israel — A Focal Point in Israelite Historiography. *IEJ* 27: 103–109.
Kochavi, M. 1972. The Land of Judah. In: Kochavi, M. ed. *Judaea, Samaria and the Golan,* Archaeological Survey 1967–1968. Jerusalem: 17–89. (Hebrew).
Kochavi, M. 1974. Khirbet Rabûd = Debir. *Tel Aviv* 1: 2–33.
Lapp, P.W. 1960. Late Royal Seals from Judah. *BASOR* 158: 11–22.
Lemaire, A. 1972. L'ostracon "Ramat-Négeb" et la topographie historique du Négeb. *Semitica* 23: 11–26.
Lemaire, A. 1975a. Mmšt = Amwas, vers la solution d'une énigme de l'épigraphie Hébraïque. *RB* 82: 15–23.
Lemaire, A. 1975b. Remarques sur la datation des estampilles *"lmlk." VT* 25: 678–682.
Lemaire, A. 1977. *Inscriptions hébraïques.* I. *Les ostraca.* Paris.
Lemaire, A. 1981. Classification des estampilles royales Juéennes. *Eretz Israel* 15: 54*–59*.
Macdonald, J. 1976. The Status and Role of the *Na'ar* in Israelite Society. *JNES* 35: 147–170.
Mazar, A. and Kelm, G.I. 1980. Canaanites, Philistines, and Israelites at Timna/Tel Batash. *Qadmoniot* 13: 89–97. (Hebrew).
Mazar, B. 1960. The Cities of the Priests and the Levites. *Supplement to VT* 7: 193–205.
Mettinger, T.N.D. 1971. *Solomonic State Officials. A Study of the Civil Government Officials of the Israelite Monarchy* (Coniectanea Biblica, Old Testament Series 5) Lund.
Miller, J.M. 1966. The Elisha Cycle and the Accounts of the Omride Wars. *JBL* 85: 441–454.
Mittmann, S. 1977. Ri. 1, 16f and das Siedlungsgebiet der kenitischen Sippe Hobab. *ZDPV* 93: 213–235.
Mommsen, H., Perlman, L., and Yellin, J. 1984. The Provenience of the *lmlk* Jars. *IEJ* 34: 89–113.
Na'aman, N. 1974. Sennacherib's "Letter to God" on His Campaign to Judah. *BASOR* 214: 25–39.
Na'aman, N. 1979a. Sennacherib's Campaign to Judah and the Date of the *lmlk* Stamps. *VT* 29: 61–86.
Na'aman, N. 1979b. The Brook of Egypt and Assyrian Policy on the Border of Egypt. *Tel Aviv* 6: 68–90.
Na'aman, N. 1980. The Inheritance of the Sons of Simeon. *ZDPV* 96: 136–152.
Na'aman, N. 1982. A New Look at the List of Levitic Cities. *Zion* 47: 237–252. (Hebrew).
Oren, E.D. 1982. Ziklag — A Biblical City on the Edge of the Negev. *BA* 45: 155–166.
Rainey, A.F. 1965. Royal Weights and Measures. *BASOR* 179: 34–36.
Rainey, A.F. 1966. Private Seal-Impressions: A Note on Semantics. *IEJ* 16: 187–190.
Rainey, A.F. 1967. The Samaria Ostraca in the Light of Fresh Evidence. *PEQ* 99: 32–41.
Rainey, A.F. 1982. Wine from the Royal Vineyards. *BASOR* 245: 57–62.
Reade, J. 1976. Sargon's Campaigns of 720, 716 and 715 B.C.: Evidence from the Sculptures. *JNES* 35: 95–104.
Rothstein, J.W. and J. Hänel. 1927. *Das erste Buch der* Chronik. (Kommentar zum Alten Testament 18/2). Leipzig.
Rudolph, W. 1955. *Chronikbücher.* (Handbuch zum Alten Testament 21). Tübingen.

Šanda, A. 1912. *Die Bücher der Könige übersetzt und erklärt*. 2. Das zweite Buch der Könige. (Exegetisches Handbuch zum Alten Testament 9/2). Münster.

Seger, J.D. 1980. Tel Ḥalif. *IEJ* 30: 223–226.

Sellers, O.R., Funk, R.W., McKenzie, J.L., Lapp, P. and Lapp, N. 1968. *The 1957 Excavation at Beth-zur.* (AASOR 38). Cambridge, MA.

Sellin, E. 1943. Die palästinischen Krughenkel mit den Königsstempeln. *ZDPV* 66: 216–232.

Stern, E. 1975. Israel at the Close of the Period of the Monarchy: An Archaeological Survey. *BA* 38: 26–54.

Tadmor, H. 1958. The Campaigns of Sargon II of Assur: A Chronological-Historical Study. *JCS* 12: 22–40, 77–100.

Tadmor, H. 1982. Traditional Institutions and the Monarchy: Social and Political Tensions in the Time of David and Solomon. In: Ishida, T. ed. *Studies in the Period of David and Solomon and Other Essays*. Tokyo.

Timm, S. 1980. Die territoriale Ausdehnung des Staates Israel zur Zeit der Omriden. *ZDPV* 96: 20–40.

Ussishkin, D. 1976. Royal Judean Storage Jars and Private Seal Impressions. *BASOR* 223: 1–13.

Ussishkin, D. 1977. The Destruction of Lachish by Sennacherib and the Dating of the Royal Judean Storage Jars. *Tel Aviv* 4: 28–57.

Ussishkin, D. 1978. Excavations at Tel Lachish — 1973–1977. *Tel* Aviv 5: 1–97.

Ussishkin, D. 1980. The "Lachish Reliefs" and the City of Lachish. *IEJ* 30: 174–195.

Welten, P. 1969. *Die Königs-Stempel. Ein Beitrag zur Militärpolitik Judas unte Hiskia and* Josia (Abhandlungen des Deutschen Palästinavereins). Wiesbaden.

Welten, P. 1973. *Geschichte and Geschichtsdarstellung in den Chronikbüchern* (Wissenschaftliche Monographien zum Alten and Neuen Testament 42). Neukirchen-Vluyn.

Yadin, Y. 1961. The Fourfold Division of Judah. *BASOR* 163: 6–12.

New Light on Hezekiah's Second Prophetic Story (2 Kings 19:9b–35)[1]

The biblical story of Sennacherib's campaign to Judah has been discussed in a great number of books, articles and commentaries. The list of publications is so long that we may well wonder whether it is still possible — on the basis of the extant sources — to significantly advance our understanding of any aspect of the story.

The majority of scholars agree that the text of Isaiah had its original context in Kings (see recently Konkel 1993:462–482; Williamson 1996:477–483; Person 1997:5–79). B. Stade suggested that the account of Sennacherib's campaign was built of two sources: a chronistic record (18:13–16) and two prophetic stories (18:17–19:9a, 37; 19:9b–20, 30–37) (Stade 1886:172–186). His arguments were accepted by some early scholars (A. Šanda is an exception) (for early scholars who discussed Stade's suggestion, see Šanda 1912:289–291; Gonçalves 1986:351–354). B.S. Childs revised this suggestion and proposed that the first prophetic story (Account B_1) included 18:17–19:9a, 36–37, and the second story (Account B_2) included 19:9b–35 (Childs 1967:69–103; see Gonçalves 1986:355–363, 376–394, 449–455, with earlier literature). Most scholars adopted this revision, and scholarly disagreements have been confined largely to the problem of the original scope of the two prophetic stories and, in particular, to the scope of Account B_2.[2]

It is the purpose of this article to re-examine some elements in Account B_2 that have not been satisfactorily explained by scholars, in an effort to shed more light on the date and place in which it was composed. The results of this re-examination will also be applied to the discussion of Account B_1. I will not discuss the complicated problem of the original scope of the two stories, because it is external to this discussion. I will also try to avoid repetition of what has already been said by other scholars and to concentrate on some new suggestions that I wish to present.

---

1. Reprinted with permission. *Biblica* 81 (2000), 393–402.

2. See the list of authors cited by Long 1991:200; Person 1997:76, n. 8. For recent detailed discussion of Account B_2, see Gonçalves 1986:449–477, with earlier literature.

The List of Conquered Places in 2 Kings 19:12–13

The key for dating Account B_2 (2 Kgs 19:9b–35) is the list of cities mentioned in vv. 12–13. The text runs as follows:

> Did the gods of the nations save them whom my ancestors destroyed, Gozan, Harran, Rezeph, and the people of Eden who were in Telassar? Where is the king of Hamath and the king of Arpad and the king of Lair, Sepharvaim, Hena, and Ivvah?

This text may be compared with 2 Kgs 18:33–34, which is part of the second speech of the Rabshakeh in Account B_1:

> Did any of the gods of the nations ever save his land from the king of Assyria? Where are the gods of Hamath and Arpad? Where are the gods of Sepharvaim? [ ][3] <Where are the gods of Samaria?>[4] Did they save Samaria from me?

Hamath, Arpad and Samaria participated in the anti-Assyrian rebellion that broke out in Syria-Palestine upon the death of Shalmaneser V, when Sargon II ascended the throne in 722 BCE (Tadmor 1958:33–39; Saggs 1975: 14, line 20; Fuchs 1994:89, line 25, 200–201, line 33). After he crushed the rebellion in 720 BCE, Sargon annexed Hamath and Samaria to the Assyrian territory. Arpad had been an Assyrian province since 738 BCE and after the rebellion was probably re-organized.[5] Sepharvaim appears in 2 Kings 17,24 as the origin of settlers whom Sargon deported to the province of Samerina in his late years (for the date of the Assyrian deportation to the province of Samerina, see Na'aman and Zadok 2000:177–179) and is identified in the area of eastern Babylonia. (For the identification of places mentioned in 2 Kgs 17:24, see Zadok 1976:115–116.) It is mentioned before Samaria, the re-

---

3. Hena and Ivvah are missing from Isaiah 36:19 and the LXX of 2 Kgs 18:34, and many scholars suggested that they entered the text from 19:13. See Orlinsky 1939:18, 62, with earlier literature in note 53. For a different opinion, see Barthélemy 1982:411.

4. The end of the verse requires a preceding question, like the one found in the Lucianic and Vulgate versions. For the restoration, see Burney 1903:342; Šanda 1912:260; Orlinsky 1939:46; Anbar 1990. For a different opinion, see Montgomery 1951:503; Barthélemy 1982: 411; Person 1997:63, no 69.

5. It should be noted that among the six places mentioned in Isa 10:9, four participated in the anti-Assyrian alliance that fought Sargon in 720 BCE (Hamath, Arpad, Damascus and Samaria). Carchemish was annexed by Sargon three years later, in 717 BCE. Only Calno/ Calneh (Assyrian Kullani), the capital of the former kingdom of Unqi/Patina that was annexed by Tiglath-pileser III in 738 BCE, is not mentioned in Sargon's inscriptions. However, Sargon's annals for the year 720 are broken, and details of the anti-Assyrian rebellion in the west in this year are incomplete. Thus, it is possible that Kullani/Calneh participated in the anti-Assyrian coalition that fought Sargon in 720 BCE, but is missing from the extent corpus of Sargon's inscriptions. Isaiah could have deliberately selected six central cities conquered and annexed (or re-annexed) by Sargon II in his early years, because his audience/readers had heard of the conquest of the cities not long before the prophecy was said/written.

gion where the deportees were settled. The text of 2 Kgs 18:33–34 refers to three cities that participated in the rebellion against Sargon in 720 BCE and to a place in eastern Babylonia that was conquered by Sargon during his campaigns against Babylonia in the years 710–709 BCE. (For the Babylonian campaigns of Sargon II, see Brinkman 1964:309–405.) It is evident that the four toponyms mentioned in Account B_1 are drawn from the western and eastern campaigns of Sargon II, Sennacherib's father.

The list of cities in 2 Kgs 19:12–13 is almost entirely different both from the list in 2 Kgs 18:33–34 and from the list of peoples settled by Sargon II in Samaria according to 2 Kgs 17:24. Most scholars agree on the identification of the places mentioned in vv. 12–13. (For the identification of the list of towns, see Šanda 1912:260, 272–273; Driver 1958; Zadok 1976; Gonçalves 1986: 458–461.) Some of these places (Gozan, Harran, Rezeph-Raṣappa and Eden-Bīt Adini) are located in northern Mesopotamia and were conquered and annexed by Assyria in the time of Ashurnaṣirpal II (883–859) and the early years of Shalmaneser III (858–824). Why did the author of Account B_2 select places that were conquered and annexed hundreds of years before his time to exemplify the Assyrian conquests? Another group of places (Telassar, Lair, Sepharvaim, Hena and Ivvah) is probably located in eastern Babylonia. Again, why did the author include these remote and unimportant eastern places in his list of conquered towns? Hamath and Arpad are located in Syria, and their location and history differ from the other places in this list. The selection of these places requires an explanation, and we shall first examine some suggestions offered by scholars for this enigmatic list.

H. Wildberger doubted whether the narrator had any clear idea about the time and circumstances in which these places fell to the hands of Assyria and suggested that the author simply expanded the list of Isa 36:19 (Wildberger 1982:1424). F.J. Gonçalves suggested that some cities are connected with the deportation to Samaria (Hamath, Sepharvaim, Ivvah), whereas Gozan is one of the places to which inhabitants of the Northern Kingdom were deported (Gonçalves 1986:462). E. Ben Zvi assumed that v. 12 refers to places where deportees from the Northern Kingdom were settled, and v. 13 refers to places from which came the deportees who were settled in Samaria (Ben Zvi 1990:89–91). However, only one name (Gozan) is common to v. 12 and the list of Israelite deportees settled in Assyria (2 Kgs 17:6), and only two names (Sepharvaim and Ivvah/Avva) appear in v. 13 and the list of deportees to Samaria (2 Kgs 17:24).[6] The assumption that the author of Account B_2 was bet-

6. The city of Hamath mentioned in 2 Kgs 17:24 is located in eastern Babylonia (Zadok 1976:117–120), whereas the Hamath of 2 Kgs 19:13 is located in central Syria.

ter acquainted with the Assyrian deportations of the time of Sargon II than the Deuteronomist (the author of 2 Kgs 17:6, 24) is unconvincing. Moreover, the text of vv. 12–13 refers to conquests rather than deportations, although deportees could have arrived from/at these places.

S.W. Holloway suggested that Harran must be treated separately from all the other places mentioned in vv. 12–13 (Holloway 1995:311–312). He discussed at length the history and cult of Harran in the Neo-Assyrian period and concluded that it is unlikely that an Assyrian referred to the cult center of Harran as a city destroyed by his forefathers. Harran was conquered by the Babylonians in 610–609 BCE, and this is the background for its inclusion in the list of conquered places (Holloway 1995:276–314 [especially pp. 312–314]). Adopting Hardmeier's suggestion that the description of Sennacherib's blockade of Jerusalem was patterned on the Babylonian siege of Jerusalem in 588 BCE (Hardmeier 1990:392–408), Holloway suggested that the inclusion of Harran's name in Rabshakeh's speech should be interpreted in the context of the 588 BCE war against the Babylonians.

As for the other places, Holloway adopted the widely held view that Sennacherib boasted of the victories of his forefathers over them. He offered no explanation for excluding Harran from the list of places. Nevertheless, I believe that he was on the right track in suggesting that the conquest of Harran reflects the Babylonian campaigns of the years 610–609 BCE. It seems to me that the list of cities in vv. 12–13 reflects the conquests of Nabopolassar and Nebuchadrezzar in the late seventh century BCE and that some of these conquests are mentioned in the Babylonian chronicles, the only source that we have for the emergence of the Babylonian Empire.

Following is a discussion of the list of towns in light of this suggestion.

(a) Harran held an important place in the late Assyrian empire. Sargon, Esarhaddon and Ashurbanipal built the city and its temple, and Ashurbanipal (668–631) nominated his younger brother as high priest (*šešgallu*) in the temple of Sin of Harran (Streck 1916:250, lines 17–18). Ashur-uballiṭ, the last king of Assyria, ascended the throne in Harran in 611 BCE (Grayson 1975: 94–95, lines 49–50). In the following year (610), the Babylonian army under Nabopolassar and the Median troops besieged Harran and captured it, and "carried off the vast booty of the city and the temple." In the next year (609), the Babylonian garrison stationed in Harran was attacked by Assyrian-Egyptian troops, but fought back until the withdrawal of the attacking force (Grayson 1975:95–96, lines 58–70; Zawadzki 1988:121–126).

According to the inscriptions of Nabonidus (556–539), the city of Harran suffered heavy damage and declined for many years, until he restored it to its former glory. The temple of Sin was plundered during the Babylonian conquest, and the city was partly destroyed, because of its prominent place in the late Assyrian Empire. The words "did the gods of the nations save them whom my ancestors destroyed" in 2 Kgs 19:12 may allude to the destruction of Harran and the despoliation of its temples by the Babylonians (Baltzer 1973; Beaulieu 1989:58–61, 104–115; Lee 1993; Mayer 1998).

(b) After the conquest of Nineveh in 612 BCE, the Babylonian troops advanced westward, conquered Naṣibin and brought a heavy booty and exiles "[from the lands of GN] and Ruṣapu" (Grayson 1975:94, lines 47–49). Ruṣapu-Raṣappa is located in the Sindjar plain of Upper Mesopotamia and was the capital of an Assyrian province (Forrer 1920:12; Dalley 1968:150–151; Cogan and Tadmor 1988:235). Its identification with biblical Rezeph (*reṣep*) is self-evident.

(c) In the following year (611) Nabopolassar marched against the city of Ruggulitu, captured it and killed its inhabitants (Grayson 1975:95, lines 56–57). Ruggulitu is mentioned in the annals of Shalmaneser III as an important city of the kingdom of Bīt Adini, which he captured and annexed to Assyria (856 BCE) (Forrer 1920:25). In 611 BCE, about 250 years later, it was conquered and annexed by the Babylonians.

In the following years, Nabopolassar conquered all the Assyrian territories up to the Euphrates, so that in 607 he was able to cross the Euphrates and conquer the city of Kimuḫu (modern Samsat) (Grayson 1975:97–98, lines 12–15).

We may conclude that Nabopolassar conquered the cities of Gozan, Harran, Raṣappa and the land of Bīt Adini in the course of his conquest of Upper Mesopotamian in the years 612–610 BCE. Captives were taken from the conquered areas and settled in Babylonia. Among them were probably the Edenites, whom the Babylonians settled at Telassar-Til Aššuri.

(d) Til Aššuri is located on the Diyala river, near the border between Babylonia and Media (Zadok 1976:123–124; Tadmor 1994:72–73). Shilḫazi, a place near Til Aššuri, is called by Tiglath-pileser III "fortress of the Babylonians" and was probably a Babylonian fort on the border with Media. Babylonians apparently lived in Til Aššuri in the time of Tiglath-pileser III and worshiped Marduk, their national god, in the local temple. When the Babylonians regained their territories, they established their border with Media along the same line. Deportees from Bīt Adini were probably brought to this place, which must have been the central Babylonian city in this area, and these deportees are mentioned by the author of Account B_2.

(e) The district (*pīḫatu*) of Hamath was conquered by Nebuchadrezzar after he defeated the Egyptian troops in Carchemish (605 BCE) (Grayson 1975: 99, lines 6–10). Arpad was captured in the course of this campaign. The combination of Hamath and Arpad is influenced by the references to the cities in Account B_1 (2 Kgs 18:34) and Isa 10:9. However, for the readers of B_2, the reference to the gods of Hamath points to its recent capture by Nebuchadrezzar, rather than to its conquest by the Assyrians a long time earlier (as correctly noted by Hardmeier) (Hardmeier 1990:404).

(f) Telassar, Lair, Sepharvaim and Ivvah are located in eastern Babylonia (for Sepharvaim and Avva/Ivvah, see Zadok 1976:115, 120–123). The place of Hena is unknown, but it possibly may be sought in the same area.[7] Sepharvaim and Ivvah (Avva) are included in the list of peoples settled by Sargon in the province of Samerina (2 Kgs 17:24), and Sepharvaim is mentioned in Account B_1 (18:34) (see note 6 above). Lair is identical with Laḫiru, a city located in northeastern Babylonia. It was an Assyrian province under the Sargonids and is mentioned in numerous Neo- and Late-Babylonian texts (Brinkman 1968:178, n. 1093; Zadok 1985:208).

The late date in which Account B_2 was written and the author's poor knowledge of the policy of Assyria is also revealed in 2 Kgs 19:17–18: "It is true, O YHWH, that the kings of Assyria have laid waste the nations and their lands, and put their gods to fire. . . ." It is well known that the Assyrians usually treated the gods of the conquered nations with respect. Often the divine statues were brought to Assyria, where they were installed in chapels until sent home, and only seldom were they actually destroyed (Cogan 1974:9–41; Cogan and Tadmor 1988:236; cf. Beaulieu 1993).

Is it possible that this passage reflects the Babylonian practice of destroying cult statues during their conquest of Assyria, and did the author again select an example familiar to his audience to illustrate his theology? In light of the long bitter enmity between Assyria and Babylonia, along with the utter destruction of the royal cities of Assyrian (e.g., Nineveh, Ashur, Calah, Dur-sharrukin, Arbela) by the Babylonian-Median armies, the suggestion is certainly possible. Unfortunately, we do not know enough about the Babylonian cultic policy toward the gods of Assyria. The main source we have is the Babylonian chronicle series, and although the chronicles appear objective, in reality, their pro-Babylonian bias is revealed throughout their text (Zawadzki 1988:114–143; Na'aman 1991:260–261). Even if the Babylonians destroyed Assyrian cult statues, the author would avoid mentioning it in his work.

7. Some scholars suggested transposing the letters of Hena (*Hēna'*) and reading it 'Anah, i.e., the city of 'Anat (modern 'Āna) located on the middle Euphrates. See Šanda 1912:260; Loewenstamm 1954:852; Wildberger 1982:1424. The city of 'Anat was conquered by Nabopolassar when he subdued a rebellion that broke out in 613 BCE. See Grayson 1975: 93–94, lines 35–36. However, there is no textual evidence for this suggestion, and we had better follow the MT and versions and assume that Hena is an unknown place in eastern Babylonia.

It is well known that an earlier Mesopotamian cult statue that has been lost could be fashioned only on the basis of some model of the lost one. T.G. Lee (1993) demonstrated that Nabonidus reconstructed the lost statue of Sin of Harran by the image that was engraved on Ashurbanipal's cylinder seal, which he dedicated to the god Sin. This may indicate that Assyrian statues were indeed destroyed during the Babylonian conquest. The scope of destruction of cult statues is unknown, but the fact that the kings of Babylonia never mentioned the fate of captured Assyrian statues may indicate that the author of Account B_2 referred to events that happened not long before his time.

The Date and Place of Accounts B_1 and B_2

An analysis of the place names mentioned in Account B_2 indicates that its author knew some details of the Babylonian campaigns to northern Mesopotamia and Syria in the years 612–605 BCE. Moreover, he had specific knowledge of certain places in eastern Babylonia, such as the settlement of the Edenites in Telassar-Til Aššuri and the sites of Laḫiru and Hena. The attachment of Ivvah and Sepharvaim — the origin of the settlers in the province of Samerina — to Laḫiru and Ḥena may suggest that he was aware of their location in eastern Babylonia. We may safely assume that the author of Account B_2 lived in eastern Babylonia, where some other deportees from the places he mentioned lived, and they must have been his sources for the Babylonian campaigns to northern Mesopotamia.

Noteworthy also is the reference to the gods of the nations "whom my ancestors destroyed (*šiḫātû*)" (v. 12). Ostensibly, the author is referring to Sennacherib's predecessors, the kings of Assyria. Assuming that, in reality, the text refers to the kings of Babylonia who conquered these places, the term "my ancestors" indicates that Account B_2 was written after the time of Nabopolassar and Nebuchadrezzar, i.e., after 562 BCE. We may conclude that the author of the second prophetic story was a descendant of a Judahite deportee living in Babylonia. He must have written his story after the death of Nebuchadrezzar, either in the time of the late Babylonian Empire or in the early Persian period. A date after the sixth century BCE is unlikely, because the author would then have drawn the historical episodes from more recent events, and the details of the Babylonian conquests in the late seventh century BCE would not have been memorized so accurately.

The author of Account B_2 expanded and elaborated the early story of Sennacherib's campaign and the "miraculous deliverance" of Jerusalem (2 Kgs 18:13–19:9a, 36–37), in accordance with his experience in the new place and the message he was trying to convey to his audience, the Judahite deportees in Babylonia. The updating of the list of conquered cities is part of his revision. He did not know much about the Assyrian conquests, which happened long before his time, apart from what he had read in the Deuteronomistic history. He, therefore, wrote a new list of places that were conquered not long before his time and were better known to his audience than the list of places that appears in Account B_1 (18:33–34). The exact historical background of the conquests and deportations was less important to him than the theological conclusions drawn from these events. The updated list of places suited his theological lesson of the helplessness of the foreign gods and the need to trust in YHWH in times of crisis and danger.

The attribution of an exilic date for Account B_2 is commonly accepted among scholars, but my suggestions for the location of the author and a possible date for his composition are new elements in the discussion. The marked difference between the authors of Accounts B_1 and B_2 is worth noting: The former selected his examples of the Assyrian conquests from Sargon II's campaigns, and the latter selected his examples from the Babylonian campaigns of the late 7th century BCE. In what follows, I will suggest three other differences between Accounts B_1 and B_2, which also indicate the enormous chronological gap between their respective messages.

(a) The second speech of the Rabshakeh in Account B_1 (2 Kgs 18:29–35) underlines the difference between YHWH of Jerusalem and the gods of Samaria. It could have been written only in the pre-exilic time, when Jerusalem and the temple were still intact and the memory of the destruction of the Northern Kingdom was very much alive. The author of Account B_1 drew conclusions from the "miraculous deliverance" of Jerusalem in 701 BCE and conveyed the message that Jerusalem was different from all recently conquered places, including Samaria, because YHWH guarantees its safety.

The comparison between the fate of Samaria and Jerusalem is missing in Account B_2, having lost its validity after the destruction of Jerusalem in 587/6 BCE. Instead, the later author expanded the list of conquered places and contrasted the inability of their gods to protect their citizens with the power of YHWH to protect his people and their city.

(b) A second point of comparison is the emphasis on Assyria's power and impending threat in Account B_1, as against an abstract depiction of the enemy in B_2. Reading Account B_1, it is clear that the story was written when the memory of Assyria's enormous military power and its threat to the existence of the Kingdom of Judah was still very much alive. In Account B_2, on the other hand, Assyria appears as an abstract power, representing more the concept of a strong military power than a concrete historical entity. The story will remain the same if we replace the name Assyria with the name of another power (e.g., Babylonia, Persia). Here, only the theological messages are considered important, hence, the arena for the scene and details of the situation are described in the shortest and in a schematic manner.

(c) A third point is the remarkable change in the role of Hezekiah in the two stories. In Account B_1 Hezekiah first made a rite of mourning by tearing his garments, putting on sackcloth and entering the temple (19:1). He then selected distinguished officials and priests and sent them to the prophet to request his intercession in face of the severe crisis. Hezekiah's conduct in the crisis is closely related to Josiah's conduct in 2 Kgs. 22:11–12: Like Hezekiah, Josiah tore his clothes and sent officials and priests to the prophetess Huldah. The sending of a delegation and the request for prayer, which is followed by a prophecy, are paralleled in Jer. 37:3, 6–8. In Account B_1, Isaiah appears as an intercessor between the king and the God, and only he is capable of addressing YHWH in prayer; Hezekiah acts piously and shows his trust in YHWH and his prophet, but has no power to address the God directly.

The description of Hezekiah and Isaiah in Account B_2 is entirely different. Let me cite the observation of B.S. Childs on the way that the author presented the king and the prophet in this story (1967:100–101):

> In B_2 Hezekiah does not even inform Isaiah, but enters the temple, approaches the very presence of God, and offers as a royal priest the prayer of his people. Here the parallel with David (II Sam. 8.18), and Solomon (I Kings 8.14–61) is striking. Hezekiah has become the type of the righteous king whose heart is perfect before God. The writer is already far removed from the Hezekiah of II Kings 18.13–19.9a. . . . The message of the prophet with its immediate fulfilment is closely attached to the preceding prayer. The prophet plays no independent role nor is his person significant. He is merely a bearer of the divine message. The emphasis falls fully on the power of God in his word which then effects its task. The larger form is, therefore, not the prophetic legend which centers in the prophet's role, but a similar genre which focuses on a picture of the pious king.

P.R. Ackroyd has demonstrated the growth of the figure of Hezekiah from a king of absolute faith and trust in YHWH in the face of the Assyrian onslaught (in Account B_1), to an ideal figure, a kind of a new David and a new Solomon, in the Book of Chronicles, and finally, a figure who gave rise to messianic speculations and hopes in rabbinical literature (Ackroyd 1987:105–120, 152–192; see Williamson 1977:119–131; Thronveit 1987: 121–124). Hezekiah's figure in Account B_2 is closer to that of the Book of Chronicles than to that of Account B_1. The new elevation of his figure is the outcome of the destruction of Jerusalem and the exile, a catastrophe that gave rise to a new evaluation of the course of the history of Israel. Following the destruction and exile, Hezekiah's conduct in face of the Assyrian threat, as described in the early story (B_1), was contrasted with the failure of the last kings of Judah to counter the Babylonian threat. The first stage in the process of the growth of Hezekiah's figure after the exile appears in Account B_2. Its author attributed to the king the kind of power that, in Account B_1 (and in other prophetic stories as well), was attributed only to prophets and great kings (David and

Solomon). The marked difference in the portrayal of Hezekiah in Accounts B_1 and B_2 is best explained by the assumption that they were composed with different perspectives in different historical circumstances.

Account B_1 was no doubt composed in the pre-exilic period. It seems to me that the author of 2 Kgs 18:13–19:9a, 36–37 (the Deuteronomist) combined two early sources that were available to him: a chronistic text (the source of Account A), and a prophetic story of the "miraculous deliverance" of Jerusalem (Account B_1). The chronistic text was written shortly after the conclusion of the Assyrian campaign, which is why its contents so accurately match the text of Sennacherib's inscriptions (for a good summary, see Dion 1989:5–25). It may have been included in the so-called "chronicles of the kings of Judah." The story was probably transmitted orally for some time, but was composed in writing at a time when the memory of the power and impending threat of Assyria to the very existence of Judah was still very much alive. The reference to Tirhakah "king of Egypt" in connection with the Assyrian withdrawal from Judah (18:9a, 19:36) indicates that when the story was written, Tirhaka's name was memorized in connection with the Assyrian-Egyptian struggle over the domination of Palestine.[8] The vivid memory of the murder of Sennacherib by his sons (2 Kgs 19:37), including the names of the murderers, the circumstances of the murder, the place where they found shelter, and the name of Sennacherib's successor, all point to a relatively early date of composition. The struggle of Tirhaka (690–664) with Assyria and the murder of Sennacherib (681) are the earliest possible dates for the composition of Account B_1, which could have been written at any time after these dates.

Dating the composition of the Deuteronomistic history is disputed among scholars, and this is not the place to enter the discussion. (For short surveys of the different schools of thought, see Eynikel 1996:7–31; van Keulen 1996: 3–52.) I have already suggested some arguments in support of a Josianic date of composition (Na'aman 1995a; 1996:180–183; 1997a:76–80; 1998) and will restate here my conviction that the early comprehensive history of Israel was written in the time of Josiah.

The Deuteronomist combined the chronistic and narrative texts (Accounts A and B_1) into a continuous history and integrated them into his composition of the history of Israel. He worked the chronistic source and fitted it into the pattern of other closely related texts that described the campaigns of foreign

8. J. von Beckerath (1992) suggested that Tirhakah could not have taken part in the 701 BCE campaign, because he arrived in Palestine no earlier than 700 BCE and, possibly, only in 696 BCE. See von Beckerath 1993:7–9. However, the Egyptian chronology of the 25th Dynasty is still uncertain, as indicated by the new inscription of Sargon II discovered in Iranian Kurdistan. See Frame 1999:52–54; Redford 1999:58–60.

kings and the payment of tribute (e.g., 1 Kgs 14:25–26; 2 Kgs 12:18–19; 15:19–20; 16:5, 7–9). He copied almost verbatim the prophetic story, as he did with many other prophetic stories that were available to him (Na'aman 1997b). His main contribution to Account B_1 is the insertion of 2 Kgs 18:22, which he wrote in order to support and corroborate his description of Hezekiah's cultic reform (18:4) (Na'aman 1995b:183). The note on Hezekiah's cultic reform is the only place where a clear Deuteronomic/Deuteronomistic feature appears in the speech. It supports my suggestion that Account B_1 is a pre-Deuteronomistic prophetic story and that — like many other prophetic stories — it was integrated by the Deuteronomist into his work of the history of Israel.

The Deuteronomist attached Account B_1 after Account A and omitted any reference to the subjugation of Judah to Assyria from 701 BCE to the Assyrian retreat from Palestine, thereby depicting Hezekiah's revolt against Assyria as an unqualified success. Anyone reading the Hezekiah-Josiah pericope in the Book of Kings would have to conclude that Judah was subjugated in the reign of Ahaz and was freed during the reign of Hezekiah. This is an exemplary case of the decisive role of the Deuteronomist in shaping the history of Judah, according to his ideological and theological considerations, although he cited his two sources almost verbatim and added very little to the early texts.

Account B_2 was written in Babylonia, either in the late years of the Babylonian Empire, or the early Persian period, and in many ways is a revised theological version of the first account. The prophetic story of the "miraculous deliverance" of Jerusalem had a prominent place in the theology of the Deuteronomistic history. However, the Deuteronomist left many parts of the Rabshakeh address virtually unanswered. As P. Machinist (2000:156–158) observed, there is no critique like the Rabshakeh's letter-address in the rest of the Deuteronomistic History. "Every one of its points has echoes in or provides a sharp counter to activities and theological positions elsewhere recorded in the Bible of Judah." The author of Account B_2 found it necessary to update the early prophetic story, both to counter the critique and respond to the Rabshakeh's political and theological claims and to fit the messages of the story to the new experience of the Jewish community in Babylonia in the second half of the sixth century BCE.

References

Anbar, M. 1990. *Kai pou eisin oi theoi tēs choras Samareias*; et où sont les dieux du pays de Samarie? *Biblische Notizen* 51: 7–8.

Ackroyd, P.R. 1984. The Biblical Interpretation of the Reigns of Ahaz and Hezekiah. In: Barrick, W.B. and Spencer, J.R. eds. *In the Shelter of Elyon. Essays on Ancient Palestinian Life and Literature in Honor of G.W. Ahlström*. (Journal for the Study of the Old Testament, Supplement 31). Sheffield: 247–259.

Ackroyd, P.R. 1987. *Studies in the Religious Tradition of the Old Testament*. London.

Baltzer, D. 1973. Harran nach 610 "medisch"? Kritische Überprüfung einer Hypothese. *WO* 7: 68–95.

Barthélemy, D. 1982. *Critique textuelle de l'Ancien Testament. 1. Josué, Juges, Ruth, Samuel, Rois, Chroniques, Esdras, Néhémie, Esther* (Orbis Biblicus et Orientalis 50/1). Fribourg.

Beaulieu, A. 1989. *The Reign of Nabonidus, King of Babylonia, 556-539 BCE*. (Yale Near Eastern Research 10). New Haven and London.

Beaulieu, P.E. 1993. An Episode in the Fall of Babylonia to the Persians. *JNES* 52: 243–261.

von Beckerath, J. 1992. Ägypten und der Feldzug Sanheribs im Jahre 701 v.Chr. *Ugarit-Forschungen* 24: 3–8.

von Beckerath, J. 1993. Die Nilstandsinschrift vom 3. Jahr Schebiktus am Kai von Karnak. *Göttinger Miszellen* 136: 7–9.

Ben Zvi, E. 1990. Who Wrote the Speech of the Rabshakeh and when? *JBL* 109: 79–92.

Brinkman, J.A. 1968. *A Political History of Post-Kassite Babylonia 1158-722 BCE*. (Analecta Orientalia 43). Rome.

Brinkman, J.A. 1964. Merodach-Baladan II. In: Biggs R.D. and Brinkman J.A. eds. *Studies Presented to A. Leo Oppenheim*. Chicago: 6–53.

Burney, C.F. 1970. *Notes on the Hebrew Text of the Books of Kings with an Introduction and Appendix*. (Oxford 1903; reprint New York 1970).

Childs, B.S. 1967. *Isaiah and the Assyrian Crisis*. (Studies in Biblical Theology, Second Series 3). London.

Cogan, M. 1974. *Imperialism and Religion: Assyria, Judah and Israel in the Eighth and Seventh Centuries B.C.E.* (Society of Biblical Literature Monograph Series 19). Missoula.

Cogan, M. and Tadmor, H. 1988. *II Kings. A New Translation with Introduction and Commentary*. (The Anchor Bible). Garden City.

Dalley, S. 1968. A Stela of Adad-nirari III and Nergal-ereš from Tell al Rimah. *Iraq* 30: 139–153.

Dion, P.E. 1989. Sennacherib's Expedition to Palestine. *Église et Théologie* 20: 5–25.

Driver, G.R. 1958. Geographical Problems. *Eretz Israel* 5: 16*–20*.

Eynikel, E. 1996. *The Reform of King Josiah and the Composition of the Deuteronomistic History*. (Oudtestamentische Studiën 33). Leiden.

Forrer, E. 1920. *Die Provinzeinteilung des assyrischen Reiches*. Leipzig.

Frame, G. 1999. The Inscription of Sargon II at Tang-i Var. *Orientalia* 68: 31–57.

Fuchs, A. 1994. *Die Inschriften Sargons II. aus Khorsabad*. Göttingen.

Gonçalves, F.J. 1986. *L'expédition de Sennachérib en Palestine dans la littérature Hébraïqe ancienne*. Louvaine-la-neuve.

Grayson, A.K. 1975. *Assyrian and Babylonian Chronicles*. (Texts from Cuneiform Sources 5). Locust Valley.

Hardmeier, C. 1990. *Prophetie im Streit vor dem Untergang Judas*. Erzählkommunikative Studien zur Entstehungssituation der Jesaja- und Jeremiaerzählungen in II Reg 18–20 und Jer 37–40. (Beiheft zur ZAW 187). München: 392–408.

Holloway, S.W. 1995. Harran: Cultic Geography in the Neo-Assyrian Empire and its Implications for Sennacherib's 'Letter to Hezekiah' in 2 Kings. In: Holloway, S.W. and Handy, L.K. eds. *The Pitcher is Broken. Memorial Essays for Gösta W. Ahlström.* (Journal for the Study of the Old Testament Supplement Series 190). Sheffield: 276-314.

van Keulen, P.S.F. 1996. *Manasseh through the Eyes of the Deuteronomists. The Manasseh Account (2 Kings 21:1-18) and the Final Chapters of the Deuteronomistic History.* (Oudtestamentische Studiën 38). Leiden.

Konkel, A.H. 1993. The sources of the Story of Hezekiah in the Book of Isaiah. *VT* 43: 462-482.

Lee, T.G. 1993. The Jasper Cylinder Seal of Aššurbanipal and Nabonidus' Making of Sîn's Statue. *RA* 87: 131-136.

Loewenstamm, S.E. 1954. Hena. *Enc. Miqr.* 2: 852 (Hebrew).

Long, B.O. 1991. *2 Kings.* (Forms of Old Testament Literature 10). Grand Rapids.

Machinist, P. 2000. The *Rab Šāqēh* at the Wall of Jerusalem: Israelite Identity in the Face of the Assyrian "Other." *Hebrew Studies* 41: 151-168.

Mayer, W. 1998. Nabonidus Herkunft. In: Dietrich, M. and Loretz, O. eds. *DUBSAR ANTA-MEN, Studien zur Altorientalistik. Festschrift für Willem H.Ph. Römer.* Münster: 245-261.

Montgomery, J.A. 1951. *A Critical and Exegetical Commentary on the Books of Kings* (ICC) Edinburgh.

Na'aman, N. 1991. Chronology and History in the Late Assyrian Empire (631-619 B.C.). *ZA* 81: 243-267.

Na'aman, N. 1995a. Historiography, the Fashioning of the Collective Memory, and the Establishment of Historical Consciousness in Israel in the Late Monarchial Period, *Zion* 60: 449-472 (Hebrew).

Na'aman, N. 1995b. The Debated Historicity of Hezekiah's Reform in the Light of Historical and Archaeological Research. *ZAW* 107: 175-195.

Na'aman, N. 1996. Sources and Composition in the History of David. In: Fritz, V. and Davies P.R. eds. *The Origins of the Ancient Israelite States.* (Journal for the Study of the Old Testament Supplement Series 228). Sheffield: 170-186.

Na'aman, N. 1997a. Sources and Composition in the History of Solomon. In: Handy, L.K. ed. *The Age of Solomon — Scholarship at the Turn of the Millennium.* Leiden: 57-80.

Na'aman, N. 1997b. Prophetic Stories as Sources for the Histories of Jehoshaphat and the Omrides. *Biblica* 78: 153-173.

Na'aman, N. 1998. Royal Inscriptions and the Histories of Joash and Ahaz, Kings of Judah. *VT* 48: 333-349.

Na'aman, N. and Zadok, R. 2000. Assyrian Deportations to the Province of Samerina in the Light of two Cuneiform Tablets from Tel Hadid. *Tel Aviv* 27: 159-188.

Orlinsky, H.M. 1939. The Kings-Isaiah Recensions of the Hezekiah Story. *Jewish Quarterly Review* 30: 33-49.

Person, R.E. 1997. *The Kings — Isaiah and Kings — Jeremiah Recensions.* (Beiheft zur ZAW 252). Berlin.

Redford, D.B. 1999. A Note on the Chronology of Dynasty 25 and the Inscription of Sargon II at Tang-i Var. *Orientalia* 68: 58-60.

Saggs, H.W.F. 1975. Historical Texts and Fragments of Sargon II of Assyria. I. The "Aššur Charter." *Iraq* 37: 11-20.

Šanda, A. 1912. *Die Bücher der Könige übersetzt und erklärt.* 2. Das zweite Buch der Könige. (Exegetisches Handbuch zum Alten Testament 9/2). Münster.

Stade, B. 1886. Miscellen. 16. Anmerkungen zu 2 Kö. 15-21. *ZAW* 6: 156-189.

Streck, M. 1916. *Assurbanipal und die letzten assyrischen Könige bis zum Untergange Niniveh's* II. Leipzig.

Sweeney, M.A. 1996. *Isaiah 1-39 with an Introduction to Prophetic Literature* (Forms of Old Testament Literature 16). Grand Rapids.

Tadmor, H. 1958. The Campaigns of Sargon II of Assur: A Chronological-Historical Study. *JCS* 12: 22–40, 77–100.

Thronveit, M.A. 1987. *When Kings Speak: Royal Speech and Royal Prayer in Chronicles.* (Society of Biblical Literature Dissertation Series 93). Atlanta.

Wildberger, H. 1982. *Jesaja. 3. Jesaja 28-39* (Biblischer Kommentar X/3). Neukirchen-Vluyn.

Williamson, H.G.M. 1977. *Israel in the Books of Chronicles.* Cambridge.

Williamson, H.G.M. 1996. Hezekiah and the Temple. In Fox M.V. et al. eds. *Texts, Temples, and Traditions: A Tribute to Menahem Haran.* Winona Lake: 47–52.

Zadok, R. 1976. Geographical and Onomastic Notes. *Journal of the Ancient Near Eastern Society of Columbia University* 8: 113–126.

Zadok, R. 1985. *Geographical Names According to New- and Late-Babylonian Texts.* (Repertoire Géographique des Textes Cunéiformes 8; Beihefte zum Tübinger Atlas des Vorderen Orients, Reihe B Nr. 7/8). Wiesbaden.

Zawadzki, S. 1988. *The Fall of Assyria and the Median-Babylonian Relations in Light of the Nabopolassar Chronicle.* Poznan and Delft.

Esarhaddon's Treaty with Ba'al and Assyrian Provinces along the Phoenician Coast[1]

1. Text and Interpretation of Paragraph III 18–30

What remains of the treaty between Esarhaddon, king of Assyria, and Ba'al, king of Tyre, is preserved in two fragments, one large and the other small. The text, edited several times in the past (Weidner 1932–33:29–34; Borger 1956:pp. 107–9, with earlier literature; Reiner 1969:533–34; Pettinato 1975:145–60), has recently been collated, transliterated and translated by Parpola and Watanabe as part of a comprehensive edition of all Neo-Assyrian treaties (Parpola and Watanabe 1988:xxix, xlvii, 24–27; Pl. VI). This new edition will serve as a point of departure for my analysis of the text.

A key passage for the discussion of the development of the Assyrian provincial system along the Phoenician coast is column III, lines 18–30 of the treaty. I will open the discussion by suggesting a somewhat different reconstruction and translation of the text.[2]

18 *an-nu-te* KAR^{meš} KASKAL^{meš} *šá* ^{m}*Aš-šur*-PAB-A MAN KUR *Aš-šur a-na* ^{m}*Ba-a-lu* ARAD-*šú ip-qi-*[*du-ni*]

19 *a-na* ^{uru}*A-ku-u* ^{uru}*Du-u'-ri ina na-ge-e* KUR *Pi-liš-te gab-*[*bu*]

20 *ù ina* URU^{meš} *ta-ḫu-me šá* KUR *Aš-šur*^{ki} *šá ši-di tam-tim gab-*[*bu*]

21 *ù ina* ^{uru}*Gu-ub-lu* KUR *Lab-na-*[*na*] URU^{meš} *šá ina* KUR-*i gab-*[*bu*]

"These are the ports of trade and the trade routes which Esarhaddon, king of Assyria, en[trusted] to his servant Ba'al: to Acco, Dor, to the entire district of the Philistines, and to all the cities within Assyrian territory on the seacoast, and to Gubla, the Lebanon, all the cities in the mountains."

---

1. Reprinted with permission. *Rivista di Studi Fenici* 22 (1994), 3-8.

2. Col. III, lines 11-12 may tentatively be reconstructed thus: "[If a ship carrying a messenger$^{?}$], which comes to you, [shall contact you], do not listen to his (the messenger's) [wo]rds; without the royal deputy [do not meet him]."

22 am-mar URU^{meš} [šá ^{m}Aš-š]ur-PAB-AŠ MAN KUR *Aš-šur* ^{m}Ba-a-lu URU^{meš} [šá$^{?}$]
23 KUR Ṣur-ra-a-a pit-ti šá ^{m}*Aš-šur*-PAB-AŠ MAN KUR *Aš-šur*[^{ki}] i-din [am-mar$^{?}$ *šá*$^{?}$]
24 ina ŠÀ ^{giš}MÁ^{meš}-šú-nu

"Of all the cities of Esarhaddon, king of Assyria, he gave Ba'al the cities of the Tyrians (located) in the territory of Esarhaddon, king of Assyria, [and everything that is] on their ships."

24 ù am-mar e-r[a]b-u-ni ina ŠÀ URU^{meš} šá ^{m}[Ba-a-lu]
25 URU^{meš}-šú URU.E^{meš}-šú KAR^{meš}-šú šá a-na na-še-e [x x x x x x x]
26 am-mar a-ḫi-ta-te-šú-nu-u-ni ki-i šá ina la-bi-[ri KUR Ṣi-du-na-a-a]
27 in-na-ga-ru-u-ni me-me-ni pi-ir-k[u x x x x x x x x]
28 ina ŠÀ ^{giš}MÁ^{meš}-šú-nu la I-ḫa-ṭi

"And everyone who enters into the towns of [Ba'al] — his cities, his villages, his ports of trade — for carrying [beams$^{?}$ of cedar$^{?}$ and juniper$^{?}$] in all their outskirts, as [the Sidonians] have agreed in the past, nobody [will cause them] injustice [and] nobody will do harm to their ships."

28 ina ŠÀ K[UR ṣur-ri URU^{meš}-šú ù KAR^{meš}-šú]
29 ina na-ge-ú URU.E^{meš}-šú e-kil$^{?}$-tu [šá . . .]
30 ki-i šá la-bi-ri KUR ṣi-du-[na-a-a in-na-ga-ru-u-ni x x x x]

"In the la[nd of Tyre — his cities and his ports of trade], in his district (and) in his villages — expended$^{???}$ [. . .], as the Sido[nians have agreed] in the past [. . .]."

Notes:

Line 23: For the restoration, see lines 16–17.

Line 25: The restoration is *ad sensum*. The carrying of logs of trees fits well the context. What else may be carried from the outskirts of all the towns of the land of Tyre?

Line 26: The restoration is based on the text of line 30.

Line 28: The restoration is based on the text of lines 24–25.

Line 29: The interpretation of the line is extremely tentative, assuming that *ekiltu* is a variant form of *akiltu* "expended goods."

Line 30: The restoration is based on lines 26–27.

The translated passage may be divided into two parts. The first section (lines 18–21) refers to the free access that Esarhaddon granted (verb *paqādu)* Ba'al to all Assyrian ports of trade along the eastern coast of the Mediterranean. The second section (lines 22–30) refers to former Assyrian cities that Esarhaddon gave (verb *nadānu*) to Ba'al and the regulations that are applied to this new Tyrian territory. Its first clause (lines 24–28) regulates the operation of groups entering the land of Tyre for cutting and carrying logs of trees. Its second clause (lines 28–30) is fragmentary; only tentatively (with a big question mark) may one assume that it refers to the obligation of the Tyrians to supply perishables to Assyrian expeditions.

The two clauses refer to the entire area of the continental Tyrian territory, and the stipulations are contracted "as the Sidonians have agreed in the past." This is an indication that the territory was part of the kingdom of Sidon before it was transferred to Ba'al. Indeed, the inscriptions of Esarhaddon explicitly state that areas of the former kingdom of Sidon were annexed to the territory of Tyre:

"From among those cities which belonged to him (i.e., Abdi-milkutti) I assigned Ma'rubbu and Ṣariptu in the hands of Ba'al, king of Tyre, and imposed upon him, in addition to the previous yearly tax, a tribute of my lordship" (Borger 1956:49, lines 15–19).

The increase of the yearly tax is not mentioned in the surviving parts of the treaty. The above-mentioned two clauses, rather, suggest that with the transfer of the area from the former kingdom of Sidon to Tyre certain obligations remained unchanged. The past agreement of the Sidonians probably refers to the treaty of Sennacherib with Ithoba'al (Tuba'il), king of Sidon, a treaty concluded when the continental areas of Luli (Eloulaios), king of Tyre, were separated and assigned to the newly established kingdom of Sidon (Katzenstein 1973:246–252). It seems that the transfer of territories in the days of Sennacherib and Esarhaddon was accompanied by the conclusion of treaties, each treaty establishing the relation of Assyria with the newly delineated kingdom.

The date of the treaty being considered here can be determined accurately. In the Prism class Nin. B, composed in year 676 BCE, only the building of Kār-Esarhaddon, the transfer of deportees there and the nomination of officers as governors in the new city are mentioned (Heidel 1956:12, lines 31–37; Borger 1956:49). The annexation of the district of Sidon, the deportation to the towns of the new province and the cession of Ma'arubbu and Sarepta to Ba'al are mentioned only in the Prism class Nin. A, written in 673 BCE (Borger 1956:48–49, III 1–9, 15–19).[3] It is evident that the reorganization of the new province, the transfer of deportees to its towns and the assignment of the two towns to Ba'al took place in 675–674 BCE, a few years after the destruc-

3. For the identification of Ma'arubbu at Ma'arub, 14 km northeast of Tyre and three km south of the Liṭani river, see Lipiński 1993:161*.

tion of the city of Sidon and the foundation of Kār-Esarhaddon. The treaty of Esarhaddon with Baʿal, in which the cession of the former Sidonian territory is mentioned, must have been concluded at that time.

2. The System of Assyrian Provinces along the Phoenician Coast

The development of the system of Assyrian provinces along the Phoenician coast can be re-examined against this background. Two inferences may be made from the above-cited passage:

(a) The two towns granted to Baʿal in 675/74 are located north of the Liṭani river, and this may indicate that the town of Ushu and its area were already included within the territory of the kingdom of Tyre. Otherwise, the transfer of towns located north of the Liṭani, far away from the island of Tyre, does not make territorial sense. Ushu was already part of the kingdom of Tyre in the Late Bronze Age and served as a source of supply for the island. When Ushu fell into the hands of the king of Sidon, the king of Tyre, Abi-Milku, wrote to the Pharaoh as follows (*EA* 148:26–34): "May the king give attention to his servant, and may he charge his commissioner to give Usu to his servant for water, for fetching wood, for straw, for clay." It seems probable to me that sometime after Sennacherib's campaign of 701 BCE, Baʿal of Tyre submitted to him and received in exchange the area around Ushu. One must remember that there are no Assyrian sources for the history of Syria-Palestine for most of Sennacherib's reign, so that the non-mention of the relations of Baʿal with Assyria in Sennacherib's late years is understandable.

(b) The cities of Acco and Dor are mentioned among the ports of trade that the Tyrian ships may enter. This is a clear indication that Acco was not included in the territory of Baʿal (Alt 1937:69 n. 2). Alt suggested both that it was annexed to the province of Megiddo, which, thereby, acquired an exit to the Mediterranean and that Acco may have become that province's capital (Alt 1937:68–71). The suggestion seems quite unlikely to me. Acco had been a city of the kingdom of Tyre from the tenth century BCE onward and was never part of the district of Galilee. Furthermore, an examination of the system of Assyrian provinces in Syria-Palestine reveals that the coastal districts were systematically separated from the interior, without exception. Therefore, I would suggest that, like the province of Dor, Acco became the seat of an Assyrian governor, either in the late years of Sennacherib or in the early days of Esarhaddon. It seems that the geo-physical structure of the coastal region, which is cut by river estuaries and along which several important cities were located, led to the establishment of a chain of relatively small provinces, just as the same environmental conditions had led to the development of a chain of city-states of medium size in the second millennium BCE.

The treaty of Esarhaddon and Ba'al did not last long. Ba'al was accused of cooperation with Taharqa, king of Egypt, and, on its way to Egypt in 671 BCE, the Assyrian army blockaded the island of Tyre (Borger 1956:112, lines 12–14). Following Assyria's successful campaign in Egypt, Ba'al surrendered and was severely punished: "I took away from him his cities on the mainland, [my officers as governors I pl]aced [over them] and turned it into Assyrian territory" (Borger 1956:110, rev. 9–10). In another text, these events are described thus: "I conquered Tyre . . . and took away from its king Ba'al, who relied on Taharqa, king of Egypt, all his cities and possessions" (Borger 1956:86, lines 7–8).

To which province were the former areas of Ba'al annexed? There can be no certainty in this matter. A certain Bel-shadu'a, "prefect (*šaknu*) of Tyre," is mentioned in the colophon of an oracular text (K 1292) (Zimmern 1910:169, n. 12; Ungnad 1938:446), and Forrer suggested identifying him with Bel-ḫarran-shadu'a, the prefect of Kār-Esarhaddon (Forrer 1920:66, 70; Ungnad 1938:428, 446; Elayi 1983:56). He, thus, assumed that the areas of Ba'al were added to the province of Kār-Esarhaddon. However, the identification of the two figures is quite unlikely, as they differ in name and district. Another possibility is that the area of Tyre was organized as an independent province bordering the districts of Acco and Kār-Esarhaddon. It seems preferable, however, to assume that the former areas of Ba'al were attached to the Assyrian territories in the Acco plain and that "Tyre" in the prefect's title is the official name of the new province. It would have covered the area between Mount Carmel in the south and either the Liṭani river, or Nahr Zahrani in the north, bordering on the province of Kār-Esarhaddon, whose territory reached northward up to Nahr Beirut or Nahr el-Kalb. The latter river delineated the southern border of the kingdom of Gubla, and one may tentatively suggest that the small kingdom of Samsimuruna was situated not far away from its estuary.[4]

The reorganization of the new province took place either in the late years of Esarhaddon or in the early years of Ashurbanipal and, as far as we know, was the final step in the Assyrian annexation of the former Phoenician territories. Only two mainland kingdoms, Gubla and Samsimuruna, survived the thrust of Assyrian annexation and, alongside them, the tiny kingdoms of Tyre and Arvad whose islands protected them.

Following his campaign against the Arabs ca. 644 BCE, Ashurbanipal suppressed a rebellion in the towns of Ushu and Acco. He killed the rebels and

4. This may be inferred from letter ND 2370, lines 3-6. See Saggs 1963: 76-77; Parpola 1970: 303. The name of the town of Ḫariṣu was possibly preserved in the village's name, Ḥariṣṣa, about 2.5 km. east of Jounie; cf. Baer 1960: 155-58.

deported many of the towns' inhabitants (Streck 1916:80–83, lines 115–128). The simultaneous rebellion and severe punishment of the two towns may corroborate my assumption that both were included in the same province and were possibly the central towns in its northern and southern regions.[5]

Overall, six Assyrian provinces were located along the eastern Mediterranean coast in the late Assyrian empire. The northern provinces of Kullani and Ṣimirra were founded by Tiglath-pileser III in 738 BCE (Kessler 1975:49–63). The province of Kār-Esarhaddon was established by Esarhaddon in 676/75, and the province of Tyre was reorganized either by Esarhaddon in his late years or by Ashurbanipal in his early years. The province of Dor, bounded by the Yarkon river in the south and Mount Carmel in the north, was founded by Tiglath-pileser III in 732 BCE (Forrer 1920: 52, 54, 59–60, 69; Alt 1929:234–237; Na'aman 1986: 184–186 and n. 28). The province of Ashdod was annexed by Sargon II in 711 BCE, possibly as the first step in a plan to create a corridor to the Egyptian border. His death in the battlefield (705 BCE) brought his plans to an end. His heir, Sennacherib, adopted a different policy and restored a king to the throne of Ashdod. Thus, Ashdod remained an isolated Assyrian province on the Philistine coast, having an Assyrian governor side by side with a local king (Alt 1945:141–146; Na'aman 1979:71–72, n. 7). It is obvious that no overall plan guided the Assyrian kings in their handling of the coastal districts and that the system of Assyrian provinces along the Mediterranean coast developed in stages, according to the individual policies of successive Assyrian rulers.

References

Alt, A. 1929. Das System der Assyrischen Provinzen auf dem Boden des Reiches Israel. *ZDPV* 52: 220–242. (Reprint: Alt 1953: 188–205).

Alt, A. 1937. Galiläische Probleme. *PJB* 33:52–88. (Reprint: Alt 1953: 363–395).

Alt, A. 1945. Neue assyrische Nachrichten über Palästina und Syrien. ZDPV 67: 128–159. (Reprint: Alt 1953: 226–241).

Alt, A. 1953. *Kleine Schriften zur Geschichte des Volkes Israel* II. München.

Baer, A. 1960. Un cylindre d'offrande à Sennachérib. *RA* 54: 155–58.

Borger, R. 1956. *Die Inschriften Asarhaddons Königs von Assyrien.* Graz.

Elayi, J. 1983. Les cités Phéniciennes et l'empire Assyrien à l'époque d'Assurbanipal. *RA.* 77: 45–58.

5. A fragment of clay tablet was found at Tell Keisan, southeast of Acco. It records the distribution of rations to persons whose names are not preserved intact. See Sigrist 1982: 32-35. The tablet may reflect provisioning of foreign deportees at the site, either by Esarhaddon or by Ashurbanipal. See Na'aman 1993: 117.

Forrer, E. 1920. *Die Provinzeinteilung des assyrischen Reiches.* Leipzig.

Heidel, A. 1956. A New Hexagonal Prism of Esarhaddon (676 B.C.). *Sumer* 12: 9–37.

Katzenstein, H.J. 1973. *The History of Tyre, from the Beginning of the Second Millennium B.C.E. until the Fall of the Neo-Babylonian Empire in 538 B.C.E.* Jerusalem.

Kessler, K. 1975. Die Anzahl der assyrischen Provinzen des Jahres 738 v. Chr. in Nordsyrien. *WO* 8: 49–63.

Lipiński, E. 1991. The Territory of Tyre and the Tribe of Asher. In: Lipiński, E. ed. *Phoenicia and the Bible. Proceedings of the Conference Held at the University of Leuven on the 15th and 16th March 1990.* (Orientalia Lovaniensia Analecta 44; Studia Phoenicia XI). Leuven: 153–166.

Na'aman, N. 1979. The Brook of Egypt and Assyrian Policy on the Border of Egypt. *Tel Aviv* 6: 68–90.

Na'aman, N. 1986. *Borders and Districts in Biblical Historiography.* Jerusalem.

Na'aman, N. 1993. Population Changes in Palestine following Assyrian Deportations. *Tel Aviv* 20: 104–124.

Parpola, S. 1970. *Neo-Assyrian Toponyms.* (AOAT 6). Kevelaer and Neukirchen-Vluyn.

Parpola, S. and Watanabe, K. 1988. *Neo-Assyrian Treaties and Loyalty Oaths.* (State Archives of Assyria II). Helsinki.

Pettinato, G. 1975. I rapporti politici di Tiro con l'Assiria alla luce del "trattato tra Asarhaddon e Baal." *Rivista di Studi Fenici* 3: 145–60.

Reiner, E. 1969. Akkadian Treaties from Syria and Assyria. In: *ANET*: 531–541.

Saggs, H.W.F. 1963. The Nimrud Letters, 1952 — Part VI. *Iraq* 25: 70–80.

Sigrist, M. 1982. Une tablette cuneiforme de Tell Keisan. *IEJ* 32: 32–35.

Streck, M. 1916. *Assurbanipal und die letzten Assyrischen Könige bis zum Untergange Niniveh's* II. Leipzig.

Ungnad, A. 1938. Eponymen. *RLA* II: 412–457.

Weidner, E.F. 1932–33. Der Staatsvertrag Aššurnirâris VI. von Assyrien mit Mati'ilu von Bît-Agusi. *AfO* 8: 17–34.

Zimmern, H. 1910. Gilgameŝ-Omina und Gilgsameŝ-Orakel. *ZA* 24: 166–178.

Population Changes in Palestine Following Assyrian Deportations[1]

Mass deportations employed by the Assyrians for various ends (e.g., political, military, demographic, economic) have been studied many times in the past and are the subject of a special monograph (Oded 1979). Assyrian and biblical references to "two-way" deportations — from Palestine to foreign countries and/or from foreign countries to Palestine — likewise have been discussed in detail. Nevertheless, there is still the need for a comprehensive historical discussion of the role these deportations played within the policy of Assyrian kings and the effect of the deportations on the land, its districts and its inhabitants. To achieve a better understanding of these issues, a number of points must be clarified:

(1) How did the geo-political position of Palestine influence the Assyrian policy of deportation into this area?

(2) Did different Assyrian rulers employ a consistent policy over time, or are there differences of policy between various rulers?

(3) What are the numerical ratios between deportations to the land and from it? Was "two-way" deportation consistently carried out, or were there areas in which only "one-way" deportations took place?

(4) What effects did the deportations have on the demographics and economics of the various regions of the land?

The many new excavations and surveys that have been conducted throughout Israel recently comprise an important source for the discussion. The archaeological work enables us, for the first time, to suggest a reasonable estimation of the population size in various parts of the land (Broshi and Finkelstein 1990) and to analyze the demographic and settlement changes that took place throughout history. The archaeological evidence can be combined now with the data derived from the written sources (Assyrian, biblical and epigraphic documents) for a much better understanding of the effects that the Assyrian deportations had on the demography, economy and culture of Palestine in the late 8th–7th centuries BCE.

---

1. Reprinted with permission. *Tel Aviv* 20 (1993), 104–124.

Deportations in the Time of Tiglath-pileser III (745–727 BCE)

Southern Syria and Palestine were conquered by Tiglath-pileser III during his campaigns in 734–732 BCE. Parts of the occupied areas were annexed to Assyria, and other parts became vassal kingdoms of Assyria. Deportations from captured territories took place following their conquest. The deportation is described in the book of Kings (2 Kgs. 15:29) as follows: "In the days of Pekah, king of Israel, Tiglath-pileser, king of Assyria, came and captured Ijon, Abel-beth-maacah, Janoah, Kedesh, Hazor, Gilead, and Galilee, all the land of Naphtali; and he carried the people captive to Assyria." Further references to the capture of Galilee and Gilead appear in Judg. 18:30 and 1 Chr. 5:6, 26.

These deportations must have comprised the first stage in the process of annexation and the establishment of new Assyrian provinces in the areas of Galilee, Dor and Gilead (Forrer 1920:59–63; Alt 1929). No clear reference to such annexation appears in the surviving inscriptions of Tiglath-pileser III, and some scholars have expressed doubts as to the date of the foundation of the three Assyrian provinces (Eph'al 1979:285–286; Tadmor 1982:424). However, one of Tiglath-pileser's summary inscriptions (Rost 1893:38 lines 227–228; Na'aman 1986a:72 and n. 5) may help resolve this matter. The inscription is badly broken, but may safely be restored thusly: "[The land of Bit Ḫumri, which] in my former campaigns I razed [to the ground all its cities, all its people and] its [ca]ttle I had carried away as booty, the town of Samaria I le[ft] alone. [Pekah], their king, [they . . .]." This is a transparent allusion to an annexation that took place at the same time as the annexation of Damascus, Israel's northern neighbor and ally in the rebellion against Assyria (Tadmor 1962). Noteworthy is the fact that, in the inscriptions of Sargon II, only the annexation of Samaria is mentioned, which fits well the assumption that the rest of the kingdom was already part of the Assyrian provincial system. We may conclude that, following the campaigns of 734–732, Tiglath-pileser annexed the northern areas of the Israelite kingdom and only the hill country of Samaria remained in the hands of Hosea, its last king.

In two badly broken, parallel (but not identical) passages in the annals of Tiglath-pileser III, the following descriptions appear:

(a) "[I razed to the gr]ou[nd xx cities] of the 16 districts of the land of Bit [Ḫumri . . . xx captives of the city of Da]bara, 625 captives of the city [of GN, . . . xx captives of the city of] Ḫinatuna, 650 captives of the city of Ku[. . .,[2] . . . xx Captives of the city of Ya]tbite, 650 captives of the city of Sa[mḫuna, . . .],

2. A possible restoration for the toponym is Chisloth-tabor/Chesulloth (Josh. 19:12,18), which is located near Daberath (Josh. 19:12).

Aruma, Marom, [. . .]." (Rost 1893:38, 229–234, Pl. XVIIIb; Forrer 1920:60–61; Tadmor 1967:62–64; Na'aman 1986a:73).

(b) ". . . 13,520 [people . . .] together with their possessions, [their cattle and sheep I had carried away as booty. I had them cross?] difficult mountains [and brought them to the land of . . .]." (Rost 1893:Pl. XVIIIa; Tadmor 1967:64, 66; Na'aman 1986a:73).

The relation of the number 13,520 to the other small numbers is unknown. Following Tadmor (1967:66–67), we may assume that this is the overall number of the exiles carried from the entire area.

All the towns mentioned in the text are situated in Lower Galilee and along the margins of the Jezreel valley: Dabara (i.e., biblical Daberath) is located near Mt. Tabor; Samḫuna (i.e., biblical Shimᶜon/Shimron) is located on the northwestern margins of the Jezreel valley; Marom is identified with Tell Qarnei Ḥiṭṭin in Lower Galilee (Na'aman 1986b:122–25); and Ḫinatuna (Ḫannathon), Yatbite (Yoṭbah) and Aruma (Rumah) are all located near the Beth-neṭophah valley (Sahl el-Baṭṭof). The toponyms cover a well-defined area, and, if 13,520 is indeed the overall number of exiles, then a considerable part of the population of this area was deported by Tiglath-pileser.

The evidence from the detailed survey conducted in Lower Galilee corresponds well with our historical data. There is a remarkable decline of settlement in Lower Galilee in the late 8th–7th (and possibly 6th) centuries BCE (Gal 1988–89, 56–64). The excavations conducted at Hazor and Chinnereth (Tell el-'Oreimeh) have indicated a significant destruction and a long period of desolation at this time (Yadin 1972; Fritz 1986:22–26). (For the survey of Abel-beth-maacah, see Dever 1986:215–21.)

Why did the Assyrians not resettle the Galilee region, as they did in other parts of the country? The answer may be sought in the marginality of the area within the confines of the Assyrian empire and the relatively poor economic potential of the area. The city of Megiddo, the capital of the province of Galilee, was rebuilt and restored on a large scale, and a large "Assyrian residence"was built there (Lamon and Shipton 1939:69–74; Amiran and Dunayevsky 1958; Fritz 1979:64–67). Deportees may well have been settled in the newly rebuilt city. Other Assyrian residences have been discovered both at Ayyelet ha-Shaḥar near Tel Hazor (Reich 1975; Lipschitz 1990:96–99) and at Tell el-ᶜOreimeh (Fritz 1986:30–31). Additional buildings may well be discovered in the future. However, the Assyrians apparently regarded most of the area of Galilee as unimportant — both economically and politically. Thus, following deportation of part of the population, the Galilee was left in a state of partial abandonment and desolation.

Deportations under Sargon II (721–705 BCE)

(A) Deportations from Palestine:

Upon the death of Shalmaneser V and the accession of Sargon II, rebellions broke out in various parts of the empire, and well-established provinces in the west joined Yaubi'di of Hamath in his war against Assyria. Sargon first quashed the internal revolt in Assyria and secured his throne. He then conducted a short campaign against the Elamites, who had come to the aid of Merodach-baladan. In the same year (720 BCE), he moved into Syria to quell the rebellion. Near Qarqar, Sargon vanquished Yaubi'di and his allies and conquered the rebellious Syrian provinces. He then moved southward, captured Gaza, and, near Raphia, smote the Egyptian troops that had hastened to help the alliance. In the course of the campaign, he captured Samaria, which had joined the rebellion against Assyria, deported its people, and turned it into an Assyrian province. (For the controversy over the date of the conquest of Samaria by the Assyrians, see Tadmor 1958:33–40; Na'aman 1990; Becking 1992:21–59; Hayes and Kuan 1991, with earlier literature.) The capture of Samaria is described in the Nimrud prism (Gadd 1954:179, 181–82 and pls. XLV–XLVI; Tadmor 1958:34):

> I fought with them (the Samarians) and I counted as spoil 27,280 people who lived therein, with their chariots and the Gods of their trust. 200 chariots for my royal bodyguard I mustered from among them, and the rest of them I settled in the midst of Assyria. The city of Samaria I resettled and made it greater than before. People of the lands conquered by my own hands I brought there. My courtier I placed over them as a governor and I counted them with Assyrians.

According to biblical tradition (2 Kgs. 17:6; 18:11), the deportees were settled "in Halah, and on the Habor, the river of Gozan, and in the cities of the Medes." Halah (Assyrian Ḫalaḫḫa) was a district north of Nineveh, and Gozan was situated on one of the branches of the Habor river in northern Mesopotamia. The cities of the Medes were located in the Zagros region, where Sargon had conducted campaigns in 716–713 BCE (Na'aman and Zadok 1988:38–40; Diakonoff 1991:16–18). The large number of deportees (27,280) indicates that they were taken from the district of Samaria, rather than the city itself.[3]

Following his victory over the Egyptian troops near Raphia, Sargon deported the rebellious king of Gaza, destroyed and burned the city of Raphia, and led away 9,033 of its people as prisoners. The large number indicates that

3. For the Samarians deported to Assyria, see Dalley 1985: 31–48; Zadok 1985: 567; Eph'al 1991: 40–45, with earlier literature.

the deportees were taken from the district of Raphia, rather than the city itself.

In 711 BCE, the Assyrian army again marched to the coast of Philistia to suppress the rebellion of Yamani, king of Ashdod (Alt 1945:141–146; Tadmor 1958:79–80, 83–84; Spalinger 1973; Kapera 1972–73; 1987). The result of the revolt is described in one of Sargon's summary inscription, as follows:

> I besieged and conquered the cities of Ashdod, Gath and Ashdod-Yam. His gods, his wife, his children, all the possessions and the treasures of his palace as well as the inhabitants of his country I counted as spoil. These cities I rebuilt anew and settled therein people from the regions of the east that I had conquered. I installed an officer of mine over them and counted them with the inhabitants of Assyria and they bore my yoke.

Samaria and Ashdod suffered the same consequences of Assyrian conquest and annexation: "two-way" deportation and the rebuilding of the captured city as a provincial center. The number of exiles led from Samaria is accurately recorded, but the origin of the deportees transferred to the new province is missing. Conversely, the number of deportees taken from Ashdod is not recorded, but it is stated explicitly that deportees from the eastern regions were transferred to Ashdod. Inasmuch as Sargon had conducted campaigns to the Iranian plateau in the years that preceded his campaign against Ashdod, the exiles settled in the province of Ashdod most probably came from these eastern areas.

(B) Deportations to Palestine

In two badly broken prisms from Nineveh and Ashur, a partially reconstructable description appears in a passage that concludes the campaign of 716 BCE to the Zagros region (Weidner 1941–41:44; Tadmor 1958:77–8; Na'aman 1979:71):

> . . . (people) from the land [GN I deported and in] a land whose [place they have never known, in the city of GN_2] situated on the border of the Brook of Eg[ypt, territory which is located on the shore of the] Western [Sea] I set[tled them. Into the hand of PN], the sheikh of Laban, [I entrusted them].

Elsewhere, I have suggested both that Naḥal Besor (Wādi Ghazzeh and Wādi Shelaleh) should be identified with the Brook of Egypt mentioned both in the Bible and the Assyrian royal inscriptions, and that exiles were settled by Sargon II in its vicinity, possibly at Arza (Tell Jemmeh) (Na'aman 1979: 71, 74–77).[4] Some new epigraphic data that was recently discussed in detail

4. In his book of the history of Israel, Donner (1984–86:306, n. 18) writes: "N. Na'aman . . . idenzifiert den 'Bach von Ägypten' mit dem in 1. Sam 30,9f.21 genannten Naḥal Besor, von

(Na'aman and Zadok 1988) may now be added in support of this view and will be presented here briefly.

During the renewed excavations at Tell Jemmeh, a site located on the Besor river, 10 km. south of Gaza, two ostraca were unearthed, dated stratigraphically to the late 8th–early 7th century BCE, and published by Naveh (1985:11–15, 20–21). Both ostraca contain name lists. Each line has two names that represent a patronymic relationship: PN_1 (son of) PN_2. On ostracon No. 2, the first name in each line is broken. The second name is followed by quantities of goods. On ostracon No. 1, five of the first names are West Semitic, and all the other names, many of which end with *shin*, are etymologically non-Semitic. Thus, the West Semitic names can be determined to be names of sons, and all 11 patronyms occurring on the two ostraca are non-Semitic. This pattern of name distribution is typical in immigrant communities: the parents bear names of their homeland, but the second generation has local names, adapted to the new environment.

Tell Jemmeh was an important Assyrian center in the 7th century BCE, which probably served as the seat of the military governor of the area of the Besor river (Van Beek 1973; 1977:171–76; 1983:12–19; Amiran and Van Beek 1976:547–48). As Tell Jemmeh was an Assyrian military and administrative center, it is logical to assume that the non-Semitic immigrants whose names end with *shin* were deportees brought to the place by the Assyrians. The two prisms cited above mentioned the settlement of exiles near the Brook of Egypt as the last episode of Sargon II's campaign of 716 BCE to the Zagros mountains, and it is clear that the exiles must have come from these newly conquered areas. The episode illustrates the motif of transferring people from the easternmost border of the empire (the Zagros regions) to its southwesternmost limit (the Brook of Egypt).

When the name lists on the Tell Jemmeh ostraca are analyzed in this light, at least three names could be Iranian, and three others may be Kassite. The number of non-Indo-Iranian names originating in the Zagros mountains may be higher (Na'aman and Zadok 1988:40–42). Information on the Iranian and pre-Iranian ethnic composition of the Zagros region in the 8th century BCE is scanty, and, thus, the number of identifiable names is quite remarkable. We may conclude that in 716 BCE (or shortly afterwards), Iranians and/or pre-Iranians were transferred and settled near the Brook of Egypt (the Besor

---

dem freilich niemand genau weisst, wo er zu suchen ist." Curiously, Donner has not realized that Naḥal Besor is the modern Hebrew name of Arabic Wādi Ghazzeh and Wādi Shallaleh. Its identification with Naḥal Besor mentioned in 1 Sam. 30 is irrelevant to the discussion.

river) and that some groups were settled in Tell Jemmeh, the main Assyrian center on its border with Egypt.

The deportation from the Zagros region to the Egyptian border was the first in a series of deportations conducted in the time of Saron II.

(a) In the Annals from Khorsabad describing his seventh *palû*, Sargon wrote the following (Lie 1929:20–23, lines 120–23):

> With the help of the god Ashur, my lord, I defeated (the tribes of) Thamud, Ibadidi, Marsimani and Ḫayapa, the far-off Arabs who are dwelling in the desert, concerning whom neither governor nor warden had any knowledge, who had not brought any king their tribute. The rest of them I removed and in Samaria I caused them to dwell.

This episode is linked with the receipt of "tribute" (that is, a gift) from the Egyptian Pharaoh; from Samsi, queen of the Arabs; and Ita'amra, the Sabaean (lines 123–25). The campaign against the Arabs and the sending of the tribute would best be dated to 715 BCE (Na'aman and Zadok 1988:43). (For dating the episode to 716 BCE, see Tadmor 1958:78; Eph'al 1982:37–39.) This passage indicates that the first deportation to Samaria took place five years after its conquest and annexation.

(b) The deportation of people "from the countries of the east that I had conquered" to Ashdod (712 BCE) was mentioned above. The deportees probably came from the Iranian plateau, where Sargon had conducted several campaigns in the years 716–713 BCE.

(c) The major deportation to Samaria is related in 2 Kgs. 17:24 thus:

> And the king of Assyria brought people from Babylonia, Cuthah, Avva, Hamath, and Sepharvaim, and placed them in the cities of Samaria instead of the people of Israel; and they took possession of Samaria and dwelt in its cities.

Some scholars have assumed that the Assyrian practice of exile was too widespread to allow the precise dating of the deportation from the reported homelands in the passage (Burney 1903:333–35; Montgomery 1951: 472). Others, however, have used the list of countries of origin to pinpoint the reign of a certain king. Winckler (1892:97–107) assigned the deportation to Ashurbanipal, assuming that the text reflects an inadvertent confusion between the exile conducted by Sargon and that by Ashurbanipal. His suggestion was accepted by other scholars (e.g., Streck 1916:CCCLXIV–CCCLXVII; see Olmstead 1908:73, n. 39). Tadmor, on the other hand (1969:137; 1983:4–8), has suggested that Sargon pursued a policy of reconciliation toward Babylonia, serving concurrently as king of Assyria and Babylonia. In his opinion, this situation precludes identification of Sargon as the anonymous king who deported people from Babylon and Cuthah. Instead, he has identified the anonymous king with Sennacherib, who exiled Babylonians in large numbers after his conquest of 689 BCE (see Cogan 1974:101, n. 23; Eph'al 1991:40).

Contrary to previous belief, Driver (1958) and Zadok (1976) have demonstrated that none of the new settlers listed in 2 Kgs. 17:24 came from Syria. Of the five places of origin named, Babylon and Cuthah are well-known Babylonian temple cities, and Avva was situated on the Uqnu river, near the Babylonian-Elamite borderland. Hamath was probably the name of both a tribe and a town situated not far from Avva. Sepharvaim was probably a settlement in the Chaldean territory of Bit Awukani. All these areas were conquered by Sargon II during his campaign against Merodach-baladan in the years 710–709 BCE. Thus, any assumption that Sargon was unable to deport people from the five toponyms listed in verse 24 is untenable. Moreover, the propagandistic tone of the royal inscriptions should not blur the historical reality: Sargon most probably took the opportunity during his campaigns to remove his opponents from the major Babylonian cities and to resettle them in remote areas of his empire, just as he deported 6,300 Assyrians and settled them in the new province of Hamath in his early years (see Finet 1973:12–13, n. 48). According to Sargon's inscriptions, 90,580 Arameans and Chaldeans were deported from the tribal areas of Babylonia to various sectors of Western Asia. Some were deported to Melid and Kummuh (Lie 1926: 72–73, lines 9–10). Postgate (1973:29) has suggested that deportees from several Babylonian temple cities (Babylon, Borsippa, Nippur) were deported to Cilicia (Que) by Sargon. The list of settlers in Samaria in 2 Kgs. 17:24, which includes people from both the Babylonian temple cities (Babylon and Cuthah) and from the peripheral areas (Avva, Hamath and Sepharvaim), fits well with all the known data of Sargon's campaigns against Babylonia and most likely refers to his time (see Becking 1981:79–80; 1992:95–102; Brinkman 1984:52, n. 242).

It seems that 2 Kgs. 17:24 originally followed verse 6 of the same chapter and was detached by a later author, who wrote a polemical composition against the Samarians (Na'aman 1990:222 and n. 50). Verse 6b described the deportation of people from Israel, following the conquest of Samaria by Sargon II (vv. 5–6a), and verse 24 proceeded to describe the deportation of people to the newly founded province (Na'aman 1990:218–25). Thus, verses 6 and 24 originally recounted Sargon's conquest of Samaria and the subsequent "two-way" deportation: from Samaria to northern Mesopotamia and Media and from Babylonia and its peripheral areas to Samaria.

Certain names in the town list of Benjamin in Josh. 18:21–24 reflect the settlement of group(s) of deportees in southern Mt. Ephraim. Avvim in verse 23 was obviously named for the exiles from Avva who had been settled in the district of Bethel (Na'aman 1986:229–30, n. 47). It is also possible that *kpr* *h*^{c}*mny* and *h*^{c}*pny* in verse 24 are settlements named after groups of exiles who were brought in from some distant places (Na'aman 1991:25, n. 25). The town list of Benjamin may be dated safely to the time of King Josiah (Na'aman: 23–33, with earlier literature), reflecting the deportation conducted by Sargon to the Bethel district. This deportation is referred to in the polemical narrative in 2 Kgs. 17:24–33. The settlement of *kpr ksdyh*, which is mentioned in the Rehob synagogue inscription of the 6th or beginning 7th century CE (modern Khirbet Kashde southwest of Ṭubas), also may have been named after Chaldean exiles ("the Chaldeans' village") who were transferred to the place by an Assyrian king, possibly Sargon II (Zadok 1985:569).

We may conclude that, in 720–708 BCE, the Assyrians deported thousands of local inhabitants from Samaria and the coast of Philistia to various parts of the Assyrian empire. In their place, Sargon transferred various population groups: peoples from the Zagros region were settled near the Besor river (the Brook of Egypt) and, possibly, also in the kingdom of Ashdod. Other groups from Babylonia and from the Syro-Arabian desert were settled in the Samaria hill country, as far south as the area of Bethel. There is a marked difference between the policy of Tiglath-pileser III and that of Sargon II. The former deported local inhabitants of the newly established provinces, but did not settle others in their places. The latter, on the other hand, conducted two-way deportations, bringing new deportees in place of the local exiles and making an effort to settle at least part of the deserted places.

Of particular importance are Sargon's efforts to ensure Assyrian control in areas near the Egyptian border. In the Nimrud prism, he wrote: "I opened the sealed har[bor] of Egypt. The Assyrians and Egyptians I mingled together and I made them trade with each other" (Tadmor 1958:34). The well-planned and fortified settlement at Ruqeish, near Deir el-Balah, south of the Besor river, extended over an area of ca. 20–25 acres. According to the excavators, it was founded in the late 8th century BCE (Oren et al. 1986), probably by Sargon II. The building of a new city necessitates the transfer of population groups to inhabit the place, and it seems that some of the deportees brought to the area of the Brook of Egypt in 716 BCE were settled here. We may, thus, suggest that Ruqeish (whose ancient name remains unknown) was founded in that year. It developed further in the 7th century, becoming an important maritime center on the southern coast of Philistia until the late Persian period.

The establishment of Assyrian military/administrative centers at Tell Jemmeh and Ruqeish was only part of the extensive building projects in southern Philistia and the western Negeb in this period. A massive fortress was excavated recently at Tel Haror, near the western end of Naḥal Gerar (Oren, Yekutieli, Nahshoni and Feinstein 1991). Its foundation is dated to the late 8th century BCE. A second fortress was built at Tel Sera[c] (Tell esh-Shari'a), on the eastern side of Naḥal Gerar, dating to the same period (Oren 1978:1060–64). Another massive building has been unearthed at Khirbet

Hoga, located on a tributary of Naḥal Shiqma (Na'aman 1979:81). The establishment of this complex of fortified military/administrative centers north of the Besor river (the Brook of Egypt), the most important east-west route in the area, which served as the main outlet for the Arabian trade to the Mediterranean, should be assigned to Sargon II. (On the economic objectives of the Assyrians on the Egyptian border, see Tadmor 1966; Elat 1978:26–30; Na'aman 1979:83–85.) Transferring deportees from far off areas to this strategically located and economically important region and settling them in the newly established Assyrian centers was an integral part of his ambitious policy in Philistia. The annexation of Ashdod was another aspect of the same policy (see Alt 1945:141–146; Na'aman 1979:71–72, n. 7).

Deportations in the Time of Sennacherib (704–681)

The conquest of Judah is related in Sennacherib's annals, where the events of the year 701 BCE are described as follows:

> As for Hezekiah, the Judean, who did not submit to my yoke, I laid siege to 46 of his strong cities, walled forts and to the countless small villages in their vicinity, and conquered them . . . I drove out (of them) 200,150 people, young and old, male and female, mules, donkeys, camels, big and small cattle beyond counting, and considered (them) booty.

An analysis of Sennacherib's inscription lends support to the assumption that the aim of his campaign against Hezekiah, the leader of the anti-Assyrian coalition, was to break and weaken Judah, the strongest kingdom that remained near the Egyptian border. To achieve this goal he systematically destroyed as many Judahite sites as possible and deported thousands of their inhabitants to unknown places in the empire. Notable also are the words of the Rabshakeh near the walls of Jerusalem (2 Kgs. 18:31–32):

> Do not listen to Hezekiah; for thus says the king of Assyria: "Make your peace with me and come to me; then every one of you will eat his own vine, and every one of you will drink the water of his own cistern; until I come and take you away to a land like your own land, a land of grain and wine, a land of bread and vineyards, a land of olive trees and honey, that you may live, and not die."

The text reflects a plan for mass deportation, as was already taking place in the Shephelah and, possibly, other regions. It goes without saying that the speech of the Rabshakeh is a late literary composition written many years after the events described therein. It echoes the fears of the besieged inhabitants of Jerusalem in the face of the Assyrian deportation policy and campaign against Hezekiah.

Annexation of Judah, on the other hand, was not part of Sennacherib's plans and is not mentioned in any source relating to the 701 campaign.

Rather, he intended to create a balance of power among the various small, weak (and weakening) kingdoms located in the buffer zone between Assyria and Egypt. The destruction of the towns of Judah and the deportation of its people directly served this aim. In my opinion, Sennacherib's campaign was a great success from the Assyrian point of view and, for this reason, was described in great detail in the king's royal inscriptions and reliefs. The fact that no western alliances or another campaign against Judah are mentioned in the inscriptions of Esarhaddon or Ashurbanipal is the best proof of the success of the campaign of 701 BCE.

Excavations conducted in Judah have provided plenty of evidence for the thoroughly destructive nature of the Assyrian campaign. Large sites in the Shephelah that were destroyed in the course of the Assyrian campaign (Beth-shemesh, Tel ᶜEton, and Tell Beit Mirsim) remained deserted during the 7th century BCE (Aharoni and Aharoni 1976; Ayalon 1985; Zimhoni 1985). The number of 8th century sites discovered in the recently conducted survey of the Shephelah is several times higher than the number of the 7th century sites (Broshi and Finkelstein 1990:12; Na'aman 1991:31; Dagan 1992:242–263). Furthermore, the overall inhabited area and estimated population size of settlements dating to the 8th century BCE are about four times higher than those of the settlements dating to the 7th century BCE (Dagan 1992: 252–263). The destructive results of Sennacherib's campaign remained remarkably clear even in the last years of Josiah's reign (639–609 BCE), almost a century later. The kingdom of Hezekiah was considerably stronger than the kingdom of Josiah, with more extensive borders, larger and stronger settlements, larger population, and greater military power and economic capability (Na'aman 1991).

Contrary to the situation in Judah, there was an increase in building activity and growth in population and economic prosperity on the coastal plain of Philistia in the 7th century BCE. This is particularly clear at Ekron, Judah's closest western neighbor. In the 9th–8th centuries BCE, Ekron was a small town situated mainly on the tell's northeastern acropolis. In the 7th century, it suddenly expanded, covering an area of 60 acres and becoming a major industrial city (Gitin 1989). The massive growth of Ekron in the 7th century is the direct result of Judah's decline, the destruction and mass deportation of 701 BCE, and Assyrian counter support of its western neighbor. Ekron took the place of Judah in the northern Shephelah, exploiting some of Judah's agricultural territories, developing its economy, and possibly attracting many refugees from the destroyed and desolated Judahite towns. Ekron's strength is one of the reasons for Judah's continuous weakness along its western border and, particularly, in the northern Shephelah during the 7th century BCE (Na'aman 1991:44–51).

In his inscription, Sennacherib wrote that he deported 200,150 people from Judah. The number may well be exaggerated, but it is much closer to historical reality than scholars have assumed in the past (see, e.g., Olmstead 1923:305; Ungnad 1942–43; von Soden 1972:44; Sauren 1985).[5] A large number of settlements were destroyed in the Shephelah, in Benjamin, around Jerusalem, and in the southern hills of Judah, and these settlements remained deserted for decades or even for hundreds of years. Consequently, tens of thousands of people must have been deported by Sennacherib, causing the extreme weakness of the kingdom of Judah in the 7th century (see, recently, Halpern 1991:28–49). The kingdom was relatively small with a limited reservoir of manpower. The territory of Judah had been sparsely inhabited in Iron Age I, and it took approximately 200 years — from the 10th to the 8th century BCE — to settle and populate it. Following the massive Assyrian deportation in 701 BCE, the kingdom lacked the human resources needed to resettle the destroyed and deserted areas. The period of *pax Assyriaca* in the 7th century enabled Judah to recover gradually, restore some of its settlements and strengthen its economy. However, the time span of less than a century that separated the Assyrian campaign of 701 from the death of Josiah (609) was too short for more than a partial recovery. Josiah's political, military and economic weakness is explained fully by the disastrous results of Sennacherib's campaign of 701 BCE (see Na'aman 1991).

It must be remembered that Judah was never an Assyrian province, and, therefore, its prosperity and welfare was not the concern of the Assyrians. Moreover, Sennacherib radically changed his father's external and internal policy, reducing Assyrian intervention in the affairs of the southwestern and northwestern fronts of the empire (Landsberger 1948:83; Na'aman 1974:35–36; Hawkins 1979:152–57; Elayi 1985). Instead, he concentrated on the Babylonian front (Levine 1982; Brinkman 1984:54–70) and, particularly, on Assyria's internal affairs (Reade 1978:47–72, with earlier literature; Winter 1982:367–68). Thus, no further Assyrian campaign to the west or conflict with Egypt is known from his later years. Also, no deportations to the west are mentioned in documents from his reign. A clear sign of the change of policy on the southwestern front was the re-establishment of the monarchy in Ashdod, in marked contrast to the policy of his father (Na'aman 1979:71–72, n. 7, with earlier lit-

5. Stohlmann (1983) has noted, correctly, that a sizeable number of people were deported in 701 BCE, certainly in the thousands. However, his onomastic evidence (Stohlmann 1983:167–68) is not convincing, and it is hardly conceivable that thousands of Judahites were deported to Nineveh (or other major Assyrian cities), in light of the absence of Hebrew names in the onomastica. Instead, we may assume that the people of Judah were transferred to some remote area(s), rather than the royal cities of Assyria.

erature). Sennacherib, likewise, conducted a lenient policy toward the rebellious kingdoms of Ashkelon and Ekron. He neither destroyed them nor exiled their populations. The change of policy may have brought Sargon's impetus for development on the empire's border with Egypt to a halt. Sennachrib's innovative policy on the southwestern front of his empire established a balance of power and preserved what was already gained, replacing the previous Assyrian policy of offensive and initiative in the region.

Deportations in the Time of Esarhaddon and Ashurbanipal

A new offensive on the southwestern front began with the accession of Esarhaddon to the throne in 680–669 BCE. During his second year, he undertook a campaign to the coast of Philistia. Two years later, he attacked Sidon and destroyed it. His main enemy, however, was Tirhaka (Taharqa), the Nubian king, and Esarhaddon conducted three campaigns against Egypt. In 674, he was defeated, but, in 671, he crossed the Sinai peninsula and conquered Lower Egypt. During his third campaign (669), Esarhaddon died and was replaced by Ashurbanipal.

The new king conducted two campaigns to Egypt to quell rebellions. In the second campaign of 663 BCE, he succeeded in conquering Thebes, the capital of Egypt. However, the Assyrian domination of Egypt was short-lived, and, in 656, Psammetichus I, who ascended the throne with Assyrian support, was able to unite all of Egypt under his rule (Kitchen 1973:391–406, 455–61; Spalinger 1974:316–326; 1976:133–42). It appears that the Assyrian retreat took place following the conclusion of an agreement with Psammetichus, and there was no armed struggle between Assyria and Egypt at that time (Na'aman 1991:38–39, with earlier literature).

Despite the extensive involvement of Assyria in the west in the time of Esarhaddon and Ashurbanipal, no deportations to Palestine are related in their inscriptions. Two reasons can be offered for this lack of reference. First, as Palestine had already been subjected to Assyrian rule and had experienced two-way deportation, any further deportation would not have been exceptional and so might not have been deemed worthy of comment. Second, there appears to have been a change in the scribal tradition for writing royal inscriptions that de-emphasized the motif of deportation (see Oded 1979:19–22).

Deportations under Esarhaddon and Ashurbanipal are mentioned in the book of Ezra. According to Ezra 4:1–2, the "adversaries of Judah and Benjamin" demanded thus: "Let us build with you, for we have been sacrificing to him ever since the days of Esarhaddon king of Assyria who brought us here." The background of the deportation remains unknown. According to Ezra 4:9–10, Asnappar = Ashurbanipal (*As<rb>npr*; see Streck 1916:CCCLXIV–CCCLXV) deported Babylonians (men of Erech, Babylon and possibly Sippar) and Elamites (men of Susa) and settled them "in the cities of Samaria and in the rest of the province Beyond the River (*ᶜbr nhrh*)." Ashurbanipal deported the Babylonians after quashing the revolt of Shamash-shum-ukin in 648 BCE. He transferred the Elamites after he conquered the land of Elam and destroyed its capital Susa in 647–646 BCE (Winckler 1892:97–99; Streck 1916: CCCLXIV–CCCLVII). Thus, it is evident that, during the 640s, the Assyrians were still assiduously active in developing their southernmost province by settling new groups of deportees in its area.

Two cuneiform documents found during the excavations at Gezer (Macalister 1911:22–29; Becking 1981; 1992:114–118, with earlier literature) are sale contracts dating to 651 and 649 BCE, which include 21 complete names. All the names, except one, are non-Israelite. Twelve are Akkadian, five are West Semitic and one is Egyptian (Zadok 1985:568–69). The Akkadian names belong primarily to Babylonians, who were probably transferred to Gezer from Babylonia (Galling 1935:82–84; Becking 1981:88–89). The deportees were resettled either by Sargon II or Ashurbanipal; there is no way to determine between the two alternatives. Zadok (1985:569–70) has further suggested that Sanballat, the governor of the satrapy of Samaria in the time of Nehemiah, was called *ha-Ḥoroni* because he originated from Beth-horon, a site near Gezer. In view of his Akkadian name (Sin-uballiṭ), it is likely that Beth-horon was one of the sites in which Babylonian exiles were settled.

The two cuneiform tablets appear to have been found inside an Assyrian administrative building dating to the mid-7th century BCE (Reich and Brandl 1985). Various other objects of Mesopotamian origin were also discovered at the site, supporting the assumption that Gezer was an Assyrian administrative center. At the same time that it served as the seat of Assyrian officials, it became home to newly arrived Babylonian deportees.

As noted above, exiles were settled in the areas of Samaria and Bethel. When this fact is considered with the evidence of resettlement of non-native deportees in the northern Shephelah, it becomes evident that a considerable part of the population of the Assyrian province of Samaria was subjected to deportation and that various foreign elements (Babylonians, Elamites, and Arabians), mostly of Mesopotamian origin, were resettled there. These findings are important for the study of historical developments in Samaria in the post-exilic period.

Finally, we should note the small clay tablet that was found at Tell Keisan, southeast of Acco (Sigrist 1982). It records the distribution of rations to persons whose names were not preserved intact. As the Acco Plain was annexed by Esarhaddon in 671 BCE, it is possible that the tablet reflects rationing to foreigners deported to Tell Keisan, either by Esarhaddon or Ashurbanipal, until they became self-supporting. Other finds from Tell Keisan includes a scaraboid and an engraving on a sherd, both decorated with the symbol of Sin, the moon-god, standing on a pedestal (Spycket 1973). These finds seem to indicate that the site was the seat of deportees who worshiped the moon-god of Harran.

Summary

In conclusion, I would like to emphasize the following four points:

(a) There were differences in the deportation policies of various Assyrian kings. Tiglath-pileser III was the first to annex large areas of Israelite territory. He implemented "one-way" deportation to weaken the national spirit and reduce the possibility of rebellion against the Assyrian government. Sargon II conducted a different policy, aimed at integrating Palestine into the Assyrian empire by way of "two-way" deportation that concentrated on two regions: the province of Samaria and the region north of the Besor river (the Brook of Egypt). Sennacherib changed his father's policy considerably: He implemented a massive "one-way" deportation from the kingdom of Judah to create a balance of power among the small weak kingdoms situated near his border with Egypt. Esarhaddon renewed the offensive on the southwestern front of the empire. Following his campaigns and the conquest of Egypt, the importance of Palestine as a front station on the way to Egypt increased. The deportations to Palestine by Esarhaddon and Ashurbanipal, along with the intensive building activity in the province of Samaria and the southern coast of Philistia and western Negeb, clearly indicate the Assyrian interest in the land. This involvement continued at least until the middle of Ashurbanipal's reign, as is evident from the deportation of Babylonians and Elamites to the region in the 640s BCE.

(b) Considerable changes in the composition of the population of Palestine took place in the period under discussion. Large population groups were transferred to new homes throughout the empire. Two areas in particular suffered from the deportations: the Galilee, particularly the Lower Galilee, and the Shephelah of Judah. Surveys conducted in both areas have revealed a dramatic reduction in the number and scope of settlements during the 7th century. In other areas, "two-way" deportations took place, and Assyrian involvement was less destructive — in some instances, even serving as an impetus for prosperity. The extensive surveys conducted in the hill country of Manasseh and Ephraim are as yet unpublished (for Manasseh, see Zertal 1990), and we are unable to appreciate the effect of the Assyrian population transfers on the area. It is clear, however, that Assyrian deportation and building activity near its border with Egypt brought about an unprecedented prosperity.

The kingdom of Edom also reached its height of prosperity during the period of vassaldom to Assyria in the 7th century. This flourishing was due mainly to Assyrian involvement in Arabian trade and possibly, in copper mining in the Arabah (Bennett 1982; Knauf and Lenzen 1987; Bartlett 1989:128–143; Bienkowski 1990). It is unclear whether deportation played any role in the prosperity of Edom. We may conclude that Assyrian deportation, when combined with planned development, could create settlement growth and economic prosperity.

(c) The demographic changes in the late 8th and 7th centuries BCE had only a marginal effect on the material culture of Palestine. Assyrian residences have been discovered at several sites (Amiran and Dunayevsky 1958; Reich 1975; Fritz 1979, with earlier literature), and artifacts of Assyrian origin have been uncovered in centers like Samaria, Gezer and Tell Jemmeh. However, this is only part of the picture. Thus, for example, no evidence of the presence of deportees from the Iranian plateau or from Elam have been detected in any of the excavations and extensive surveys conducted up to the present time. Moreover, relatively little evidence for the presence of either deportees or the Assyrian bureaucracy have been detected at the new provincial centers of Megiddo, Dor and Ashdod. Archaeological evidence may demonstrate the presence of a group of deportees; however, it cannot be used as "negative" evidence. A certain group may arrive from outside and leave material traces of its land of origin; another group may be assimilated entirely and leave no trace of its original material culture. It is possible that new scientific techniques may help us overcome some of these limitations in the field of archaeology. However, in the present state of research, documentary evidence must remain the primary source of information for identifying new ethnic elements that entered a certain region.

(d) The considerable changes in the ethnic composition of the population may well have brought similar changes in society, economy, cult, etc. It must be emphasized that following the *pax Assyriaca*, the borders between kingdoms were open. As a result, international and local trade developed, and contacts took place among the districts included within the empire or located on its periphery. The available evidence relating to the material culture of Judah in the 8th century BCE, for example, attests that the borders of the kingdom were largely closed and that contacts with neighboring states were limited. In the 7th century BCE, on the other hand, contacts with neighboring regions are manifold (Zimhoni 1990:47–49). Various questions may be posed in this light. How did Sennacherib's mass deportation of 701 BCE influence the social structure of the kingdom of Judah? (See Halpern 1991:49–58.) How did the emergence of the new center of Ekron influence the economy of the land of Judah? Did "foreign" cults only enter the national temple of Jerusalem, or did they also influence the local cult places? These and many other questions deserve extensive discussion, and the issue of deportation must be taken into consideration in all future discussions of the kingdom of Judah and its neighbors in the 7th century BCE.

References

Aharoni, M. and Aharoni Y. 1976. The Stratification of Judahite Sites in the 8th and 7th Centuries BCE. *BASOR* 224: 73–90.

Alt, A. 1929. Das System der assyrischen Provinzen auf dem Boden des Reiches Israel. *ZDPV* 52:220–42. (Reprint: Alt 1953: 188–205).

Alt, A. 1945. Neue assyrische Nachrichten über Palästina und Syrien. *ZDPV* 67: 128–159. (Reprint: Alt 1953: 226–241).

Alt, A. 1953. *Kleine Schriften zur Geschichte des Volkes Israel* II. München.

Amiran, R. and Dunayevsky, I. 1958. The Assyrian Open Court Building and its Palestinian Derivatives. *BASOR* 149: 25–32.

Amiran, R. and Van Beek, G.W. 1976. Jemmeh, Tell. In: *Enc. Arch. Exc.* II: 545–549.

Ayalon, E. 1985. Trial Excavation of Two Iron Age Strata at Tel ʻEton. *Tel Aviv* 12: 54–62.

Bartlett, J.R. 1989. *Edom and the Edomites* (Journal for the Study of the Old Testament, Supplement 77). Sheffield.

Becking, B. 1981. The Two Neo-Assyrian Documents from Gezer in their Historical Context. *Jaarbericht van het Vooraziatisch-Egyptisch Genootschap Ex Oriente Lux* 27: 76–89.

Becking, B. 1992. *The Fall of Samaria: An Historical and Archaeological Study.* (Studies in the History of the Ancient Near East II). Leiden.

Bennett, C.M. 1982. Neo-Assyrian Influence in Transjordan. In: Hadidi, A. ed. *Studies in the History and Archaeology of Jordan* I. Amman: 181–187.

Bienkowski, P. 1990. Umm el-Biyara, Tawilan and Buseirah in Retrospect. *Levant* 22: 91–109.

Brinkman, J.A. 1984. *Prelude to Empire. Babylonian Society and Politics, 747-627 BCE.* Philadelphia.

Broshi, M. and Finkelstein, I. 1990. The Population of Palestine in 734 BCE. *Cathedra* 58: 3–24. (Hebrew).

Burney, C.F. 1903. *Notes on the Hebrew Text of the Books of Kings with an Introduction and Appendix*. Oxford. (Reprint 1970. New York).

Cogan, M. 1974. *Imperialism and Religion: Assyria, Judah and Israel in the Eighth and Seventh Centuries BCE.* (Society of Biblical Literature Dissertation Series 19). Missoula.

Dagan, Y. 1992. *The Shephelah during the Period of the Monarchy in Light of Archaeological Excavations and Survey* (M.A. Thesis). Tel Aviv University. (Hebrew).

Dalley, S. 1985. Foreign Chariotry and Cavalry in the Armies of Tiglath-Pileser III and Sargon II. *Iraq* 47: 31–48.

Dever, W.G. 1986. Abel-Beth-Maʻacah: "North Gateway of Ancient Israel." In: Geraty, L.T. and Herr, L.G. eds. *The Archaeology of Jordan and Other Studies Presented to Siegfried H. Horn.* Berrien Springs: 207–222.

Diakonoff, I.M. 1991. The Cities of the Medes. In: Cogan, M. and Ephʻal, I. eds. *Ah, Assyria . . . Studies in Assyrian History and Ancient Near Eastern Historiography Presented to Hayim Tadmor.* (Scripta Hierosolymitana 33). Jerusalem: 13–20.

Donner, H. 1984–86. *Geschichte des Volkes Israel und seiner Nachbarn in Grundzügen* I–II. Göttingen.

Driver, G.R. 1958. Geographical Notes. *Eretz-Israel* 5: 16*–20*.

Elat, M. 1978. The Economic Relations of the Neo-Assyrian Empire with Egypt. *JAOS* 98: 20–34.

Elayi, J. 1985. Les relations entre les cités phéniciennes et l'empire Assyrien sous le règne de Sennachérib. *Semitica* 35: 19–26.

Eph'al, I. 1979. Assyrian Domination in Palestine. In: Malamat, A. ed. *The Age of the Monarchies: Political History.* (The World History of the Jewish People). Jerusalem: 276–289, 364–368.

Eph'al, I. 1982. *The Ancient Arabs. Nomads on the Borders of the Fertile Crescent 9th–5th Centuries BCE.* Jerusalem and Leiden.

Eph'al, I. 1991. "The Samarian(s)" in the Assyrian Sources. In: Cogan, M. and Eph'al, I. eds. *Ah, Assyria . . . Studies in Assyrian History and Ancient Near Eastern Historiography Presented to Hayim Tadmor.* (Scripta Hierosolymitana 33). Jerusalem: 36–45.

Finet, A. 1973. Le trône et la rue en Mésopotamie: l'exaltation du roi et les techniques de l'opposition. In: Finet, A. ed. *La voix de l'opposition en Mésopotamie.* (Colloque organisé par l'Institut des Hautes Etudes de Belgique). Bruxelles: 2–27.

Forrer, E. 1920. *Die Provinzeinteilung des assyrischen Reiches.* Leipzig.

Fritz, V. 1979. Die Paläste während der assyrischen, babylonischen und persischen Vorherrschaft in Palästina. *MDOG* 111: 63–74.

Fritz, V. 1986. Kinneret: Vorbericht über die Ausgrabungen auf dem Tell el-'Oreme am See Genezaret in den Jahren 1982–1985. *ZDPV* 102: 1–39.

Gadd, C.J. 1954. Inscribed Prisms of Sargon II from Nimrud. *Iraq* 16: 173–201.

Gal, Z. 1988–89. Lower Galilee in the Iron Age II: Analysis of Survey Material and its Historical Interpretation. *Tel Aviv* 15–16: 56–64.

Galling, K. 1935. Assyrische und persische Präfekten in Geser. *PJb* 31: 75–93.

Gitin, S. 1989. Tel Miqne-Ekron: A Type Site for the Inner Coastal Plain in the Iron Age II Period. In: Gitin, S. and Dever, W.G. eds. *Recent Excavations in Israel. Studies in Iron Age Archaeology.* (*AASOR* 49). Winona Lake: 23–58.

Halpern, B. 1991. Jerusalem and the Lineages in the Seventh Century BCE: Kinship and the Rise of Individual Moral Liability. In: Halpern, B. and Hobson, D.W. eds. *Law and Ideology in Monarchic Israel.* (Journal for the Study of the Old Testament, Supplement 124). Sheffield: 11–107.

Hawkins, J.D. 1979. Some Historical Problems of the Hieroglyphic Luwian Inscriptions. *AnSt* 29: 153–167.

Hayes, J.H. and Kuan, J.K. 1991. The Final Years of Samaria (730–720 BC). *Biblica* 72: 153–181.

Kapera, Z.J. 1972. Was *ya-ma-ni* a Cypriote? *Folia Orientalia* 14: 207–218.

Kapera, Z.J. 1987. The Oldest Account of Sargon II's Campaign against Ashdod. *Folia Orientalia* 24: 29–39.

Kitchen, K.A. 1973. *The Third Intermediate Period in Egypt (1100–650 B.C.).* Warminster.

Knauf, E.A. and Lenzen, C. 1987. Edomite Copper Industry. In: Hadidi, A. ed. *Studies in the History and Archaeology of Jordan* III. Amman: 83–88.

Lamon, R.S. and Shipton, G.M. 1939. *Megiddo I. Seasons of 1925–34 Strata I–V.* Chicago.

Landsberger, B. 1948. *Sam'al. Studien zur Entdeckung der Ruinenstaede Karatepe.* Ankara.

Levine, L.D. 1982. Sennacherib's Southern Front: 704–689 BCE. *JCS* 34: 28–58.

Lie, A.G. 1929. *The Inscriptions of Sargon II King of Assyria.* Part I: *The Annals.* Paris.

Lipschits, O. 1990. The Date of the "Assyrian Residence" at Ayyelet ha-Shaḥar. *Tel Aviv* 17: 96–99.

Macalister, R.A.S. 1911. *The Excavations of Gezer* I. London.

Montgomery, J.A. 1951. *A Critical and Exegetical Commentary on the Books of Kings* (ICC). Edinburgh.

Na'aman, N. 1974. Sennacherib's "Letter to God" on his Campaign to Judah. *BASOR* 214: 25–39.

Na'aman, N. 1979. The Brook of Egypt and Assyrian Policy on the Border of Egypt. *Tel Aviv* 6: 68–90.

Na'aman, N. 1986a. Historical and Chronological Notes on the Kingdoms of Israel and Judah in the Eighth Century BCE. *VT* 36: 71–92.

Na'aman, N. 1986b. *Borders and Districts in Biblical Historiography. Seven Studies in Biblical Geographical Lists.* (Jerusalem Biblical Studies 4). Jerusalem.

Na'aman, N. 1990. The Historical Background of the Conquest of Samaria (720 BC). *Biblica* 71: 206–225.

Na'aman, N. 1991. The Kingdom of Judah under Josiah. *Tel Aviv* 18: 3–71.

Na'aman, N. and Zadok, R. 1988. Sargon II's Deportations to Israel and Philistia (716–708 BCE). *JCS* 40: 36–46.

Naveh, J. 1985. Writing and Scripts in Seventh-Century BCE. Philistia: The New Evidence from Tell Jemmeh. *IEJ* 35: 8–21.

Oded, B. 1979. *Mass Deportations and Deportees in the Neo-Assyrian Empire.* Wiesbaden.

Olmstead, A.T.E. 1908. *Western Asia in the Days of Sargon of Assyria, 722-705 BCE.* New York.

Olmstead, A.T.E. 1923. *History of Assyria.* Chicago.

Oren, E.D. et al. 1986. A Phoenician Emporium on the Border of Egypt. *Qadmoniot* 19: 83–91. (Hebrew).

Oren, E.D., Yekutieli, Y., Nahshoni, P. and Feinstein, R. 1991. Tell Haror — After Six Seasons. *Qadmoniot* 24:2–19. (Hebrew).

Oren, E.D. 1978. Esh-Shari'a Tell (Tel Sera'). In: *Enc. Arch. Exc.* IV: 1059–1069.

Postgate, J.N. 1973. Assyrian Texts and Fragments. *Iraq* 35: 13–36.

Reade, J.E. 1978. Studies in Assyrian Geography. Part I: Sennacherib and the Waters of Niniveh. *RA* 72: 47–72, 157–180.

Reich, R. 1975. The Persian Building at Ayyelet ha-Shahar: The Assyrian Palace of Hazor? *IEJ* 25: 233-237.

Reich, R. and Brandl, B. 1985. Gezer under Assyrian Rule. *PEQ* 117: 41–54.

Rost, P. 1893. *Die Keilschrifttexte Tiglath-Pilesers III, nach den Papierabklatschen und Originalen des Britischen Museums* I–II. Leipzig.

Sauren, H. 1985. Sennachérib, les Arabes, les déportés Juifs. *WO* 16: 80–99.

Sigrist, M. 1982. Une tablette cuneiforme de Tell Keisan. *IEJ* 32: 32–35.

von Soden, W. 1972. Sanherib vor Jerusalem 701 v. Chr. In: *Antike und Universalgeschichte. Festschrift Hans Erich Stier zum 70. Geburtstag.* Münster: 43–51.

Spalinger, A. 1973. The Year 712 BCE and its Implications for Egyptian History. *Journal of the American Research Center in Egypt* 10: 95–101.

Spalinger, A. 1974. Esarhaddon and Egypt: An Analysis of the First Invasion of Egypt. *Orientalia* 43: 295–326.

Spalinger, A. 1976. Psammetichus, King of Egypt: I. *Journal of the American Research Center in Egypt* 13: 133–147.

Spycket, A. 1973. Le culte du dieu-lune à Tell Keisan. *RB* 80: 384–395.

Stohlmann, A. 1983. The Judaean Exile after 701 B.C.E. In: Hallo, W.W., Moyer, J.C. and Perdue, L.G. eds. *Scriptures in Context II. More Essays on the Comparative Method.* Winona Lake: 147–175.

Streck, M. 1916. *Assurbanipal und die letzten assyrischen Konige bis zum Untergange Niniveh's* I–III. Leipzig.

Tadmor, H. 1958. The Campaigns of Sargon II of Assur: A Chronological-Historical Study. *JCS* 12: 22–40, 77–100.

Tadmor, H. 1962. The Southern Border of Aram. *IEJ* 12: 114–122.

Tadmor, H. 1966. Philistia under Assyrian Rule. *BA* 29: 86–102.

Tadmor, H. 1967. The Conquest of Galilee by Tiglath-Pileser III, King of Assyria. In: Hirschberg, H.Z. ed. *All the Land of Naphtali.* (The Twenty-Fourth Archaeological Convention). Jerusalem: 62–67. (Hebrew).

Tadmor, H. 1969. The First Temple and the Return to Zion. In: Ben Sasson, H.H. ed. *History of the Jewish People. I. The Ancient Times.* Tel Aviv: 91–173. (Hebrew).

Tadmor, H. 1982. Tiglath-Pileser III. *Enc. Miqr.* VIII: 415–430. (Hebrew).

Tadmor, H. 1983. Some Aspects of the History of Samaria during the Biblical Period. *The Jerusalem Cathedra* 3: 1–11.

Ungnad, A. 1942–43. Die Zahl der von Sanherib deportierten Judäer. *ZAW* 59: 199–202.

Van Beek, G.W. 1973. Assyrian Vaulted Buildings at Tell Jemmeh. *Qadmoniot* 6: 23–26. (Hebrew).

Van Beek, G.W. 1977. Tell Gamma. *IEJ* 27: 171–176.

Van Beek, G.W. 1983. Digging up Tell Jemmeh. *Archaeology* 36: 12–19.

Weidner, E. 1941–44. Šilkan(ḫe)ni, König von Muṣri, ein Zeitgenosse Sargons II. *AFO* 14: 40–53.

Winckler, H. 1892. Die samaritanischen Ansiedler. In: Winckler, H. *Alttestamentliche Untersuchungen.* Leipzig: 97–107.

Winter, I.J. 1982. Art as Evidence for Interaction: Relations between the Assyrian Empire and North Syria. In: Nissen, H.J. and Renger, J. ed. *Mesopotamien und seine Nachbarn.* Berlin: 355–382.

Yadin, Y. 1972. *Hazor.* (The Schweich Lectures of the British Academy 1970). London.

Zadok, R. 1976. Geographical and Onomastic Notes. *The Journal of the Ancient Near Eastern Society of Columbia University* 5: 113–126.

Zadok, R. 1985. Samarian Notes. *BiOr* 42: 567–572.

Zertal, A. 1990. The Pahwah of Samaria (Northern Israel) during the Persian Period. Types of Settlement, Economy, History and New Discoveries. *Transeuphratène* 3: 9–30.

Zimhoni, O. 1985. The Iron Age Pottery of Tel ᶜEton and its Relation to the Lachish, Tell Beit Mirsim and Arad Assemblages. *Tel Aviv* 12: 63–90.

Zimhoni, O. 1990. Two Ceramic Assemblages from Lachish Levels III and II. *Tel Aviv* 17: 3–52.

Province System and Settlement Pattern in Southern Syria and Palestine in the Neo-Assyrian Period[1]

1. The Assyrian Provincial System

1.1. The Political System Prior to Tiglath-pileser's Conquest

On the eve of Tiglath-pileser III's conquest, the political system in the area under discussion included two relatively large territorial kingdoms (Aram Damascus and Israel) and numerous small kingdoms. The power of the two large kingdoms is evident from their leading role in the history of the region and their struggle for hegemony during the tenth-eighth centuries BCE.

The small kingdoms included the Phoenician, Philistine and Transjordanian kingdoms as well as Judah. Among the Phoenician kingdoms were Tyre (which included the island of Tyre and the continental area of Sidon), Byblos and the island of Arvad. Among the Philistine kingdoms were the three city-states of Ashdod, Ashkelon and Gaza situated along the coast, and Ekron in the northern Shephelah, near the border of Judah. The three Transjordanian kingdoms were Ammon, Moab and Edom. Arab tribes living along the eastern and southern frontiers of these kingdoms participated in the anti-Assyrian alliances of the ninth-eighth centuries BCE.

1.2. The Provincial System in Southern Syria

In three successive campaigns (734–732), Tiglath-pileser defeated the Syro-Ephraimite coalition under the leadership of Rezin of Damascus and subjugated the entire area up to the Egyptian border. He annexed Damascus in its entirety and most of the territory of Israel, thereby breaking the backbone of any future anti-Assyrian local alliance. All the small kingdoms, including the reduced kingdom of Israel, became vassals of Assyria (Eph'al 1979; Weippert 1982).

The extent of the annexed "widespread land of Bīt Ḫazaili" is indicated in one of Tiglath-pileser's summary inscriptions as follows: "[From] the town

1. Reprinted with permission. In Liverani, M. ed., *Neo-Assyrian Geography*, Rome 1995: 103–115.

of Kashpuna which is on the shore of the Upper Sea [as far as the town of *mi*?*-in*?]*-ni-te*, the town of *ga-al-'a-/a/-*[*di*] and the town of *a-bi-il-šiṭ-ṭi* which is on the border of Bīt Ḫumri" (III R 10,2; see Tadmor 1962:114–15; Walker in Ottoson 1969:20, n. 30; Weippert 1972:152, 154–155). In another inscription (ND 4301+), the borders are delineated as follows: "From the t[own of Kashp]una as far as the town of Gilea[d and the town of Abel-šiṭṭi which is on the bor]der of Bīt Ḫumri" (Tadmor 1962:117–119; Weippert 1982:405, n. 21).

It is clear that the northwestern border of Aram Damascus did not reach the Mediterranean. Kashpuna may possibly be identified with the site of Kusba, near Nahr Qadisha, about 15 km. south of Tripoli. This is evident from letter ND 2715, in which it is stated that the water supply of Kashpuna was established in the town of Immiu, i.e., modern Tell Amyun (Na'aman 1978: 230–231; Weippert 1982:405–406, n. 21; Sapin 1990:80–81). Nahr Qadisha (and Nahr Abu ᶜAli) formed the southern border of the province of Ṣimirra, and Kashpuna was probably that province's southernmost town. The northwestern border of Damascus must have reached the eastern side of Mount Lebanon.

According to the textual restorations suggested above, the southern border of Aram Damascus reached the towns of [Min]nite, Gilead and Abel-šiṭṭi. The latter, described as a town which borders Bīt Ḫumri, is the same as biblical Abel-shittim, located on Wādi el-Kefrein, east of Jericho. Biblical Abel-shittim appears as the last station in the "plains of Moab" before the crossing of the Jordan and the entrance into Canaan (Num. 25:1; 33:49; Josh. 2:1; 3:1; Mic. 6:5). It is clear that the town was located on the northern border of Moab, overlooking the cisjordanian Israelite territories. The town of Gilead should most likely be identified with biblical Mizpeh-gilead, located on the Jabbok river, near the northwestern border of the kingdom of Ammon (Gen. 31:48–49; Judg. 10:17; 11:29). Minnite (if this is the correct restoration) is the same as Minnith of the Jephthah story (Judg. 11:33), located at Umm el-Ḥanafish (Umm el-Basatin), near the southwestern border of Ammon. According to these site identifications, the "widespread land of Bīt Ḫazaili" encompassed the Israelite Transjordanian territories up to the boundaries of Ammon and Moab. This would make Gilead a Damascene land, contrary to 2 Kgs. 15:29, according to which the Gilead was taken from Pekah king of Israel.

My analysis of the Assyrian texts clashes with scholarly consensus about the borders of Israel in the third quarter of the eighth century BCE. It calls for a new evaluation of the role of Rezin in the events that preceded the Syro-Ephraimite war and raises additional biblical literary-historical questions that, naturally, cannot be discussed here (see Na'aman 1995). Leaving for the moment the problem of Transjordan, the areas of Aram Damascus were divided into four provinces: Dimashqa, Ṣūbat/Ṣūbite, Qarnini and Manṣuate.

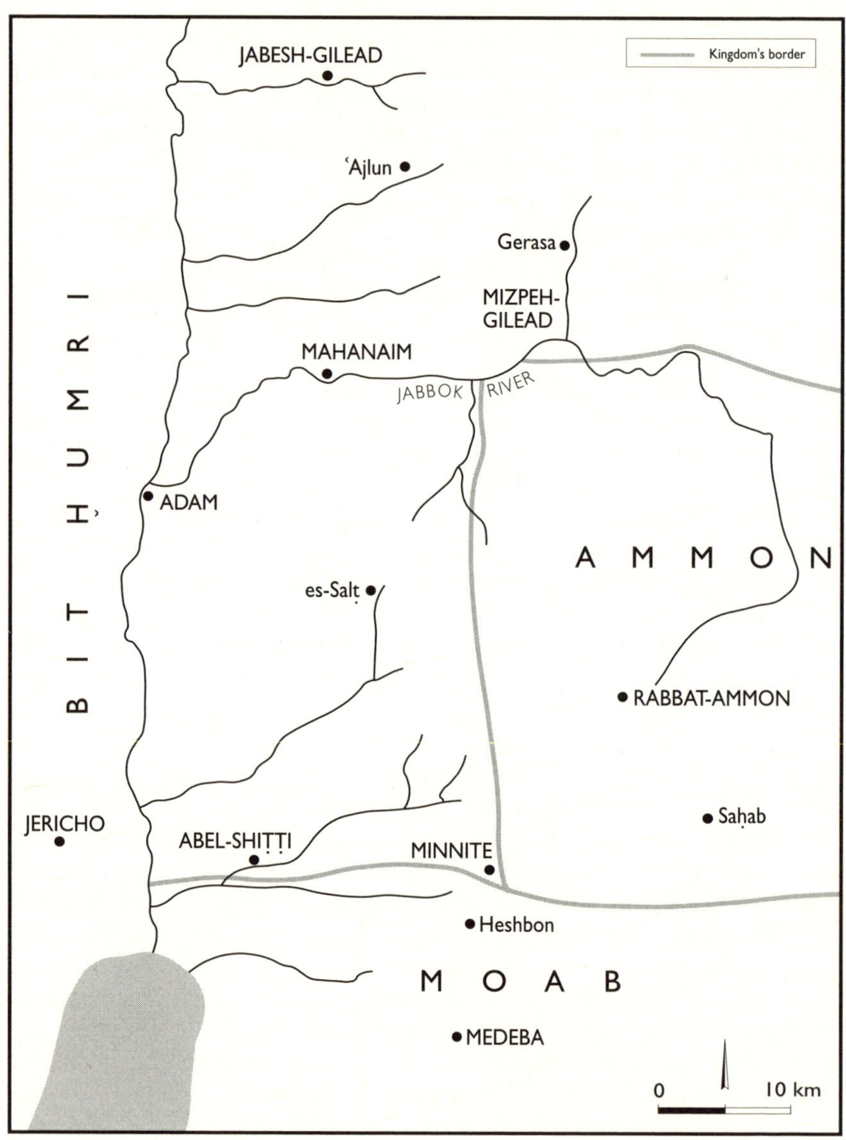

Province system in southern Syria and Palestine

Qarnini encompassed the Bashan and Hauran. Dimashqa covered the area east of the Anti-Lebanon.

Two conflicting locations have been proposed for Manṣuate: either in the Beqa[c] of Lebanon or in the southern territory of Hamath (Lipiński 1971; Weippert 1992:49–53). The campaign against Manṣuate in 796 BCE attested in the Eponym Chronicle is probably associated with Adad-nirari III's attack on Damascus and its submission. Thus, Manṣuate may be sought in the Damascene territory. Moreover, in light of the close relations of the governors of Hamath and Ṣūbat in the time of Sargon II, it is evident that the two provinces have a common border. This is further confirmed by biblical references in which Hamath appears as Damascus' northern neighbor (note in particular, Ezek. 47:16–17; 48:1). It seems that Manṣuate extended along the Beqa[c] from the sources of the Liṭani river (south of Lab'u) in the north to the western slopes of Mount Hermon in the south, covering the territory of the former Aramean kingdom of Beth Rehob. The location of its capital remains unknown.[2] Ṣūbat must be sought in the northern Beqa[c] and the northern Anti-Lebanon areas, bordering on its south with the provinces of Manṣuate and Dimashqa and in the north with the province of Hamath. The location of its capital Ṣūbat remains unknown. Among its towns were Lab'u, Rable and Qidisi in the Beqa[c] and the road stations of Ḫesa, Argite and Sazana on the eastern frontier.

1.3. The Provincial System in the Former Israelite Areas

The territory of Israel west of the Jordan was divided by Tiglath-pileser into three parts: Magidû and Du'ru became the centers of Assyrian provinces, whereas the hill country of Samaria remained in the hands of a vassal king. Twelve years later, in 720 BCE, Samaria was annexed by Sargon II.

Du'ru is mentioned both in an Assyrian administrative list that records only the names of provinces (ADD 919) and in a geographical list, where the Assyrian provinces were enumerated together with kingdoms located near the borders of the empire (K 4384) (Forrer 1920:52, 54, 69; Alt 1929:234–236). The Assyrian province must have replaced the Israelite district of Dor (1 Kgs. 4:11), which, in turn, had succeeded the small city-state established by the Sea Peoples in the twelfth century BCE. It encompassed a narrow stretch of coast between Mount Carmel in the north and the Yarkon river in the south.

---

2. In an article recently published (Na'aman 1999:427–428), I discussed once again the location of Manṣuate and concluded that it should be located in the area of present-day Maṣyāf/Maṣyāt, in the southern territory of Hamath. The southern Beqa' of Lebanon was probably included in the province of Damascus.

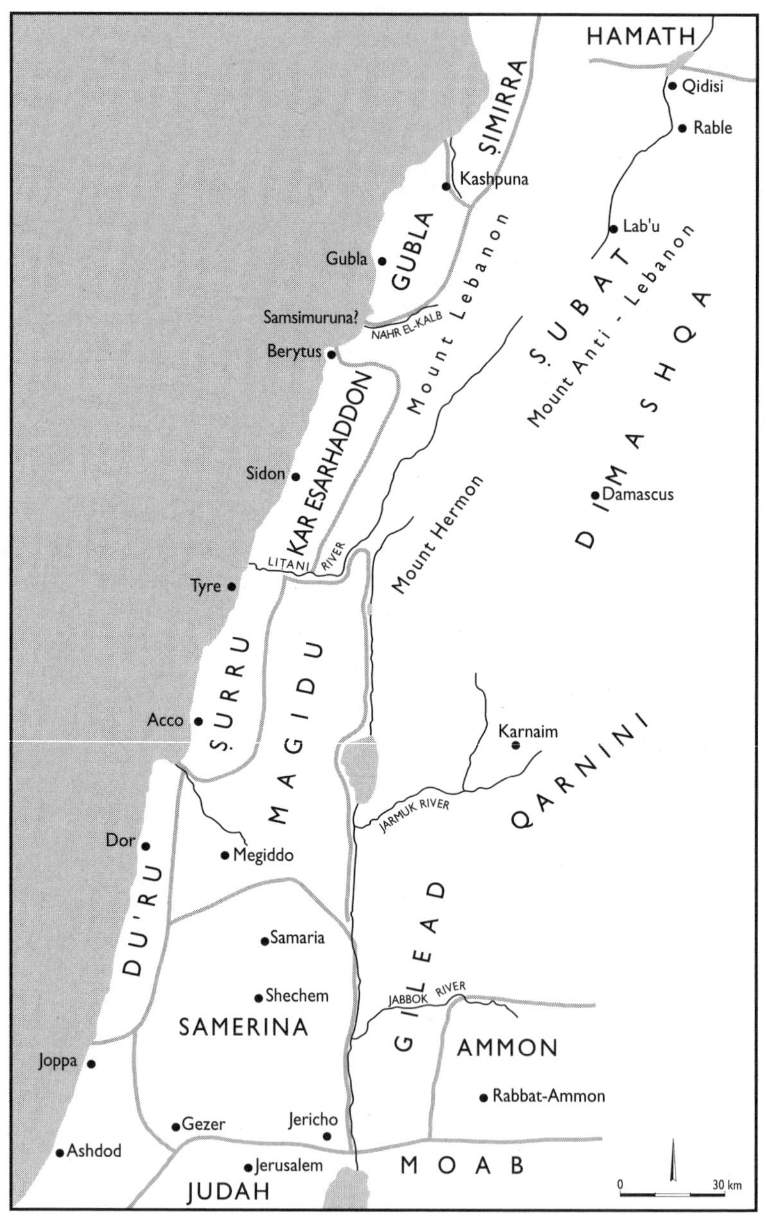

The boundary system in central Transjordan

The population was concentrated mainly in and around the center of Dor and in small hamlets along the coast. Recent excavations at Dor indicate that the Israelite city was utterly destroyed in the eighth century BCE and that soon afterwards the site was fortified and a new gate built. Two Assyrian seals and Assyrian "Palace Ware" have been discovered at the site, supporting the claim that Dor was the seat of an Assyrian governor (Stern 1990).

The province of Magidû encompassed Upper and Lower Galilee and the Beth-shean and Jezreel plains. Its center was at Megiddo, at the southern end of the district. The royal Israelite city situated here in the ninth-eighth centuries was leveled, and a well-planned fortified city with a large residence for the seat of the governor was built on its ruins.

Samaria was the capital of the hill country north of the kingdom of Judah. The town of Aphek, located on the outlet of the main north-south road that connected the northern plains of Beth-shean and Jezreel with the northern Shephelah, was part of the district of Samerīna according to Esarhaddon's inscription. The town of Socoh, located north of it on the same road, was likewise part of the hill country district in the Solomonic district system (l Kgs. 4:10). Thus, it is evident that the eastern Sharon was part of the province of Samerīna, bordering on the west with the province of Du'ru.

Establishing the number and name or names of the Assyrian province(s) in Transjordan remained an unresolved problem. Alt (1953) has suggested that Tiglath-pileser's conquests and annexations of 733/32 are the historical background to the mention of "the way of the sea, Transjordan, and Galilee of the nations" in Isa. 8:23b. He has identified "the way of the sea" and "Galilee of the nations" with the provinces of Du'ru and Magidû, reconstructing, accordingly, a single Transjordanian district called Gilead (Alt 1929:238–41). His suggestion was followed by all scholars (e.g., Tadmor 1962; Aharoni 1967:331–332; Weippert 1982:398; Miller and Hayes 1986:332–333), with the exception of Oded (1970). However, there is no textual support for the assumption that Gilead was the name of an Assyrian province.

Forrer (1920:64), on the other hand, holds that, at a later date, the province of Gilead was split into two provinces: Gilead in the north and Hamath in the south. He bases his suggestion on an analysis of the list in K 4384, which mentions two different provinces called Hamath (obv. col. II lines 13, 17). He identifies one of them with Amathus, the center of a toparchy in the Second Temple period, today Tell el-'Amtah on Wādi Rajib, north of the Jabbok river (see Oded 1970:181). Unfortunately, the location of Hamath of list K 4384 in Transjordan cannot be verified. We are left with no concrete evidence as to the system of provinces in Transjordan under the Assyrian empire.

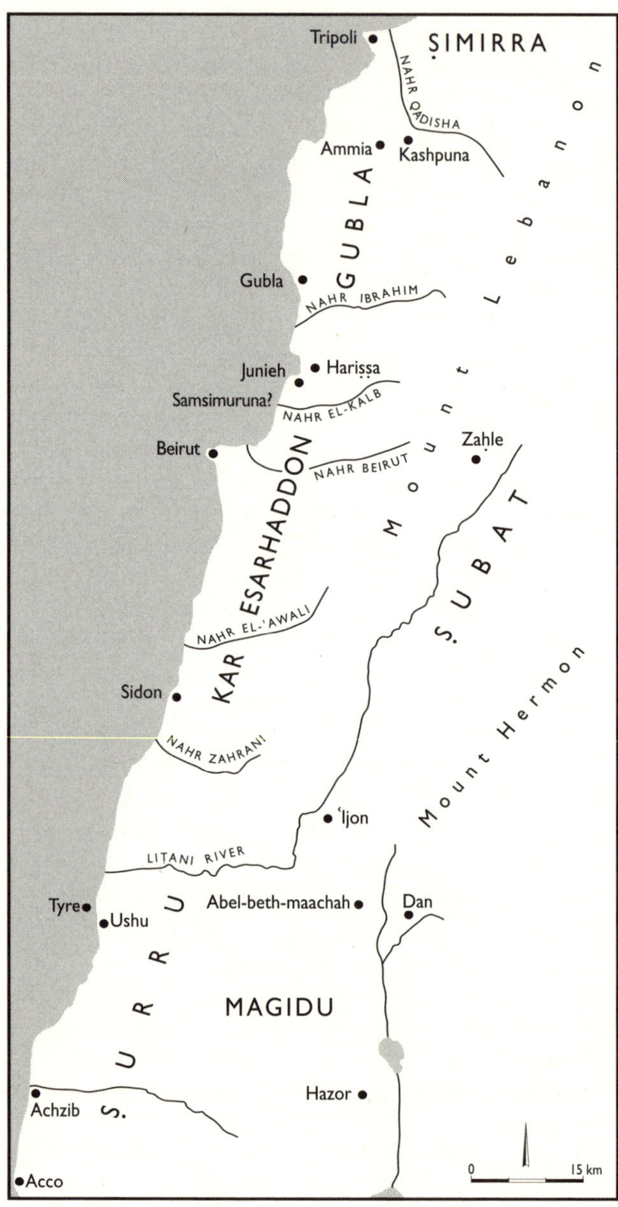

The provincial system along the Phoenician coast

1.4. Later Developments in the Assyrian Provincial System

In 712 BCE, Sargon II conquered Ashdod and its towns, deported its inhabitants and annexed the area to Assyria. A governor of Ashdod was the eponym of year 669, thus, supporting the evidence of Sargon's inscription. On the other hand, a king of Ashdod is mentioned in the description of Sennacherib's 701 campaign. It seems that Sargon's annexation of Ashdod was only the first step in his plan to annex all of Philistia. Lack of territorial contiguity with the nearby province of Samerīna has parallels in Sargon's annexation of the Anatolian kingdoms: first the remote kingdoms of Bit-Burutash and Kammanu (713/12) and only later the kingdoms of Gurgum (711) and Kummuḫ (709/8). The death of Sargon in 705 brought the Assyrian plans for the Philistine coast to an end. His son Sennacherib had a different policy, and, thus, Ashdod remained an isolated province, having both a local king and an Assyrian governor (Alt 1945:141–146; Na'aman 1979:71–72, n. 7).

In his campaign of 701, Sennacherib punished the rebellious king of Tyre, Lulî (Eloulaios), by severing his continental areas and assigning them to Tuba'lu (Ethbaal), thus, creating the kingdom of Sidon. But the new kingdom did not last long. In the year 677, Esarhaddon conquered Sidon, destroyed it, deported its people and established a new province called Kār-Esarhaddon on its territory. Two of its towns were transferred to Baal, king of Tyre, and a vassal treaty was signed with him. It may further be recalled that the treaty lists the cities of Acco and Dor as among the ports that the Tyrian ships may enter for trade. This is a clear indication that Acco was not included in the territory of Baal. It may be suggested that, like the province of Du'ru, Acco became the seat of an Assyrian governor, either in the late years of Sennacherib, or in the early days of Esarhaddon.

The treaty of Esarhaddon and Baal lasted only a few years. Baal was accused of cooperation with Taharqa, king of Egypt, and on its way to Egypt in 671 BCE, the Assyrian army blockaded the island of Tyre. Following the successful Assyrian campaign, Baal surrendered and was severely punished: his cities on the continent were taken from him and annexed to the Assyrian territory in the Acco plain. A certain Bel-shadu'a is known to have held the title of "prefect of Tyre" (Ungnad 1938:446); "Tyre" may have been the official name of the new province. It covered the area between Mount Carmel in the south and either the Liṭani river, or the Zahrani river in the north. It bordered on the province of Kār-Esarhaddon, whose area reached northward as far as Nahr el-Kalb, the southern border of the kingdom of Gubla.

The reorganization of the new province took place either in the late years of Esarhaddon or in the early years of Ashurbanipal and, as far as we know, was the final step in the Assyrian annexation of the former Phoenician areas.

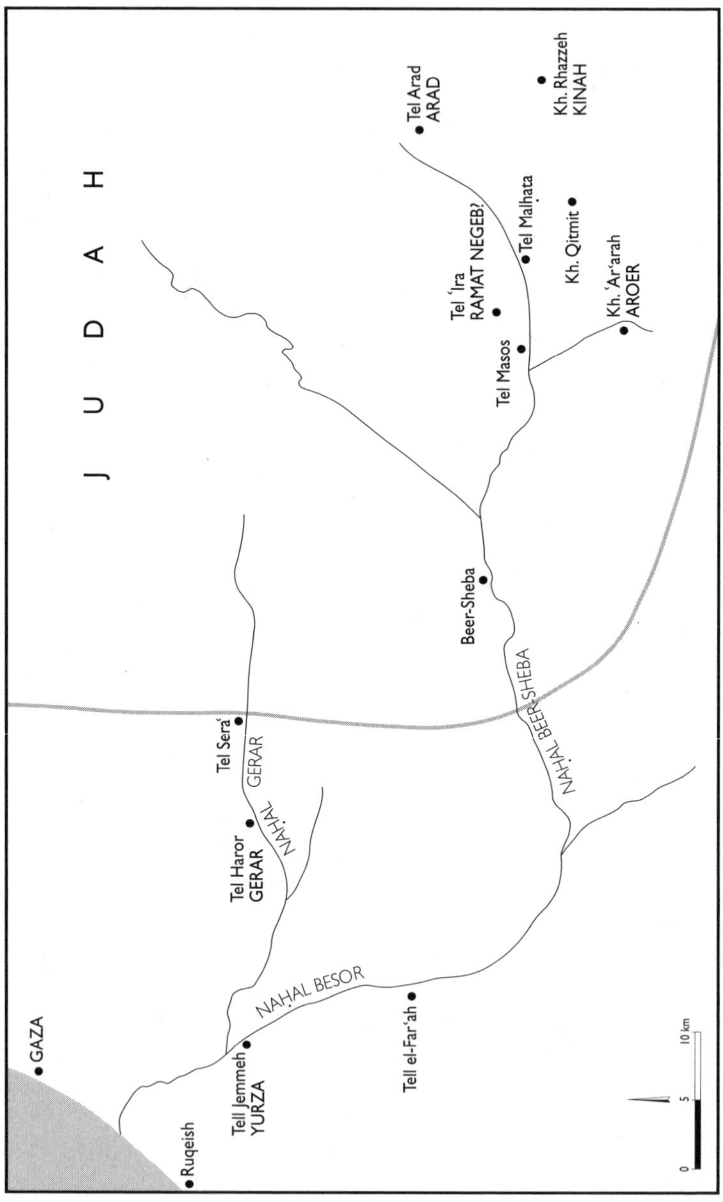

Settlements along Naḥal Besor and Its Tributaries

Only two continental kingdoms, Gubla and Samsimurūna, survived the thrust of Assyrian annexation, together with the two island kingdoms of Tyre and Arvad.

The location of Samsimurūna may be discussed briefly. The key document is letter ND 2370 (Saggs 1963:76–77). Qurdi-Ashur-lāmur informs the king that the people of Yauna, i.e., the Greeks, have raided Samsimurūna, Ḫariṣu, and a third town, whose name is not intact. The name Ḫariṣu may have been preserved in that of the modern village Ḥarissa, about 2.5 km. east of modern Jounie. We may assume that Samsimurūna was located on the southern border of the kingdom of Gubla, not far from the outlet of Nahr el-Kalb to the sea.

Overall, six Assyrian provinces were located along the eastern Mediterranean coast in the late Assyrian empire. The northern provinces of Kullani and Ṣimirra were founded by Tiglath-pileser in 738. The province of Kār-Esarhaddon was established by Esarhaddon in 677, and the province of Tyre was reorganized, either by Esarhaddon in his late years, or by Ashurbanipal in the early years of his reign. The province of Du'ru was founded by Tiglath-pileser in 732. The province of Ashdod was annexed by Sargon II in 712. It is obvious that no overall plan guided the Assyrian kings in their handling of the coastal districts and that the system of Assyrian provinces along the coast developed in stages, according to the individual policy of each Assyrian ruler.

2. Population Changes and Settlement Distribution Following Assyrian Deportations

"Two-way" mass deportations from/to Syria-Palestine are amply attested in contemporaneous sources. Assyrian royal inscriptions and biblical references indicate the areas from which the deportees were uprooted or to where they were resettled. Assyrian documents indicate the steps taken to build towns and fortresses, transfer the deportees and settle them in new locations. However, the documentary evidence, important as it is, reflects only part of the overall activity and can hardly supply the data necessary for estimating the effect of the deportations and resettlements on the Assyrian provinces and vassal kingdoms. But archaeological evidence may fill in some of the missing data and, when combined with the written sources, may help us understand the impact of Assyrian activity on demography, settlement distribution and economic activity. Although such data, unfortunately, as yet are lacking for southern Syria and the Phoenician coast, they are particularly rich for the area of modern Israel, where detailed surveys and many excavations have been carried out over a long period, enabling us to arrive at a reasonable estimate of the overall built-up area and population size in various parts of the land. Extensive field work and surveys were also recently conducted in Transjordan, making it possible to draw some preliminary conclusions about the Transjordanian kingdoms.

My discussion will concentrate mainly on the different areas of modern Israel and will be presented geographically, rather than chronologically (for a detailed discussion, see Na'aman 1993).

2.1. The Area of Galilee

Assyrian and biblical sources indicate that following his campaigns of 733/32, Tiglath-pileser III deported people from Upper and Lower Galilee and, in particular, from Lower Galilee and the margins of the Jezreel Valley (Na'aman 1993:105–106). The 13,520 exiles mentioned in one inscription (Rost 1893:Pl. XVIIIA:9) may be the overall number of deportees from Lower Galilee.

The evidence from the detailed survey conducted in Lower Galilee indicates a decline of settlement in the late eighth-seventh (and possibly sixth) centuries. Significant destruction in the late eighth century BCE and a long period of desolation were observed in the excavations conducted at Hazor, Chinnereth (Tell el-ᶜOreimeh) and Marom (Tel Qarnei Ḥiṭṭin). We may conclude that the "one-way" deportation conducted within the area of Galilee left it in a state of partial abandonment and desolation.

In addition to the provincial capital (Megiddo), the Assyrians built residencies at Ayyelet ha-Shahar, near Tel Hazor, and at Chinnereth (Tell el-ᶜOreimeh). Additional residencies may well be discovered in the future. The pattern of government as indicated by the archaeological research is clear: a central provincial capital for the governor and his court and numerous secondary strategically located centers where local officials and small military units were stationed.

2.2. The Province of Samerīna

During his 720 campaign, Sargon deported 27,290 people from the hill country of Samaria and settled them in Halah, on the Habor and in Media (2 Kgs. 17:6; 18:11). The first deportation to the new province took place in 715, when north Arabian tribes were settled there. The major deportation to Samerīna, mentioned in 2 Kgs. 17:24, took place in 710/9, following Sargon's Babylonian campaigns against Merodach-baladan. The deportees were brought from both the major Babylonian cities (Babylon and Cuthah) and from the peripheral Aramean and Chaldean areas. One of these groups, the Avvim, settled in the district of Bethel as is attested by the name of a settlement there (Josh. 18:23). Another group of deportees was settled in northern Samerīna as is evident from the name *kpr ksdyh* ("the Chaldeans village";

modern Khirbet Kashde southwest of Ṭubas) mentioned in the Rehob synagogue inscription of the sixth century CE.

Deportations under Esarhaddon and Ashurbanipal are mentioned in the book of Ezra. According to Ezra 4:9–10, Asnappar (= Ashurbanipal) deported Babylonians (men of Erech, Babylon and possibly Sippar) and Elamites (men of Susa) and settled them "in the cities of Samaria and in the rest of the province Beyond the River." The deportation took place in years 648–646, after the quashing of Shamash-shum-ukin's rebellion and the conquest of Susa. Thus, it is evident that, during the 640s, the Assyrians were still actively developing the province and settling new groups of deportees there.

Two cuneiform documents found during the excavations of Gezer are dated to 651 and 649 BCE. More than half of the names mentioned therein (12 out of 21) are Babylonian, and it is evident that deportees were settled there, either by Sargon or Ashurbanipal.

A detailed survey was conducted in the hill country of Samaria, and some of the results have been published. The eighth century population of this area is estimated to have been about 95,000–100,000 persons (the hill country of Manasseh — 50,000; the city of Samaria — 15,000; the hill country of Ephraim — 33,000). Thus, the 27,290 persons deported by Sargon would have constituted more than a quarter of the entire estimated population.

In studying the settlements of the deportees, the main problem is to distinguish the pottery of the eighth century from that of the seventh century. Zertal (1989; 1990:11–14) suggests that the so-called "wedge-shaped indented bowl," fragments of which were found in sites located in the area to the north and east of the city of Samaria, was brought by exiles from southern Mesopotamia and should be dated to the seventh century. Fragments of this bowl were found in 34 hill country sites, and, thus, he concludes that these are places in which deportees were settled. However, neither the date of the pottery nor its origin are satisfactorily established (London 1992). The areas and scope of settlement in the hill country of Samaria must await further investigation.

2.3. The Southern Coast of Philistia

During his 720 campaign, Sargon deported 9,033 people from the Raphia area, south of Naḥal Besor. In 712, he conquered Ashdod and its towns and deported their inhabitants. Esarhaddon in his second year (679) conducted a campaign against the city of Arza, which is described as situated "on the border of the Brook of Egypt," and deported its king and its inhabitants.

In two badly broken prisms, it is stated that Sargon settled people on the borderland of the Brook of Egypt. The deportation of people "from the countries of the east" to Ashdod is mentioned in Sargon's inscriptions of 712. I have suggested that the Brook of Egypt should be identified with Naḥal Besor, a remarkable, deep, long wādi that, in many periods, marked (with its tributaries) the limits of permanent settlement in southern Palestine (Na'aman 1979:74–86). Excavations and surveys conducted in southern Philistia and along Naḥal Besor give considerable support to this identification, as against an earlier suggestion that the Brook of Egypt be identified with Wādi el-'Arish. It is evident that the area of Naḥal Besor experienced an unprecedented demographic boom in the seventh century, whereas the area near Wādi el-'Arish was sparsely inhabited at that time (see Oren 1993).

The most remarkable site established on the coast of Philistia in the late eighth-seventh centuries is Tell er-Ruqeish (in the vicinity of Deir el-Balaḥ). It is a fortified site, 20–25 acres in size, founded on virgin soil (Oren et al. 1986). The site was recently identified with Ienysos, which, according to Herodotus (III 5), was the southernmost coastal emporia that belonged to the king of the Arabs in the fifth century BCE (Lemaire 1990:44). A fortified stronghold uncovered at Tel Haror (Oren et al. 1991) and a second Assyrian citadel unearthed at Tel Sera^{c} were both located along Naḥal Gerar, north of Naḥal Besor. Two small sites in southern Philistia — one near the outlet of Naḥal Shiqma to the sea and the other at Ḥorvat Hogah — seem to be small Assyrian forts. Another site, apparently with an Assyrian temple, was unearthed at Tell Abu Seleimeh, on the northwestern coast of the Sinai Peninsula (Reich 1984).

An Assyrian administrative center, with mudbrick barrel-vaulted building and a considerable amount of Assyrian "Palace Ware," was unearthed at Tell Jemmeh, about 12 km. south of Gaza. Two ostraca with names apparently of deportees brought to the place from the Zagros area were found at the site (Na'aman and Zadok 1988). Tell Jemmeh, which is possibly identical with the city of Arza, apparently served as the seat of the military governor of the area of Naḥal Besor. Seventh century Aramaic ostraca from Tell Sera^{c}, Tell Jemmeh and Tell el-Far^{c}ah may have been written either by deportees or by Assyrian garrisons stationed in the area (Naveh 1985:20).

It should be noted both that the area of southern Philistia was not annexed by Assyria and that, nevertheless, Assyria operated there intensively, regardless of its legal status. The importance of the area as a bridge to Egypt and as the outlet of the Arabian trade is well-known (Tadmor 1966; Na'aman 1979; Finkelstein 1992). Direct Assyrian involvement in the area began in the time of Tiglath-pileser III, who entrusted the sheikh of the Arab tribe Idibi'ilu with the task of "gatekeepership over Egypt." Sargon and Esarhaddon deported rural and pastoral groups from the areas of Raphia and Arza (Tell Jemmeh), bringing others to replace them. Sargon entrusted deportees to the Sheikh of Laban, and Esarhaddon cooperated with the Arabs in his Egyptian campaign in 671. The policy of "divide and rule" is typical of the Assyrian handling of their desert frontiers, and the flourishing of the southern coast of Philistia testifies to the success of their policy.

2.4. The Kingdom of Judah

In his annals, Sennacherib wrote that he laid siege to 46 of Hezekiah's walled cities and to the countless small villages in their vicinity, conquered them and drove out 200,150 people. Excavations and surveys conducted in Judah have provided much evidence of the destructive nature of the Assyrian campaign. All sites that have been excavated in the Shephelah were destroyed, and major sites remained deserted during the seventh century BCE. The number of eighth century sites discovered in the survey of the Shephelah and the estimated number of population are several times greater than those of the seventh century (Dagan 1992). A somewhat similar, though less drastic, picture emerges from the new surveys conducted in the hill country of Judah and in Benjamin (Finkelstein and Magen 1993; Ofer 1993). Late eighth century Judah was much stronger than the late seventh century kingdom, with larger and stronger settlements, a larger population, and greater military power and economic capability.

Broshi and Finkelstein (1992) recently estimated that the overall population of the kingdom of Judah in the late eighth century was about 110,000 persons. In light of the new surveys of the Shephelah and the hill country, the number should be raised to about 130,000 persons. The number of exiles reported by Sennacherib (200,150) is certainly exaggerated, but it is much closer to historical reality than scholars have assumed in the past. Sennacherib's aim to weaken the rebellious kingdom of Judah by systematic destruction and massive deportation met with lasting success. Judah lacked the human resources needed to resettle the destroyed and deserted areas, and the results of the Assyrian campaign were felt everywhere, even a hundred years later (Na'aman 1993:112–115, with earlier literature).

The weakness of Judah opened the way for the rise of Ekron, its closest neighbor to the west. In the ninth-eighth centuries BCE, Ekron was a small, weak town. The massive growth of Ekron in the seventh century is the direct result of Judah's decline. It took the place of Judah in the northern Shephelah, attracted refugees from the destroyed Judean towns, expanded its territory and developed its economy (Gitin 1989).

Only one district of the kingdom of Judah flourished in the seventh century, namely, the Beer-sheba Valley. New sites were established, and the overall built-up area of sites is about double that of the eighth century (Na'aman 1987; Finkelstein 1992:161). The prosperity of the southern frontier of the kingdom of Judah is the direct result of the *pax Assyriaca* and the growth of the Arabian caravan trade that stemmed from the economic activity of the Assyrian empire.

2.5. The Transjordanian Kingdoms

Edom, Moab and Ammon are listed among the southern Syrian and Transjordanian cities and districts, which were attacked by the Qedarites in the time of Ashurbanipal and defeated by the Assyrian troops (Eph'al 1982: 147–155). Defending the eastern frontier was essential for Assyrian military and economic interests, and, for this reason, the Transjordanian vassal states stood under the Assyrian military umbrella. No wonder that the three kingdoms thrived during this period, as is evident from the archaeological work conducted in their areas.

Of particular interest is the situation in Edom. Recent excavations and surveys have demonstrated that extensive settlement in this peripheral zone occurred no earlier than the eighth century BCE (Bienkowski 1992) and that the highlands of Edom experienced a wave of settlement in the seventh century (Hart 1987:292; Bienkowski 1990). The direct relation between the rise of the Assyrian empire and the settlement and prosperity of Edom is self-evident. The Assyrians defended the land, because it served both as a buffer zone against the desert tribes and as a link in the Arabian overland trade. Edom dominated the trade routes to Elath and Arabia and was able to enjoy the economic fruits of its position. The *pax Assyriaca* and economic prosperity brought about, for the first time in history, the emergence of a territorial kingdom in this remote arid zone.

The extent of Assyrian involvement in the affairs of Edom remains unknown (Weippert 1987:99–100; Millard 1992). Assyrian influence is evident in the two major buildings unearthed on the acropolis of Buseirah, although the function of the buildings is unclear. Further influence is revealed by an analysis of the material culture (Bennett 1978; Bienkowski 1990:193–196). It is possible that the Assyrians installed their own official(s) to supervise and co-ordinate with the local rulers, as they did in Phoenicia and Philistia (Bennett 1978:170). However, it must be emphasized that political reality must have been far more important than the formal status of the representatives of the empire.

The settlement pattern and material culture of Moab in the seventh century is not clear. On the other hand, a flourishing of settlement may be observed in the land of Ammon. It has recently been suggested that the so-called "Rujm el-Malfuf buildings" should mainly be dated to the seventh century and that their outer limits reflect the western boundary of the kingdom. These sites indicate the extensive Ammonite settlement along their borders in the time of the *pax Assyriaca*, similar to the flourishing of other frontier areas (southern Philistia, the Negeb and Edom) discussed above (Kletter 1991; see Hübner 1992:137–46).

2.6. Babylonian Policy Near the Egyptian Border

Comparison may contribute to a better perception of history, and I would like to conclude this article with a short presentation of the Babylonian strategy on the southwestern front of the empire, *vis-à-vis* that of Assyria.

In the course of his conquest of Palestine, Nebuchadnezzar destroyed the cities of Ashkelon and Ekron (604 BCE). In the year 601/600 he tried to conquer Egypt and failed. The military failure brought in its wake the renewal of Egyptian efforts to regain a foothold in Asia and the eruption of rebellions in the Babylonian vassal states. Nebuchadnezzar responded drastically to the threat in the buffer zone with Egypt. Step by step, he conquered all the kingdoms and annexed them to his territory, with some kingdoms suffering severe destruction. Moreover, unlike the Assyrians, the Babylonians neither tried to develop their new provinces, nor tried to defend them against Arabian raiders. The trade network in southern Palestine and Transjordan was neglected, and areas participating in the Arabian trade suffered economic recession. As a result, the eastern and southern frontiers shrank westward and northward. Archaeological excavations and surveys conducted in Palestine and Transjordan indicate a drastic reduction during the sixth century in the number of settlements and their size, in economic activity and in material culture. It is evident that its overall policy can have crucial consequences for people living on the frontier of the empire and that a change of policy may bring about drastic change in the fortune of peoples living under imperial sway.

References

Aharoni, Y. 1967. *The Land of the Bible: A Historical Geography.* Philadelphia.

Alt, A. 1929. Das System der assyrischen Provinzen auf dem Boden des Reiches Israel. *ZDPV* 52: 220–42. (Reprint: Alt 1953: 188–205).

Alt, A. 1945. Neue assyrische Nachrichten über Palästina und Syrien. *ZDPV* 67: 128–159 (Reprint: Alt 1953: 226–241).

Alt, A. 1953. Jesaja 8,23–9,6. Befreiungsnacht und Kronungstag. In Alt 1953: 206–225.

Alt, A. 1953. *Kleine Schriften zur Geschichte des Volkes* Israel II. München.

Bennett, C.-M. 1978. Some Reflections on Neo-Assyrian Influence in Transjordan. In: Moorey, R. and Parr, P. eds. *Archaeology in the Levant. Essays for Kathleen Kenyon.* Warminster: 164–171.

Bienkowski, P. 1990. Umm el-Biyara, Tawilan and Buseirah in Retrospect. *Levant* 22:91–109.

Bienkowski, P. 1992. The Date of Sedentary Occupation in Edom: Evidence from Umm el-Biyara, Tawilan and Buseirah. In: Bienkowski, P. ed. *Early Edom and Moab. The Beginning of the Iron Age in Southern Jordan* (Sheffield Archaeological Monographs 7). Sheffield: 99–112.

Broshi, M. and Finkelstein, I. 1992. The Population of Palestine in Iron Age II. *BASOR* 287: 47–60.

Dagan, Y. 1992. *The Shephelah during the Period of the Monarchy in Light of Archaeological Excavations and Survey* (M.A. Thesis). Tel Aviv University. (Hebrew).

Eph'al, I. 1979. Assyrian Domination in Palestine. In: Malamat, A. ed. *The Age of the Monarchies: Political History.* (The World History of the Jewish People). Jerusalem: 276–289, 364–368.

Eph'al, I. 1982. *The Ancient Arabs. Nomads on the Borders of the Fertile Crescent 9th–5th Centuries B.C.* Jerusalem and Leiden.

Finkelstein, I. 1992. Horvat Qitmit and the Southern Trade in the Late Iron Age II. *ZDPV* 108: 156–170.

Finkelstein, I. and Magen, Y. (eds.). 1993. *Archaeological Survey of the Hill Country of Benjamin.* Jerusalem. (Hebrew).

Forrer, E. 1920. *Die Provinzeinteilung des assyrischen Reiches.* Leipzig.

Gitin, S. 1989. Tel Miqne-Ekron: A Type-Site for the Inner Coastal Plain in the Iron Age II Period. In: Gitin, S. and Dever, W.G. *Recent Excavations in Israel: Studies in Iron Age Archaeology* (AASOR 49). Winona Lake: 23–58.

Hart, S. 1987. The Edom Survey Project 1984–85: The Iron Age. In: Hadidi, A. ed. *Studies in the History and Archaeology of Jordan* III. Amman: 287–290.

Hübner, U. 1992. *Die Ammoniter. Untersuchungen zur Geschichte, Kultur und Religion eines transjordanischen Volkes im 1. Jahrtausend v. Chr.* Wiesbaden.

Kletter, R. 1991. The Rujm el-Malfuf Buildings and the Assyrian Vassal State of Ammon. *BASOR* 284: 33–50.

Lemaire, A. 1990. Populations et territoires de la Palestine à l'époque perse. *Transeuphratène* 3: 31–74.

Lipiński, E. 1971. The Assyrian Campaign to Manṣuate, in 796 B.C., and the Zakir Stela. *Annali dell'Istituto Orientale di Napoli* 31: 393–399.

London, G. 1992. Reply to A. Zertal's "The Wedge-shaped Decorated Bowl and the Origin of the Samaritans." *BASOR* 286: 89–90.

Millard, A. 1992. Assyrian Involvement in Edom. In: Bienkowski, P. ed. *Early Edom and Moab. The Beginning of the Iron Age in Southern Jordan* (Sheffield Archaeological Monographs 7). Sheffield: 35–39.

Miller, J.M. and Hayes, J.H. 1986. *A History of Ancient Israel and Judah.* Philadelphia.

Na'aman, N. 1977–78. Looking for KTK. *WO* 9: 220–239.

Na'aman, N. 1979. The Brook of Egypt and Assyrian Policy on the Border of Egypt. *Tel Aviv* 6: 68–90.

Na'aman, N. 1987. The Negev in the Last Century of the Kingdom of Judah. *Cathedra* 42: 3–15. (Hebrew).

Na'aman, N. 1993. Population Changes in Palestine Following Assyrian Deportations. *Tel Aviv* 20: 104–24.

Na'aman, N. 1995. Rezin of Damascus and the Land of Gilead. *ZDPV* 111: 105–117.

Na'aman, N. 1999. Lebo-Hamath, Ṣubath-Hamath, and the Northern Boundary of the Land of Canaan. *Ugarit-Forschungen* 31: 417–441.

Na'aman, N. and Zadok, R. 1988. Sargon II's Deportations to Israel and Philistia (716–708 B.C.). *JCS* 40: 36–46.

Naveh, J. 1985. Writing and Scripts in Seventh-Century B.C.E. Philistia: The New Evidence from Tell Jemmeh. *IEJ* 35: 8–21.

Oded, B. 1970. Observations on Methods of Assyrian Rule in Transjordania after the Palestinian Campaign of Tiglath-Pileser III. *JNES* 29: 177–186.

Ofer, A. 1993. *The Highland of Judah during the Biblical Period* I–II. (Ph.D. Thesis). Tel Aviv University. (Hebrew).

Oren, E.D. 1993. Ethnicity and Regional Archaeology: The Western Negev under Assyrian Rule. In: Biran, A. and Aviram, J. eds. *Biblical Archaeology Today* II. Jerusalem: 102–105.

Oren, E.D. et al. 1986. A Phoenician Emporium on the Border of Egypt. *Qadmoniot* 19: 83–91. (Hebrew).

Oren, E.D. et al. 1991. Tel Haror — After Six Seasons. *Qadmoniot* 24: 2–19. (Hebrew).

Ottoson, M. 1969. *Gilead: Tradition and History.* (Coniectanea Biblica, Old Testament Series 3). Lund.

Reich, R. 1984. The Identification of the "Sealed *karu* of Egypt." *IEJ* 34: 32–38.

Rost, P. 1893. *Die Keilschrifttexte Tiglath-Pilesers III., nach den Papierabklatschen und Originalen des Britischen Museums* I–II. Leipzig.

Saggs, H.W.F. 1963. The Nimrud Letters, 1952 — Part VI. *Iraq* 25: 70–80.

Sapin, J. 1990. Essai sur les structures geographiques de la toponymie araméenne dans la Trouée de Homs (Liban-Syrie) et sur leur signification historique. *Transeuphratène* 2: 73–108.

Stern, E. 1990. Hazor, Dor and Megiddo in the Time of Ahab and under Assyrian Rule. *IEJ* 40: 12–30.

Tadmor, H. 1962. The Southern Border of Aram. *IEJ* 12: 114–122.

Tadmor, H. 1966. Philistia under Assyrian Rule. *BA* 29: 86–102.

Ungnad, A. 1938. Eponymen. *RLA* II: 412–57.

Weippert, M. 1972. Simo Parpola, Neo-Assyrian Toponyms. *Göttingische gelehrte Anzeigen* 224: 150–161.

Weippert, M. 1982. Zur Syrienpolitik Tiglatpilesers III. In: Nissen, H.J. and Renger, J. eds. *Mesopotamien und seine Nachbarn. Politische und kulturelle Wechselbeziehungen im Alten Vorderasien vom 4. bis 1. Jahrtausend v. Chr.* (Berliner Beiträge zum Vorderen Orient 1). Berlin: 395–408.

Weippert, M. 1987. The Relations of the States East of the Jordan with the Mesopotamian Powers during the First Millennium BC. In: Hadidi, A. ed. *Studies in the History and Archaeology of Jordan* III. Amman: 97–105.

Weippert, M. 1992. Die Feldzüge Adadniraris III. nach Syrien: Voraussetzungen, Verlauf, Folgen. *ZDPV* 108: 42–67.

Zertal, A. 1989. The Wedge-shaped Decorated Bowl and the Origin of the Samaritans. *BASOR* 276: 77–84.

Zertal, A. 1990. The Pahwah of Samaria (Northern Israel) during the Persian Period. Types of Settlement, Economy, History and New Discoveries. *Transeuphratène* 3: 9–30.

The Brook of Egypt and Assyrian Policy on the Border of Egypt[1]

The extensive archaeological activity conducted recently in the western Negev and the southern coast of Philistia poses a challenge to the historian studying the ancient history of the Land of Israel. Although the archaeological evidence alone cannot throw direct light on these historical processes and events, the combination of excavations and surveys produces many clues that — if correctly combined with the written sources — may fill in the gaps of several sketchy chapters in the history of the country.

This article is devoted mainly to the events that occurred in southern Philistia during the late eighth-seventh centuries BCE, based on the relevant Assyrian texts, as well as the archaeological findings from this region, supplemented, wherever necessary, by sources from earlier and later periods.

The problem of the location of the Brook of Egypt, mentioned both in the Bible and Assyrian inscriptions, will be central to the discussion, because this is crucial for the correct understanding of the area in which the events under discussion took place.

A. The Evidence of the Assyrian Inscriptions

According to the eponym chronicle, the first Assyrian campaign to the coast of Philistia was conducted in the year 734 BCE.[2] The annals describing the events of that year have not yet been found, but several summary inscriptions[3] of Tiglath-pileser III mention a campaign against Gaza that resulted in

---

1. Reprinted with permission. Tel Aviv 6 (1979), 68–90.

2. For detailed description of the Assyrian campaigns to Philistia during the reign of Tiglath-pileser III, see Alt 1953a; Tadmor 1964:263 –269; 1972.

3. The term "summary inscription" is differentiated here from the "annals" in that the latter are year-by-year narratives of events arranged according to their chronological sequence, and, in the summary inscriptions, the sequence of events is not maintained, but arranged according to geographical — or even associative — order. Another term frequently used to express the non-chronological character of the summary inscriptions is "display inscriptions" (German Prunkinschriften, first introduced by Schrader 1880:13); but, this term should, in my opinion, be reserved for monumental inscriptions accessible to the

the flight of Hanunu, king of Gaza, to Egypt. The Assyrian king entered the city, erected his stele in the palace, carried its booty to Assyria and imposed payment of an annual tribute. In his most detailed summary inscription (ND 400)[4] a campaign to the Brook of Egypt (Naḫal Muṣur) and the setting up a stele there is mentioned immediately after the conquest of Gaza.

The determinative URU that usually precedes a toponym appears before "Naḫal Muṣur." Therefore, several scholars have translated this toponym as "the city of the River of Egypt" (Wiseman 1951:23; Alt 1953a:157; Tadmor 1966:88; Borger in Galling 1968:56). But the phrase "as far as the town of Raphia, to the border zone of the Brook of Egypt" (for the translation see below) is repeated in two inscriptions of Esarhaddon, once with the determinative URU preceding "Naḫal Muṣur" (*adi Rapiḫi ana itê Naḫal māt Muṣur*) (Borger 1956:112, line 17) and second, without it ([. . . *ana it*]*ê* ^{uru}*Naḫal Muṣur*) (Borger 1956:113, Frt. G, line 6). Thus, it is clear that the determinative URU in the inscription of Tiglath-pileser is employed in its more generalized sense and that the toponym is to be transliterated as ^{uru}*na-ḫal mu-ṣur* and translated as "the Brook of Egypt" (see Weidner 1941–1944: 42–44; Alt 1945:129–130). The word *naḫal* (meaning "river," "stream," "wâdi") is already included in the toponym, so it is possible that the scribe felt it redundant to use the determinative ÍD (river) and preferred the more general determinative URU. Moreover, ^{uru}*na-ḫal mu-ṣur* is followed by the noun "river" (*nā*[*ru*]), which is an apposition to the Brook of Egypt, not to a place called by this name. The passage of Tiglath-pileser, thus, is to be translated: "[I erected] my royal stele at the Brook of Egypt, a ri[ver that . . .]."

ND 400 is a duplicate (or perhaps even a *long-distance join*) of the detailed summary inscription II R 67, published in the edition of Tiglath-pileser's inscriptions (Rost 1893:pls. 35–38).[5] Its text was arranged according to geographical, rather than chronological, order. It is, therefore, questionable

public eye, as opposed to "building inscriptions" found on objects buried in the foundations; neither of them should be applied to the content of the inscriptions.

4. ND 400 was published by Wiseman (1951:21 24); for translation, see Borger in Galling 1968:56; for discussion, see Alt 1953a:150, 162; Tadmor 1966:88 90; 1972:222–228.

5. For the text of II R 67, see Rost 1893:54–76. Wiseman (1951:21, n. 2) has already commented on the similarity in script between II R 67 and ND 400. Tadmor (1972:223 and n. 6) has noted that "originally ND 400 was part of a large tablet like K 3751 (= II R 67) representing the detailed 'display inscription' written in ornate literary style (not to be confused with the summary 'display inscription' like ND 4301 + 4305)." Furthermore, the text of II R 67 comes to an end exactly where the text of ND 400 opens. Hence, the two texts should be combined, because it seems that they are either duplicates or even two fragments of the same tablet.

whether the Assyrian ruler reached the Brook of Egypt immediately after the conquest of Gaza in his campaign of 734 BCE or whether he arrived there only during a later campaign, the Brook of Egypt becoming associated with the Gaza episode due to its geographical proximity. To clarify this matter, we must examine the passages dealing with the southern Philistine coast in tablet ND 400 and its (direct) continuation in the inscription II R 67.

After the campaign to the River of Egypt, the summary inscription mentions the payment of tribute by an (unknown) Arab ruler and by "Siruatti the Me'unite, whose [territory is] below Egypt" (Tadmor 1966:89; 1972:223–224). The expression "below Egypt" refers to the intermediate region between southern Palestine and Egypt (for a more precise location, see below). Therefore, it is tempting to connect these two episodes with the campaign to Gaza and the Brook of Egypt and to date all of them to the year 734. However, the annals of Tiglath-pileser mention a second campaign to the Philistine coast in 733–732, in the course of which the Assyrian king replaced the ruler of Ashkelon and entrusted the sheikh of the Arab tribe Idibi'ilu (see Gen. 25: 13 Adbe'el) with the task of "gatekeepership over Egypt" (Rost 1893:38–40, lines 235–240; see Rost 1893:38, line 226; 70, line 6; 82, line 34; Oppenheim 1969:282, n. 2; *pace* Garelli 1971:45–46). Thus, there is a possibility of dating all the Assyrian activity in the vicinity of the Brook of Egypt to this second campaign. However, pending the discovery of new material on the subject, there is no definite solution to these two possibilities.

The nomination of the sheikh of the tribe of Idibi'ilu to "gatekeepership over Egypt," as well as the reference to the Me'unites dwelling "below (i.e., at the foot of) Egypt," shows that there was a region to the south of Philistia considered (from a northern point of view) to be part of Egypt. This was the area south of the River of Egypt, on the fringes of which the Me'unites were dwelling. Locating their seat, therefore, is essential for defining its borders.

The Me'unites are mentioned twice in the Bible. The verse related to Uzziah (2 Chr. 26:7) is of no help to us, but 1 Chr. 4:39–41 Is of great importance:

> They [the sons of Simeon] went to the entrance of Gedor, to the east side of the valley, to seek pasture for their flocks, where they found rich, good pasture, and the land was very broad, quiet, and peaceful; for the former inhabitants there belonged to Ham. These, registered by name, came in the days of Hezekiah, king of Judah, and destroyed their tents and the Me'unites who were found there, and exterminated them to this day, and settled in their place, because there was pasture there for their flocks.

The sons of Simeon had settled in the western Negev; therefore, the Septuagint version "entrance of Gerar" (instead of Gedor) is certainly correct and is to be identified with either Naḥal Gerar (Wâdi esh-Shari'a) or Naḥal Besor (Wâdi Shelaleh and Wâdi Ghazzeh; see Albright 1924:147–150; Alt 1935:

301–302; Aharoni 1967:337). According to biblical tradition, this region was occupied by the ʿAvites (Deut. 2:23; Josh. 13:3) belonging to the sons of Ham (1 Chr. 4:40), who were counted among the people of Egypt (Albright 1921: 187–190). The above verses describe events that occurred during the reign of Hezekiah, king of Judah, shortly after Tiglath-pileser's campaigns, when the sons of Simeon smote the desert tribes, including the Me'unites, living in the territory southeast of Gaza adjacent to the Besor river. Hence, this is probably the same area that Tiglath-pileser reached and where he forced the tribes to pay him tribute.

As we shall see below, there are additional indications that the region south of the Besor river was considered as "Egypt" in the eyes of the northerners, thus, supplying the first clue to the location of the Brook of Egypt.

The next Assyrian king who campaigned against the southern Philistine coast was Sargon II. After his victory over Hamath and its allies (720 BCE), the Assyrian ruler led his troops towards Philistia. Probably the cities of Gibbethon and Ekron were the first to be conquered (with El-Amin 1953:35–40; Reade 1976:99–102; *pace* Tadmor 1958: 83, n. 243); Sargon then continued his march to Gaza, whose king, Hanunu, fled for the second time to Egypt. But on this occasion, Egyptian troops came to his aid, as seen from the following passage from the annals of Sargon (Lie 1921:8–9, lines 53–54; Luckenbill 1927: §5; Oppenheim 1969:285): "[. . .] he gave him Re'u, his [commander], to his aid, and set out against me in order to wage battle." Nevertheless, the Assyrian army won the battle near Raphia, the Egyptian commander fled to Egypt, and Hanunu was taken into captivity. Sargon destroyed the city of Raphia, seized "9033 people together with their many possessions" and deported them to Assyria.

Four years later (716 BCE), the Assyrian army returned to southern Philistia. The details of this campaign are known only from a prism fragment, for which the following reconstruction is suggested:

> . . . (people) from the land [GN I deported and in] a land whose [place they have never known, in the city GN_2] situated at the border zone of the Brook of Eg[ypt, territory which is located on the shore of the] Western [sea] I set[tled them. In the hands of so and so], the sheikh of Laban, [I entrusted them].[6]

6. The prism was published by Weidner (1941–1944:41–46) and subsequently discussed by Alt (1945:128–132), Tadmor (1958:77–78; 1966:91–92), Ephʿal (1969:149–151) and Garelli (1971: 45). Following is my suggested transliteration:

(3) *ul-tu qé-reb* [*KUR GN as-su-ḫa-am-ma ù*] (4) *i-na ma-a-ti ša* [a?-šar?-ša? *la i-du-ú i-na* [uru]GN_2] (5) *ša paṭ-ṭi* [uru]*Na-ḫal M*[*u-ṣur na-gi-i ša a-ḫi tam-tim*] (6) *ša šul-mu* [d]*šam-ši u-ša-a*[*ṣ-bit-ma i-na* ŠU[II] PN] (7) [lú]na-si-ku *ša* [uru]*La-ba-an* [*am-nu-šu-nu-ti*]

A fragmentary text, published by Winckler (1899 PI. 45, No. 79–7–8, 14) and restored

In attempting to identify the site of resettlement of these deportees on "the border of the Brook of Egypt," Alt (1945:130–137) suggested that it was in or near Raphia and that they were placed under the supervision of the sheikh of Laban. Tadmor (1958:77; 1966:91–92) has argued that the exiles were settled around Wâdi el-ʿArish and that the entire region was given over to the sheikh of Laban. (For the author's proposal, based on a different location of the River of Egypt, see Section B below).

Further Assyrian campaigns to Philistia were conducted in 712–711 BCE. This time they were directed against Ashdod, whose main cities were conquered, its inhabitants deported and the kingdom annexed to Assyria (Alt 1945:138–146; 1953a:160–162; Tadmor 1958:79–84; 1966:94–95; Na'aman 1974: 32–33).[7]

---

by Tadmor (1958:77 n. 182), helps to fill the lacunae in lines 6–7 of the prism. It seems that more signs are needed to fill the gap at the beginning of line 2 of this fragment, and, according to the facsimile published by Winckler, I would like to suggest restoring lines 1–2 of it as follows: (1) [*ú-ša-aṣ-bit-ma i-na* ŠU]^{II} ^{m}x [. . .] (2) [^{lú}*na-si-ku ša* ^{uru}*La-ba-an*] *am-nu-šu*-[*nu-ti*]. Thus, the two texts are parallel in all their lines.

The restoration "whose [place they have never known]" in line 4 is tentative; another possibility would be "whose [name they have never heard]."

7. When discussing the campaign of 711 BCE against Ashdod, Tadmor (1966:95) has suggested several other places where there was the same kind of dual existence of local king and Assyrian governor, i.e., Egypt, Que and Tabal (see Postgate 1973:28; Elat 1975). Granted that Tadmor has a valid argument regarding Egypt (see detailed discussions by Spalinger 1974:307-326; 1976:133–137), this was, in any event, an exceptional case. Regarding Tabal, however, it is clear that only the northern kingdom of Bit Burutash was annexed; the others remained vassals of Assyria (Postgate 1973:30–32), and, thus, Tabal is not a relevant example. As for Que, I have suggested (Na'aman 1976:89–90) that only its coastal parts were annexed to Assyria, the northern mountainous regions remaining under their local rulers (Urikki in the reign of Sargon and Sanduari under Esarhaddon). Hence, we are left with no certain parallel to this "dual system" from the reign of Sargon.

As for Ashdod, Alt (1945:141–146) has suggested that Sargon's annexation of Ashdod was only the first step in his plan to annex all of Philistia, but he was killed before he could do so. His son Sennacherib had a different policy, and, thus, Ashdod remained an isolated province surrounded by vassal states. Contrary to my previous opinion (Na'aman 1974:33, n. 34), I now think that Alt's hypothesis is basically acceptable. It seems that the Assyrians planned to create a corridor to the Egyptian border and to isolate the Philistine coast from Judah. As the first stage towards this goal, they annexed Ashdod (711), still lacking any territorial contiguity with the nearby province of Samaria — exactly like Sargon's annexation of the Anatolian kingdoms at that time: first the remote kingdoms of Bit Burutash and Kammanu (713–712) and only later the kingdoms of Gurgum (711) and Kummuh (709/8), thus, creating territorial continuity with the two isolated western provinces. The death of Sargon in 705 brought the Assyrian plans for the Philistine coast to an end. Thus. the existence of an Assyrian governor side by side with a local king in Ashdod was, in my opinion, the result of an historical accident and not representative of any particular model of government current at the time in the Assyrian empire.

In a summary inscription written during the last years of Sargon, the range of his conquests are described as extending "from the land of Rashi near the Elamite border . . . as far as the Brook of Egypt" (Winckler 1889:pl. 43, lines 12–13).

The next Assyrian king whose inscriptions mention the region between Philistia and Egypt is Esarhaddon. According to the Babylonian chronicle, this ruler conducted a campaign against the city of Arza in his second year (679 BCE), plundered the town and deported its king, his son and all the inhabitants (Borger 1956:122; see Tadmor 1966:97–98), This event is described several times by Esarhaddon, who refers to the city as "Arza situated at the border zone (*ša pāṭi/itê*) of the Brook of Egypt" (Borger 1956:130 s.v. Arza; cf, Weissbach 1928–1929).[8]

Concerning the location of Arza: In documents from the second half of the second millennium BCE and in Shishak's topographical list, a city called Yurza is mentioned. Mazar (1952) placed it at Tell Jemmeh (Tel Gamma) on the banks of the Besor river. Although Mazar noted the similarity between "Yurza" of the second millennium and "Arza" of the first millennium (see Yeivin 1934–1935:156, n. 14), he did not pursue this equation, which was eventually proposed by Grintz (1961:16). Following the recent excavations at Tell Jemmeh, several scholars have taken up Grintz' proposal (Van Beek 1972: 246; Aharoni 1974:90; Mazar 1975:146). Nevertheless the equation has difficulties. Yurza was identified with Tell Jemmeh, situated on the banks of the Besor river, because this site lies at the southernmost limit of the Canaanite city-states; Arza was sought previously "at the border zone of the Brook of Egypt," commonly identified with Wâdi el-'Arish. However, it is most unlikely that Esarhaddon would have used such a precise expression as "at the border zone of the Brook of Egypt" to designate the broad area of 75 km. separating the two rivers, Naḥal Besor, on whose banks Tell Jemmeh is located, and Wâdi el-'Arish. It is even more unlikely that a city located near one river would be described by him as lying near the banks of another. We are left, then, with two diametrically opposed postulations: (a) to treat Yurza and Arza as two different places, or (b) to equate Yurza with Arza by identifying the Brook of Egypt with the Besor river.

My proposal to identify the Brook of Egypt with Naḥal Besor will be discussed hereunder. In the meantime, to maintain the equation of Yurza with Arza, the philological identity of the two names must be examined. The

8. Arza appears once with the determinative for country (KUR; Heidel 1956:14, line 57), but, in the parallel version (Borger 1956:50, line 55), it appears with the determinative for town (URU). The determinative KUR is best viewed here as a scribal error. For Arza in the Neo-Babylonian documents, see Eph'al 1978:80.

Egyptian transcription of Yurza is *yrḏ*. As we know, Egyptian *ḏ* may reflect either ṣ (*ḥḏr* = *Haṣor*) or z (*qḏr* = Gezer) in ancient Hebrew (Aharoni 1967:103), and the toponym might be transcribed as Yurza or Yurṣa. In light of Mazar's suggestion (1951:41) that the toponyms Yarda and Orda reflect the late transcription of ancient Yurza,[9] it is better transcribed with z. This shift from *z* to *d* finds a parallel in the very same area in the name "Gaza" written as Kadytis (Herodotus II 159).

According to the well-known rule that *yod* at the beginning of a word is preserved as a consonant before a long vowel. while it often shifts to a vowel before a short vowel (Aharoni 1967:111), the name Yurza may have been assimilated to *Urza (see Jordan/Urdunu; Jericho/er-Riḥa) and finally to Arza. Another possibility is that Arza is merely a shortened form, for which there are parallels both in biblical Hebrew (Jibleam/Bileam; Jabneel/Jabneh; Jekabzeel/Kabzeel; see Alt 1932:135, n. 14; Lipiński 1974:42) and Akkadian (Yalman/Alman; see Grayson 1975:242).

Summing up, it is clear that despite the difference in transcription between *Yurza* and *Arza* (and later also *Yarda* and *Orda*), these names might refer to one and the same place.

Coming back to the inscriptions of Esarhaddon: After his failure in the first campaign against Egypt (674 BCE), Esarhaddon marched again in the year 671. From Aphek, near the southwestern border of the province of Samaria, the Assyrian army advanced southward. In the words of annals of Esarhaddon: 30 *bēru qaqqar ultu Apqu ša pāṭi māt Same(ri)na adi Rapiḫi ana itê Naḫal māt Muṣur ašar nāru la išu* (Borger 1956:112, lines 16–17; Luckenbill 1927: §557; Oppenheim 1969:290; Tadmor 1964:281). In Raphia, the army took on as much water as might be carried and continued on its way to Egypt.

In order to translate the Akkadian passage cited above, the expression *ana itê GN*, needs to be clarified. There is no problem regarding the entity *ša pāṭi/ itê* GN, "at the border region of toponym so-and-so"; but the use of the preposition *ana* (instead of *ša)* deserves a short discussion. To the best of my knowledge, the expression *ana itê GN* appears in only one other royal inscriptions, i.e., that of Sargon II, where it is said of Yamani of Ashdod that when he heard of the approach of the Assyrian army, "*ana itê māt Muṣuri ša pāṭ māt Meluḫḫa innabitma*" (Winckler 1889:pl. 26, No. 56, lines 102–103; Weissbach 1918:178, line 12; Luckenbill 1927:§62; Oppenheim 1969:286b; Spalinger 1973: 97, n.

9. In this article, Mazar identified Yarda of Josephus with Yurza. However, subsequently (1957:66), he identified Yarda with *yrdn* of the Shishak inscription, although Yurza also appears in this inscription. Only one of the two identifications can be correct. Thus, it is preferable to connect Yurza with Yarda (and Orda of the Madeba map), with *yrdn* being located elsewhere.

17).[10] Subsequently, Yamani was detained by the Nubian ruler and extradited to Assyria. It is, thus, clear that Yamani crossed through Egypt and reached the border zone of Nubia in his attempt to gain support there. Accordingly, the translation "to the Egyptian border zone" for the phrase *ana itê māt Muṣri* would suit the context of the passage. ("He [Yamani] fled to the Egyptian border zone, which is at the border of Nubia.") Hence, the above-cited passage from the annals of Esarhaddon is to be translated: "A distance of thirty 'miles' from the town of Aphek which is at the border of Samaria as far as the town of Raphia, to the border zone of the Brook of Egypt, a place without (flowing) river." The Brook of Egypt was the best known landmark on the southern border of Philistia, and the scribe selected it in order to define the location of Raphia.

All of the above discussion is overshadowed by the question to be discussed hereunder: Which of the rivers on the border of Sinai was the Brook of Egypt?

B. The Location of The Brook of Egypt

From the outset of modern research, the equation Naḥal Mizraim = Wâdi el-'Arish was accepted without reservations. This equation was based on the Septuagint, where Naḥal Mizraim in Isa. 27:12 was translated by Greek Rhinocorura (Qal'at el-'Arish) and on the testimony of Rabbi Se'adya Gaon, who identified Naḥal Mizraim with Wâdi el-'Arish (Loewenstamm 1968; Abel 1939:546). But these references are of very late date, compared with the Assyrian and biblical sources, and should be treated with great caution.

Regarding the ancient borders between the Land of Israel and Egypt, the Egyptian sources provide us with the following background.

Traditionally, in the eyes of the Egyptians, the Nile or the Isthmus fringes were considered to be their *northern* boundary, the Sinai peninsula being regarded as part of Asia (Gardiner 1920; Grintz 1961; Kees 1961:190–211; Ḳallai 1975:28–29). This view is diametrically opposite to the northern point of view, according to which, the southern limits of Gaza, the southernmost city along the coast of Philistia, and the edges of the urban settlements on its eastern side were thought of as the southern border of Canaan, the intervening desert of Sinai being regarded by the northerners as part of Egypt (Albright 1921:187–190; Eph'al 1971). In the Late Bronze Age, as the Egyptians

10. CAD I 313b translated "He fled across the Egyptian border at the border region of Meluhha." For criticism of Oppenheim's translation, see Spalinger 1973:97, n. 17. The expression *ana itê* GN in the sense of "to the (end of the) border of GN" appears also in several Neo-Babylonian texts (CAD I 313b 6') and fits well the meaning of the Assyrian inscriptions.

came into closer contact with the north, they also became aware of the fact that the Sinai desert is not part of Canaan. Thus, when their scribes were concerned with the southern coastal area exclusively, they considered its border to be the southernmost limits of the urban settlements in this region, Sinai having the status of a kind of "no-man's land."

According to the annals of Thutmose III, Yurza was considered to lie at the southernmost end of Canaan; thus, when the Egyptian ruler wanted to emphasize the maximal limits of the rebellion confronting him, he used the phrase "from Yurza to the ends of the land" (Wilson 1969:235; Helck 1968–69: 27). In the Amarna archive, there are also three letters of the ruler of Yurza (*EA* 314–316) showing that Yurza was a Canaanite city-state located in the southern part of the country. After a gap of several centuries, Yurza is again mentioned in the inscription of Shishak (see recently Kitchen 1973a:432–447). In the ninth column, the following list of names appears (Kitchen 1973a: 440–441): *yrz, 'Ir[m?], ml[ḥ],*[11] *[b]'r [m]lḥt, 'dm, [g]rn, 'lmtn, šrḥ[n]/šlḫ[m], bt 'nt, b'r l/rz, 'bl, fltm*. The numerous toponyms typical of a desert region (Melaḥ, Be'er Milḥat, Be'er *l/rz*, Goren) and personal names used as toponyms (El-ram, El-mat(t)tan, Pelet) as well as the position of the ninth column within the list, clearly points to the Negev. This accords well with the suggestion of Mazar (although he did not refer to Shishak's inscription) to locate Yurza at Tell Jemmeh.[12]

Therefore, it may be concluded that during the reign of Thutmose III, when Yurza was considered to be at the southernmost end of the Land of Canaan, the Besor river was likewise considered the southern border of the country.

Gaza appears as the southern border of Canaan in two New kingdom sources describing the road from Egypt to Asia. According to Papyrus Anastasi I, this route began at Sile and ended at Gaza, with Raphia as the penultimate station (Gardiner 1920:103–104; Wilson 1969:478). The same road is depicted on the reliefs of Seti I as opening at Sile and terminating at Raphia, followed

---

11. For the toponym *mlḥ* in an Egyptian inscription, see Edel 1966:22–23.

12. The exact position of column IX of the Shishak inscription is dependent on the location of No. 125 *šrḥ*[n] *šlḫ*[*m*]. In a forthcoming article (Na'aman 1983), I have suggested that the Hyksos stronghold Shirḥon (sic!) and biblical Sharuhen/Shilhim/Shaaraim are to be treated separately. Shirḥon is to be located (with Kempinski 1974 and Stewart 1974: 62–63) at Tell el-'Ajjul, while the biblical toponym should be sought near the border between Judah and Philistia in the western Negev. Accordingly, if Shirḥon = Tell el-'Ajjul is the site mentioned in column IX, the other places in this column should be located along the Besor river between Tell Jemmeh and the Mediterranean. Alternatively, if it is Sharuhen/Shilhim that is mentioned, the associated places would lie along Naḥal Gerar between Tell Jemmeh and the western border of Judah.

by an inscription stating that in his first year Seti smote the Shasu from the fortress of Sile to *p3* Canaan (= Gaza); the conquest of Gaza is described at the left of the reliefs (Gardiner 1920; Wreszinski 1935:pls. 41–43; Helck 1971:310–313). The same concept is implied in the annals of Thutmose III, where Gaza is mentioned immediately after the departure from Sile. Gardiner (1920:100) has concluded, accordingly, that after the stretch from Sile to Raphia, Gaza was regarded as the first city in Canaan.

This concept of Gaza as lying near the southernmost border of Canaan is confirmed by the archaeological finds as well. A line of fortified cities of the Middle Bronze IIB was found along the banks of the Besor river, three in its western stretches (Tell el-'Ajjul, Tell Jemmeh and Tell el-Far'ah) and one in the Beer-sheba Valley at its east (Tel Malḥata). Only the three western sites survived into the beginning of the Late Bronze Age (Tel Malḥata evidently having been abandoned), and with the destruction of Shirḥon (Tell el-'Ajjul; see note 12), the city of Gaza took its place. This line-up of three southern cities (Tell el-Far'ah, Tell Jemmeh and Gaza) endured throughout the Late Bronze Age, and it is important to note that there were no Canaanite cities south of this line. Thus, the pattern of settlement created in the Middle Bronze IIB when Naḥal Besor was the southern limit of urban settlement in Canaan continued to exist until the end of the second millennium BCE, The annals of Thutmose III describing rebellion "from Yurza to the end of the land" are referring to this array of urban settlement.

Turning to the Bible, one can immediately find expression reflecting the same territorial concept. For example, Gen. 10:19: "And the territory of the Canaanites extended from Sidon, in the direction of Gerar, as far as Gaza, and in the direction of Sodom, Gomorrah . . ." shows that Gaza was regarded as the southern limit of the Canaanite settlement, from whence the border turned eastwards. And indeed, according to biblical tradition (1 Chr. 4:40; see Deut. 2:23; Josh. 13:3), the region south of Gaza was settled by the sons of Ham. When summing up the conquest of the southern parts of Canaan in Jos. 10: 41a, the verse says: "And Joshua defeated them from Kadesh-barnea to Gaza," reflecting his conquest of biblical Canaan from its southernmost limit to the borders of the settled area at Gaza. The same concept appears in Judges 6:4 (Kallai 1975:31). Even more important is the passage of 1 Kgs, 4:21–24 [MT 5: 1–4]: "Solomon ruled over all the kingdoms from the River [i.e., Euphrates] to the land of the Philistines and to the border of Egypt. . . . For he had dominion over all the region west the River [i.e., Euphrates] from Tiphsah to Gaza." Gaza is clearly regarded here as the southern limit of the kingdom of Solomon and is adjacent to the "border of Egypt," i.e., the Brook of Egypt. Finally, there is Josh. 15:47, in which three cities of Philistia — Ekron, Ashkelon and Gaza — are mentioned, with Gaza at the end of the list: "Gaza its towns and its villages; to the river of Egypt." Obviously, Naḥal Besor, only slightly south of Gaza, fits well into this geographical context; Wâdi el-'Arish is much less suitable because of its remoteness and the paucity of settlements in the area between it and the Besor river.

The River of Egypt marks the southwestern border of the land of Canaan in two more passages (Num. 34:4–5; Josh. 15:3–4). The above-cited verse, Josh. 15:47, might well be connected with the overall concept of the Land of Canaan in the Bible. According to 1 Kgs. 8:65, King Solomon celebrated the consecration of the temple "and all Israel with him, a great assembly, from Lebo Hamath to the Brook of Egypt," again reflecting the northern and southern boundaries of the Land of Canaan. The passage in 2 Kgs. 24:7 describes the borders of the territories conquered by Nebuchadrezzar in Syria/Israel: "From the Brook of Egypt to the river Euphrates," thus, leaving a buffer zone between the River of Egypt and the Isthmus. The last verse is Isa. 27:12: "In that day from the River [i.e., Euphrates] to the Brook of Egypt the Lord will thresh out the grain. . . ." This prophecy reflects the borders of the Promised Land of Israel in the days to come.

Of these six biblical passages mentioning the Brook of Egypt, four are related to the borders of the Land of Canaan stretching from Lebo Hamath to the River of Egypt. The same set of borders appears in Ezek. 47:20. Mazar (1946: 93) has suggested that the boundaries of biblical Canaan reflect the border of the Egyptian province in Asia as it was demarcated during the Egyptian 19th dynasty, a proposal that is supported by both the literary and archaeological data of the second millennium. These borders, however, are alien to both the political disposition and pattern of settlement created after the Israelite occupation at the end of the 13th century BCE (de Vaux 1968:28; 1971:126–127). The urbanization of the Late Bronze Age did not spread eastward beyond the Jordan Valley; indeed, the Transjordanian area is not included in the borders of the Land of Canaan. However, the Israelites settled intensively on both sides of the Jordan (Glueck 1940:144–157; Mittmann 1970:208–209; Epstein and Gutman 1972:249; Ibrahim Sauer and Yassine 1976).[13] It is clear, therefore, that the biblical concept of the Land of Canaan was borrowed from the pre-existing native population of the country and was stamped onto a period for which it was no longer suited.

As has been shown above, the line of the Besor river marks the southern border of Canaan, both in the Egyptian documents and the biblical sources,

13. The exclusion of Transjordan from the borders of Canaan clearly proves that the boundaries of Canaan described in Num. 34 cannot be dated to the United Monarchy, as was suggested by Elliger (1936:59–73).

as well as in the archaeological finds from the second millennium BCE. The borders of Canaan designated in the Bible reflect the political disposition and the pattern of settlement prevailing at the end of the Late Bronze Age. Accordingly, the Brook of Egypt, which marks the southwestern border of the Land of Canaan, is better to be identified with Naḥal Besor, rather than with the remote and unsettled Wâdi el-ʻArish, particularly in view of the lack of evidence for any connection between this area and the Land of Canaan during the Late Bronze Age, when the biblical concept of Canaan crystallized.

In light of this tentative conclusion, the Assyrian documents discussed in Section A should be reconsidered. The Me'unites dwelt "below (= at the foot of) Egypt," and their dwelling place, according to the Book of Chronicles, was in the vicinity of Naḥal Gerar or Naḥal Besor. It appears, therefore, that the territory south of Naḥal Besor (= the Brook of Egypt) was considered "Egypt" by the scribes of Tiglath-pileser III. This viewpoint is in conformity with the *northern* concept of the borders of Egypt, as reflected in several biblical passages, including the "ethnographic" evidence specifying that the sons of Ham occupied this area. The coastal strip south of Gaza — the gateway to Egypt — was entrusted to the sheikh of the tribe Idibi'ilu and to the sheikh of Laban during the reigns of Tiglath-pileser and Sargon, respectively.

The above-suggested identification of the Brook of Egypt with Naḥal Besor enables us to identify Yurza (Tell Jemmeh), lying on the banks of the Besor river, with Arza situated near the Brook of Egypt. The exiles settled by Sargon in the year 716 BCE near the Brook of Egypt are to be sought now in the vicinity of the Besor river. The deportation of the king of Arza and his subjects might then be interpreted as an act intended to provide living space for the Assyrians in that area, and Arza was possibly transformed into an Assyrian administrative center. As we shall see below, there is ample support for this suggestion in the archaeological finds from Tell Jemmeh (Yurza/Arza). Moreover, the translation "as far as the town of Raphia, to the border zone of the Brook of Egypt" for the above-discussed passage from the annals of Esarhaddon concurs well with the supposition that it refers to a river north of Raphia.

Finally, we should like to present a direct argument against identifying the Brook of Egypt with Wâdi el-ʻArish: In none of the surveys conducted up to the present in the Qalʻat el-ʻArish area have either pre-Hellenistic ruins, or even pre-Hellenistic pottery been found (Cledat 1923:141, 143; 1924:58; Margovski 1969:46; Aharoni 1974:88, 90). Obviously, if Wâdi el-ʻArish was the actual border between the Land of Israel and Egypt in the Late Bronze and Iron Ages, we would expect some signs of occupation here.

As the "devil's advocate," we must note that there are two counterclaims that could be raised against my hypothesis that the River of Egypt is

Naḥal Besor. The first might be that the southern border of Canaan ran from Kadesh-barnea on a northwestern axis and that its natural continuation would therefore be Wâdi el-ʿArish, instead of Naḥal Besor. The second, and more serious, argument would be based on the Septuagint and later sources, which clearly show that from the Hellenistic period (at least) and onwards, there was a tradition identifying the Brook of Egypt with Wâdi el-ʿArish. Even such late traditions cannot be brushed aside, as they may preserve folk memories transmitted from very ancient times. Inasmuch as these arguments apparently contradict my thesis, it is important to establish what historical factors may have intervened between the beginning and end of the first millennium BCE to cause the Brook of Egypt to become identified with Wâdi el-ʿArish. Therefore, we shall try to weigh the importance of these two possible claims in comparison with the other data presented in our discussion.

Kadesh-barnea is mentioned as the southernmost point of Canaan in two border descriptions of the Promised Land (Num. 34:4; Ezek. 47:19; 48:28), as well as being the southern boundary of the tribe of Judah (Josh. 15:3). Most of the biblical stories mentioning Kadesh-barnea are connected with the wanderings in the desert, so it seems reasonable to assume that this oasis was a center for the tribes, before their settlement in Canaan (Aharoni 1976). The concept of Kadesh-barnea as the southernmost point in the Land of Canaan appears also in Josh. 10:41 (see above). Nevertheless, the inclusion of Kadesh-barnea within the borders of Canaan is problematic, because Kadesh and its surrounding deserts were entirely outside the area of urban settlement of the Late Bronze Age.[14] I would suggest, therefore, that Kadesh was added to the borders of biblical Canaan on account of its importance in the pre-history of the Israelite tribes. And indeed, in Gen. 10:19, where the line of settlement passes directly from Gaza to the Dead Sea, Kadesh-barnea is clearly *outside* the limits of Canaanite settlement. The southern boundaries of the Promised Land, however (Num. 34:4, etc.), pass almost directly from the Dead Sea to Kadesh-barnea; by drawing the opposite line up to the Besor river, an isosceles triangle, whose vertex is Kadesh-barnea, is created. It may be argued, reasonably, that the triangle is an artificial "addition" to the actual borders of historical Canaan in order to include Kadesh-barnea in the inheritance of the tribes; thus, this southwestern boundary line from Kadesh to Naḥal Besor is not a real obstacle to my suggested identification of Naḥal Besor with the Brook of Egypt.

14. Those scholars who believe that the boundaries of biblical Canaan reflect the borders of the Egyptian province in Asia during the 19th dynasty have overlooked the difficulties created by the inclusion of Kadesh-barnea in the borders of the Promised Land.

Last, the toponym Azmon, mentioned in Num. 34:5 and Josh. 15:4 in juxtaposition with the Brook of Egypt, should be recalled. Musil (1907:47, 73, 246) has suggested identifying Azmon with the Simeonite town of Ezem (Josh. 15:29; 19:3; 1 Chr. 4:29), which also appears (No. 66) in the list of Shishak. Such identification would support the identification of the Brook of Egypt with Naḥal Besor, because the towns of Simeon were situated in the western Negev. However, we hesitate to use this argument, because of the uncertainty of the equation of Azmon/Ezem (see Aharoni 1971; Tsafrir 1971).

As for the second possible counterclaim: To understand correctly the origin of the late tradition identifying the Brook of Egypt with Wâdi el-ʿArish, the location of the border between Egypt and Palestine in later periods must be examined.

According to Herodotus III 5, the border of the Syrians extended up to Gaza in the 5th century BCE. The area between Gaza and Ienysus, located in the vicinity of Sheikh Zuweid, according to Abel (1939:535–545), was under control of the Arabs, and the territory west of Ienysus was again Syrian. This description reflects a certain degree of continuity in the history of the western coast of Sinai from the 8th–7th centuries BCE. At that time, the territory south of the Brook of Egypt was controlled by Arab tribes with which the Assyrian kings found it necessary to cooperate. However, at the same time, there was also a marked increase in the presence of the Arabs along the western coast of Sinai. The conquest of Egypt by Assyria (although only for a short period) and, especially, its annexation by the Persian empire increased the importance of the coastal road, making it mandatory to cooperate with the Arabs, who controlled both the road and other means of transportation (see Borger 1956:112 rev., lines 1–2; Herodotus III 5–9; Spalinger 1976:138). According to Herodotus, the mooring places (*emporia*) along the coast from Gaza to Ienysus were in the hands of the Arabs at that time. The intensification of settlement along the western coast of Sinai, therefore, already had begun in the Persian period. (For recent surveys of northern Sinai, see Margovski 1969; 1971; Oren 1973; 1977).

The question of the location of the boundary between Palestine and Egypt from the Persian period onward has been treated extensively (Alt 1926; Abel 1939; 1940; Avi-Yonah 1966:151; Barag 1973). Herodotus (II 158; III 5) wrote that the borderline between the fifth satrapy of the Persian empire (*eber nāri*= "Beyond the River") and the sixth (Egypt) ran close to Mt. Casius. Abel (1939:541–542) suggested that coast between Gaza and Ienysus, i.e., Sheikh Zuweid, was in the hands of the Arabs. At the time of the battle of Raphia (217 BCE), the border passed at Bytyl, identified with Bitolion of the Byzantine period, also situated near Sheikh Zuweid (Alt 1926; Abel 1939:227–228, 544–546). After some minor shifts in the boundary resulting from the strengthening of the Nabatean and Hashmonean kingdoms, it was again established between Raphia and Wâdi el-'Arish under the Romans, at least from the time of Gabinius (57–55 BCE) (Abel 1939:546–547). In the 4th century CE, according to Eusebius, the borders of Syria-Palaestina were located at Bethaffu, 14 miles from Raphia, i.e., in the vicinity of Sheikh Zuweid (Abel 1939:547; Barag 1973:51; see Schwabe 1954). And, indeed, in an inscription dated to 233 BCE found near Raphia, the distance from this border point was recorded (Barag 1973). During the Byzantine period the situation was similar: the main site in this region was Bitolion, located by Dalman (1924:57) and Alt (1926) at Sheikh Zuweid. The borderline of Syria-Palaestina ran, according to the Madeba map, a bit west of Bitolion (Avi-Yonah 1954:75, No. 120; pl. 9). The location of both Bethaffu and Bitolion in the neighborhood of Sheikh Zuweid shows the general stability of the border during the Roman and Byzantine periods.

Summing up, it becomes clear that, at least from the Hellenistic period (and probably already under the Persians) until the end of the Byzantine period (with the exception of short intervals resulting from specific political events), the border between Palestine and Egypt was more or less permanently located near Sheikh Zuweid, with Rhinocorura and Wâdi el-'Arish included in Egyptian territory. This shifting of the borders from their 2nd–1st millennia locations resulted, in my opinion, from the unification of Syria-Palestine and Egypt under the rule of the Persian empire, which increased the importance of the coastal region connecting these two political units.

The question now arises as to whether it was not this new southern border of Palestine that explains the late tradition that "shifted" the Brook of Egypt to Wâdi el-'Arish. Like so many other places in Palestine that were forgotten during the period of desolation and exile following the Babylonian conquest, the site of the Brook of Egypt may have dropped into oblivion. The name Rhinocorura has been found (as far as we know) only in Hellenistic sources, when it was an important center on the coastal road to Egypt (Abel 1939:545–548; 1940:228–230). The Egyptian border ran to its north, and Rhinocorura was the first important town inside the borders of Egypt.[15] It was, therefore, only natural to identify the great wâdi nearby, Wâdi el-'Arish, with the biblical Brook of Egypt, the southernmost limit of biblical Canaan. Naḥal Besor lay far to the north, and its identification with the Brook of Egypt did not match the new political reality. This southward shift of the border resulting from political developments and new pattern of settlement on the coast of Sinai in the Hellenistic (and perhaps even in the Persian) pe-

15. Rhinocorura was evidently under Egyptian administration in the Roman period; see Jones 1971: 342–343, 549, and the map after 294.

riod very likely created a new tradition, current from the Hellenistic period onward in all sources, according to which the brook of Egypt was identified with Wâdi el-ʿArish.

C. The Objectives and Policy of The Assyrians on the Egyptian Border

The location of the Brook of Egypt in the general vicinity of Gaza enables us to reevaluate the Assyrian activity in southern Philistia, because all Assyrian inscriptions mentioning it and other nearby places may now be linked with the western Negev. This is especially significant from the archaeological aspect, because all findings from surveys and excavations conducted in southern Philistia and the western Negev now can be integrated with Assyrian source material.

Most important for our subject are the recent excavations conducted at Tell Jemmeh, lying on the banks of Naḥal Besor. A detailed excavation report is still to be published, so we must rely on the preliminary reports (Van Beek 1972:245–246; 1973; 1974: 138–139, 274–275; 1977:172–174; Amiran and Van Beek 1976:544–549). A large structure, characterized by Assyrian building techniques, that was exposed during the excavations is regarded by the excavator as the seat of the Assyrian military governor and referred to as the governor's residence. Assyrian pottery, of the type known as "palace ware," was found in quantities in this building (Van Beek 1973:25–26; 1974:139, 274), perhaps indicating occupancy by people originating in Assyria. In a second building of the same period situated east of the residency, three different phases were distinguished, pointing toward a rather lengthy period of Assyrian activity at the site. However, the residency itself was built only at a late stage, perhaps in the course of the Assyrian preparations for the campaign against Egypt in the reign of Esarhaddon (Van Beek 1977:172).

A second recently excavated site of importance is Tel Seraʿ (Tell esh-Shariʿa) on the banks of Naḥal Gerar (Wâdi esh-Shariʿa). Again, only preliminary reports have been published (Oren 1974; 1976a; 1976b). In Stratum VI, belonging to Iron Age III, an "Assyrian fortress" (excavator's term) was excavated; it had 4-m. thick walls and a paved courtyard at one side. Assyrian palace ware and other finds of Assyrian origin were discovered in its destruction level (Oren 1974:266; pl. 57; 1976a:35; 1976b:52). Pits dug into this destruction level yielded fragments of Greek wine jars, thus, supplying a *terminus ante quern* for the fortress. Underneath this Assyrian fortress, there was a monumental building that had been destroyed in a terrible conflagration (Oren 1976b: 52–53). We suggest that the earlier building was destroyed by the Assyrians in one of their campaigns to Philistia and replaced by a military/administrative base. This Assyrian fortress came to an end approximately in the third quarter of the 7th century BCE, prior to the importation of Greek pottery during the last quarter of this century.

In the excavations recently conducted at Khirbet Hoga, on a tributary of Naḥal Shiqma, a massive building was unearthed that may also have been an Assyrian fortress (Porath 1976). Another possible Assyrian fortress was discovered by R. Gophna during his survey of 1965 around the Mediterranean outlet of Naḥal Shiqma on the conjectured borderline between the territories of Gaza and Ashkelon.[16]

In the excavations at Tell Abu Salima ("Anthedon") near Sheikh Zuweid, a building was unearthed that Petrie (1937:6; pls. II, X, XXXI) compared with a temple at Khorsabad (Dur-Sharrukin).[17] Here as well, Assyrian palace ware was found, indicating that this was a military/administrative base built by the Assyrians to control the route to Egypt. Aharoni (1967:290, 334; 1974: 90) has suggested identifying Laban, which is mentioned in the inscription of Shishak and on one of the prisms of Sargon II, with Tell Abu Salima. In Shishak's inscription, Laban appears next to Raphia, but, nevertheless, their exact geographical relationship is unknown. The passage in the inscription of Sargon refers to the "Sheikh of Laban" (see note 6 above), thus, Alt (1945:133) suggested that Laban was more likely a tribal center than a town. Actually, the data concerning Laban is so flimsy that its identification with any specific site is no more than a guess.[18] The erection of an Assyrian center in Tell Abu Salima might have been connected with the Assyrian campaigns against Egypt during the reigns of Esarhaddon and Ashurbanipal, when the Assyrians were obliged to maintain several strategic military posts on the road leading from Philistia to Egypt.

The results of the extensive excavations recently conducted over a number of seasons at the main sites along Naḥal Beer Sheva shed additional light on the subject at hand. This is particularly true of Tel Beer-sheba, the westernmost mound along this line, where the destruction of Stratum II was attributed by the excavator to the campaign of Sennacherib in 701 BCE (Aharoni 1973a: 5–6). Surprisingly, however, only one *lmlk* seal impression (stamped on a "non-standard" type of storage jar; see Aharoni 1973b:76–

16. I am grateful to my colleague R. Gophna for informing me of this site.

17. I would like to thank R. Reich for drawing my attention to these Assyrian finds at Tell Abu Salima.

18. Laban is not mentioned in any Egyptian source describing the route along the Sinai coast during the 19th dynasty, and there is no evidence that it existed prior to the first millennium BCE. On the other hand, in the excavations of Tell Abu Salima a Late Bronze settlement was discovered. In the light of my proposal to identify the Brook of Egypt with Naḥal Besor, I would prefer to locate Laban (whose sheikh was appointed to supervise the relocation of the deportees near Naḥal Mizraim) between Raphia and Gaza, rather than in the more southernly Tell Abu Salima.

77) was found during the excavation, nor did a single sherd of Assyrian origin come to light. The renewed excavations at Lachish now definitely prove that the majority of the *lmlk* seal impressions, found in enormous quantities in the destruction level resulting from Sennacherib's 701 campaign to Judah, are to be dated to the end of the 8th century BCE (Ussishkin 1977; Na'aman 1979). Hence, the lack of *lmlk* seal impressions in Tel Beer-sheba, destroyed in the same campaign, according to the excavator, is rather conspicuous. The Assyrian holdings on the Philistine coast opposite Tel Beer-sheba began to be established about 30 years before Sennacherib's campaign, and, thus, the lack of any Assyrian finds on Tel Beer-sheba is not without difficulties.[19]

At Tel Arad on the eastern fringes of Naḥal Beer Sheva, the strata belonging to the monarchical period were almost entirely unearthed, but, nevertheless, only five *lmlk* seal impressions were found, two in Stratum VII; the rest were without any clear archaeological context (Aharoni 1964:138; pl. 33c). At Tel Masos (Khirbet el-Meshâsh) and Tel Malḥata (Tell el-Milḥ), both situated in the Beer Sheva Valley between Arad and Tell Beer-sheba, no *lmlk* seal impressions were found at all. In the survey conducted on Tel 'Ira (Khirbet Gharreh) near Tel Masos, only a single *lmlk* seal impression was found (Aharoni 1958:36–38).

The above findings from the Beer Sheva basin lead to the following interpretation: the sites lying along the course of the wâdi (Tel Beer-sheba II, Arad VIII, Malḥata) were destroyed even before 701 BCE. Settlement on Tel Beer-sheba was not restored, and, thus, there are no *lmlk* jars on Assyrian finds.[20] Only at those sites that were rebuilt and occupied at the end of the 8th century (Arad VII, Tel 'Ira), when the *lmlk* jars were already diffused throughout Judah, a few seal impressions of the *lmlk* type have come to light. In my opinion, it was Sargon II who brought about the destruction of the sites, in the process of entrenching his holding on the Philistine coast.

---

19. The suggestion of Yadin (1976) to date the destruction of Tel Beer-sheba Stratum II to the reign of Josiah involves enormous difficulties, because, according to this theory, the town would have existed during an entire century of Assyrian rule on the Philistine coast without any evidence showing this co-existence. Although the late Iron Age strata on the tell were almost completely excavated, not a single Assyrian vessel, or even an imitation thereof, was discovered, but other sites, located much further from the Assyrian centers than Tel Beer-sheba and dug on a much smaller scale, have yielded at least some of this Assyrian ware. This fact, as well as the lack of *lmlk* seal impressions at Tel Beer-sheba, is in direct contradiction to the dates assigned by Yadin to the last stages of the Iron Age there (see Herzog, Rainey and Moshkovitz 1977).

20. The dates proposed here, according to which Stratum II at Tel Beer-sheba was destroyed before Stratum III at Lachish, correspond very well with the conclusions of Kenyon (1976), based on a comparative analysis of the pottery from both sites.

To understand the background for this severe act, the policy of the Assyrians in Philistia must be examined. Throughout the ages, this region has been of foremost strategic importance, either as a springboard for the conquest of Egypt from the north, or as a basis for capturing Syria-Palestine from the south. From the Assyrian point of view, the seizure of the Philistine coast meant pushing the Egyptians back to their homeland, with the intervening expanses of Sinai preventing any immediate threat to their holdings in Philistia. From the outset of the Assyrian campaigns to Philistia, Egypt was the main threat to Assyria from the south. The menace gathered strength with the unification of Egypt and Nubia under the hegemony of the 25th (Nubian) dynasty during the reign of Shabako (see Kitchen 1973b; Spalinger 1973; Baer 1973). The annexation of Ashdod to the Assyrian territories in 712 BCE was, thus, motivated as a counter-measure to the unification of Egypt. In light of this background, we may also understand the erection of military and administrative bases on the southern coast of Philistia, the transference of deportees there to create population groups dependant on Assyria, and the close contacts with powerful tribal leaders living in the buffer zone between the two powers.

In addition to military considerations, there was also a distinctive economic-commercial aspect to the Assyrian policy (Tadmor 1966: *passim*; 1972: 230; Eph'al 1969:146–151; Elat 1977:132–135). Tiglath-pileser relates that after the conquest of Gaza he "counted the city of Gaza as a custom-house (*bīt kāri*) of Assyria,"[21] by which he meant that he settled Assyrian officials there to collect duties in the harbor. The same type of intervention into the affairs of another vassal kingdom on the coast of the Mediterranean is seen at Tyre.

In a letter from Calah (Nimrud), dated to the reign of Tiglath-pileser III, there appears the following passage (Postgate 1974:393):

> With regard to the ruler of Tyre, of whom the king said that I was to speak kindly to him, all the quays (*kārrāni*) are open to him, (and) his subjects enter and leave the custom houses (*bīt kārrāni*) as they wish, (and) sell and buy. Mount Lebanon is at his disposal, and they go up and down as they wish, and bring down the wood. I levy taxes (*miksē*) on anyone who brings down wood, and I have appointed tax collectors (*mākisāni*) over the quays of all Mount Lebanon. I appointed a tax-collector (*mākisu*) over those who come down to the quays which are in Sidon, but the Sidonians chased him off. Then I sent the Itu'aeans into Mount Lebanon, and they made the people grovel. Afterwards, they sent to me, and they brought the tax-collector (back) into Sidon.

The text makes it clear that Assyria compelled its vassals to pay customs and that the payment was levied when the timber was brought to the

21. This translation is based on three almost identical summary inscriptions of Tiglath-pileser III. See Rost 1893:80, line 14; Wiseman 1951:23, line 18; 1956:126, line 16.

Mediterranean quays (see Saggs 1955;149–150; Tadmor 1966:88; Postgate 1974:131; Oded 1974:48; Elat 1977:130–132, 166–167).

I would further suggest that Tiglath-pileser appointed two Assyrian officials bearing the title *qēpu* to serve, respectively, on the Phoenician coast (Qurdi-Ashur-lāmur)[22] and in the eastern fringes of the desert (Rost 1893:82, line 26), both regions lying outside of the Assyrian provincial system. The purpose of these appointments is clear: to tighten the supervision over these economically important areas to increase the share of Assyria in their revenues. We may safely assume that such a *qēpu* was also appointed to supervise the coast of Philistia and its southern border and that Assyrian custom collectors were set to work in the port of Gaza.

Another way by which Assyria tried to increase its share in the profits of the Mediterranean ports is illustrated by a letter (*ABL* 992), probably dating to the reign of Esarhaddon, which reads as follows (lines 14–21; Pfeiffer 1935: 137; see *CAD* E 118b; *CAD* K 232b):

> The king my lord knows that Ikkilu does not release the boats (so that) they cannot land at the quay (*kāru*) of the king my lord; he made the whole mooring place (*kāru*) go over to his side. Anyone who comes to him he opens his way; (but) anyone who wants to land at the quay (*kāru*) of Assyria he kills and smashes his boat.

The Ikkilu mentioned in this letter is Yakinlu, king of Arvad, and the text clearly shows that an Assyrian quay existed near the Arvadite moorage, with competition and tension prevailing between them (see Meissner 1914; Hirschberg 1932:63–64; Elat 1977: 168–169).[23] Possibly in their attempt to get a maximal share of the revenues of Gaza, the Assyrians used both of these methods: collecting duties on the quays of Gaza and constructing their own quay or moorage, whose revenues went directly to the Assyrian treasury.

Sargon II wrote in his inscription: "I opened the sealed h[ar]bour of Egypt, mingled Assyrians and Egyptians together and made them trade with

22. One of the clauses in the treaty of Esarhaddon with Ba'al, king of Tyre (Borger 1956: 108, lines 13–14) forbids the ruler of Tyre to open a letter unless the Assyrian *qēpu* is present, showing that this official had wide powers of supervision over the affairs of Tyre during the reign of Esarhaddon. Presumably, Qurdi-Ashur-lāmur, who fulfilled similar missions on the Phoenician coast under Tiglath-pileser, bore the same title. For the *qēpu*, see Godbey 1905; Landsberger 1965:30, 36, 59; Garelli 1971:46, n. 1; Postgate 1974:194–195; Spalinger 1974:314 and n. 65.

23. An extraordinary measure designed to enable him to put his hands on the Phoenician trade was taken by Esarhaddon when he destroyed the city of Sidon and founded an Assyrian commercial center nearby, which he named Kar-Esarhaddon. This new port was obviously built to replace Sidon in the Mediterranean trade (see Tadmor 1966:98).

each other" (Gadd 1954:179, lines 46–49; Tadmor 1958:34; 1966:92; see *CAD* K 153a). This passage illustrates another important aspect of Assyrian imperialistic policy, i.e., an effort to maintain commercial relations with Egypt. The commerce was conducted both by sea and by land, making it necessary for Assyria to control the southern coast of Philistia, which was the gateway for both types of transport. In addition to their military objectives, this may have been a second motive behind the efforts expended by the Assyrians to strengthen their control over the region.

During the reign of Tiglath-pileser and the first years of Sargon, these efforts were concentrated around Gaza, which, being the southernmost of the Philistine cities, controlled the entrance to Egypt and maintained a close relationship with her. Furthermore, Gaza was the western terminal for one of the major trade routes over which spices and valuable luxuries were transported from the Arabian peninsula to the Fertile Crescent. This route passed along the Besor river and its tributaries (Naḥal Gerar and Naḥal Beer Sheva) from earliest times, which may explain the growth of towns along this line from the Middle Bronze Age IIB onwards. Evidently Tell el-ʿAjjul (= Shirḥon) was the main gateway for this commerce in the MB IIB, with a share of the revenues going to the other towns along the route (Tel Malḥata, Tel Seraʿ, Tel Haror, Tell el-Farʿah and Tell Jemmeh). After the fall of Shirḥon, Gaza became the main port for this trade and continued to maintain this position even in the first millennium BCE. The Assyrian rulers, in trying to realize the maximum gains out of this commerce, made an effort to dominate the entire length of route. To achieve this, they, presumably, conducted a campaign against the fortresses blocking their access to the Arabah (Arad, Tel Malḥata, Tel Beer-sheba and Tel Seraʿ) and the tribes living along the Besor river. To gain control of the route leading to Egypt as well, the Assyrians apparently destroyed Raphia and subjugated the nomads dwelling there. At key points on several of the destroyed sites, they erected military and administrative centers (Tell Jemmeh, Tel Seraʿ and perhaps also at Khirbet Hoga and near the border between Gaza and Ashkelon); later(?), an additional center may have been created at Tell Abu Salima. In addition to these measures, Assyria tried to strengthen the power of the local tribal leaders (the sheikh of the Idibi'ilu tribe during the reign of Tiglath-pileser and the sheikh of Laban in the reign of Sargon), probably by paying them various types of compensation in the hope that their tribes would support the Assyrian military and economic aims.

There is no doubt that these policies had already been set into motion during the reign of Tiglath-pileser. However, the Assyrian king who developed them in full was Sargon. During his reign, not less than four campaigns were conducted to the Philistine coast (720, 716, 712, 711 BCE), thereby, firmly entrenching the Assyrian holdings in that region and resulting in the annexation of Ashdod. I am inclined, therefore, to date the destruction of the above-mentioned Judean settlements along Naḥal Beer Sheva and Naḥal Gerar, as well as the foundation of the Assyrian administrative centers in Tell Jemmeh and Tel Sera', to the years 720–711 BCE. The same military and economic policy was continued under Sennacherib and during most of the reign of Esarhaddon. Only in the last years of Esarhaddon, as a result of the conquest of Lower Egypt, did the center of activity shift to the south, while the Philistine coast lost some of its importance as a major military base and center for continental and maritime trade with Egypt. However, we may safely assume that the strong Assyrian presence in southern Philistia continued without interruption until the retreat of Assyria, probably at the beginning of the reign of Josiah in Judah.

Addendum: Further Remarks on the Brook of Egypt

The following notes originally appeared in Na'aman 1980:105–106. They are intended to supplement the discussion on some of the topographical and linguistic problems with which this article dealt.

(1) Whether URU *Naḫal Muṣur* should be translated as "the city of the Brook of Egypt" or "the Brook of Egypt" (p. 69) is a question requiring further elaboration. In Sargon's and Esarhaddon's inscriptions, the correct transcription is undoubtedly [URU]*Naḫal Muṣur* ("the Brook of Egypt"); it is only in Tiglath-pileser's inscription that the transcription is problematic. We know that the Assyrian kings were accustomed to leaving their inscriptions and reliefs in places other than the conquered sites themselves. For example, Shalmaneser III erected his royal steles in two remote juxtaposed border points of the kingdom of Que after his campaign of 839 BCE to Cilicia, when, for the first time in history, an Assyrian king crossed the Amanus range (Michel 1954:41, lines 30–33). For Tiglath-pileser, the Brook of Egypt was the southernmost point reached in his campaign; therefore, perhaps he likewise erected a stele on its banks to commemorate this great achievement. According to this explanation, URU served as a determinative, and the correct translation is "the Brook of Egypt." This translation is confirmed by the next sign in this line, which seems to be a broken ÍD, thus, opening an appositional sentence to be rendered as "a river [which . . .] ."

(2) As against the claim that an *ō* vowel appears at the beginning of the toponym Yurza, it should be noted that if Yurza really was the former name of Jarda/Orda (Na'aman 1979a:73), it must have opened with a short vowel, because the initial *yôd* would have been preserved if the *o* were a long vowel (as against Orda) and the *o*-vowel would have been preserved (as against Jarda). The transliteration of Yurza in Shishak's inscription (No. 133: *yw-rw-d*3),

which is parallel to the transliterations of other names in the same list, such as Rehob (No. 17: *rw-ḥ3-b3)* and Jeroham (Nos. 112, 139: *yw-r(3)-ḥ(w)-m*), does not indicate a long ō vowel.

(3) Recently, Eph'al (1978:80) has pointed out the name Arzā in several Neo-Babylonian documents. However, Zadok (1977:112–113, 151) has demonstrated that the Arzā of those documents cannot be a toponym and that the second element in the combination URU*Bīt* m*Arzā* can be only a private name. Thus, the two explanations offered for the shift from Yurza to Arza (Na'aman 1979a:73) may be supplemented with a third. Sometimes, the Assyrian scribes transcribed a toponym in a certain way and continued using this spelling even when they knew it to be at variance with the correct rendering (e.g., Tilgarimmu vs. Tegarama/Togarma; Kinalua/Kunalia vs. Calneh). The name Arza may be just this kind of formalistic spelling, imitating the name as the Assyrians first heard it pronounced by the local population.

4) The word *'ad* appearing in Gen. 10:19 and Deut. 2:23 (see Na'aman 1979a: 70, 76) might be interpreted, following Ginsberg (1951), in the sense of "near," "by." If so, the southern border of the Canaanites would have spread out from Gerar, which was *near* Gaza, unto the cities of the plain, which were *near* Lasha (Gen. 10:19), and the 'Avites would have dwelt *near* Gaza (Deut. 2:23).

[R. Zadok (1996:730–731) noted that already Japheth ben 'Ali in the early Middle Ages identified Naḥal Mizraim with Wâdi *'ltk'w* near Gaza, slightly south of Wâdi Ghazzeh.]

References

Abel, F.M. 1939. Les Confins de la Palestine et de l'Égypte sous les Ptolémées. *RB* 48: 207–236, 530–548.

Abel, F.M. 1940. Les Confins de la Palestine et de l'Égypte sous les Ptolémées (cont.). *RB* 49: 55–75, 224–239.

Aharoni, Y. 1956. The Land of Gerar. *IEJ* 6: 26–32.

Aharoni, Y. 1958. The Negeb of Judah. *IEJ* 8: 26–38.

Aharoni, Y. 1964. Excavations at Tel Arad. Preliminary Report on the First Season, 1962. *IEJ* 14: 131–147.

Aharoni, Y. 1967. *The Land of the Bible: A Historical Geography.* Philadelphia.

Aharoni, Y. 1971. Ezem. *Enc. Miqr.* VI: 334. (Hebrew).

Aharoni, Y. 1973a. The Stratification of the Site. In: Aharoni, Y. ed. *Beer-sheba I, Excavations at Tel Beer-sheba, 1969–1971 Seasons.* (Publications of the Institute of Archaeology of Tel Aviv University 2). Tel Aviv: 4–8.

Aharoni, Y. 1973b. The Hebrew Inscriptions. In: Aharoni, Y. ed. *Beer-sheba I, Excavations at Tel Beer-sheba, 1969–1971 Seasons.* (Publications of the Institute of Archaeology of Tel Aviv University 2). Tel Aviv: 4–8.

Aharoni, Y. 1974. Survey between Raphia and the Brook of Egypt. A. The Survey. *'Atiqot* 7: 88–90. (Hebrew Series). English summary: 14*.
Aharoni, Y. 1976. Kadesh, Kadesh-barnea. *Enc. Miqr.* VII: 39–42. (Hebrew).
Albright, W.F. 1921. A Colony of Cretan Mercenaries on the Coast of the Negeb. *JPOS* 1: 187–194.
Albright, W.F. 1924. Egypt and the Early History of the Negeb. *JPOS* 4: 131–161.
Alt, A. 1926. Bitolion and Bethelea. *ZDPV* 49: 236–242, 333–335.
Alt, A. 1932. Beiträge zur historischen Geographie and Topographie des Negeb: II. Das Land Gari. *JPOS* 12:126–141. (Reprint Alt 1959: 396–409).
Alt, A. 1935. Beiträge zur historischen Geographie and Topographie des Negeb: III. Saruhen, Ziklag, Horma, Gerar. *JPOS* 15: 294–324. (Reprint Alt 1959: 409–435).
Alt, A. 1945. Neue Assyrische Nachrichten über Palestina. *ZDPV* 67:128–146. (Reprint Alt 1953: 226–241).
Alt, A. 1953. *Kleine Schriften zur Geschichte des Volkes Israel* II. München.
Alt, A. 1953a. Tiglathpilesers III. erster Feldzug nach Palästina. Alt 1953: 150–162.
Alt, A. 1959. *Kleine Schriften zur Geschichte des Volkes Israel* III. München.
Amiran, R. and Van Beek, G.W. 1976. Jemmeh, Tell. *Enc. Arch. Exc.* II: 545–549.
Avi-Yonah, M. 1954. *The Madeba Mosaic Map, with Introduction and Commentary.* Jerusalem.
Avi-Yonah, M. 1966. *The Holy Land from the Persian to the Arab Conquest (536 B.C. to A.D. 640); A Historical Geography.* Grand Rapids.
Baer, K. 1973. The Libyan and Nubian Kings of Egypt: Notes on the Chronology of Dynasties XXII-XXVI. *JNES* 32: 4–25.
Barag, D. 1973. The Borders of Syria-Palaestina on an Inscription from the Raphia Area. *IEJ* 23: 50–52.
Borger, R. 1956. *Die Inschriften Asarhaddons, Königs von Assyrian.* (AfO Beiheft 9). Graz (reprint 1967. Osnabrück).
Cledat, J. 1923. Notes sur l'Isthme de Suez (Suite). *Bulletin de l'Institut Français d'Archéologie Orientale* 22: 135–189.
Cledat, J. 1924. Notes sur l'Isthme de Suez (Suite). *Bulletin de l'Institut Français d'Archéologie Orientale* 23: 27–84.
Dalman, G. 1924. Durch die Ägyptische Wüste nach Palästina. *PJb* 20:41–68.
EA = Knudtzon, J.A. 1915. *Die El Amarna-Tafeln.* (Vorderasiatische Bibliothek 2). Leipzig.
Edel, E. 1966. *Die Ortsnamenlisten aus dem Totentempel Amenophis III.* Bonn.
El-Amin, M. 1953. Die Reliefs mit Beischriften von Sargon II. in Dûr Sharrukîn. *Sumer* 9: 35–59, 214–228.
Elat, M. 1975. The Political Status of the Kingdom of Judah within the Assyrian Empire in the 7th Century BCE. In: *Aharoni*, Y. ed. *Investigations at Lachish. The Sanctuary and the Residency. (Lachish V).* Tel Aviv: 61–70.
Elat, M. 1977. *Economic Relations in the Lands of the Bible c. 1000–539 B.C.* Jerusalem. (Hebrew).
Elliger, K. 1936. Die Nordgrenze des Reiches David. *PJb* 32: 34–73.
Eph'al, I. 1969. The Penetration of Arab Tribes to the Periphery of Palestine and Southern Syria in the 8th Century B.C. *Proceedings of the Fifth World Congress of Jewish Studies.* Jerusalem: 141–152, 243. (Hebrew).
Eph'al, I. 1971. Gaza. *Enc. Miqr.* VI: 116–122. (Hebrew).
Eph'al, I. 1978. The Western Minorities in Babylonia in the 6th–5th Centuries B.C. *Orientalia* 47: 74–90.
Epstein, C. and Gutman, S. 1972. The Golan. In: Kochavi, M. ed. *Judaea, Samaria and the Golan, Archaeological Survey 1967–1968.* Jerusalem: 243–295. (Hebrew).

Gadd, C.J. 1954. Inscribed Prisms of Sargon II from Nimrud. *Iraq* 16: 173–201.
Galling, K. 1968. *Textbuch zur Geschichte Israels.* (2nd ed.). Tübingen.
Gardiner, A.H. 1920. The Ancient Military Road between Egypt and Palestine. *JEA* 6: 99–116.
Garelli, P. 1971. Nouveau coup d'oeil sur Muṣur. In: *Hommages à André Dupont Sommer.* Paris: 37–48.
Ginsberg, H.L. 1951. A Preposition of Interest to Historical Geographers. *BASOR* 122: 12–14.
Glueck, N. 1940. *The Other Side of the Jordan.* New Haven.
Godbey, A.H. 1905. The Ḳêpu. *AJSL* 22: 81–88.
Grayson, A.K. 1975. *Assyrian and Babylonian Chronicles.* (Texts from Cuneiform Sources 5). New York.
Grintz, Y.M. 1961. The South-Western Border of the Promised Land. In: *Yehezkel Kaufmann Jubilee Volume.* Jerusalem: 7–19. (Hebrew).
Heidel, H. 1956. A New Hexagonal Prism of Esarhaddon (676 B.C.). *Sumer* 12:9–37.
Helck, W. 1968–69. Zur Staatlichen Organisation Syriens im Beginn der 18. Dynastie. *AfO* 22: 27–29.
Helck, W. 1971. *Die Beziehungen Ägyptens zu Vorderasien im 3. and 2. Jahrtausend v Chr.* (2nd ed.). Wiesbaden.
Herzog, Z., Rainey, A.F. and Moshkovitz, S. 1977. The Stratigraphy at Beer-sheba and the Location of the Sanctuary. *BASOR* 225: 49–58.
Hirschberg, H. 1932. *Studien zur Geschichte Esarhaddons König von Assyrian* (681–669). Ohlau in Schlesien.
Ibrahim, M., Sauer, J. and Yassine, K. 1976. The East Jordan Valley Survey, 1975. *BASOR* 222: 41–66.
Jones, A.M.H. 1971. *The Cities of the Eastern Roman Provinces.* (revised ed.). Oxford.
Kallai, Z. 1975. The Boundaries of Canaan and the Land of Israel in the Bible. *Eretz Israel* 12: 27–34. (Hebrew).
Kees, H. 1961. *Ancient Egypt, A Geographical History of the Nile.* Chicago.
Kempinski, A. 1974. Tell el-'Ajjul - Beth-Aglayim or Sharuḥen? *IEJ* 24: 145–152.
Kenyon, K.M. 1976. The Date of the Destruction of Iron Age Beer-sheba. *PEQ* 108: 63–64.
Kitchen, K.A. 1973a. *The Third Intermediate Period in Egypt (1100-650 B.C.).* Warminster.
Kitchen, K.A. 1973b. Late-Egyptian Chronology and the Hebrew Monarchy. *Journal of the Ancient Near Eastern Society of Columbia University* 5: 225–233.
Landsberger, B. 1965. *Brief des Bischofs von Esagila an König Asarhaddon.* (Mededelingen der Koninklijke Nederlandse Akademie van Wetenschappen, afd. Letterkunde, Nieuwe Reeks 28/6). Amsterdam.
Lie, A.G. 1929. *The Inscriptions of Sargon II King of Assyria.* Part I: *The Annals Transliterated and Translated with Notes.* Paris.
Lipiński, E. 1974. 'Anaq — Kiryat 'Arba' — Hébron et ses sanctuaires tribaux. *VT* 24: 41–55.
Loewenstamm, S.E. 1968. Naḥal Mizraim. *Enc. Miqr.* V: 813–814. (Hebrew).
Luckenbill, D.D. 1927. *Ancient Records of Assyria and Babylonia* II. Chicago.
Margovski, Y. 1969. The Survey of North Western Sinai. *Had. Arkh.* 28–29: 43–47. (Hebrew).
Margovski, Y. 1971. The Archaeological Survey of Sinai. *Had. Arkh.* 37: 31–34. (Hebrew).
Mazar (Maisler), B. 1946. Lebo-Hamat and the Northern Boundary of Canaan. *BJPES* 12: 91–102. (Hebrew).
Mazar (Maisler), B. 1951. Yurza — Tell Jemmeh. *BJPES* 15: 38–41. (Hebrew).
Mazar, B. 1952. Yurza: The Identification of Tell Jemmeh, *PEQ* 84, 48–51.
Mazar, B. 1957. The Campaign of Pharaoh Shishak to Palestine. *Supplement* to *VT* 4: 57–66.
Mazar, B. 1975. *Cities and Districts in Eretz-Israel.* Jerusalem. (Hebrew).

Meissner, B. 1914. Jakinlû von Arwad. *OLZ* 17: 422–424.
Michel, E. 1954. Die Assur-Texte Salmanassars III. (858–824). 6. Fortsetzung. *WO* 2/1: 27–45.
Mittmann, S. 1970. *Beiträge zur Siedlungs- and Territorialgeschichte des nördlichen Ostjordanlandes.* Wiesbaden.
Musil, A. 1907. *Arabia Petraea II.* Wien.
Na'aman, N. 1974. Sennacherib's "Letter to God" on his Campaign to Judah. *BASOR* 214: 25–39.
Na'aman, N. 1976. Que. *Enc. Miqr.* VII: 87–93. (Hebrew).
Na'aman, N. 1979. Sennacherib's Campaign to Judah and the Date of the LMLK Stamps. *VT* 29: 61–86.
Na'aman, N. 1980. The Shihor of Egypt and Shur that is Before Egypt. Tel Aviv 7: 95–109.
Na'aman, N. 1983. The Inheritance and Settlement of the Sons of Simeon in the South of Eretz Israel. In Rofé, A. and Zakovitch, Y. eds. *Isac Leo Seeligmann Volume* I. Jerusalem: 111–136. (Hebrew).
Oded, B. 1974. The Phoenician Cities and the Assyrian Empire in the Time of Tiglath-pileser III. *ZDPV* 90: 38–49.
Oppenheim, A.L. 1969. Babylonian and Assyrian Historical Texts. In *ANET*: 265–317.
Oren, E.D. 1973. The Overland Route between Egypt and Canaan in the Early Bronze Age. *IEJ* 23: 198–205.
Oren, E.D. 1974. Tel Sera' (Tell esh-Shari'a). *IEJ* 24: 264–266.
Oren, E.D. 1976a. Tel Shera (Shari'a) — 1975. *Had. Arkh.* 57–58: 33–35. (Hebrew).
Oren, E.D. 1976b. Tel Shera (Shari'a) — 1976. *Had. Arkh.* 59–60: 50–53. (Hebrew).
Oren, E.D. 1977. Pithat Rafiah — Fort. *Had. Arkh.* 61–62: 49. (Hebrew).
Petrie, W.M.F. 1937. *Anthedon*. London.
Pfeiffer, R.H. 1935. *State Letters of Assyria.* (American Oriental Series 6). New Haven.
Porath, J. 1976. Khirbet Hoga. *Had. Arkh.* 59–60: 41–42. (Hebrew).
Postgate, J.N. 1973. Assyrian Texts and Fragments. *Iraq* 35: 13–36.
Postgate, J.N. 1974. *Taxation and Conscription in the Assyrian Empire.* (Studia Pohl, Series Maior 3). Rome.
Reade, J. 1976. Sargon's Campaigns of 720, 716 and 715 B.C.; Evidence from the Sculptures. *JNES* 35: 95–104.
Rost, P. 1893. *Die Keilschrifttexte Tiglat-Pilesers III., nach den Papierabklatschen und Originalen des Britischen Museums* I-II. Leipzig.
Saggs, H.W.F. 1955. The Nimrud Letters 1952, Part II. *Iraq* 17: 126–160.
Schrader, E. 1880. *Zur Kritik der Inschriften Tiglath-pileser's II., des Asarhaddon and des Asurbanipal.* Berlin.
Schwabe, M. 1954. Documents of a Journey through Palestine in the Years 317–323 C.E. *Eretz Israel* 3: 181–185. (Hebrew).
Spalinger, A. 1973. The Year 712 B.C. and its Implications to Egyptian History. *Journal of the American Research Center in Egypt* 10: 95–101.
Spalinger, A. 1974. Esarhaddon and Egypt; An Analysis of the First Invasion of Egypt. *Orientalia* 43: 295–326.
Spalinger, A. 1976. Psammetichus, King of Egypt: I. *Journal of the American Research Center in Egypt* 13: 133–147.
Stewart, J.R. 1974. *Tell el-'Ajjul.* (Studies in Mediterranean Archaeology 38). Göteborg.
Tadmor, H. 1958. The Campaigns of Sargon II of Assur; A Chronological-Historical Study. *JCS* 12: 22–40, 77–100.

Tadmor, H. 1964. The Assyrian Campaigns to Philistia. In: Liver, J. ed. *The Military History of the Land of Israel in Biblical Times.* Tel Aviv: 261–285. (Hebrew).
Tadmor, H. 1966. Philistia under Assyrian Rule. *BA* 29: 86–102.
Tadmor, H. 1972. The Me'unites in the Book of Chronicles in the Light of an Assyrian Document. In: Uffertheimer, B. ed. *Bible and Jewish History. Studies in Bible and Jewish History Dedicated to the Memory of Jacob Liver.* Tel Aviv. (Hebrew).
Tsafrir, Y. 1971 Azmon. *Enc. Miqr.* VI: 334–335. (Hebrew).
Ussishkin, D. 1977. The Destruction of Lachish by Sennacherib and the Dating of the Royal Judean Storage Jars. *Tel Aviv* 4: 28–60.
Van Beek, G.W. 1972. Tel Gamma. *IEJ* 22: 245–246.
Van Beek, G.W. 1973. Assyrian Vaulted Buildings at Tell Jemmeh. *Qadmoniot* 6: 23–26. (Hebrew).
Van Beek, G.W. 1974. Tel Gamma. *IEJ* 24: 138–139, 274–275.
Van Beek, G.W. 1977. Tel Gamma, 1975–1976. *IEJ* 27: 171–176.
de Vaux, R. 1968. Les Pays de Canaan. *JAOS* 88: 23–30.
de Vaux, R. 1971. *Histoire Ancienne d'Israel. Des Origines à l'Installation en Canaan.* Paris.
Weidner, E.F. 1941–1944. Šilkan(ḫe)ni, König von Muṣri, ein Zeitgenosse Sargons II. *AfO* 14: 40–53.
Weissbach, F.H. 1918. Zu den Inschriften der Säle im Palaste Sargon's II. von Assyrien. *Zeitschrift der Deutschen Morgenländischen Gesellschaft* 72: 161–185.
Weissbach, F.H. 1928–29. Der Assyrische Name von Qal'at al-'Ariš. *ZA* 38: 108–110.
Wilson, J.A. 1969. Egyptian Historical Texts. In *ANET*: 227–264.
Wilson, J.A. 1969. An Egyptian Letter. In *ANET*: 475–479.
Winckler, H. 1889. *Die Keilschrifttexte Sargons nach den Papierabklatschen and Originalen neu herausgeben* I-II. Leipzig.
Wiseman, D.J. 1951. The Historical Inscriptions from Nimrud. *Iraq* 13: 21–26.
Wiseman, D.J. 1956. A Fragmentary Inscription of Tiglath-pileser III from Nimrud. *Iraq* 18: 117–129.
Wreszinski, W. 1935. *Atlas zur Altägyptischen Kulturgeschichte II.* Leipzig.
Yadin, Y. 1976. Beer-sheba: The High Place Destroyed by King Josiah. *BASOR* 222: 5–17.
Yeivin, S. 1934–35. The Annals of Thutmose III. In: Slousch, N. ed. *Journal of the Jewish Palestine Exploration Society III.* Dedicated to the Memory of Dr. A. Mazie. Jerusalem: 145–174. (Hebrew).
Zadok, R. 1977. *On West Semites in Babylonia during the Chaldean and Achaemenian Periods. An Onomastic Study.* Jerusalem.
Zadok, R. 1996. Notes on Syro-Palestinian History, Toponymy and Anthroponymy. *Ugarit-Forschungen* 28: 721–749.

The Shihor of Egypt and Shur That is Before Egypt[1]

In a previous article (Na'aman 1979a), I tried to demonstrate that the Brook of Egypt of the Assyrian inscriptions and the Bible should be identified with Naḥal Besor and that it is only since the time of the Second Temple that it has been considered to be Wādi el-'Arish. It was then, in the wake of the destruction and desertion of the land following the downfall of the First Temple and the ensuing change in the pattern of settlement in northern Sinai during the Persian period that the old tradition passed into oblivion. My main concern, then, was the Assyrian policy on the Egyptian border; thus, I did not include all of the biblical data pertaining to the southern border. This article is intended to complement my previous thesis by examining several toponyms pertaining to this border, in an attempt to clarify the main issue: What were the biblical concepts of the southern border between the Land of Israel and Egypt? I shall begin with the location of the Shihor, which is mentioned several times in conjunction with the southern border of Canaan as being על-פני מצרים (Josh. 13:3), i.e., "before Egypt" (or "east of Egypt," in some English translations), and proceed to the location of Shur, also described as על-פני מצרים (Gen. 25:18; 1 Sam. 15:7) and similarly translated.

A. The Shihor of Egypt and the Southern Border of the Land of Canaan

Shihor is mentioned five times in the Bible (Josh. 13:3; 19:26; Isa. 23:3; Jer. 2:1.8; 1 Chr. 13:5). Undoubtedly, the word was borrowed from Egyptian *š-ḥr*, "the waters of Horus." In Egyptian inscriptions *š-ḥr* denotes "pools" or "lakes" in the northeastern delta and, in the opinion of many scholars, it may designate the Pelusic branch of the Nile or the lakes in the same region (Lambdin 1962; Ahituv 1976:619–620; Saebø 1974:29–31; Wüst 1975:33–35).

For two of the biblical verses, there is scholarly unanimity. In Jer. 2:18, where the Shihor appears as a counterpart to the Euphrates (see Gen. 15:18), it is certainly the Nile, and in Isa. 23:3 the parallelism Shihor-*Ye'ôr* also signifies the Nile — but here the consensus ends. Undoubtedly, it was under the influence of these two verses, backed up by the Egyptian etymology of the

1. Reprinted with permission. *Tel Aviv* 7 (1980), 95–109.

word, that most scholars were led to consider the Shihor as a branch of the Nile in the other three verses as well (Delitzsch 188'1:311–312; Meyer 1906: 457; Cooke 1918:118; Japhet 1977:304–305; Lipschitz 1978:48, n. 25).

In the first of these problematic references to the Shihor, the borders of "the land that yet remains" are described as extending "from the Shihor which is before Egypt even unto the borders of Ekron northward" (Josh. 13:3). The basic geographical problem of this verse was already sensed in Dillmann's commentary (1886:508), thus, we shall translate his remarks in full:

> The Shihor . . . in Isa. 23:3 and Jer. 2:18 without any doubt denotes the Nile or one of its branches and therefore cannot be here Wādi el-'Arish (the Brook of Egypt), which denotes in [source] A the southern border of the land (Num. 34:5; Josh. 15:4, 47); but it is just as unlikely that it is the Nile itself, since it is not the Nile that runs "before Egypt" (see Gen. 25:18; 1 Sam. 15:7) but only its easternmost branch.

As noted above, most commentators have been influenced by both the Egyptian etymology of the word and the passages from Isaiah and Jeremiah in locating the Shihor of Josh. 13:3 along the eastern Egyptian delta, but there are still those who prefer to identify it with the Brook of Egypt (Curtis 1910: 205; Rudolph 1955:110; Simons 1959:27; see Wüst 1975:32–38). The main difficulty caused by identifying the Shihor with a branch of the Nile, as pointed out by Meyer (1906:457, n. 1), is that the whole of northern Sinai would then lie within the borders of the land of Canaan.[2] Inasmuch as the external borders of "the land that yet remains" (Josh. 13:2–6), both in the north and northeast, are the same as the boundaries of the Land of Canaan in Num. 34 (Kallai 1967: 90–96; 1975:32–33), why would the biblical historiographer have depicted the southern frontier as lying far beyond the traditional limits of Canaan and encompassing the Sinai desert? Kallai (1975:28–29) tried to resolve this incongruity by assuming that the biblical authors borrowed their border concepts from the Egyptians, an interpretation that is open to debate.

First, let us review the concept of "the Land of Canaan." In my previous article (1979a:76–78), I pointed out that the eastern borders of Canaan reflect mainly the Late Bronze Age pattern of settlement, a pattern that no longer

2. In an attempt to solve this difficulty, Meyer suggested amending the "Shihor" to "Shur," a proposal that has no textual support.

3. Kallai (1975:27; 1977:107, n. 10) has raised several doubts concerning the eastern border of Canaan. In reply, it should be noted that Piḫilu is the only Transjordanian city-state mentioned in any Late Bronze Age document, and Zaphon should be dropped altogether, because there is no textual ground for the emendation to EA 274 suggested by Albright (Na'aman 1979b:680 n. 33). However, even more important, we should realize that the Jordan Valley was the eastern limit of Canaanite settlement and culture, regardless of whether or to what extent the 19th dynasty Egyptians were active on the other side of the river.

existed in the Iron Age (de Vaux 1968:28–29; Kallai 1975:32–33);[3] moreover, the entire Kadesh-barnea triangle was considered to be outside of the limits of historical Canaan, whose southern border passed from the Dead Sea to Naḥal Besor.[4] As for the northern boundary, Mazar (1946:93) has argued that it was identical to the borders of the province of Canaan under the Egyptian 19th dynasty. However, this territorial unit was known even earlier, as may be seen in the list of 119 cities conquered by Thutmose III in his first campaign to Canaan (Aharoni 1967:142–152). It is even possible that these are the same territorial limits reflected in the second (early 18th century) group of Execration texts (Mazar 1947:68). This northern boundary is also marked by the *ā>ō* phonetic difference in the dialects of Canaan and "Amurru" in the second half of the second millennium BCE and perhaps even earlier (Gelb 1961: 42–44; Zadok 1977:38–44). Consequently, the biblical concept of Canaan reflects not only the political situation of the 13th century BCE, but goes back to much earlier times. The Israelites adopted this long-established border concept from the local Canaanite population — not from the Egyptians. Furthermore, the Egyptian idea that the eastern delta of the Nile was their border (demarcated by the frontier station at Sile), with the Sinai peninsula belonging to Asia, was alien to both the inhabitants of Canaan of the second millennium and to their Israelite heirs; for these peoples, the southernmost line of urban settlement marked their border in that direction and they — contrary to the Egyptians — regarded Sinai as part of Egypt.

As contacts between Egypt and Canaan increased during the course of the second millennium, the Egyptians seemed to become more aware of the fact that the Sinai peninsula was not really part of Canaan (Na'aman 1979a:74–76), an attitude that is expressed in several New kingdom inscriptions. The Egyptians began to look upon Sinai from two — ostensibly — contradictory points of view: traditionally, they continued to regard it as part of Asia, but, at the same time, they seemed to consider it a kind of buffer zone between themselves and the inhabited regions of Canaan, demarcated by a southern border running south of Gaza.

The conclusion we should draw from the above discussion is clear. Any thesis that includes Sinai within Canaanite territory on the basis of the traditional Egyptian border concept is untenable, because such an Egypto-centric perspective did not have any bearing on the Canaanite/Israelite views. Inasmuch as the only textual support for "adding" the Sinai peninsula to the

4. Sensing this difficulty, Alt (1925:108, n.1) proposed that the inclusion of Kadesh-barnea within the southern boundaries of Canaan was merely a theoretical claim on this region.

Land of Canaan is the identification of the Shihor of Josh. 13:3 as the easternmost branch of the Nile, another location for the Shihor that corresponds with the overall evidence should be sought.

Parenthetically, it should be remembered that there is a second and broader border concept than that based on the boundaries of historical Canaan. I refer to the "Patriarchs' borders" (Gen. 15:18), extending "from the river of Egypt unto the great river, the river Euphrates" (see Saebø 1974:20–21; Kallai 1975 :29). But these borders do not belong to the same category as those of Canaan, in that they were never described in detail and are defined only by the "from . . . unto . . ." formula. On no account can they be regarded as an expression of the maximal territory held by the Egyptians during the New Kingdom (Aharoni 1967:61; Saebø 1974:36; Kallai 1975:29–30), if for no other reason than that Egyptian rule over this entire area was nothing more than a brief episode at the beginning of the 18th dynasty, but also because the biblical border concepts are not applicable to Egyptian historiographic patterns. These maximal borders seem to reflect a late pattern that developed after the Assyrians had formulated the geographical/administrative term *Ebir nāri* ("beyond the river") following the unification of the Fertile Crescent during the last third of the 8th century BCE.[5] It is, therefore, my opinion that the Bible contains three basic territorial concepts, each with its own set of borders: (a) the Land of Canaan, which was adopted from the local inhabitants at the time that the Israelites first settled; its northern border was the same as that of David and Solomon at the height of empire and included their vassal states (Elliger 1936); (b) the kingdom of David and Solomon, excluding the vassal states, reflected by the borders of the tribes of Israel (Kallai 1977); to account for the gaps between (a) and (b), the borders of the land that remains were devised; (c) the kingdom promised by the Deuteronomist for the end of days, which embodied the "Patriarchs' borders" and envisioned the Israelite nation extending over all the territory of "beyond the River" from the Nile to the Euphrates; there are several verses (e.g., Exod. 23:31; Deut. 11:24; Josh. 1:4) that try to reconcile the incongruities between (b) and (c) (*pace* Saebø 1974:17–20).

We may now return to the problem of the Shihor. Commentators on 1 Chr. 13:5 were inclined to identify the "Shihor of Egypt" of this verse with the Brook of Egypt, on account of its similarity with 1 Kgs. 8:65 (= 2 Chr. 7:8). Noth (1955:70) tried to explain this reference to the Shihor by suggesting that it was used learnedly — but inaccurately — as an appelative, an explanation

5. For the. Abrahamic covenant (Gen. 15), see the detailed study by Anbar (1978), who dated its composition to the end of the First Temple.

that was adopted by several others (Rudolph 1955:110; see Simons 1959:27, 68–69; Wüst.1975:36–38). I would suggest that, in this verse, the Chronicler paraphrased the words of 1 Kgs. 8:65 (=2 Chr. 7:8), intentionally using an archaic form (Shihor). By this device, he claimed that David's shifting of the ark from Kiriath-jearim to Jerusalem was equal to Solomon's consecration of the Temple.

In the third problematic reference to the Shihor (Josh. 19:26), the border of the tribe of Asher is described as reaching "to the Carmel westward and to Shihor-libnath." The LXX and Eusebius treated Shihor and Libnath as two different places, but in modern research the Massoretic text was unanimously accepted (Dillmann 1886:560; Noth 1955:117; Aharoni 1967:237–238). Broshi (1962:430) suggested that, in this case, "Shihor" was used metaphorically for "wādi" or "river," thereby, rendering Shihor-libnath as "the waters of Libnath" or "the river of Libnath." Surprisingly, most scholars do not refer at all to Shihor-libnath in their discussion of the biblical toponym Shihor (an exception is Simons 1959:27, 190, n. 178).

Summing up, the following picture emerges: biblical *Shihor,* originally borrowed from the Egyptian language, was used in the two prophetic passages to denote a specific watercourse, perhaps a branch of the Nile. In the course of time, however, it developed into a more figurative term for "river," "stream" or "wādi" and, in this sense, it appears in all three verses dealing with border delineation. The same semantic development may be traced in biblical *Ye'or,* also borrowed from the Egyptian and originally denoting the Nile, but sometimes used in its more general meaning of "river" (Simons 1959:68–69; see Lambdin 1953:151).

Once we eliminate a term originally denoting a branch of the Nile from the discussion of the boundaries of the Land of Canaan, we may draw the following picture: In the Bible there are two closely related demarcation lines for the south. The first, crossing from the Dead Sea to Naḥal Besor, is the border of historical Canaan and corresponds to the southernmost limit of urban settlement. The second adds Kadesh-barnea and the Negev highlands to this territory. In my previous article (1979a:78), I suggested that it was due to its importance in the early history of the Israelite tribes that Kadesh-barnea was included within these borders, but a more comprehensive explanation suggests itself. This remote stronghold, first fortified under the United Monarchy (Meyers 1976; Cohen 1976a; 1978), was built to guard the rich springs in its vicinity and to protect the caravans *en route* to the Gulf of Eilat via Darb el-Ghazzeh. At about the same time or slightly earlier, many villages and fortresses were founded in the Negev highlands (Cohen 1976b; Meshel 1977). The eastern line of these settlements corresponds with the southeastern border described in Num. 34:3–4a and Josh. 15:2–3a (Cohen

1976b:49–50), and, in the west, they extend up to the main road leading from Kadesh-barnea to Naḥal Besor, i.e., the same line that delineated the southwestern border of the Land of Canaan (Na'aman 1979a:78–79). All this area, with Kadesh as its southern stronghold, was apparently conquered by David and, therefore, was "allotted" to the tribe of Judah in the system of the twelve tribes.

The descriptions of the southern border of the Land of Canaan (Num. 34: 3–5) and that of the Israelite tribes (Josh. 15:2–4), which, unlike the northern and eastern borders, are identical in the south, were reciprocally influenced. It was probably under the influence of the boundaries of the Israelite tribes that the biblical historiographers included Kadesh-barnea and the Negev highlands within the Land of Canaan, just as their knowledge of the scope of the Land of Canaan caused them to include the Philistine coast within the territory of the Israelite tribes, despite the fact that this coastal strip never was annexed by the Israelite kings (and, therefore, was relegated to the "land that yet remains" of Josh. 13:2–3). By synthesizing these two originally separate traditions into a unified border scheme, the biblical historiographers created a boundary that may seem somewhat strange to us when looking at a detailed map, but we must remember that the ancients were accustomed to visualizing geographical areas in terms of roads, settlements and directions. Perhaps the southern border was demarcated by desert trails leading to Kadesh from the northwest and northeast, with the result that the main road from Kadesh to Naḥal Besor was regarded as the southwestern boundary of Canaan. The four toponyms, Hezron, Adar, Karkaa and Azmon (Josh. 15:3–4) must be sought along this line.

The biblical historiographers did not seem to take into account territorial gaps. In their eyes, for example, the entire country was divided among the twelve tribes, and if any areas were not completely settled or were inhabited by other peoples, these areas were simply ignored. It is perhaps this psychology that caused them to regard the zone south of the Brook of Egypt as part of Egypt (just as the Egyptians originally looked upon the area north of the Pelusic branch of the Nile as part of Asia). This, in my opinion, is the origin of the "Brook of Egypt": it was the river demarcating the border with Egypt from the point of view of the peoples living north of this line. The description of Shihor (= Brook of Egypt) as being "before Egypt" (Josh. 13:3) should therefore be interpreted in this light.

B. Shur That is Before Egypt

The fact that exactly the same expression, "על-פני מצרים" ("that is before Egypt") is used for biblical Shur in two verses (Gen. 25:18; 1 Sam. 15:7) seems to imply that Shur was also located on the southern border of Canaan.

Inasmuch as this is at variance with commonly held views as to the location of Shur, let us examine the data very carefully.

Altogether, Shur is mentioned seven times in the Bible, including the references to the "way of Shur" (Gen. 16:7) and the "wilderness of Shur" (Exod. 15:22). In early Aramaic translations of the Bible, *Shur* was rendered as *ḥagrā*, meaning a place surrounded by a wall. The noun *shur is* indeed identical with the Aramaic *šwr* ("wall") and as such appears twice in biblical poetry (Gen. 49:22; 2 Sam. 22:30 = Ps. 18:30). From the earliest days of modern research, Shur has been regarded as a term designating the chain of forts in the eastern delta defending Egypt against potential invasion from Sinai (the "Wall of the Ruler" in the story of Sinuhe). The "wilderness of Shur," therefore, was thought to lie east of this fortified line, with the "way of Shur" running along the line Beer-sheba — Ḥaluṣa - Quseima — Bir el-Ḥasana — Ismailia (Simons 1959:217, 251, 317–318; Lipschitz 1978:51–52, 155–157).

However, it is hard to find any justification for interpreting "Shur" as a fortified line, an interpretation based mainly on analogy to the Roman *limes* (Mazar 1950; 1957:64). Not only is this concept unknown in the Bible, but the *ḥgrm* of Shishak's topographical list are all individual enclosed settlements. The use of Aramaic *ḥagrā* to denote a line of fortifications is of late origin, influenced by the western concept of the *limes.* "Shur" would better be interpreted, like other biblical toponyms (such as Bezer, Geder, Hazor and Migdal), as the name of a town or settlement. This would explain the lack of the defining article in front of the word, which we would expect if it were a descriptive noun referring to a topographical feature such as the limes (see Mihelic 1962).

In two passages (1 Sam. 15:7 and 27:8), Shur is mentioned in clear contexts. In 1 Sam. 15, Saul mustered his army at Telaim (probably the Telem of Josh. 15:24) and subsequently attacked the city of Amalek. After smiting the Amalekites "from Havilah as far as Shur," Saul returned to Carmel in the southern Judean hill country. The site of Havilah is unknown, but the geographical context requires a locale in the eastern Negeb, and not in north Arabia as sometimes proposed (Driver 1913:123; Winnett 1970:175–179; Stoebe 1973:285). The same geographical scope — "from Havilah unto Shur" — is repeated in Gen. 25:18 in a passage dealing with the Ishmaelites.[6] The Ishmaelites were "the main tribal confederation south of Palestine at a cer-

6. The continuation of v. 18, "as thou goes *aššurāh*," is a repetition of the aforementioned phrase "unto Shur" (see Meyer 1906:321). In spite of being rendered as "toward Assyria" or "on the way to Ashur" in most English translations of the Bible, there is no support for this assumption, nor is there any evidence that this Ashur was the name of a nomadic tribe dwelling in northern Arabia.

tain period prior to the mid-tenth century," while "other, possibly unrelated tribes, such as the Amalekites, were considered also to be Ishmaelites" (Eph'al 1976:226). Therefore, we may conclude that "from Havilah unto Shur" refers to two points roughly aligned from east to west along Naḥal Beer Sheva and Naḥal Besor, at either end of the main route of the nomads then living on the southern periphery of the country.

Shur is mentioned once again in 1 Sam. 27:8, describing David's raids from his base in Ziklag against the neighboring tribes (Geshurites, Gerizites and Amalekites), "for these were the inhabitants of the land *m'wlm* as far as Shur to the land of Egypt" (see Stoebe 1973:474). Structurally, this verse is parallel to Gen. 10:19, although it lacks geographical directions. Our main difficulty here lies in the interpretation of *mē'ôlām* (translated in most English versions of the Bible as "of old"). The proposal to read it as "from Elam" (Seebass 1965: 389–391) is questionable. On the basis of several LXX manuscripts, Driver (1913:211–212) suggested rendering it "from Telam" (and, indeed, *The New English Bible* (1970) reads "from Telaim"). As noted above, Telaim/Telem appears in Josh. 15:24 and 1 Sam. 15:4 as the site in the Negeb where Saul organized his troops prior to attacking the Amalekites. Tentatively (and with a large question mark), we may suggest locating Telem/Telaim in the area of Tel Malḥata (Tell el-Milḥ), on the eastern side of Naḥal Beer Sheva, because this area suits the geographical context. Presumably, however, Saul would have mustered his troops on Israelite territory, and it seems rather curious to use the name of an Israelite town or village to define the range of the non-Israelite tribes. Another possibility is to locate both 'Olam? ("from *'ôlām*") and Shur in the western Negeb, in the territory of the Geshurites (Josh. 13:2). According to this hypothesis, David would have directed his raids against the non-Israelite tribes in the vicinity, abstaining from attacks on the Israelites, who, for the most part, dwelt in the eastern Negeb (see 1 Sam. 27:10–11).

In Gen. 20:1 we read that "From there Abraham journeyed toward the territory of the Negeb and dwelt between Kadesh and Shur; and he sojourned in Gerar." To understand the geographical implications of this verse, the term "Negeb" must first be clarified (Simons 1959:67; Aharoni 1968:749–752; 1976a: 55–56; Meshel 1974:6–14). As the southernmost region of historical Canaan in several verses (e.g., Gen. 10:19; Num. 13:17, 29; 21:1; Judg. 1:9), the Negeb was well differentiated from the wilderness *(midbar)* in that it supported some agriculture; the wilderness was suitable only for pasture. Naḥal Beer Sheva and Naḥal Besor, together with their tributaries, were the backbone of the biblical Negeb; the question is whether Kadesh-barnea was also considered part of it. Simons (1959:67), for example, believes that the southern borders of Canaan, including the Kadesh triangle, were identical to the boundaries of the Negeb, but, against this assumption, there are several verses (e.g., Gen. 21:14; Num.

13:26; 34:4; 1 Kgs. 19:3–4) showing that Kadesh was considered part of the wilderness (Meshel 1974:8). By studying all the Bible references to the Negeb, we see that it is only Gen. 20:1 (and to a certain extent also Josh. 15:23)[7] that gives any grounds for the claim that the southern borders of the Negeb are poorly defined in the Bible (Noth 1935:36; Fritz 1975:31). According to Gen. 20:1, Abraham dwelt in the area between Kadesh and Shur, which is commonly interpreted to mean between Kadesh and the Egyptian delta, thereby, implying that the Negeb extended far to the south of Kadesh (Speiser 1964: 148). However, the difficulty disappears once we realize that the places in this verse are listed from south to north (instead of *vice versa, as* commonly assumed), which puts Shur north of Kadesh on the main road leading to Gerar. Alt (1935) located Gerar within the Roman-Byzantine *Saltus Gerariticus,* and Aharoni (1956) identified it with Tel Haror (Tell Abū Hureireh) on the western bank of Naḥal Gerar (Wādi esh-Shari'ah) (Aharoni 1977). "Towards the Negeb country," therefore, states the general direction in which Abraham was headed, Gerar being his final destination. The words "from there" at the beginning of the verse, which have always troubled the commentators, refer to the land of Egypt where Abraham "went down" during the famine, according to Gen. 12. Gen. 20:1 is, therefore, a second tradition of Abraham coming out of Egypt, parallel to Gen. 13:1 "And Abram went up out of Egypt . . . into the Negeb."

In the story of the birth of Ishmael, we read that when Hagar fled from Sarah, "the angel of the Lord found her by a spring of water in the wilderness, the spring on the way to Shur" (Gen. 16:7); in v. 14 the location is pinpointed: "Therefore the well was called Beer-lahai-roi; it is between Kadesh and Bered."[8] In a slightly different story (Gen. 21:14) Hagar wandered "in the wilderness of Beer-sheba", i.e., the area south of the Beer Sheva valley. If we coalesce these two narratives, we see that Beer-lahai-roi should be sought somewhere in the area of Beer-Mash'abim (Bir 'Asluj), on the road leading to Naḥal Besor through Ḥaluṣa (el-Khalassa). This site is fairly close to Beer-

7. As for the Kadesh listed in Josh. 15:23 under the Negeb district of Judah, Alt (1925: 108, n.1) was certainly correct in divesting it of any connection with Kadesh-barnea by arguing that the Negeb district of Judah did not extend beyond the settled area of the south (see Aharoni 1976b:36; *pace* Kallai 1967:318, n. 99). Not only is the town list of Josh. 15:21–32 clearly divided into two groups, eastern and western, with Kadesh belonging to the eastern group, but several of the other toponyms appearing in this verse are also mentioned in the Arad inscriptions (Aharoni 1975:145–147), so Kadesh must have been located somewhere in the eastern Negeb.

8. As it is expressly stated that the well was situated in the wilderness, it tends to confirm our thesis that the more southerly Kadesh-barnea was considered part of the desert.

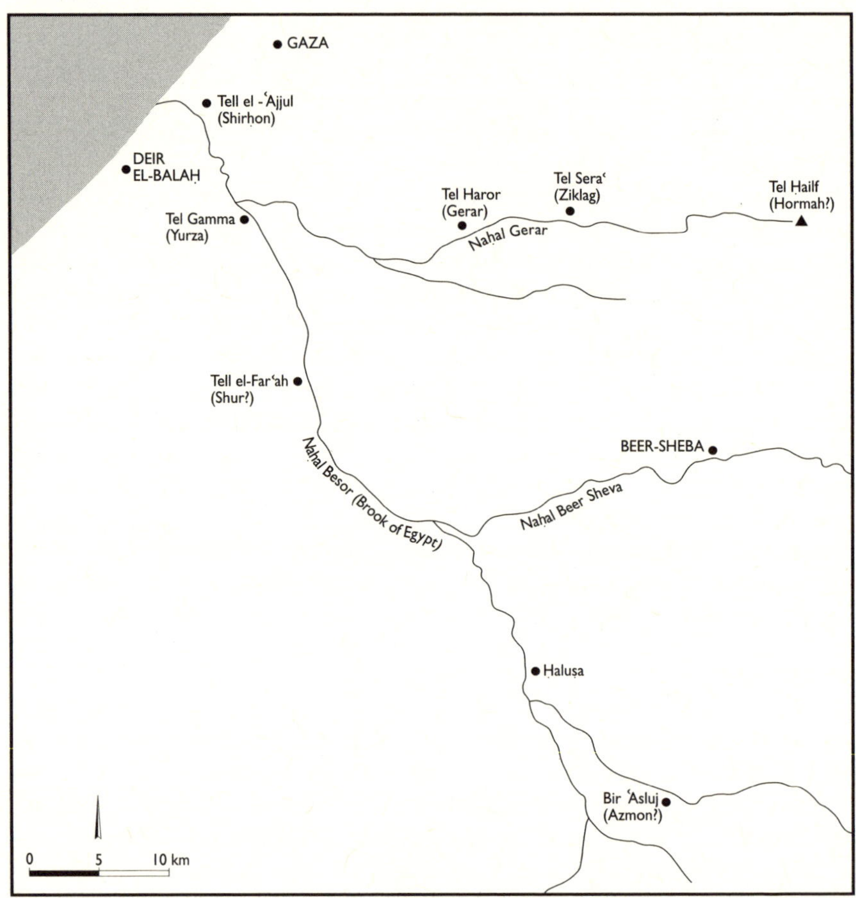

Proposed site identification along Naḥal Besor

sheba, the center of the Isaac traditions in which Beer-lahai-roi is twice mentioned (Gen. 24:62; 25:11).[9]

Finally, we come to the story of Exod. 15:22. Without going into the vexing problem of identifying the places mentioned in the Exodus narrative, we

9. It has often been suggested that the story of Hagar refers to the birth of the eponymous father of the Ishmaelites and that their cultic center was in the vicinity of the well where the angel of the Lord found Hagar (Meyer 1906:322–323; Loewenstamm 1954:6; White 1975:303–305). The location of this well at Beer Mash'abim, thus, has important implications for resolving the question of who built the settlements in the Negev highlands in the 11th–10th centuries BCE (see Aharoni 1967:273, 278; Rothenberg 1967:92–96; Cohen

may assume that "the wilderness of Shur" covered most of the northern Sinai desert lying west of Shur.

Summing up, "Shur" is a place name, marking in two biblical passages the western limits of the wanderings of the Ishmaelites and Amalekites. From the stories of David at Ziklag, we know that Shur marked the border for the nomads then dwelling in the south and, therefore, should be sought in the western Negeb. Abraham's itinerary indicates that Shur lay on the main road from Kadesh-barnea to Gerar (Tel Haror), and, according to the story of Hagar, "the way of Shur" crossed the desert on its way from Kadesh, going in the direction of Naḥal Besor. Therefore, we must look for a site on Naḥal Besor at the southern edge of the settled area. The best candidate would be Tell el-Far'ah, the southernmost of the big mounds lying along Naḥal Besor (see Yisraeli 1978). There, in the level belonging to the 19th–20th dynasties, a large building (the "Residency") built according to Egyptian-Canaanite plan was uncovered, and among the small finds was a wooden box with ivory inlays depicting Egyptian scenes. In Cemetery 900, other objects of this period were found, including several scarabs, the latest one dating to Ramesses IV. In one of the tombs, there were some fragments of anthropoid coffins, testifying to the presence of Egyptian soldiers or officials (Dothan 1979:101–104). All this is evidence that the site was under Egyptian hegemony at the time. The Iron Age I city lay south of the "Residency"; among the many tombs of this period are Petrie's "graves of the five lords of the Philistines," rich in finds, including quantities of Philistine pottery (Yisraeli 1978:1077, 1081; Dothan 1979: 101–102).

Tell el-Far'ah has generally been identified as the Hyksos city of Sharuhen. A few years ago, however, it was proposed that this Hyksos center was located at Tell el-'Ajjul (Kempinski 1974; Stewart 1974:62 f.), a proposal that I readily accept (Na'aman 1979a:75, n. 12). This leaves Tell el-Far'ah unidentified, and it is my opinion that Shur has all the necessary requirements to fill this vacuum.[10]

1976b:49–50; Meshel 1977:132–135), because this cultic center would have been located in the same area as these settlements. The confederation of the Ishmaelites with related tribes such as the Amalekites and Midianites is well known from the biblical narratives pertaining to the settlement period and early days of the United Monarchy, but absent from all later traditions (Eph'al 1976:226; see Mazar 1969:77–79). Inasmuch as this chronological framework corresponds well with the archaeological data of the settlements in the Negev highlands, these settlements and fortresses should be attributed to the above-mentioned tribes. If these were *not* the settlements of these tribes, then where else could they have been located?

10. In the Negeb section of Shishak's list, the names *š3-rw-n-rw* (No. 104) and *š3-rw-d-d-*[?] (No. 1 bis), appear; either might represent Shur-xx (see No. 15 in this list *š3-n-m* for Shunem). But this is no more than a hypothesis.

Five of the six passages mentioning Shur come from either the Book of Genesis or Samuel. Mazar's theory (1969:78) that the stories of Abraham, Isaac and Abimelech in Genesis contain "transparent allusions to the relations between the Judeans and their sub-groups in the Negev and the Philistine kingdoms during the last quarter of the eleventh century" presupposes that these passages were composed at one and the same time. In my opinion, the short time-span allocated by this theory for the background of Genesis may be open to debate, but, if these stories are perceived as a telescopic contraction of all the experiences and historical memories of the southern tribes, the problem may be resolved. As an example, one might cite Gerar, which was an actual city (rather than a region, as Mazar proposed; see Alt 1935:295–303, and particularly the description in Gen. 26:6–8), whose place in these stories reflects a period when Gerar played an important role on the southern coast. The traditions concerning Shur also had their roots in the conditions prevailing during this period when "Shur that is before Egypt" held a key position on the southern border and lent its name to the road entering the land from Kadesh-barnea, "the way of Shur," analogous to "the way of the land of the Philistines" for the northern road, both terms denoting the point of view of someone entering the country from outside.

Conclusion

The Bible is remarkably consistent in its concept of the southern border of the country. Whether in the patriarchal legends, the sagas of conquest and settlement or the narratives of Saul and David, Naḥal Besor and Naḥal Beer Sheva are invariably presented as being the southern limits of the permanently inhabited land. The only exception is the oasis of Kadesh-barnea, and for a short time also the Negev highlands. Obviously the ancient authors were well acquainted with the geographical and cultural reality of those areas they so vividly described, and regardless of the historical validity of each and every story, these traditions may be safely used to draw a concrete historical-geographic picture.

References

Aharoni, Y. 1956. The Land of Gerar. *IEJ* 6: 26–32.

Aharoni, Y. 1962. Negev. *Enc. Miqr.* V: 749–752. (Hebrew).

Aharoni, Y. 1967. *The Land of the Bible: A Historical Geography.* Philadelphia.

Aharoni, Y. 1975. *Arad Inscriptions.* (Judean Desert Studies). Jerusalem. (Hebrew).

Aharoni, Y. 1976a. Nothing Early and Nothing Late: Re-writing Israel's Conquest. *BA* 39: 55–76.

Aharoni, Y. 1976b. Kedesh. *Enc. Miqr.* VII: 36. (Hebrew).

Aharoni, Y. 1977. Tel Haror. *Eretz Israel* 13: 106–107. (Hebrew).

Ahituv, S. 1976. Shiḥor. *Enc. Miqr.* VII: 619–620. (Hebrew).

Alt, A. 1925. Judas Gaue unter Josia. *PJb* 21: 100–116. (Reprint: Alt 1953: 276–288).

Alt, A. 1935. Beiträge zur historischen Geographie und Topographie des Negeb: III. Saruhen, Ziklag, Horma, Gerar. *JPOS* 15: 294–324. (Reprint: Alt 1959: 409–435).

Alt, A. 1953. *Kleine Schriften zur Geschichte des Volkes* Israel II. München.

Alt, A. 1959. *Kleine Schriften zur Geschichte des Volkes Israel* III. München.

Anbar, M. 1978. Abrahamic Covenant — Genesis 15. *Shnaton. An Annual for Biblical and Ancient Near Eastern Studies* 3: 34–52. (Hebrew).

Broshi, M. 1962. Libnath, Shihor-libnath. *Enc. Miqr.* IV: 430. (Hebrew).

Cohen, R. 1976a. Kadesh-Barnea, 1976. *IEJ* 26: 201–202.

Cohen, R. 1976b. Excavations at Ḥorvat Ḥaluqim. *'Atiqot* 11: 34–50.

Cohen, R. 1978. Kadesh-Barnea, 1978. *IEJ* 28: 197.

Cooke, G.A. 1918. *The Book of Joshua.* (The Cambridge Bible for Schools and Colleges). Cambridge.

Curtis, E.L. 1910. *A Critical and Exegetical Commentary on the Books of Chronicles.* (ICC). Edinburgh.

Delitzsch, F. 1881. Wo *lag das Paradies?* Leipzig.

Dillmann, A. 1886. *Numeri, Deuteronomium und Josua.* (Kurzgefasstes exegetisches Handbuch zum Alten Testament). Leipzig.

Dothan, T. 1979. *Excavations at the Cemetery of Deir el-Balah.* (Qedem 10). Hebrew University of Jerusalem.

Driver, S.R. 1913. *Notes on the Hebrew Text and the Topography of the Books of Samuel.* (2nd ed. revised and enlarged). Oxford.

Elliger, K. 1936. Die Nordgrenze des Reiches Davids. *PJb* 32: 34–73.

Eph'al, I. 1976. "Ishmael" and "Arab(s)": A Transformation of Ethnological Terms. *JNES* 35: 225–235.

Fritz, V. 1975. Erwägungen zur Siedlungsgeschichte des Negeb in der Eisen I-Zeit (1200–1000 v. Chr.) im Lichte der Ausgrabungen auf der Ḫirbet el-Mšāš. *ZDPV* 91: 30–45.

Gelb, I.J. 1961. The Early History of the West Semitic Peoples. *JCS* 15:27–47.

Japhet, S. 1977. *The Ideology of the Book of Chronicles and its Place in Biblical Thought.* Jerusalem. (Hebrew).

Kallai, Z. 1967. *The Tribes of Israel: A Study in the Historical Geography of the Bible.* Jerusalem. (Hebrew).

Kallai, Z. 1975. The Boundaries of Canaan and the Land of Israel in the Bible. *Eretz Israel* 12: 27–34. (Hebrew).

Kallai, Z. 1977. The United Monarchy of Israel — A Focal Point in Israelite Historiography. *IEJ* 27: 103–109.

Kempinski, A. 1974. Tell el-'Ajjûl — Beth-Aglayim or Sharuḥen? *IEJ* 24: 145–152.

Lambdin, T.O. 1953. Egyptian Loan Words in the Old Testament. *JAOS* 73: 145–155.

Lambdin, T.O. 1962. Shihor. *The Interpreter's Dictionary of the Bible* IV. New York: 328.

Lipschitz, O. 1978. *Sinai.* Jerusalem.

Loewenstamm, S.E. 1954. Beer-lahai-roi. *Enc. Miqr*. II: 6. (Hebrew).

Mazar (Maisler), B. 1946. Lebo-Hamath and the Northern Boundary of Canaan. *BJPES* 12: 91–102. (Hebrew).

Mazar (Maisler), B. 1947. Palestine in the Time of the Middle Kingdom in Egypt. *Revue de l'Histoire Juive en Égypte* 1:33–68.

Mazar (Maisler), B. 1950. *Ha-reqem* and *Ha-ḥeger. Tarbiz* 20 (J.N. Epstein Jubilee Volume): 316–319. (Hebrew).

Mazar, B. 1957. The Campaign of Pharaoh Shishak to Palestine. *Supplement* to *VT* 4: 57–66.

Mazar, B. 1969. The Historical Background of the Book of Genesis. *JNES* 28: 73–83.

Meshel, Z. 1974. *A History of the Negev in the Time of the Kings of Judah.* (Ph.D. Thesis). Tel-Aviv. (Hebrew).

Meshel, Z. 1977. Ḥorvat Ritma — An Iron Age Fortress in the Negev Highlands. *Tel Aviv* 4: 110–135.

Meyer, E. 1906. *Die Israeliten and ihre Nachbarstämme.* Halle.

Meyers, C. 1976. Kadesh Barnea: Judah's Last Outpost. *BA* 39: 148–151.

Mihelic, J.L. 1962. Shur, Wilderness of. *The Interpreter's Dictionary of the Bible* IV. New York: 342.

Na'aman, N. 1979a. The Brook of Egypt and Assyrian Policy on the Border of Egypt. *Tel Aviv* 6: 68–90.

Na'aman, N. 1979b. The Origin and Historical Background of Several Amarna Letters. *Ugarit-Forschungen* 11: 673–684.

Noth, M. 1935. Zur historischen Geographie Südjudäas. *JPOS* 15:35–50. (Reprint: 1971. *Aufsätze zur biblischen Landes- und Altertumskunde* I. Neukirchen-Vluyn: 197–209).

Noth, M. 1955. *Das Buch Josua.* (2nd revised ed.). (Handbuch zum Alten Testament I/7). Tübingen.

Rothenberg, B. 1967. *Negev, Archaeology in the Negev and the Arabah.* Ramat-Gan. (Hebrew).

Rudolph, W. 1955. *Chronikbücher.* (Handbuch zum Alten Testament I/21). Tübingen.

Saebø, M. 1974. Grenzbeschreibung und Landideal im Alten Testament mit besonderer Berücksichtigung der *min-'ad*-Formel. *ZDPV* 90: 14–37.

Seebass, H. 1965. Der Ort Elam in der südlichen Wüste und die Überlieferung von Gen. XIV. *VT* 15: 389–394.

Simons, J. 1959. *The Geographical and Topographical Texts of the Old Testament.* Leiden.

Speiser, E.A. 1964. *Genesis: Introduction, Translation, and Notes.* (The Anchor Bible). New York.

Stewart, J.R. 1974. *Tell el-'Ajjul.* (Studies in Mediterranean Archaeology 38). Göteborg.

Stoebe, H.J. 1973. *Das erste Buch Samuelis.* (Kommentar zum Alten Testament VIII/1). Stuttgart.

de Vaux, R. 1968. Le Pays de Canaan. In: Hallo, W.W. ed. *Essays in Memory of E.A. Speiser.* (American Oriental Series 53). New Haven: 23–30.

White, H.C. 1975. The Initiation Legend of Ishmael. *ZAW* 87: 267–305.

Winnett, F.V. 1970. The Arabian Genealogies in the Book of Genesis. In: Frank, H.T. and Reed, W.L. eds., *Translating and Understanding the Old Testament. Essays in Honor of H.G. May.* New York: 171–196.

Wüst, M. 1975. *Untersuchungen zu den Siedlungsgeographischen Texten des Alten Testaments. 1. Ostjordanland.* (Beiheft zum Tübinger Atlas des Vorderen Orients. Reihe B [Geisteswissenschaften] Nr. 9). Wiesbaden.

Yisraeli, Y. 1978. Sharuhen, Tell. *Enc. Arch. Exc.* IV: 1074–1082.

Zadok, R. 1977. Historical and Onomastic Notes. *WO* 9: 31–56.

An Assyrian Residence at Ramat Raḥel?[1]

The proposal of Finkelstein and Singer-Avitz (2001) that Tel Ashdod was not inhabited in the 7th century BCE and that Ashdod-Yam took its place, if correct, opens new perspectives for evaluating the Assyrian intervention in the territories of vassal kingdoms. According to the suggestions of these scholars, after he conquered Ashdod in 711 BCE, Sargon II built Ashdod-Yam, settled deportees in the new city and made it both the seat of his governor and the capital of the kingdom. Sargon's building activity on the southern coast also included the sites of Blakhiyeh, Ruqeish and Tell Abu Salima. Indeed, as recognized long ago by scholars (Alt 1945:138–146; Tadmor 1958:77–84; 1966: 90–93; Na'aman 1979:68–74, 80–86; 1993:111–112), Sargon was the dominant figure behind the Assyrian imperial policy in southern Palestine. It remains to be seen whether it was Sargon who started this policy, or whether the policy was initiated and implemented by Tiglath-pileser III (745–727), the king who conquered the areas of Syria and Palestine and established a network of Assyrian provinces in the territories of former independent kingdoms.

In the following four sections, I will examine the available evidence of the Assyrian building activity near the centers of vassal kingdoms, first along the Mediterranean coast and, second, in Judah and Transjordan. I will also examine some other building operations located along Naḥal Besor and the southern Palestinian desert areas. It is not my aim to present a detailed picture of the Assyrian settlements and buildings in southern Palestine, a topic that has been discussed several times by scholars (see Na'aman 1979:80–82; 1995:111–113; Reich 1992:214–222; Finkelstein 1992:160–161; Oren 1993; Stern 2001:25–27, 32). Rather, I will investigate the textual and archaeological evidence in an effort to better understand the Assyrian building operations in the territories of their Syrio-Palestinian vassals and to clarify the Assyrian aims in areas located near the borders of the empire in the late 8th–7th centuries BCE.

1. Assyrian Centers along the Mediterranean Coast

Tiglath-pileser's conquest of Gaza is related in three summary inscriptions (see the synoptic table in Tadmor 1994:222–225). All three inscrip-

---

1. Reprinted with permission. *Tel Aviv* 28 (2001), 260-280.

tions have the statement, "[The city of Ga]za ([URUHa-az-z]u-tú) I turned into an Assyrian emporium (*bīt kāri*)" (for the restoration, see Frahm 1997/1998: 403 ad p. 188f). The establishment of an Assyrian emporium at Gaza was designed to promote Assyrian control of commerce on the coast of Philistia. In his stele erected in Iran, Tiglath-pileser describes the city of Aḫta, perhaps modern el-Mina (Zadok 1996a:No 17), as "emporium (*bīt kāri*) on the seashore, a royal store-house" (Tadmor 1994:104–105, line 13). The text might refer to the installing of Aḫta as an Assyrian emporium. Finally, a letter from Calah (Nimrud), sent to Tiglath-pileser by Qurdi-Aššur-lāmur, probably the Assyrian governor of the province of Ṣimirra, indicates that Assyria compelled its Phoenician vassals to pay custom on the timbers cut on Mount Lebanon (Postgate 1974:131, 390–391; Na'aman 1979:83–84, with earlier literature). It is evident that, by the time of Tiglath-pileser III, Assyria operated in the Phoenician and Philistine ports of trade in an effort to direct part of their revenues to the Assyrian treasury.

How should we interpret Tiglath-pileser's statement that he turned Gaza into an Assyrian emporium? I suggest that soon after his conquest, the Assyrian king began constructing emporiums near Gaza and, possibly, along the Phoenician coast. The inscriptions probably refer to the construction of the heavily fortified late Iron Age II settlement of Blakhiyeh, situated near the city of Gaza (for the recent excavations of the site, see Humbert and Sadeq 2000). The Assyrian building project near the port of Gaza explains why Hanunu, king of Gaza, rebelled against Assyria in the early days of Sargon II, although Gaza had no real military power that could stand the impending Assyrian attack on the city. The project threatened to deprive Gaza of its gains from the maritime trade, and Hanunu sought Egyptian aid in a desperate effort to escape the growing Assyrian hold on its territory and its income.

I further suggest that Sargon founded the harbor at Ashdod-Yam immediately after he crushed the anti-Assyrian rebellion that broke out upon the death of Shalmaneser V, defeated the Egyptian task force that was sent to support the rebels, and conquered the coast of Philistia (720 BCE). This might explain why the kingdom of Ashdod — which did not participate in the coalition that fought Assyria in 720 BCE — rebelled 8 years later. Before the Assyrian intervention, Ashdod-Yam was a small port of trade that served the capital city of Ashdod. Sargon's building operations at this site threatened to block Ashdod's way to the sea and deprive it of all revenues gained from the maritime trade. The two revolts that Sargon describes in his inscriptions are the direct outcome of this building project (for the annals and summary inscriptions, see Fuchs 1994:425 s.v. Asdūdu; for the prism, see Fuchs 1998: 44–46, 73–74, 124–131). The rebels probably seized and fortified the recently built harbor. Contrary to the large-scale rebellion of the early days of Sargon,

Ashdod's rebellion was a local event. No other kingdom joined the rebels, despite their efforts to gain support from neighboring kingdoms and from the Egyptian Pharaoh (Na'aman 1994a:239–247; Frahm 1997:229–232). Sargon took advantage of the revolt, destroyed Ashdod, brought his building activity at Ashdod-Yam into completion and made it the capital of the newly established province. Sennacherib, his heir, adopted a different policy and let the royal house of Ashdod rule over the kingdom, side by side with the Assyrian governor (Alt 1945:144–146; Na'aman 1979:71–72, n. 7). The city of Ashdod remained desolated — although not entirely deserted — during the 7th century, and Ashdod-Yam took its place as the kingdom's capital (Finkelstein and Singer-Avitz 2001).

As noted by Finkelstein and Singer-Avitz, the well-planned and heavily fortified settlement of Ruqeish was probably founded by Sargon II and served as the main Assyrian port on the coast south of Gaza. Sargon's statement that he "opened the sealed h[arb]our of Egypt, mingled Assyrians and Egyptians together and made them trade with each other" (Fuchs 1994:88 lines 17–18) may possibly refer to Ruqeish. The site is located south of the Brook of Egypt (Wâdi Ghazzeh and Wâdi Shelaleh = Naḥal Besor), which the Assyrians conceived as the southern border of Palestine, and Sargon's scribe might have considered it as a port (*kāru*) situated in the Egyptian territory (for the "northern" concept of the Egyptian border, see Na'aman 1986:237–251).

Dor was already established as an Assyrian province in 732 BCE, and its port served as the main Assyrian harbor in central Palestine.[2] As for Joppa, I recently suggested that Tiglath-pileser transferred it to Rukibtu, king of Ashkelon, in 732 BCE, hence, the appearance of an Ashkelonite enclave east of Joppa in the time of Sennacherib's campaign in Palestine (Na'aman 1998: 219–223). After the rebellion of Ashkelon in 701 BCE, the area of Joppa was transferred to Padi, king of Ekron, and served as a main port of trade for his kingdom (Na'aman 1998:223–225).

In Esarhaddon's treaty with Ba'al, king of Tyre, the following passage appears (Parpola and Watanabe 1988:25; Na'aman 1994b:3–4):[3]

> These are the ports of trade (*kārāni*) and the trade routes which Esarhaddon, king of Assyria, en[trusted] to his servant Ba'al: to Acco, Dor, to the entire district of the Philistines, and to all the cities within Assyrian territory on the seacoast, and to Gubla, the Lebanon, all the cities in the mountains.

---

2. Finkel and Reade (1998:253) suggested that the governor of Dor was possibly the eponym in the year 693 BCE. For the material culture of Dor under the Assyrians, see Gilboa 1996.

3. My division of the passages in lines 18-24 of Esarhaddon's treaty and my translation of lines 22-24 differ from the division and translation of Parpola and Watanabe.

It seems that Esarhaddon granted Ba'al free access to ports where Assyrian emporiums were established along the coast of the Mediterranean and to routes in Mount Lebanon where Assyrian custom houses were built. If this interpretation is correct, we may add Acco and Gubla to the list of harbors where Assyria established its emporiums side by side with the local ports. The rebellion of the cities of Ushu and Acco against Ashurbanipal (ca. 644 BCE) (Katzenstein 1973:293–294) probably broke out as a result of the Assyrian imperial policy that threatened to deprive the two cities of their gains from the maritime trade.

Letter ABL 992, probably dating to the reign of Esarhaddon (Pfeiffer 1935: 137; Na'aman 1979:84, with earlier literature), illustrates the situation in the first half of the 7th century BCE in the city of Arvad. Lines 14–21 run as follows:

> The king my lord knows that Ikkilu does not release the boats (so that) they cannot land at the harbor of the king (*kāru ša šarri*), my lord. He made the whole harbor (*kāru*) go over to his side. He opens his way to anyone who comes to him; (but) he kills anyone who wants to land at the harbor of Assyria (*kāru ša* KUR *Aššur*) and smashes his boat.

It is clear that two harbors, one controlled by the king of Arvad and the other by an Assyrian official, co-existed side by side in the island of Arvad. The letter shows the competition and enmity prevailing between the two ports and the efforts made by Yakinlu (Ikkilu), king of Arvad, to shift the boats to his side to gain his share in the profits.

We may conclude that Tiglath-pileser initiated the policy of constructing Assyrian emporiums near the major Philistine and Phoenician ports of trade and that Sargon and that his heirs greatly expanded these building operations in vassal territories. The many anti-Assyrian rebellions that broke out in kingdoms situated along the Mediterranean coast are the outcome of the Assyrian imperial activity. They reflect the reaction of the Phoenician and Philistine cities to a policy that threatened to take most of the revenues of the maritime trade and to deprive the inhabitants of their main source of income.

2. An Assyrian Centre on Naḥal Besor

Assyrian intervention was not confined to ports of trade. Tell Jemmeh is situated on Naḥal Besor, about 10 km south of Gaza, on the important trade route that leads from Arabia — via Kadesh-barnea or the Beersheba Valley — to the coast of Philistia. This site exemplifies the effect of Assyrian building projects on the local pastoral groups in a peripheral area (for the Arabian trade along the Beersheba Valley, see, recently, Finkelstein 1992; Singer-Avitz 1999, with earlier literature).

The site of Tell Jemmeh was excavated in the 1970s by Van Beek (1983; 1993). He uncovered a large mudbrick building with at least six rooms. The cellar stores of the building have been preserved, including part of the vaulted ceiling of each room. The plan of the building is similar in design to a series of buildings that Petrie excavated at Tell Jemmeh and that have close parallels in the Assyrian cities of Calah, Khorsabad and Nineveh. The vaults were constructed with voussoirs, which makes it possible to flatten their upper part, and these are the oldest known vaults built of wedge-shaped bricks discovered so far. The doorways between rooms were covered by rib vaulting, a technique that is confined mainly to the Iranian plateau and that was employed extensively at Nush-i Jan (Van Beek 1987:84–85; for the excavations of Nush-i Jan, see Stronach 1985, and the literature cited on p. 925).

Sealed deposits of pottery were found in the cellar stores, including a large amount of the so-called "Assyrian Palace Ware." It is clear that the vaulted building was the seat of the Assyrian official who supervised the Naḥal Besor area. Esarhaddon, in his second year (679 BCE), conducted a campaign against Arza, a city located in the border zone of the Brook of Egypt (*ana itê Naḫal Muṣur*), plundered the city and deported its king and inhabitants (Borger 1956:130 s.v. Arza). On the basis of the identification of Arza with Tell Jemmeh, Van Beek (1993:672; see Wapnish 1996:287–288) dated the foundation of the strata of the vaulted building to the time of Esarhaddon.

Two Aramaic ostraca were found in the excavations of Tell Jemmeh and published by Naveh (1985). He interpreted the two ostraca as name lists. Although some of the names are West Semitic, all other names, many of which end with *shin*, are etymologically non-Semitic. Naveh (1985:14, 21) questioned whether the names belong to local inhabitants (i.e., Philistines), or perhaps to foreign mercenaries of Anatolian or Greek origin, who served in the Assyrian army. Kempinski (1987) analyzed the names and suggested that they were local Philistines. Zadok and this author, on the other hand, suggested that the names belong to deportees brought to the place by Sargon II in about 715 BCE (Na'aman and Zadok 1988). Our suggestion rested on two bases: an analysis of the name lists, and Sargon's statement in his prism that he deported people from the east and settled them in a city (whose name is broken) situated in the border zone of the Brook of Egypt (Naḥal Besor).

The use of rib vaulting over the doorways between the rooms in the vaulted building is a technique mainly confined to sites located in the Iranian plateau. Van Beek (1987:85) suggested that "the technique may have been brought to Tell Jemmeh by a Median builder in the service of the Assyrian forces." However, in light of the registration of deportees from the Zagros mountains on the ostraca from Tell Jemmeh, the suggestion that a Median builder was specifically brought to the place is redundant. Some deportees were doubtless employed in the construction of the public buildings at Tell Jemmeh and used the vaulting technique, which was common in their homeland, for constructing the doorways. Text and archaeology go hand in hand in this case, and both fit well my suggestion that the Brook of Egypt should be identified at Naḥal Besor (Na'aman 1979:74–80). Indeed, most of the Assyrian building activity in southern Palestine is confined to the area on both sides of Naḥal Besor. Wâdi el-ʿArish, on the other hand, which some scholars identified with the Brook of Egypt (Rainey 1982:131–132; Eph'al 1982:103–105; Ahituv 1984:203 n. 631; Stern 2001:114; see Hooker 1993), is located in a sparsely inhabited area, where no settlements that date to this period were found.[4]

Sargon II built the Assyrian center at Tell Jemmeh soon after he brought deportees from the Iranian plateau (ca. 715 BCE) to the area of Naḥal Besor. Leaders of the local pastoral groups probably lived in the place side by side with the Assyrian official and his staff. The marked influence of the newly built Assyrian center on the local market is indicated by the faunal evidence, as was demonstrated by Wapnish (1996:289–293) in a penetrating analysis of the sheep and goats bones uncovered in the excavations of Tell Jemmeh. The Assyrians must have competed with the pastoral groups who lived in this area for the revenues gained from the long-distance trade and from the sale of sheep and goats to the local and remote markets.

Against this background, we can suggest an interpretation for the anti-Assyrian rebellion that broke out in Arza upon the death of Sennacherib (Borger 1956:126 s.v. Asuḫili). Asuḫili, king of Arza, was a local chief, leader of the pastoral groups who lived in the Naḥal Besor area. His status in this area was probably similar to that of the sheikh of the city of Laban in the time of Sargon II (see Eph'al 1982:93–94). The growing intervention of the Assyrians in the overland trade and the regional economy must have endangered the subsistence of the local population and must have brought about a growing tension and unrest in the region. Asuḫili's "rebellion" was probably no more than either a struggle with the local Assyrian official and a refusal to pay the tribute, or raids on Arab caravans protected by the Assyrians. The "rebellion" was soon crushed (679 BCE), the rebel's possessions plundered and he and his supporters deported to Assyria. It is evident that the dynamics of the political and economic relationship between Assyria and its vassals was not dissimilar in coastal and internal regions, all emanating from the imperial policy and economic objectives of Assyria in the peripheral areas of the empire.

---

4. For the identification of the Brook of Egypt near Gaza in the early Middle Ages, see Zadok 1996b:730-731.

Before proceeding to discuss the foundation of some other Assyrian centers, it is worth examining textual evidence of the construction of an Assyrian fortress in a peripheral area. Parker (1997) recently discussed, in detail, a letter (ND 2666; NL 67) sent by Duri-Aššur, governor of Tušḫan (an Assyrian province situated on the Upper Tigris, southeast of modern Diyarbakir), to Tiglath-pileser III. The new fortress was built beside the Tigris river. In the first stage, a defensive wall with a gate was erected, so that work could continue with relative safety, and building materials and tools were stored within the walls. Later, the inner courtyard was prepared, and the drains were sealed with bitumen. Two main living quarters were constructed, one for the garrison and the other for the commander and, possibly, his officers. Stores were built in the two quarters and yards for livestock were associated with the barracks of the soldiers. Whether it was intended for the horses or for other animals is unknown. A chapel for the goddess Ishtar was also erected within the fortress.

Thousands of workers were recruited to construct the fort. The toponyms mentioned are situated along the Habur river, in Jebel Sinjar, the Lower Zab and modern Kirkuk. Thus, workers from all over the empire were mobilized, not only for building the Assyrian royal cities, but also for projects on the periphery of the empire.

In spite of the many climatic and environmental differences between the Assyrian province of the upper Tigris and vassal kingdoms in southern Palestine, the letter sheds valuable light both on the way that Assyria organized construction works in peripheral areas of the empire and on the stages in which the building project were executed. The Assyrian authorities in the western Euphrates areas must have forced the vassal kings and the leaders of the pastoral groups to supply construction workers. For major projects, they probably mobilized workers from several kingdoms and from the pastoral groups living on the periphery.

Massive walls and a gate were probably erected everywhere in the first stage of building projects. Leveling of the courtyard and construction of the living quarters, the stores and, possibly, the yards for the horses occurred in the second stage. In light of the power of the empire to recruit hundreds, and, if necessary, thousands of workers, construction must have taken a relatively short time and could have ended within months or a few years. No wonders that the building projects constructed by the Assyrians (like Blakhiyeh, Ashdod-Yam and Ruqeish) are so remarkable in dimension and the quantity of manual work invested in their execution.

3. Assyrian Fortresses in Edom and the Negev

Excavations conducted at Buseirah, the capital of Edom, uncovered two buildings whose plans are unique to Transjordan. One building is located on the acropolis (Building B in Area A) and the other in area C, southeast of the acropolis (Bennett 1974:2). The two buildings are similar in construction and were dated to the 7th century BCE. Bennett (1978:169; 1982:184–187; see Bienkowski 1995:139–141) noted the close similarity of Building B to the so-called Assyrian "open court" buildings and the resemblance of the lavatory of the building in area C to installations found at Khorsabad and Nineveh. She suggested that "the Neo-Assyrians installed their own official or military commander to coordinate tactics in the event of threat of invasion. At the same time, they brought in architects to erect buildings worthy of them" (Bennett 1978:170; see 1982:187). Reich (1992:219–220) suggested that the two large public buildings at Buseirah were erected by the Assyrians, "one serving as a residence, the other as a temple" (see Stern 2001:29; for a different interpretation, see Bienkowski 1995:140–142; 2000:52–53).

The interpretation of Bennett and Reich fits well with what is known of Assyrian building projects in or near the centers of vassal kingdoms. The Assyrians must have mobilized the local population and built a center of government where an Assyrian official and his staff and guard were installed. This official must have supervised the caravans that arrived from Arabia, regulated the payment of duties and tribute to the Assyrian treasury and kept an eye on the nomadic Arab tribes. Troops and chariots probably were entrusted to his command, so that he could send them to defend the Assyrian interests in this remote area.

Three Assyrian fortresses were built in the peripheral desert areas of southern Palestine, in sites located on the trade routes that connected Arabia with Transjordan, Judah and the southern coastal plain. A large fortress was erected at ʿEn Ḥaṣeva, a site situated in Wâdi ʿArabah, near the copper mines of Wâdi Feinan, on the road to the Gulf of Eilat (Cohen and Israel 1995:18–22; 1996:79–83). The fortress of stratum 5 covers an area of 2.5 acres (100 by 100 m.). An offsets-insets casemate wall built of dressed stones, with four towers at the corners, surrounds an enormous courtyard. A four-room gate was built near the northeastern corner of the fortress leading to an inner courtyard surrounded by casemate walls, where storehouses and granaries were uncovered. No floors were found, either in the stores, or in the casemate walls, and complete vessels were found only in two of the casemate rooms near the gate and in the granaries. It is clear that only the foundations of the large fortress were left intact, and the remains above the floors were removed or eroded. The foundations display the enormous amount of work invested in the construction of the fortress and indicate the importance of the fortress, built on a juncture of roads leading west to the Philistine coast, south to the Gulf of Eilat and Arabia, and east to the neighboring kingdoms of Edom and Moab.

Cohen and Yisrael (1995:22; 1996:82–83) attributed the building of the fortress to Uzziah, king of Judah. In light of the dimension of the site and the amount of work involved in the construction, their proposal is highly unlikely. I have suggested attributing the construction of the fortress to the Assyrians in the late 8th century BCE (Na'aman 1997a).

A second fortress was probably built by the Assyrians in the late 8th century BCE, near the oasis of Kadesh-barnea, on the western caravan route leading from the coastal plain to the Gulf of Eilat and Arabia (Darb el-Ghazzeh) (Na'aman 1991:48–49; for the stratigraphy of the site, see Ussishkin 1995).

A third fortress (covering about 1 acre) was built at Tell el-Kheleifeh, about 500 m. from the northern shore of the Gulf of Eilat, on the trade route that connected Arabia with the Beersheba Valley and the southern coastal plain (for the stratigraphy of the site, see Pratico 1985; 1993). An offsets-insets square casemate wall, with four-room gate, surrounded a large courtyard. The stratigraphy of the buildings uncovered within the courtyard is not clear. Pratico (1985:22–27; 1993:26–34) suggested that the offsets-insets fortress was settled between the 8th and the early 6th centuries. In light of its date of construction, the overall similarity to the fortresses erected at 'En Haṣeva, the large assemblage of imitations of Assyrian vessels (Pratico 1993:41–43), the large assemblage of vessels stamped by a royal official and brought to the place,[5] and the distribution of the Assyrian centers in all areas of southern Palestine, it is logical to attribute the construction of the fortress at Tell Kheleifeh to the Assyrians.

An example of recruiting workers from the eastern periphery for a building project in the province of Ṣūbat appears in a letter from Nimrud (ND 2437; NL 20), sent by Adda-ḫati of Hamath to Sargon II (Parpola 1987:138 lines 34–39; see Watanabe 1991:194 ad Nr. 176):

> As to what the king, my lord, ordered: "The people living on the mounds should come down and build down," they have come down. Should these ten fortified towns in the desert come down as well? What does the king, my lord, say?

We may assume that similar measures were taken to build the Negevite fortresses. The local pastoral groups and probably the kingdoms in their

5. About 22 seal impressions with the text "belonging to Qaus'anal, servant of the king" (i.e., the king of Edom) were uncovered in the excavations of the site (Pratico 1993:53-55). They indicate that contributions were brought to the place in vessels stamped by a royal official and consumed by the local governor and his staff.

neighborhood were most likely ordered to mobilize workers and to construct the three fortresses.

Tiglath-pileser III wrote that, after his victory on Samsi, queen of the Arabs, he installed *qīpu* to supervise her territory (Tadmor 1994:142–143 line 26). This official probably operated from the Assyrian peripheral fortresses built on the eastern front of the Assyrian provinces in Syria. On other occasions, the Assyrians reached agreement with leaders of Arab tribes situated on the periphery of Sinai and "nominated" them as Assyrian supervisors over their tribal territories (Eph'al 1982:93–94). These Arab leaders are Idibi'ilu and Siruatti the Me'unite in the time of Tiglath-pileser III (for the texts, see Tadmor 1994:291 s.v. Idibi'ilu, 292 s.v. Siruatti; Na'aman 1997b), and the sheikh of the city of Laban in the days of Sargon II (for the text, see Fuchs 1998:28 lines 6–7). For how long these agreements continued remain unknown (for parallels in the Roman and Byzantine periods, see Mayerson 1986; 1989). It is evident that the Assyrians used various strategies in different parts of the empire and that their policy might have changed in the course of time. By combining text and archaeology, we can clarify these measures and evaluate the steps taken by the Assyrians in the southern frontier of the empire.

Assyrian Building operations in the kingdoms of Moab and Ammon are unknown. Weippert (1987:100 n. 42) suggested that Ayya-nūri of the land of D/Ṭabila, who sent a letter to Qurdi-Aššur-lāmur, possibly the governor of the province of Ṣimirra, in which he complained of the raid of the Gidiraeans on an unnamed Moabite city, was an Assyrian *qīpu*. Following a suggestion by Mittmann (1973:16–18), Weippert identified the land of D/Ṭabila with modern aṭ-Ṭafilah, located in southern Edom, and suggested that this was the seat of the Assyrian official. However, the identification of the two toponyms is unlikely, because aṭ-Ṭafilah is located far south of the land of Moab (for other suggested identifications, see Lipiński 1979:97–100; Timm 1989:321–329, with earlier literature). The Gidiraeans must be sought in the territory that Tiglath-pileser annexed in 732 BCE in Transjordan. Ayya-nūri, who complained of the raid of Assyrian "citizens" on Moabite territory, most probably lived in Moab. It may be speculated that Ayya-nūri was an Assyrian *qīpu*, who was installed in Moab and who sent messages to the Assyrian authorities in Phoenicia about what happened in the area under his supervision. However, the assumption is highly uncertain, and the administrative apparatus by which the Assyrians supervised the kingdoms of Ammon and Moab remains unknown.[6]

---

6. Prof. I. Finkelstein reminded me of the four Proto-Aeolic capitals discovered at Khirbet el-Mudeibi'a, a site located in the southeastern frontier of Moab, whose deco-

4. An Assyrian Centre in the Kingdom of Judah?

We have already observed the Assyrian policy of constructing emporiums and centers of government at sites located near the capitals of vassal kingdoms and the posting of officials and troops in these places. What can be said about the Assyrian permanent presence in the territory of the kingdom of Judah? The question has never been raised, and no answer has been suggested. Once the question *is* posed, however, an immediate answer comes to mind: The Assyrian center in the kingdom of Judah was located at Ramat Raḥel, about 4 km. southwest of its capital, Jerusalem.

Five seasons of excavations at Ramat Raḥel (ancient Beth-haccerem) were directed by Aharoni in the years 1954 and 1959–1962 (Aharoni et al. 1962; 1964; Aharoni 1993), and another season was conducted by Barkay in 1984 (for details, see Vaughn 1999:39–40). Two Iron Age II strata (VB and VA) were differentiated, both badly damaged by later building activity at the site. Very few architectural elements of stratum VB were uncovered, because it had been almost completely removed during construction work carried out by the builders of Stratum VA. Aharoni uncovered a few remains of casemate wall belonging to this stratum, and Barkay found a wall and some building remains.

Most of the finds of stratum VB came from the fill used to level the ground in the construction work of stratum VA. Approximately 162 jar handles stamped by the *lmlk* seals were found, and scholars have debated whether all of them should be attributed to stratum VB (as suggested by Vaughn 1999: 40, 102–105, 189), or whether a certain portion should be attributed to stratum VA (Mazar in Mazar, Amit and Ilan 1996:208–209, with earlier literature). Vaughn (1999:95–110) demonstrated that the *lmlk* jars were not manufactured after Sennacherib's campaign to Palestine (701 BCE). However, his conclusion that the use of *lmlk* jars came to an end in the 7th century is arbitrary. There is no securely dated destruction level in 7th century Judahite sites, and there is no way to establish how long the jars may have been re-used in the cities. Sennacherib's campaign provides a *terminus ante quem* for the use of *lmlk*-stamped jars in non-destroyed sites; the jars must have been re-used

ration is almost identical to the capitals unearthed at Ramat Raḥel (Negueruela 1982). A large fortress with monumental gate was built there, possibly in the 8th century BCE, and was finally destroyed only in the Hellenistic period. Khirbet el-Mudeibi'a was an important Moabite fortress, commanding the important eastern road that connected northern and southern Moab. The similarity of the Proto-Aeolic capitals from Khirbet el-Mudeibi'a and Ramat Raḥel is indeed striking. However, not enough is known of the fortress to date its construction and to establish whether it was part of the system built by the Assyrians to control the caravan roads leading from Arabia to the Levant.

during the 7th century until broken and thrown away. Jerusalem survived the Assyrian campaign of 701 BCE and was the source of supplies delivered to the center at Ramat Raḥel in the 7th century. Mazar's suggestion that *lmlk* jars were transported to Ramat Raḥel in the early 7th century BCE and should be attributed to the early years of stratum VA is well founded.

Aharoni (1993:1263) dated stratum VB to the 8th–7th centuries BCE, but it is commonly accepted today that the site was destroyed in the time of Sennacherib's blockade of Jerusalem (701 BCE). Barkay (1993:1267; in Vaughn 1999:40) suggested that the site of Ramat Raḥel was built by Hezekiah in the late 8th century. After the destruction, it was restored either by Hezekiah, or by Manasseh, his successor.

The new citadel (stratum VA), which was probably built in the early 7th century BCE, comprises a palace surrounded by a large fortified courtyard (see Reich 1992:207–208, 211–213). The ground was leveled, and a massive wall (3–4m thick) encompassed an area of about 5 acres. The palace, measuring approximately 70 by 50 m., was constructed in the Phoenician-Israelite architecture style and ornamentation. It is the best example of Phoenician architecture discovered at a 7th century BCE site lying outside the Phoenician coast (Stern 1992; 2001:167–168). Moreover, the quality of the workmanship and ornamentation is without parallel in other 7th century Judahite sites excavated so far. Same-sized stones were carefully cut and laid in header-and-stretcher fashion, and the floor pavement consists of a heavy layer of limestone waste. Architectural ornamentation includes about a dozen proto-Aeolic capitals, window balustrades, and stones cut in a pyramidal shape, which were probably used as crenellations on top of the city wall or the roofs. Proto-Aeolic capitals and window balustrades were also uncovered in the excavations of the City of David, which may indicate the origin of the architect and stone workers who built Ramat Raḥel.

The small finds of stratum VA include — in addition to an unknown number of *lmlk* seal impressions (see above) — about 60 rosette seal impressions and several Assyrian-style goblets, the most elaborate examples of Assyrian palace ware found so far in Judah. Matthiae (1964) interpreted sherds of black and red painted jars, depicting a ruler seated on a throne, as a possible local imitation of an Assyrian prototype. Other scholars (Aharoni 1962:42–43; Keel and Uehlinger 1998:357; Stern 2001:35, 168) also noted the Assyrian influence on the depiction of the figure.[7]

7. The pointed protruding beard of the figure is not an Assyrian feature (see Aharoni (1962:43; Matthiae 1964:90). Aharoni (1962:43) was probably correct in observing a Syrian influence on the fashioning of the figure. Matthiae's suggestion that it served as a small-

The remains of stratum IVB, dated to the Persian-early Hellenistic period, are also relevant for the discussion. The plan of the site in this period is unclear; only a few massive and various fragmentary walls were attributed to stratum IVB (see Aharoni et al. 1964:fig. 2). The most outstanding feature of this stratum is the large number of seal impressions (ca. 270 altogether) of almost all known types from other sites in Judah, some without parallel. This collection is the largest and most varied group of impressions found in one site from this period. In light of this exceptionally rich epigraphic material of the Persian period, Aharoni (in Aharoni et al. 1964:122; Aharoni 1967:364) suggested that the site served as an administrative center of a sub-district of the province of Yehud (see Stern 2001:436–437).

The close proximity of Ramat Raḥel to Jerusalem was always an obstacle for the assumption that a royal palace of the kings of Judah stood there in the 8th–7th centuries BCE. I could not find any ancient Near Eastern parallel for the assumed impressive palace built so close to the capital city. Why should a king of Judah build this magnificent palace near his royal palace at Jerusalem? And how can we explain the construction of the assumed elaborate royal residence in the early 7th century BCE (stratum VB), immediately after the severe crisis of Sennacherib's campaign, when a large number of Judahite cities were destroyed and thousands of its inhabitants deported to Assyria? Moreover, why should the Judean authorities of the Persian period build a major administrative center near the temple-city of Jerusalem? Finally, it is certainly not a coincidence that the early edifice of Ramat Raḥel was built about the same time that Judah became an Assyrian vassal. Interpreting the buildings unearthed at Ramat Raḥel as administrative centers built for the seat of Assyrian and Persian officials would immediately explain their dates (late 8th–7th and 5th–4th centuries BCE) and function. The site is located in an ideal place for supervising the capital city of Jerusalem without staying within its walls, and no wonder that the Assyrian, and later the Persian authorities, selected it for residence[8]

The early edifice at Ramat Raḥel (stratum VB) was probably built in the early years of Sargon II for the seat of an Assyrian official appointed to su-

---

scale model for a larger painting that was drawn on one of the palace's wall is possible, but cannot be verified.

8. The location of Ramat Raḥel near Jerusalem may be compared with the location of Meṣad Ḥashavyahu *vis à vis* Yavneh-Yam. The latter site was the major port in this area, and the Egyptians built the fortress for their Greek or Cypriot mercenaries in its vicinity (Na'aman 1991:44-47), in a place that enabled them to supervise the neighboring port city and to keep the mercenaries in isolation from the local inhabitants.

pervise the affairs of the kingdom of Judah and, in particular, the city of Jerusalem. Its construction must have been one of the main reasons for the rebellion that broke out in Judah in the time of Hezekiah, just as the construction of other residencies near the capitals/ports of vassal kingdoms accelerated rebellions in these kingdoms. We may recall that Ahaz, king of Judah, refused to join the anti-Assyrian coalition that fought Tiglath-pileser III and surrendered to Assyria. Judah remained a loyal Assyrian vassal during the reign of Ahaz (734–715/14), and Hezekiah (715/14–686 BCE) apparently continued his father's policy in the first decade of his reign (Na'aman 1994a). The change in the policy of Judah and Hezekiah's rebellion against Assyria after Sargon's death in the battlefield (705 BCE) was probably motivated by the construction of an Assyrian center near Jerusalem and the growing Assyrian intervention in the affairs of Judah.

As a result of Hezekiah's rebellion against Assyria, the early edifice built in Ramat Raḥel (stratum VB) was either destroyed or abandoned. After the suppression of the rebellion in 701 BCE, the site was rebuilt on larger scale, with more elaboration and extravagance.

The task of building the new residence was imposed on the king of Judah, and he mobilized his subjects and executed this task in a quality that befitted the seat of an imperial representative. The plan of the building probably followed a Judahite architectural design and was modeled after the royal palace of Jerusalem. The residence was the seat of an Assyrian official, and the large courtyard possibly served for his guard. The stores of the palace were built for tribute and provisions. Some local Judahites probably lived in the place, functioning as part of the staff that maintained the place. The many stamped handles discovered in the site were part of the contributions brought to the place and consumed by the Assyrian representative, his staff and guard. As suggested above, some of the *lmlk*-stamped jars unearthed at Ramat Raḥel were delivered in the early 7th century BCE to the Assyrian official stationed at the site.[9]

On the basis of the discovery of rosette-stamped handles at Tel Batash, a site that was probably destroyed at 604 BCE, Cahill (1995:247–248) dated the production of these jars to the reign of Jehoiakim (608–598/7), king of Judah. However, no secure destruction level is known from 7th century Judahite sites, and the destruction of Tel Batash provides no more than a *terminus ad quem* for the production of the jars (Fox 2000:239–240). The five dozen ro-

9. The supply of jars stamped by the royal Judahite seal (*lmlk*) at Ramat Raḥel may be compared with the supply of jars stamped by a high Edomite royal official (Qaus'anal) to the Assyrian official at Tell el-Kheleifeh (see above).

sette-stamped jars discovered in Ramat Raḥel must have been part of the supply delivered to the Assyrian center. Thus, they should be dated, at least partly, to the time of Judah's vassalage to Assyria in the 7th century BCE.

As noted above, local Judahite workers built the residence according to the architectural plan and artistic design of the palace of Jerusalem. Almost all the artifacts discovered at Ramat Raḥel are Judahite (the few Assyrian-style goblets might be exceptional). This is not surprising. Foreigners, who lived abroad, far away from their homeland, usually used local products. Moreover, from the time of Sargon II (or even Tiglath-pileser III) onward, the administration of the west Euphrates areas (*Ebir nāri*) was conducted mainly in Aramaic (Parpola 1981:123, 132). Thus, the absence of cuneiform tablets in Assyrian centers in Syria-Palestine is not surprising. Finally, the number of Assyrians who stayed in vassal kingdoms was very small. Their safety was guaranteed by the might of the empire and the fear of its severe reaction to any attack on its delegations. Thus, the lack of direct evidence for the presence of the representative of an empire in edifices built in vassal kingdoms is not an obstacle to identification.[10] The architecture and material culture discovered in some edifices might be of a local nature, and, yet, the building could have been erected as the seat of imperial officials who lived there as long as the empire was in power.

When was the site of Ramat Raḥel deserted? The Assyrians may have retreated from Palestine in the 620s (Na'aman 1991:33–41). Did the Assyrians destroy the site before their withdrawal? Was the site deserted in the last days of the kingdom of Judah? Until now, scholars dated the end of stratum VA to the Babylonian conquest of 587 BCE. Assuming that Josiah and his successors on the throne of Judah occupied the deserted site, this remains a possibility. Exact dating for the destruction/desertion of sites on the basis of archaeological data alone is possible only in cases in which the strata supply definite clues for dating. Nothing of the kind was discovered at Ramat Raḥel, and no exact date for the destruction/desertion of stratum VA can be fixed with certainty.

The *raison d'être* of constructing the center at Ramat Raḥel was the supervision of Jerusalem, the capital city of Judah. Desertion of the site in the sixth century, when Jerusalem lay in ruins, is self-evident (Lipschits 1998:473–476). The Persian authorities must have rebuilt and resettled the site some time after the resettlement of Jerusalem in the 5th century BCE,

10. For this kind of criticism of my suggestion that Meṣad Ḥashavyahu was built at an Egyptian initiative and that the Greek mercenaries and Judahite workers were employed by the Egyptians, see Waldbaum and Magness 1997:38-39.

transferring their center of government from Mizpah (Tell en-Naṣbeh) to Beth-haccerem (Ramat Raḥel). The transfer of the administrative center is indicated by the relative number of *mwṣh* (Mozah) and *yhwd* (Yehud) seal impressions at the two sites. The Mozah seal impressions are dated to the sixth century BCE, and 71.4% of their overall number were unearthed at Tell en-Naṣbeh, as against 2.4% at Ramat Raḥel. The Yehud seal impressions are dated to the 5th–4th centuries BCE, and 4.6% of their overall number were found in Tell en-Naṣbeh, as against 47.1% at Ramat Raḥel (Lipschits 1997: 362). The new administrative center at Ramat Raḥel must have functioned in a way not dissimilar to that of the Assyrian center of the 7th century BCE.

Therefore, the buildings erected in Ramat Raḥel in the late 8th–7th and the 5th–4th centuries BCE, as well as the rich assemblage of Iron Age II and Persian period artifacts discovered in the excavations, are best explained by the assumption that the site functioned as an Assyrian and Persian administrative center and that Assyrian and Persian officials, with their staff and guard, lived there at that time.

Summing up the discussion, it is suggested that the Assyrians established their officials not only in provinces, but also in vassal kingdoms. Although the prefects of provinces held the title of *bēl pīḫati*, at least some of the officials appointed for vassal kingdoms carried the title of *qīpu*. The presence of Assyrian officials in vassal kingdoms is known, or may be inferred, for Arvad, Byblos, Tyre, Ashdod, Gaza, Edom and Judah. Military officers were probably installed in desert settlements and fortresses, such as Tell Jemmeh, 'En Ḥaṣeva, Kadesh-barnea, Tell el-Kheleifeh and other sites not discussed in this paper (for details, see Na'aman 1979:81–82; Finkelstein 1992:160–161). Economic considerations played a major role in the Assyrian operations in the territories of vassal kingdoms and pastoral groups, and Assyria competed with its vassals for the revenues gained from the maritime and continental commercial activity. No wonder that anti-Assyrian rebellions broke out from time to time by kingdoms that were severely damaged by the Assyrian relentless imperialism. But Assyria was strong enough to curb them and was able to continue its imperial policy for about a century, from the time of Tiglath-pileser III until its withdrawal in the 620s.

References

Aharoni, Y. 1962. *Excavations at Ramat Raḥel 1, Seasons 1959 and 1960.* (Università di Roma – Centro di Studi Semitici, Serie Archeologia 2). Rome.

Aharoni, Y. 1964. *Excavations at Ramat Raḥel 2, Seasons 1961 and 1962.* (Università di Roma – Centro di Studi Semitici, Serie Archeologia 6). Rome

Aharoni, Y. 1967. *The Land of the Bible. A Historical Geography.* Philadelphia.

Aharoni, Y. 1993. Ramat Raḥel. *New Enc. Arch. Exc.* IV. Jerusalem: 1261–1267.
Ahituv, S. 1984. *Canaanite Toponyms in Ancient Egyptian Documents.* Jerusalem and Leiden.
Alt, A. 1945. Neue assyrische Nachrichten über Palästina und Syrien. *ZDPV* 67: 128–159. (Reprint: Alt 1953: 226–241).
Alt, A. 1953. *Kleine Schriften zur Geschichte des Volkes* Israel II. München.
Bennett, C.-M. 1974. Excavations at Buseirah, Southern Jordan, 1972: Preliminary Report. *Levant* 6: 1–24.
Bennett, C.-M. 1978. Some Reflections on Neo-Assyrian Influence in Transjordan. In Moorey, P.R.S. and Parr, P.J. eds. *Archaeology in the Levant. Essays for Kathleen Kenyon.* Warminster: 164–171.
Bennett, C.-M. 1982. Neo-Assyrian Influence in Transjordan. In: Hadidi, A. ed. *Studies in the History and Archaeology of Transjordan* 1. Amman: 181–187.
Bienkowski, P. 1995. The Architecture of Edom. In: Tell, S. et al. eds. *Studies in the History and Archaeology of Transjordan* 5. Amman: 135–143.
Bienkowski, P. 2000. Transjordan and Assyria. In: Stager, L.E. at al. eds. *The Archaeology of Jordan and Beyond. Essays in Honor of James* A. Sauer. Winona Lake: 44–58.
Borger, R. 1956. *Die Inschriften Asarhaddons, Königs von Assyrien.* (AfO Beiheft 9). Graz. (Reprint 1967. Osnabrück).
Cahill, J.M. 1995. Rosette Stamp Seal Impressions from Ancient Judah. *IEJ* 45: 230–252.
Cohen, R. and Yisrael, Y. 1995. *On the Road to Edom. Discoveries from En Ḥaẕeva.* The Israel Museum Catalogue No. 370. Jerusalem.
Cohen, R. and Yisrael, Y. 1996. The Excavations at 'Ein Haẕeva/Israelite and Roman Tamar. *Qadmoniot* 29: 78–92 (Hebrew).
Eph'al, I. 1982. The Ancient Arabs. *Nomads on the Borders of the Fertile Crescent 9th-5th Centuries B.C.* Jerusalem and Leiden.
Finkel, I.L. and Reade, J.E. 1998. Assyrian Eponyms, 873–649 BC. *Orientalia* 67: 248–254.
Finkelstein, I. 1992. Ḥorvat Qiṭmīt and the Southern Trade in the Late Iron Age II. *ZDPV* 108: 156–170.
Frahm, E. 1997. *Einleitung in die Sanherib-Inschriften.* (AfO Beiheft 26). Horn.
Frahm, E. 1997/98. Rezensionen. H. Tadmor, The Inscriptions of Tiglath-pileser III King of Assyria. Jerusalem 1994. *AfO* 44–45: 399–404.
Finkelstein, I. and Singer-Avitz, L. 2001. Ashdod Revisited. *Tel Aviv* 28: 231–259.
Fox, N.S. 2000. *In the Service of the King. Officialdom in Ancient Israel and Judah.* (Monographs of the Hebrew Union College 23). Cincinnati.
Fuchs, A. 1994. *Die Inschriften Sargons II. aus Khorsabad.* Göttingen.
Fuchs, A. 1998. Die Annalen des Jahres 711 v. Chr. nach Prismenfragmenten aus Ninive und Assur. (State Archives of Assyria Studies 8). Helsinki.
Gilboa, A. 1996. Assyrian-Type Pottery at Dor and the Status of the Town during the Assyrian Occupation Period. *Eretz Israel* 25: 122–135. (Hebrew).
Hooker, P.K. 1993. The Location of the Brook of Egypt. In: Graham, M.P. et al. eds. *History and Interpretation. Essays in Honour of John H. Hayes.* (Journal for the Study of the Old Testament Supplement 173). Sheffield: 203–214.
Humbert, J.-B. and Sadeq, M. 2000. Fouilles de Blakhiyah — Anthédon. In: Humbert, J.-B. ed. *Gaza. Méditerranéenne. Histoire et archéologie en Palestine.* Paris: 105–120.
Katzenstein, H.J. *The History of Tyre, from the Beginning of the Second Millennium B.C.E. until the Fall of the Neo-Babylonian Empire in 538 B.C.E.* Jerusalem.
Keel, O. and Uehlinger, C. 1998. *Gods, Goddesses, and the Images of God in Ancient Israel.* Minneapolis.
Kempinski, A. 1983. Some Philistine Names from the Kingdom of Gaza. *IEJ* 37:20–24.

Lipiński, E. 1979. Aram et Israël du Xe au VIIIe si cle av. *N.é. Acta Antiqua Academiae Scientiarum Hungaricae* 27: 49–101.

Lipschits, O. 1997. *The "Yehud" Province under Babylonian Rule (586–539 B.C.E.): Historic Reality and Historiographic Conceptions.* (Ph.D. Thesis). Tel Aviv University. (Hebrew).

Lipschits, O. 1998. Nebuchadrezzar's Policy in "Ḫattu-Land" and the Fate of the Kingdom of Judah. *Ugarit-Forschungen* 30: 467–487.

Matthiae, P. 1964. The Painted Sherd of Ramat Raḥel. In: Aharoni 1964: 85–94.

Mayerson, P. 1986. The Saracens and the Limes. *BASOR* 262: 35–47.

Mayerson, P. 1989. Saracens and Romans: Micro-Macro Relationship. *BASOR* 274: 71–78.

Mazar, A., Amit, D. and Ilan, D. 1996. Hurvat Shilhah: An Iron Age Site in the Judean Desert. In: Seger, J.D. ed., *Retrieving the Past. Essays on Archaeological Research and Methodology in Honor of Gus W. Van Beek.* Winona Lake: 193–211.

Mittmann, S. 1973. Das südliche Ostjordanland im Lichte eines neuassyrischen Keilschriftbriefes aus Nimrud. *ZDPV* 89: 15–25.

Na'aman, N. 1979. The Brook of Egypt and Assyrian Policy on the Border of Egypt. *Tel Aviv* 6: 68–90.

Na'aman, N. 1986. *Borders and Districts in Biblical Historiography. Seven Studies in Biblical Geographical Lists* (Jerusalem Biblical Studies 4). Jerusalem.

Na'aman, N. 1991. The Kingdom of Judah under Josiah. *Tel Aviv* 18: 3–71.

Na'aman, N. 1993. Population Changes in Palestine following Assyrian Deportations. *Tel Aviv* 20: 104–124.

Na'aman, N. 1994a. Hezekiah and the Kings of Assyria. *Tel Aviv* 21: 235–254.

Na'aman, N. 1994b. Esarhaddon's Treaty with Baal and Assyrian Provinces along the Phoenician Coast. *Rivista di Studi Fenici* 22: 3–8.

Na'aman, N. 1995. Province System and Settlement Pattern in Southern Syria and Palestine in the Neo-Assyrian Period. In: Liverani, M. ed. *Neo-Assyrian Geography.* (Quaderni di Geografia Storica 5). Rome.

Na'aman, N. 1997a. Notes on the Excavations at 'Ein Haṣeva, *Qadmoniot* 30: 60. (Hebrew).

Na'aman, N. 1997b. Siruatti the Me'unite in a Second Inscription of Tiglath-pileser III. *Nouvelles Assyriologiques Br ve et Utilitaires* 1997/4: No 150.

Na'aman, N. 1998. Two Notes on the History of Ashkelon and Ekron in the Late Eighth-Seventh Centuries B.C.E. *Tel Aviv* 25: 219–227.

Na'aman, N. and Zadok, R. 1988. Sargon II's Deportations to Israel and Philistia (716–708 B.C.). *JCS* 40: 36–46.

Naveh, J. 1985. Writing and Script in Seventh-Century B.C.E. Philistia: The New Evidence from Tell Jemmeh. *IEJ* 35: 8–21.

Negueruela, I. 1982. The Proto-Aeolic Capitals from Mudeibi'a, in Moab. *ADAJ* 26: 395–401.

Oren, E.D. 1993. Ethnicity and Regional Archaeology: The Western Negev under Assyrian Rule. In: Biran, A. and Aviram, J. eds. *Biblical Archaeology Today, 1990: Proceedings of the Second International Congress on Biblical Archaeology.* Jerusalem: 102–105.

Parker, B.J. 1997. Garrisoning the Empire: Aspects of the Construction and Maintenance of Forts on the Assyrian Frontier. *Iraq* 59: 77–87.

Parpola, S. 1981. Assyrian Royal Inscriptions and Neo-Assyrian Letters. In: Fales, F.M. ed. *Assyrian Royal Inscriptions: New Horizons in Literary, Ideological, and Historical Analysis.* Rome: 117–142.

Parpola, S. 1987. *The Correspondence of Sargon II, Part I: Letters from Assyria and the West.* (State Archives of Assyria 1). Helsinki.

Parpola, S. and Watanabe, K. 1988. *Neo-Assyrian Treaties and Loyalty Oaths* (State Archives of Assyria 2). Helsinki.

Pfeiffer, R.H. 1935. *State Letters of Assyria*. (American Oriental Series 6). New Haven.

Postgate, J.N. 1974. *Taxation and Conscription in the Assyrian Empire* (Studia Pohl, Series Maior 3). Rome.

Pratico, G.D. 1985. Nelson Glueck's 1938–1940 Excavations at Tell el-Kheleifeh: A Reappraisal. *BASOR* 259: 1–32.

Pratico, G.D. 1993. Nelson Glueck's *1938-1940 Excavations at Tell el-Kheleifeh: A Reappraisal.* (American Schools of Oriental Research Archaeological Reports), Atlanta.

Rainey, A.F. 1982. Toponymic Problems (cont.). *Tel Aviv* 9: 130–136.

Reich, R. 1992. Palaces and Residencies in the Iron Age. In: Kempinski, A. and Reich, R. eds. *The Architecture of Ancient Israel from the Prehistoric to the Persian Period*. Jerusalem: 202–222.

Singer-Avitz, L. 1999. Beersheba — A Gateway Community in Southern Arabian Long-Distance Trade in the Eighth Century B.C.E. *Tel Aviv* 26: 3–74.

Stern, E. 1992. The Phoenician Architectural Elements in Palestine during the Late Iron Age and the Persian Periods. In: Kempinski, A. and Reich, R. eds. *The Architecture of Ancient Israel from the Prehistoric to the Persian Period.* Jerusalem: 302–309.

Stern, E. 2001. *Archaeology of the Land of the Bible.* II: *The Assyrian, Babylonian and Persian Periods 732-332 BCE*. New York.

Stronach, D. 1985. Tepe Nūsh-i Jān: The Median Settlement. In: Gershevitch, I. ed. *The Cambridge History of Iran. 2. The Median and Achaemenian Periods.* Cambridge: 832–835, 925.

Tadmor, H. 1958. The Campaigns of Sargon II of Assur: A Chronological-Historical Study. *JCS* 12:22–40, 77–100.

Tadmor, H. 1966. Philistia under Assyrian Rule. *BA* 29: 86–102.

Timm, S. 1989. *Moab zwischen den Mächten. Studien zu historischen Denkmälern und Texten.* (Ägypten und Altes Testament 17). Wiesbaden.

Ussishkin, D. 1995. The Rectangular Fortress at Kadesh-barnea. *IEJ* 45: 118–127.

Van Beek, G.W. 1983. Digging up Tell Jemmeh. *Archaeology* 36: 12–19.

Van Beek, G.W. 1987. Arches and Vaults in the Ancient Near East. *Scientific American* 257/1: 78–85.

Van Beek, G.W. 1993. Jemmeh, Tell. *New Enc. Arch. Exc.* II. Jerusalem: 667–674.

Vaughn, A.G. 1999. *Theology, History, and Archaeology in the Chronicler's Account of Hezekiah.* Atlanta.

Waldbaum, J.C. and Magness, J. 1997. The Chronology of Early Greek Pottery: New Evidence from Seventh-Century B.C. Destruction Level in Israel. *AJA* 101: 23–40.

Wapnish, P. 1996. Is ṣēnī ana lā māni an Accurate Description or a Royal Boast. In: Seger, J.D. ed., *Retrieving the Past. Essays on Archaeological Research and Methodology in Honor of Gus W. Van Beek*. Winona Lake: 285–296.

Watanabe, K. 1991. Review: Simo Parpola, The Correspondence of Sargon II, Part I, Letters from Assyria and the West, Helsinki 1987. *BiOr* 48: 183–202.

Weippert, M. 1987. The Relations of the States East of the Jordan with the Mesopotamian Powers during the First Millennium BC. In: Hadidi, A. ed. *Studies in the History and Archaeology of Jordan* III. Amman: 97–105.

Zadok, R. 1996a. Geographical and Onomastic Remarks on H. Tadmor, The Inscriptions of Tiglath-Pileser III King of Assyria (Jerusalem 1994). *Nouvelles Assyriologiques Br ve et Utilitaires* 1996/1:No 17.

Zadok, R. 1996b. Notes on Syro-Palestinian History, Toponymy and Anthroponymy. *Ugarit-Forschungen* 28: 721–749.

Ḫabiru-like Bands in the Assyrian Empire and Bands in Biblical Historiography[1]

The term ^{lú}*urbī* for a certain kind of troops or band is mentioned three times in the Assyrian royal inscriptions: They are, in translation and in chronological order:

(1) Sennacherib's first campaign after he conquered the cities of the Chaldeans (703 BCE):

> The *urbī* (^{lú}*ur-bi*), Arameans (^{lú}*Aramu*) (and) Chaldeans (^{lú}*Kaldu*) who were in Uruk, Nippur, Kish (and) Ḫursagkalamma, together with the citizens (*mārē āli*), the rebels, I brought forth and counted as spoil (Luckenbill 1924:54, line 52).

(2) Sennacherib's third campaign against Judah (701 BCE):

> Hezekiah himself, the awe-inspiring splendor of my lordship overwhelmed him, and he sent me after my (departure) to Nineveh, my lordly city, the *urbī* (^{lú}*úr-bi*) and his elite troops (^{lú}*ṣābē-šu damqūti*), which he had brought in to strengthen (*ana dunnun*) Jerusalem, his royal city, and were auxiliary troops (*iršû tillāti*), together with 30 talents of gold . . . (Luckenbill 1924:33, lines 37–48).

(3) Assurbanipal's third campaign against Elam (653 BCE):

> I brought as spoils from the land of Gambulu to the land of Ashur the rest of Bel-iqisha's sons, his kinsmen, the members of his family . . . together with the *urbī* (^{lú}*ur-bi*), the rebels (^{lú}*tēbê*), the inhabitants (*nišē*) of the land of Gambulu, cattle, sheep and goats . . . (Streck 1916:28, lines 61–67).

Scholars have offered two main lines of interpretation for *urbī*: an ethnic group, i.e., Arabs, and a designation of a type of warrior. The first was dismissed long ago by I. Eph'al (1974:110, n. 160; see Bauer 1993:1), and is best abandoned. The second interpretation has many variants. H. Winckler (1906:333–34) and T. Bauer (1933:1) suggested that *urbī* means "fugitives" or "bandits." A.L. Oppenheim (1969:288; cf. *CAD* B 176b) translated it "irregular troops." H. Tadmor (1982:454; 1988:175–77; Cogan and Tadmor 1988:247, n. 2) has translated it as "a special type of soldiery" or "elite troops," and considered a possible West Semitic derivation (from the Hebrew verb *'rb*, "lie in wait"). Finally, E. Frahm (1997:104–105) has suggested combining the two

1. Reprinted with permission. *JAOS 120* (2000), 621-624.

ethnic and military interpretations. He assumed that *urbī* is a designation of elite troops named after an assumed Arab tribe, 'Urbu.

It seems to me that *urbī* is an Assyrian form, which (as suggested by Winckler and Bauer) is derived from the verb *nērubu* ("to flee, run away, escape") and which is closely related to other derivatives of this verb, such as *arbu* ("fugitive, person without family"), *arbūtu* ("flight"), *munnarbu* ("runaway") and *nērubtu* ("flight"). The term *urbī* refers to groups of fugitives who, in the face of Assyrian military campaigns, destructions or annexations, fled from their homeland and found shelter in peripheral areas. These uprooted people tried to adapt themselves to new circumstances by forming a band under the command of a prominent leader. The bands were independent armed bodies, restricted in number and characterized by their predatory nature and military ability. Often they became dangerous to sedentary and pastoral societies. Thanks to their military ability, they served on occasion as mercenaries in the armies of neighboring rulers.

All these characteristics are typical of the bands of Ḫabiru, which are so well known from late third- and second-millennium BCE ancient Near Eastern documents (Bottéro 1954; 1972–75:14–27; 1980:201–13; Greenberg 1955; Liverani, 1965:315–36; Loretz 1984 with earlier literature; Lemche 1992: 6–10). It seems to me that the Assyrians coined the collective denomination *urbī* to describe the Ḫabiru-like bands that emerged in marginal areas of their empire. According to the first reference, uprooted bands were mobilized by the rebellious Babylonian cities (Uruk, Nippur and Kish), together with Aramean and Chaldean tribal groups, and after the capture of these cities they were deported to Assyria. According to the second reference, a band (or bands) of *urbī* served as mercenaries in Hezekiah's army, side by side with his elite troops and, following the failure of the rebellion, were transferred and deported to Assyria. According to the third reference, uprooted bands participated in the struggle of the Gambulaeans against the invading Assyrian troops, and, following the defeat, both bands (*urbī*) and Gambulaean rebels (*^{lú}tēbē*) were deported to Assyria.

It is clear that the Assyrians made efforts to eradicate these unstable and predatory elements, who joined their enemies either as individual mercenaries or as independent bands and must have given trouble to the inhabitants of peripheral areas. The Assyrians fought these tribes and, whenever possible, deported them to Assyria. The scope and distribution of bands at this period is unknown, because our sources do not sufficiently illuminate the situation in marginal areas, where bands of refugees must have found shelter.

The above discussion sheds an interesting light on the description of bands in the Old Testament. As was recognized long ago, the bands of Jephthah and David were socially identical to the Ḫabiru-bands of the second millennium (see for example Buccellati 1962:95–99; Mazar 1963:310–12; Mendenhall 1973: 133–36). In fact, the best descriptions of bands in ancient Near Eastern literature appear in the biblical narratives of these leaders. They portray the background of the flight, the emergence of the bands, their ways of survival, and the manner in which they were reintegrated into Israelite society. However, in addition to these clear examples, there are other episodes in which Ḫabiru-like bands are portrayed (Na'aman 1986:278–85, with earlier literature).

(a) Abimelech came to power by hiring "worthless and reckless fellows," who followed him and killed all his brothers (Judg. 9:4–5). The author of the story is doubtless referring to the hiring of a band of uprooted men as a means of gaining political and military power.

(b) Gaal, the son of Ebed, and his "kinsmen" are also portrayed as refugees who formed a band and found shelter in the city of Shechem, under the protection of the "lords" of Shechem (Judg. 9:26–29). They served the city as mercenaries until they were expelled from it as a result of Abimelech's military pressure (vv. 25, 31–41) (Na'aman 1986:281).

(c) The tribe of Dan is depicted as a band of outlaws in Judg. 18. The migrating Danites are portrayed as a brigade of 600 armed men (vv. 11, 16, 17), i.e., a *g*^{e}*dūd*, exactly like the bands of David (1 Sam. 23:13; 27:2; 30:9) and Rezon (1 Kgs. 11:24), and their behavior in the plot is wholly brigand-like (Na'aman 1986:281. For the tendentious aspects of Judg. 18, see Amit 1990:2–20).

(d) Following the victory over the Philistines in the battle of Michmash (1 Sam. 14:1–20), two different groups joined the victorious side: the "Hebrews" (*'ibrîm*) who served in the Philistine camp (v. 21) and the Israelites who, in face of the Philistine onslaught, hid on Mount Ephraim (v. 22; see 1 Sam. 13: 6). This is the only biblical reference that makes the distinction between Israelites and "Hebrews." The latter term refers to a band of outlaws who served as mercenaries in the Philistine army, much like the service of David and his band in the army of Achish, king of Gath.

(e) Sheba, the son of Bichri, who revolted against King David (2 Sam. 20), is depicted as an outlaw who stayed with his band of "Hebrews" (I suggest transcribing in v. 14 *kl h<'>brym*) on Mount Ephraim. After the failure of Absalom's rebellion, he tried to incite a revolt, but failed, and was obliged to escape. He sought refuge at Abel-beth-maacah, near the northern border of Israel, but was betrayed and killed (Na'aman 1986:282–85).

(f) It seems to me that the author of the story of David's escape from Jerusalem at the time of Absalom's revolt portrays Ittai the Gittite as a leader of a band of outlaws (Na'aman 1998:22–25). Ittai led a contingent of 600 men, i.e., a *g*^{e}*dūd* "who had accompanied him from Gath" (2 Sam. 15:18b). In the discussion of David, Rezon and the migrating Danites, we have noted that a brigade/band of six hundred men is typical of the descriptions of bands in biblical narratives. Moreover, according to 2 Sam. 15:22, the band of Ittai included men and children (*ṭaf*). The combination of a contingent of warriors along with women and children is typical of bands and is mentioned in the narratives of the Danites (Judg. 18:11, 16, 17, 20) and of David's escape and wanderings (1 Sam. 27:2–3; 30:2–3, 18–19; 2 Sam. 2:2–3). Labeling Ittai a leader of a band explains why David calls him a "foreigner," addressing him as "an exile from your home," i.e., an uprooted person. Like some other leaders of bands depicted in biblical narratives (i.e., Gaal and Sheba), Ittai's figure is literary. It was created to convey a message about the concern of the king for those who served him, and about the devotion of the foreigner in contrast to the treachery of the king's son and his followers.

(g) Rezon, son of Eliada, was an officer in the army of Hadadezer, king of Zobah, who became the leader of a band (*gᵉdūd*) and subsequently seized the throne of Damascus and became king (1 Kgs. 11:23–24). The description of his rise in Damascus resembles, in outline, the depiction of David's rise to power in Israel.

The presentation of this variegated gallery of bands and their leaders in biblical historiography calls for an explanation. It is clear that the biblical narrators deliberately picked these figures of outlaws to depict the history of the pre-monarchical and early-monarchical periods. It is commonly held today that the biblical historiography of these periods was written hundreds of years after the time in which the depicted episodes supposedly took place. The depicted "events" are more literary than historical, although some episodes may reflect certain oral traditions that had come down to their authors. It is, therefore, legitimate to ask: Where did the narrators in the late monarchical period encounter bands of refugees, and why was their life-style so suitable for the depiction of the pre-monarchical and early monarchical periods?

It is well known that the term "Ḫabiru" vanished from Western Asiatic documents toward the end of the second millennium, and, in the first millennium, it is mentioned only in scholarly texts. The phenomenon of uprooted bands, on the other hand, did not vanish, although its scope was more limited in the early first millennium, following the establishment of a new array of states in many parts of Western Asia.[2] With the destruction of this system of kingdoms following the expansion of Assyria, and the emergence of a large-scale empire on their territory, many people lost their homes and property and were forced to leave their places and find shelter on the periphery of the

2. Rowton 1976:16 suggested that the term "Suteans" probably evolved in the first millennium BCE into a social ethnonym.

empire. As a result, the number of uprooted people increased considerably. The three references above to bands reflect the situation of migration and desertion, which must have been far more widespread than represented in our written sources.

The Assyrian campaigns against the kingdom of Israel were destructive; they culminated in the annexation of its territory and the deportation of tens of thousands of its inhabitants to other parts of the empire. Sennacherib's campaign against Judah was devastating, aimed at breaking the power of the kingdom, and his deportation of tens of thousands left parts of the kingdom, in particular the Shephelah, desolate (Na'aman 1991:57–58; Dagan 1992:252–63; Ofer 1993: part II:125–131). Following this campaign, the devastated areas may have attracted groups of refugees, who wandered there in search of shelter and provision. The kingdom of Judah in the first half of the seventh century was too weak either to re-settle the peripheral areas or to restore their security and order.

The band or bands (*urbī*) who served in the army of Hezekiah and were stationed in Jerusalem in 701 were recruited from among the refugees of the earlier Assyrian campaigns. The inhabitants of the city must have encountered these mercenaries. Additional bands may have served in the other fortified cities of the kingdom. Moreover, it is reasonable to assume that the mobilization of refugees — as individuals or groups — to serve in the army was not limited to particular situations and that they served in the army of Judah in the seventh century. The inhabitants of peripheral areas of the kingdom must have encountered individuals as well as groups of outlaws. Thus, it is evident that the phenomenon of Ḫabiru-like bands was well known in Judah in the late eighth-seventh centuries BCE.

With this background in mind, we can explain the many descriptions of bands and their leaders in the biblical historiography of the pre-monarchical period. Later sources may reflect the concerns of the times in which they were written, and texts may be investigated in search of the environment in which their authors operated and of their historical knowledge of ancient reality. I suggest that the biblical descriptions of bands in the narratives of the periods of the Judges and the early monarchy were "borrowed" from the situation in their authors' time. The condition of destruction and desolation, and the emergence of groups of refugees, suggested to the narrators that similar situations had prevailed in the pre-monarchical period, before the rise of urban centers and the establishment of army and administration to control the peripheral areas. Bands symbolized the absence of central control, hence, the widespread use of this motif in stories that refer to pre-monarchical situations.

Scribes in the court of Jerusalem may even have portrayed episodes of the early history of Israel in light of actual events and historical figures of their own time. Thus, for example, the Shephelah and the southern highlands of Judah were affected badly by Sennacherib's campaign. The narratives about the wanderings of David and his band in these areas, in search of shelter and provisions, pursued from time to time by the king and his army, finally escaping to Philistia and serving there as mercenaries, may have reflected an unknown historical episode of the time of their author. Unfortunately, the history of Judah in the seventh century is unknown, and there is no way to confirm such an hypothesis. Be that as it may, the reality of bands and their leaders must have been well known to scribes in Jerusalem in the late eighth and seventh centuries, and this reality influenced their shaping of narratives and figures in the early history of Israel. These narratives came down to the Deuteronomistic historian, and he incorporated them in the history of Israel in the pre-monarchical and early monarchical periods.

References

Amit, Y. 1990. Hidden Polemic in the Conquest of Dan: Judges xvii-xviii. *VT* 40: 2–20.

Bauer, T. 1933. *Das Inschriftenwerk Assurbanipals vervollständigt und neu Bearbeitet* II. Leipzig.

Bottéro, J. 1954. *Le problème des Ḫabiru à la 4e Rencontre Assyriologique Internationale.* Paris.

Bottéro, J. 1972–75. Ḫabiru. *RLA* IV: 14–27.

Bottéro, J. 1980. Entre nomades et sédentaires: Les Ḫabiru. *Dialogues d'Histoire Ancienne* 6: 201–13.

Buccellati, G. 1962. La 'carriera' di David e quella di Idrimi, re di Alalac. *Bibbia e Oriente* 4: 95–99.

Cogan M. and Tadmor, H. 1988. *II Kings. A New Translation with Introduction and Commentary.* (The Anchor Bible). Garden City.

Dagan, Y. 1992. *The Shephelah during the Period of the Monarchy in Light of Archaeological Excavations and Surveys.* (M.A. Thesis). Tel Aviv University. (Hebrew)

Eph'al, I. 1974. "Arabs" in Babylonia in the 8th Century B.C. *JAOS* 94: 108–115.

Frahm, E. 1997. *Einleitung in die Sanherib-Inschriften* (AfO Beiheft 26). Horn.

Greenberg, M. 1955. The Ḫab/piru (*American Oriental Series* 39). New Haven.

Lemche, N.P. 1992. Ḫabiru, Ḫapiru. *The Anchor Bible Dictionary* 3. New York: 6–10.

Liverani, M. 1965. Il fuoruscitismo in Siria nella tarda età del Bronzo. *Rivista storica italiana* 77: 315–36.

Loretz, O. 1984. *Habiru-Hebräer. Eine sozio-linguistische Studie über die Herkunft des Gentiliziums 'ibrî vom Appelativum ḫabiru* (Beiheft zur ZAW 160). Berlin and New York.

Luckenbill, D.D. 1924. *The Annals of Sennacherib.* (Oriental Institute Publications 2). Chicago.

Mazar, B. 1973. The Military Elite of King David. *VT* 13: 310–320.

Mendenhall, G.E. 1973. *The Tenth Generation. The Origins of the Biblical Tradition.* Baltimore.

Na'aman, N. 1986. Ḫabiru and Hebrews: The Transfer of a Social Term to the Literary Sphere. *JNES* 45: 271–286.

Na'aman, N. 1991. The Kingdom of Judah under Josiah. *Tel Aviv* 18: 3–71.

Na'aman, N. 1998. Ittai the Gittite. *Biblische Notizen* 94: 22–25.

Ofer, A. 1993. *The Highland of Judah during the Biblical Period* 1. (Ph.D. Thesis). Tel Aviv University. (Hebrew).

Oppenheim, A.L. 1969. Babylonian and Assyrian Historical Texts. In: *ANET*: 265–317.

Rowton, M.B. 1976. Dimorphic Structure and the Problem of the *'Apirû-'Ibrîm*. *JNES* 35: 13–20.

Streck, M. 1916. *Assurbanipal und die letzten assyrischen Könige bis zum Untergange Niniveh's* II. Leipzig.

Tadmor, H. 1982. The Aramaization of Assyria: Aspects of Western Impact. In: Nissen, H.-J. and Renger J. eds. *Mesopotamien und seine Nachbarn: Politische und kulturelle Wechselbeziehungen im Alten Vorderasien vom 4. bis 1. Jahrtausend v. Chr.* (Berliner Beiträge zum Vorderen Orient 1). Berlin: 449–470.

Tadmor, H. 1988. The *urbi* of Hezekiah. *Beer-Sheva* 3: 171–178. (Hebrew).

Winckler, H. 1906. Besprechungen: Erasmus Nagel, Die nachdavidische Königsgeschichte Israels. Ethnographisch und geographisch beleuchtet. *OLZ* 9: 266–272, 330–336.

Chronology and History in the Late Assyrian Empire (631–619 BCE)*[1]

The chronology of the last kings of Assyria and the historical reconstruction of the events during the eighth decade of the 7th century BCE have been the subject of numerous works.[2] All the historical reconstructions that have been suggested so far involve either the rejection of certain evidence or hypotheses that are not compatible with what is known about the history of the Assyrian Empire in former times. Readers may well ask themselves why another reconstruction should be offered, when so many works have already been written on the same subject, or in other words, what are the chances that yet another scholar might be able to suggest a solution for a complex problem where many others before him have failed?

The answer to this question is that many new chronological data have recently been published. and these data form a much better basis for investigation of the period under discussion.[3] It is suggested that when arranged according to data and place of origin, the new data lead us to a specific chronological scheme, one that conforms well to all other documentary evidence (with one exception — see below) and enables us to present a reasonable description of the events which led to the final withdrawal of Assyria from southern Mesopotamia.

1. *The Chronology of the Last Kings of Assyria*

I will open the discussion by presenting the data of those kings whose dates can be accurately determined, i.e., Kandalānu (Knd.), Nabopolassar

---

* The following royal names will be used in abbreviated form: Ašb. = Ashurbanipal; Aei. = Ashur-etil-ilāni; Knd. = Kandalānu; Npl. = Nabopolassar; Sši. = Sin-šar-iškun; Sšl. = Sin-šum-līšir.

1. Reprinted with permission. *Zeitschrift für Assyriologie* 81 (1991), 243–267.

2. Fundamental studies are: Falkner 1952–53; Wiseman 1956:5–11, 89–94; van Dijk 1962:40–43, 53–57; von Soden 1957:316–319; 1967; Borger 1959; 1965; 1969; 1974–77; von Voigtlander 1963:1–37; Oates 1965; Reade 1970; Zawadzki 1988:23–63.

3. Brinkman and Kennedy 1983:1–90; 1986:99–106; Kennedy 1986:172–244; Leichty 1986; Leichty and Grayson 1987; Leichty, Finkelstein and Walker 1988.

(Npl.) and Ashurbanipal (Ašb.). The data concerning the other rulers are integrated subsequently into this chronological scheme. The Babylonian and Assyrian regnal years are equated to the Gregorian (e.g., year 630 is Gregorian 630/629). No reference is given when the dates are taken from the list of dated Babylonian economic texts recently published by Brinkman/Kennedy[4] and by Kennedy.[5]

Knd.'s latest date in his 21st year is 8/III (627 BCE). His 21st year is represented on tablets written in Babylon (26/I; 6/II), Sippar (5/II; 13/II) and Borsippa (?/I; 25/II). He died before the eighth month of this year as is evident from a tablet written in Babylon that is dated 1+x/VIII "*arki* [. . .] Kandalānu."Another tablet written in 626 BCE is dated 2/VIII 22nd year "*arki* Kandalānu."

Npl.'s earliest date is 22/VI of his accession year. Unfortunately, the city name is not recorded on the tablet.[6] Two other tablets from his accession year are known: one from Uruk (date damaged) and one from an unknown place.

Seven tablets dated in Npl.'s first year and three from his second year were written in Uruk. Only one Urukean tablet is dated in his third year (22/IV) and another, most probably from Uruk, is dated in his forth year (26/I).[7] Only one Uruk tablet bearing his name is dated in his fifth (16/V) and sixth (19/IX). From his seventh year, on the other hand, there are four tablets (14/III; 23/VI; 25/VII; 11/VIII). It, therefore, seems that Npl. held Uruk from his accession year (626) until the first half of his third year (623). The situation in years 622–620 is not immediately clear, but it is certain that he ruled the city in his seventh year (619).

Npl.'s earliest dates from Babylon are 18/XII and 25/XIIb (intercalary month) of his first year. Three tablets are dated in his second (4/II; 30/II;

4. There are certain inconsistencies in dates, between the catalogues of the British Museum and the list of dated texts published by Brinkman and Kennedy. Four significant dates were kindly collated for me by C.B.F. Walker, with the following results (letter of 24/XI 1989): BM 49165 Knd. -/II/21 (rev.? (1) *x zib tum šá ina* ITU GU_4 (2) [M]U 21 KÁM *kan-da-la* (ruling) (3) [. . .] *sin šá* UD 2 KÁM); BM 54153 Sšl. 15/-/acc. (This date effectively has to be taken from the duplicate BM 54608, because year designation and royal name are all but illegible); BM 60838 Knd. 12/II/20; BM 67313 Sšl. -/-/acc. (Sin-M[U-. .]) [see recently Brinkman 1995:97].

5. There are certain inconsistencies in dates, between the catalogues of the British Museum and Kennedy's list of dated texts. Two significant dates have been collated: BM 49883 Npl. 9/II/3; BM 79253 Npl. 24/IV/5 [see recently Brinkman 1995:97].

6. Kennedy 1986:178. The text (BM 49656) was formerly assigned to the Sippar tablets; see Wiseman 1956:93–94.

7. Kennedy 1986:181.

?/XIIb) and four tablets in his fourth year. Since then, there is an unbroken sequence of tablets dated by his regnal years.

Relatively few tablets are known from Borsippa. Significantly, there is a sequence of tablets dated in Npl.'s third (15/VIII), fourth (11/V), fifth (20/IX) and sixth (15/V) years. Furthermore, no Assyrian king is mentioned in the Borsippa tablets of these years.

Analyzing the evidence from Sippar is more complicated. Knd.'s latest dated tablets are from the 5/II and the 13/II of his 21st year (627). Npl.'s earliest dated tablets, on the other hand, are from his fifth year (24/IV)[8] and his sixth (6/XII) year. It should, however, be recalled that the place of origin is not recorded on many tablets dated to Npl.'s second year and to his seventh to twenty-first years; also, many of the British Museum tablets dated to his reign came from illicit excavations at Sippar. Only after the full publication of these tablets will we be able to establish accurately the history of the city in the time of Npl.

Ašb. last dated tablet from Nippur is from his 38th year (20/III), i.e., 631 BCE. Npl.'s earliest dated tablet is from his 17th year (607) and does not really indicate the time when he conquered the city.

Bearing these data in mind, we can eliminate, first of all, certain chronological schemes suggested in the past for the last Assyrian kings. It is clear that Sin-šar-iškun's (Sši.) first year cannot antedate the last year of Knd. (627 BCE), because tablets with his dates would then fall within the same years as those of Knd.[9] The chronological scheme suggested by Oates, according to which Sši. ascended the throne only in 623 BCE and his first full year was 622, is likewise unacceptable.[10] The Uruk tablets dated to his years 5–7 would then fall in 618–616 BCE, several years after the unification of Babylonia by Npl.; Sši.'s rule in Sippar as late as 621–620 BCE is unlikely, and his accession date on a tablet from Babylon (21/XII), which, according to this chronological scheme would be 623, would break the uninterrupted sequence of tablets bearing the dates of Npl. Also, her dating of Ashur-etil-ilāni (Aei.) to 627–623 is unlikely, becuase his royal inscriptions would have been written in Babylonian cities occupied by Npl. after his revolt of 626 BCE (see below).

8. For the date, see note 5 above.

9. The chronological schemes suggested by Wiseman, von Soden, Borger, von Voigtlander and Zawadzki, according to which Sši's first year was earlier than 626 BCE, therefore, are unacceptable.

10. For a criticism of the chronological and historical reconstruction suggested by Oates, see Zawadzki 1988:37–42.

Dating the accession year of Sši to 627 on the other hand fits the dates of Knd. and Npl. The former king must have died between 8/III (his latest known date) and 1/VII (Sši.'s earliest known date), the "*arki* Kandalānu" date of 1+x/VIII fits well into this scheme. In his accession year, Sši. is attested in Sippar (8/VII), Uruk (6/XI) and Babylon (21/XII), cities whose tablets until then were dated by Knd.'s regnal years, and in Nippur (1/VII).[11] His first year (626) appears only on one tablet (11/II). His years are not attested again on tablets from the city of Babylon, but tablets bearing his name appear in Sippar in his second and the beginning of his third year (625–624 BCE). His first year is not represented in Nippur, but from his second year (earliest date 17/V) until his fifth year (latest date 9/VI) there is an uninterrupted sequence of tablets bearing his name.

After Sši's accession date (6/XI) there is a gap of four years in his Uruk dates; his fifth year (622) is attested on two tablets (4/VIII, 12/VIII). In between these years there is a sequence of tablets, all dated by Npl.'s years from accession (month and day are broken) to the beginning of his fourth year (26/I). Five Uruk tablets of Sši. are from his sixth year (621) and two are from his seventh year (620), the latest tablet being dated 12/X. Two dates of Npl. (16/V year 5; 19/IX year 6) are also attested on tablets from these years. Since the reconstruction of the history of Uruk during these years involves the problem of the "siege documents," the sequence of events is discussed in more detail in the fifth part of this article.

Only the accession year of Sin-šum-lišir (Sšl.) is attested on tablets written in Nippur, Babylon and Ru'a. Unfortunately, of the eight tablets bearing this date only two have the month name (12/ III and 15/V), so the exact number of months during which he was in power remains uncertain.[12] Dating his reign in 627 as suggested by some scholars (van Dijk 1962:55; Reade 1970:3, 5) creates difficulties, since Knd.'s latest date falls in the second (days: 5, 6, 13,

11. The date appears on the Nippur tablet published by Krückmann 1933:Nr. 35 = San Nicolò 1951:Nr. 63. The tablet is a compendium written at the end of Sši's second year and it recorded a list of debts to the creditor Remût-Gula. Most of the loans were agreed in this year (lines 1–4, 12–26), but two loans were contracted earlier. The loan mentioned in lines 8–11 was given in 1/VIII of Aei.'s first year and the creditor noted that the interest for the first 2 years has already been paid (see Borger 1965:66b; Brinkman and Kennedy 1983:53 [M11]). The second loan mentioned in lines 5–7 was given in 1/VII of Sši's accession year. The broken line 7 was discussed by Borger 1965:65–66; von Soden 1967:245–246. I would suggest restoring it [*a-di* M]U 3 KÁM [MÁŠ *inaddin kim*]*a šá-ṭir* – "[He will pay the interest until the] third year [a]s was contracted." The loan was given for 3 years; it bears interest of 20% (line 1) and should be paid in the next year (Sši's third year).

12. Borger 1969. For the dates of tablets BM 54153 and BM 67313 see note 1.

25) and the third (8th day) months of the year, while Sši.'s earliest date falls four days later, on the 12/III. It also does not fit the Uruk King List, according to which Sšl. and Sši. reigned in Babylonia for one year (between Knd.'s and Npl.'s reigns) (van Dijk 1962:53; Grayson 1980–83:97). Dating Sšl to 626 , on the other hand, fits the words of the latter source, falling in the year which, according to the description of chronicle BM 25127, was "the first year in which there was no king in the land."[13] Significantly, only one tablet of Sši.'s first year (dated to 11/II) is known so far. We may safely assume that, early in 626, Sšl. rebelled and dominated northern Babylonia for several months; at approximately the same time, Npl. rebelled in southern Babylonia.

There are several clues for dating Aei. Tablets dated with his name are restricted to Nippur, whereas his royal inscriptions have been found in several Babylonian cities (Sippar, Babylon, Dilbat, Nippur).[14] The direct continuity from the time of Ašb., his father, is self-evident. The pattern of documentation for Sši. is the reverse of this: None of his inscriptions have so far been discovered in Babylonia — they were all found in Assyria. On the other hand, many tablets dated with his years were found in various Babylonian cities. It is, thus, clear that Aei. and Sši. reigned in entirely different historical situations and that the former ruled prior to the rebellion of Npl. and was able to construct buildings and dedicate objects in various Babylonian centers.

Aei.'s earliest known date is 20/VII of his accession year, and the latest known date is 1/VIII of his fourth year. In his royal grant tablet, he mentions that he ascended the throne after his father *illiku nammušīšu*, i.e., "died" (Postgate 1969:Nos. 13–14; CAD N/2, 235b). We may safely assume that Ašb. died between 20/III (his latest date) and 20/VII (Aei.'s earliest date) of year 631 and that Aei ruled Assyria in the years 631–627 BCE. There is a one-month discrepancy in the dates of Aei. and Sši, because, according to the chronological scheme suggested above, Sši. already had ascended the throne on 1/VII 627, whereas Aei.'s latest date is 1/VIII. Such a clerical error in far-off Nippur immediately after the ruler's death in Assyria, however, is understandable. Therefore, it is suggested that Aei. died shortly before Tishri 627.

The synchronism between the deaths of Aei. and Knd. was possibly recorded in KAV 182 r. 5–7.[15] The three last lines before the colophon may be restored as follows:

---

13. Grayson 1975:14. Sši. was dated (with question mark) by Brinkman and Kennedy (1983) 626 BCE.

14. For the inscriptions of Aei., see Borger 1965:67a; 1975:27; Leichty 1983:217–220.

15. See recently Grayson 1980–83:122–125, with earlier literature.

(5) [Šamaš-šum-ukin ....]	Ashur-bāni-apli	Ištar-šuma-ēreš
(6) [Kandalānu . . .]	DITTO	DITTO
(7) [DITTO . . .]	Ashur-etil-ilāni	

It seems to me that death of the two kings in one year provided the immediate incentive for the composition of a synchronistic list in which the kings and their *ummānus* in Babylonia and Assyria were arranged against one other. The scribe who composed the list was probably Aei.'s *ummānu*, and his name is possibly mentioned in the colophon.[16]

The dates now suggested for the Assyrian kings are as follows:

Ashurbanipal 669–631	Ashur-etil-ilāni 631–627
Sin-šar-iškun 627–612	Sin-šum-līšir 626 (only in Babylonia)

Table 1

The table illustrates the change of rulers in Mesopotamia in years 631–620 BCE. The earliest known date of each king appears in brackets.

631	Ašb. 38	Aei. acc.	Knd. 17			
		(20/VII)				
630		Aei. 1	Knd. 18			
629		Aei. 1	Knd. 19			
628		Aei. 3	Knd. 20			
627		Aei. 4	Knd. 21	Šši. acc.		
				(1 /VII)		
626				Šši. 1	Npl. acc.	Ššl. Acc.
					(10/IV)	(12/III)
625				Šši. 2	Npl. 1	
624				Šši. 3	Npl. 2	
623				Šši. 4	Npl. 3	
622				Šši. 5	Npl. 4	
621				Šši. 6	Npl. 5	
620				Šši. 7	Npl. 6	

This set of dates is similar to the dates suggested by Falkner (1952–53: 310) and van Dijk (1962:18, 57). This is no coincidence: Falkner wrote her article before the publication of the Harran inscription of Nabonidus' mother,

16. For the colophon and the name of the scribe, see Hunger 1968:Nr. 238.

and van Dijk (1962:55 n. 170) ignored it in his discussion. Indeed, it is this inscription with its chronological data that has confused many scholars who believed that its dates could provide a sound basis for their respective chronological schemes.

According to the Harran inscription, Adda-guppi' was born in Ašb.'s 20th year (649) and died in Nabonidus' ninth year (547), altogether 104 years; there is, thus, a two-year discrepancy in this calculation (Gadd 1958:69–72; Borger 1965:60–62; Oates 1965:141–142). Col. i 29–31 of the inscription states that she lived under Ašb. until his 42nd year, under Aei. until his 3rd year, under Npl. until his 21st year, etc. Ašb.'s assumed 42 years (669–627) clashed with the above suggested chronological scheme. Ostensibly, there is one way to avoid this contradiction: the assumption of a co-regency of four years of Ašb. and Aei.[17] However, not only does this assumption contradict the plain words of Aei.'s royal grant tablet cited above, coregency is not attested elsewhere in the history of Assyria. Such an *ad hoc* solution with no historical precedent is best avoided. The solution for the 42 years assigned to Ašb. must be sought in the sources of the scribe who composed the inscription.

First, it should be noted that the inscription (or its *Vorlage*) was originally written in Babylonia, as is evident from the close similarity between many of its phrases and those of Nabonidus' other inscriptions (Tadmor 1965:351–363; Zawadzki 1988:55–57). It may well be possible to account for the three years assigned to Aei. by assuming that this was the time when Adda-guppi' moved from Harran to Babylonia (Oates 1965:142). All other data were apparently borrowed from king list(s) current at that time in Babylonia. Inasmuch as the Babylonian scribe knew that Ašb. ruled in Assyria concurrently with Šamaš-šum-ukīn and Knd. in Babylonia, he probably added together the years of the latter kings (21+21), getting 42 years for Ašb. The procedure of borrowing the throne tenures from king list(s) and then adding them together also produced the two-years' error in the total. It must be recalled that Mesopotamian scribes always calculated the time-spans to past events by a combination of the regnal years borrowed from king lists (Na'aman 1984: 115–120). The calculation of the years of Adda-guppi' in the Harran inscription is easily interpreted in the light of this long-established tradition of Mesopotamian scribes.

17. Van Dijk 1962:57; see the critical remarks by Oates 1965:138–39. J. Reade's suggestion (1970:l, 5) that Ašb. had abdicated in 631 and was succeeded by his son Aei., but that until his death in 627 was still recognized (under the name Knd.) as King of Babylonia, is unlikely.

Table 2

The table illustrates the change of power in four Babylonian cities. The earliest and the latest known dates of each king in each city were recorded accurately.

	Babylon	Sippar	Nippur	Uruk
628	Knd. 20		Knd. 20	Aei. 3
627	Knd. 21 21/II		Knd. 21 13/11	Aei. 4 1/VIII
	arki Knd. VIII			
	Sši. acc. 21/XII	Sši. acc. 8/VII	Sši. acc. 1/VII	Sši. acc. 6/XI
626	Sši. acc. 15/V	-	Sšl. acc.	
	Npl. acc. 26/VII			Npl. acc.
625	Npl. 1	Sši. 2	Sši. 2 17/V	Npl. 1
624	Npl. 2	Sši. 3 11/I	Sši. 3	Npl. 2
623	-	-	Sši. 4	Npl. 3
622	Npl. 4	-	Sši. 5 9/VI	Npl. 4 26/I
				Sši. 5 4/VIII
621	Npl. 5	Npl. 5 24/IV	-	Sši. 6
620	Npl. 6	Npl. 6	-	Sši. 7 12/X
619	Npl. 7	Npl. 7	-	Npl. 7 14/III

2. *Ashurbanipal and Kandalānu*

The assumed identification of Ašb. with Knd. should be briefly discussed now. This suggestion has recently been defended in detail by Zawadzki in his book on the fall of Assyria (1988:57–62). Before dealing with his new evidence, let me present the main arguments, most of which have already been raised in the past, against equating the two kings.[18]

(A) All the Assyrian kings who ruled Babylonia appear on Babylonian tablets with their "Assyrian" names. The assumption of the use of two different names for the same king has no parallel in the history of Assyria.

(B) There is a marked difference in the documents unearthed in Babylonia between the numbering of Ašb.'s and Knd.'s years. Ašb.'s years in his royal inscriptions and in the Nippur tablets are counted from his first year (668 BCE), whereas Knd.'s years are counted from 647 BCE. Thus, for example, Ašb.'s prism from the temple of Gula in Babylon is dated in his 30th year (639 BCE), and an economic tablet written in the same year and in the same place is

18. Smith 1928, with earlier literature in n. 1; Dubberstein 1944:39–41; Shea 1971:62–64; Brinkman 1976–80:368–69; 1984:105–106.

dated Knd.'s ninth year (Nassouhi 1924–25:104; Brinkman and Kennedy 1983: 42).

(C) In their inscriptions, all Assyrian kings who ruled Babylonia bear the title "King of Babylonia." Although many of the royal inscriptions of Ašb. were composed after 648 BCE, in no inscription does he bear this royal title.[19]

(D) In the synchronistic king list from Ashur written immediately after the death of Ašb., his name appears twice vis-à-vis the names of Šamaš-šum-ukīn and Knd. Such a presentation in a contemporaneous text can be explained only by the assumption that the scribe regarded them as two different kings.

(E) There is no trustworthy Babylonian source that refers to Ašb. as King of Babylonia. The text of Eusebius, presented by Zawadzki as a sound basis for the identification of Ašb. with Knd., lacks authority and cannot be considered a reliable source for such identification (this was emphasized by Smith 1928:623–624).

Of all the evidence that Zawadzki (1988:61–62) presents to support the identification, the office held by Šamaš-danninanni deserves a special discussion. According to his analysis, in 647 BCE he was appointed governor over all Babylonia; his nomination is incongruous with the coronation of a new king in the same year, in the same territory. To clarify the problem, I have analyzed in detail BIN 2, 132, the text in which Šamaš-dinanni's office in Babylonia is mentioned.[20]

BIN 2, 132 is a judicial report describing an extended dispute over a group of Puqudu people who were consecrated by Sargon and Sennacherib to the service of Ishtar and Nana of Uruk. The case was first decided through a *ḫuršān*-ordeal by Esarhaddon and the temple won the case (lines 1–7).

The rest of the obverse is severely damaged and until now has not been discussed in detail. I will first suggest a tentative translation for lines 7–27 and then will discuss the role of Šamaš-dinanni in the case:

> (7) Afterwards (8) Kudurru, governor of Uruk, the . . . of Uruk, (9) with the Urukeans [ga]ve them. (10) Into [Uruk?] Šamaš-dinanni, governor of Akkad, (11) with the šandabakku [of Nippu]r? (*it-ti ša-da-bak-k*[*i* NIBR]U?.KI) to[ok the ro]ad? (*ḫu-l*[*i*? *il-l*]*i-ku-ú*). (12) Šamaš-dinanni, governor of Akkad, against Kudurru, governor of Uruk, (13) brought] a lawsu[it saying] (*di-n*[*am*] *ig-r*[*e-e-ma um-ma*]): "Why ([*m*]*i-nam-ma*) the Puqudeans (14) are [. . . Sargon and] Sennaeherib wi[th?] their [son]s? (15) gave (them) to

19. Seux 1967:301–302. However, Ašb. bore the broader title of *šakkanakku Bābili šar māt Šumeri u Akkadî*, formerly held by his brother and rival Šamaš-šum-ukin (ibid., 278).

20. The text was published by Nies and Keiser 1920:No. 132. For earlier discussions of the text, see Borger 1967:216; Frymer-Kensky 1985:406–410; Brinkman 1984:75 n. 368; 105–106 n. 526; cf. Kümmel 1979:139 n. 226.

> [Ishtar-Uruk] and Nanâ. (16) I[n the house? of Ishtar-Uruk and] Nanâ they stayed, and (17) a[fter? that . . . ga]ve them, (18) Nabû-[ú]-š[e-zib? son of Apla-adi?] against them (19) [. . . The Puq]udeans, (20) who in the [time? of Esarhaddon? for a ḫuršān?] with Nabû-ušēzib (21) [went and were cleared] and afterwards (22) [Kudurru?, governor of Uruk?, wit]h? the . . . (23) [gave? them? . . . (24) . . . Ashurbani]pal? ([AN.ŠÁR.DÙ.]IBILA?), king of A[ssyria], who (25) [. . .] they went (26) [. . . to the ḫuršān? he] sent them ([*i*]*š-pur-šu-nu-ti-m*[*a*] *(27)* [and they were cleared. Ashurbanipal? to] Ishtar-Uruk [and Nanâ released them].

The next part (lines 28–41) enumerates 28 names described (line 42) as "28 Puqudeans who were cleared in the ḫuršān-ordeal." It certainly refers to the judicial proceedings that took place in the time of Ašb. (and not to the earlier ordeal), emphasizing that these 28 men, who must have been the offspring of the originally consecrated Puqudeans, were cleared of the claims of the Urukeans. The tablet bears an Assyrian official seal reserved for such documents.[21]

It is clear that the Assyrian kings and their officials consistently supported the claim of the temple of Ishtar and Nanâ, and the Urukeans contested the claim that the Puqudeans formed part of the temple personnel. The role of Šamaš-dinanni, "the governor (*šakin māti*) of Akkad" must be examined against this background. He may well be the same as Šamaš-danninanni, who bore the title "governor of Akkad" or "provincial official of Babylon" and was an eponym in Assyria in 643/42, when Edition A of the annals was written.[22] Inasmuch as Kudurru is mentioned in tablets dated 647–646 BCE (Dietrich 1970:98; Brinkman 1977:309–312; Kümmel 1979:139), the case under discussion was probably written in the mid–40s of the seventh century. Šamaš-d(ann)inanni acted in the case as representative of the Assyrian government, but there is no indication that he held executional administrative authority over all Babylonia (contra Zawadzki). Marduk-xx, who bore the title "provincial official (*bēl pīḫāti*) of Babylon," appears in a list of witnesses only in the fourth place, and another official who also bore the title of *bēl pīḫāti* is mentioned as witness only in the sixth places.[23] Very little is known of the officials bearing the title "governor of Babylon/Akkad," and it is quite possible that their power and actual authority were less than that of the Assyrian *šaknus*.

---

21. The seal impressed on the tablet has been compared by Borger (1957–58:117) with the Assyrian royal seal. For the latter seal, see Sachs 1953; Millard 1965.

22. For the date of the composition of Ašb.'s Edition A, see Tadmor 1962:240; Grayson 1980:231–232, 245. For the titles of Šamaš-danninanni, see Brinkman 1984:107 n. 534.

23. Pinches 1939–40:52: rev. 5; Weidner 1952–53:41, line 14. For a general discussion, see Frame 1982.

When describing his arrangements in Babylonia after the conquest, Ašb., in his annals, wrote: "I established over them (i.e., the people of Babylonia) governors and officials whom I selected" (Streck 1916:40, iv 103–105). Knd.'s authority must have been very limited, which is why nothing is known about his activities as king. He was probably a Babylonian who had supported Ašb. during the war against his rebellious brother, afterwards raised to the nominal rank of king, but without any political or military authority.[24] True power was in the hands of the Assyrians and their supporters among the Babylonians; they exercised this power as long as they were strong enough to hold the land under their sway.

3. *The Accession of Sin-šar-iškun*

The chronological framework established in the preceding section is the basis for the historical discussion. Only the main outlines are discussed in the following sections with emphasis on the major problems.

Aei. ascended the throne after the death of his father Ašb. (631 BCE). Upon his accession he met certain opposition, which he overcame with the help of Sšl.[25] It is well known that, from the middle of the eighth century BCE onward, a change of sovereign in Assyria was frequently associated with rioting and revolts, which sometimes lasted quite a long time. Aei.'s accession is no exception, and there is nothing to suggest that the assumed troubles were more than a short-lived episode. The distribution of Aei.'s inscriptions in the major Babylonian cities (Babylon, Dilbat, Sippar and Nippur), the letter sent to him from Babylon (ABL 469), and the dating of the Nippur tablets by his years all suggest that he continued to rule Babylonia and exercised the same authority as his father had exercised there in his later years.

The circumstances of Aei.'s death and the transfer of power to his brother Sši. are so far unknown. There is no evidence that the latter was promoted by a *coup d'état* or that he deposed his brother and took his throne, as some scholars have suggested.[26] The statement in his inscriptions — that the gods selected him *ina birīt maššija/maššišu* — can hardly refer to Aei., because *birīt*

---

24. The closest parallel to the enthronement of Knd. is that of Bēl-ibni. He is described in the inscriptions of Sennacherib (Luckenbill 1924:54, line 54; 57, line 13) as "a native of Babylon who like a young puppy grew up in my palace" who was placed over the Babylonians as king. See Brinkman 1973:91.

25. Postgate 1969. The treaty that was imposed by an Assyrian king over three persons and was erroneously assigned to Sšl. should be assigned to Sši.; see Parpola and Watanabe 1988:xxxiii, 72–73.

26. Von Soden 1957:317–319; 1967:250–253; Tadmor 1962:241; 1983:52; Oates 1965:146–148; Reade 1970:4–5.

requires a plural object. Worthy of note are the following semantic parallels: (1) *ina birīt maššija uttûnnima* (Böhl 1936: 35, line 17), as compared with *ina puḫur aḫḫēja rabûti kīniš luttânima* (Borger 1956:16, line 14) and with *ina napḫar malikī kīniš luttânima* (Lie 1921:42, line 270); (2) *ina birīt maššišu kīniš ippalsūšuma* (Borger 1965:76, line 5), as compared with *ina kullat malikī kīniš ippalsanima* (Luckenbill 1924: 85, lines 3–4). Thus, it is clear that Sši. was selected "from among my/his equals," i.e., his brothers, who were also candidates for the Assyrian throne.[27]

Sši. ascended the throne in the middle of 627 BCE, shortly after the death of Knd. Tablets bearing his accession year have been discovered in Babylon, Sippar, Nippur and Uruk; it seems that he was regarded as King of Assyria and Babylonia. This situation, however, did not last long: At the beginning of the following year (626) his general, Sšl., rebelled and was able to take control of Babylon, Nippur and, probably, other North Babylonian cities. The background for the revolt is not clear. Sšl. was Aei.'s chief supporter, and during the latter's reign may well have been the strong man in the Empire. The transfer of power may have endangered his position, particularly because the new king decided to hold Assyria and Babylonia under his own direct control. Be that as it may, it is clear that Sšl. rebelled and tried to strengthen his own position in Babylonia against his rival's center of power in Assyria.

Was Npl., at this stage, Sšl.'s ally? This important question has no clear answer, because hardly anything is known of the early career of Npl. (Brinkman 1984:110 n. 551, with earlier literature). Hellenistic tradition — according to which Npl. was an official who had served under Sarakos (i.e., Sši.), before Npl. revolted and became King of Babylonia — is of questionable value. There is one tablet dated 22/VI of Npl.'s accession year and another from his 20th year that mentions 10/IV as his accession year (Brinkman 1984:110 n. 551, with earlier literature; Kennedy 1986:213 [T. 20.48]). These dates fall within the throne tenure of Sšl. Therefore, it may be suggested both that the two formed an alliance against the new ruler who had declared himself king of Assyria and Babylonia and that the scribes in various Babylonian cities were able to date tablets by either name. However, it is equally possible that Npl. had taken advantage of the Sšl.'s revolt to strengthen his own position, and, with the fall of the latter, Npl. had rebelled. The second alternative has the advantage of requiring fewer assumptions, but who knows?

27. Borger 1959:73 n. 41; Grayson 1972:167 (to line 5), 168; CAD B 250b and the parallel passages there. The reference to *māšu* in KAR 25 i 8 (see CAD M/1, 402a) also should be translated "equals" rather than "twins" (contra CAD).

There are no details concerning the armed struggle between Sši. and Sšl. or of the first stage of Npl.'s revolt, because our main source, chronicle BM 25127, begins shortly before 12/VI 626 (see below). From the concentration of tablets between the third and the fifth month of Sšl.'s accession year (626) and the total absence of any of a later date, it may be inferred that, around this time, Sšl. was crushed by Sši. Thus, when Npl.'s troops attacked Babylon shortly before 12/VI 626, they fought the garrison left behind by Sši. These two rivals remained in the historical arena, and their struggle, which lasted 15 years, decided the history of Mesopotamia for many years to come.

4. Chronicle BM 25127 and Nabopolassar's Rise to Power

626 BCE, the year in which three rivals fought for hegemony in Babylonia, was treated differently in various Babylonian chronological and chronographic texts. The Ptolemaic Canon assigned Shamash-shum-ukin and Knd. 42 years and Npl. 21 years, ignoring the problematic year altogether (Bickerman 1980:108; Grayson 1980–83:101). The Uruk King List assigned the year to Sši. and Sšl., thereby acknowledging the legitimacy of both Assyrian rivals. Chronicle BM 25127 refers to 626 as "the first year in which there was no king in the land" (line 14) (for the translation, see Brinkman 1984:110 n. 550), emphasizing that Npl. ascended the throne on 26/VIII. Npl.'s claim that months VIII-XII formed his *rēš šarrūti*, thus, was accepted, whereas the claims by the Assyrian contenders were rejected. In another Babylonian chronicle, the rebellions and the intensive fighting of 626 are described thus: "After Kandalānu, in the accession year of Nabopolassar, there were insurrections in Assyria and Akkad. There were hostilities and warfare continued" (Grayson 1975:132, lines 24–27). Year 626 is described as the *rēš šarrūti* of Npl. with no reference to his Assyrian rivals.

The interpretation of the first paragraph in chronicle BM 25127 (lines 1–17) is disputed among scholars. Following the interpretation of Wiseman, the editor of the chronicle, many scholars have assumed that the first paragraph refers to a single year (Wiseman 1956:5–7; Oates 1965:143–146; von Voigtlander 1963:18–20). Others, however, suggested that the events of two years were combined in this paragraph: lines 1–9 referring to year 627, and lines 10–17 refer to year 626 (van Dijk 1962:55–56; Brinkman 1984:108–110). Zawadzki (1988:48–54) recently defended the latter suggestion at length, and it should be examined in detail.

The basic fault of the two-years hypothesis is that it is not in accordance with the consistent structure of the chronicle: the customary horizontal dividing line between years and the introductory chronological phrase indicating a specific year are both missing (Borger 1965:70 n. 10; von Voigtlander 1963:33 n. 70; cf. Brinkman 1984:109 n. 546). Furthermore, the chronological statement in line 14 ("the first year in which there was no king in the land") refers to an aforementioned year-unit and fits only the one-year assumption. No explanation for these anomalies has been offered by the supporters of the two-years hypothesis, nor have they been able to fit the Babylonian tablet dated to 21/XII of Sši.'s accession year (which would be six months after the capture of the city by the troops of Npl.) into their chronological schemes. The arguments raised in support of their claim are: (1) the listing of one month out of order if the year refers only to 626 BCE, and (2) the sequence of events that can hardly be integrated within one year. In the following discussion, I will try to show, instead, that the sequence of events in the passage is not in accordance with the assumption that two years have been combined in it.

(A) According to the chronicle, the Babylonian army conquered the city of Babylon before 12/VI (lines 1–4), so Npl.'s enthronement in the city shortly afterwards (on the 26/VIII) would be only natural. Yet, according to the two-years hypothesis, he waited a very long time (15 months) before ascending the throne of the city, which had been occupied by his troops uninterruptedly.

(B) Assyrian campaigns were usually conducted during the spring and summer; only in exceptional situations were campaigns conducted in autumn or winter. Their offensive in the sixth and seventh months (lines 4–13) — as a continuation to the bitter summer fighting that culminated in the capture by the enemy of Babylon, the capital — is self-evident: an immediate attack on Babylon shortly after its capture is what one would expect in this situation. Yet, according to the two-years hypothesis, the Assyrians were very slow in their reaction to the fall of the city (before Tishri 627): they returned to Babylonia only in the second month of year 626, waited all summer long and attacked the occupied city in autumn, fourteen months after its fall.

(C) The Assyrian commanders were well aware of the fact that their best chance of quelling the rebellion was an immediate offensive, before their rival was able to strengthen his position and marshall his forces. Yet, according to the above hypothesis, no Assyrian campaign was conducted between Tishri 627, when the Assyrians failed to conquer Uruk (lines 7–9), and Tishri 626, when they were defeated near Babylon (lines 10–13); instead they gave their rival a whole year in which to prepare everything required for future battles.

It is clear that the two-years hypothesis creates many more problems than it solves and is best abandoned. As has been suggested by scholars, the chain of events as described in the chronicle is best explained by the assumption that the Assyrians (as well as the Babylonians) split their army and fought simultaneously in different places (Wiseman 1956:5–7; Oates 1965:143–146; von

Voigtlander 1963:18–20) This was not unusual: on many other campaigns the Assyrian army was also divided into task forces, each with its specific mission. Only the large-scale battles conducted in the open field demanded the concentration of all the task forces, to form a mass of power and to decide the battle.[28] We may conclude that lines 1–17 of the chronicle refer to the events that took place in year 626 and that should be interpreted within this chronological framework.

The opening lines of the chronicle are partly damaged, but may possibly be reconstructed as follows (Grayson 1975:87–88):

(1) [In the month of xx], when [Nabopolassar] had sent [troops t]o Babylon, at night
(2) [they entered the city an]d did battle within the city all day
(3) [(and) inflicted a defeat. The garri]son of Sin-šar-iškun fled to Assyria.
(4) He (Npl.) stationed [troops? with]in the city. On the twelfth day of the month of Elul the army of Assyria
(5) [went down], entered Shasnaku, set fire to the temple
(6) [(and) carried of the booty]. And in the month of Tishri the gods of Kish went to Babylon.
(7) [On the xx day the army] of Assyria went to Nippur . . .

Notes:

Line 2 was kindly collated for me by C.B.F Walker. In his words: "ù is possible but it is very damaged. There is certainly not enough *now* to justify Wiseman's *ki*."

Line 3: [*ŠI.ŠI GAR.MEŠ* [lú]*šu-lu*]-*tu*.

Line 4: [ERÍN.MEŠ *ina lib*]*bi*. The stationing of troops is what one expects after the conquest of the city.

Line 5: [*it-tar-da-nu*] (compare line 9).

Line 6: [NÍG.GA È.ME] (compare line 20). Note the similarity between lines 5–6 and lines 20–21 of the chronicle: in both cases the conquest and the plundering of a city brought about the transfer of the city gods to a safer place.

Line 7: For the restoration, see Borger 1965:63b.

The conquest of Babylon by the troops of Npl. is described in the first episode (lines 1–4). The garrison of Sši. must have been stationed in the city after his victory over Ššl. in the first half of year 626. The details of the fighting between Sši. and Ššl., as well as of Npl.'s early operations, were apparently described on another tablet that ends with the events of summer 626. Npl. took the city of Babylon by surprise, sending part of his army to conquer the city

28. On the battle in the open field, see Eph'al 1983:91–94.

while he himself attacked the city of Nippur. The Assyrians immediately reacted: A part of the army was sent to Nippur, they succeeded in driving Npl. from the city and pursued him up to Uruk, but failed to conquer the city (lines 4–9); a second task force was sent to re-conquer Babylon, but was defeated (lines 10–13). The Assyrian failure to conquer either Uruk or Babylon in autumn 626 had far-reaching consequences: It enabled Npl. to ascend the throne of Babylon (lines 14–15) and to consolidate his power in the land.

A curious remark appears in line 10 of the chronicle: "In the month of Iyyar the army of Assyria went down to Akkad." It interrupts the sequence of events and is either a scribal mistake or an intentional repetition of what has already been said, to emphasize that this was the same army that had operated (against Sšl?) at the beginning of the year.

In the years 625–624, the Assyrians tried, with little success, to quell the rebellion. They concentrated their efforts on northern Babylonia, in the areas of Sippar and Babylon. The chronicle of year 625 (Npl.'s first year) reports that on 17/I "a panic overcame the city (of Sippar), Šamaš and the gods of Shapazzu went to Babylon" (lines 18–19). On 21/II, the Assyrian army conquered Shallat, and on the previous day (20/II) "the gods of Sippar went to Babylon" (line 21)[29]. It is clear that the scribe erred in line 18 and that the reference was to the city of Sippar, against which the Assyrian onslaught was directed. Furthermore, it is evident that, in this campaign, the Assyrians conquered the city, as indicated by five Sippar tablets dated to Sši.'s second and third years (I/II year 2 to II/I year 3). This constitutes remarkable evidence for the tendentiousness of the chronicler, who had concealed the fact that Sippar was captured by the Assyrians, recording only that the gods of Sippar, most prominent of which was Šamaš, were brought to Babylon in fear of the impending Assyrian attack.

The tendentiousness of the author of the chronicle is revealed throughout his composition. It has already been noted that he refused to admit Assyrian rule in Babylonia in year 626, describing it as a year in which there was no king in the land (line 14). He further omitted from his description the failure of the Babylonians to conquer Nippur in Sši.'s third year, as is known from the "siege documents" unearthed in the city.[30] One wonders whether the

29. Grayson's emendation of the text in line 21 (1975:89:21 and note) is redundant. One should rather follow Wiseman 1956:52–53, line 21.

30. Oppenheim 1955. It is possible that Nippur was also besieged in Sši's second year. This may be inferred from an analysis of the last paragraph of Krückmann 1933:Nr. 35 = San Nicolò 1951:Nr. 63, a text briefly discussed in n. 10 above. The passage includes three different loans: lines 18–20 (sic!), 21–23 and 24–26. The latter section deals with a loan of one shekel of silver bearing no interest and to be repaid "at the opening of the gate." A part of

Assyrians conquered the city of Kish in the month of Tishri 626, shortly before their attack on Babylon in the same month, as might be inferred from the statement that the gods of the city "went" to Babylon (line 6). Acts of sacrilege by the Assyrians are deliberately emphasized (lines 4–6), and this impression is magnified by the references to the flight of the Babylonian gods for fear of the Assyrians (lines 6, 18–19, 21). Npl., on the other hand, acted piously and the city gods, which the Assyrians had previously despoiled, he returned to Susa (lines 16–17). The chronicler's pro-Babylonian outlook further explains why it is always Babylonian successes that are emphasized, whereas the many campaigns conducted by the Assyrians ended in failure. Although the data the writer presented may well be authentic, the selection of events that are introduced and the manner in which they are presented are remarkably pro-Babylonian and anti-Assyrian.[31]

5. Rebellion in the West and the Assyrian Withdrawal from Babylonia

Year 623 was crucial for the struggle between Assyria and Babylonia. Unfortunately, the chronicle's description of the chain of events is badly broken. Following is a suggested reconstruction of the text (Grayson 1975:89–90):

(29) [The third year]: On the eighth [day of the month xx] Der rebelled against Assyria. On the fifteenth day of the month of Tishri

(30) [Itti-ili? Attacked? Nippur?. In th]at year the king of Assyria and his army went down to Akkad,

(31) [captured? Der?, carried] off [the booty] and brought (it) into Nippur. After Itti-ili

(32) [he went, the city of Uruk? he rava]ged and stationed a garrison in Nippur.

(33) [In the month of xx PN] went upstream [from] *Ebir-nāri* and towards

(34) [the land? of Assyria? he proceeded. The city of G]N he ravaged and set out for Nineveh.

(35) [The army of Sin-šar-iškun, king of Assy]ria, who had come to battle against him

(36) [. . . whe]n they saw him they bowed down before him.

Notes:

Line 30: The restoration [MU].BI was suggested by Wiseman 1956:79, note on line 30.

the first loan was also free of interest (see CAD Ṣ 161a), but the remainder possibly bears the usual interest of 20%. A suggested translation: (18) "[x . . . silver are debited on PN] son of PN_2 without interest. (19) He will pay back [at the opening of the gat]e. (20) [x . . . silver to his debit] with interest, in the month Tammuz, the second year of Sši." The loan was given in the third month of 625 and at that time Nippur must have been under siege.

31. For the problem of source criticism of chronicle BM 21901, see Zawadzki 1988:114–143. In my opinion, however, the tendentiousness of the text should be attributed to the author of the chronicle and not to some hypothetical editor, as suggested by Zawadzki.

Line 31: [. . . *makkūra ušēṣ*]*î-ma*; compare line 20. For *arki*, compare line 8.

Line 32: For the restoration, see von Soden 1957:319; Borger 1965:64 b. For the restoration of the city name see below.

Line 33: The mention of *Ebir nāri* (i.e., the areas west of the Euphrates) indicates that the usurper came from Syria. The verb šaqû refers to the route along the Euphrates or along one of its tributaries (i.e., the Balih or the Habur rivers). Tentative restoration: [*ina* MN PN TA (KUR)] *e-bir* ÍD *iš-qa-am-ma.*

Line 34: Originally I restored [. . . [uru]*Ḫar-r*]*a-nu.* The broken sign was kindly collated by Walker, who noted (letter of 23 March 1988) that "the sign is as copied by Wiseman except that one can detect the lower side of a preceding horizontal at the middle level (i.e., as the first wedge of LA)." Although "[*r*]*a* is not altogether impossible," it is far from certain. The ravaged city was probably situated on the way from Syria to Nineveh.

Line 35: The reading [. . . *Aš*]-*šur* was confirmed by collation.

In year 623, the Assyrian army launched a major campaign into Babylonia in an effort to break the Babylonian power and to quell local rebellions. It was lead by the Assyrian king, i.e., Sši., who was not mentioned in the chronicle description of the 625–624 campaigns. The Assyrian success in the early stages of the campaign is recorded in the chronicle (lines 29–32). Furthermore, the drastic reduction in the number of tablets dated in this year, reflecting a regression in economic activity, is a good indication of the seriousness of the situation as a result of the Assyrian onslaught.

The offensive, however, was halted abruptly. The absence of the king and his troops from Assyria was exploited by a contender to the throne who attacked Sši. from the rear by launching a campaign against his capital. A hastily organized army was sent out against him, but surrendered without a battle (lines 35–36), and the rebel was able to reach Nineveh and ascend the throne. The chronicler designated him "an usurper king" (*šarru ḫamma'u*). This designation and the surrender of the Assyrian troops before him without a battle indicate that he was an Assyrian, possibly the commander of the Assyrian army in the West and not a foreign prince (Cavaignac 1957:28–29). Whether he was a son of the royal house of Assyria is still unknown.

For the years from late 623 to 617 we have no chronicle account and in order to gain some idea of the chain of events we must rely on the economic tablets. It is clear that Sši. was able to put down the rebellion, possibly after 100 days (line 39), and that he ruled Assyria until 612 BCE. The rebellion, however, had a serious effect on the Assyrian position, both in the west and in the southeast. It is no coincidence that Josiah's cultic reform began in the eighteenth year of the king, i.e., 622 BCE (2 Kgs. 22:3; 23:23); only at that point did he feel sufficiently secure to conduct a comprehensive purge throughout the kingdom and eradicate the "foreign" cults, including those that had come in under Assyrian political and cultural influence (Na'aman 1989:45–53, 68–69). It may be suggested further that the alliance between Sši. and Psammetichus King of Egypt as reflected in chronicle BM 21901 ("Gadd chronicle") was concluded in the late 620s; in these years, the Assyrians retreated from *Ebir-nāri*, and Egypt (gradually or rapidly) took their place. Sši. won both an assurance of military aid and free reign to handle the immediate threat in the southeast.

The rebellion of the western commander severely shook the Assyrian's position in Babylonia. According to the chronological scheme suggested above, Uruk came under siege not later than 4/VIII 622 (Sši. year 5). Zawadzki (1979:175–184) has demonstrated that *šattu ša edēl bābi* ("the year when the gate was closed") is identical to the fourth year of *edēl bābi*. He has shown further that all the local officials mentioned in the *edēl bābi* texts belonged to the pro-Sši. faction (1988:37). It is, thus, clear that the city was held by the troops of Sši. and was besieged by the army of Npl.

When did Uruk fall into the hands of the Assyrians? Tentatively, I suggest that it was conquered by Sši. in the course of his offensive of autumn 623 (lines 31–32 of the chronicle). According to this reconstruction Itti-ili, probably a commander of Npl., attacked the city of Nippur (lines 29–30) and when he retreated the Assyrian troops followed him and conquered Uruk (for a somewhat similar situation, compare lines 7–9 of the chronicle). The rebellion, however, turned things upside-down: Not only did the Assyrian offensive come to an immediate halt, but Sši. was forced to organize his troops and leave Babylonia to fight the usurper king. Thus, Npl. was able to besiege Uruk in the following year (622), not later than the 4/VIII (which is the date on the earliest "siege document").

As *šattu ša edēl bābi* refers to the same date as the fourth year of *edēl bābi*, it is reasonable to suggest that the "fourth year" refers to a king's year. To which of the two rival kings does this date refer? There is no definite answer to this question, but it seems preferable to assume that it refers to Npl. and that, in this indirect manner, the scribes were able to express their recognition of the legitimacy of the Babylonian king. There is one *edēl bābi* text that is dated the 16/V of Npl. year 5 and isolated texts that are dated during his reign (19/IX Npl. 6 and possibly 26/1 Npl. 4). In the fluid political situation of that time, these anomalies are understandable. Accordingly, I suggest that Uruk fell into Assyrian hands after the month of Tishri 623, was besieged by Npl. before 4/VIII 622 and fell into his hands at the end of 620. That the city was in his hands in 619 is evident from four tablets of his seventh year written in Uruk (the earliest is dated 14/III).

Sši.'s latest date from Nippur is 9/VI year 5. Significantly, this date falls shortly before the earliest "siege document" from Uruk. We cannot establish whether the city fell during this year or shortly afterward, because there is a gap in the Nippur tablets in years 621–607 BCE. The gap in documentation may well be explained by the assumption that Nippur was partly destroyed when it was conquered by Npl.'s troops. Thus, it is clear that Nippur and Uruk were captured by Npl. no later than the end of year 620; that since 619, Assyria had lost its last foothold in Babylonia; and Npl. was master of the entire land.[32]

6. Concluding Remarks

In conclusion I would like to emphasize the following four points:

(A) The history of the later years of the Assyrian Empire can be written on the basis of our knowledge of the history of the Empire. No conjectures of a double name, a co-regency, divided rule over parts of the Empire, or a rapid change of sovereignty over Babylonian cities is necessary to interpret the documents.

(B) The hypothesis of a long civil war in Assyria as an explanation for the fall of the Empire is not supported by the evidence.[33] There is no text that mentions a struggle between Aei. and Sši., though the background for the death of the former remains unknown. Rebellions that broke out following the deaths of rulers and the enthronement of their heirs are well-documented throughout the history of the Assyrian Empire, and the rebellion that broke out upon Sši.'s accession to the throne was no exception: It did not last long, and, in itself, it cannot be regarded as a decisive event that lead to the fall of the Empire. The rebellion that broke out in the fourth year of Sši. (623 BCE) was indeed a novelty, emerging as the direct outcome of the inability of the new king to crush the Babylonian revolt. It seems that the rebellion did not last long and was possibly put down after 100 days. It brought about the loss of the areas of *Ebir-nāri* and their transfer to Egypt in exchange for an alliance and military support, as well as an immediate deterioration of the Assyrian position in Babylonia. However, one must not forget that even before 623 most of Babylonia was in the hands of Npl.; the rebellion enabled him to conquer the Assyrian strongholds in central Babylonia and drive Assyria out of the country.

(C) The fall of Assyria was, in the first place, the result of her failure to solve the "Babylonian problem" and Sši.'s inability to crush the rebellion. For

32. For a reference to the "workmen of Enlil (i.e., Nippur)" in the early inscriptions of Nabopolassar, see Al-Rawi 1985:2, 4, line 31, with earlier literature.

33. For an emphasis on the long civil war as a central element in the fall of the Assyrian Empire, see von Soden 1957:318; 1967:242, 259–53. See also von Soden 1957:317–319; 1967: 250–253; Tadmor 1962:241; 1983:52; Oates 1965:146–148; Reade 1970:4–5.

many years, Babylonia had been a thorny problem for the Sargonids, and many different strategies were put into effect in an effort to provide a suitable solution to the problem. Rebellions, however, broke out again and again; the last one, that of Npl., succeeded where all former revolts had failed. Year after year, Sši. tried to quell the rebellion (626–623); his inability to accomplish it, the revolt of 623, and his subsequent withdrawal from Babylonia immediately endangered his own kingdom.[34]

However, Npl. was unable to vanquish Assyria and conquer it alone. At this point the Medes, the other major power directly involved in the fall of Assyria, entered the historical arena. For many years Assyria fought against Indo-Iranian groups appearing on its northern and eastern borders in an effort to prevent the emergence of major political formations that would endanger her borders. Her failure to prevent the crystallization of the Median kingdom had fatal consequences for Assyria's continued existence.

(D) Empires, by nature, are complex entities and the causes of their dissolution and fall are manifold. The Assyrian Empire was no different, and there are many aspects that could be brought into the discussion in connection with its fall. It has sometimes been suggested that Assyria suffered a gradual loss of pieces of her territory and that the loss of Babylonia was a link in a chain of territorial losses that had gradually begun in the later years of Ašb. However, there is no concrete evidence to support this assumption, common particularly among biblical historians in conjunction with the doubtful concept of Josiah's great kingdom.[35] It seems, instead, that Assyria was able to maintain most of her territory until the rise of Sši. and that the fall of the Empire was primarily the direct result of the emergence of the independent kingdoms of Babylonia and Media, willing and able to cooperate and unite forces against the common enemy. The disruption and fall of the first ancient Near Eastern empire may be described as a relatively short process of a military nature, which started with the Babylonian revolt of 626 BCE and came to completion with the fall of Nineveh in 612 BCE.

34. Noteworthy is the recently published document including a sort of declaration of war by a Babylonian king (possibly Npl.) against an Assyrian king (possibly Npl.). See Gerardi 1986.

35. Cross and Freedman 1953; Smirin 1952:11–35; Noth 1960:272–273; Tadmor 1966: 101–102; Malamat 1973:270–271; Cogan 1974:70–71; Spalinger 1978:49–51; Eph'al 1979:281–282; Miller and Hayes 1986:381–385. For a criticism of the assumption of an early Assyrian withdrawal from Palestine and of the concept of Josiah's great kingdom, see Na'aman 1989: 54, 45–71.

References

Al-Rawi, F.N.H. 1985. Nabopolassar's Restoration Work on the Wall *Imgur-Enlil* at Babylon. *Iraq* 47: 1–13.

Bickerman, E.J. 1980. *Chronology of the Ancient World*. London.

Böhl, F.M.Th. de Liagre. 1936. *Assyrische en Niew-Babylonische Oorkonden 1100-91 v. Chr.* (Mededeelingen uit de Leidsche verzameling van spijkerschrift-inscripties). Amsterdam.

Borger, R. 1956. *Die Inschriften Asarhaddons, Königs von Assyrien*. (AfO Beiheft 9). Graz. (Reprint 1967. Osnabrück).

Borger, R. 1957–58. Die Inschriften Asarhaddons (AfO Beiheft 9), Nachtrag und Verbesserungen. *AfO* 18: 113–118.

Borger, R. 1959. Mesopotamien in den Jahren 629–621 v. Chr. *Wiener Zeitschrift für die Kunde des Morgenlandes* 55: 62–76.

Borger, R. 1965. Der Aufstieg des neubabylonischen Reiches. *JCS* 19: 59–78.

Borger, R. 1967. *Handbuch der Keilschriftliteratur* I. Berlin.

Borger, R. 1969. Zur Datierung des assyrischen Königs Sinšumulišir. *Orientalia* 38: 237–239.

Borger, R. 1974–77. Zur Königsliste aus Uruk. *AfO* 25: 165–166.

Borger, R. 1975. *Handbuch der Keilschriftliteratur* III. Berlin.

Brinkman, J.A. 1976–80. Kandalānu. *RLA* V: 368–369.

Brinkman, J.A. 1973. Sennacherib's Babylonian Problem: An Interpretation. *JCS* 25: 89–95.

Brinkman, J.A. 1977. Notes on the Arameans and Chaldeans in Southern Babylonia in Early Seventh Century B.C. *Orientalia* 46: 304–325.

Brinkman, J.A. 1984. *Prelude to Empire. Babylonian Society and Politics, 747-627 B.C.* Philadelphia.

Brinkman, J.A. 1995. Notes on the Dates of Late Seventh-Century Babylonian Economic Texts. *Nouvelles Assyriologiques Brèves et Utilitaires* 1995/4: 96–97.

Brinkman, J.A. and Kennedy, D.A. 1983. Documentary Evidence for the Economic Base of Early Neo-Babylonian Society: A Survey of Dated Neo-Babylonian Economic Texts, 721–626 B.C. *JCS* 35: 1–90.

Brinkman, J.A. and Kennedy, D.A. 1986. Supplement to the Survey of Dated Neo-Babylonian Economic Texts, 721–626 B.C. *JCS* 38: 99–106.

Cavaignac, E. 1957. Sur un passage de la tablette B.M. 25127. *RA* 51: 28–29.

Cogan, M. 1974. 1974. Imperialism and Religion: Assyria, Judah and Israel in the Eighth and Seventh Centuries BCE. (Society of Biblical Literature Monograph Series 19). Missoula.

Cross, F. M. and Freedman, D. N. 1953. Josiah's Revolt against Assyria. *JNES* 12: 56–58.

Dietrich, M. 1970. *Die Aramäer Südbabyloniens in der Sargonidenzeit (700-648)*. (Alter Orient und Altes Testament 7). Kevelaer and Neukirchen-Vluyn.

van Dijk. J. 1962. Die Inschriftenfunde. In: Lenzen, H.J. XVIII. *Vorläufiger Bericht über die von dem Deutschen Archäologischen Institut und der Deutschen Orient-Gesellschaft aus Mitteln der Deutschen Forschungsgemeintschaft unternommenen Ausgrabungen in Uruk-Warka*. Berlin: 39–62.

Dubberstein, W. H. 1944. Assyrian-Babylonian Chronology (669–612 B.C.) *JNES* 3: 38–42.

Eph'al, I. 1979. Assyrian Dominion in Palestine. In: Malamat, A. ed. *The Age of the Monarchies: Political History*. (The World History of the Jewish People). Jerusalem: 276–289, 364–368.

Eph'al, I. 1983. On Warfare and Military Control in the Ancient Near Eastern Empires: A Research Outline. In: Tadmor, H. and Weinfeld, M. eds. *History, Historiography and Interpretation. Studies in Biblical and Cuneiform Literature.* Jerusalem: 88–106.

Falkner, M. 1952–53. Neue Inschriften aus der Zeit Sin-šarru-iškuns. *AfO* 16: 305–310.

Frame, G. 1982. Another Babylonian Eponymy. *RA* 76: 157–166.

Frymer-Kensky, T. 1985. *The Judicial Ordeal in the Ancient Near East.* (Ph.D. Thesis). Ann Arbor.

Gadd, C. J. 1958. The Harran Inscriptions of Nabonidus. *AnSt.* 8: 35–92.

Gerardi, P. 1986. Declaring War in Mesopotamia. *AfO* 33: 30–38.

Grayson, A.K. 1972. Cylinder C of Sîn-šarra-iškun, a New Text from Baghdad. In: Wevers, J.W. and Redford, D.B. eds. *Studies on the Ancient Palestinian World, Presented to Professor F.V. Winnett.* University of Toronto: 157–168.

Grayson, A.K. 1975. *Assyrian and Babylonian Chronicles.* (Texts from Cuneiform Sources 5). Locust Valley, NewYork.

Grayson, A.K. 1980. The Chronology of the Reign of Ashurbanipal. *ZA* 70: 227–245.

Grayson, A.K. 1980–83. Königslisten und Chroniken. B. Akkadisch. *RLA* VI: 86–135.

Hunger, H. 1968. *Babylonische und Assyrische Kolophone.* (Alter Orient und Altes Testament 2). Kevelaer and Neukirchen-Vluyn.

Kennedy, D.A. 1986. Documentary Evidence for the Economic Base of Early Neo-Babylonian Society. Part II: A Survey of Dated Neo-Babylonian Economic Texts, 626–605 B.C. *JCS* 38: 172–244.

Krückmann, O. 1933. *Neubabylonische Rechts- und Verwaltungstexte.* (Texte und Materialen der Frau Professor Hilprecht Collection in Eigentum der Universität Jena 2/3). Leipzig.

Kümmel, H.M. 1979. *Familie, Beruf und Amt im spätbabylonischen Uruk. Prosopographische Untersuchumgen zu Berufsgruppen des 6. Jahrhundert v. Chr. in Uruk.* Berlin.

Leichty, E. 1983. An Inscription of Aššur-etel-ilani. *JAOS* 103: 217–220.

Leichty, E. 1986. *Catalogue of the Babylonian Tablets in the British Museum. VI: Tablets from Sippar* 1. London.

Leichty, E., Finkelstein J.J. and Walker, C.B.F. 1988. *Catalogue of the Babylonian Tablets in the British Museum. VIII: Tablets from Sippar* 3. London.

Leichty, E. and Grayson, A.K. 1987. *Catalogue of the Babylonian Tablets in the British Museum. VII: Tablets from Sippar* 2. London.

Lie, A.G. 1921. *The Inscriptions of Sargon II King of Assyria.* Part I: *The Annals.* Paris.

Luckenbill, D. D. 1924. *The Annals of Sennacherib.* (Oriental Institute Publications 2). Chicago.

Malamat, A. 1973. Josiah's Bid for Armageddon. *Journal of the Ancient Near Eastern Society of Columbia University* 5: 267–279.

Millard, A.R. 1965. The Assyrian Royal Seal Type Again. *Iraq* 27: 12–16.

Miller, J.M. and Hayes, J.H. 1986. *A History of Ancient Israel and Judah.* Philadelphia.

Na'aman, N. 1984. Statements of Time-Spans by Babylonian and Assyrian Kings and Mesopotamian Chronology. *Iraq* 46: 115–123.

Na'aman, N. 1989. The Town Lists of Judah and Benjamin and the Kingdom of Judah under Josiah. *Zion* 54: 17–71. (Hebrew).

Nassouhi, E. 1924–25. Prisme d'Assurbânipal daté de sa trentième année, provenant du temple de Gula à Babylone. *Archiv für Keilschriftforschung* 2: 97–106.

Nies, J.B. and Keiser, C.E. 1920. Historical, Religious and Economic Texts and Antiquities. (Babylonian Inscriptions in the Collection of J.B. Nies 2). New Haven.

Noth, M. 1960. *The History of Israel.* London.

Oates, J. 1965. Assyrian Chronology, 631–612 B.C. *Iraq* 27: 135–159.
Oppenheim, A. L. 1955. "Siege Documents" from Nippur. *Iraq* 17: 69–89.
Parpola, S. and Watanabe, K. 1988. *Neo-Assyrian Treaties and Loyalty Oaths.* (State Archives of Assyria 2). Helsinki.
Pinches, T.G. 1939–40. Ein babylonischer Eponym. *AfO* 13: 51–54.
Postgate, J.N. 1969. *Neo-Assyrian Royal Grants and Decrees.* (Studia Pohl, Series Maior 1). Rome.
Reade, J. 1970. The Accession of Sinsharishkun. *JCS* 23: 1–9.
Sachs, A.J. 1953. The Late Assyrian Royal-Seal Type. *Iraq* 15: 167–170.
San Nicolò, M. 1951. *Babylonische Rechtsurkunden des ausgehenden 8. und des 7. Jahrhunderts v. Chr.* (Abhandlungen der Bayerischen Akademie der Wissenschaften, philosophisch-historische Klasse, Neue Folge Heft 34). München.
Seux, M.-J. 1967. *Épithètes royales Akkadiennes et Sumériennes.* Paris.
Shea, W.H. 1971. An Unrecognized Vassal King of Babylon in the Early Achaemenid Babylonia (I). *Andrews University Seminary Studies* 9: 51–67.
Smirin, S. 1952. *Josiah and His Age.* Jerusalem. (Hebrew).
Smith, S. 1928. Dating by Ashurbanipal and Kandalanu. *Journal of the Royal Asiatic Society of Great Britain and Ireland*: 622–626.
von Soden, W. 1957. Review of Wiseman, D.J.: Chronicles of Chaldean Kings (626–556 B.C.) in the British Museum, London 1956. *Wiener Zeitschrift für die Kunde des Morgenlandes* 53: 316–321.
von Soden, W. 1967. Aššuretellilāni, Sinšarriškun, Sinšum(u)lišer und die Ereignisse im Assyrerreich nach 635 v. Chr. *ZA* 58: 241–255.
Spalinger, A.J. 1978. Psammetichus, King of Egypt: II. *Journal of the American Research Center in Egypt* 15: 49–57.
Streck, M. 1916. *Assurbanipal und die letzten assyrischen Könige bis zum Untergang Niniveh's* I-III. (Vorderasiatische Bibliothek 7). Leipzig.
Tadmor, H. 1962. Tri poslednich desatiletija Assirii. *Proceedings of the 25th International Congress of Orientalists* 1. Moskva: 240–241.
Tadmor, H. 1965. The Inscriptions of Nabunaid: Historical Arrangement. In: Güterbock, H.G. and Jacobsen, T. eds. *Studies in Honor of Benno Landsberger on his Seventy-Fifth Birthday.* (Assyriological Studies 16). Chicago: 351–363.
Tadmor, H. 1966. Philistia under Assyrian Rule. *BA* 29: 86–102.
Tadmor, H. 1983. Autobiographical Apology in the Royal Assyrian Literature. In: Tadmor, H. and Weinfeld, M. (eds.) *History, Historiography and Interpretation. Studies in Biblical and Cuneiform Literature.* Jerusalem: 36–57.
von Voigtlander, E. 1963. *A Survey of Neo-Babylonian History* (Ph.D. Thesis). University of Michigan.
Weidner, E.F. 1952–53. Keilschrifttexte nach Kopien von T.G. Pinches. Aus dem Nachlass veröffentlicht und bearbeitet. 1. Babylonische Privaturkunden aus dem 7. Jahrhundert v. Chr. *AfO* 16: 35–46.
Wiseman, D.J. 1956. *Chronicles of Chaldean Kings (626–556 B.C.) in the British Museum.* London.
Zawadzki, S. 1979. The Economic Crisis in Uruk during the Last Years of Assyrian Rule in the Light of the So-Called Nabu-ušallim Archives. *Folia Orientalia* 20: 175–184.
Zawadzki, S.1988. *The Fall of Assyria and Median-Babylonian Relations in Light of the Nabopolassar Chronicle.* Poznan-Delft.

The Kingdom of Judah Under Josiah[1]

Introduction

King Josiah acceded to the throne of Judah following the murder of Amon (who had reigned only briefly) by his courtiers. The court rebellion was quickly suppressed; following the execution of the conspirators, Josiah, the young son of the late ruler, was crowned at the tender age of eight (2 Kgs. 21: 23–24; 22:1). It may be assumed that during the first years of his reign, the young king was supported by his mother and by those circles that had ensured his accession, and that he assumed full authority only upon reaching maturity. He reigned for 31 year (639–609 BCE), and was killed at Megiddo by Pharaoh Necho II of Egypt.

Whereas Josiah's accession to the throne, as well as his death and the crowning of his heir, Jehoahaz (2 Kgs. 23:29–30; 2 Chr. 35:20–24; 36:1), are described in considerable detail, our information on his foreign policy, his relations with both neighboring countries and the great powers then struggling for hegemony throughout the fertile crescent is drawn entirely from non-Biblical sources. Following Sennacherib's campaign against Judah during Hezekiah's reign, in 701 BCE, Assyria is not mentioned at all in the Book of Kings; also, Egypt did not take part in the chain of events before the episode of Josiah's death. None of Judah's near neighbors, in fact, is mentioned in the description of Josiah's time. That description focusses on the restoration of the Temple and the discovery of the "Book of the Law," as well as on the reform enacted by Josiah throughout his kingdom; the passages in question include little on the extent of his kingdom and/or his activities during his reign (2 Kgs. 23:8a, 15, 19–20; 2 Chr. 34:6). This difficulty is aggravated by the total lack of details concerning the state of affairs in Judah between Sennacherib's campaign in 701 and Josiah's coronation in 639 BCE. It should be remembered that Sennacherib's campaign was a disastrous event for the kingdom, bringing about the destruction of dozens of its cities and the deportation of many thousands of its inhabitants. Vast districts were grievously damaged;

1. Reprinted with permission. *Tel Aviv* 18 (1991), 3–71.

their resettlement was a slow and gradual process. Many of the refugees certainly fled to the capital, Jerusalem, which, since the eighth century, had become a metropolis immeasurably larger (in both area and population) than any other city in Judah. The campaign greatly increased the degree of subjugation to Assyria, as well as of Assyrian involvement in the internal affairs of the kingdom, and gave rise to significant "foreign" influences in the spheres of cult and culture. Sennacherib's campaign represented a historical turning point of the utmost significance to the Kingdom of Judah, following which the kingdom underwent a series of profound demographic, social, economic, and cultural changes. The paucity of information on the six decades between Sennacherib's campaign and Josiah's accession, and on the latter king's activities, present a difficulty when attempting to sketch the outline and contemporary history of Josiah's kingdom.

The limited nature of the source material has not prevented scholars from investigating the period of Josiah's rule, due to its crucial importance in the history of the Jewish People. It is commonly accepted that "the Book of the Law" (2 Kgs. 22:8, 11) — otherwise known as "the Book of the Covenant" (23:2, 21) — was written in the seventh century BCE, perhaps even during Josiah's early reign, and that its composition gave rise to a comprehensive cultic reform throughout the kingdom and to the initial widespread influence and literary activity of the Deuteronomistic school. The years of Josiah's reign constitute an important starting point for the study of developments in Jewish religion, cult, law, and literature and, therefore, have gained the attention of a considerable number of scholars, starting in the earliest days of Biblical research. The scarcity of Biblical data invited a wide variety of opinions concerning the extent of the kingdom, its internal structure, economy, etc. Some scholars have concluded that Josiah's kingdom consisted mainly of the area between the Beer-sheba Valley and Bethel; others, by contrast, have suggested that Josiah attempted to restore the kingdom of David in all its glory and that he controlled much of the Cisjordanian areas.

In the framework of this Introduction, let me emphasize the importance of the archaeological findings to the discussion of Josiah's kingdom and the vast progress made in this field since the early 1970s. It was the new excavations and surveys conducted throughout the area of the Kingdom of Judah that first pointed out the destructive consequences of Sennacherib's campaign and the many changes that occurred in the kingdom during the seventh century BCE. The considerable progress made in archaeological research is reflected in the discussion of the *lmlk* seal impressions. For many years, dating these impressions to the seventh century was accepted widely and, specifically, to Josiah's day. For that reason, archaeologists tended to date the layers of settlement in which such impressions were unearthed to the seventh century, and to use their distribution as a basis for determining the extent of Josiah's kingdom. However, recent studies have indicated that the jars bearing the *lmlk* seal impressions were manufactured in the late eighth century BCE and that their production and distribution apparently are related to the preparations for Sennacherib's campaign against Judah. These conclusions led to the redating of levels in many sites in Judah and eliminated the basis for the assumption that any direct connection might have existed between the *lmlk* jars and Josiah's kingdom. These stratigraphic conclusions also provided additional clarification of the relationships between the Kingdom of Judah and its near neighbors in the area of material culture. It appears that, in the eighth century BCE, the borders of Judah were largely closed, and contacts with neighboring states to the east and west were limited. On the other hand, in the seventh century, following the *pax Assyriaca*, the borders were opened, and the available evidence of material culture attests to manifold contacts with various regions within the Assyrian empire (Zimhoni 1990:47–49). Thus, recent archaeological research has provided us with new data pertinent to the study of this period — data that were not at the disposal of those scholars who discussed Josiah's kingdom in the past — enabling a re-evaluation of the written sources. It appears that, by re-integration of all these sources, we may now suggest a fairly new picture of Josiah's kingdom — including its territorial extent, population, economic power, and international status — a picture based on firmer foundations than previous reconstructions.

It is not my intention to deal here with all the aspects of Josiah's kingdom. Religious and cultic matters within the kingdom, as well as the development of the Deuteronomistic school and its effect on the reform, require extensive discussions that have no place within the present work. It is hoped that the conclusions reached in this study will provide a sounder basis for the study of these central issues; primarily, however, my intention is to review Josiah's kingdom and its contemporary history in a new historical perspective and, thus, to attempt to make an additional contribution to the study of the last hundred years of the Kingdom of Judah.

I. Josiah's Kingdom and the Town Lists of Judah and Benjamin

1. Previous Discussions of the Town Lists

Much of the research on the town lists in the Book of Joshua is founded on A. Alt's basic work, "Judas Gaue unter Josia" (Alt 1925). In that article, Alt proposed the separation of the town lists from the system of borders and the independent discussion of each of these two groups. Although he dates the system of tribal allotments at the end of the period of the Judges, he felt that the town lists of the southern tribes (Josh.15:21–62; 18:21–28; 19:2–8, 40–46) more properly belonged to King Josiah's time. In his opinion, originally there had existed a single list encompassing all the towns within the Kingdom of Judah; a later editor had divided that list into four parts and assigned each section to the tribe within whose inheritance it was geographically located. Due to inattention on the part of that editor, certain place names are mentioned twice, as belonging to two different tribes (Zorah and Eshtaol appear within the inheritances of Dan and Judah; Kiriath-jearim and Beth-arabah, within the allotments of Judah and Benjamin). The towns of Simeon are also mentioned in the town list of Judah; the two lists appear to have a common source. Alt considered the internal division of the list into sections, separated by a count of towns in each section, as reflecting the array of districts — 12 in all — within the Kingdom of Judah (Alt 1925:105–106). He also attempted to ascertain the course of development of each district by examining its affinity to the patterns of settlement existing in Late Bronze Age Canaan and the settlement in the mountain regions during the Iron Age I. The array of ten districts first developed after the division of the kingdom; the conquered districts of Bethel and Ekron (the inheritance of Dan) were added during Josiah's reign. Some of the districts persisted into the Persian period and served as administrative districts of the province of Yehud.

The article by Cross and Wright (1956), published some thirty years later, constitutes an additional milestone in the study of the town lists. Cross and Wright maintained that the town list of Dan matches the gap left between the borders of neighboring tribes (Judah, Benjamin, Ephraim). This list includes a passage comprising a border description and, thus, belongs to the "mixed" lists in which border descriptions were appended to town lists. The appearance of Zorah and Eshtaol in both the town list of Judah and the inheritance of Dan also indicates that those towns do not belong to the same boundary system. In view of the above, Cross and Wright reached the conclusion that the town list of Dan should be considered as part of the array of tribal allotments and, thus, should be detached from the town list of the other southern tribes (Judah, Simeon, Benjamin). The scope of towns reviewed in those three lists corresponds to the area of the Kingdom of Judah; the lists themselves were originally included in a document written in King Jehoshaphat's day, describing the division of the kingdom into twelve districts. In contrast to Alt, who appended the wilderness district of Judah (Josh. 15:61–62) to the eastern district of Benjamin (Josh. 18:21–24), Cross and Wright distinguished between the two, classifying them as neighboring districts. In this manner, they also reached a total of twelve districts for the kingdom.

Cross and Wright's statement that the town list of Dan should be detached from the other southern town lists has been generally accepted by scholars.[2] Several scholars have later tended to consider it as independent of the boundary system (B. Mazar 1960; Strange 1966; Aharoni 1979:311–313; Galil 1985; Kallai 1986:361–371). I have attempted to show that Cross and Wright's conclusions are correct and that there are weighty reasons in favor of appending that list to the system of tribal allotments (Na'aman 1986a:75–117).

An article by Kallai, published two years after Cross and Wright's study, raises an exceptional hypothesis: the division of the southern towns into four separate lists, each of which belonging to a different period in the history of Israel (Kallai-Kleinmann 1958; Kallai 1986:372–404). The principal justification given for this division is that of the duplications in the town lists, which would never have occurred in a single, orderly system of records. In view of this consideration, Kallai believes that the town list of Simeon was drawn up during the reign of King David; that of Dan, under King Solomon; that of Benjamin, under King Abijah; and that of Judah, under King Hezekiah.

The separation of the town lists of Dan and Simeon from the other town lists is accepted by many scholars; moreover, the differences of opinion regarding their extent and dates are not my concern in the framework of this article. However, the definition of the town list of Benjamin as an independent section in its own right, reflecting a special historical situation, changes the entire picture. If this were the case, we could no longer speak of one ancient document that includes all the towns in the kingdom, but, rather, of documents of varying origin and date, assembled and compiled by a later editor.

The date specified by Kallai for the town list of Benjamin (Josh. 18:21–28) is puzzling. In another work published at about the same time, Kallai reconstructed the extent of the borders of Josiah's kingdom; set its northern border (in the first stage of that king's expansionist activity) at Geba-Ephraim, north of Bethel and Ophrah; and claimed that this border became stable in the late First Temple period (Kallai 1960:74–78). This northern border is identical in every detail to the northern border of the town list of Benjamin, as traced by Kallai in his first article (see Kallai 1986:398–404 and map no. 2). It is difficult to understand why Kallai ascribed the town list to Abijah (it is doubtful whether that king had undertaken a campaign to the Bethel area, as related in 2 Chr. 13 — [Klein 1983] - and he certainly did not annex it to his territory) and not to Josiah, as his own discussion (and Alt's basic work) would seem to warrant.

2. Auld (1980:52–67) claimed that the lists of towns and tribal allotments of the ten tribes west of the Jordan were composed at the same time, in the seventh century BCE. Auld, however, contented himself with a textual discussion, and did not deal with any of the topographical or geographical-historical problems related to those lists.

Another of Kallai's innovations is his ordering of the Shephelah sections listed in Josh. 15:33–44. Alt (1925:105–106, 117), and later, Noth (1953:91, 95–96; also Cross and Wright 1956:213, 217–219) believed that the three Shephelah sections were listed in order from north to south. By contrast, Kallai claimed that the third and fourth sections were located alongside each other on the north-south axis: the third (Josh. 15:37–41) in the lower Shephelah to the west and the fourth (Josh. 15:42–44) in the higher Shephelah to the east (Kallai-Kleinmann 1958:155–156; Kallai 1986:379–386). Both these proposals have additional adherents and will be discussed further below.

Additional studies of the southern town lists, published since the early 1960s, primarily have addressed the problem of identification of individual towns — a significant factor in the analysis of the lists. The dating of the lists has remained controversial; the arguments advanced by these studies have neither changed the situation, nor enabled a decisive settlement of the question. Scholars are generally agreed upon two basic assumptions: that the lists reflect the original documents from whence they were extracted and that, in their present form, they portray the administrative districts of the kingdom. This concept was expanded upon in the works of Galil, who divided all the sections appearing in the hills of Judah, the Shephelah of Judah, and the northernmost Shephelah (in the inheritance of Dan) into small sub-districts, each of which included several settlements and functioned as an administrative section (Galil 1984; 1985; 1987).

Notwithstanding the great number of discussions of the southern town lists, several of the basic problems have not yet been solved, and a number of central questions are still the subjects of dispute. It now seems possible to discuss these questions yet again; to present arguments not yet advanced in prior publications; and, by means of these arguments, to reach a better understanding of the lists. The problems that I intend to address are as follows:

(1) Do the town lists of Judah and Benjamin constitute two lists dating from different times, or were they originally part of a single list?

(2) Does the internal division of these lists really reflect the administrative system of the Kingdom of Judah?

(3) In what order are the sections of the Shephelah towns arranged?

(4) To which period should the town lists of Judah and Benjamin be dated?

The answers to these questions are complex and call for balanced, multifaceted discussion. It seems, nevertheless, that such a discussion can reach clear conclusions concerning the dating, composition, and nature of the town lists, thus enabling a better use of the lists in historical research.

2. *The Town Lists of Judah and Benjamin and the System of Tribal Allotments*

Two towns are mentioned twice in the town lists of Judah and Benjamin: Beth-arabah (Josh. 15:61; 18:22) and Kiriath-jearim (Josh. 15:60; 18:28). Some scholars have claimed that this duplication exists only in one instance — that of Beth-arabah — and that the second instance actually refers to two separate settlements: Kiriath-jearim in Judah (Josh. 15:60) and Gibeath-kiriath-jearim in Benjamin (Josh. 18:28) (Mazar [Maisler] 1947:319; Mazar 1976:271; Aharoni 1959:228–229; 1979:350–351, 356; Kallai 1960:34–35, n. 82; 1986:134–135, 400, n. 152,403; Galil 1984:222). This question should be investigated before discussing the affinity between the two groups of towns.

The argument in favor of distinction between the two settlements is based on the fragmented passage of Josh. 18:28, whose original Hebrew reads *gbʿt qryt ʿrym ʾrbʿ ʿśrh wḥṣryhn* and is translated in the Revised Standard Version as "Gibeah and Kiriath-jearim — fourteen cities with their villages." Scholars have postulated that the document originally read *gbʿt qryt <yʿrym> ʿrym . . .* and was subsequently miscopied. Corroboration for this claim is found in the mention of "Gibeah" in the account of the Ark of the Covenant, which was halted at Kiriath-jearim and brought up from that town by David (1 Sam. 7:1; 2 Sam. 6:3). This hypothesis, however, engenders great difficulty. In the tradition concerning the Ark of the Covenant, the names of Kiriath-jearim and Gibeah have obviously been interchanged (compare 2 Sam. 6:2–3). It appears that "Gibeah" (literally, "[the] hill") was the name used for the cultic site in Kiriath-jearim, where the Ark of the Covenant was placed — in accordance with the custom by which cultic sites in ancient Israel were given distinct names (Na'aman 1987a:19–21). The Gibeah mentioned in the Ark of the Covenant cycle has nothing to do with the Gibeah cited in the town list of Benjamin. Moreover, the versions of the LXX of Josh. 18:28 read: *wgbʿt wqryt yʿrym ʿrym . . .* (in the A and Luciani manuscripts), or: *wqryt wgbʿt yʿrym ʿrym . . .* (in the B manuscript). The hypothetical existence of a settlement called "Gibeath-Kiriath-jearim" has not been corroborated by any ancient source. As this name is not mentioned in the Bible, and especially as tripartite place names are extremely rare in the toponomy of Palestine, this possibility should be viewed as dubious. It, thus, seems best to assume (as do most scholars) that the original document mentioned two places — Gibeah and Kiriath-jearim (Steuernagel 1900:224–225; Holmes 1914:68; Albright 1924b: 32; Noth 1953:108). In discussing the affinity between the town lists of Judah and Benjamin, the duplication of the names Beth-arabah and Kiriath-jearim should he clarified.

In my opinion, the reason for these duplications lies in the efforts made by the author of the Book of Joshua to adapt the town lists to the border between Judah and Benjamin as it appears in the description of the tribal allotments. In the latter system, Beth-arabah was included within the inheritance of Judah, Jerusalem was considered part of Benjamin, and Kiriath-jearim was part of Judah. On the other hand, the Jericho area, including Beth-arabah and Hoglah to the south, became part of the Northern Kingdom until its collapse. Jerusalem, as the capital of the Kingdom of Judah, gradually grew in size and importance. During the eighth and seventh centuries BCE, it expanded considerably, becoming the largest city in the kingdom; at its zenith, its area and population were many times larger than those of any other city. Metropolitan Jerusalem, with its surrounding agricultural areas, must have encompassed vast areas of the tribal inheritances of both Judah and Benjamin. By contrast, Kiriath-jearim, which appears in the system of tribal allotments as a sort of salient at the northern edge of the inheritance of Judah, formed a ramified network of connections with neighboring towns to the north, until it was eventually considered as part of Benjamin; for this reason, it appears alongside the towns of Benjamin in lists composed at the time (Josh. 9:17b;[3] 18: 28; Ezra 2:25; Neh. 7:29). When the author of the Book of Joshua attempted to integrate the document containing the town lists into his work, he encountered a series of discrepancies between the system of tribal allotments and the situation prevailing in his own day. In an effort to make the ancient border conform to the later array of settlements, the author apparently reworked the town list in the following manner:

(1) Beth-arabah and Hoglah, which, as stated above, belonged to the Northern Kingdom, were listed in the document among the eastern towns of Benjamin. To adapt the phrasing of the document to the ancient border, he added Beth-arabah to the town list of Judah, thus, creating the duplication mentioned above.

(2) Jerusalem was added to the town list of Benjamin, in accordance with the ancient border, although at the time the town list was composed, the city was already totally detached from the ancient district of Benjamin.

(3) Kiriath-jearim was listed in the document among the western towns of Benjamin. In an attempt to adapt the town list to the ancient border, the author appended Kiriath-jearim to Rabbah, its southern neighbor in the hill country, thus, creating a miniature "district" comprising only two towns,

3. It appears to me that this later reality is reflected in Josh 9:17b ("Now their cities were Gibeon, Chephirah, Beeroth, and Kiriath-jearim") and that this half-verse was stuck into the tale of the Gibeonites at a later date, apparently in the post-exilic period. The fact that very little pottery from the Iron Age I was found at Khirbet Kefireh, the site of Chephirah, despite the painstaking survey conducted there, is discussed by Vriezen (1975).

which scholars have found so difficult to explain.[4] Thus, the town of Kiriath-jearim appears twice: once in Benjamin, to which it belonged in the author's day, and once in Judah, to which it had belonged in former times.

The effort to adapt the area of Judah as defined in the system of tribal allotments to the town list also elucidates the appearance of Philistine cities (Josh. 15:45–47) among the towns of Judah — a fact that some scholars have had difficulty in explaining and who have attempted to relate to special historical circumstances. The author of the system of tribal allotments appended the Philistine coast to the area of Judah (although, in reality, it was never a part of Judah), as part of an overall trend to expand and glorify his tribe (Na'aman 1986a:62–66). The town list of Judah in the original document did not, of course, include the Philistine cities. For the sake of congruence between the two systems, the author of the Book of Joshua also appended the Philistine cities to the town list of Judah.

It is not impossible that the attachment of Kedesh to the cities of the south (Josh. 15:23) — assuming that town is to be identified with Kadesh-barnea — was added to adapt the southern border of the inheritance of Judah to the town list. (For additional discussion of the status of Kadesh-barnea, see Section 8, below.)

Another — by no means coincidental — similarity between the boundary system (and the traditions of conquest as set forth in the Book of Joshua) and the town list lies in the appearance of archaic appellations beside the names of some towns: "Kerioth-hezron (that is, Hazor)" (Josh. 15:25); "Kiriath-sannah (that is, Debir)" (Josh. 15:49) (Orlinsky 1939); "Kiriath-arba (that is, Hebron)" (Josh. 15:54); "Kiriath-baal (that is, Kiriath-jearim)" (Josh. 15:60); "Ephrathah (that is, Bethlehem)" (LXX, following Josh. 15:59, in a district

4. A number of scholars have solved the problem of the tiny two-town section by attaching it to the western section of the towns of Benjamin (Alt 1925:105–106; Noth 1953: 91, 99; Cross and Wright 1956:213, 221–222; Galil 1984:219–221). By contrast, other scholars have included the two towns in the framework of a separate, independent district (Aharoni 1979:346–355; Kallai 1986:394–395 and map no. 2; but, compare Kallai 1971:251). The attempt to identify Rabbah within the northern Shephelah is dubious, as is the addition of areas in the Shephelah to the framework of the mountain districts (Aharoni 1969:137–141;1979:346–355; Galil 1984:219–223). The town lists make a clear and sharp distinction between the mountain districts and those of the Shephelah, and there is no justification for the formation of an artificial district including both mountain and Shephelah towns. Rabbah is to be sought in the mountain district, not far from Kiriath-jearim. In this connection, let me recall the B manuscript of the LXX mentioning the town of Sotheba, which may be identified with Ṣubah, southeast of Kiriath-jearim (Kallai 1986:392–395).

omitted in the Hebrew);[5] "Jebus (that is, Jerusalem)" (18:28). We cannot assume that these archaic appellations appeared to the original document (or, more correctly, administrative list) from which the author of the Book of Joshua obtained the town names. The additional appellations are to be ascribed to the author of the Book of Joshua, who attempted to reconcile the town list with descriptions appearing in the system of tribal allotments, thus instilling in the former an odour of antiquity.

Finally, let us consider the different attitudes evidenced by the author toward the tribes of Judah and Ephraim. While the inheritance of Judah is reflected in its complete and unabridged dimensions, in accordance with its description in the system of tribal allotments, the author does not follow the same policy with that of Ephraim, and does not "correct" reality by concealing the encroachment upon its territory by the northern towns of Benjamin.[6] This preferential attitude toward the tribe of Judah is also reflected in additional descriptions in the Book of Joshua (see Na'aman 1986a:62–66), thus, indicating the tendentiousness of its author.

Generally speaking, it seems that the author's tendentiousness and "literary" considerations played an important role in the formulation of the town lists of Judah and Benjamin as they now stand. The lists are not exact copies of administrative documents incorporated word for word into the Book of Joshua, as Kallai assumed in his proposal to separate them and assign them different dates.[7] Moreover, the practice of reworking ancient documents is familiar to us from the analysis of other lists in the Book of Joshua and other books of the Bible; the town lists discussed here are not the only topographi-

5. For the reconstruction of the missing section in Josh. 15:60 see Hollenberg 1881:99–100; Steuernagel 1900:214; Noth 1953:99; Kallai 1986:392–393.

6. Auld (1980:87, n. 50) examined the possibility that the border of the tribal allotment of Benjamin described in Josh. 18:12–14 is secondary to the town list of Benjamin. This is not the appropriate framework for a detailed discussion of this original proposition. However, it should be emphasized that the problem of incompatibility between the northern border of the tribal allotment of Benjamin and the scope of the town list is not solved in this way: if the town list were indeed at the disposal of the author who traced the border of Benjamin, why is there no compatibility between the two? Concerning the theory that the southern border of tribal allotment of Benjamin is no more than an adaptation of the northern border of that of Judah, see Schmitt 1980:39–42; Na'aman 1986a:102–104.

7. One of Kallai's basic hypotheses, reflected in all his works, is that documents that served the administration of the kingdom were reproduced in the Bible word for word, with no attempt at modification or adaptation to suit the author's tendencies. This approach is also reflected in his discussions of the town lists in the Book of Joshua (Kallai-Kleinmann 1958; Kallai 1986:346–348). This basic hypothesis (which Kallai shares with other scholars) is criticized by Auld (1980:37–42). It is important to stress that a simplistic approach of this type is not at all appropriate to a discussion of the Biblical material and

cal documents to have undergone reworking in view of literary and theological considerations.[8]

Given the above conclusions, we may again examine the affinity between the town lists of Judah and Benjamin. As it seems, we have to reject the assumption that, at the time of composition of the original lists, the ancient division still existed between the two main sections comprising the kingdom (Judah and Benjamin), and that later administrative town lists were drawn up on that basis. This assumption constitutes the basis for Kallai's hypothesis that the lists of Judah and Benjamin should be separated and assigned to different periods. The very assumption that the author had in his possession a separate list of towns within the area of ancient Judah, at least two hundred years after the establishment of the kingdom and the merging of Judah and Benjamin, seems far from plausible. The separation between the two sections is artificial and was implemented by the author of the book. Apparently, a single town list had existed originally, covering the entire Kingdom of Judah, and the author, who ascribed that list to Joshua's time — a period governed (according to his description) by tribal regime — was responsible for dividing it between the tribal allotments of Judah and Benjamin. Any discussion of the original town lists should be based on the combination of both lists: Josh. 15:21–62 and 18:21–28.

3. *The Districts of the Kingdom of Judah and the Town Lists*

Garfinkel presented arguments against the concept that the town lists reflect the administrative districts of the Kingdom of Judah (Garfinkel 1987). He argued that administrative procedure, as reflected in documents discovered at Arad, Ḥorvat 'Uza, Lachish, and Tel Beer-sheba, is not in line with the commonly held interpretation of the system of districts. In a detailed rebuttal, Galil (1984; 1985; 1987) attempted to defend both the accepted concept regarding the affinity of the town lists to the administrative districts of the kingdom, and his own concept, which goes so far as to hold that the town lists actually reflect sub-sections within the framework of those districts. It should be stated that the paucity of documents discovered to date throughout Judah, their fragmented nature, their incomplete preservation and deciphering, and their brief and concise phrasing, all preclude any definitive ob-

that it is impossible to deal with the geographical lists in the Bible without considering the tendencies of their authors. To illustrate the great importance of discussion of these tendencies, see Na'aman 1986a:55–58, 64–66, 84–91, 116–117, 174–176, 216–236, 244–251.

8. See the works cited in the previous note, as well as the following additional examples: Auld 1975; Williamson 1979; 1981; Na'aman 1986b:5–11.

servations concerning the *modus operandi* of the administrative system then in force. A few of the settlements mentioned in the Arad archive were possibly located in the hill country (Maon; concerning the others, see notes 28–29, below); nevertheless, there is no way to determine either their administrative status in the period during which the document was written, or their historical situation at the time (as it may be claimed that they reflect an exceptional state of affairs). This is also the situation regarding the reference to the men of Moladah, *rntn* (or *rptn*) and Makkedah in the Ḥorvat ʻUza ostracon, and Azekah, Lachish and Beth-achzib in the Lachish ostraca. Garfinkel is correct in stating that the tiny sub-districts reconstructed by Galil are nowhere reflected in the administrative documents from the First Temple period. In any event, the division into "mini-districts" is not supported by any evidence from the administration of neighboring countries or from the Bible; it is entirely the result of an artificial process of re-grouping, based on the town lists in the Book of Joshua. Internal groupings may be created in any list drawn up in any kind of geographical order, without constituting evidence of the status of those groups within the administration of the kingdom.[9] The few documents discovered to date in excavations do not permit us to determine the then-existing array of districts within the Kingdom of Judah; we must, accordingly, seek other means of handling this complex problem.

It seems to me that the key to this problem maybe found by examining the status of Jerusalem in the framework of the town lists. As stated above, Jerusalem expanded considerably during the eighth century BCE and became a metropolis occupying approximately 600 dunams and housing thousands of residents — several times larger than the area and population of any other city in the kingdom. Jerusalem was located in the center of a sort of district, which encompassed the capital and its periphery, including the agricultural areas of the city's residents, as well as satellite settlements directly connected to Jerusalem proper (Barkay 1985:399–401). A similar situation prevailed in every metropolis of the ancient Near East. The city's exceptional, singular status in the framework of the kingdom is indicated by the phrase "Judah and Jerusalem." Furthermore, in the array of districts in force in the post-exilic period — an array parallel in some respects to the town lists of Judah and Benjamin (Alt 1925:115–116; Aharoni 1956:152–155; Kallai 1960: 92–94) — Jerusalem is included as an independent district (Neh. 3:9,12). The special status of Jerusalem in the Kingdom of Judah is not reflected in the

9. For criticism (with which I wholeheartedly agree) of Garfinkel (1987), see Eph'al and Naveh 1988.

town lists; this fact cannot be reconciled with the hypothesis defining them as lists of the districts of the Judahite kingdom.

An additional difficulty encountered by that hypothesis becomes evident when we consider the location of the central cities in the southern areas of the Judean hill country.[10] Hebron is situated near the eastern edge of the area within which it is mentioned; by contrast, Debir lies on the northern border of the area within which it is included, and Debir's two near neighbors, Arab and Dumah, are listed one "district" to the north. Galil correctly noted that the internal division of the hill country does not fit the information at our disposal concerning the places of residence of the main families occupying the hill country (Galil 1984:210–211, 213–216, 224). This is obvious in the case of the sons of Caleb, whose families dwelt in three different "districts"; even Hebron itself, the most important Calebite city, is detached from its "descendants" (Jorkeam, Maon, and Beth-zur; see 1 Chr. 2:44–45), which are listed in separate "districts." The family of Othniel also resided in two different "districts." The present order of the town lists in Josh. 15 is not based on any genitive principle. Yet, the discrepancy ostensibly existing between the main families of the Judean hill country and the town lists results entirely from the hypothesis that the division of those lists reflects districts within the kingdom. A different explanation for the division of the town lists into groups of towns may resolve this discrepancy.

A special problem is posed by the settlement of Zior, mentioned in the framework of "district VI" (Josh. 15:54). The site, which has preserved its name, Si'ir, is located one "district" to the north, and pottery from the Iron Age II was found there (Kochavi 1972:21, 54, site 100; Galil 1984:212; Kallai 1986:389). In view of its location, some scholars have rejected the identification of Si'ir with Zior, claiming that it is irreconcilable with the identification of other sites listed in the same "district" and that the similarity between the names is purely coincidental (Noth 1953:97–98; Kochavi 1972:21, 54; Galil 1984:212). Admittedly, acceptance of this identification creates a conspicuous deviation in the descriptions of the settlements in the Judean hill country, as these are usually grouped in well-defined geographical areas. Nevertheless, this identification should not be rejected out of hand; its acceptance would constitute additional evidence that the internal division in the hill country does not reflect a system of districts.

In view of this discussion, it may be hypothesized that the town lists were based on an administrative document listing the settlements of the kingdom,

10. See the maps published in Kochavi 1972:22; Aharoni 1979:346; Kallai 1986: map no. 2.

in accordance with a division into broad geographical-administrative territories. The town list in Josh. 15 features the headings *bngbh* (in the Negeb — Josh. 15:21), *bšplh* (in the Shephelah — 15:33), *bhr* (in the hill country — 15:48), *bmdbr* (in the wilderness — 15:61); that in Josh. 18 is headed "of the tribe of Benjamin" (Josh. 18:21). It should be noted that the conquest descriptions in Joshua, written by the Deuteronomist during a period not distant from that of the lists discussed here (see Section 5, below), frequently mention a similar geographical division prevailing in Judah (10:40; 11:2, 16; 12:8; see also Deut. 1:7). Even more striking is the fact that Jeremiah, a contemporary of our list as well as that of the Deuteronomist, makes use of the same division as that appearing in our list in describing the entire Kingdom of Judah. Jer. 17:26 — "And people shall come from the cities of Judah and the places round about Jerusalem, from the land of Benjamin, from the Shephelah, from the hill country, and from the Negeb . . ."; Jer. 32:44 — "in the cities of the hill country, in the cities of the Shephelah, and in the cities of the Negeb . . ."; Jer. 33:13 — "in the cities of the hill country, in the cities of the Shephelah, and in the cities of the Negeb, in the land of Benjamin, the places about Jerusalem, and in the cities of Judah. . . ." It may be postulated that this division into broad geographical territories (Negeb, hill country, Shephelah, Jerusalem and vicinity, Benjamin) reflects the administrative division of the Kingdom of Judah and that this was the external framework for the preparation of the original document on which our town lists are based.

One may further ask whether the numerical totals of towns accompanying the list were also copied from the original document, or were added up by the later author. On the one hand, it may be shown that some contradictions exist between the totals given and the number of towns actually listed — a fact that may attest to the originality of the numerical totals. On the other hand, we know of cases in which the sum total was secondarily added to an existing list of towns.[11] Scholars have ascertained that the division of the broad territories into sub-sections generally corresponds to the natural topography; this may reinforce the hypothesis that the totals of towns comprised an integral part of the original document. Nonetheless, it may just as easily be claimed that these totals were added by the later author, who was familiar with the topography of the kingdom; if this is the case, that author, when breaking down the list into separate groups, could have simply re-

11. See Noth 1953:93. For the attempt to reconcile the contradiction between the total number of Negeb towns (36 in all) and the summation (15:32) "in all, twenty-nine cities, with their villages," see Talmon 1965. For the secondary nature of the summations in the list of Levitical cities, see Na'aman 1986a:209, 214.

corded the total number of places listed in each group. In any event, even if the numerical totals were drawn from the original document, this does not prove the existence of administrative sub-districts; the figures may merely have been technically recorded as sub-totals, as part of the grand total of towns in the list.

In closing, we may state that the division of the town lists of Judah and Benjamin into sub-groups does not reflect the administrative division of the kingdom; likewise, it is not certain that these groups of towns constituted administrative sub-districts within the kingdom. The broad geographical areas apparently corresponded to the districts of the kingdom and constituted distinct organizational-administrative units; they included Benjamin, Jerusalem, the Judean hill country, the Shephelah, the Negeb, and possibly the Wilderness. It appears to me that, at the time of Sennacherib's campaign, when it became necessary to organise a supply system for times of war and siege, the kingdom was organised on a slightly different basis and was divided into four "districts": three in the hill country and one in the Shephelah (Yadin 1961; Aharoni 1962:53–56; 1979:398–399; Na'aman 1986b:14–17). It may be postulated that the division into districts had been initiated a short while after the emergence of the Kingdom of Judah, when it became necessary to adapt administrative procedure to the newly established kingdom, and was maintained throughout the First Temple period.

4. The Composition of the Town Lists and the Order of the Shephelah Sub-districts

Included in the Shephelah town list are three groups: one in the north and two in the south. The location of the first group (known in professional literature as "district II" — Josh. 15:33–36) in the northern Shephelah is universally accepted; opinions differ, however, regarding the location of the other two groups ("district III" — Josh. 15:37–41; and "district IV" — Josh. 15:42–44). Some scholars believe one to be situated north of the other, and others believe one to be situated east of the other.[12] The dispute results principally from the small number of sites identified within "district III": out of the 16 settlements in that group, only Migdal-gad (Khirbet el-Mejdeleh) and Lachish have been positively identified, whereas controversy exists over the location

12. See Alt 1925; 1953; Noth 1953; Cross and Wright 1956; Kallai-Kleinmann 1958:155–156; Kallai 1986:379–386. Also supporting the west-east arrangement of the Shephelah sections, as proposed by Kallai, are the following works: Kochavi 1972:22; Aharoni 1979:346, 353–354; Galil 1987:64–71. Rainey has defended the arrangement of the districts along a north-south axis (Rainey 1980:194–202; 1983:6–11).

of Eglon and Makkedah. Supporters of the north-south arrangement identify Makkedah at Khirbet el-Qôm, near Khirbet Beit Maqdûm (about nine kilometers southeast of Mareshah), and Eglon with Tell Beit Mirsim or Tell ʿAiṭûn (Tel ʿEton);[13] Ether, mentioned in proximity to Libnah, is identified by proponents of that school with Khirbet el-ʿAter (about three kilometers northwest of Mareshah). Those who favor the east-west arrangement base their arguments on the mention of Ether and Ashan both in the northernmost group of towns in Simeon (Josh. 19:7) at the southern edge of the Shephelah and in "district IV" of the Shephelah (Josh. 15:42), and emphasize the absence of these towns from the Negebite town list of Judah, which (for the most part) parallels the town list of Simeon. This would seem to indicate that "district IV," within which the two towns are mentioned, should be considered as extending out to the southern edges of the Shephelah, from Keilah in the north to the edge of the Negeb district. Proponents of this view reject the above-mentioned identifications of Makkedah, Eglon, and Ether, proposing alternative locations for those towns.

The location of Libnah constitutes a difficulty for those supporting the east-west arrangement. The town is mentioned in the town lists alongside Ether and Ashan; the attempt to situate it in the southern Shephelah cannot be reconciled with its place in the order of conquest as listed in Josh. 10. Accordingly, supporters of this method detach Libnah from Ether and Ashan to the south, and locate it north of Lachish.[14] Galil attempted to overcome that obstacle by suggesting that the order of appearance of the towns in Josh. 10 is not geographical and that Libnah should be identified with Tell ʿAiṭûn in the southern Shephelah.[15] Unfortunately, he was unaware of the findings of the excavations at Tell ʿAiṭûn and its adjacent cemetery, which indicate that the site was not inhabited during the seventh century BCE (Ussishkin 1974:

13. In his basic article, Elliger proposed the identification of Makkedah with Khirbet Beit Maqdûm and Eglon with Tell Beit Mirsim (1934a:55–68). Noth (1953:95) came to no definitive conclusions regarding the identification of Makkedah (although he tended to support Elliger's opinion); as for Eglon, he proposed that it be identified with Tell ʿAiṭûn (Tel ʿEton), located just south of Tell Beit Mirsim (Noth 1937:32–34). The identification of Eglon with Tell ʿAiṭûn is also accepted by Rainey (1980:197). Lately, it has been suggested that Makkedah should be identified with Khirbet el-Qôm, near Khirbet Beit Maqdûm, where rich findings from the Iron Age II have been unearthed (Kellermann 1978:428 and n. 24; Dorsey 1980).

14. On the identification of Libnah with Tell Bornâṭ, see Elliger 1934a:58–63; Noth 1937: 34–35; 1953:91, 95; Aharoni 1979:332, 353; Rainey 1980:198. On the identification of Libnah with Tell el-Judeideh, see Kallai 1962; 1986:379–382.

15. Galil 1987:67–71. Kallai 1971:249 tentatively suggested the identification of Tell ʿAiṭûn with Moresheth-gath; Aharoni (1979:261–262,353–354) suggested identifying it with Etam; for its identification with Eglon, see above, n. 12.

118–120; Ayalon 1985; Zimhoni 1985). This fact is not in line with the mention of Libnah as the birthplace of Hamutal, wife of Josiah and mother of Jehoahaz (2 Kgs. 23:31) and Zedekiah (2 Kgs. 24:18), indicating that, during that time, Libnah was a town of some importance in the Judahite kingdom. Moreover, the claim that no consistent geographical order can be found in Josh. 10:28–39 is unfounded; it is difficult to ascertain the basis for the statements that the author "did not claim to describe a continuous campaign, but sought to portray a representative description," and that the order of appearance is "artificial, and came into being as a result of the combination of several traditions, some of them unrelated to one another" (Galil 1984:67–70). The passage has a well-formed, consistent structure and was undoubtedly written by an author familiar with the Shephelah and the hill country. The description of their conquest in the framework of a single military campaign was dictated, above all, by the topography of the area, rather than by historical memory or the existence of previous traditions.[16] It seems best to establish Libnah's location north of Lachish, thus, casting doubt on the plausibility of an east-west arrangement for the town "districts."

Discussions regarding the identity of the Shephelah towns have usually led to a blind alley. Despite the protracted debate on this issue, little actual progress has been made since the publication of the basic works by Elliger (1934a; 1934b) and Noth (1937). Accordingly, the question of the order of the town groups has remained unresolved; each of the two proposals displays conspicuous weak points.

I would like to propose a new angle, unexplored in professional literature to date, for studying the scope of the Shephelah "districts." This proposal is based on study of the method used in drawing up the southern town lists (of Judah, Benjamin and Dan). These lists seem to share a common and consistent unifying factor — the method by which the towns are recorded within "districts," which appears to be in accordance with the geographical lines of the areas themselves. At first glance, this proposal would seem difficult, as the location of many towns is unknown or doubtful. However, the number of places definitely (or nearly definitely) identified is sufficient to enable a fairly certain determination of the order of recording in most places in the Kingdom of Judah (Fig. 1).

(1) The Negeb district ("district I") is shaped like a rectangular strip, extending along an east-west longitudinal axis. The list of Negeb towns is drawn

16. For a discussion of Josh. 10:28–39 and its evaluation as a historical source, see Elliger 1934a; Noth 1937; 1953:60–66; Weippert 1971:29–33; de Vaux 1978:627–631.

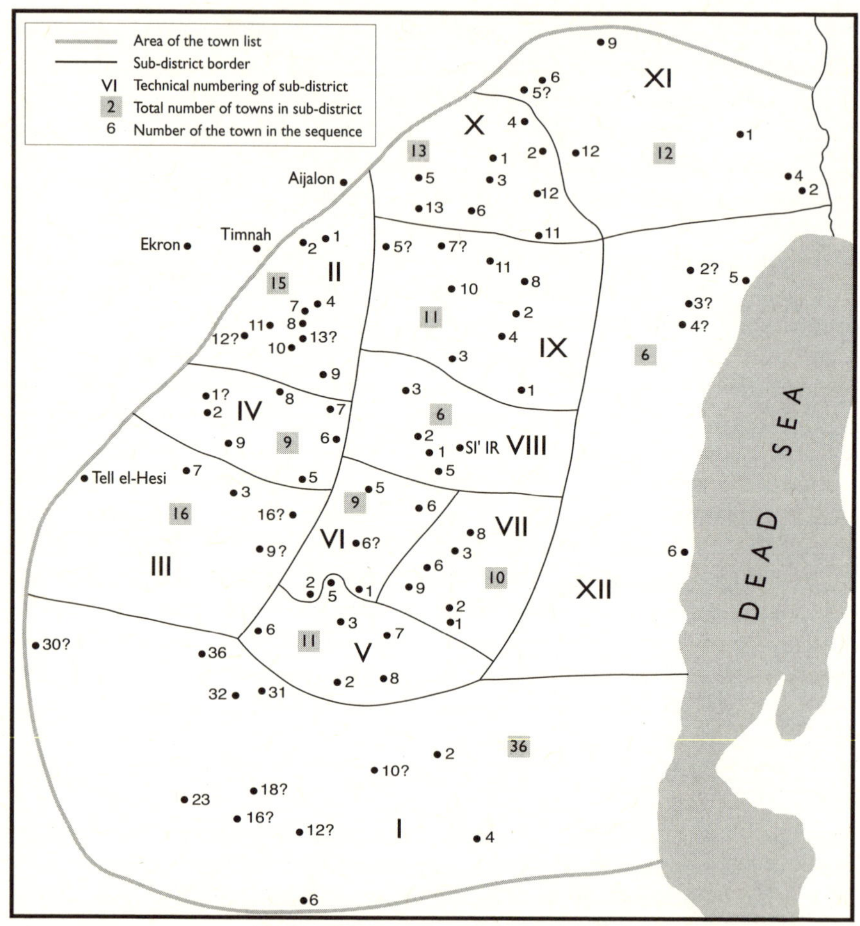

Fig. 1. The order of listing of the towns of Judah and Benjamin in "districts."

Legend: The numbers standing for the names of towns represent their relative location in the framework of their listing in "districts." For example: town No. 2 in the Negeb district represents Arad; town No. 4, Kinah; and town No. 6, Ararah. The total number of towns in that "district" is 36. In the eastern "district" of Benjamin, Jericho is represented by No. 1; Beth-hoglah, by No. 2; and Beth-arabah, by No. 4. The total number of towns in that "district" is 12.

up, generally speaking, from east to west; the first towns listed (Eder/Arad, Kinah) have been identified in the east, and the last (Ziklag, Sansannah, Madmannah, Ein-Rimmon) in the northwest.

(2) The wilderness district ("district XII") is shaped like an elongated strip, extending along a north-south longitudinal axis. The list of wilderness towns runs from north to south (from Beth-arabah to En-gedi).

(3) The Judean hill country follows an elongated contour, extending along a north-south longitudinal axis. The hill country lists are divided into five "districts," generally arranged along the longitudinal axis, from south to north. The first town listed in each group is located on its southern edge; for the most part, the towns in each group are arranged in accordance with the hill country's longitudinal axis. As the longitudinal axis of the southernmost group ("district V") runs from west to east, the towns in that group are arranged accordingly, with the last towns located in the east. The next two sections ("districts VI-VII") run along a north-south longitudinal axis, and their towns are ordered accordingly. The next group ("district VIII") runs along a west-east longitudinal axis, and its towns are apparently arranged in accordance with that axis. The northernmost group ("district IX") occupies a rectangular area, with its towns arranged from south to north.

The overall south-north orientation, in accordance with the contour of the Judean hill country, is quite conspicuous in the town lists of Judah, as regards the order in which the "districts" are arranged, the starting point of each group of towns, and the internal order of the towns within each "district."

(4) The district of Benjamin is shaped like a strip, running along an east-west longitudinal axis. The district is divided into two sub-districts, eastern ("district XI") and western ("district X"). The first towns listed in each group of towns are located on the eastern edge of that group. In the eastern sub-district, which is elongated in shape and runs along an east-west longitudinal axis, the towns are arranged from east to west. In the western sub-district, the order is less absolute; however, it begins in the northeast (Gibeon, Ramah, Mizpah, Beeroth) and ends in the southwest (Kiriath-jearim).

The overall east-west orientation, in accordance with the contour of the Benjamin district, is quite striking in all aspects of the town lists of Benjamin.

(5) The northern sub-district ("district II") of the Shephelah is elongated in shape, with its longitudinal axis running from north to south. The towns in this section, generally speaking, are arranged from north to south; the first towns listed are located in the north (Eshtaol, Zorah), and the last are located in the south, along the Valley of Elah and its tributaries.[17]

---

17. For the location of Shaaraim in the Valley of Elah, west of Socoh and Azekah, see 1

(6) Last in my discussion is the town list of Dan (Josh. 19:40–46), which, though admittedly not a true part of the town system of Judah, follows a similar pattern of ordering. The allotment of Dan is elongated in shape, extending along a southeastnorthwest longitudinal axis. The town list is ordered in accordance with this axis; the first towns are located in the southeast of the inheritance, and the last are located in the northwest.

It may be stated that all the southern town lists (including that of Simeon[18]) were recorded in a consistent order, in accordance with the overall contour of the area. The author of the original town list always selected a starting point at one end of the narrow dimension of the "district" and continued by recording the towns in groups, concluding at the other end of the narrow dimension of the "district." This is especially conspicuous in the narrow, elongated territories, such as the Negeb, the wilderness, Benjamin, and the inheritance of Dan.

This conclusion is of great importance in considering the problem of the two southern "districts" of the Shephelah. Were one of these two sections located to the east of the other, both would have had long and narrow contours; it could then be expected that, in both sections, the town names would be listed parallel to the longitudinal axis. Even a superficial study of the places identified in both sections reveals that this is not the case and that the towns included can by no means be listed in that kind of order. On the other hand, if we arrange one "district" to the north of the other, we find a consistent order of recording. Admittedly, only a few towns have been identified in "district III"; nevertheless, the first ones listed (Migdal-gad and Lachish) seem to be located at its northern end. "District IV" is rectangular in shape, with its longitudinal axis running from east to west; therefore, the first towns mentioned are at its northern end, and the others around its perimeter. Also conspicuous is a possible continuity between the last town of each section and the first town in the neighboring section. Libnah (Tell Bornâṭ?) is apparently close to the last group of cities mentioned in "district II" (see note 18); on the other hand, Migdal-gad (and probably also Zenan and Hadashah) is close to Mareshah, the last town in "district III." This may indicate that "district IV"

Sam. 17:52. For the identification of Gederah (or Gederothaim) with Khirbet Judrayah, approximately two kilometers northeast of Socoh, see Alt 1934:12–13; Kuschke 1971:299, 312–313. The preservation of the name, the proximity to Socoh, Azekah, and Shaaraim, and the archaeological findings — all tend to corroborate this identification. In my opinion, the location of Gederah near Laṭrûn, and the array of sub-districts in the northern Shephelah as described by Galil (1987:56–63), are erroneous.

18. Concerning the internal order of the town list of Simeon, see Na'aman 1980:145–147.

was originally listed before "district III," and that the present order was dictated by the author of the book, who chose to append the Philistine towns (Josh. 15:45–47) to the end of the Shephelah town list, after the southernmost section (Rainey 1980:195).

Why, then, are Ether and Ashan listed in the town list of Simeon and in "district IV," but not in the Negeb district? I will not review the solutions that have been proposed to this question (Albright 1924:159–160; Noth 1953:96, 110, 113–114; Fritz 1975:35–37; Rainey 1980:199–200), but will limit the discussion to presenting the solution that seems appropriate to me.

Let me first call attention to the spelling of the place names appearing in the Negeb town list. In I Sam. 30:30, Athach (thus, also in the A manuscript of the LXX); in Josh.19:7, Ether (in the LXX, Iether); in 1 Chr. 4:32, Tochen. There appear to be grounds for the assumption that the original place name was Athach, that both "Tochen" in 1 Chr. 4:32 and "Ether" in Joshua 19:7 are miscopyings (the latter influenced by Ether in the Shephelah), and that no place by the name of Ether existed on the northern edge of the Negeb.[19] The explanation for the appearance of "Ether" in the latter quotation results from its proximity to Ashan, a city mentioned by its full name of Borashan in I Sam. 30:30 (thus, also in Hebrew manuscripts and in the LXX) (Driver 1913:226–227; Fritz 1975:34–35). The linking of Ether and Ashan in the Shephelah resulted in the miscopying of Athach alongside (Bor)ashan in Josh. 19:7, just as in Josh. 15:42 of the B manuscript of the LXX, the name "Ether" is miscopied as "Ithak," due to the influence of the Negeb list.

Why do these towns appear only in the town list of Simeon, in Josh. 19:7, and not in the Negeb town list in Josh. 15:31? This appears to result from the changes that occurred in the condition of the Shephelah settlements between the respective periods during which the two lists were composed (for discussion of the dates, see Section 5 below). The town list of Simeon is probably the earlier; for this reason, it features a considerable degree of resemblance to the list of towns to which, accoring to biblical history, David sent the spoils of Amalek (1 Sam. 30:27–30; cf. Bethel/Bethul; Hormah; Borashan/Ashan; Athach/Ether). It appears that Sennacherib's campaign in Judah brought about the destruction of many Shephelah towns. Of those appearing in the list of Simeon, only Ain and Rimmon (or Ein-Rimmon) were restored; Athach, (Bor)ashan, and Etam (1 Chr. 4:32) were not inhabited in the seventh century BCE and, therefore, are not included in Josh. 15.[20] This hypothesis is corrobo-

19. Noth 1953:110, 113–114. Several scholars have expressed the opinion that this question cannot be definitively resolved. See Steuernagel 1900:225; Driver 1913:227.

20. For this reason, it appears to me that the Levitical town of Ashan (1 Chr. 6:59; LXX

rated by excavations in the southern Shephelah, which revealed no findings from the seventh century BCE in the two most important sites in the area, Tell Beit Mirsim and Tell 'Aiṭûn. Naturally, we cannot ignore the fact that the town list in Josh. 15 includes many small settlements; the two sites may have been inhabited by individual families (a possibility difficult to prove or disprove in archaeological research) and, for that reason, were included in the list. It should, however, be assumed that a large number of settlements were destroyed in Sennacherib's campaign and never again resettled (see Section 5, below). Athach, (Bor)ashan, and Etam were among these abandoned settlements and, therefore, are not mentioned in the later list of Negeb towns.

5. The Dating of the Town Lists

In his seminal study of the southern town lists in Joshua, Alt proposed that they be dated to Josiah's reign (Alt 1925:106–112). He argued that the town list of Benjamin includes Bethel, Ophrah, and Jericho — towns that had been controlled by Israel up to its conquest by Assyria — and did not pass into Judah until Josiah's day. Alt even explained that the town list of Dan reflects the westward expansion of the Kingdom of Judah at that time. In view of the assumption that the exiles returned to the places from which they had been exiled by the Babylonians, he suggested that the the mention of Lod, Hadid, and Ono in the lists of the "Returning Captives" (the "Gola List") indicates that those places belonged to Judah in the last stages of the kingdom's existence. This date has been accepted by other, principally German, scholars (Proksch 1928:45–46; Noth 1953:13–14; 1960:273–274; Welten 1969:93–102; Soggin 1984:245). The present writer has raised additional arguments in its favor (Na'aman 1986a:229–230; 1986b:18, n. 6).

On the other hand, some scholars have dated the list to an earlier time. Cross and Wright (1956:212–226) dated it to Jehoshaphat's reign. Mazar initially supported this date; however, following his excavations at En-gedi, he apparently changed his opinion and began to favor a later date.[21] Aharoni also assumed that the initial division into districts was accomplished under Jehoshaphat, but that the list in its present form (except for Josh. 18:21–24)

translation of Josh. 21:16) should be located near Libnah, and not on the edge of the Negeb district. For the dating of the Levitical town list, see Na'aman 1986a:227–234.

21. Mazar initially distinguished between the town list of Judah, which he ascribed to Jehoshaphat's reign, and that of Benjamin, which he ascribed to Josiah's day (Mazar [Maisler] 1944:74, n. 9; 1950:718). He later viewed both town lists as having been composed under Jehoshaphat (1958:566). After directing the Tel Goren (En-gedi) excavations, he again changed his opinion concerning the dating of these lists (1967:223).

reflects the situation in Uzziah's reign (Aharoni 1959:239–246; 1979:268–272). Schunck dated the list to Uzziah's time, but considered the lists in Josh. 18: 21–24 and 19:41–46 as supplements from Josiah's reign (Schunck 1962:141–145, n. 18; 1963:153–168). Kallai dated the town list of Benjamin to Abijah's reign and ascribed that of Judah to the reign of Hezekiah (Kallai 1960:24–26, 33–34; 1986:372–377); his view was accepted by Galil (1984:223; 1985:12; 1987: 55, 60).

As observed above, the separation of the town lists of Judah and Benjamin into two distinct periods does not withstand the test of criticism. The date proposed by Kallai for the town list of Judah is based principally on the omission of Beth-shemesh, Timnah, and Aijalon — towns that the Philistines conquered from Ahaz (2 Chr. 28:18). On the other hand, Hezekiah conquered Philistia (2 Kgs.18:8), which Kallai believes explains the inclusion of the Philistine towns in the town list of Judah (Josh. 15:45–47). It seems, however, that these arguments can be easily disproved. A significant number of *lmlk* seal impressions were uncovered in the excavations of both Beth-shemesh and Timnah (Tel Batash), indicating that these towns belonged to the Kingdom of Judah on the eve of Sennacherib's campaign (Na'aman 1986a:11–17). Additionally, there is no basis for the assumption that Hezekiah annexed the Philistine towns mentioned in Josh. 15:45–47, as his entire intention was to form an alliance headed by him and in cooperation with Egypt, not to conquer or annex. Moreover, as suggested above (see Section 2), the addition of the Philistine towns to the list was implemented by the author of the book, and they did not appear in the original document.

The arguments raised in favor of dating the town list to the ninth or eighth century BCE are not convincing, and it now seems appropriate to focus the discussion on the most likely alternative datings: the second half of the eighth century, or the second half of the seventh century. Significantly, during the 200 years after the establishment of the Kingdom of Judah (the late tenth century BCE), there was continuity of settlement and material culture in the kingdom, with no destruction or disruption of culture. Thus, we are unable to make a detailed study of the situation prevailing in Uzziah's reign, as, with the exception of several verses in 2 Chronicles (26:6–15) whose reliability is doubted by some scholars,[22] nearly nothing is known of his time, and there is no way of isolating archaeological findings from his period. This continuity of settlement was interrupted by Sennacherib's campaign in 701 BCE, when many cities were destroyed, causing a significant break in the his-

22. For the reliability of the descriptions of Uzziah's reign in Chronicles, see Welten 1973:153–163, with earlier literature; Knauf 1985:116–119, 122.

tory of the Kingdom of Judah for the first time since its establishment. The cultural characteristics of Judah in the seventh century and the geographical distribution of its settlements differ considerably from those in the eighth century. The choice of the "Hezekiah or Josiah" alternative (or rather, the second half of the eighth or the second half of the seventh century BCE) is the most fruitful for discussion, as their reigns are also covered by considerable documentation, in addition to archaeological findings. Obviously, dating the list in the eighth or seventh century will require us to re-examine the rulers who reigned at that time, in an attempt to determine whose rule is more appropriate to the dating of the town list.

Following are a number of points to be considered in analysing the proposed alternatives:[23]

(1) The Benjamin district (Josh. 18) includes the town of Avvim (verse 23) — a settlement named for a group of deportees brought in from Avva (a town located on the border between Elam and Babylon; see 2 Kgs. 17:24, 31; 18:34; 19:13) and settled in the Bethel district by King Sargon II of Assyria in approximately 708 BCE.[24] If this assumption is correct, the town list dates, at the earliest, to Hezekiah's reign, several years before Sennacherib's campaign to Judah.

(2) The appearance of Bethel, Ophrah, and Jericho in the town list — as observed by Alt (1925:109–110; see also Klein 1983) — is appropriate only to Josiah's time. From the foundation of the Kingdom of Israel, these cities were located in its territory; after the Assyrian conquest, they were annexed to the Assyrian province of Samaria. Only after the Assyrian retreat was Josiah able to expand northward, to conquer Bethel and annex it, as well as other nearby cities (e.g., Jericho), to his kingdom. The town of Geba mentioned in this group (Josh. 18:24) is Geba of Benjamin, which, being located near the northern border of the Kingdom of Judah since its establishment, had protected the vital eastern route running from Baal-hazor through Ophrah to Jerusalem. Thanks to its important strategic status, Geba was fortified, along with Mizpah, by Asa (1 Kgs. 15:22); in the description of Josiah's reforms (2 Kgs. 23:8), it is mentioned (in the phrase "from Geba to Beer-sheba") as de-

---

23. I will not compare here the lists of Judah and Benjamin either to the genealogies appearing in Chronicles, or to additional lists appearing in those books and ascribed to the period of the Monarchy, as they have no direct relevance to the issue under discussion.

24. Na'aman 1986a:229–230, n. 47; Na'aman and Zadok 1988:45–46. It is possible that the name "Ophni" (Josh. 18:24) is that of a settlement named for a group of exiles brought in from some distant place bearing that name. No suitable identification has as yet been suggested for this toponym (Noth 1953:108; Schunck 1962:152–153; Kuschke 1965:108–109; Kallai 1972).

noting the northern border of the kingdom. The latter passage explicitly relates to the reform implemented in "the cities of Judah," and the author clearly differentiates between this early reform and the reform later implemented in Bethel (2 Kgs. 23:15–18). Accordingly, it seems to me that there is no basis either for the suggested location of Geba as far north as et-Tell in the hill country of Ephraim, or for setting the border of the kingdom that far north.[25] The northern border of the Benjamin district (Josh. 18:21–28) should be set along the Bethel-Ophrah line; this deviates northward from the traditional border of the Kingdom of Judah, which, from Asa's time to the beginning of Josiah's rule, had been set along the line Geba-Mizpah.

(3) Conspicuously absent from the town list of Benjamin are many cities mentioned in Isaiah (10:28–32). The only towns common to both lists are Ramah, Geba, and Gibeah (= Gibeah of Saul; for determination of the phrasing in Josh. 18:28, see Section 2, above); missing are Aiath, Migron, Michmash, Maabara ("the Pass"), Bat-gallim ("Daughter of Gallim"), Laishah, Anathoth, Madmannah, Gebim, and Nob (admittedly, some of these are not towns, but toponyms located along the route). Kallai noted that a group of places in Benjamin was missing from the town list and suggested that an entire district had been omitted from the list (Kallai 1960:33; 1986:399–400, map no. 2). By refraining from identifying either Geba (Josh. 18:24) with Geba of Benjamin, or Gibeah (Josh. 18:28) with Gibeah of Saul, Kallai artificially expanded the "missing area." In fact, what is missing is not a "district," but simply a group of towns, notably Michmash, Anathoth, and Alemeth, all located northeast of Jerusalem. Possibly, this group was initially listed after Gibeath (verse 28) and was mistakenly omitted. The original text may be restored thus: "Gibeah <of Saul . . . > and Kirjath-jearim" (Na'aman 1986a:229, n. 45). The absence of this group of towns from Josh. 18:21–28 prevents us from determining whether any correspondence exists between the town list of Benjamin and the group of places mentioned in Isa. 10:28–32, or whether the two lists belong to diffefrent periods; the latter supposition would allow for the possibility that some of the towns mentioned in the prophecy were destroyed in Sennacherib's campaign and not inhabited at the time of composition of the town list.

25. Mazar (Maisler) 1941; 1954; Smirin 1952:91; Liver 1958:420; Kallai 1960:75–76; 1986: 400–401 and map no. 2; Cogan and Tadmor 1988:286. Aharoni distinguished between the Geba mentioned in Josh. 18:24, which he identified with Geba (Ephraim) (1959:232–233; 1976:12), and the Geba mentioned in 2 Kgs. 23:8, which he identified with Geba (Benjamin) (1979:404). See Aharoni 1985. Demsky proposed the identification of the Geba mentioned in 2 Kgs. 23:8 with Gibeon (Demsky 1973:30–31).

(4) There is a considerable difference between the Shephelah town list in Josh. 15 and that cited in Micah (1:10–16), which reflects the period of Sennacherib's campaign to Judah. The only towns common to both lists are Zenan, Lachish, Achzib, Mareshah, and Adullam. On the other hand, the towns of Gath, Beth-leaphrah, Shaphir, Eriah ("Nakedness"), Maroth, and Moresheth-gath are missing from the list in Josh. 15. It is difficult to avoid the conclusion that the two lists belong to different periods of time and that some of the places destroyed in Sennacherib's campaign were not inhabited at the time of composition of the town list.

(5) The lack of correspondence between the Shephelah town list and the state of affairs in that area during Hezekiah's rule is also evident when comparing the list with the distribution of *lmlk* seal impressions. The storage jars bearing these impressions were manufactured in a central royal pottery, sent to various districts of the kingdom to be filled with agricultural produce, and then brought to the towns as reserve rations for use in time of war and siege (Na'aman 1986b:15–17; see Mommsen et al. 1984; Garfinkel 1988a: 70; Eshel 1989). Their distribution reflects both the preparations for siege and the array of settlements in the Kingdom of Judah under Hezekiah, immediately prior to Sennacherib's campaign. Fairly large numbers of *lmlk*-impressed handles were found in Gezer (37), Beth-shemesh (28), Tel 'Erani (14), Tel Batash (9), and Tell es-Ṣâfi (6); all of the above (except Beth-shemesh) are located west of the area included in the list of Shephelah towns in Josh. 15. There is also a conspicuous degree of discrepancy on the northern border; the northern cities (Bethel and Ophrah) are not included in the logistical array of the *lmlk* jars.

(6) Among the other towns that may be linked to Hezekiah's day, the name of *mmšt* — one of the four towns whose names appear in the *lmlk* seal impressions — is conspicuously absent from our list. I proposed that the list of "cities for defense" mentioned in 2 Chr. 11:6–10 be detached from Rehoboam, to whom it is ascribed, and linked to the preparations made by Hezekiah to meet the Assyrian attack in 701 BCE (Na'aman 1986b:5–11). The towns appearing in this list, but missing from the town list of Judah, include Adoraim in the hill country and Aijalon and Gath in the Shephelah. Acceptance of this suggested date would provide additional confirmation that the number and distribution of the towns of Judah in Hezekiah's day differ from those reflected in our town list.

(7) The genealogical lists in 1 Chr. 4:21–23 mention the following places in the Shephelah: Lecah, Mareshah, Beth-ashbea, Cozeba, Lahem(?), Netaim, and Gederah. The proposals for the identification of Lecah with Lachish and Lahem with Lahemas (Yeivin 1962; Demsky 1966:213, n. 15; Galil 1987:64) are unsupported and should be rejected. The town list includes Mareshah,

Cozeba-Achzib, and Gederah, which appear in the genealogical lists, but the remaining places, Lecah, Beth-ashbea, Lahem(?), Netaim, are unknown. The mention of "the house of linen workers" (verse 21) and "the potters . . ." who "dwelt there with the king for his work" (verse 23) indicate that these lists date from the time of the Monarchy and may refer to royal potteries and workshops established in the region by the kings of Judah during that kingdom's great expansion in the eighth century BCE (Demsky 1966; Aharoni 1968: 168–169, n. 29; Lemaire 1977:136–137, n. 123; Mommsen et al. 1984:111–112). If this conclusion is correct, it provides additional testimony to the striking difference in settlement patterns in the Shephelah between the town list and the lists reflecting settlement in the eighth century.

(8) Let me now consider the correspondence between the town list and the state of settlement in Judah in the seventh century, beginning with the testimony on the marriages of the kings of Judah. Manasseh married a woman from Jotbah (2 Kgs. 21:19); Amon married a woman from Bozkath (22: 1); Josiah married women from Libnah (23:31; 24:18) and Rumah (23:36); and Jehoiakim married a woman from Jerusalem (24:8). One of these women, then, came from the capital and two of the others from the Shephelah (Bozkath and Libnah). The origin of the remaining two is disputed. Some scholars have proposed that they came from towns in the Galilee, and their marriages to kings of Judah reflected a policy of intentional efforts on the part of those kings to achieve rapprochement with the Galilean population (Smirin 1952: 56; Aharoni 1957:132; Broshi 1958; Yeivin 1960:254–55; Liver 1968; Cogan 1974: 91). Such a policy, however, was by no means appropriate to Manasseh, a vassal to Assyria throughout his reign; moreover, it is doubtful whether Rumah and Jotbah in the Valley of Beth-netophah could have been settled in the seventh century. Both towns were destroyed in the campaign of Tiglath-pileser III in 733–732 BCE and their population exiled (Tadmor 1967), and there is no evidence of the town having been resettled by exiles from other places. The archaeological survey attests to a significant decrease in settlement in the Lower Galilee in the seventh century, as a direct result of the Assyrian campaign and the subsequent Assyrian policy in that area (Gal 1988–89). Accordingly, the assumption that the kings of Judah married women from that distant and desolate area is difficult to accept. Ginsberg (1950:350) has proposed an emendation reading "Juttah" (for "Jotbah") and "Dumah" (for "Rumah"), enabling the location of both these places in the southern Judean hill country. Given the many *resh-daleth* substitutions in the Bible, the emendation "Dumah" appears possible (though certainly not compulsory) and may refer to the Dumah mentioned in the town list (15:52). The emendation "Juttah," however, is not corroborated by any other ancient version and should be rejected. Thus, those scholars who sought to locate it outside

Judah, possibly on the Idumaean border, may well be correct; the Idumaean location would be appropriate to Manasseh's rule and to the *pax Assyriaca.*[26]

(9) Both 2 Kings and the town list in Joshua mention Geba and Beer-sheba (2 Kgs. 23:8), Bethel (23:17), and Mizpah (25:23, 25). Both the Book of Jeremiah and the town lists mention Tekoa and Beth-haccerem (Jer. 6:1), Kiriath-jearim (26:20), Gibeon (28:1; 41:12, 16), Ramah (31:14), Lachish and Azekah (34:7), Mizpah (chapters 40–41), and Bethlehem (41:17). Moreover, I have already discussed the similarity between the names of the regions in the town list and in Jeremiah (Section 3, above). Anathoth, Jeremiah's home town, is missing from the town list; following Kallai, I have suggested that Anathoth and other towns were inadvertently omitted from the town list of Benjamin (paragraph 3, above). Also missing from the town list are Netophah, home of Seraiah and the sons of Ephai (2 Kgs. 25:23; Jer. 40:8); and Nehalim, which — as some scholars have postulated — may have been the home town of Shemaiah of "Nehelam" (Jer. 29:24–32) (Kochavi 1972:28, Site 32; Galil 1984:218, n. 64). It should be noted that additional towns mentioned in lists ascribed to David's time (Harod, Hushah, Atroth-beth-joab) are missing from the town list pertaining to the Bethlehem area ("district IX"). Was this group of towns omitted from the list, as in the case of the town list of Benjamin? This assumption, of course, is by no means compulsory; the absence of Netophah (and, perhaps, of Nehalim) may also result from the fact that the town list is not complete, and that individual places were omitted (see below).

(10) Let me now compare the town list with a number of seventh century inscriptions found in excavations in various towns in Judah.

Ostraca of the Arad archive[27] mention Beer-sheba, Yanum[28], Kinah, Arad, Maon, Hazar-susah, and Baalath[29], all of which appear in the town list. On the other hand, Ramath-negeb — which appears in an Arad ostracon, in the town list of Simeon (Josh. 19:8), and in the list of towns to which David sent

26. Montgomery 1951:521; Gray 1970:711; McKay 1973:23–25; Williamson 1982:390, 395. It should also be remembered that a place named Arumah was located close to Shechem (Judg. 9:41), and that the root *rwm* is quite common in ancient Palestinian toponyms (Isserlin 1957:141–143).

27. For publication of the inscriptions from Arad, see Lemaire 1977:145–235; Aharoni 1981. Three place names mentioned by Aharoni (*'nym, zp, ygwr*) have been left out, as the transliteration of their names cannot be ascertained (see notes by Aharoni and Lemaire to inscriptions 17, 25, 42).

28. There can be no certainty that the word *ynm* indeed denotes a place-name. See the literature cited in Aharoni 1981: inscription 19.

29. Lemaire (1977:216–217) read inscription No. 60 (lines 1–2) as *kprh hb'lty* — that is, a certain person originating from Baalath. However, his suggested rendering is quite uncertain.

the spoils of Amalek (1 Sam. 30:27), is missing from the Negeb town list in Josh. 15.

Inscriptions from Lachish[30] mention Achzib, Azekah, Lachish, and perhaps also Ashan (Ussishkin 1978:83–84), all of which appear in the town list. On the other hand, Beth-harapid, if this is in fact a name of a town (see Lemaire 1977:110–112), does not appear in the town list.

A Ḥorvat ʿUza ostracon (Beit-Arieh 1986–87) mentions Moladah and Makkedah, both of which appear in the town list; on the other hand, *rptn* is not mentioned.

A considerable degree of correspondence seems to exist between the seventh century epigraphic findings and the town list. However, a few individual towns (Ramath-negeb, *rptn*, and perhaps also Beth-harapid) do not appear in the list, and this problem should be examined before summing up the chronological details.

(11) Turning to the archaeological excavations and surveys conducted in Judah, we see that the large number of settlements mentioned in the town list exceeds the number of contemporary sites discovered by archaeological research. A good example of this trend is provided by the Negeb district, for which the list mentions 35 towns, a number greater than that of the sites discovered in the area over many years. Accordingly, it may be assumed that the list also included a number of small sites inhabited by several households each. This situation makes it difficult to discuss the archaeological findings. Let me illustrate this difficulty by means of the excavations in various Shephelah sites. Several large sites in this area (Beth-shemesh, Tell ʿAiṭûn, Tell Beit Mirsim) revealed no pottery from the seventh century BCE (Ussishkin 1974:118–120; Aharoni and Aharoni 1976; Aharoni 1982:261–264; Ayalon 1985; Zimhoni 1985). Are we to conclude that these places were not included in the list (on the assumption that the list indeed belongs to that period)? Could these places have been inhabited by a few individual families and, thus, were included in the list, but not discerned in archaeological investigations, as their material remains are located near the surface of the mound, making them extremely difficult to trace?

This example illustrates how careful one has to be to avoid reaching negative conclusions on the basis of archaeological findings; as observed above, all the archaeological arguments raised thus far concerning the dating of the town lists were based on the absence of layers of settlement from certain periods at sites supposedly belonging to those periods. Nor should we forget that a prerequisite for any historical interpretation of archaeological find-

30. The Lachish inscriptions are quoted according to Lemaire 1977: 83–143.

ings is the certain identification of the site(s) under discussion. Thus, for example, there is no real historical basis for the archaeological discussions concerning Tell el-Far'ah in the south, as its identification with Sharuhen/Shilhim is not well founded, and it was apparently located outside the borders of the Kingdom of Judah (Na'aman 1980:147–148). Given those limitations, it may be stated that stratigraphic evidence from the sites cannot provide a definitive dating of the town lists and, at best, that such evidence may serve as auxiliary tools, alongside the historical evidence and the distribution of special findings (such as *lmlk* seal impressions, or "rosette" jar handles).

The Tel Goren (En-gedi) excavations showed that the settlement here was established in the seventh century BCE; this, at first glance, supposedly constituted evidence that the town list did not date from before that period.[31] However, surveys conducted around En-gedi have shown that the oasis was also settled in the eighth century; therefore, the Tel Goren findings cannot be used to settle this issue (Aharoni 1979:351). None of the pottery found at Ramat Raḥel dates from before the eighth century; if the identification of that site with Beth-haccerem is correct, this information — like the En-gedi findings — may be used to set an upper limit to the list (Aharoni 1956:152–155; 1979:351). A similar situation is reflected in the Aroer excavations: the findings indicate that the site was established in the eighth century, perhaps even in the second half of that century (Biran and Cohen 1981:270–273); the identification of Aroer with Adadah (i.e., Ararah, by *resh-daleth* substitution), a town appearing in the town list, enables the setting of an upper limit to the list. Finally, let me mention Ḥorvat 'Uza, a site on the southeastern border of the Kingdom of Judah, which some scholars have identified with Kinah, a town appearing in the town list and in an Arad document (Lemaire 1973: 18–22; Mittmann 1977:234–235; Na'aman 1980:145). The excavations here revealed no pottery dating to before the seventh century (Beit-Arieh 1986; Beck 1986). If we accept the proposed identification, this will constitute the first evidence that the town list does not date from before the seventh century BCE.

Noteworthy also is the enormous difference between the number of settlements found in the recent surveys of the Shephelah and the number of settlements in the town list: 92 settlements have been discovered in the incomplete survey conducted so far (Broshi and Finkelstein 1990:12), whereas the overall number mentioned in Josh. 15:33–44 is 40. The discrepancy in numbers is another indication that the town list should not be dated to the eighth century BCE.

31. See n. 21 above.

(12) Of the many seventh-century archaeological finds unearthed in the Judean hill country, it is important to examine the distribution of one particular type of artifact, the "rosette" seal impression. These impressions appear on the handles of a jar type that developed from jars bearing *lmlk* seal impressions. Neutron activation analysis of two jars bearing rosette impressions found in Jerusalem and Tel Batash (Timnah) showed that both jars were manufactured in the Shephelah, probably at the same pottery center that manufactured the *lmlk* jars (Mommsen et al. 1984:106–107). Were the rosette jars manufactured by a royal authority, as were those that were inscribed *lmlk*? Scholarly opinions differ: Some believe the rosette to have been a royal symbol (Albright in Mendelsohn 1940:21, n. 51; Barkay 1978:213, n. 27; Aharoni 1979:400); others, the trade-mark of a group of potters (Mendelsohn 1940:20–21; Welten 1969:32–33; Cross 1969:22b). In any event, given the striking discrepancy between the distribution of the jars marked *lmlk* and the town list (see paragraph (5), above), it is especially interesting to examine the affinity between the distribution of rosette jars and the town list.

Following is a list of the sites in which rosette-stamped jar handles were found, arranged by districts, with the number of stamped handles found at each site appearing in parentheses (see Welten 1969:191; Barkay 1978:212–213, nn. 16–22; 1985:416–418 and n. 11; A. Mazar 1985:317; Nadelman 1989: 132):

Benjamin: Tell el-Ful (3), Gibeon (1)
Jerusalem (59)
Judean hill country: Ramat Raḥel (42), Nebi Daniel (1), Beth-zur (5)
Negeb: Tel Malhata (1), Arad (1), Tel ʿIra (3)
Wilderness: En-gedi (5)
Shephelah: Lachish (23), Azekah (9), Tell Bornâṭ (1), Tell el-Beidah (1), Tel Batash (5), Gezer (1)

It may be stated that the distribution of rosette-stamped jar handles corresponds, to a great extent, to that of the town list, as all the districts in the kingdom are represented; the towns mentioned in the list correspond more closely to the distribution of rosette jars than to the distribution of jars bearing *lmlk* seal impressions. It should be borne in mind that the number of *lmlk* jar handles found to date (about 1,200) is approximately 7.5 times greater than the number of rosette jar handles (about 160) and that, for this reason, any comparison should be cautiously undertaken.[32] Both jar types are

32. *lmlk* seal impressions were frequently stamped on several handles of the same jar (see Ussishkin 1976), whereas rosette seal impressions were stamped on two handles at

well represented in the Benjamin district; not a single specimen of either type has been found to date in the southern hill country of Ephraim (except for one *lmlk* jar handle from Bethel; see Eshel 1989). In the west, however, there is a nearly complete correspondence between the town list and the distribution of rosette jars, in contrast to the *lmlk* jars. The two exceptions in the Shephelah are Tel Batash (Timnah) and Gezer, which are not included in the town list, although rosette jars were found there. In the seventh century, Timnah was apparently part of the kingdom of Ekron (see Section 7, below); the presence of rosette jars at sites located outside the borders of the Kingdom of Judah constitutes an obvious exception. Could this possibly result from the proximity of Timnah and Gezer to the place where the jars were manufactured, and/or their close economic connections with the Shephelah towns of Judah at the time?

In summary, the information at our disposal reveals that there is little correspondence between the names and distribution of the towns in the list, on one hand, and the state of affairs prevailing in eighth-century Judah (especially in Hezekiah's day), on the other. This information also indicates the great degree of destruction and desolation that befell the Kingdom of Judah following Sennacherib's campaign; clear testimony, from both documents and archaeological findings, attests to the fact that many settlements were not inhabited in the kingdom's later stages of existence.

The inclusion of the Jericho and Bethel areas in the town list also weighs the dating question in favor of Josiah's day, as Alt claimed. The great majority of towns existing in the seventh and early sixth centuries BCE, and mentioned in the Bible or in epigraphic documents, also appear in the town list of Joshua. Conspicuous is the absence of Beth-shemesh, located on the western border of Judah, which was apparently not inhabited in the seventh century BCE. Among the other towns not mentioned in the town list are Netophah, Ramath-negeb, *rptn*, and, perhaps, also Nehalim and Beth-harapid. Thus, we see that individual towns in the kingdom, for one reason or another, may have been omitted from the list. Notable among the above mentioned omissions is Ramath-negeb, mentioned in an Arad ostracon, in a list seemingly dating from David's day (1 Sam. 30:27) and in the town list of Simeon; if this town were to be identified with Tel 'Ira, as some scholars have proposed, it was both inhabited and fortified in the late eighth and seventh centuries BCE.[33] The dis-

most (A. Mazar 1985:317 and n. 44). This factor should be taken into account when attempting to compute the total number of jars bearing impressions.

33. For the excavations at Tel 'Ira, see Beit-Arieh 1985; Biran 1985. For the identification of the site, see Lemaire 1973:21–22; Na'aman 1980:146, with earlier literature in n. 48.

tribution of rosette jars — which date from the seventh century BCE — corresponds to the scope of the town list, providing additional corroboration of my conclusion as to its proper dating.

II. Josiah's Kingdom and His Political Status

6. The Geopolitical Background and Date of the Assyrian Retreat from Palestine.

Josiah is usually considered as a strong and independent ruler, who was active for many years in the vacuum formed by the Assyrian retreat from Palestine and who succeeded in expanding considerably the borders of his kingdom. This view has many variants, concerning such points as the date of release from Assyrian bondage, the number and distribution of towns conquered by Josiah and annexed to his kingdom, and his relations with Egypt. My conclusions regarding the limited borders of the Kingdom of Judah under Josiah are of extreme importance in evaluating his achievements; these conclusions clash with many generally accepted conventions pertinent to the history of his reign.

I will now examine the sources relevant to Josiah's time and activity, to determine how they may be integrated with the conclusions obtained from analysis of the town list. I will first examine the date of the Assyrian retreat from Palestine. Some scholars have claimed that the Assyrian domination of Palestine collapsed several years before the death of Ashurbanipal in 631 BCE, and that, at the time of Josiah's rise to power, the Assyrian presence had become so weak as to be scarcely noticeable, enabling Josiah to operate for many years in the vacuum thus created (Ginsberg 1950:351–353 and n.19; Smirin 1952:13–14,31–32, 57–58, 62–63; Cross and Freedman 1953; Noth 1960: 272–273; Cogan 1974:71; Malamat 1974:270–271; Spalinger 1978a:49–51; Eph'al 1979:281–282; Spieckermann 1982:37; Miller and Hayes 1986:381–385; Halpern 1987:97). According to those scholars, the premature Assyrian retreat from Palestine was occasioned by pressure on the part of northern tribes, especially the Scythians — whose campaigns, according to Herodotus, reached as far as the Egyptian border — as well as by the erosion of Assyria's own power following the protracted wars against Babylonia, Elam, and the Arabs in 652–645 BCE. Thus, Eph'al claimed that the Gezer cuneiform tablet dated to 651 BCE, from which the name of the eponym then in office is lacking, indicates "serious breakdowns in communication and control in Palestine and perhaps in other parts of the western region of the Assyrian empire." According to his view, the revolt of the towns Ushu and Acco in ca. 644, and Manasseh's revolt as described in 2 Chr. 33:11, indicate that Assyrian control of the West began to wane in the early second half of the seventh century, and "seems to have declined rapidly thenceforward and to have ended within a few years" (Eph'al 1979:281–282). However, in a document from Gezer written in 649 BCE, the name of the eponym then in office appears; therefore, we may state that, even if there had been a brief lapse in communications in 651, following the revolt of Shamash-shum-ukin in Babylonia, it was rapidly remedied. Revolts along the coast of Lebanon recurred frequently under Sennacherib, Esarhaddon, and Ashurbanipal; the revolt of Ushu and Acco, which was suppressed by Ashurbanipal, was no exception. The account of Manasseh's revolt conceals a good deal more than it reveals (to the point that many scholars believe that no such revolt took place)[34]; even if it did happen, it was quickly overcome and the rebel ruler exiled, a fact that certainly does not indicate any Assyrian weakness.

Cogan claimed that the omission of any reference to Assyria in the account of the murder of Amon, king of Judah (2 Kgs. 21:23–24), indicates that by that time (640 BCE), Judah had already begun to free itself of the Assyrian yoke (Cogan 1974:70–71). However, the Assyrians are not mentioned throughout the description of the reigns of Manasseh, Amon, and Josiah; thus, by the same reasoning, the continuity of the Book of Kings should lead readers to conclude that Judah had freed itself of the Assyrian yoke as early as Hezekiah's day (see below). The author of the book, in describing Amon's murder, focused on the ascension of a descendant of the House of David to the throne and did not go into detail regarding the background of the deed. The Assyrians may have supported the measures enacted by those circles who placed the heir of the ancient dynasty of Judah on the throne. As their own interests were, in any event, not damaged by this development, they might have preferred not to intervene. On the other hand, the Assyrians may have intervened, and the author of the Book of Kings may have ignored this, because he described the progression of events without reference to the Assyrian presence.

Faced with these scholarly claims, we must, nonetheless, emphasize that during the decade from 650 to 640 BCE, the Assyrians were still assiduously active in the defence and development of the southwestern provinces. Evidence to that effect may be found in Ezra 4:9–10: Following the campaigns against Babylonia (652–648 BCE) and Elam (647–646), Ashurbanipal exiled residents of those remote areas and resettled them in the province of Samaria. In addition, once Ashurbanipal was no longer occupied with

34. Wellhausen 1899:206–207; North 1974:383–386; Spieckermann 1982:35–37. For a survey of scholarly opinions concerning the reliability of the description of Manasseh's exile and return, see Cogan 1974:67, n. 15; Williamson 1982:391–393.

the wars in the southern and eastern regions of his empire, he launched a campaign against the Arabs dwelling on the edge of the Syro-Arabian desert, striking them down in numbers and, thus, protecting the border areas of Syria and Palestine (Eph'al 1982:157–164). A year later (ca. 644 BCE), the Assyrian army again played a major role in the area, suppressing the revolt that had had erupted in the province of Tyre.[35] Thus, it may be seen that, during the decade 650–640 BCE, the Assyrians were still active in the Syro-Palestinian arena, suppressing elements that endangered their rule and ensuring security and prosperity throughout the region.

The last of Ashurbanipal's annals was written in 639 BCE. From that time until the appearance of the Babylonian chronicles describing the revolt in Babylonia in 626–623 BCE, we have no "historical" documents enabling the reconstruction of the history of the Assyrian empire. The Babylonian documents inform us that the years 647–627 BCE were years of peace and economic growth, characterised by continuous and uninterrupted Assyrian rule in Babylonia (Brinkman 1984:105–111). In 609–607 BCE, when all the major cities of Assyria had already fallen into his hands, King Nabopolassar of Babylonia launched campaigns into districts south of the kingdom of Urartu; this leads us to conclude that, throughout its existence, the Assyrian empire maintained control of its northern districts, up to its border with Urartu (Wiseman 1956:19–20, 45–46, 62–65). Are we to assume that a different state of affairs prevailed on its southwestern front and that Assyria had previously withdrawn from that front? The answer to this question is related to two central problems that have been extensively discussed in research to date: the evaluation of Herodotus' testimony concerning the Scythian invasion of Syria and Palestine and the date of the Egyptian expansion north of the Sinai peninsula.

Herodotus describes the Scythians as having played a major role in the chain of events throughout Western Asia in the second half of the seventh century BCE. He states (1:103–106) that, following their victories over the Cymmerians and the Medes, the Scythians continued southward into Egypt; when they reached Syria and Palestine, "Psammetichus king of Egypt met them and persuaded them with gifts and prayers to come no further." On

35. Oppenheim 1969:300b; Katzenstein 1973:293–294; Oded 1974:42, n. 55; Eph'al 1982: 157; Elayi 1983:56. The excavations at Tell Keisan unearthed a fragment of a Neo-Assyrian cuneiform tablet listing an allotment of food rations to various persons whose names are not preserved. As the Acco Plain was annexed by the Assyrians only in the last years of Esarhaddon's reign, it may be assumed that those mentioned in the tablet were exiles brought there by Ashurbanipal (Sigrist 1982; cf. Spycket 1973).

their way back, some of them robbed the temple of "Divine Aphrodite"; the Scythians then "ruled in Asia for twenty-eight years," until their defeat by the Medes under Cyaxares.[36]

Although a great deal of ink has been expended on the subject of the Scythian invasion and the Scythian's protracted control of Asia, this issue remains obscure and puzzling. Among the Indo-Iranian groups mentioned in seventh-century Assyrian documents, the Scythians may be identified with the Ishguzans, whose leader Protothyes has been identified with Partatua, a contemporary of Esarhaddon, king of Assyria (681–669 BCE).[37] Thus, Partatua's son Madyes would be the Scythian ruler who vanquished the Cymmerians and the Medes and ruled Asia. However, the reign of Esarhaddon (in whose time Protothyes ruled) and that of Cyaxares (in whose time Madyes was active) are separated by more than 50 years, a fact that makes it difficult to integrate the two sources from a chronological standpoint. Moreover, during the reign of Esarhaddon's heir Ashurbanipal, the Ishguzans had no role in the chain of events. Thus, the Assyrian sources do not help to clear up the historical picture drawn by Herodotus.[38]

The fantastic description of a huge Scythian campaign (which reached as far as the Egyptian border and, yet, within a short time, retreated and disappeared into the north, leaving no impression on the region through which its vast forces supposedly passed) is hardly plausible.[39] The overall form of the account bears some resemblance to the description of the "Hyksos" invasion given by Manetho (Josephus, *Contra Apion*, 1:14); in that passage, the Hyksos were also described as having come "from the eastern lands" to Egypt and, following a protracted period of rule, as having retreated into Syria. It should

36. The quotations are cited from the edition in *The Loeb Classical Library* (1946).

37. For the problem of the affinity between the Scythians and Ishguzans (and the Biblical Ashkenaz), see Wilke 1913:230–232; Loewenstamm 1950; Cazelles 1967: 29–30; Kammenhuber 1976–80, with earlier literature.

38. For attempts to date the Scythian activities and to reconstruct their course, see Labat 1961; Cavaignac 1961; Cogan and Tadmor 1977:80–81, n. 26; Spalinger 1978a; 1978b: 406–409; Millard 1979.

39. Many scholars have considered the Scythian invasion of the Philistine coast to be a historical event, and some have even attempted to date that event and to integrate it into a historical context (Malamat 1951:154–59; Rowley 1962–63:206–212, with earlier literature on p. 211, n. 3; Spalinger 1978a; Millard 1979; Miller and Hayes 1986:390). Cazelles (1967) proposed that the Scythians mentioned in Herodotus be considered as a garrison sent by the Assyrians to Ashdod, to stand against the Egyptian invasion of the Philistine coast. This garrison held out for 29 years (638–609 BCE), until repulsed by Pharaoh Necho II. In this way, Cazelles distinguished between the Scythians acting from the lands north of the Assyrian empire and their brethren who assisted Assyria in its struggle against Egypt.

be remembered that invasions by such nomad groups always leave a distinctive mark, because they not only overthrow the ruling power in the area, but also generate widespread havoc and destruction. Neither documents or material culture attest either to such an Assyrian defeat, or to its disastrous consequences; accordingly, those scholars who cast doubt on Herodotus' tale of the Scythian invasion of Syria and Palestine appear to have been correct (Wilke 1913:225–233, Hyatt 1940:501–502; Avi-Yonah 1962:123–127; Otzen 1964:92–95; Vaggione 1973; Cogan and Tadmor 1988:301, n. 35). Possibly, the Scythians played a certain role in the struggles between the large Indo-Iranian nomad groups then present north and northwest of the Assyrian empire and perhaps even in the crystallisation of the kingdom of Media.[40] Nonetheless, no ancient Near Eastern documents now in our possession can confirm this hypothesis; our evaluation of Herodotus' descriptions is largely based on an overall evaluation of the reliability of the information appearing in his writings on Western Asia.[41]

Generally speaking, it seems that no one managed to oust Assyria from Syria and Palestine before Ashurbanipal's death in 631 BCE and the outbreak of the revolt in Babylonia in 626 BCE.[42] It seems that the revolt that arose in Assyria following the accession of Ashur-etel-ilani in 631 BCE was no more than an episode, no different from similar rebellions following the rise of various rulers in Assyria (e.g., Tiglath-pileser III, Sargon II, and Esarhaddon) during the eighth and seventh centuries BCE. The great crisis in the Assyrian empire did not begin until after the outbreak of the revolt in Babylonia (which Assyria — despite repeated attempts — did not manage to crush between 626 and 623 BCE) and reached its zenith following the outbreak of the civil war between Sin-shar-ishkun and one of his generals in 623 BCE (Na'aman 1991: 262–264). It is no coincidence that Josiah's cultic reform began in the following year, 622 BCE, in the eighteenth year of the king's reign (2 Kgs. 22: 3; 23:23), as only at that point did he feel sufficiently secure to implement a comprehensive purge throughout the kingdom, eradicating "foreign" cults

40. See the articles cited in nn. 36–37, above. Concerning the role of Assyria in the formation of the Median Kingdom, see Brown 1986.

41. For the problem of the historical reliability of the information on Mesopotamia and Egypt given in Herodotus, see, e.g., de Meulenaere 1951; Lewy 1952; Baumgartner 1959; Africa 1963; Otzen 1964:50–51, including a listing of additional literature in n. 28; Brown 1965; Wilson 1970; Lloyds 1975; Armayor 1978; Diakonoff 1985:149–199; Zawadzki 1988:64–98, with earlier literature; Fehling 1989.

42. For a cautious and considered discussion of the problem of the Assyrian retreat from Palestine, see Barth 1977:242–250; Nelson 1983:177–184; Cogan and Tadmor 1988:291–293.

and concentrating worship of the God of Israel in the Temple in Jerusalem. Although the Chronicler's account (2 Chr. 34:3) ostensibly indicates that the reform had begun in the twelfth year of Josiah's reign, the entire description of that reform in 2 Chr. 34 does not seem plausible. Moreover, the specified date was artificially created, in view of the special doctrine of retribution held by the author of the book: Being a righteous king, Josiah would have had to demonstrate his devotion to the God of Israel immediately on attaining maturity and independence at the age of 20, as otherwise he could have been accused of tolerating idolatry in his kingdom and capital until the age of 26 (the eighteenth year of his reign).[43]

Last to be discussed is the Egyptian factor. We know that Pharaoh Psammetichus I ascended the throne of Egypt with the support of Assyria, which assisted him in thwarting the attempted re-taking of Egypt by the rulers of the Nubian (twenty-fifth) Dynasty and which took pains to maintain his senior status among the Delta princes (Kitchen 1973:391–406; Spalinger 1974a:316–326; 1974b:322–325; 1976). In 656 BCE, Psammetichus I managed to unite all of Egypt under his rule and to dethrone his competitors among the Delta princes. Neither Egyptian nor classical sources attest to any rivalry between Assyria and Egypt (Kitchen 1973:399–400, 455–461; Spalinger 1976:133–142; 1982). Only once is Egypt even mentioned in the later Assyrian sources: King Gyges of Lydia is accused of having "sent his troops to aid Tushamilki/Pishamilki, king of Egypt, who had thrown off my yoke" (Cogan and Tadmor 1977:79–80). The said military support is no more than a dispatch of mercenaries from Lydia to Egypt, which is in line both with Herodotus' report (II: 152) that Psammetichus I enlisted the aid of Ionian and Carian mercenaries and with the mention in Jeremiah (46:9) of "men of Lud" in the Egyptian army. The beginning of hostilities between Gyges and Assyria should, it seems, be dated in the mid-650s (Cogan and Tadmor 1977:78–79, n. 25, 84; Spalinger 1978b) — which is apparently when Psammetichus I freed himself from the Assyrian yoke. The Assyrian, Egyptian and Greek sources tell us nothing about hostile relationships between Assyria and Egypt; it appears that the Assyrian retreat took place following the conclusion of an agreement with Psammetichus I, Assyria's protégé-turned-ally (Gyles 1959:20–23; Spalinger 1978a:51; 1978b:402–403).

43. Gressmann 1924:313–316; Rudolph 1955:321; Mosis 1973:195–200; Cogan 1980:169–170. A number of scholars have adopted the chronology given by the author of Chronicles as the cornerstone of their own works (Oestreicher 1923:60–65; Proksch 1928:20–27; Smirin 1952:58–65; Cross and Freedman 1953; Liver 1958:418–420; Jepsen 1959:104–108; Nicholson 1967:7–14; Aharoni 1979:401–404).

The next testimony that has come down to us concerning the relations between Assyria and Egypt is from a later period: In 616 BCE, the Egyptian army was sent to the aid of king Sin-shar-ishkun of Assyria, then at war with the Babylonian army (Wiseman 1956:11–13, 44, 54–55). Two questions now arise: When did the Egyptians enter Asia, and when had Egypt become so close to Assyria as to be willing to send its army to assist its sorely beset ally? These questions have no unambiguous answers. As it seems, the Egyptian entry into Asia was not a forcible conquest, but part of an Assyrian retreat by agreement, with Egypt (gradually or rapidly) taking the place of Assyria in the vacated areas. It appears that the alliance between the two powers became especially close during the reign of Sin-shar-ishkun, after he had crushed the rebellion of his general (end of year 623 BCE) and was willing to pay a heavy territorial price in the west in order to overcome the severe danger facing him and his kingdom in the south and east.[44] Thus, the renewed alliance between Assyria and Egypt may have been concluded in the late 620s; this, in turn, would mean that only then did Assyria retreat from (and Egypt enter) the territories beyond the Euphrates (for Jer. 2:18, see Holladay 1981:64).

Herodotus states that Psammetichus I besieged Ashdod (Azotus) for twenty-nine years before finally taking the city (II:157). Tadmor attempted to interpret this passage as meaning that the siege took place, and the city fell, in 635 BCE, the twenty-ninth year of Psammetichus I's reign. He then went on to conclude that Assyria had retreated from the coast of Philistia even before 635 BCE (Tadmor 1966:101–102; Miller and Hayes 1986:383–384; Cogan and Tadmor 1988:300). This assumption, however, is not compatible with the meaning of Herodotus' statement ("Of all the cities, that Azotus, to the best of our knowledge, held out the longest time in the face of the siege"[45]); those scholars who linked the twenty-nine years mentioned in this context with Herodotus' former comment (I:106) on the twenty-eight years of Scythian rule in Asia (Wilke 1913:229; de Meulenaere 1951:30–33; Gyles 1959:22–23; Cazelles 1967:24–27, 38–39, 44) appear to have been correct. It seems that the "twenty-nine years of siege" grew out of chronological speculation on Herodotus' part: According to his calculations, the siege began when Psammetichus I set out to meet the Scythians on the coast of Philistia and persuaded them to retreat (I:105), end-

---

44. Na'aman 1991:257–267; see also Borger 1965; Zawadzki 1988, with earlier literature. Noteworthy is a document that includes a sort of declaration of war by a Babylonian king (possibly Nabopolassar) against an Assyrian king (possibly Sin-shar-ishkun) (Gerardi 1986:30–38).

45. See note 36, above.

ing immediately after the Scythian defeat by the Medes twenty-eight years later, putting an end to their rule in Asia. It seems that this is not a date enabling exact chronological dating. Apparently, Herodotus merely wished to state that Ashdod was conquered after the Scythian defeat by Cyaxares — that is, in the late seventh century BCE.

To conclude, it seems that no element endangered the Assyrian control of Syria and Palestine prior to the death of Ashurbanipal and the outbreak of the revolt in Babylonia in the 620s and that Assyrian rule continued until that time in Palestine as well. Although Egypt may have attained a foothold on the Philistine coast in some prior period, this cannot be effectively proven. Neither do we know whether Egypt was forced to conquer some of the places evacuated by Assyria, as there may well have been resistance (like that of Ashdod) or even revolts at the critical stage of the change of sovereignty. In principle, the Assyrian retreat was implemented in coordination with Egypt, which could, from all possible standpoints, be considered as a sort of "successor state" for the territories vacated by Assyria.[46] Thus, it may be concluded that Josiah was a vassal of Assyria during the first half of his reign, and that, even after freeing himself from the Assyrian yoke, he became (at least nominally) a vassal of Egypt. Still, Egypt was tied up with obligations at that time, both because it had to ensure its control of the coast and maritime transportation routes that had fallen into its hands and because of its commitment to assist Assyria in return for the territories that it had obtained west of the Euphrates.[47] Also, we should not forget the pattern of Egyptian rule dating from the period of the New Kingdom, when the main emphasis was placed on control of the valley districts and the coast, with the mountain areas being considered of secondary importance. This state of affairs gave Josiah considerable freedom of action in the internal regions of the country, and there can be no doubt that he exploited this freedom to gather strength, to unify and crystallise his kingdom (the cultic reform played a major role in these trends), and, to a certain extent, even to expand his borders.

In my opinion, the kingdom's subjugation to Assyria during the first half of Josiah's reign, and the formal subordination to Egypt during the second half, explain the way in which the author of the Book of Kings presented the relationship of the Kingdom of Judah with Assyria and Egypt. According to the description in that book, Judah freed itself from the Assyrian yoke fol-

46. See the literature cited above, and Na'aman, 1987b:11–12. For the term "successor state," taken from international law, see: Malamat 1982:195, with earlier literature in n. 17.

47. Miller and Hayes (1986:383–385, 388–390) came to the conclusion that Judah was under Egyptian dominance and probably an Egyptian vassal throughout Josiah's reign.

lowing Sennacherib's campaign, and did not become an Egyptian vassal until after Josiah's death. This extraordinary presentation, so different from the historical reality of the seventh century BCE, is (among other motives) intended to mask the fact that Josiah, the ruler of unparalleled loyalty to God and His precepts (2 Kgs. 23:25), was subordinate to foreign rulers for most of his days — a subordination perceived in the Deuteronomistic outlook as unfitting the righteous king.[48] By selecting only specific material, the author was able to present a different picture of the past, thus, portraying Josiah as having acted independently of foreign dictates throughout his rule and having been capable of implementing the necessary reforms without the intervention of a foreign element (for a comprehensive discussion of this subject, see Summary in Section 10, below).

7. The Extent of Josiah's Expansion in the East and North

In beginning the discussion of the extent of Josiah's conquests, we should make the distinction between the kingdom proper and the conquered areas outside its borders. Although it is impossible to state with any certainty the original purpose of the document in which the town lists were recorded and from which the author of the Book of Joshua drew the data for his composition, it may be assumed that it was used by the administration of the kingdom as a basis for the obligations and charges imposed by the king on his subjects. The town lists of Judah and Benjamin, then, reflect the area that was subordinate to the regular administration of the kingdom. Included in this area was the Kingdom of Judah in its old borders, "from Geba to Beer-sheba" (2 Kgs. 23:8), plus a number of additional cities (including Jericho, Zemaraim, Bethel, Ophrah), which were conquered and appended to its territory.

We shall attempt below to determine which additional areas Josiah conquered up to his death in 609 BCE. This question is one of profound controversy among scholars, and various solutions have been proposed. In the following discussion, we shall deal separately with each border of the kingdom.

In an article never published, but quoted by others, Alt proposed that Josiah expanded into Transjordan, and that his territorial claims on the districts of Israel in that area are reflected in the town lists of Gad and Reuben (Num. 32; Josh. 13). This gave rise to hostility between Jehoiakim son of Josiah and the kingdoms of Moab and Ammon (2 Kgs. 24:2) (Alt in Proksch 1928:47–48). Noth hypothesized that Josiah attempted to expand into Transjordan

48. For the associative affinity between the sins of Ahaz and Judah's subjugation to Assyria in his day (a subjugation viewed as punishment for his sins), see Ackroyd 1968:25–26; Tadmor and Cogan 1979:498–499, 506–508.

and that the thirteenth district of Josiah's kingdom included a series of towns whose list is now submerged in Joshua 13 (17b–20, 27a[a]) (Noth 1935:252–255; 1944:48–57). Ginsberg, on the other hand, suggested that Josiah conquered districts of Transjordan and, in the process, clashed with the Ammonites (see Bardtke 1936:250–251; Ginsberg 1950:362–363; Aharoni 1979:404). However, none of these hypotheses have any solid textual basis; in fact, they are nothing more than bold reconstructions.[49]

Based on the existence of Galilean town lists in Josh. 19, Alt assumed that Josiah realized his claim on areas of the kingdom of Israel, conquered Galilee (in which there still remained a significant Israelite population), and annexed it to his territory (Alt 1927). From the absence of town lists pertaining to Samaria, he concluded that Josiah skipped that area deliberately — apparently in view of the considerable non-Israelite population there — and contented himself with the destruction and annexation of Bethel. This hypothesis has not been supported, even by Alt's own students, and is of no real validity.[50]

Most scholars agree that, following the Assyrian retreat, Josiah conquered all of the Samarian hill country; some even believe that he included that area within his cultic reform (see, e.g., Smirin 1952:63–64; Milgrom 1971:26–27; Malamat 1974:271). This assumption is based on the text of 2 Kgs, 23:19, "And all the shrines also of the high places that were in the cities of Samaria, which kings of Israel had made, provoking the Lord to anger, Josiah removed; he did to them according to what he had done at Bethel." It seems, however, that verses 19–20 (or, more correctly, the entire section, from verse 16 to verse 20) are a later expansion, written by an author who edited the description of the destruction of the altar at Bethel (verses 16–17a) (Welten 1969:163, n. 21; Ogden 1978:31–33; Spieckermann 1982:116–119,427–428; Rofé 1982:145–146). It may be assumed that Josiah could then act without hindrance throughout the province of Samaria, which, following its annexation and reorganisation and the "two way" mass deportations by the Assyrians, had lost a great deal of its former national identity, and, after the Assyrian retreat, no longer had the strength and internal cohesion to compete with him. Possibly, he tried to uproot Assyrian cult in that province — a cult that was practiced throughout the Assyrian provinces and constituted a vital factor in their unification

49. For criticism of these hypotheses, see Smirin 1952:90; Liver 1958:420–421; Kallai 1986:413–414.

50. Proksch (1928:46–47) supported this hypothesis; Noth (1935:215–230), however, rejected it. See Kallai 1986:405–410.

into a single, well-formed group.[51] However, we must cast doubt upon the assumption that he implemented a reform in Samaria similar to that implemented in Judah and Jerusalem, in whose wake all the local centers of cult were cancelled. Unfortunately, we do not know which sources the author had at his disposal when composing the description in verses 19–20 — whether he developed and expanded the tale of reform at Bethel without benefit of additional sources, or based his narrative on additional written material covering Josiah's reign.

The problem of the scope of Josiah's action and the extent of his presence in the area involves two further questions: (1) Did he also expand his influence into Galilee? and (2) What were the circumstances that led him to his death at Megiddo? The second question will be covered in a separate section; the first will be discussed here.

Many scholars have used the text of 2 Chr. 34:6–7, 33 as a basis for arguing that Josiah's expansion extended into Galilee and that that area was even included in his cultic reform (Smirin 1952:90; Cross and Freedman 1953:57–58; Liver 1958:421; Noth 1960:274, 278; Kallai 1960:75–76; Aharom 1979:309–310). This is the origin of the radical view that holds that Josiah had concrete claim to the entire territory of the kingdom of Israel and that he attempted to reinstate the great kingdom of David, in theory and in practice, throughout the territory of Israel, up to its remotest borders (Proksch 1928:48; Ginsberg 1950: 362; Smirin 1952:63, 97; Cross and Freedman 1953:56; Noth 1960:274; Otzen 1964:62–123; Aharoni 1979:310; Clements 1984:96). To illustrate this, let me quote Cross' work: "He (Josiah) attempted to restore the kingdom or empire of David in all detail. The cultus was centralized according to the ancient law of the sanctuary, and Passover was celebrated as it had not been 'since the days of the Judges.' The story of the renewal of the covenant and the resurrection of the Davidic empire by the reincorporation of the North is told at a length not given to the labors of other approved kings after David" (Cross 1973:283; see von Rad 1958:89).

These reconstructions, however, are built on shaky foundations, and the presentation of a cultic reform that encompassed all of the Cisjordanian areas is mainly the result of the deliberately tendentious description given by the author of Chronicles, in light of his special perception of the last period in the history of the kingdoms of Judah and Israel, from Hezekiah's day to the destruction of the kingdom (Williamson 1977:119–131; Japhet 1977:

51. For the role played by Assyrian cult in the formation of the provinces, see Cogan 1974:49–55.

254–255, 282–284). Although the content of Chronicles is indicative of its author's unique historiography, we must not use this material as the basis for a description of Josiah's rule. It is, of course, possible that the fall of Assyria may have aroused hopes and longings for a return to the glorious past. Nonetheless, hopes and longings are often incompatible with historical reality, and there are no grounds for the assumption that Josiah attempted to conquer the entire North and to impose his reforms throughout the territory of Palestine.

In summary, it is definitely possible that Josiah expanded in the Samarian hill country, although the information on this is not sufficiently clear and there is no way to determine the actual extent of his activity in the area. On the other hand, his expansion certainly ran no further north than the central hill country, and there is no basis for the hypothesis that either Galilee or the Jezreel Valley was also included within the boundaries of his kingdom.

8. The Extent of Josiah's Expansion in the West and his Relations with Egypt

In light of the assumption that the town list of Dan (Josh. 19:41–46) belongs to the original town list document, Alt assumed that Josiah conquered and annexed the northern Shephelah area, as far south as Joppa (Alt 1925: 109–111, 115). For hundreds of years, this area had been controlled by foreign kingdoms; when Josiah acquired sufficient strength, he conquered it, as well as the neighboring kingdom of Ekron. Alt found corroboration for this theory in the list of those returning from Babylonia (Ezra 2:33; Neh. 7:37), which mentions men from Lod, Hadid, and Ono. In Alt's opinion, those settlements were included within the borders of the Kingdom of Judah from the time of their conquest by Josiah and up to the destruction of the kingdom; their inhabitants were then exiled by the Babylonians (Alt 1925:110–111).

The assumption that the town list of Dan reflects Josiah's expansion to the west has not been accepted by most scholars (see above); nevertheless, several scholars have considered the list of those returning from Babylonia as attesting to the westward expansion of the kingdom (Smirin 1952:97; Liver 1958:420; Kallai 1960:77; Barth 1977:256–259). This view celebrated its victory with the discovery of the Meṣad Ḥashavyahu fortress in northern Philistia, near Yavneh-Yam (for the excavations of the site, see Naveh 1977:862–863; Reich 1989). Found there were ostraca, whose text, written in the Hebrew alphabet, is in a language close to Biblical Hebrew and includes a number of Yahwistic names (Hosha'yahu, Ḥashavyahu, 'Obadyahu). In light of the above, it has been assumed that Meṣad Ḥashavyahu was built by Josiah during his takeover of the coastline south of Joppa; these findings have been presented as conclusive proof of the argument that Josiah conquered vast areas in the northern Shephelah, down to the coast itself.[52]

Was Meṣad Ḥashavyahu indeed built by the king of Judah? It seems to me that the data must be interpreted in a manner different from previous interpretations. First, we must emphasize that the plan of the fortress is unparalleled by any other fortress excavated to date in Judah and that its roots must apparently be sought elsewhere. Typical Eastern Greek pottery, originating in the eastern Greek islands and in Asia Minor, was discovered on the site in large quantities, indicating the presence of mercenaries of western origin. By contrast, only a few sherds of this type of pottery have been found to date in other excavations in Judah.[53] There is no evidence of western mercenaries having served in the army of Judah during this period, and the assumption that Josiah enlisted such mercenaries into his army is largely based on interpretation of the findings at Meṣad Ḥashavyahu.[54] On the other hand, there is clear evidence that mercenaries from Asia Minor served in the Egyptian army and even occupied fortresses built within Egypt. In the annals of Ashurbanipal, King Gyges of Lydia is accused of having sent his army to the assistance of King Psammetichus I of Egypt (cf. Jer. 46:9); this evidence is contemporary (mid-seventh century) with the service of mercenaries from western Anatolia in the Egyptian army (Cogan and Tadmor 1977: 79–80; Spalinger 1978b). Herodotus (II:152) states that Psammetichus I took control of Egypt with the aid of Ionian and Carian mercenaries. In another place (II:30), Herodotus mentions three border fortresses staffed with Greek mercenaries during Psammetichus I's reign: Elephantine on the Nubian border, Daphnae (Tahpanhes) on the Arabian border, and Marea on the Libyan border. Excavations at Tell Defenneh have revealed clear ceramic evidence, including locally manufactured Eastern Greek pottery, attesting to the set-

52. Naveh 1960:136–139; 1977:863; Tadmor 1966:102; Strange 1966:134–139; Welten 1969:66, 100–102; Malamat 1974:272, 277; Barth 1977:257–259; Aharoni 1979:312, 403; Spieckermann 1982:145. Miller and Hayes (1986:389), on the other hand, suggested that Greek and Judahite contingents were stationed by the Egyptians at Meṣad Ḥashavyahu and were employed to guard the coast south of Joppa. For a similar suggestion, see Na'aman 1987b:12–14.

53. For the distribution of Eastern Greek pottery in Palestine, see Stern 1982:283–286; Biran 1985:27.

54. Frequently mentioned in the Arad ostraca are the Kittim. Aharoni (1981:12–13) regarded them as "Greek or Cypriot mercenaries serving in the Judahite army, perhaps especially in garrisons of the more remote fortresses." He further noted the Eastern Greek pottery found at Meṣad Ḥashavyahu, suggesting that "here was a garrison of Greek mercenaries working for Josiah." This hypothesis had already been raised by Aharoni in the original publication of the ostraca (1966:4–5 and n. 9).

tlement of mercenaries from Asia Minor. Also discovered, in the foundation layer, were cartouches of Psammetichus I, indicating the date of establishment of the site (Petrie 1888; Boardman 1980:133–134; Oren 1984:12–13, 37–38). The site of Migdol, called Stratopeda by Herodotus (II:152), close to the Pelusian arm of the Nile, has been excavated, revealing Eastern Greek pottery alongside Phoenician and Palestinian pottery (Oren 1984). In the opinion of the excavator, the non-Egyptian pottery (Eastern Greek, Phoenician, and Palestinian) had been brought there by foreign mercenaries, who had settled on the site.

In this context, let me also recall the words of Jeremiah (44:1; 46:14) regarding the settlement of Jews in Migdol, Tahpanhes, and Memphis. This evidence is in line with the evidence from Elephantine regarding the settlement of Jewish mercenaries there (Porten 1968:3–27), and with additional evidence of Phoenicians having served as mercenaries and garrisons in Egypt (Katzenstein 1978; Oren 1984:36). It may be stated that, in the days of the Twenty-sixth Dynasty, starting in the reign of Psammetichus I, mercenaries from Asia Minor, Phoenicia, and Judah served in the Egyptian army, took part in campaigns, and even dwelt in fortresses built by the Egyptians (de Meulenaere 1951:22–43; Kienitz 1953:35–47; Otzen 1964:51–62; Spalinger 1976:137–138, 145–146, nn. 30–43; Oren 1984:30–38).

In view of the above, the Meṣad Ḥashavyahu findings should be re-examined. I have already pointed out that mercenaries of western origin were posted on the site and that the findings there included ostraca bearing Yahwistic names; however, another ostracon found at Meṣad Ḥashavyahu bears an obviously Phoenician name (with the theophoric element of 'Ba'al') unknown in Judah in the seventh century BCE (Naveh 1962:30–31; Lemaire 1977:268–269). Thus, it appears that the fortress was built by the Egyptians, perhaps according to an Egyptian plan (therefore, its plan is alien in comparison to that of fortresses in Judah), and was staffed by mercenaries of mixed origin — Greek, Phoenician, and Judahite — similar to the situation that prevailed in other sites at the time of the Saitic (Twenty-sixth) Dynasty in Egypt. It seems that, following their takeover of Palestine after the Assyrian retreat, the Egyptians felt a need to ensure the route running from the Philistine coast to the port of Joppa and the north, and, for this reason, they built a fortress near the border of Philistia and populated it with foreign garrisons.

At this point, we should inquire: What was the background for the service of Judahites in the fortress and in the fields of a nearby place called Ḥaṣar Asam, and what is the situation reflected by the letter of complaint found on the site? To answer these questions, let me first examine the manner in which the Egyptians ran their administrative centers in the conquered lands.

The best source available for the study of this problem is the Amarna archive, which admittedly reflects a period hundreds of years before the Saitic Dynasty. The Amarna documents indicate that the Egyptians relied, to a great extent, on their vassals in Canaan to manage their administrative centers (Helck 1971:246–255; Na'aman 1981:177–181, 184–185; 1982:195–212, 241–251; Hachmann 1982). The vassals were required to serve as garrisons in the cities, guarding their walls, gates, and installations; to plough and reap the fields adjoining those cities; and to repair the damage caused to them. Enlisted to work the land were workers from nearby or even distant kingdoms, and the responsibility for performance of that work was imposed on the rulers of those kingdoms (Na'aman 1988).

The picture reflected in the Amarna letters is well in line with the Meṣad Ḥashavyahu findings; the presence of a garrison from Judah in the fortress and of corvée workers in the adjoining fields (see below) are best explained in light of the assumption that Judah was then subject to Egypt. If this is so, we may attempt to reconstruct the situation reflected in the letter of complaint as follows:[55] The group of reapers, including the complainant, was working in Ḥaṣar Asam near the fortress. Each worker had to reap a certain quota of land during the period allotted for the work, and then to store the harvested grain. As the complainant did not complete his quota in time, he was punished by having his garment taken away by his superior, Hosha'yahu. As scholars have shown, this punishment is suitable for corvée workers, who were not paid for their labor, but not for paid workers, tenant farmers, or sharecroppers, who could be punished by reducing their salary or share in the harvest (Amusin and Heltzer 1964:154–157; Talmon 1964; Pardee 1978:55–57). After some time, when his garment had not been returned to him, the punished worker complained to the officer of the fortress. The latter was certainly appointed by the king of Judah and in charge of all the recruits — both military personnel and corvée workers — serving in that area; we have seen that the Amarna documents also indicate that the responsibility for implementation of works was imposed upon the Canaanite rulers. Thus, the officer was able to order Hosha'yahu to restore the complainant's garment to him.[56]

The exact date of the Meṣad Ḥashavyahu ostraca is unknown, and we cannot determine whether they belong to Josiah's day (and, thus, indicate his subordination to Psammetichus I), or to those of his sons Jehoahaz

55. For the interpretation of the Meṣad Ḥashavyahu ostracon, see Naveh 1960:129–139; Lemaire 1977:259–269, including a listing of additional literature on pp. 259–260; Sasson 1978; 1984; Pardee 1978; 1980; Suzuki 1982.

56. For the term *śr* ("officer"), see Rüterswörden 1985.

or Jehoiakim, both of whom were vassals to Necho II. The desertion of the fortress by the mercenaries may be dated at 604 BCE, the year in which Nebuchadrezzar launched a campaign to the Philistine coast, thrust out the Egyptians, and destroyed Ashkelon (Wiseman 1956:28, 47, 68–69, lines 18–20; Malamat 1975:130–131).

The subordination of Judah to Egypt is also indicated by the findings at Arad. In a series of ostraca, the Arad fortress commander Elyashib is ordered to transfer large quantities of supplies to members of a group referred to as Kittim (*ktym*). Aharoni noted that the reference is to Greek or Cypriot mercenaries, but interpreted this as evidence that such mercenaries served in the Judahite army.[57] It is, however, more likely that these were mercenaries in the Egyptian or Babylonian army and that the king of Judah, then subordinate to either Egypt or Babylonia, was obligated to transfer supplies to these units, which were surely either en route through the Beer-sheba Valley, or encamped in fortresses along the roads (Miller and Hayes 1986:389, 417). It is difficult to determine the extent of the Kittim units, in view of the uncertainty concerning the quantities of bread and wine consumed by one soldier in one day, as well as the exact volume of the measuring units mentioned in the documents (*bath*, *homer*, etc.); nevertheless, these units apparently consisted of several tens of soldiers each.[58] The transfer of supplies to the mercenaries of Egypt or Babylonia was implemented by the Arad fortress commander, and certainly by other local commanders, and was a considerable burden on the kingdom.

The findings from the fortress at Kadesh-barnea may also indicate the service of Judahites in a local garrison. The fortress, constructed in the late eighth or seventh century, is rectangular in shape; its casemate walls rest on massive underground offset/inset foundation walls (Dothan 1965:134–143; contra Cohen 1981; 1983). In my opinion, Egyptian control of the site during the last phase of the fortress' existence is hinted at by the presence of ostraca

---

57. See the literature cited in n. 54, above; Lemaire 1977:159–161, 229–230,233. For the Kittim (Kittiyim) in the Bible, see Loewenstamm 1962, with earlier literature.

58. Lemaire 1977:229–230; Aharoni 1981:15–16, 144–145. Lemaire (1977:159–160) considered the possibility that the Kittim were merchants of Greek origin, but preferred the hypothesis that they were Greek mercenaries. Rainey suggested that the Kittim were convoy leaders from the town of Kition in Cyprus and were, therefore, Phoenicians and not Greeks. Their supplies were provided in the framework of the duties imposed on the Kingdom of Judah as vassal to the Neo-Babylonian Empire then controlling the area (Rainey 1986:25; see Herzog et al. 1984:31). Notwithstanding the above, the hypothesis of dozens of convoy leaders marching along the Beer-sheba Valley under the protection of the Neo-Babylonian Empire seems unlikely. Garfinkel has proposed that the *qrsy* mentioned in ostracon No. 18 from Arad was also of western origin (Garfinkel 1988b).

in hieratic writing, bearing various figures (from 1 to 10,000) and dimension units commonly in use in the area at the time (Lemaire and Vernus 1980; 1983). These may have been used by pupils of Semitic origin, for practice in the Egyptian method of record-keeping then in force; this would explain the few Semitic words appearing on the ostraca. Some of the pottery vessels discovered on site were made by hand ("Negebite" pottery) and others on a potters' wheel; the latter resemble vessels from Judah and coastal sites. Some examples of coloured "Idumaean" pottery, originating in southern Transjordan, were also found (Cohen 1983:12: E. Mazar 1985:264) Additional ostraca discovered at the site are written in alphabetic writing. Admittedly, only after complete publication of the material will it be possible to formulate a considered opinion of the cultural relations between the site and the neighboring kingdoms during that period. Nevertheless, as a "working hypothesis," I would like to propose that the building of the casemate fortress with wide offset/inset foundation walls at Kadesh-barnea was initiated by the Assyrians and that the last phase of this fortress was controlled by the Egyptians. It was staffed by garrisons either from the vassal kingdoms, or perhaps by Semitic mercenaries from the surrounding kingdoms.

Why, in any event, did Josiah go no further westward than the edges of the northern Shephelah and refrain from penetrating the Biblical inheritance of Dan? An unequivocal answer to this question has been given by archaeological research. Excavations at Tel Miqne (Ekron) have shown that a very large town, more than 200 dunams in area, flourished there during the seventh century, and that its economy was principally based on the production of olive oil (Gitin 1989). The sudden growth of Ekron, following a period of decline that had lasted approximately 200–250 years — since the destruction of the Iron I city in about the mid-tenth century BCE — indubitably resulted from Sennacherib's campaign to Judah. Following that campaign, most of the Shephelah towns were razed and a considerable portion of their inhabitants exiled to Assyria. This state of affairs permitted Ekron to take the place of its stronger neighbor to the east, to exploit some of its agricultural territories, to expand its area and population, and to develop its economy. Judah's obvious weakness along its western border following Sennacherib's campaign, no less than Ekron's rise to power, prevented Josiah from expanding westward. It should be remembered that Egypt had always had interests on the Philistine coast and that any strike against one of the more important Philistine kingdoms was considered a direct strike against Egyptian interests. This was the reason for the destruction of Philistine cities, Egypt's protégés, by the Babylonians during their conquest of the area. The territory of Judah in the northern Shephelah, as reflected in the town-list in Joshua, included only Zorah and Eshtaol: to the west extended the territory of the Kingdom of

Ekron, with Timnah (Tel Batash), and certainly also all of the Biblical inheritance of Dan included therein.[59]

How can we explain the appearance of residents of Lod, Hadid, and Ono in the list of those returning from Babylonia? As we recall, Alt proposed that those places were included in the Kingdom of Judah on the eve of the Babylonian conquest, following which their inhabitants were exiled, a proposal supported by additional scholars. Are we indeed to assume that every place mentioned in the list of those returning from Babylonia belonged to the Kingdom of Judah in the last years of the First Temple?

To clarify this problem, let me (briefly) examine the tribal genealogies of Benjamin (Rudolph 1955:77–79; Kallai 1960:38–40; Williamson 1982:84–85). Mentioned in those lists is Elpaal, who built Ono and Lod (1 Chr. 8:12); also mentioned are Beriah and Shema, "heads of fathers' houses of the inhabitants of Aijalon" (8:13). Noteworthy is the appearance of Beriah in the genealogies of Benjamin. The family of Beriah was originally an important Ephrathite family (7:23). Following the fall of the Northern Kingdom, as families from Benjamin migrated westward and settled in Aijalon, formerly an Ephrathite city, they mingled with families there, including that of Beriah. Thus, the latter family was listed in the tribal genealogies of Benjamin.

It seems to me that this migration of the Benjaminite families to Aijalon, Lod, and Ono belongs to the period of the *pax Assyriaca* in the seventh century BCE, when borders were opened and relations strengthened between the various districts in and around the empire.[60] During that period, groups left Benjamin and wandered outside the borders of the Kingdom of Judah, to settle in areas that promised them a better living. During the Babylonian conquest, residents of those places, as well as members of many other groups in the area, may have been exiled in circumstances unknown to us.[61] Their Benjaminite origin may have caused them to strengthen their relations with

59. For the role of Tel Batash in the border system of the seventh century, see Na'aman 1987b:14, n. 21.

60. Dating the westward migration of the Benjaminites in Josiah's period is in line with the dates proposed by Rudolph (1955:77) and Kallai (1960:40). Concerning the *pax Assyriaca* and its effects on economics and settlement, see Na'aman 1987b:8–15.

61. A fitting example of a deportation whose background remains obscure is given by Josephus, quoting the third-century Chaldean historian Berossus (*Ant.* X:232; *Contra Apion* I:136–137): Following Nebuchadrezzar's defeat of the Egyptians at Carchemish in 605 BCE, "the prisoners — Jews, Phoenicians, Syrians, and those of Egyptian nationality" were conducted to Babylonia (Stern 1976:58). For a discussion of this passage and its historical background, see Katzenstein 1973:306–307, with earlier literature; Malamat 1975:130; Miller and Hayes 1986:389. The settling of exiled groups belonging to various nations in Babylonia

the Judahite exiles in Babylonia; during the Post-exilic period, they came back to their places of origin in Palestine.

One may likewise assume that the lists of those "who came up out of the captivity" in Ezra 2 and Neh. 7 in fact combine those who returned (listed by family association) and those who had remained in the land (listed by their place of residence) (Galling 1951:157; Japhet 1983:114; Williamson 1987a:31). The inhabitants of Lod, Hadid and Ono lived outside the confines of Judah in the pre-exilic and post-exilic periods, but, nevertheless, were considered as Israelites by the author of the Books of Ezra and Nehemiah, due to their Benjaminite origin.

In my opinion, the lists of those returning from Babylonia cannot provide a solid basis for determining the extent of the Kingdom of Judah in its last years. Thus, for example, there is no way to ascertain whether Bethel remained within the borders of Judah after the Babylonian conquest, or was returned to the Babylonian province of Samaria. Only a careful examination of all the sources enables us to attempt to determine which places were included within the territory of Judah on the eve of the Babylonian deportations at the beginning of the sixth century BCE, as well as the territorial affinity between these places and the places mentioned in the list of those returning from Babylonia.

9. *The Circumstances Leading to Josiah's Death*

In the discussions of the relationship between the Kingdom of Judah and Egypt, an important role is occupied by the death of Josiah near Megiddo in 609 BCE. A great deal of literature has been written on this subject, with the main difference of opinion centering on the question whether to give credence to the version related in 2 Chr. 35:20–24, despite its drastic deviation from that given in 2 Kgs. 23:29–30 (Spieckermann 1982:138–153; Višaticki 1987:121–128; Begg 1987; Williamson 1987b; Cogan and Tadmor 1988:300–302). In 609 BCE, Pharaoh Necho II (610–595 BCE) launched a campaign to northern Syria, in an effort to assist his ally, Ashur-uballiṭ II, who was sorely beset by the Babylonians and Medes and was about to lose his last foothold in western Mesopotamia. Many scholars tend to accept the hypothesis that, on his way north with his army, Necho II passed through Palestine and encountered Josiah near Megiddo. In this context, let me pose a question not hitherto sufficiently discussed: Why did the Pharaoh and his army have to pass

---

during the sixth and fifth centuries BCE is indicated by the documents unearthed in the excavations; however, only in a very few instances have actual historical sources for deportations been preserved.

through Palestine on their way to northern Syria? Why did Necho II not adopt the tactics of the Egyptian kings at the time of the New Kingdom, who often sailed as far as the Lebanese coast and launched campaigns from there, via the Nahr el-Kebir (Eleutheros), to the Orontes River?[62] In this way, Necho II could have gone by sea to the Lebanese coast and set out from there on foot, by way of his military base at Riblah on the Orontes, to northern Syria, shortening the travel time and refraining from exhausting his forces in a grueling forced march from the Egyptian border to the battlefield near the Euphrates.

In this context, we note that Egypt controlled Phoenicia during the years prior to the campaign of 609 BCE. Indicative of Egypt's control of the Lebanese coast at that time is a stele dated to Psammetichus I's fifty-second year (612 BCE), which records the burial of an Apis and mentions the tax paid by the Phoenician kings to Egypt and the appointment of an Egyptian inspector over them (Freedy and Redford 1970:477; Spalinger 1977:228–229; 1978a: 55, n. 27). A stele of Psammetichus I was discovered in Arvad; a fragment of an inscription, perhaps dating from that king's reign, was found in Tyre; and a stele of Necho II was found in Sidon (Otzen 1964:90–91; Katzenstein 1973:299, n. 24, 313, n. 100). The Nebuchadrezzar inscription from Wādi Brisa mentions "the evil enemy," undoubtedly the King of Egypt, who controlled the mountains of Lebanon until his eviction by the Babylonian ruler.[63]

It appears to me that the reason why Necho II chose to travel via Palestine lies in the transfer of power that had taken place in Egypt not long before. Psammetichus I had died between July and September of 610 BCE, and 609 was the second regnal year of his successor, Necho II (Freedy and Redford 1970:474, nn. 47–48). Helck has pointed out that Egyptian officials customarily took an oath of fealty to the reigning Pharaoh; when the king died, the oath became invalid, and the officials had to swear an oath to his successor. In view of this fact, Helck raised the hypothesis that during the period of the New Kingdom the Canaanite kings also had to swear fealty to every new ruler and gave this as the explanation for campaigns made by several Egyptian

62. Alt 1950; Helck 1971:137–156; Na'aman 1986a:131. Several scholars have assumed that, on previous campaigns, the Egyptians conveyed their forces to Syria by sea (Smirin 1952:100; Liver 1958:421; Yoyotte 1960:372, 375). For the development of marine transportation under the Twenty-Sixth Dynasty, see de Meulenaere 1951:60–63; Gyles 1959:29–30; Spalinger 1978c:20–21, with earlier literature.

63. For a translation of the inscription, see Oppenheim 1955:307. For a discussion of it, see Spalinger 1977:227–229, with earlier literature in nn. 18–19. It should be emphasized that Egypt controlled the coast of Lebanon at the time and that this was not merely a case of trade relations, as was assumed by Katzenstein (1973:298–304). See also Otzen 1964:78–95.

kings to Canaan in the first year of their rule (Helck 1971:247; see Lorton 1974:passim; Redford 1985:7 n. 2).[64] Necho II apparently came to Palestine in 609 BCE for that very reason: to administer an oath of fealty to his vassals, whose previous oath had become invalid on his father's death. There is, then, no need to assume that the entire Egyptian army passed through Palestine on the way north; it is even probable that Necho II reached Palestine by sea on his way to the Lebanese coast and stopped in Palestine only briefly. Moreover, one may wonder whether he did not take the opportunity to enlist an army from among his vassals and append them to the Egyptian expeditionary force on its way north. It should be remembered that, at various times during the time of the New Kingdom, auxiliary forces were enlisted from among the vassals to assist the Egyptian army in its wars (Na'aman 1981:180–181, n. 46). This may also have been the case in 609 BCE: Necho's vassals may have been ordered to dispatch army units to assist in the northward campaign.

It is against this background that we should re-examine the Biblical description of the events of 609 BCE. Let me first cite the passage from 2 Kgs. 23: 29: "In his days Pharaoh Necho king of Egypt went up to the king of Assyria to the river Euphrates. King Josiah went to meet him; and Pharaoh Necho slew him at Megiddo, when he saw him." The verse opens with the word *bymyw* ("in his days") — a typical editorial opening formula that introduces a chronistic account (cf. 1 Kgs. 16:34; 2 Kgs. 8:20; 24:1) (Montgomery 1934: 49; Spieckermann 1982:139; Cogan and Tadmor 1988:96, 291). The account that follows does not give the slightest hint of a battle. Therefore, it is possible that Josiah reported to the Egyptian ruler, his lord, at Megiddo, to swear an oath of fealty to him and that, in the critical situation of the new ruler's impending first campaign to the north, Josiah was suspected or accused of disloyalty and slain on the spot.[65] Immediately afterward, Necho II continued on his northward campaign, and Jehoahaz son of Josiah was crowned in

---

64. For a different opinion, see Morschauser 1988.

65. Some scholars, rejecting the version given in Chronicles and viewing it as a sort of later interpretation arising from an attempt to fill in the gaps in Kings, have proposed various reconstructions for the account of Josiah's death. According to one supposition, Josiah was executed because his responses did not satisfy the Egyptian ruler before whom he was brought to trial (Welch 1925; Boehmer 1933:203); another hypothesis states that Josiah controlled Megiddo, but, by some unknown means, fell into Necho's hands and was put to death (Noth 1960:278–279); or Josiah may have controlled Megiddo, set out to greet Necho as he passed through the town, and was thus caught and killed (Pfeifer 1969:305–306); or the two rulers may have met as allies, in an attempt to reach a mutual understanding, but Necho traitorously slew Josiah in the course of that meeting (Nelson 1983:186–189). A few scholars have discussed this incident without suggesting solutions of their own (Frost 1968: 376; Miller and Hayes 1986:402; Cogan and Tadmor 1988:301).

Judah (2 Kgs. 23:30). Nevertheless, although he failed in his campaign against Babylonia and was forced to retreat from Mesopotamia,[66] Necho II was still in absolute control of Judah: He was able to arrest the Judahite ruler who appeared before him, in Riblah, to swear an oath of fealty and to obtain Necho's permission to rule in Judah, to crown another ruler (Jehoiakim) according to his own choice, and to impose a heavy tax on the kingdom (2 Kgs. 23:31–35). During the implementation of these measures, Necho II remained in Riblah in Syria and, to the best of my knowledge, required no military means to impose his will. This is enough to confirm the conclusion that, as early as Josiah's day, Judah was at least formally subordinate to Egypt and that the slaying of Josiah was intended to intimidate the Judahites into abiding by the Egyptian ruler's instructions.

Did Josiah perhaps try to change the status quo and rebel against Egypt? Did he take advantage of the transfer of power and of the crucial situation of 609 BCE to attack the new ruler when he passed through Palestine? This is the conjecture made by several scholars, who rejected the evidence given in Kings and preferred the detailed account in 2 Chr. 35:20–24.[67] I will not analyze this problematic account, the wide range of opinions expressed concerning it, or the complex historiographic problems that it raises.[68] It seems to me that the entire description is no more than a far-ranging, speculative interpretation, given by the author of Chronicles to the brief and unenlightening description in Kings, in an attempt to adapt it to his own special doctrine of retribution, while integrating descriptions of the deaths of two rulers — Ahab, king of Israel (1 Kgs. 22:29–36), and Ahaziah, king of Judah (2 Kgs. 9:27–28) — which he found in his source, the Book of Kings (Welch 1925:255; Welten 1969:164–166).

66. For the Egyptian campaign against Haran in 609 BCE, see Wiseman 1956:18–19, 45, 62–63, lines 66–69; Grayson 1975:96, lines 66–69. In the course of that campaign, a large Egyptian army crossed the Euphrates and set out for Haran. On the way, it conquered a town occupied by a Babylonian garrison (this, in my opinion, is the correct restoration of line 67), and encamped opposite Haran. Line 69: "Until the month of Elul they did battle against the city but achieved nothing. [They turned (?) and] withdrew" (*mim-ma ul il-[qu-ú issuḫūma(?) ana arki-šu]-nu iḫḫisu*). Wiseman's and Grayson's translation for the end of the line ("they did not withdraw") is mistaken. Rather, we must adopt the reconstructions suggested by Lewy (1925:76–77, line 69) and Landsberger and Bauer (1926:88 and n. 2).

67. For the theological interpretation of the war and its consequences, see Augustin 1988.

68. Williamson (1987b) attempted to prove that the author of Chronicles had at his disposal an independent source, in addition to the Book of Kings, from which to drew his description. The main reason for this claim was the order of writing used to describe this incident in Chronicles, which differs from that in Kings, whereas, in other descriptions, the

It is important to emphasize that the assumption of a battle near Megiddo raises a number of difficulties. Why would the ruler of a small kingdom choose to fight the ruler of a great power in battle on an open field, in circumstances giving the larger, stronger army all possible advantages?[69] Why would he make a stand in a place so far from his kingdom, which did not provide him with any advantage at all?[70] Furthermore, if Josiah was such a strong ruler as to dare to report for battle on an open field against the king of Egypt, why did his kingdom surrender unconditionally, so soon after his death, enabling Necho II to assume absolute control? Why did king Jehoahaz of Judah not trust his fortresses and his army — in those districts where the Egyptian army was obviously weak and where he could have enjoyed a significant advantage over his rival — especially as the king of Egypt had just failed in his campaign and was hard pressed by the Babylonians? Why did he report, of his own will, to distant Riblah, even though he could easily have guessed the king of Egypt's reaction (cf. Jer. 22:10–12)?

In view of these considerations, it seems preferable to adopt the brief, untendentious testimony in the Book of Kings, rather than the detailed and colourful description in the Book of Chronicles, and to assume that Necho II slew Josiah when he appeared before him, perhaps to swear an oath of fealty. The background for this deed is unknown, and any possible hypothesis in this

order of writing in the two books is more or less the same. It may be, however, either that a later editor intervened, changing the order of writing in Kings after that book had been used as a source by the author of Chronicles, or that the latter author had at his disposal a different version of Kings, in which the incidents were recorded in inverse order (for this problem, see Lemke 1965). The argument proposing the existence of an independent source that antedated Chronicles obviously does not prove the reliability of that hypothetical source; in my opinion, the evidence cited by Williamson seems hardly sufficient to confirm his hypothesis concerning the existence of a source of this type.

69. On reporting for battle in an open field, see Eph'al 1983:91–94.

70. Some doubt should be cast upon the multi-level "structure" erected by Malamat (1973), in his effort to explain why Josiah reported for battle, of all places, in distant Megiddo. His reconstruction is founded on the assumption that the king of Judah launched a surprise attack on the Egyptian army, which was then headed northward, toward the Euphrates (1973:274–278). Nonetheless, those accepting the testimony in 2 Chr. 35:20–24 cannot simultaneously accept this hypothesis: According to the Chronicler's description, negotiations initially took place between the parties and only after that did the two armies take up positions opposite each other and commence the battle, in the course of which Josiah was killed by the Egyptian archers (just as Ahab had been killed, in a similar situation, by the Aramean archers). The assumption of a surprise attack and of springing "an ambush on his enemy in the Plain of Megiddo . . . before the Egyptian army could deploy on the plain or find protection within Megiddo" (*ibid.*:277) has no basis in the Chronicler's description of the event.

regard (dissatisfaction at the independence shown by the king of Judah and evidenced by his reforms; his activity in Samaria, outside the borders of his kingdom; his refusal to send an army to assist the king of Egypt in his campaign) will remain unproven.[71]

10. Summary: Josiah in Historiography and in Historical Reality

The picture of Josiah's reign, as reflected in this discussion, is far removed from the description of those years as reflected in the Book of Kings, and no less distant from the sketch of his period presented in modern historiography.

By utter contrast to historical reality, the author of the Book of Kings presented Hezekiah's revolt against Assyria as an impressive success and the Assyrian campaign into Judah as having ended in the failure and retreat of the Assyrian ruler, following the dramatic intervention of the God of Israel. To reinforce this picture of the revolt as a success, the author omitted any mention of Assyria from that point on. Anyone reading the history of Manasseh, Amon, and Josiah in the Book of Kings, and finding there no hint of the Assyrian domination, would have to conclude — in view of the internal sequence of events of the Book of Kings — that Judah fell under the yoke of Assyria in the reign of Ahaz and was freed during that of Hezekiah. In this way, the author of the Book of Kings avoided having to describe the external reality in Josiah's day — a reality in which Judah was subjugated to one great power for many years and, following the retreat of that power, became subordinate (at least nominally) to another, a reality far out of line with the image of the righteous king. Instead, the author concentrated on internal affairs and described in great detail the implementation of the reforms, by which all foreign cults were eradicated, leaving only the sacred worship of the God of Israel, centered in the Temple in Jerusalem. Not until the account of Josiah's death, and even then with deliberate brevity, did the author make any further reference to Judah's foreign affairs; from that point on, the great powers and external politics assume a central role in his work. According to the description in the Book of Kings, Judah became subjugated to Egypt during the reign of a sinful king (Jehoahaz), just as it had become subjugated to Assyria

71. Based on 2 Kgs. 23:29, Yoyotte (1960:380) assumed that Necho II's campaign in late 609 BCE was directed against Assyria, Egypt's long-time ally, and that Ashur-Uballiṭ II, last king of Assyria, was killed during that campaign. It is, of course, possible that Necho II decided to get rid of the Assyrian king, who had lost all his lands and was no longer useful, and, therefore, put him to death. There is, however, certainly no reason to assume that Assyria, rather than Babylonia, was the prime target for the Egyptian campaign.

under another sinful king (Ahaz), and had won its liberty under a righteous king (Hezekiah). Neither should we marvel that all of the last kings of Judah, who were dominated by foreign powers (first Egypt, then Babylonia), were described in the Book of Kings as having done "what was evil in the sight of the Lord," a phrase that may not represent the actual state of affairs in their time.

The gaps in the Book of Kings have been filled in by the works of various scholars; the manifold nuances of these works have repeatedly been pointed out in the course of this discussion. Many scholars have assumed that Josiah freed his kingdom from the Assyrian yoke in the early stages of his reign, enjoyed many years of independent rule, and expanded his kingdom over vast areas. A few have gone so far as to assume that he controlled most of the Israelite territory, and even to ascribe to him the tendency to restore David's kingdom to its former glory.

By contrast, I have attempted to show that Josiah was subjugated to Assyria throughout the first portion of his reign and that, following the Assyrian retreat, Egypt entered the scene and took over Assyria's territories and, to a not insignificant extent, its status. The idea of rival pro-Assyrian and pro-Egyptian factions operating in Judah in Josiah's time seems, in my opinion, to be divorced from reality and based on an erroneous analogy with the state of affairs at a later period, when Babylonia and Egypt were struggling for control of Palestine.[72] In Josiah's time, Assyria and Egypt were allies, not rivals. Accordingly, it might be possible to speak of nationalist circles calling for political daring, as against more conservative circles that, in light of the lessons learned from Sennacherib's campaign, advocated compromise with the great powers and restraint from measures that might endanger the well-being of the kingdom; yet, it is certainly not correct to speak of opposite Assyrian and Egyptian orientations.

We do not know whether or not Egypt gained a foothold on the coast of Philistia even before the Assyrian retreat from Palestine. In any case, the main change in the state of affairs in the area took place only after Assyria failed in its efforts to suppress the Babylonian revolt, which began in 626 BCE, and after the outbreak of civil war in 623 BCE. Following these developments, Assyria retreated from *Ebir nāri* ("Beyond the River") and turned those territories over to Egypt in exchange for military aid. In subsequent years, Egypt occupied itself with reinforcing its status in the evacuated regions and with

72. Malamat 1953; 1973:271; 1975:125–126; Milgrom 1955:65–67; Cazelles 1967:92. For a critique of the concept of "pro-Assyrian" or "anti-Assyrian" policy as implemented by the kings of Judah (Manasseh, Amon, and Josiah), see Nelson 1983:177–183.

military assistance to Assyria; therefore, Judah enjoyed a considerable measure of independence, despite being formally subordinate to Egypt.

Josiah took advantage of this situation to implement comprehensive reforms in his kingdom, focused on the extirpation of "foreign" cults and the concentration of worship in the Temple in Jerusalem; in this, he was assisted by the awakening of nationalist consciousness in extensive circles throughout the kingdom, although other, oppositionist circles no doubt did all in their power to prevent the implementation of the reforms. Some time later, Josiah expanded northward; he captured Bethel, the cult center that had been Jerusalem's great rival throughout the days of the Kingdom of Judah, destroyed the site of worship, and annexed the area to his kingdom. He may have extended his rule into Samaria also, outside the range of Egypt's immediate political interests, in which there was no well-formed body to assume control and concentrate independent power following the Assyrian retreat. The extent of Josiah's activity in the former Assyrian province of Samaria is not known; however, he surely did not dare to annex the entire region, in view of the expected Egyptian response to such a deed and because of the great difficulties foreseen in attempting to assimilate its population into his kingdom. Throughout their history, Israel and Judah were two different kingdoms, and, following its conquest, Samaria became an Assyrian province. Samaria's annexation would have been regarded as an act of aggression and the assimiliation of its vast population was probably beyond the power of the small Kingdom of Judah.

Josiah was unable to expand westward, both due to the danger of conflict with Egypt and to the growth and strengthening of his neighbor Ekron, which became a sort of buffer state between the coastal area and the Kingdom of Judah.

The extent of the Kingdom of Judah in Josiah's time is reflected in the town lists of Judah and Benjamin in the Book of Joshua. These lists, their meaning and date, constitute a starting point for the discussions in the second part of this study. The information at our disposal on the period of Josiah's reign, drawn from the descriptions in the Books of Kings and Chronicles, is surprisingly limited and does not enable us to determine the extent of his kingdom, let alone its strength and economic power. The dating of the town lists in Josiah's time and the integration of the date with the archaeological data on the extent of settlement, strength, and deployment in Judah in the seventh century BCE provide the foothold so vital to our discussion.

The combination of textual and archaeological information enables us to state that, in all matters related to the extent of its borders, its strength of settlement and economic power, Josiah's kingdom was considerably weaker than the kingdom that had existed in the eighth century BCE. The destructive results of Sennacherib's campaign remained evident even in the last years of Josiah's reign, almost a century after the end of the campaign; many sites that had been destroyed in 701 BCE and whose inhabitants had been exiled were still unsettled. The period of *pax Assyriaca* enabled Judah to recover gradually, restore some of its settlements, and strengthen its economy (Na'aman 1987b: 9–15). Not only Judah enjoyed a period of tranquility and prosperity at this time. Its eastern and western neighbors, whose expansion was to exert considerable influence on Judah's fate in the last stages of its existence, did as well.

Josiah enjoyed a protracted period of peace throughout his rule; following the Assyrian retreat, he took energetic action toward the stabilization of his kingdom, and perhaps also toward its northward expansion. There can be no doubt that these actions were accompanied by a burst of popular enthusiasm and the awakening of nationalist ambitions, along with hopes for expansion and prosperity. In reality, however, things were different: Egypt strengthened its presence in the region, and Josiah's activity within his kingdom and beyond its northern border irritated the great power. The details of the occurrences cannot be reconstructed precisely, and we cannot state why Necho II decided to rid himself of Josiah when the latter appeared before him at Megiddo. In any event, Josiah's death cooled the recently awakened hopes, and Egyptian intervention in the internal affairs of the Judahite kingdom became an established fact.

Would it have been possible to expect great things of Josiah, had he not been killed before his time? We cannot reconstruct historical events that did not actually take place; any discussion of what might have been is necessarily hypothetical. However, it can be seen that the hopes of great expansion and glory could not have been realized in the conditions prevailing in the late seventh century. Within a few short years, Babylonia was to take the place of Assyria and Egypt as the ruling power in the area, and attempts by the kings of Judah to demonstrate an independent policy led Judah directly into destruction and exile. It seems that many scholars were deceived by the false similarity between Josiah's reign and the biblical description of the days of the United Monarchy. By placing emphasis on the hopes and longings based on the assumed distant past, they managed to reconstruct a concrete reality in which those hopes and longings were achieved in fact. It is important to remember that the period in which Josiah lived and acted was different in every characteristic from that of his forefathers, as his hands were constantly tied and his ability to realize his ambitions was limited. Accordingly, there is no basis to compare the achievements attained in his day with the earlier reality.

My historical conclusions are in line with the lack of descriptive material concerning conquests and expansions in Palestine under Josiah — a lack that has puzzled and perplexed many scholars and that has engendered many and varied explanations. Even the argument in favor of a "conspiracy of silence," supposedly formed about Josiah's death, seems unfounded to me (Frost 1968). Those reading the enthusiastic, pro-Josiah description in the Book of Kings will naturally be surprised at the fate of the righteous king; those presenting a historic picture that emphasizes Josiah's great achievements by contrast to the weakness of his successors will be no less surprised by the near-absence of any reflection of his death in the words of scribes and prophets active at the time.[73] Indeed, the above-mentioned "conspiracy of silence" argument is based primarily on the assumption that the king's death was a fateful event in the history of the Kingdom of Judah and one that cast the kingdom from the topmost heights into the lowest depths. The presentation here of a different historical picture casts this "silence" of his contemporaries in a different light. The grief at the king's sudden death was certainly heavy, and the feeling of immediate crisis was surely no less acute. Nevertheless, it is doubtful whether this episode drastically altered the course of events, and anyone observing the event from a slightly later perspective might not even have perceived it as fateful. It appears that the impression made on contemporaries by the slaying of Josiah was less profound than assumed by modern scholars and, for that reason, was so sparingly mentioned in works dating from after Josiah's time.

The author of the Book of Kings emphasized the scope of Josiah's actions in the fields of religion and cult, which won him an unprecedentedly favorable evaluation (probably awarded by a later editor):[74] "Before him there was no king like him, who turned to the Lord with all his heart and with all his soul and with all his might, according to all the law of Moses; nor did any like him arise after him" (2 Kgs. 23:25). Studying the history of Josiah from an overall historical perspective, it seems that this evaluation is acceptable; even though his modest political and territorial achievements were wiped out by his death, his actions in the areas of religion and cult remained engraved in the hearts of his supporters from among the members of the Deuteronomistic school for generations and exerted considerable influence on the development of Judaism during the Babylonian exile and the post-exilic period.

73. Compare the history of Josiah and his heirs as presented in detailed articles by Malamat (1973; 1975; 1988).

74. The paragraph in 2 Kgs. 23:25–27 belongs to a later stratum of Deuteronotrlistic historiography. See (from various viewpoints): Seeligmann 1969–74:279–280; Cross 1973:285–287; Spieckermann 1982:43–46, with earlier literature.

References

Ackroyd, P.R. 1968. Historians and Prophets. *Svensk Exegetisk Årsbok* 33: 18–54.
Africa, T.W. 1963. Herodotus and Diodorus on Egypt. *JNES* 22: 254–258.
Aharoni, M. and Aharoni, Y. 1976. The Stratification of Judahite Sites in the 8th and 7th Centuries BCE. *BASOR* 224: 73–90.
Aharoni, Y. 1956. Excavations at Ramat Rahel, 1954. Preliminary Report. *IEJ* 6: 102–111, 137–155.
Aharoni, Y. 1957. The Settlement of the Israelite Tribes in Upper Galilee. Jerusalem. (Hebrew).
Aharoni, Y. 1959. The Province List of Judah. *VT* 9: 225–246.
Aharoni, Y. 1962. *Excavations at Ramat Rahel, Seasons 1959 and 1960.* Rome.
Aharoni, Y. 1966. Hebrew Ostraca from Tel Arad. *IEJ* 16: 1–7.
Aharoni, Y. 1968. Trial Excavation in the "Solar Shrine" at Lachish. Preliminary Report. *IEJ* 18: 157–169.
Aharoni, Y. 1969. Rubute and Ginti-kirmil. *VT* 19: 137–145.
Aharoni, Y. 1976. The Solomonic Districts. *Tel Aviv* 3: 5–15.
Aharoni, Y. 1979. *The Land of the Bible: A Historical Geography.* (2nd revised ed.). Philadelphia.
Aharoni, Y. 1981. *Arad Inscriptions.* (Judean Desert Studies). Jerusalem.
Aharoni, Y. 1982. *The Archaeology of the Land of Israel.* Philadelphia.
Aharoni, Y. 1985. From Geba to Beer-sheba. In: Luria, B.Z. ed. *Studies in the Book of Kings.* Jerusalem: 321–330. (Hebrew).
Albright, W.F. 1924a. Egypt and the Early History of the Negeb. *JPOS* 4: 131–161.
Albright, W.F. 1924b. *Excavations and Results at Tell el-Fûl (Gibeah of Saul).* (AASOR 4). New Haven.
Alt, A. 1925. Judas Gaue unter Josia. *PJb* 21: 100–116. (Reprint: Alt 1953: 276–288).
Alt, A. 1927. Eine galiläische Ortsliste in Jos. 19. *ZAW* 45: 59–81.
Alt, A. 1934. Das Institut im Jahre 1933. *PJb* 30: 5–31.
Alt, A. 1950. Das Stützpunktsystem der Pharaonen an der phönikischen Küste and im syrischen Binnenland. ZDPV 68: 97–133. (Reprint: Alt 1959: 107–140).
Alt, A. 1953. *Kleine Schriften zur Geschichte des Volkes Israel* II. München.
Alt, A. 1959. *Kleine Schriften zur Geschichte des Volkes Israel* III. München.
Amusin, J.D. and Heltzer, M.L. 1964. The Inscription from Meṣad Ḥashavyahu: Complaint of a Reaper of the Seventh Century B.C. *IEJ* 14: 148–157.
Armayor, O.K. 1978. Did Herodotus Ever Go to Egypt? *Journal of the American Research Center in Egypt.* 15: 59–73.
Augustin, M. 1988. The Literary Form of the "Constructed War Chronicle with Theological Interpretation" in the Books of Chronicles. *Proceedings of the Ninth World Congress of Jewish Studies. Panel Sessions: Bible Studies and Ancient Near East.* Jerusalem: 133–140.
Auld, A.G. 1975. Judges 1 and History: A Reconsideration. *VT* 25: 261–285.
Auld, A.G. 1980. Joshua, *Moses and the Land. Tetrateuch-Pentateuch-Hexateuch in a Generation since 1938.* Edinburgh.
Avi-Yonah, M. 1962. Scythopolis. *IEJ* 12: 123–134.
Ayalon, E. 1985. Trial Excavation of Two Iron Age Strata at Tel 'Eton. *Tel Aviv* 12: 54–62.
Bardtke, H. 1936. Jeremia der Fremdvölkerprophet. *ZAW* 54: 240–262.
Barkay, G. 1978. A Group of Iron Age Scale Weights. *IEJ* 28: 209–217.
Barkay, G. 1985. *Northern and Western Jerusalem in the End of the Iron Age.* (Ph.D. Thesis). Tel Aviv University. (Hebrew).

Barth, H. 1977. *Die jesaja-Worte in der Josiazeit.* (Wissenschaftliche Monographien zum Alten und Neuen Testament 48). Neukirchen-Vluyn.

Baumgartner, W. 1959. Herodots Babylonische and Assyrische Nachrichten. In: Baumgartner, W. *Zum Alten Testament und seiner Umwelt*: Ausgewählte Aufsätze. Leiden: 282–331.

Beck, P. 1986. A Bulla from Ḥorvat 'Uzza. *Qadmoniot* 19: 40–41. (Hebrew).

Begg, C.T. 1987. The Death of Josiah in Chronicles: Another View. *VT* 37: 1–8.

Beit-Arieh, I. 1985. Tel 'Ira — A Fortified City of the Kingdom of Judah. *Qadmoniot* 18: 17–25. (Hebrew).

Beit-Arieh, I. 1986. Ḥorvat 'Uzza — A Border Fortress in the Eastern Negev. *Qadmoniot* 19: 31–40. (Hebrew).

Beit-Arieh, I. 1986–87. The Ostracon of Ahiqam from Ḥorvat 'Uza. *Tel Aviv* 13–14: 32–38.

Biran, A. 1985. Tel 'Ira. *Qadmoniot* 18: 25–28. (Hebrew).

Biran, A. and Cohen, R. 1981. Aroer in the Negev. *Eretz Israel* 15: 250–271. (Hebrew).

Boardman, J. 1980. *The Greeks Overseas: Their Early Colonies and Trade.* New York.

Boehmer, J. 1933. König Josias Tod. *Archiv für Religionswissenschaft* 30: 199–203.

Borger, R. 1965. Der Aufstieg des neubabylonischen Reiches. *JCS* 19: 59–78.

Brinkman, J.A. 1984. *Prelude to Empire. Babylonian Society and Politics, 747–627 B.C.* Philadelphia.

Broshi, M. 1958. Jotbah. *Enc. Miqr.* III: 672. (Hebrew).

Broshi, M. and Finkelstein, I. 1990. The Population of Palestine in 734 BCE. *Cathedra* 58: 3–24. (Hebrew).

Brown, S.C. 1986. Media and Secondary State Formation in the Neo-Assyrian Zagros: An Anthropological Approach to an Assyriological Problem. *JCS* 38: 107–119.

Brown, T.S. 1965. Herodotus Speculates about Egypt. *American Journal of Philology* 86: 60–76.

Cavaignac, E. 1961. À propos du début de l'histoire des Médes. *Journal Asiatique* 249: 153–162.

Cazelles, H. 1967. Sophonie, Jérémie, et les Scythes en Palestine. *RB* 74: 24–44.

Clements, R.E. 1984. *Isaiah and the Deliverance of Jerusalem: A Study of the Interpretation of Prophecy in the Old Testament* (Journal for the Study of the Old Testament Supplement 13). Sheffield.

Cogan, M. 1974. *Imperialism and Religion: Assyria, Judah and Israel in the Eighth and Seventh Centuries B.C.E.* (Soiety of Biblical Literature Monograph Series 19). Missoula.

Cogan, M. 1980. Tendentious Chronology in the Book of Chronicles. *Zion* 45: 165–172. (Hebrew).

Cogan, M. and Tadmor, H. 1977. Gyges and Ashurbanipal: A Study in Literary Transmission. *Orientalia* 46: 65–85.

Cogan, M. and Tadmor, H. 1988. *II Kings. A New Translation with Introduction and Notes.* (The Anchor Bible). Garden City.

Cohen, R. 1981. The Excavations at Kadesh-Barnea (1976–1978). *BA* 44: 93–104.

Cohen, R. 1983. Excavations at Kadesh-Barnea, 1976–1982. *Qadmoniot* 16: 2–14. (Hebrew).

Cross, F.M. 1969. Judean Stamps. *Eretz Israel* 9: 20*–27*.

Cross, F.M. 1973. *Canaanite Myth and Hebrew Epic. Essays in the History of the Religion of Israel.* Cambridge.

Cross, F.M. and Freedman, D.N. 1953. Josiah's Revolt against Assyria. *JNES* 12: 56–58.

Cross, F.M. and Wright, G.E. 1956. The Boundary and Province Lists of the Kingdom of Judah. *JBL* 75: 202–226.

Demsky, A. 1966. The Houses of Achzib. A Critical Note on Micah 1: 14b. *IEJ* 16: 211–215.

Demsky, A. 1973. Geba, Gibeah, and Gibeon — An Historico-Geographic Riddle. *BASOR* 212: 26–31.

Diakonoff, I.M. 1985. Media. In: Gershevitch, I. ed. *The Cambridge History of Iran 2. The Median and Achaemenian Periods.* Cambridge: 36–148.

Dorsey, D.A. 1980. The Location of Biblical Makkedah. *Tel Aviv* 7: 185–193.

Dothan, M. 1965. The Fortress at Kadesh-Barnea. *IEJ* 15: 134–151.

Driver, S.R. 1913. *Notes on the Hebrew Text and the Topography of the Books of Samuel.* Oxford.

Elayi, J. 1983. Les cités phéniciennes et l'empire assyrien à l'époque d'Assurbanipal. *RA* 77: 45–58.

Elliger, K. 1934a. Josua in Judäa. *PJb* 30: 47–71.

Elliger, K. 1934b. Die Heimat des Propheten Micha. *ZDPV* 57: 81–152.

Eph'al, I. 1979. Assyrian Dominion in Palestine. In: Malamat, A. ed. *The Age of the Monarchies: Political History.* (The World History of the Jewish People). Jerusalem: 276–289, 364–368.

Eph'al, I. 1982. *The Ancient Arabs. Nomads on the Borders of the Fertile Crescent 9th–5th Centuries B.C.* Jerusalem.

Eph'al, I. 1983. On Warfare and Military Control in the Ancient Near Eastern Empires: A Research Outline. In: Tadmor, H. and Weinfeld, M. eds. *History, Historiography and Interpretation.* Jerusalem: 88–106.

Eph'al, I. and Naveh, J. 1988. The Use of Epigraphical Sources for the Study of Biblical History. *Zion* 53: 211–213. (Hebrew).

Eshel, H. 1989. A *lmlk* Stamp from Bethel. *IEJ* 39: 60–62.

Fehling, D. 1989. *Herodotus and His "Sources."* (Arca 21). Leeds.

Freedy, K.S. and Redford, D.B. 1970. The Dates in Ezekiel in Relation to Biblical, Babylonian and Egyptian Sources. *JAOS* 90: 462–485.

Fritz, V. 1975. Erwägungen zur Siedlungsgeschichte des Negeb in der Eisen I-Zeit (1200–1000 v. Chr.) im Lichte der Ausgrabungen auf der îirbet el-Mšāš. *ZDPV* 91: 30–45.

Frost, S.B. 1968. The Death of Josiah: A Conspiracy of Silence. *JBL* 87: 369–382.

Gal, Z. 1988–89. The Lower Galilee in the Iron Age II: Analysis of Survey Material and Its Historical Interpretation. *Tel Aviv* 15–16: 56–64.

Galil, G. 1984. The Administrative Districts of the Judean Hill Area. *Zion* 49: 205–224. (Hebrew).

Galil, G. 1985. The Land of Dan. *Tarbiz* 54: 1–19. (Hebrew).

Galil, G. 1987. The Administrative Division of the Shephelah. Shnaton. *An Annual for Biblical and Ancient Near Eastern Studies* 9: 55–71. (Hebrew).

Galling, K. 1951. The "Gola-List" according to Ezra 2/Nehemiah 7. *JBL* 70: 149–158.

Garfinkel, Y. 1987. The City-List, Epigraphic Evidence and the Administrative Division of the Kingdom of Judah. *Zion* 52: 489–494. (Hebrew).

Garfinkel, Y. 1988a. 2 Chr. 11:5–10 Fortified Cities List and the *lmlk* Stamps — Reply to Nadav Na'aman. *BASOR* 271: 69–73.

Garfinkel, Y. 1988b. MLṢ HKRSYM in Phoenician Inscriptions from Cyprus, the QRSY in Arad, HKRSYM in Egypt, and BNY QYRS in the Bible. *JNES* 47: 27–34.

Gerardi, P. 1986. Declaring War in Mesopotamia. *AfO* 33: 30–38.

Ginsberg, H.L. 1950. Judah and the Transjordan States from 734 to 582 B.C.E. In: Lieberman, S. ed. *Alexander Marx Jubilee Volume.* New York: 347–368.

Gitin, S. 1989. Tel Miqne-Ekron: A Type-Site for the Inner Coastal Plain in the Iron Age II Period. In: Gitin, S. and Dever, W.G. eds. *Recent Excavations in Israel: Studies in Iron Age Archaeology.* (AASOR 49). Winona Lake: 23–58.

Gray, J. 1970. *I & II Kings. A Commentary.* (Old Testament Library). Philadelphia.

Grayson, A.K. 1975. *Assyrian and Babylonian Chronicles.* Locust Valley, New York.

Gressmann, H. 1924. Josia and das Deuteronomium. *ZAW* 42: 313–337.

Gyles, M.F. 1959. *Pharaonic Policies and Administration, 663-323 B. C.* Chapel Hill.

Hachmann, R. 1982. Die ägyptische Verwaltung in Syrien während der Amarnazeit. *ZDPV* 98: 17–49.

Halpern, B. 1987. “Brisker Pipes than Poetry”: The Development of Israelite Monotheism. In: Neusner, J., Levine, B.A. and Frerichs, E.S. eds. *Judaic Perspectives on Ancient Israel.* Philadelphia: 77–115.

Helck, W. 1971. *Die Beziehungen Ägyptens zu Vorderasien im 3. and 2. Jahrtausend v. Chr.* Wiesbaden.

Herzog, Z., Aharoni, M., Rainey, A.F. and Moshkovitz, S. 1984. The Israelite Fortress at Arad. *BASOR* 254: 1–34.

Holladay, W.L. 1981. A Coherent Chronology of Jeremiah’s Early Career. In: Bogaert, P.-M. ed. *Le Livre de Jérémie. Le Prophète et son milieu; les oracles et leur Transmission.* (Bibliotheca Ephemeridum Theologicarum Lovaniensium 54). Leuven: 58–73.

Hollenberg, J. 1881. Zur Textkritik des Büches Josua and des Büches der Richter. *ZAW* 1: 97–105.

Holmes, S. 1914. *Joshua, the Hebrew and Greek Texts.* Cambridge.

Hyatt, J.P. 1940. The Peril from the North in Jeremiah. *JBL* 59: 499–513.

Isserlin, B.S.J. 1957. Israelite and Pre-Israelite Place-Names in Palestine: A Historical and Geographical Sketch. *PEQ* 89: 133–144.

Japhet, S. 1977. *The Ideology of the Book of Chronicles and Its Place in Biblical Thought.* Jerusalem. (Hebrew).

Japhet, S. 1983. People and Land in the Restoration Period. In: Strecker, G. ed. *Das Land Israel in biblischer Zeit.* Göttingen: 103–125.

Jepsen, A. 1959. Die Reform des Josia. In: Herrmann, J. ed: *Festschrift Friedrich Baumgärtel zum* 70. Geburtstag. Erlangen: 97–108.

Kallai-Kleinmann, Z. 1958. The Town Lists of Judah, Simeon, Benjamin and Dan. *VT* 8: 134–160.

Kallai, Z. 1960. *The Northern Boundaries of Judah from the Settlement of the Tribes until the Beginning of the Hasmonean Period.* Jerusalem. (Hebrew).

Kallai, Z. 1962. Libnah. *Enc. Miqr.* IV: 421–423. (Hebrew).

Kallai, Z. 1971. The Kingdom of Rehoboam. *Eretz Israel* 10: 245–254. (Hebrew).

Kallai, Z. 1972. Ophni. *Enc. Miqr.* VI: 321–322. (Hebrew).

Kallai, Z. 1986. *Historical Geography of the Bible. The Tribal Territories of Israel.* Jerusalem and Leiden.

Kammenhuber, A. 1976–80. Kimmerier. *RLA* V: 594–596.

Katzenstein, H.J. 1973. *The History of Tyre, from the Beginning of the Second Millennium B.C.E. until the Fall of the Neo-Babylonian Empire in 538 B.C.E.* Jerusalem.

Katzenstein, H.J. 1978. The Camp of the Tyrians at Memphis. *Eretz Israel* 14: 161–164. (Hebrew).

Kellermann, D. 1978. Überlieferungsprobleme Altestamentlicher Ortsnamen. *VT* 28: 423–432.

Kienitz, F.K. 1953. *Die politische Geschichte Ägyptens vom 7. bis zum 4. Jahrhundert vor der Zeitwende.* Berlin.

Kitchen, K. A. 1973. *The Third Intermediate Period in Egypt (1100-650 B.C.).* Warminster.

Klein, R.W. 1983. Abijah’s Campaign Against the North (II Chr. 13) — What Were the Chronicler’s Sources? *ZAW* 95: 210–217.

Knauf, E.A. 1985. Mu’näer and Mëuniter. *WO* 16: 114–122.

Kochavi, M. 1972. The Land of Judah. In: Kochavi, M. ed. *Judaea, Samaria, and the Golan. Archaeological Survey 1967-1968.* Jerusalem: 17–89. (Hebrew).

Kuschke, A. 1965. Historisch-topographische Beiträge zum Buche Josua. In: Reventlow, H. Graf ed. *Gottes Wort and Gottes Land, Festschrift für H. H. Hertzberg*. Göttingen: 90–109.

Kuschke, A. 1971. Kleine Beiträge zur Siedlungsgeschichte der Stämme Asser and Juda. *Harvard Theological Review* 64: 291–313.

Labat, R. 1961. Kaštariti, Phraorte et les débuts de 1'histoire Mède. *Journal Asiatique* 249: 1–12.

Landsberger, B. and Bauer, T. 1926. Zu neuveröffentlichten Geschichtsquellen der Zeit von Asarhaddon bis Nabonid. *ZA* 37: 61–98.

Lemaire, A. 1973. L'ostracon "Ramat Negeb" et la topographie historique du Negeb. *Semitica* 23: 11–26.

Lemaire, A. 1977. *Inscriptions Hébraïques* I. *Les Ostraca*. Paris.

Lemaire, A. and Vernus, P. 1980. Les ostraca paléo-hébreux de Qadesh-Barnéa. *Orientalia* 49: 341–345.

Lemaire, A. and Vernus, P. 1983. L'ostracon paléo-hébreu N° 6 de Tell Qudeirat (Qadesh-Barnéa). In: Görg, M. ed. *Fontes atque Pontes. Eine Festgabe für Hellmut Brunner*. Wiesbaden: 302–326.

Lemke, W.E. 1965. The Synoptic Problem of the Chronicler's History. *Harvard Theological Review* 58: 349–363.

Lewy, J. 1925. *Forschungen zur alten Geschichte Vorderasiens* (Mitteilungen der Vorderasiatischen Gesellschaft 29/2). Leipzig.

Lewy, H. 1952. Nitokris-Naqî'a. *JNES* 11: 264–286.

Liver, J. 1958. Josiah. *Enc. Miqr.* III: 417–424. (Hebrew).

Liver, J. 1968. Manasseh. *Enc. Miqr.* V: 41–45. (Hebrew).

Lloyd, A.B. 1975. *Herodotus Book II: Introduction*. Leiden.

Loewenstamm, S.E. 1950. Ashkenaz. *Enc. Miqr.* I: 762–763. (Hebrew).

Loewenstamm, S.E. 1962. Kittim. *Enc. Miqr.* IV: 394–398. (Hebrew).

Lorton, D. 1974. *The Juridical Terminology of International Relations in Egyptian Texts through Dynnasty XVIII*. Baltimore and London.

McKay, J. 1973. *Religion in Judah under the Assyrians 732-609 BC*. (Studies in Biblical Theology, Second Series 26). London.

Malamat, A. 1951. The Historical Setting of Two Biblical Prophecies on the Nations. *IEJ* 1: 149–159.

Malamat, A. 1953. The Historical Background of the Assassination of Amon King of Judah. *IEJ* 3: 26–29.

Malamat, A. 1973. Josiah's Bid for Armageddon. *Journal of the Ancient Near Eastern Society of Columbia University* 5 (T. H. Gaster Festschrift): 267–279.

Malamat, A. 1975. The Twilight of Judah in the Egyptian-Babylonian Maelstrom. *Supplement to VT* 28: 123–145.

Malamat, A. 1982. A Political Look at the Kingdom of David and Solomon and Its Relations with Egypt. In: Ishida, T. ed. *Studies in the Period of David and Solomon and Other Essays*. Tokyo: 189–204.

Malamat, A. 1988. The Kingdom of Judah between Egypt and Babylon: A Small State within a Great Power Confrontation. In: Classen, W. ed. *Text and Context. Old Testament and Semitic Studies for F.C. Fensham* (Journal for the Study of the Old Testament Supplement 48). Sheffield: 117–129.

Mazar, A. 1985. Between Judah and Philistia: Timnah (Tel Batash) in the Iron Age II. *Eretz Israel* 18: 300–324. (Hebrew).

Mazar (Maisler), B. 1941. Topographical Studies 1: From Geva to Beer-sheba. *BJPES* 8: 35–37. (Hebrew).

Mazar (Maisler), B. 1944. Topographical Studies III: The Hill of God. *BJPES* 10: 73–75. (Hebrew).
Mazar (Maisler), B. 1949. Kiriath-arba which is Hebron. In: Baer, Y.F., Gutman, I. and Schwabe, M. eds. *Dinaburg Jubelee Volume: Studies Presented to Ben-Zion* Dinaburg. Jerusalem: 310–325. (Hebrew).
Mazar (Maisler), B. 1950. Eretz Israel. *Enc. Miqr.* I: 667–741. (Hebrew).
Mazar, B. 1954. Geba. *Enc. Miqr.* II: 412. (Hebrew).
Mazar, B. 1958. Jehoshaphat son of Asa. *Enc. Miqr.* III: 565–570. (Hebrew).
Mazar, B. 1960. The Cities of the Territory of Dan. *IEJ* 10: 65–77.
Mazar, B. 1967. En-Gedi. In: Thomas, D.W. ed. *Archaeology and Old Testament Study.* Oxford: 223–230.
Mazar, B. 1976. Kiriath-jearim. *Enc. Miqr.* VII: 270–273. (Hebrew).
Mazar, E. 1985. Edomite Pottery at the End of the Iron Age. *IEJ* 35: 253–269.
Mendelsohn, I. 1940. Guilds in Ancient Palestine. *BASOR* 70: 17–21.
Meulenaere, H. de. 1951. *Herodotus over de 26ste Dynastie (II, 147- III, 15).* (Bibliothèque du Muséon 27). Leuven.
Milgrom, J. 1955. The Date of Jeremiah, Chapter 2. *JNES* 14: 65–69.
Milgrom, J. 1971. Did Josiah Take Over Megiddo? *Beth Mikra* 16: 23–27. (Hebrew).
Millard, A.R. 1979. The Scythian Problem. In: Ruffle, J. et al. eds. *Glimpses of Ancient Egypt. Studies in Honour of H.W. Fairman.* Warminster: 119–122.
Miller, J.M. and Hayes, J.H. 1986. *A History of Ancient Israel and Judah.* Philadelphia.
Mittmann, S. 1977. Ri. 1,16f and das Siedlungsgebiet der kenitischen Sippe Hobab. *ZDPV* 93: 213–235.
Mommsen, H., Perlman, I. and Yellin, J. 1984. The Provenience of the *lmlk* Jars. *IEJ* 34: 89–113.
Montgomery, J.A. 1934. Archival Data in the Book of Kings. *JBL* 53: 46–52.
Montgomery, J.A. 1951. *A Critical and Exegetical Commentary on the Books of Kings* (International Critical Commentary). Edinburgh.
Morschauser, S.N. 1988. The End of the *Sdf(3)-Tr(yt)* "Oath." *Journal of the American Research Center in Egypt* 25: 93–103.
Mosis, R. 1973. *Untersuchungen zur Theologie des chronistischen Geschichtswerkes.* (Freiburger theologiche Studien 92). Freiburg.
Na'aman, N. 1980. The Inheritance of the Sons of Simeon. *ZDPV* 96: 136–152.
Na'aman, N. 1981. Economic Aspects of the Egyptian Occupation of Canaan. *IEJ* 31: 172–185.
Na'aman, N. 1982. Palestine in the Canaanite Period: The Middle and the Late Bronze Ages. In: Eph'al, I. ed. *The History of Eretz Israel I.* Jerusalem: 131–275. (Hebrew).
Na'aman, N. 1986a. *Borders and Districts in Biblical Historiography.* Seven Studies in Biblical Geographical Lists. (Jerusalem Biblical Studies 4). Jerusalem.
Na'aman, N. 1986b. Hezekiah's Fortified Cities and the *LMLK* Stamps. *BASOR* 261: 5–21.
Na'aman, N. 1987a. Beth-aven, Bethel and Early Israelite Sanctuaries. *ZDPV* 103: 13–21.
Na'aman, N. 1987b. The Negev in the Last Century of the Kingdom of Judah. *Cathedra* 42: 3–15. (Hebrew).
Na'aman, N. 1988. Pharaonic Lands in the Jezreel Valley in the Late Bronze Age. In: Heltzer, M. and Lipiński, E. eds. *Society and Economy in the Eastern Mediterranean (c. 1500-1000 B.C.).* (Orientalia Lovaniensia Analecta 23). Leuven: 177–185.
Na'aman, N. 1991. Chronology and History in the Late Assyrian Empire (631–619 B.C.). *ZA* 81: 243–267.
Na'aman, N. and Zadok, R. 1988. Sargon II's Deportations to Israel and Philistia (716–708 B.C.). *JCS* 40: 36–46.

Nadelman, Y. 1989. Hebrew Inscriptions, Seal Impressions and Markings of the Iron Age II. In: Mazar, E. and Mazar, B. *Excavations in the South of the Temple Mount.* (Qedem 29). Jerusalem: 128–137.

Naveh, J. 1960. A Hebrew Letter from the Seventh Century B.C. *IEJ* 10: 129–139.

Naveh, J. 1962. More Hebrew Inscriptions from Meṣad Ḥashavyahu. *IEJ* 12: 27–32.

Naveh, J. 1977. Meṣad Ḥashavyahu. In: Enc. *Arch. Exc.* III: 852–863.

Nelson, R. 1983. Realpolitik in Judah (687–609 BCE). In: Hallo, W.W., Moyer, J.C. and Perdue, L.G. eds. *Scriptures in Context* II. More Essays on the Comparative Method. Winona Lake: 177–189.

Nicholson, E.W. 1967. *Deuteronomy and Tradition.* Philadelphia.

North, R. 1974. Does Archaeology Prove Chronicles Sources? In: Bream, H.N, Heim, R. and Moore, C. eds. A Light unto My Path. *Old Testament Studies in Honor of Jacob M. Myers.* Philadelphia: 375–401.

Noth, M. 1935. Studien zu den historisch-geographischen Dokumenten des Josuabuches. *ZDPV* 58: 185–255. (Reprint: 1971. *Aufsätze zur biblischen Landes- und Altertumskunde* I. Neukirchen-Vluyn: 229–280).

Noth, M. 1937. Die fünf Könige in der Höhle von Makkeda. *PJb* 33: 22–36. (Reprint:1971. *Aufsätze zur biblischen Landes- und Altertumskunde* I. Neukirchen-Vluyn: 281–293).

Noth, M. 1944. Israelitische Stämme zwischen Ammon and Moab. *ZAW* 60: 11–57. (Reprint: 1971. *Aufsätze zur biblischen Landes- und Altertumskunde* I. Neukirchen-Vluyn: 391–433.)

Noth, M. 1953. *Das Buch Josua.* (2nd revised ed.). Tübingen.

Noth, M. 1960. *The History of Israel.* London.

Oded, B. 1974. The Relation between the City-States of Phoenicia and Assyria in the Reigns of Esarhaddon and Ashurbanipal. *Studies in the History of the Jewish People and the Land of Israel* 3. Haifa: 31–42. (Hebrew).

Oestreicher, T. 1923. *Das deuteronomische Grundgesetz.* (Beiträge zur Förderung christlicher Theologie 27/4). Gütersloh.

Ogden, G.S. 1978. The Northern Extent of Josiah's Reforms. *Australian Biblical Review* 26: 26–34.

Oppenheim, A.L. 1955. Babylonian and Assyrian Historical Texts. In: *ANET*: 265–317.

Oren, E.D. 1984. Migdol: A New Fortress on the Edge of the Eastern Nile Delta. *BASOR* 256: 7–44.

Orlinsky, H.M. 1939. The Supposed Qiryat-Sannah of Joshua 15 49. *JBL* 58: 255–261.

Otzen, B. 1964. *Studien über Deuterosacharja.* Copenhagen.

Pardee, D. 1978. The Judicial Plea from Meṣad Ḥashavyahu (Yabneh-Yam): A New Philological Study. *Maarav* 1: 33–66.

Pardee, D. 1980. A Brief Note on Meṣad Ḥashavyahu Ostracon, l. 12: *W'ML'. BASOR* 239: 47–48.

Petrie, W.M.F. 1988. *Tanis. Part II: Nebesheh (Am) and Defenneh (Tahpanhes).* London.

Pfeifer, G. 1969. Die Begegnung zwischen Pharao Necho and König Josia bei Megiddo. *Mitteilungen des Instituts für Orientforschung* 15: 297–307.

Porten, B. 1968. *Archives from Elephantine: The Life of an Ancient Jewish Military Colony.* Berkeley and Los Angeles.

Proksch, O. 1928. König Josia. In: *Festgabe für Theodor Zahn.* Leipzig: 19–53.

von Rad, G. 1958. *Theologie des Alien Testaments* I. München.

Rainey, A.F. 1980. The Administrative Division of the Shephelah. *Tel Aviv* 7: 194–202.

Rainey, A.F. 1983. The Biblical Shephelah of Judah. *BASOR* 251: 1–22.

Rainey, A.F. 1986. Arad in the Latter Days of the Judean Monarchy. *Cathedra* 42: 16–25. (Hebrew).

Redford, D.B. 1985. Sais and the Kushite Invasions of the Eighth Century B.C. *Journal of the American Research Center in Egypt* 22: 5–15.
Reich, R. 1989. The Third Season of Excavations at Meṣad Ḥashavyahu. *Eretz Israel* 20: 228–232. (Hebrew).
Rofé, A. 1982. *The Prophetical Stories. The Narratives about the Prophets in the Hebrew Bible. Their Literary Types and History.* Jerusalem. (Hebrew).
Rowley, H.H. 1962–63. The Early Prophecies of Jeremiah in Their Setting. *Bulletin of the John Rylands Library.* 45: 198–234.
Rudolph, W. 1955. *Chronikbücher.* (Handbuch zum Alten Testament, I/21). Tübingen.
Rüterswörden, U. 1985. *Die Beamten der israelitischen Königszeit. Eine Studie zu śr und vergleichbaren Begriffen.* Stuttgart.
Sasson, V. 1978. An Unrecognized Juridical Term in the Yabneh-Yam Lawsuit and in an Unnoticed Biblical Parallel. *BASOR* 232: 57–63.
Sasson, V. 1984. A Matter to be Put Right: The Yabneh-Yam Case Continued. *Journal of Northwest Semitic Languages* 12: 115–120.
Schmitt, G. 1980. Bet-Awen. In: Cohen, R. and Schmitt, G. *Drei Studien zur Archäologie und Topographie Altisraels.* Wiesbaden: 33–76.
Schunck, K.D. 1962. Bemerkungen zur Ortsliste von Benjamin (Jos. 18,21–28). *ZDPV* 78: 143–158.
Schunck, K.D. 1963. *Benjamin: Untersuchungen zur Entstehung und Geschichte eines israelitischen Stammes.* (Beiheft zur ZAW 86). Berlin.
Seeligmann, I.L. 1969–74. From Historical Reality to Historiographic Conception in the Bible. *P'raqim* II. Jerusalem: 273–313. (Hebrew).
Sigrist, R.M. 1982. Une tablette cuneiforme de Tell Keisan. *IEJ* 32: 32–35.
Smirin, S. 1952. *Josiah and His Age.* Jerusalem. (Hebrew).
Soggin, J.A. 1984. A History of Israel: from the beginnings to the Bar Kochba Revolt, *AD* 135. London.
Spalinger, A. 1974a. Esarhaddon and Egypt: An Analysis of the First Invasion of Egypt. *Orientalia* 43: 295–326.
Spalinger, A. 1974b. Assurbanipal and Egypt: A Source Study. *JAOS* 94: 316–328.
Spalinger, A. 1976. Psammetichus, King of Egypt: I. *Journal of the American Research Center in Egypt* 13: 133–147.
Spalinger, A. 1977. Egypt and Babylonia: A Survey (c. 620 B.C.–550 B.C.). *Studien zur Altägyptischen Kultur* 5: 221–244.
Spalinger, A.J. 1978a. Psammetichus, King of Egypt: II. *Journal of the American Research Center in Egypt* 15: 49–57.
Spalinger, A.J. 1978b. The Date of the Death of Gyges and its Historical Implications. *JAOS* 98: 400–409.
Spalinger, A.J. 1978c. The Concept of the Monarchy during the Saite Epoch — An Essay of Synthesis. *Orientalia* 47: 12–36.
Spalinger, A. 1982. Psammetichus I. *Lexikon der Ägyptologie* IV. Wiesbaden: 1164–1169.
Spieckermann, H. 1982. *Juda unter Assur in der Sargonidenzeit.* (Forschungen zur Religion und Literatur des Alten und Neuen Testaments 129). Göttingen.
Spycket, A. 1973. Le culte de Dieu-Lune à Tell Keisan. *RB* 80: 384–395.
Stern, E. 1982. *The Material Culture of the Land of the Bible in the Persian Period 538-332 B.C.* Warminster.
Stern, M. 1976. *Greek and Latin Authors on Jews and Judaism I. From Herodotus to Plutarch.* Jerusalem.

Steuernagel, C. 1900. *Übersetzung and Erklärung der Bücher Deuteronomium and Josua und Allgemeine Einleitung in den Hexateuch.* (Handkommentar zum Alten Testament). Göttingen.

Strange, J. 1966. The Inheritance of Dan. *Studia Theologica* 20: 120–139.

Suzuki, Y. 1982. A Hebrew Ostracon from Meṣad Ḥashavyahu: A Form-Critical Reinvestigation. *Annual of the Japanese Biblical Institute* 8: 3–49.

Tadmor, H. 1966. Philistia under Assyrian Rule. *BA* 29: 86–103.

Tadmor, H. 1967. The Conquest of Galilee by Tiglath Pileser III, King of Assyria. In: Hirschberg, H.Z. ed. *All the Land of Naphiali.* (The Twenty-Fourth Archaeological Convention October 1966). Jerusalem: 62–67. (Hebrew).

Tadmor, H. and Cogan, M. 1979. Ahaz and Tiglath-Pileser in the Book of Kings: Historiographic Considerations. *Biblica* 60: 491–508.

Talmon, S. 1964. The New Hebrew Letter from the Seventh Century B.C. in Historical Perspective. *BASOR* 176: 29–38.

Talmon, S. 1965. The Town Lists of Simeon. *IEJ* 15: 235–241.

Ussishkin, D. 1974. Tombs from the Israelite Period at Tel ʻEton. *Tel Aviv* 1: 109–127.

Ussishkin, D. 1976. Royal Judean Storage Jars and Private Seal Impressions. *BASOR* 223: 1–13.

Ussishkin, D. 1978. Excavations at Tel Lachish — 1973–1977. *Tel Aviv* 5: 1–97.

Vaggione, R.P. 1973. Over All Asia? The Extent of the Scythian Domination in Herodotus. *JBL* 92: 523–530.

de Vaux, R. 1978. *The Early History of Israel.* London.

Višaticki, K. 1987. *Die Reform des Josija and die religiöse Heterodoxie in Israel.* (Dissertationen theologische Reihe 21). St. Ottilien.

Vriezen, K.J.H. 1975. Ḥirbert Kefīre — eine Oberflächenuntersuchung. *ZDPV* 91: 135–158.

Weippert, M. 1971. *The Settlement of the Israelite Tribes in Palestine.* London.

Welch, A.C. 1925. The Death of Josiah. *ZAW* 43: 255–260.

Wellhausen, J. 1899. *Prolegomena zur Geschichte Israels.* (5th ed.). Berlin.

Welten, P. 1969. *Die Königs-Stempel. Ein Beitrag zur Militärpolitik Judas unter Hiskia und Josia.* (Abhandlungen des Deutschen Palästinavereins). Wiesbaden.

Welten, P. 1973. *Geschichte und Geschichtsdarstellung in den Chronikbüchern.* (Wissenschaftliche Monographien zum Alten und Neuen Testament 42). Neukirchen-Vluyn.

Wilke, F. 1913. Das Skythenproblem im Jeremiabuch. In: Alt, A. et al. eds. *Alttestamentliche Studien Rudolf Kittel zum 60. Geburtstag dargebracht.* (Beiträge zur Wissenschaft vom Alten und Neuen Testament 13). Leipzig: 222–254.

Williamson, H.G.M. 1977. *Israel in the Books of Chronicles.* Cambridge.

Williamson, H.G.M. 1977. Sources and Redaction in the Chronicler's Genealogy of Judah. *JBL* 98: 351–359.

Williamson, H.G.M. 1981. "We Are Yours, O David." The Setting and Purpose of I Chronicles xii 1–23. *Oudtestamentische Studiën* 21: 164–176.

Williamson, H.G.M. 1982. *1 and 2 Chronicles.* (The New Century Bible Commentary). Grand Rapids and London.

Williamson, H.G.M. 1987a. *Ezra and Nehemiah.* (Old Testament Guides). Sheffield.

Williamson, H.G.M. 1987b. Reliving the Death of Josiah: A Reply to C.T. Begg. *VT* 37: 9–15.

Wilson, J.A. 1970. *Herodotus in Egypt.* Leiden.

Wiseman, D.J. 1956. *Chronicles of Chaldean Kings (626–556 B. C.) in the British Museum.* London.

Yadin, Y. 1961. The Fourfold Division of Judah. *BASOR* 163: 6–11.

Yeivin, S. 1960. *Studies in the History of Israel and His Country.* Tel Aviv. (Hebrew).

Yeivin, S. 1962. Lecah. *Enc. Miqr.* IV: 503–504. (Hebrew).
Yoyotte, J. 1960. Néchao. *Dictionnaire de la Bible*, Supplement VI. Paris: 363–393.
Zawadzki, S.1988. *The Fall of Assyria and Median-Babylonian Relations in Light of the Nabopolassar Chronicle.* Poznan.
Zimhoni, O. 1985. The Iron Age Pottery of Tel 'Eton and Its Relation to the Lachish, Tell Beit Mirsim and Arad Assemblages. *Tel Aviv* 12: 63–90.
Zimhoni, O. 1990. Two Ceramic Assemblages from Lachish Levels III and II. *Tel Aviv* 17: 3–52.

Nebuchadrezzar's Campaign in the Year 603 BCE[1]

The historical evaluation of the events of years 604–603 BCE is entirely dependent on the Babylonian chronicle series. According to the chronicle (BM 21946), in his first year (604 BCE) Nebuchadrezzar marched to Syria-Palestine and "all the kings of Hatti came into his presence and he received their vast tribute." Then he marched to the city of Ashkelon, captured and destroyed it and carried its king, its prisoners and its spoil to Babylonia (Grayson 1975: 100 lines 15–20).

The description of the chain of events of year 603 is almost entirely damaged in the chronicle. Wiseman (1956:70) estimated that about four lines are missing at the end of the tablet and about the same number are missing at the beginning of the reverse side. The description of the year covered about 12 lines and was relatively long and quite detailed.

In his *editio princeps*, Wiseman restored the first three lines as follows:

(21) "In the second [year] in the month of Iyyar the king of Akkad gathered together a powerful army and [marched to the land of Hatti]. (22) [. . .] he threw down, great siege towers he [. . .] (23) [. . .] from the month of Iyyar until the mon[th of . . . he marched about unopposed in the land of Hatti]."

This reconstruction of the 603 campaign was accepted by all scholars who discussed the Babylonian campaigns to the west in years 605–600 BCE. Wiseman himself was aware of the fact that the objective of the campaign is missing, but assumed that "since Nebuchadrezzar marched to Syria in the preceding and following years it is likely that Syria was his goal in this year also" (Wiseman 1956:29). As so often happens, later scholars sometimes tend to forget that textual restorations may be quite hazardous and should be treated with great caution. Thus, various suggestions have been offered for the name of the Palestinian or Phoenician supposedly attacked city in line 21: Jerusalem (Vogt 1957:90); Gaza (Rainey 1975:54–55); Ashdod, Ekron, or Gaza (Malamat 1975:131); Aphek (Shea 1976); Sidon or Tyre (Wiseman 1985:26–28); Ekron (Gitin 1989:46). Wiseman's reconstruction of the 603 campaign even served as the basis for dating the submission of Judah to Babylonia in that

1. Reprinted with permission. *Biblische Notizen* 62 (1992), 41–44.

same year (Pavlovsky and Vogt 1964:345–346; Malamat 1968:141–142; 1975: 129–132, 144).

Did Nebuchadrezzar march to Syria-Palestine in 603 BCE? The key for the correct understanding of the broken passage is in line 22: *ṣāpāti rabâti ušbal*[*kit*] — "Large siege towers he moved ac[ross]". Which natural obstacle (such as a mountain range) was crossed over by the Babylonians when they "moved across" their large siege towers? The entire area of Syria-Palestine was already conquered by Nebuchadrezzar during his campaigns of 605–604 BCE, and there was no need to carry siege machines from distant bases into the captured territories. Trees for siege towers were abundant all along the coast of Lebanon and the Anti-Lebanon and no natural barrier should have been traversed for siege operations, either on the Phoenician coast, or in southern Palestine. It seems that the campaign of 603 was directed at some other area not yet conquered by the Babylonians, and siege towers, therefore, should have been "moved across" in its direction from Mesopotamian bases.

Remarkable also is the relative length of the space dedicated to the events of 603 BCE in the chronicle (about 12 lines). A quick glance at the Babylonian chronicle series reveals that campaigns conducted either within the area of Mesopotamia, or to neighboring countries are usually described in detail, whereas campaigns to Syria-Palestine are described in relative brevity. This is the result of the interest of the author who lived in Babylonia and was Mesopotamian-centric in his culture and historical outlook. He, thus, delineated the western campaigns of Nebuchadrezzar only schematically and summarily, omitting various details that looked redundant from his Babylonian point of view. Thus, the relatively long description of year 603 better suits a country bordering on Mesopotamia than the area of Syria-Palestine.

In my opinion, the most likely target for Nebuchadrezzar's campaign of 603 is the land of Kimuḫu and, possibly, some other Anatolian countries. Babylonian operations against Kimuḫu are first related in the chronicle's description of year 607 BCE. In the course of this campaign, Nabopolassar crossed the Euphrates and captured the city of Kimuḫu (modern Samsat). He placed a garrison there and returned to Babylonia (Wiseman 1956:20–21; Grayson 1975:97–98 lines 5–15). In the next year (606), the Egyptians attacked the city, besieged it for four months and conquered it. Nabopolassar reacted by crossing the Euphrates north of Carchemish and plundering three cities in the land of Kimuḫu. He left a garrison in Qurumati, a city located somewhere on the eastern bank of the Euphrates, and returned to Babylonia. Soon afterwards, the Egyptian troops at Carchemish crossed the Euphrates, attacked the Babylonian garrison and pushed them back (Wiseman 1956:21–23; Grayson 1975:98, lines 16–26). The Babylonians, thus, failed in their efforts to conquer the land of Kimuḫu, and, as late as the end of year 606 BCE, it remained in their rivals' hands.

This is the background against which we must understand the Babylonian campaign of 603 BCE. In years 605–604, Nebuchadrezzar defeated the Egyptians, drove them out of *Ebir-nāri* and subjugated all the Syro-Palestinian kingdoms. In 603, he returned to the northwestern front and completed what he failed to accomplish in the campaigns of 607–606 BCE. With the help of some parallel passages (Grayson 1975:93–94 lines 35–36, 42–43; 98, lines 19–20) we may restore the beginning of the campaign of 603 thus:

(21) [*šattu ša*]*nitu* ^{iti}*Aiiaru šàr Akkadi*^{ki} *ummāni-šú kabittu*^{tu} *ik-ṣur-ma* [*ina* ^{uru}*Ki*$^{?}$-*mu*$^{?}$-*ḫu*$^{?}$]
(22) [*karas-s*]*u id-di ṣa-pa-a-ti rabâti*^{meš} *uš-bal-k*[*it-ma a-na dūri*]
(23) [*uq-ta-rib ultu* ^{iti}*A*]*iiari adi* ^{iti}[*. . . ṣal-tu ana libbi āli īpuš . . .*]

Translation: "The second year: In the month of Iyyar the king of Akkad assembled a large army and pitched h[is camp in the city of Kimuḫu(?)]. Large siege towers he moved ac[ross and brought it up to the wall(?). From the month of] Iyyar until the month [of MN he subjected the city to a siege(?) . . .]."

The broken parts of the description may well have included details of the conquest of the city and the expansion of the campaign against some other Anatolian cities. The end of the 603 campaign (Grayson 1975:101 line 1) may tentatively be restored [. . . *ú-maš-š*]*ir-ma x* [. . .]; "[In the month of MN the king of Akkad le]ft [troops(?) . . .] and [. . .]" (compare Grayson 1975:95 line 64; 97 line 8).

We may conclude that no Babylonian campaign to *Ebir-nāri* was conducted in year 603 BCE and that the most likely date for Jehoiakim's submission to Babylonia is 604 BCE (as suggested by the majority of scholars). The destruction of Ekron by the Babylonians (Gitin 1989:45–48) may tentatively be dated to either 604 BCE, or after Nebuchadrezzar's failure on the Egyptian border in his fourth year (601/600 BCE).

References

Gitin, S. 1989. Tel Miqne-Ekron: A Type-Site for the Inner Coastal Plain in the Iron Age II Period. In: Gitin, S. and Dever, W.G. eds. *Recent Excavations in Israel. Studies in Iron Age Archaeology.* (AASOR 49). Winona Lake: 23–58.

Grayson, A.K. 1975. *Assyrian and Babylonian Chronicles.* Locust Valley, New York.

Malamat, A. 1968. The Last Kings of Judah and the Fall of Jerusalem. *IEJ* 18: 137–156.

Malamat, A. 1975. The Twilight of Judah in the Egyptian-Babylonian Maelstrom. *Supplement to VT* 28: 123–145.

Pavlovsky, V. and Vogt, E. 1964. Die Jahre der Könige von Juda und Israel. *Biblica* 45: 321–347.

Rainey, A.F. 1975. The Fate of Lachish during the Campaigns of Sennacherib and Nebuchadrezzar. Aharoni, Y. ed. *Investigations at Lachish. The Sanctuary and the Residency* (Lachish V). *Tel Aviv*: 47–60.

Shea, W.H. 1976. Adon's Letter and the Babylonian Chronicle. *BASOR* 223: 61–64.

Vogt, E. 1957. Die neubabylonische Chronik über die Schlacht bei Karkemisch und die Einnahme von Jerusalem. *Supplement to VT* 4: 67–96.

Wiseman, D.J. 1956. *Chronicles of Chaldaean Kings (626-556 B.C.) in the British Museum.* London.

Wiseman, D.J. 1985. *Nebuchadrezzar and Babylon.* (The Schweich Lectures of the British Academy 1983). Oxford.

Royal Vassals or Governors? On the Status of Sheshbazzar and Zerubbabel in the Persian Empire[1]

Many scholars accept the suggestion that, following the destruction of Jerusalem and the temple in 587/6 BCE, Judah became a Babylonian province, and Gedaliah was nominated to the office of governor.[2] The status of Judah did not change after the Persian conquest, and Sheshbazzar and Zerubbabel held the office of governors of the province of Yehud in the early Persian period. The nomination of Davidic descendants as governors resembled the nomination of members of other local dynasties in other districts of the Persian empire. These governors enjoyed a high esteem among the inhabitants of the province, thanks to the prestige of their dynasties. The Persian king and his officials took advantage of their prestige, sent them executive orders and let them enforce them upon their subjects.

Contrary to this picture, some scholars have suggested that during the sixth century BCE, the province of Yehud either enjoyed a semi-independent status as a vassal kingdom, or that it enjoyed a status that was close to that of a vassal kingdom. J. Liver (1958:115–116) was the first to suggest that the land of Judah remained a tributary state after the destruction of Jerusalem in 587/6 BCE. "The status of Judah in the Restoration Period was politically and administratively identical to its position after the destruction of the monarchy and Zedekiah's deportation." In his opinion, Yehud became a province in the time of Darius I, probably as part of his administrative reform. In support of this assumption, Liver mentions both Jehoiachin's royal status in his 37th year (2 Kgs. 25:27–30) and the fact that the Babylonians did not bring deportees to the areas of Judah. However, unlike the Assyrians who conducted "two-way" mass deportations, the Babylonians transferred uprooted deport-

1. Reprinted with permission. Henoch 22 (2000), 35–44.

2. Alt (1934; 1935) suggested that Yehud was an administrative part of the province of Samaria and not a separate province within the satrapy of Transeuphrates. Only under Nehemiah did Yehud become an independent district. His opinion has been accepted by some scholars; see, e.g., Weinberg 1972:50–52; 1992:113–115, 135; McEvenue 1981:353–364. However, the suggestion lacks concrete foundations and was criticized by many scholars; see Smith 1971:147–153; Williamson 1988:59–82; 1998:151–154; Hoglund 1992:69–86.

ees only to Babylonia proper. "One-way" deportation was conducted in all the districts of the Babylonian empire and does not indicate the administrative status of the conquered areas.

About 30 years later, P. Sacchi (1989:131–148) and F. Bianchi (1991:133–156; 1994:153–165) renewed this line of thought. They argued that Jehoiachin retained the title "king of Judah" after his deportation to Babylonia as indicated by the ration lists of the time of Nebuchadrezzar II (Weidner 1939: 923–935). His release from prison and his position in the Babylonian court in the time of Evil-Merodach (Amēl-Marduk), as related in 2 Kgs. 25:27–30, further indicate that his royal status was retained until his death. His status as a vassal king fitted the structure of the Neo-Babylonian and Persian empires, where the dynastic model was kept in peripheral districts of the empire and, particularly, in the west (i.e., in Phoenicia, Cilicia and Cyprus).

According to this line of thought, Sheshbazzar and Zerubbabel were, like Jehoiachin, both Judean kings and Persian governors. Sheshbazzar is called *peḥâ* ("governor") and *nāśîʾ* ("prince"), the first title referring to his administrative office and the second designated his royal status ("the prince of Judah"). Zerubbabel was of Davidic descent, and, although Haggai calls him "governor" (1:1, 14; 2:2), the prophecies of Haggai (2:23) and Zechariah (6:9–15) ascribed to him a royal status. It was Darius I, possibly as part of his administrative reform, who abolished the status of vassal kings for the governors of Yehud, a status that continued from the Babylonian conquest down to the late sixth century BCE.[3]

A. Lemaire took a more moderate position (Lemaire 1996:48–57). He first demonstrated that *Ṣemaḥ* (Zech. 3:8; 6:12) was not an appellation of Zerubbabel, but his Hebrew proper name. Zerubbabel had two names: one Babylonian (Zēr-bābili = "seed of Babylon") and another Hebrew (Ṣemaḥ, "sprout"). The identification of the names gives more emphasis to Zechariah's messianic expectations from the Davidic descendant who was appointed governor of the province of Yehud. In light of Lemaire's suggestion, we may ask whether Sheshbazzar (Šaššu-aba-uṣur = "May Shamash protect the father") is not the Babylonian name of Shealtiel ("I consulted El/God"), Zerubbabel's father, so that Sheshbazzar and Zerubbabel were father and son, the latter succeeding the former in the office of governor (for a comprehensive discussion, see Japhet 1982:66–98; 1983:218–229; Eskenazi 1992:1207–1209).

As for the alternative, province versus vassal kingdom, Lemaire supported a middle course: "province proche d'un royaume vassal" (Lemaire

3. The suggestion of Sacchi and Bianchi was adopted by Niehr 1999:229–231.

1996:53). On the one hand, he noted that the title "king" does not appear among the titles of persons who held the office of governor of Yehud, but, on the other hand, he emphasized that the dynastic principle was quite common in Persian provinces, particularly in the west. The local population regarded the same person as a Persian officer and as a local king. The province of Judah in the early Persian period enjoyed political autonomy, and the Persian authority deliberately appointed descendants of the House of David to the office of governor.

Are there any indications of an exceptional status of the province of Yehud in the exilic and early post-exilic periods? Did descendants of the Davidic dynasty hold the status of vassal kings in this period? I believe that the answer to the two questions is no, and that the evidence does not support even Lemaire's moderate position. To demonstrate this contention, let me analyze some of the arguments brought forward by supporters of the vassal kingdom hypothesis.

I

The references to Jehoiachin and his sons in the Babylonian ration lists of the time of Nebuchadrezzar II are the point of departure for all studies of Jehoiachin's status in the Babylonian court after his deportation in 598 BCE. He is designated "the king of the land of Judah," and once he is called "the son of the king of Judah." His five sons are recorded as "sons of the king of Judah" (Weidner 1939. For a recent discussion and literature, see Gerhards 1998:64–66). In addition to Jehoiachin, two other kings are mentioned in the ration lists: the king of Lydia (whose name is unfortunately broken) and "the 2+x sons of Aga', the king of Ashkelon" (Weidner 1939:pl. I, line 4; pl. III, line 6). The tablet in which the sons of Aga' are mentioned is dated to Nebuchadrezzar's 13th year (592 BCE). According to a Babylonian chronicle, in 604 BCE, Nebuchadrezzar destroyed the city of Ashkelon (Grayson 1975: 100, lines 18–20). Archaeological excavations at Ashkelon have uncovered evidence of the Babylonian devastation all over the site. Moreover, there is a gap of occupation in the site in the sixth century BCE, and the city only began to be rebuilt in the Persian period (Stager 1996). It is clear that in the year 592 BCE, when the tablet was recorded, the city of Ashkelon was in ruins. The title "king of Ashkelon" is only an honorific, defining the identity of the sons of Aga' in the court by the palace administration, but conveys no political-administrative status regarding their homeland.

The same conclusion should be drawn regarding Jehoiachin and his sons: the honorific "king of Judah" defines their identity in the Babylonian court, but it does not imply a political-administrative authority of the deported king and his sons. Nomination of the descendants of the royal house of Judah for the post of governor was an option for the Babylonian kings (and for their successors, the Persian kings, as well). However, as long as they stayed in Babylonia, they held neither office nor power in the administration of the newly founded province of Yehud.

Following the destruction of Jerusalem in 587/6, Judah became a Babylonian province, and a governor of non-Davidic origin was nominated to administer it.[4] The identity of Gedaliah's successors escapes us, and we do not know if members of the house of David, or a non-Davidic nominee, were chosen for the post of Babylonian governor. We may conclude that the Babylonian ration lists shed no light on the administrative-political status of Judah in the time of Nebuchadrezzar.

II

The description of Jehoiachin's release from prison by Evil-Merodach in 562 BCE (2 Kgs. 25:27–30) is sometimes interpreted as an indication of Jehoiachin's influence in the Babylonian court (Sacchi 1989:137–141; Bianchi 1994:155–156). The passage has been discussed in many articles and commentaries, and opinions differ concerning its message and historical significance. (In addition to the commentaries, see Zenger 1968:16–30; Levenson 1984:353–361; Begg 1986:49–56; Becking 1990:283–293; Gerhards 1998:52–67.) There is no doubt that the release was an act of clemency on the occasion of Evil-Merodach's accession to the throne (Becking 1990:286). There are no elements of treaty or covenant in the text, as suggested by some scholars,[5] and there is no support for the assumption that a treaty was then concluded between Evil-Merodach and Jehoiachin. Moreover, 2 Kgs. 25:27–30 neither refers to a return to the land, nor does it convey a message of hope for the

4. The suggestion of Miller and Hayes (1986:421–424) that Gedaliah was made a king and replaced Zedekiah on the throne of Judah is unlikely. Gedaliah is never called "king," and the assumption that the royal rank was suppressed by the final editors of the Book of Jeremiah because Gedaliah was not of Davidic descent is arbitrary. Moreover, the title "king" in Jeremiah 40–41 refers to Zedekiah, and certainly not to Gedaliah (contra Miller and Hayes). The complete destruction of the city of Jerusalem, the establishment of a new center of government (Mizpah), and the nomination of a non-Davidic governor, all indicate a total change in the status of Judah and its transition from a vassal kingdom into a Babylonian province.

5. For the suggestion, see Zenger 1968:21–30; Levenson 1984:356–358. The article of Nobile (1986:207–224) is not available to me.

people as a whole (Gerhards 1998:62–63). Even if the passage depicts life in Babylonia as tolerable (as some scholars maintain) (Begg 1986:49–56; Becking 1990:291–293), its message for the community of deportees in Babylonia was limited, because it referred to the fate of Jehoiachin alone.[6]

We may further recall the prophecy of Isaiah to Hezekiah (2 Kgs. 20:18): "And some of your own sons, who are born to you, shall be taken away, and they shall be eunuchs in the palace of the king of Babylon." The role of eunuchs in the ancient world, and in particularly in the ancient Near East, has recently been discussed in detail (Tadmor 1995:317–325; Grayson 1995:87–98; Deller 1999:303–311). Scholars were able to point out that, in many civilizations, captured boys were castrated and then entered the service of the state. Eunuchs who grew up and were educated by the palace administration could reach high positions in the military and civil sectors, according to their talent and luck. Not enough is known about the Babylonian eunuchs (see the literature cited by Grayson 1995:90, note 30), but the biblical reference seems to indicate that what is known of other states was also true for the Babylonian court. In 2 Kgs. 20:18, Isaiah "predicts" the fate of the deported Davidic descendant in the Babylonian court. Whether the prophecy is a *vaticinium ex eventum* and some of Jehoiachin's sons mentioned in the ration lists were in fact castrated and served in the Babylonian court, or the prophecy was speaking in general terms about what might happen to deportees of royal descent, remains unknown. Taking 2 Kgs. 25:27–30 in conjunction with 2 Kgs. 20:18 further minimizes the positive message conveyed by the former text.

In summary, 2 Kgs. 25:27–30 neither indicates a prominent status of Jehoiachin in the Babylonian court, nor points to contacts between Jehoiachin and the Babylonian province of Yehud. There is no evidence for the role or influence of deportees in the province of Yehud during the years 586–539 BCE.

III

As noted above, the status of the province of Yehud under Davidic governors (Sheshbazzar and Zerubbabel) was compared with that of western vassal kingdoms in the Persian empire (Bianchi 1994:156–157; Lemaire 1996:53–54). Is it legitimate to compare the governors of the province of Judah with these western vassal kings?

---

6. Gosse (1996:40–47) noted the similarity between the chronological framework of the Book of Ezekiel and the date in 2 Kgs. 25:27, which take Jehoiachin's deportation (597 BCE) rather than the destruction of Jerusalem (587/6) as their point of departure. The author of 2 Kgs. 25:27–30 was probably a scribe who lived in Babylonia and whose ancestors were deported in 597 BCE.

A broken prism written in Nebuchadrezzar II's seventh year (598 BCE) indicates the political position of Philistia and Phoenicia in the Babylonian empire.[7] After describing his building operations in Babylonia, Nebuchadrezzar presented his court and administrative officials in great detail. In the last preserved part of the prism (column V lines 23–29), he recorded the names of seven unnamed kings and their kingdoms, and then the text breaks off. The list includes the kings of Tyre, Gaza, Sidon, Arvad, Ashdod, Mir[. . .] and [. . .]. The list may be compared with the list of Philistine and Phoenician kingdoms recorded in the inscriptions of Assyrian kings of the house of Sargon. In the inscriptions relating his campaign to Palestine in 701 BCE, Sennacherib mentioned the kings of Sidon, Arvad, Byblos and Samsimuruna in Phoenicia, and Gaza, Ashkelon, Ashdod and Ekron in Philistia (Oppenheim 1969:287–288). Esarhaddon, who destroyed the city of Sidon and turned the kingdom of Sidon into an Assyrian province,[8] mentioned the kings of Tyre, Arvad, Byblos and Samsimuruna in Phoenicia and Gaza, Ashkelon, Ashdod and Ekron in Philistia (Oppenheim 1969:291). An identical list of kings and their kingdoms appears in an inscription of Ashurbanipal that relates his campaign to Egypt (Oppenheim 1969:294).

In light of this comparison, I suggest restoring the broken kingdom's name in line 28 *Mir*-[*ru-na*], i.e., a shortened variant form of the Phoenician kingdom of Samsimuruna (for a possible location of Samsimuruna, see Na'aman 1995:109). The last missing name in line 29 is probably Byblos, as the list enumerates kingdoms located along the eastern Mediterranean coast. Ashkelon and Ekron — the latter destroyed by Nebuchadrezzar either in the course of his 604 BCE campaign, or a few years later — are missing from among the Philistine kingdoms.[9] Evidently, the seven kingdoms listed by Nebuchadrezzar were the former vassals of Assyria who came under his rule, including Sidon, which regained its former status as a vassal kingdom either when Assyria was still in power, or immediately after the Assyrian withdrawal from Phoenicia.[10]

---

7. Unger 1931:35–36, 282–294. For further discussions and literature, see Berger 1973: 59, 108. For the date of the prism, see Landsberger 1933:298; Berger 1973:59, 108.

8. Sidon was annexed by Esarhaddon in 676 BCE and was an Assyrian province for a relatively short period. Details of the administration of the province are missing, and we do not know how deep the Assyrian involvement in the affairs of the new province was. It is clear that the annexation had only a limited effect and that Sidon regained its independence before it was conquered by the Babylonians. For discussions and literature, see Lipiński 1993:158*–163*; Na'aman 1994:3–8.

9. For the date of Ekron's destruction, see recently Gitin 1998:276, n. 2.

10. For the interval of Egyptian control in the Phoenician coast in the late years of

In the course of his struggle with Egypt for the hegemony over south Palestine, Nebuchadrezzar progressively eliminated some kingdoms in this region (i.e., Ashkelon, Ekron, Judah, Ammon, Moab and Edom) and annexed them to his territory. However, in other areas, he did not change the status of the kingdoms he conquered and included them as vassal kingdoms in his empire. Nebuchadrezzar's policy in the west may be exemplified by his policy *vis à vis* the Kingdom of Judah. He first made it a tributary vassal state, maintaining the status it had held under the Assyrian and Egyptian empires. However, after a series of rebellions that broke out in Judah, he decided to completely destroy its capital, Jerusalem, deport its elite, and turn the kingdom into a Babylonian province.

When Cyrus conquered Babylonia, he annexed to his territory the Babylonian array of provinces and vassal kingdoms. I believe that the often-cited short passage from the Cylinder of Cyrus that mentions tributary kings refers to the former vassal kingdoms of Babylonia (Oppenheim 1969:316a; Borger 1984: 409):

> [By his (Marduk's)] august [command], all the kings of the entire world from the Upper to the Lower Sea, those who live in throne rooms, (those who) live in [. . . and] all the kings of the West who dwell in tents, brought me their heavy tributes to Babylon and kissed my feet.

As far as I am aware, the Persian array of vassal kingdoms in Phoenicia and Anatolia did not differ from the Babylonian array of kingdoms. Persia further conquered new territories in the east and west, subjugated their rulers and added them to its network of vassal kingdoms. I do not know of any case in which a former Babylonian province gained independence and became a Persian vassal kingdom. In other words, the claim that the rule of vassal kings in some parts of the Persian empire indicates that the Davidic governors were also vassal kings is erroneous. The Persian vassal kings were either former vassals of the Assyrian and Babylonian empires, or were conquered recently by the Persian kings. Judah was a former province of Babylonia, and its status did not change under the Persian empire. As noted in the introduction to the article, the nomination of governors from the House of David served the Persian interests, because they enjoyed a high esteem among the inhabitants of the province and were able to implement the orders of the Persian court and enforce them on their subjects.

Psammetichus I and the early years of Necho II, see Malamat 1975:128, n. 10, with earlier literature; Spalinger 1977:227–229.

IV

In the final part of the article, I shall add a few words about the Babylonian policy in southern Palestine and the establishment of the province of Yehud on the ruins of the Kingdom of Judah. It has already been noted that in the course of his conquest of Palestine, Nebuchadrezzar destroyed the prosperous capital cities of Ashkelon and Ekron. Ekron never recovered from the destruction, and its ancient site was abandoned forever. Ashkelon began to recover only in the late sixth century BCE. In an article published a few years ago, I emphasized the fundamental difference between the Assyrian and Babylonian imperial policies in their border zone with Egypt. Let me cite the relevant passage (Na'aman 1995:114–115):

> In the year 601/600 he [Nebuchadrezzar] tried to conquer Egypt and failed. The military failure brought in its wake the renewal of Egyptian efforts to regain a foothold in Asia and the eruption of rebellions in the Babylonian vassal states. Nebuchadrezzar responded drastically to the threat in the buffer zone with Egypt. Step by step he conquered all the kingdoms and annexed them to his territory, with some kingdoms suffering severe destruction. Moreover, unlike the Assyrians, the Babylonians did not try to develop their new provinces nor to defend them against Arabian raiders. The trade network in southern Palestine and Transjordan was neglected, and areas participating in the Arabian trade suffered economic recession. As a result, the eastern and southern frontiers shrank westwards and northwards. Archaeological excavations and surveys conducted in Palestine and Transjordan indicate a drastic reduction during the sixth century in the number of settlements and their size, in economic activity and in material culture. It is evident that its overall policy can have crucial consequences for people living on the frontier of the empire, and that a change of policy may bring about drastic change in the fortune of peoples living under imperial sway.

The Babylonian policy in southern Palestine was not correctly appreciated by Hans Barstad (1996) in his otherwise fine book about the land of Judah under the Babylonian rule (586–539 BCE). He assumed that the Babylonians endeavored to integrate Judah into their empire and to develop it, in order to gain the most profit. However, the results of the archaeological investigation in Judah and its neighbors contradict this assumption. Like Ashkelon and Ekron, the city of Jerusalem was completely destroyed in 587/6 and remained deserted for many years. The wave of destruction and desertion encompassed the Shephelah and Negeb areas, where all the known Iron II sites were destroyed and deserted. Even the highlands of Judah and Benjamin suffered considerable reduction in the number of settled sites. Barstad is certainly correct that the land of Judah was never empty and that part of its former population remained on the land. Thus, for example, some families may have lived in "exilic" period Jerusalem, as indicated by the excavations at Ketef Hinnom (Barkay 1984:94–108; 1992:139–192, with earlier literature). However, following the Babylonian conquest, urban life in the city came to an end, and all civil and cultic institutions ceased to exist.[11] If we analyze such aspects as settlement size, public buildings, luxury items and epigraphic remains, which are considered reliable criteria for estimating the sociopolitical conditions of countries at different periods (for these criteria, see Jamieson-Drake 1991), the complete breakdown of state and urban life in sixth century BCE Judah immediately becomes clear. All large cities ceased to exist (Mizpah, the center of the newly founded province, is an exception), and only a network of villages survived in the northern highlands of Judah and Benjamin and in the eastern periphery of the former kingdom of Judah (Carter 1994: 106–145; Lipschits 1997:171–336; 1999:165–185; Milevski 1996–97:7–29). Neither new fortifications, nor new large public buildings have been found in "exilic" period Judah. Imported pottery disappeared, and only a few epigraphic finds were discovered. Some typical Iron II forms continued in use during the "exilic" period, and we may assign the material culture of the sixth century to the Iron Age, rather than the Persian period (Barkay 1993: 106–109). But there is a clear reduction in forms and a decline in the quality of the pottery in this final phase of the Iron Age, comparable to the decline of urban life in the land of Judah. The results of the destructive Babylonian campaigns against Judah in the years 598 and 588–586 BCE, the deportation of the elite, and the transfer of Judah from a vassal kingdom to Babylonian province, are perceived everywhere in Judah in the "exilic" period.

In summary, the Babylonian policy in its buffer zone with Egypt was totally destructive for all the kingdoms in this area, including the Kingdom of Judah. "Exilic" period Judah differs in all components from Judah of the monarchial period and that includes the abolition of the monarchy, the annexation to Babylonian territory, the replacement of the center of government, and the nomination of governors in place of the former kings of the dynasty of David. The first governor, Gedaliah, was not of Davidic descendant, and the identity of his successors in the "exilic" period is unknown. With the rise of the Persian empire, two governors of the former royal house of Judah, Sheshbazzar and Zerubbabel, both born in Babylonia, were appointed governors in the province of Yehud. They must have enjoyed popularity among the inhabitants of the province and aroused expectations in certain circles for the renewal of the monarchy under the House of David, but their position as governors was no different from all other governors in the Persian empire. For reasons that still escape us, Darius put an end to the nomination

11. Whether some cultic activity continued on the site of the temple after the destruction remains unknown. See Jones 1963:12–31; Ackroyd 1968:25–29; Miller and Hayes 1986: 426.

of Davidic descendants as governors. The new policy was fatal for the dynasty of David, which lost its power base, and left the Zadokite priests alone in center stage in Jerusalem, but it did not affect the administrative status of the province, which basically remained the same during the time of the later Achaemenid rulers.

References

Ackroyd, P.R. 1968. *Exile and Restoration. A Study of Hebrew Thought of the Sixth Century B.C.* Philadelphia.

Alt, A. 1934. Die Rolle Samarias bei der Entstehung des Judentums. In: Alt, A. et al. eds. *Festschrift Otto Proksch zum sechzigsten Geburtstag.* Leipzig: 5–28. (Reprint: Alt 1953: 316–337).

Alt, A. 1935. Zur Geschichte der Grenze zwischen Judäa und Samaria. *PJb* 31: 94–111. (Reprint: Alt 1953: 346–362).

Alt, A. 1953. *Kleine Schriften zur Geschichte des Volkes Israel* II. München.

Barkay, G. 1984. Excavations on the Slope of the Hinnom Valley in Jerusalem. *Qadmoniot* 17: 94–108. (Hebrew)

Barkay, G. 1992. The Priestly Benediction on Silver Plaque from Ketef Hinnom in Jerusalem. *Tel Aviv* 19: 139–192.

Barkay, G. 1993. The Redefining of Archaeological Periods: Does the Date 588/586 B.C.E. indeed mark the End of the Iron Age Culture? In: Biran, A. and Aviram, J. eds. *Biblical Archaeology Today* II. Jerusalem: 106–109.

Barstad, H.M. 1996. *The Myth of the Empty Land. A Study in the History and Archaeology of Judah during the "Exilic" Period.* Oslo.

Becking, B. 1990. Jehojachin's Amnesty, Salvation for Israel? Notes on 2 Kings 25,27–30. In: Brekelmans, C. and Lust, J. eds. *Pentateuchal and Deuteronomistic Studies* (Bibliotheca ephemeridum theologicarum lovaniensium 94). Leuven: 283–293.

Begg, C.T. 1986. The Significance of Jehoiachin's Release: A New Proposal. *Journal for the Study of the Old Testament* 36: 49–56.

Berger, P.-R. 1973. *Die neubabylonischen Königsinschriften. Königsinschriften des ausgehenden babylonischen Reiches (626–539 a. Chr.).* (AOAT 4/1). Kevelaer and Neukirchen-Vluyn.

Bianchi, F. 1991. Zerobabel re di Giuda. *Henoch* 13: 133–156.

Bianchi, F. 1994. Le rôle de Zerobabel et de la dynastie davidique en Judée du VIe siècle au IIe siècle av. J.-C. *Transeuphratène* 7: 153–165.

Borger, R. 1984. Historische Texte in akkadischer Sprache. In: Kaiser, O. ed. *Texte aus der Umwelt des Alten Testaments* I/4. Gütersloh: 354–409.

Carter, C.E. 1994. The Province of Yehud in the Post-Exilic Period: Soundings in Site Distribution and Demography. In: Eskenazi, T.C. and Richards, K.H. eds. *Second Temple Studies. 2. Temple and Community in the Persian Period.* (*Journal for the Study of the Old Testament* Supplement 175). Sheffield: 106–145.

Deller, K. 1999. The Assyrian Eunuchs and Their Predecessors. In: Watanabe, K ed. *Priests and Officials in the Ancient Near East.* Heidelberg: 303–311.

Eskenazi, T.C. 1992. Sheshbazzar. *The Anchor Bible Dictionary* 5. New York: 1207–1209.

Gerhards, M. 1998. Die Begnadigung Jojachins — Überlegungen zu 2. Kön. 25,27–30 (mit einem Anhang zu den Nennungen Jojachins auf Zuteilungslisten aus Babylon). *Biblische Notizen* 94: 52–67.

Gitin, S. 1998. The Philistines in the Prophetic Texts: An Archaeological Perspective. In: Magness, J. and Gitin, S. eds. *Hesed ve-Emet: Studies in Honor of Ernest S Frerichs.* (Brown Judaic Studies No. 320). Atlanta: 273–290.

Gosse, B. 1996. Le temple dans le livre d'Ézéchiel en rapport à la rédaction des livres des Rois. *RB* 103: 40–47.

Grayson, A.K. 1975. *Assyrian and Babylonian Chronicles.* (Texts from Cuneiform Sources V). Locust Valley.

Grayson, A.K. 1995. Eunuchs in Power. Their Role in the Assyrian Bureaucracy. In: Dietrich, M. and Loretz, O. eds. *Vom Alten Orient zum Alten Testament. Festschrift für Freiherrn von Soden zum 85. Geburtstag.* (AOAT 240). Neukirchen-Vluyn: 87–98.

Hoglund, K.G. 1992. *Achaemenid Imperial Administration in Syria-Palestine and the Missions of Ezra and Nehemiah.* (Society of Biblical Literature Dissertation Series 125). Atlanta.

Jamieson-Drake, D.W. 1991. *Scribes and Schools in Monarchic Judah: A Socio-Archaeological Approach.* (The Social World of Biblical Antiquity 9). Sheffield.

Japhet, S. 1982. Sheshbazzar and Zerubbabel — Against the Background of the Historical and Religious Tendencies of Ezra-Nehemiah. *ZAW* 94: 66–98.

Japhet, S. 1983. Sheshbazzar and Zerubbabel — Against the Background of the Historical and Religious Tendencies of Ezra-Nehemiah. *ZAW* 95: 218–229.

Jones, D. 1963. The Cessation of Sacrifice after the Destruction of the Temple in 586 B.C. *Journal of Theological Studies* 14: 12–31.

Landsberger, B. 1933. Bemerkungen zu einigen in Ungers "Babylon" übersetzten Texten. *ZA* 41: 287–299.

Lemaire, A. 1996. Zorobabel et la Judée à la lumière de l'épigraphie (fin du VIe s. av. J.-C.). *RB* 103: 48–57.

Levenson, J.D. 1984. The Last Four Verses in Kings. *JBL* 103: 353–361.

Lipiński, E. 1993. Le royaume de Sidon au VIIe siècle av. J.-C. *Eretz Israel* 24: 158*–163*.

Lipschits, O. 1997. *The "Yehud" Province under Babylonian Rule (586–539 B.C.E.): Historic Reality and Historiographic Conceptions.* (Ph.D. Thesis). Tel Aviv University.

Lipschits, O. 1999. The History of the Benjaminite Region under Babylonian Rule. *Tel Aviv* 26: 155–190.

Liver, J. 1958. The Return from Babylon, Its Time and Scope. *Eretz Israel* 5: 115–116. (Hebrew).

McEvenue, S.M. 1981. The Political Structure in Judah from Cyrus to Nehemiah. *Catholic Biblical Quarterly* 43: 353–364.

Malamat, A. 1975. The Twilight of Judah in the Egyptian-Babylonian Maelstrom. *Supplement to VT* 28: 123–145.

Milevski, J. 1996–97. Settlement Pattern in Northern Judah during the Achaemenid Period, according to the Hill Country of Benjamin and Jerusalem Surveys. *Bulletin of the Anglo-Israel Society* 15: 7–29.

Miller, J.M. and Hayes J.H. 1986. *A History of Ancient Israel and Judah.* Philadelphia.

Na'aman, N. 1994. Esarhaddon's Treaty with Baal and Assyrian Provinces along the Phoenician Coast. *Rivista di Studi Fenici* 22: 3–8.

Na'aman, N. 1995. Province System and Settlement Pattern in Southern Syria and Palestine in the Neo-Assyrian Period. In: Liverani, M. ed. *Neo-Assyrian Geography.* (Quaderni di Geografia Storica 5). Rome: 103–115.

Niehr, H. 1999. Religio-Historical Aspects of the 'Early Post-Exilic' Period. In: Becking, B. and Korpel, M.C.A. eds. *The Crisis of Israelite Religion. Transformation of Religious Tradition in Exilic and Post-Exilic Times.* (Oudtestamentische Studiën 42). Leiden: 228–244.

Nobile, M. 1986. Un contributo all lettura sincronica della redazione Genesi — 2 Re sulla base del filo narrativo offerto da 2 Re 25,27–30. *Antonianum* 61: 207–224.

Oppenheim, A.L. 1969. Babylonian and Assyrian Historical Texts. In: *ANET*: 265–322.

Sacchi, P. 1989. L'esilio e la fine della monarchia Davidica. *Henoch* 11: 131–148.

Smith, M. 1971. *Palestinian Parties and Politics that Shaped the Old Testament.* New York and London.

Spalinger, A. 1977. Egypt and Babylonia: A Survey (c. 620 B.C.–550 B.C.). *Studien zur altägyptische Kultur* 5: 221–244.

Stager, L.E. 1996. Ashkelon and the Archaeology of Destruction: Kislev 604 BCE. *Eretz Israel* 25: 61*–74*.

Tadmor, H. 1995. Was the Biblical *sārîs* a Eunuch? In: Zevit, Z. Gitin, S. and Sokoloff, M. eds. *Solving Riddles and Untying Knots. Biblical, Epigraphic, and Semitic Studies in Honor of Jonas C. Greenfield.* Winona Lake: 317–325.

Unger, E. 1931. *Babylon die Heilige Stadt nach der beschreibung der Babylonier.* Berlin and Leipzig.

Weidner, E.F. 1939. Jojachin, König von Juda, in babylonischen Keilschrifttexten. In: *Mélanges Syriens offerts à Monsieur René Dussaud* II. Paris: 923–935.

Weinberg, J.P. 1972. Demographische Notizen zur Geschichte der nachexilischen Gemeinde in Juda. *Klio* 54: 45–59.

Weinberg, J. 1992. *The Citizen-Temple Community* (Journal for the Study of the Old Testament Supplement 151). Sheffield.

Williamson, H.G.M. 1982. The Governors of Judah under the Persians. *Tyndale Bulletin* 39: 59–82.

Williamson, H.G.M. 1998. Judah and the Jews. In: Brosius, M. and Kuhrt, A. eds. *Studies in Persian History. Essays in Memory of David M. Lewis.* (Achaemenid History XI). Leiden: 151–154.

Zenger, E. 1968. Die deuteronomistische Interpretation der Rehabilitierung Jojachins. *Biblische Zeitschrift* 12: 16–30.

Index of Ancient Personal Names

Index of Places

Index of Biblical References

· 200, not 2000 chariots in Ahab's army. pp. 1ff